Fritz K. Ringer

THE DECLINE

OF THE GERMAN

MANDARINS

The German Academic

Community, 1890-1933

WESLEYAN UNIVERSITY PRESS

Published by
University Press of New England
Hanover and London

WESLEYAN UNIVERSITY PRESS

Published by University Press of New England, Hanover, NH 03755

© 1969 by the President and Fellows of Harvard College

Preface to the German Translation of 1983 copyright © 1990 by Fritz K. Ringer

Printed in the United States of America   5   4   3   2

∞

Library of Congress Cataloging-in-Publication Data

Ringer, Fritz K., 1934-

The decline of the German mandarins : the German academic
community, 1890-1933 / Fritz K. Ringer

  p.   cm.

Reprint. Originally published; Cambridge, Mass.: Harvard
University Press, 1969.

Includes bibliographical references (p.) and index.

ISBN 0-8195-6235-1 (alk. paper)

1. Universities and colleges—Germany—History.   2. Germany—
Intellectual life—20th

century.   I. Title.

LA727.R47   1990

378.43—dc20   90-50315

THE DECLINE OF THE
GERMAN MANDARINS

Steven Shapin (signature)

Science Studies Unit
University of Edinburgh
Feb 1996

PREFACE TO THE GERMAN TRANSLATION OF 1983

The original edition of this book was completed in early 1968. This preface was initially written for the German translation of 1983, which, like subsequent translations, was based on a somewhat abbreviated and amended version of the English original.

The present paperback edition, however, is an unaltered reprint of the 1968 edition.

Among the critical comments on the original version of this book, three have been especially insistent. First, some of my critics have objected that I reduced the views of German scholars to mere effects of social conditions. Second, several commentators have found my generalizations inadequate to the great diversity of views among German academic intellectuals. Third, a number of commentators have felt that I exaggerated the extent to which the social conditions and the views I described were unique to Germany; they have suggested that very similar circumstances and opinions were prevalent elsewhere as well. Altogether, these criticisms have forced me to become more self-conscious about my methods and my analytical framework, and I would like briefly to set down some of what has occurred to me about these matters during the last few years.

Let me begin my describing how I selected and approached my sources on German academic opinion. I first studied printed collections of speeches given at various German universities during the Weimar period. I next made a list of all nonscientists above the rank of instructor who taught for three or more years in faculties of arts and sciences at the universities of Berlin, Munich, Freiburg, and Heidelberg between 1918 and 1933. I read everything written by these men during those years that was relatively unspecialized or methodological in character. Finally, I extended my reading of university speeches and of my authors' works backward in time to 1890, while also adding major handbooks and anthologies in several disciplines, along with writings by academics, and a few non-academics, who were not members of my original sample but who were prominently mentioned in the material I had already read.

Aiming at a rigorously empirical history of belief, I wanted to start with a "random sample" of opinion, a deliberately untutored selection and demarcation of a field of study. Avoiding tacit pre-judgments, I meant to *discover* which beliefs and believers were either influential or representative within this field, and how the various meanings that played a role in it were actually related to each other. I knew that my approach would not do justice to "individual differences . . . which would interest biographers." I was trying to chart a landscape, not to describe particular trees or glades within it. I actually made an effort to look at my sources from a certain analytical distance. Resisting the temptation to empathize with individuals, I wanted to focus on impersonal patterns of meaning, and to see these patterns, at least initially, as *unfamiliar*, problematic, and thus in need of explicit interpretation and explanation.

In any case, having selected my sources, I began by trying to interpret them, and I only partly and gradually moved from interpretation to a certain kind of explanation. I still believe this sequence to be generally characteristic of intellectual history. In our reasoning, if not in the literary presentation of our conclusions, interpretation precedes explanation. We start with an effort to "translate" a text that is literally or figuratively "foreign" into an optimally clarified version of our own language. To the extent that this proves difficult or impossible, we reach for supplementary hypotheses of a functional or causal type. We begin to ask why a particular argument "works" within the "foreign" language even though we cannot make it work in ours. We wonder how certain apparently arbitrary meanings and schemes of thought came to play a role in the "foreign" culture, whether they might have been sustained by relevant social relationships or transmitted as implicit "rules" of practice. Yet this move toward a certain kind of explanation never totally replaces the interpretive mode, just as we never come to think of the texts we study as wholly arbitrary, simply false, or mere effects of their environment.

Thus I took very seriously a brief methodological comment that I included in my Introduction. I distinguished between three different ways in which a historian may try to account for past beliefs. He may claim that certain views were held because they seemed unavoidable in view of the available evidence and the rules of right thinking; this may be called a logical or (better) *rational* explanation of beliefs. Or he may claim that certain doctrines were accepted because they were inherited from intellectual ancestors; this could be called a *traditional* explanation of beliefs. Finally, the historian could account for a man's opinions by tracing them to his psychological orientation or his social or economic position; this would be an *ideological* explanation of beliefs. Having introduced these distinctions, I insisted that, in principle, *any* of the three types of historical explanation can be applied to any set of beliefs and that no historical account of an opinion implies anything about the substantive merit of that opinion. In my own account, I proposed to emphasize ideological explanations; but I specified that "I do not and cannot mean to say that traditional or logical [explanations] would prove fruitless." The point of this specification was precisely to exclude the view that the opinions of German university professors were "merely" effects of a social situation.

On the other hand, I did indeed *emphasize* the ideological type of explanation, in that I treated "mandarin ideology" primarily as an effect of "the mandarins' position in German society." The elements of what I called mandarin ideology were not simply invented, of course; they were interpretively and inductively established, and they were rather complex. I wrote of "axioms," of "characteristic mental habits and semantic preferences." These included the consistent repudiation of instrumental or "utilitarian" knowledge, the associated contrast between "culture" and "civilization," the conviction that *Wissenschaft* can and should engender *Weltanschauung*, the widely applicable "principles of empathy and individuality," and the normative concept of the "legal and cultural state." All of these in turn were anchored in the crucial ideal of *Bildung* or "cultivation" and in the underlying vision of learning as an empathetic and unique interaction with venerated texts. Taken together, these interrelated cognitive dispositions seemed to make up at least as coherent and far-reaching a form of "middle-class ideology" as the reputedly "bourgeois" complex of *laissez-faire* individualism and utilitarian liberalism.

The definition of "the mandarins" and of their social role thus almost followed of itself. I posited "a social and cultural elite which owes its status primarily to educational qualifications, rather than to hereditary rights or wealth." This included the entire university-educated upper middle class, members of the "liberal" or "academic" professions (*akademische Berufe, Akademiker*), along with Protestant ministers, secondary school teachers, higher officials, and university professors, whom I also called "mandarin intellectuals." The use of the word *status* in the definition was a reference to Max Weber's distinction between *class* and *status*, in which class standings are objective positions in the system of production, while status is the attributed social honor associated with certain styles of life. I further specified that the mandarins thrived in an "intermediate stage" of economic development, in which "the ownership of liquid capital has not yet become either widespread or widely accepted as a qualification for social status, and hereditary titles based on landholding, while still relevant, are no longer absolute prerequisites." Finally, I stressed the close association of the mandarin elite with the higher civil service and the bureaucratic monarchy.

In proposing these general characterizations, I did not mean to imply anything like an identity of views among all German university professors. On the contrary, I gave a good deal of attention to systematic variations of outlook within the mandarin world. Rather early in the book, I noted a subtle difference between a "bureaucratic wing" and a more purely "intellectual wing" within the

German educated upper middle class, whose social position was based on its ties to the higher civil service, on the one hand, and to the system of higher education on the other. I also detected a corresponding divide between a more rational-bureaucratic and a more purely cultural vision of the legal and cultural state. I tried to make clear that "the underlying tension between the outlook of the administrative official and that of the cultivated man never totally disappeared from the German intellectual scene." I was thinking not only about the difference between high officials and university professors, but also about the homologous divide *within* the German academic community between someone like Gustav Schmoller and someone like Lujo Brentano.

At the same time, I distinguished between "orthodox" and "modernist" mandarin intellectuals. What I had in mind was not primarily a political divide into conservatives and liberals. On the contrary, I strenuously avoided the term "conservative," partly because I felt that some of the modernists, not the orthodox, could properly be called enlightened conservatives. As for the term "liberal," I considered it *relatively* appropriate only when applied to those modernists (e.g., Brentano and the brothers Weber) who "read" Humboldt somewhat as John Stuart Mill did and who were more interested in cultural vitality than in social harmony. My main point about the "orthodox mandarins" was that they "made up a majority and represented a more or less official attitude within the German academic community."

> Their position was really rather simple. . . . If one regards the mandarin heritage as the ideology of an educated elite, one has no difficulty in understanding [orthodox views]. Faced with the threat of the mass age, [the orthodox] had only to exploit the antidemocratic implications of their tradition to arrive at fairly predictable arguments. . . . They were doctrinaire, single-minded, and logically uncomplicated; they followed obvious lines of reasoning to inevitable conclusions. As a matter of fact, it was generally the less articulate, politically unsophisticated, and intellectually less distinguished

members of the German academic community who made up the rank and file of the orthodox majority.

Some of the greatest German scholars, and especially the well-known social scientists, developed more complex arguments about the problems of their time. . . . The members of this relatively progressive minority may appropriately be called "modernists" or "accommodationists." . . . Their whole approach to the political and cultural affairs of their nation was colored by the conviction that only a partial accommodation to modern needs and conditions would enable the mandarins and their values to retain a certain influence even in the twentieth century. [See pp. 129–30 this volume.]

The crucial distinction here is that between the largely unconscious reproduction of a tradition, and an intellectually more complex and selective relationship to it. As I explained elsewhere, the modernists felt that "the German cultural heritage . . . had to be translated into a language appropriate to the modern context. Radically incompatible elements had to be weeded out and inessential parts sacrificed to permit concentration on the most vital and enduring ones." Ernst Troeltsch actually claimed that the word *Bildung* could not properly be applied to the "naive passing on of a single, homogeneous tradition," for *Bildung* seemed to him to "presuppose a plurality of historical traditions, therefore complexity and a problematic nature, and finally a process of conscious selection and unification."

In other words, the orthodox were rather directly and easily "understandable" in terms of the ideal type that had been posited. Their views were more fully "predictable" than those of the accommodationists. The self-consciousness of the modernists, by contrast, intervened to *mediate* the causal action of the mandarins' social role upon their opinions. Though the orthodox and the modernists certainly shared certain common assumptions, the ideological explanation was more completely and exclusively adequate for the orthodox than for the modernists, whose more articulate beliefs called for relatively greater recourse to the rational explanation. As a matter of fact, some of the great modernists were not only my objects of study, but also my colleagues and mentors in the interpretation of their own culture. I thought *with* them, not only *about* them. I regarded them as "translators," which is also how I regarded myself. Early in the book, I noted that a number of German intellectuals after around 1890 wanted to re-examine their traditional values, and that "the more clear-sighted among them" did this "because they hoped that the fundaments of their heritage might yet be saved at the expense of its less important accretions." I characterized their work as "a kind of retrospective self-analysis," commented on its occasionally "critical spirit," and suggested that my own interpretation would be an extension of theirs.

I am convinced that self-critical reflection can be a cause of changes in belief. But I also followed another line of analysis, at least with respect to some of the most determined modernists, whom I also called "radicals" or "radical critics." I cited evidence that some of these men had "unique personal experiences which may have led them into unorthodox paths":

> Tönnies, Wiese, and some of the other modernists among the sociologists had unusual backgrounds. An early and atypically serious interest in Hobbes may have helped to make Tönnies a "positivist" in social questions. Wiese was decisively influenced by Spencer; Aster, Lederer, and Mannheim, by Marx. . . . Thus the radical was typically an outsider in some way. Very often, he had contacts in the world of the non-academic, unofficial and unconnected intelligentsia, with artists, journalists, and writers. At the same time, one cannot help but notice the relatively large proportion of Jews among the critics of mandarin orthodoxy. Jewish intellectuals were very prominent among the innovators in various disciplines, as well as among the authors of progressive social and political doctrines. . . . In part, these facts may reflect certain characteristics of the Jews' own cultural heritage, along with their international dispersion. But the more immediate effects of anti-Semitism upon the Jewish intellectual should not be

overlooked. . . . Jewish instructors found their progress
through the academic ranks hampered by their colleagues,
and they often faced less tangible social barriers as well. According to Sigmund Freud, experiences of this kind tended to
encourage "a certain independence of judgment" in many
Jewish intellectuals. [See pp. 238-39 this volume.]

My impression was that it did not much matter what kind of experience first encouraged "a certain independence of judgment."
What mattered is that the path of heterodoxy, once entered, could
quickly lead to a more fully developed outsider's position.

As a matter of fact, even moderate modernists could come to feel
so alienated from the mainstream of orthodox opinion that they
occasionally had recourse to the radical tactic of "unmasking" and
"debunking," in which the opponent's views are directly traced to
his immediate interests. This began to happen with some degree of
frequency during the bitter controversies of World War I, and it
continued unabated through the interwar period. Part of the reason was that the orthodox tended to turn the rhetoric of mandarin
political "idealism" into what Ernst von Aster called "merciless
moralizing," a "patriotic-religious ragout," and a new "metaphysic" of reaction. Since mild criticisms of this rhetoric were hard
to express, "the critic almost had to make a leap into a new vocabulary, one in which interests could be considered, groups were sums
of people, and the rule of the spirit was an ideal, not a reality. . . .
Thinking of Marx and of Bertold Brecht, of Nietzsche and of
Freud, one begins to suspect that idealism has always produced its
own enemies.

In sum, I tried to outline and partly to explain the most important *differences* of orientation *within* the German academic community. Some of my critics may have overlooked this aspect of my
analysis, or to have given it little attention. To be sure, any generalizing treatment of a body of opinion will simplify that body of
opinion to some degree and will fail to do full justice to the diversity of thought within the group under consideration. Given my

approach, in other words, I could scarcely expect to avoid all generalizing simplification.

A much more serious issue was initially raised by Jürgen Habermas and more fully developed by Sven-Eric Liedman. The issue is whether the German mandarins' attitudes were largely unique, or whether similar orientations were prevalent in other European societies as well. My initial hunch was that the German educated middle class represented a particularly pronounced instance of a possibly more pervasive pattern. I noted Karl Mannheim's view that the modern bourgeoisie consisted from the beginning of two partly distinctive wings, an educated and a propertied one, and that these two groups were by no means identical in their ideologies. I also suggested that the divergence between Anglo-French and German thought during the eighteenth century should not be exaggerated, that the educated middle class — and the theoretical issue of education — were very important west of the Rhine as well. "The peculiarity of the German social situation," I wrote, "was only a matter of degree, and so was the consequent difference in intellectual orientations." I further argued that the German intellectual tradition should not be described merely in terms of its deviation from an assumed English entrepreneurial-liberal norm, but should be studied in its own right as an alternate form of middle class consciousness. What was distinctive about Germany was just that it led the rest of Europe in creating a modern system of higher education and research, just as England led in the industrial revolution. As a result, an educated upper middle class was particularly well established in Germany long before its position was abruptly challenged by rapid industrialization and political democratization after 1870.

On the other hand, these were hunches, rather than established conclusions. I could not adequately address comparative questions when I wrote *The Decline of the German Mandarins*, because I knew too little about French and English social and intellectual history. Since completing the book, I have therefore been working toward a comparison of the educated classes and their ideologies in modern France and Germany. In the process, I have discovered some important divergences between French and German institutions and ideologies of higher education and of scholarship. Thus the French concept of *culture générale,* the closest French equivalent to the German idea of *Bildung,* was by no means identical with *Bildung* in its meanings and implications. Yet despite such differences, I have in fact been increasingly impressed with the broad similarities between modern European educational systems, with the great importance of higher education as an element in both French and German social stratification, and with the centrality of educational ideals for middle-class attitudes and for intellectual roles in both France and Germany.

In any case, my critics have forced me to pursue a rather difficult comparative analysis, and the results may be observed in my book *Fields of Knowledge: French Academic Culture 1890–1920, in Comparative Perspective* (forthcoming, Cambridge University Press).

Fritz K. Ringer

ACKNOWLEDGMENTS

This book grew out of a dissertation on "The German Universities and the Crisis of Learning, 1918–1925," which was directed by Franklin L. Ford of Harvard University. Two consecutive grants from the Social Science Research Council enabled me to work at the Bayerische Staatsbibliothek in Munich for a year and to complete the thesis in the fall of 1960. I have been back to Germany for further research since then, and I have progressively enlarged the whole conception of the book over the last seven years. During that interval, I was able to discuss my ideas with colleagues and students, always to my profit. I had specific comments upon several chapters from Crane Brinton, H. Stuart Hughes, and David S. Landes of Harvard University, and from Fritz T. Epstein and Herbert H. Kaplan of Indiana University. I gratefully acknowledge their advice. The most helpful criticism and encouragement, however, has been my wife's.

I wish to thank Heike Mitchell and Anna Strikis for their help in typing and proofreading the manuscript, and Robert Grogg, for his stamina in verifying notes and working on the index.

CONTENTS

THE DECLINE OF THE
GERMAN MANDARINS

INTRODUCTION
THE MANDARIN TYPE

This book deals with the opinions of German university professors from about 1890 to 1933, particularly with their reaction to Germany's sudden transformation into a highly industrialized nation. About 1890, the impact of an abrupt economic expansion began to be felt in Germany. A dramatic boom had started sometime before 1870. The resulting sense of change and instability was increased by the political revolution and the disastrous inflation that followed upon the First World War. To German academics, the whole period covered in this study seemed a continuous upheaval, a particularly unpleasant introduction to the problems of technological civilization.

Not only in Germany but also in other European countries at

that time, there were men of letters who feared that material progress would bring with it a whole range of serious dangers, particularly cultural ones. A certain pessimism in this respect was quite common among learned Europeans, especially during the 1890's. Perhaps it is not surprising that sensitive and highly educated individuals inclined to regard the dawn of the mass and machine age with considerable skepticism. One could try to explain their misgivings by saying that they were naturally or even justifiably afraid for their values and for traditional values generally. They suspected that their own standards of personal cultivation would come to be rejected as outmoded and irrelevant. After all, economic and political affairs in the age of technology do have a certain anonymity, an automatic quality, which defies guidance by the learned few. In the cultural field, the inevitable adjustment to mass tastes seems to result in an obtrusive vulgarity from which the individual can find no permanent refuge. Moreover, there is no room for a sage in a factory, and the role of the sage is understandably more gratifying to an intellectual than that of the technician.

In a very general way, these considerations may account for the uneasy mood of many European writers during the 1890's and thereafter. In all modern nations, some men of letters have reacted against democratic mass civilization, and they have done so as intellectuals, not as defenders of the landed aristocracy or of the entrepreneurial elite. As Karl Mannheim put it, "the modern bourgeoisie had from the beginning a two-fold social root—on the one hand the owners of capital, on the other those individuals whose only capital consisted in their education. It was common therefore to speak of the propertied and educated class, the educated element being, however, by no means ideologically in agreement with the property-owning element."[1] It would seem to me that this distinction has too often been neglected, especially in its implications for the analysis of theoretical attacks upon mass society.

On the other hand, I am not prepared to substantiate Mannheim's suggestion as applied to Europe in general. Indeed, I am convinced that the German intellectuals constitute something of a special case with respect to this whole problem. As we shall see, the German educational system of the nineteenth century had peculiar characteristics. German industrialization, once it accelerated around 1870, was particularly abrupt. The social and cultural strains it engendered were unusually severe, and above all, the German academics reacted to the dislocation with such desperate intensity that the specter of a "soulless" modern age came to haunt everything they said and wrote, no matter what the subject. By the early 1920's, they were deeply convinced that they were living through a profound crisis, a "crisis of culture," of "learning," of "values," or of the "spirit."

It would be wrong to trace the intellectual concerns they shared solely to the theoretical or philosophical antecedents which they had in common. No matter how many German intellectuals of the Weimar period read Kant or Hegel, their manner of thought was not just the product of an inherited logic. It was a certain constellation of attitudes and emotions which united them, infecting even their language and their methods of argument. We must seek to account for the mood which gripped them, not just for their scholarship, and our explanation must therefore be more often psychological than logical in character. At the same time, we must direct our attention to those responses and opinions that were prevalent among the German university professors as a group, abstracting from individual differences and idiosyncrasies which would interest biographers. We are justified in doing this, because German academics from 1890 to 1932 actually thought of themselves as a group. They considered themselves part of a threatened elite of German "bearers of culture," members of a distinct cultured segment of the nation. As we shall see, their writings testified to the existence of a highly integrated and relatively homogeneous intellectual community. Their whole situation united them, their common educational background, their social status, and the threat to their position which, in one way or another, they all felt deeply.

It is possible, then, to treat the German academic intelligentsia as a group, and one of the main purposes of this study is to point up the connections between the experiences of this group on the one hand and its common attitudes and opinions on the other. In order to shed some light on the causal links involved, I will begin by positing a heuristic model, a stylized or ideal type of intellectual. I will describe his historic origins, his educational background, and his whole social position in an effort to show that certain views were natural to him, that he understandably reacted in a characteristic way. In the next chapter and throughout the book, I will then argue that the German university professors conformed rather closely to this type, and that their attitudes in fact resembled orientations which were stipulated as natural to the model. Of course the initial characterization of the type is not to take the place of evidence in any way. It simply helps to organize the information that suggested the model to me in the first place, and it warns the reader in advance that I intend to derive the opinions of the German academic intelligentsia from its peculiar role in German society.

In order to avoid misunderstandings about my approach, I would suggest the following considerations. Historians may try to account for past beliefs in three different ways. They may say that someone held a certain view because it seemed to him unavoidable in the face of the then available evidence and in accordance with the rules of right thinking as he saw them. I would call this the "logical" sequence or explanation. Again, the historian could argue that certain doctrines were accepted at a given time because they were inherited from intellectual predecessors. This explanatory technique might be called the "traditional" sequence. Finally, one could account for a man's opinions by tracing them to his psychological orientation, his social position, his economic or his religious needs. This would be an "ideological" explanation or sequence, and it has been applied to groups as well as to individuals. Very often, the word ideology is restricted to those cases in which the nonlogical sources of a theory are thought to be economic interests. Mannheim uses the term even more narrowly, so that it refers specifically to a backward-looking mentality, to the defensive rationalizations of an outdated class. For the present essay, however, these restrictions do not seem useful. Rather, I shall work with the ideological sequence in its most general form, implying only that some German academic theories may be understood as expressions of emotional group preferences.

4

Admittedly, the method I have chosen raises a serious problem, in that it seems to imply a value judgment. In practice, we are not likely to have recourse to the ideological sequence in trying to trace the opinion that the earth is more or less round. We are most comfortable with the ideological explanation when dealing with doctrines which are either demonstrably erroneous or so vaguely stated as to be essentially unverifiable. In other words, we tend to prefer the logical sequence in the case of "facts," "discoveries," or "truths," the ideological explanation in the field of "visions," unsupportable generalizations, and "rationalizations." The difficulty is that, as historians, we are rarely qualified to make substantive judgments about the ideas we describe. That is not our task in any case. Moreover, only the philosophers could tell us whether the casual distinction between "facts" and "visions" can itself be rigorously stated. They might deny it, and that would be awkward.

There is one way to get around this problem, and that is to recognize that in principle, *any* of the three classes of historical explanations can be applied to *any* idea, and that, again in principle, no historical account of an opinion implies anything about the substantive merit of that opinion. Thus, although I intend to analyze German academic literature primarily in terms of the ideological sequence, I do not and cannot mean to say that traditional or logical sequences would prove fruitless, or that the men I discuss were all shoddy thinkers. I intend simply to emphasize one particular variety of historical explanation.

The ideal type I propose is that of the "mandarin." The word itself is not important, though it is meant to evoke the traditional elite of learned officials in China. My decision to apply the term to the German academic class was probably inspired by Max Weber's striking portrait of the Chinese literati. For the European setting, I would define "the mandarins" simply as a social and cultural elite which owes its status primarily to educational qualifications, rather than to hereditary rights or wealth. The group is made up of doctors, lawyers, ministers, government officials, secondary school teachers, and university professors, all of them men with advanced

5

academic degrees based on the completion of a certain minimum curriculum and the passing of a conventional group of examinations. The "mandarin intellectuals," chiefly the university professors, are concerned with the educational diet of the elite. They uphold the standards of qualification for membership in the group, and they act as its spokesmen in cultural questions.

Strictly speaking, German professors of physics and chemistry were as much mandarin intellectuals as their colleagues in the social studies and humanities. Yet my analysis of German academic opinion will be focused upon the nonscientists. Occasionally, the reader will encounter the views of a biologist, physician, or physicist; but he will not find a full or technical exposition of German scientific thought in this book. It is my impression that in their attitudes toward cultural and political problems, many German scientists followed the leads of their humanist colleagues. But I am unable fully to substantiate this conclusion, and it is certainly possible to imagine scientists taking a more favorable view than humanists of technological civilization. Despite the inevitable scarcity of pertinent sources, others may wish to consider this possibility. In the present study, I intend to equate the mandarin intellectuals primarily with the German academic humanists and social scientists. In other words, I mean to exaggerate, to neglect potential qualifications of my argument. Indeed, the exclusion of the natural scientists is not the only simplification I plan. After all, the mandarin intellectuals in turn were only a small segment of the mandarin elite as a whole. Here again, I mean to narrow the focus of my discussion, even at the cost of a certain one-sidedness. An effect of emphatic imbalance is implied in the typological approach.

The purpose of the mandarin model, to get back to the main argument, is to relate the opinions of the German academic humanists and social scientists to the social history of the German learned class as a whole. Typically, according to my heuristic stipulations, the mandarins can achieve a predominant role within their society only under certain specific conditions. Above all, they can become and remain a functional ruling class only during a particular phase in the material development of their country. They thrive between the primarily agrarian level of economic organization and full industrialization. At that intermediate stage, the ownership of significant amounts of liquid capital has not yet become either widespread or widely accepted as a qualification for social status, and hereditary titles based on landholding, while still relevant, are no longer absolute prerequisites. In this situation, educational background and professional status may well become the only important bases for claims upon social standing that can rival the traditional prestige of the aristocracy. To be sure, if an entrepreneurial middle class is at least beginning to grow rapidly enough to assert its independence, then educated non-nobles may choose to speak for industry and new wealth in the manner of a Daniel Defoe or a Benjamin Franklin. On the other hand, if industrialization is slow and state-controlled, if the traditional social organization persists for a long time, then burgher intellectuals are more likely to concentrate attention exclusively upon the rights of the learned. They will seek to constitute a kind of nobility of the educated to supersede the "merely traditional" ruling class, and they will try to establish a system of educational certificates which can testify to the bearers' position as men of intellect. Their leaders at the universities will speak for all graduates in demanding that public affairs be put increasingly into the hands of the educated few, rather than being managed by the untrained and intellectually as well as morally backward nobles.

Politically, it is the gradual transformation of an essentially feudal state into a heavily bureaucratic monarchy which favors the development of a strong and self-conscious mandarin elite. Practically all of the early mandarins are associated with the state administration in one way or another. There is not much room for purely private lawyers, and even the university professors are state officials. Much of the elite's history is therefore the history of a bureaucracy. A ruler who is trying to reduce the power of the traditional aristocracy has to create a more or less rational system of government, so that he can effectively extend his control into areas formerly under a regime of customary privilege. He therefore has good reason to support an emerging caste of non-noble officials, whose burgher antecedents, proven intelligence, and thorough training make them useful allies against the old nobility. The reforming monarch will hasten to cooperate with the most highly educated among his subjects to their mutual advantage. He will lend financial support to the institutions of higher learning and give his official sanction to an ever more complete and rigorous system of civil service examinations. The university professors, who control the whole configuration of qualifying standards, will find their prestige and influence increased, as will academic graduates generally. Gradually, a recognized and well-defined mandarin elite will thus advance to a position of real importance in the life of their nation.

Early in their history, as long as they are a small and relatively weak group in comparison with the nobles, the mandarins are forced to keep their own social and economic demands to a minimum. The civil servants among them are satisfied with the role of scribes in the lower ranks of the administration, content to proclaim their loyalty to the person of the prince and to display an outward deference to their aristocratic superiors. As their infiltration of the bureaucratic system increases the ruler's dependence upon them, however, they manage to fortify their position in a variety of ways. They are able to convert their administrative titles into honorific ones. Military, hereditary, and bureaucratic ranks begin to be related to each other in such a way that certain positions on one scale are recognized as equivalent to stated points on the other scales. Contacts with the traditional ruling class, even to the point of intermarriage, become possible.

Although the monarch still has a check on the loyalty of the new elite, partly because he pays their salaries, he soon discovers that the mandarins are quite prepared to use their growing bargaining power even against him. For one thing, they dare to oppose his ideal of higher education. He wants his universities to be no more than institutes for the production of useful and preferably humble administrative assistants. He has a very down-to-earth notion of practical learning. Theories that are not immediately applicable make him suspicious, although he does not mind hearing that his professors are teaching some sound and straightforward doctrine of active piety and political morality. The mandarins, on the other hand, grow tired of the purely technical role assigned to them in this scheme. Their personal and social aspirations extend beyond the standing of lower-class experts or scribes. They demand to be recognized as a sort of spiritual nobility, to be raised above the class of their origins by their learning. They think of themselves as broadly cultured men, and their ideal of personal "cultivation" affects their whole conception of learning. Seeking spiritual ennoblement from education, they tend to reject "merely practical" knowledge and the pursuit of morally and emotionally neutral techniques of analysis. Instead, they regard learning as a process in which contact with venerated sources results in the absorption of their spiritual content, so that an indelible quality of spiritual elevation is conferred upon the student. In short, as the mandarins become more powerful, their intellectual leaders turn against the rather narrow ideological platform from which they started, replacing it with an ideal of learning which can function as an honorific substitute for nobility of birth. Much as their ruler may regret the emergence of a new set of pretensions among originally humble servants of the crown, he must resign himself to the inevitable, for he needs these men as much as ever.

Concurrently with their revision of academic ideology, the mandarin intellectuals tend to develop a complex of theories to defend and to increase the elite's share in the management of the state, partly at the expense of the monarch. Thus they launch a concerted attack upon "arbitrary" government in the name of legality. They insist that government should no longer be considered a private affair between princes and aristocrats, nor the dominion the ruler's property. To combat these notions, they create the idea of an abstract and rational state which "runs itself" according to fixed and logical principles and which stands above both rulers and ruled. Their inclination in this respect is natural, for it is they who will ultimately be in a position to interpret the reason and law of the state. They supply an ever growing portion of the state officials, and the more rational and complicated administrative processes become, the more it is the mandarin bureaucrats who come to execute the abstract will of reasonable government in practice. It is the prince's purely personal rule, his unpredictable whim, that is the real target of their attack.

Legality interests the mandarins not only in their capacity as officials but also in their role as private citizens. They prefer to distinguish between a public and a private sphere of law. While urging that the state proceed even in the public sphere only according to fixed and logical principles, they also demand that it interfere in the private sphere as little as possible. In every respect, they are naturally staunch defenders of private civic rights and liberties, and in this they champion the cause of all their countrymen. This is not to say, however, that they have a strong inclination to sponsor the extension of purely political rights or to advocate anything approximating popular participation in government. They are, after all, a minority. In a voting situation, in which policy might become a sort of arithmetical compromise between the interests of various groups, they would carry little weight. They have a much better chance to make their influence felt from within a monarchical government, as long as it remains "legal" and they its guardians and interpreters. For that reason, they prefer to argue that the state should stand far above the interests of any individual, even those of the ruler. How could it follow the behests of particular interests without descending from that sphere of absolute law in which, in the mandarins' view and for their sake, it definitely must stay? And what would be the point of opposing a government of pure law?

Along with this doctrine of political legality, the mandarins develop an even more subtle rationalization of their claims upon the state. Their argument takes the following general form. As long as government merely administers its territory, even legally, it is no more than a machine, a superficial and purely organizational device without soul or higher end. It can inspire loyalty only so long as it pleases everyone. It has no hold on the past or the future; it is a shabby thing without claim to historic greatness, without the right to ask men to die for it. If interests of a more conventional sort cannot influence it, then it must have a greater, a moral and cultural goal. Its existence, and its expansion, can be justified only through the cultural and spiritual values which flourish under its care. No more than a vessel by itself, it must have content; and the more valuable the content, the greater the state's right to assert itself at home and abroad.

If we compare this theory with the legality doctrine, we notice that the two are not particularly closely related in a logical way. As expressions of the mandarins' position, as rationalizations of their political and cultural purposes, however, they complement each other very nicely. The demand that the state should embody a fixed and rational law derives especially from the strong bureaucratic wing of the elite and could be reconciled with a relatively humble civil servant's notion of practical learning. The doctrine of cultural content, on the other hand, enlarges the elite's more advanced claim upon a broader, cultural leadership. It argues that the state derives its legitimacy not from divine right, for that would stress the prince's whim, nor from the interests of the subjects, for that would suggest a voting procedure, but exclusively from its services to the intellectual and spiritual life of the nation. It clearly follows that government must give material aid to the cultural and educational program of the elite and that it must do so without demanding an immediate practical return. The whole argument may actually be considered an extension of the notion that learning means spiritual "cultivation." In contrast to the theory of legality, it corresponds especially closely to the desires of the elite's intellectual wing. The argument is accompanied by a defense of the freedom of learning and teaching, a defense which is primarily designed to combat the ruler's meddling in favor of a narrowly useful education. The spirit flourishes only in freedom, according to the argument; and its achievements, though not immediately felt, are actually the life-blood of the nation. Only "pure" learning can bring forth those cultural values that justify the very existence of government. To put it perhaps a little polemically, the state lives neither for the ruler nor for the ruled as a whole; it lives for and through the "men of culture" and their learning.

Together, the doctrines of legality and of cultural content make up the ideology of a mandarin elite that has arrived at maturity. In some ways, it seems hard to imagine that any monarch could agree to accept its terms. Since the mandarins are in control of the educational system, they dominate the very language of their nation. They greatly influence its political and social standards, and they reserve the right to announce the cultural purposes of the state. In theory at least, they constitute a potential danger for the ruler, since they need only declare his government a hindrance to culture in order to refute its claims upon popular obedience. In practice, of course, their power is not that immediate, and the ruler is not entirely helpless against them. He does need their services as administrators; but he also pays their salaries. Even in education, the state can maintain a certain degree of quiet influence upon the ideology of teachers through a host of specific arrangements dealing with salaries, promotions, and the like. In addition, the ruler can encourage loyalty among the mandarins by bestowing title and rank upon men he considers reliable.

Actually, open warfare between the mandarins and their rulers is not very likely, as long as government remains appropriately "legal," retains some degree of respect for private civic liberties, avoids excessive tampering with the freedoms of thought and learning, and makes at least a mild effort to champion the cause of national culture. In the normal course of events, both the elite and the monarch derive advantages from cooperation. They may even come to join in mutual resistance to popular forces threatening to disturb their equilibrium from below. After all, the elite needs official sanction for its all-important system of qualifying examinations and for its prestigious social position generally. In return, the ruler may expect a supply of loyal and capable civil servants and an ideological defense of a regime which he actually shares with the mandarins.

Thus all will go well for the mandarins until economic conditions around them change radically enough to introduce powerful new groups upon the social scene. As full industrialization and urbanization is approached, wealthy entrepreneurs and industrial workers are likely to challenge the leadership of the cultured elite. Sentiment in favor of a popular reform of government will grow in strength and achieve some victories. Political groups, even whole ideologies, will come to compete with the older traditions. Struggle as they will, the mandarins are likely to find their influence upon public affairs reduced. Party leaders, capitalists, and technicians will usurp their leadership. Not even the educational system will be exempt from attack. Ever growing numbers of students will come to the universities for "some sort of an education," and they will want to study such practical subjects as journalism and machine building, rather than Latin and metaphysics. The traditional schooling of the elite, designed to turn out true mandarins, heroes and symbols of a broad and mildly esoteric culture, will no longer seem practical enough to modernists. All kinds of utilitarian considerations will be brought forward to advance the cause of technology. Some of the mandarin intellectuals themselves may unwittingly slide into forsaking spiritually meaningful learning for the more certain rewards of specialization and routine research.

Clearly, the mandarins will be in danger of being ignored altogether. Their future will depend upon their ability to translate their ideology into the language of their modern competitors. If they fail to find the basis for an alliance with the new social groups, defeat will come to them in one way or another. Perhaps they will be left to express in isolation their horror of a streamlined and, they will say, shallow and materialistic age. Perhaps they will stage a rebellion in their fashion. In either case, their fate will be of a kind to interest historians.

1

THE SOCIAL AND INSTITUTIONAL BACKGROUND

Throughout the eighteenth and early nineteenth centuries, Germany was suspended in a phase of economic development which especially England traversed much more rapidly. In 1846, the Prussian coal fields, including those in the Ruhr and Saar regions, raised 3.2 million English tons of coal per year. France produced a third again as much, Belgium a great deal more; the city of London alone consumed more coal than Prussia could mine. In 1815, the twelve towns that were later to become the largest in Imperial Germany had only about 50 percent more inhabitants than Paris alone. By 1850, the more rapid growth of Paris had further narrowed that gap. As late as 1871, when the industrial boom had finally begun in

Germany, some 64 percent of Germans lived in communities of less than 2000 inhabitants.[1]

In an economic environment of this type, a strong entrepreneurial bourgeoisie could not develop. It is often thought that this circumstance helps to account for the absence of a virile tradition of middleclass liberalism in nineteenth-century Germany. British intellectuals, it is argued or implied, had their roots in an independent industrial elite, so that Anglo-American liberalism may be considered an extension or sublimation of entrepreneurial utilitarianism and laisserfaire economics. German deviations from the liberal norm may be traced to the fact that the German intellectuals did not benefit from the auspicious social contacts of their English counterparts.

This kind of reasoning undoubtedly has a certain validity; but two things, at least, are wrong with it. First, it treats English developments as a norm, whereas the context in which English industrialization took place actually appears anything but standard when compared with the subsequent experiences of the rest of the world. Secondly, and this is more important, the argument fails to make any positive assertions about the social environment which the German intellectuals did face; it tells us nothing about their origins and connections, their sources of income, and their status.

THE ORIGINS OF THE EDUCATED MIDDLE CLASS, 1700–1820

Non-nobles who sought an improved social position in eighteenth-century Germany began by getting as much education as they could afford. They then entered one of the state bureaucracies, the clergy, the teaching profession, or the fields of medicine or law, always on a subordinate level to begin with.[2] Once installed in a learned profession, they naturally encouraged their offspring to make further advances along the same route. Since universities and schools were state institutions, churches were partially state supervised, and even lawyers commonly needed official connections, a kind of noneconomic middle class was thus created which centered upon the universities on the one hand and the civil service on the other.

The new elite showed an inclination from the start to separate itself from the status of peasants and craftsmen and to seek a special position within the traditional estate system. In the ancient Imperial Town of Frankfurt on the Main in 1731, the "graduated," including doctors, lawyers, and syndics, were members of the highest-ranking of five estates, together with the most important officials.[3] In late-eighteenth-century Weimar too, the highly educated were members of a minute upper class, which was closely associated with the life of the court.[4] The Prussian General Code of 1794 did not treat the holders of academic degrees and members of learned occupations as a distinct elite.[5] It proceeded through the definitions of the noble, the burgher, and the peasant estates, describing a burgher as one who was neither a noble nor a peasant. But having devoted successive titles to the traditional triad, it followed immediately with a title on "the servants of the state." It left no doubt that this important group had duties and privileges which set its members apart from the rank and file of the estate from which they came. A new division of society by profession and education thus came to run parallel to the traditional stratification by birth.

By the end of the eighteenth century, when the General Code was published, Prussian officials had long ceased to be humble servants of an all-powerful ruler.[6] They had assimilated progressive elements from the aristocracy in the reign of Frederick the Great, gaining in strength and prestige under a monarch who acknowledged himself the "servant of the state." Their power was based upon their growing esprit de corps and upon their mastery of administrative techniques in an increasingly cumbersome government apparatus. Especially after 1786, under Frederick's less energetic successors, they showed themselves increasingly determined and able to "interpret" the ruler's general decrees as they thought best.

During much of the eighteenth century, Prussian officials were educated principally at the University of Halle.[7] Founded in 1694, this institution achieved a unique place in the intellectual life of eighteenth-century Germany, because it broke most emphatically with scholastic traditions in higher learning. Under the influence of Christian Thomasius and later of Christian Wolff, Halle emphasized the modern secular knowledge of the day. Cameralistics, the primitive science of administration and statecraft, was taught. Thomasius broke precedent by lecturing in German and did not mind describing how to write a good letter. He thought it the main task of philosophy to "advance the worldly practical purposes of men and the benefit of society."[8] His interest was accordingly focused upon the new discoveries and theories in geography, politics, mathematics, and the natural sciences. The "rational" philosophy disseminated by Thomasius and by Wolff was eminently suited to the needs and interests of future officials. Wolff's most ambitious operations with the principle of sufficient reason did get him into difficulty with Frederick William I of Prussia, who was conventionally pious and instinctively suspicious of complicated theories. On a lower level of discourse, however, there could be no permanent conflict between the common-sense rationality of the new philosophy and the emerging system of bureaucratic monarchy.

In the reign of Frederick the Great, the jurists Samuel von Cocceji and Heinrich von Carmer worked on the codification of Prussian law and tried to make possible a clearer separation of the public and private spheres of law.[9] As Hans Rosenberg points out, the distinction could really arise only in a situation in which the unchecked will of the sovereign, made operative by a completely devoted bureaucracy, had come to assert itself as public law against the customary privileges once upheld by the feudal estates. The new elite of civil servants had every incentive to support an autocratic ruler against the sphere of aristocratic tradition and "corruption." And the new law was other than arbitrary only in the sense that it was presumably consistent, that it placed certain implicit limits upon the ruler's right to contradict himself. Nevertheless, once having established the monarchy's power to override aristocratic privilege, the bureaucratic elite naturally wished to make both public and private law as regular, predictable, and rational as possible. In the newly defined sphere of private law, codification provided the ordinary burgher with a certain minimal security. In the public sphere, fixed rules of procedure strengthened the officials' own position as expert agents and interpreters of an orderly system. Altogether, it seems reasonable to see at least a natural affinity between the bureaucrats' search for predictability and the philosophic rationalism of the Halle tradition.

Along with the officials, a good many Protestant theologians and pastors received their higher education at Halle, where they came under the influence of Pietist doctrines. Indeed, the Pietism of Jakob Spener and Hermann Francke was as important an early influence upon the university as the rationalism of Thomasius and Wolff. On occasion, there were serious conflicts between the two sets of ideas; but there were substantial areas of agreement as well. The Pietists too were opposed to the formalism of the old scholastic education. Their emphasis, at least at the outset, was less upon doctrinal orthodoxy than upon inner conversion and practical charity. Thus they could sympathize with some of the rationalists' reforming zeal, even if they differed with them over the ultimate objectives of the new learning. The Pietists had a strong sense of the value and sanctity of the individual soul. To them, education meant the fullest possible development of that soul, the careful unfolding of each child's unique potential for salvation.

The idea that education should further the autonomous and integral growth of a unique personality was widely current among German educational reformers of the eighteenth century. Jean-Jacques Rousseau and Heinrich Pestalozzi, Bernhard Basedow and the "philanthropic" movement, only emphasized a theme which was never entirely absent from the pedagogical literature of that time. Through German neohumanism, this theme was adapted to the field of higher learning.[10] At the University of Göttingen, founded in 1734, the neohumanist revival began around the middle of the century. In part, it was a reaction against the rationalists' neglect of philology and classical studies. It also involved a perennial concern of German educators: the objection to the senseless and mechanical drilling of Latin vocabulary in secondary schools. Far from wishing to abandon the old languages, however, the reformers sought a more total and meaningful contact with the classical sources. Greek studies were relatively more popular with them than Roman history or Latin philology. They hoped that a feeling for the aesthetic harmony of the Greek personality and of Greek art would revitalize German learning. Joachim Winckelmann's work on Greek art furthered the cause, as did Gottfried von Herder's plea for an integral comprehension of the Greek spirit as a counterweight to French and Roman traditions.

To live with the classics at Göttingen was plainly to reject the practical rationalism of Halle, and the neohumanists embued their educational program with a certain antiutilitarian bias from the start.[11] There object was the full and harmonious training of the whole individual, the forming of aesthetically pleasing, "cultivated" personalities. Learning clearly entailed more than intellectual training in their view. Contact with the revered sources of antiquity was meant to transform the learner's whole character, to make him a new man. Undoubtedly, the neohumanists were motivated by the pure love of their subject. But their ideals, or the results they achieved with students, were not without social implications. W. H. Bruford notes that it was only with the renewal of humanistic studies at the universities that academic training became a fairly certain source of social distinction.[12] Classical learning, because it was held to elevate the whole personality and perhaps because of its very impracticality, was apparently capable of enhancing a man's status as well as his self-respect.

A passage in Goethe's *Wilhelm Meister* shows the hero in a painful dilemma.[13] He feels that a certain natural assurance, a truly dignified bearing, is possible only for the aristocrat, the man of the world and of affairs. One does not ask such a man what technical skills he possesses. Only the little burgher is forced to answer such blunt questions. For the upperclass gentleman, what counts is what he is, not what he can do. Goethe's hero is not a nobleman; but he has a profound longing for full personal self-development. He realizes that the traditional organization of his society will prevent him from achieving this aim, and his only possible escape is to go on the stage. In the artificial setting of the theater, he can at least approach his ideal in a modified form by trying on roles. The antithesis established in this fictional anecdote throws much light upon the whole situation of the burgher intellectual in eighteenth-century Germany. It also begins to suggest how classical, impractical "cultivation" could come to have a social meaning.

The non-noble bureaucrat in Prussia represented an extreme which was equaled nowhere else in Europe. The German Protestant pastor too was unique in some ways. But the most unusual figure on the European social scene during the eighteenth century was the German scholar, the man of pure learning. He had less connection than his English or even his French counterpart with an emerging entrepreneurial class; he also lacked the French intellectual's contact with the cosmopolitan world of aristocratic or magisterial salons. Separated at once from the class of petty burgher artisans and from a relatively uncivilized feudal caste, he developed an intense faith in the spiritually ennobling power of the word and an equally strong sense of its impotence in the practical sphere of technique and organization. Even Goethe sometimes doubted the possibility of socially and politically ameliorative action within the confines of a petty German state.

There was intellectual protest in eighteenth-century Germany; but its focus was upon the eternal problems of the human condition, even when it dealt by implication with the contemporary short-comings of German social arrangements. That men were treated as means, not as ends, and that the intellectually and spiritually richest individual weighed little in the scales of arbitrary power and bar-baric convention: that was the recurrent lament in eighteenth-century German literature, moral philosophy, and social theory. The remedies proposed entailed a partial withdrawal from the existing situation as well as a total revolt against it. The themes were always the same: Pure learning, the absolutely disinterested con-templation of the good and the true, is the principal vocation of man. He best serves humanity who cultivates his own spirit to the fullest possible extent; for the world has no purpose and reality itself, no meaning apart from the creative labor of the human mind and spirit. Compared to this work, everything else—the practical knowledge of everyday life, the details of social organization, and the accidents of worldly rank and station—is insignificant.

The great German poets, the neohumanists, and the Idealist philosophers of the late eighteenth century were deeply committed to these ideas.[14] Perhaps no group of men has ever proclaimed the worth of personal culture more fervently than such Idealists as Wilhelm von Humboldt and Friedrich von Schiller. At the court of Weimar and at the nearby University of Jena, a brilliant decade and a half brought together some of the leading figures of the German cultural revival. Schiller lectured at Jena in 1789; Gottlieb Fichte became a professor there in 1794; F. W. J. Schelling and Friedrich Hegel also began their teaching careers at Jena around this time. These men exalted the calling of the pure intellectual with much pride and some pathos. They were priests of the new Idealist philosophy, and later generations of Germans inevitably saw them as a new aristocracy of "cultivation" (*Bildung*). It would be silly to discover no more in their doctrines than a social situation and a social message; but it would also be wrong to insist that the ideal of pure learning had exclusively logical origins.

A difficulty for the mandarin hypothesis seems to arise from the fact that the three major groups within the eighteenth-century elite of the highly educated differed from each other in their experiences and in their ideologies. The Protestant pastor derived his authority from his religious mission and shared the Pietists' faith in the value of the emerging soul. The bureaucrat made his way on the basis of his special administrative skills and upheld the ideal of rationality and predictability in politics. The humanist scholar and the Idealist philosopher lived the life and preached the honor of impractical learning and cultivation. These differences of emphasis were noticeable in the eighteenth century, and they were never to become entirely irrelevant even during the nineteenth and twentieth centuries. On the other hand, the three groups also had much in common from the start. They met at the universities; they all based their aspirations upon the new higher education, and their pedagogical ideals were capable of reconciliation. After all, a future pastor, even a future administrator, could and often did read the classics or study Idealist philosophy during his stay at one of the new universities. Pietists and rationalists did not always get along too badly at Halle, and there was also a remarkable similarity of tone between Pietist and neohumanist conceptions of spiritual development through education. Idealist philosophy itself resembled an incompletely secularized Protestantism. As for the bureaucrat, he might indeed continue to claim special expertise on the basis of his practical training in cameralistics; but there was nothing to prevent him from simultaneously seeking the status conferred by classical or philosophical cultivation. This might help him to move from the position of the scribe toward that of the aristocratic states-man, who is asked what he is, not what he can do. Some of this is speculation; but the facts do suggest that in the hostile environment of eighteenth-century Germany, the various segments of the educated upper middle class drew together, and that something like a homogeneous ideology of the cultivated emerged from this process.

There is ample evidence of such a fusion even in the field of institutional and legal history, particularly for the years between about 1790 and 1820. These three decades witnessed a whole series of interrelated developments which jointly established a firm basis for the new elite's predominant role in nineteenth-century German social and intellectual life. In 1791, Prussia introduced regular civil service examinations, together with legal security of tenure for officials.[15] Other German states took similar steps during the late eighteenth and early nineteenth centuries. The examinations strengthened the position of educated but low-born administrators against poorly trained aristocrats, and tightened the bond between the universities and the civil service. In Prussia, according to Rosenberg, this was the period of "bureaucratic absolutism," in which the administrative elite achieved its greatest autonomy and influence. A liberal official of the 1840's described the government organization that now emerged as "a system of rulership by career bureaucrats peculiar to the Prussian state, in which the king appears to be the top functionary who invariably selects his aides from the intellectual elite of the nation, recognized as such by means of truly or allegedly rigorous examinations. He allows them great independence, acknowledges thereby their corulership and, consequently, sanctions a sort of aristocracy of experts who purport to be the true representatives of the general interest."[16]

In 1794, the Prussian General Code was finally promulgated. It did not establish any sort of civic equality; nor did it list political rights in the manner of modern constitutions. But its ordering of all classes' rights and duties in the form of properly general maxims, together with its abstract language and rational tone, made it extremely popular with the educated minority of Germans.[17] For Prussian officials, the code brought a new and systematic certification of special prerogatives and obligations. For Prussian education, it provided a basic legal framework which was to remain in force until the advent of National Socialism.[18]

Schools and universities, the code asserted, were state institutions and could be established only with official permission. The universities were guaranteed the right to manage their own purely academic affairs in accordance with special corporation charters; but the ultimate supervision and control of higher education, together with its financial support, remained with the state. The question was how immediately that control was to be exercised and how directly the teaching program of the universities was to be adjusted to the practical needs of the government. In the late 1780's and the 1790's, Prussian censorship repeatedly interfered with the freedoms of thought on an all too immediate level, especially in the name of Protestant orthodoxy. This provoked a revolt among the leading intellectuals which lasted until 1810. Before 1806, much of the stimulus for protest came from the University of Jena, then at the height of its glory as the home of the new philosophy. After 1806, the Prussia of the reform period provided the main setting, and plans for a new university at Berlin moved to the center of the stage.

In a series of programmatic memoranda, Kant, Schelling, Fichte, F. E. D. Schleiermacher, and Humboldt developed their ideal of academic freedom.[19] Idealist, neohumanist, and even Pietist motifs were united in their writings. The universities, they argued, were not to be mere training schools for officials, as Halle had been. The arts faculty (*philosophische Fakultät*), not those of law, medicine, or theology, should be at the heart of the new university. Pure learning in the Idealist sense was to be cultivated for its own sake. The state was to support this great objective without trying to exercise direct control over the materials learned and taught. The universities might continue to train future officials and teachers; but they would undertake even this task in the spirit of philosophic cultivation, not in a narrowly utilitarian way. In the long run, the state and society would surely benefit from the spiritual and moral influence of the new learning.

Ever since the late 1770's, Prussia had been gradually reorganizing and centralizing its administrative apparatus in the field of higher education. This process was completed during the period of reform which followed upon Prussia's defeat at the hands of Napoleon.[20] In 1809, Wilhelm von Humboldt himself was called to take charge of a newly created Section for Culture and Education within the Prussian Ministry of the Interior. In 1817, this section became the independent Ministry of Culture.* In accordance with a regulation of 1801, the universities were henceforth under the direct control of this ministry, which also carried out the greatly increased supervision of the central government over the secondary schools. In 1810, a state examination for teachers at secondary schools was introduced. This qualifying examination further reduced the influence of churches and local patrons upon the institutions of higher learning; it raised the status of secondary teachers to that of a learned estate, and it increased the influence of the universities by establishing, in effect, that secondary school teachers required a full course of scholarly training at the universities. Ever since 1788, graduate examinations had been given at certain secondary schools. In 1812, a thorough revision and regulation of these tests fixed the normal course of preparation for university study. The *Abitur*, as this graduate qualifying examination came to be called, was given only at those institutions that taught a full complement of Latin and Greek. Secondary schools accredited in this way now rose above

---

* *Kultusministerium* in unofficial usage; officially in Prussia from 1817 to 1918: *Ministerium der geistlichen, Unterrichts- und Medizinalangelegenheiten.*

ordinary Latin schools and took on the character of pre-universities. They were given the name "gymnasium," and their increasingly standardized classical curriculum began to emerge as a prerequisite for many important offices and a conventional measure of cultivation.

The crowning achievement of the Prussian reform period in the field of education was the establishment of a new university in Berlin. It opened in 1810 and received its statutes in 1816. Fichte was its first rector, and many of the leading neohumanists and Idealists were among its sponsors and early faculty members. Within the limits imposed by the General Code and ultimate state control, the Berlin statutes embodied the ideals of the reformers.[21] Throughout the nineteenth and early twentieth centuries, the internal organization of Berlin University came to serve as a model for all German institutions of higher learning. As new universities were founded and as older ones moved or changed their statutes, the example of Berlin exerted a tremendous influence.[22] Each of the several German states continued to administer its own separate educational system; there was no legal or formal centralization in this field until the National Socialists came to power. On the other hand, there was also very little precise and systematic legislation on matters of education in any of the German states during the nineteenth century.[23] As a result, the various governments exercised their extensive rights of supervision through a mass of ad-hoc regulations and administrative precedents. While this procedure tended to strengthen the initiative of the bureaucracy in education, it also left room for the informal influence of revered institutional and intellectual antecedents. This is how the statutes of Berlin and all the other ideas and innovations of the Prussian reform period came to be the basic pattern for a fairly homogeneous system of higher education in nineteenth-century Germany.

EDUCATION AND SOCIETY, 1820–1890

In the 1820's and 1830's, the educational innovations of the reform period were consolidated in Prussia and elsewhere in Germany.[24]

The *Abitur* regulation of 1812 had not been decisive, since it had not done away with entrance examinations at the universities. Students who could not graduate from a gymnasium had thus been left with an alternate route to the universities. This path was essentially closed in 1834 when admissions tests at the universities were canceled altogether. The curriculum of the Prussian gymnasium was more and more precisely defined during these years, and the rest of the German states adapted their own secondary school systems to the Prussian model. All over Germany, barriers rose between the privileged gymnasiums and the old Latin secondary schools. The Latin schools came to be variously labeled burgher schools, town schools, or modern schools (*Realschulen*), and it became their task to train young people for clerical and technical positions in commerce and industry. While they generally taught some Latin, they gave more curricular emphasis than the gymasiums to such "realistic"—meaning nonclassical—subjects as mathematics and the natural sciences, German and the modern foreign languages. In 1832, many of the realschulen were given the right to give graduation examinations and certificates of their own; but the holders of these nonclassical degrees were not entitled to enroll at a university or to take any of the important state examinations.

The formal elevation of the gymnasium above the rest of the secondary schools was but the beginning of a tragic process in which the ideals of the reform period were gradually routinized and transformed into defenses of social privilege. Rigid curricular specifications took the place of neohumanist enthusiasm. The theoretical claims of "cultivation" became demands for official preferment. A gulf began to open between the highly learned and the rest of the nation, and pedagogical controversies became political conflicts. Worried about signs of political and cultural unrest during the 1840's, the Prussian Ministry of Culture was particularly suspicious of the realschulen. It regarded them as the foremost breeding grounds of a dangerous tendency toward materialism, irreligiosity, and revolution.[25] A few classical philologists and gymnasium supporters shared this official opinion, arguing that the modern curriculum elevated the useful above the beautiful, reason above faith, and change above respect for authority. At the scholarly congresses of the 1840's, there were occasional outbursts by classicists against the contentious "spirit of the age" and its vulgar practicality.[26] On the whole, educated and propertied Germans stood together during the 1840's against the repressive policies of their governments. But the signs of future divisions had already begun to show themselves.

"The Revolution provided an opportunity for all hitherto repressed or suppressed tendencies, including those in the field of higher education."[27] That is Friedrich Paulsen's comment upon a whole cluster of teachers' conferences and school reform projects which sprang up in 1848. In an overwhelmingly optimistic atmosphere, some very thorough changes were proposed, and it is significant that these recommendations had the air of "democratic" attacks upon a conservative establishment. There was dissatisfaction with the exclusive concentration upon Latin at the gymnasium. It was proposed that Greek and especially German receive more attention. The cause of the nonclassical subjects, of modernism or "realism" in secondary education, was vigorously defended. According to one scheme, all secondary schools were to be integrated in such a way that their curriculum would be uniform for at least three years. Graduates of realschulen were to be admitted to the universities. It was recommended that the training, salary, and status of primary school teachers be improved, so that the gap between primary and secondary education would be reduced. Teachers in all schools wanted more freedom to vary the standard curriculum according to their own inclinations. Even the lower-ranking university lecturers demanded reforms. They sought a revision of their economic position, quicker and more regular advancement, and a more important role in academic self-government.

Unfortunately, the objectives of the education conferences of 1848 were not realized. Article 26 of the Prussian Constitution of 1850 did announce a general reform of the school system; but the promise was never kept.[28] The storm of revolution passed, and the subsequent political reaction made itself felt in the field of education too. The realschulen were especially unpopular with the restored governments. Looking back upon the events of 1848, obscurantist officials were more convinced than ever that modernism in education was among the most dangerous enemies of religion and authority. While the gymnasium henceforth enjoyed the position of an official favorite, the nonclassical schools were treated harshly indeed. In the mid-1850's, Prussia denied them the right to send their graduates to the institutes of mining and construction and put them at a serious disadvantage even in the competition for places in the postal service. In 1859, during the brief and seemingly liberal promise of the "New Era," there was a slight upturn in the fortunes of the realschulen.[29] They were organized into several classes according to curriculum, and their graduates were allowed at least to audit lectures at the universities in a few special subjects. But it was not until late in the nineteenth century that the modern curriculum began to achieve any real successes in its battle against the monopoly position of the gymnasium.

The technical institutes (*Technische Hochschulen*) were natural allies of the realschulen in this conflict.[30] They had their earliest antecedents in the eighteenth century; but even the rudimentary economic and technological advances of the 1840's brought them only minor gains in enrollment and accreditation. After the mid-1860's, however, they were ready to begin their own difficult and drawn-out quest for academic standing. Graduating from their earlier status of advanced vocational schools, they began to call themselves "polytechnical" and finally "technical" institutes, simultaneously attempting to move toward something like equality with the universities. In this effort, they met considerable opposition from the traditional champions of pure and impractical learning. Technical institutes could not confer doctoral degrees until late in the century. To some extent, they provided an outlet for the talents of students from nonclassical secondary schools; but this circumstance in turn subjected them to the disdain and the disabilities faced by the modernists in secondary education.

Since the Revolution of 1848, there had been a steady increase in the hostility of gymnasium supporters for the realschulen. The attacks on the modern curriculum, which became ever more frequent toward the end of the century, showed how thoroughly the classical ideal had become entangled with political conservatism and social snobbery. The animus against practicality sometimes reached absurd proportions. One gymnasium instructor supported the teaching of Latin on the grounds that it "accustoms students not to regard language training as a means to the end of palavering, which is what would almost invariably happen if one started with French." The nonclassical schools were condemned as *Nützlichkeitskramschulen,* which means "schools of useful junk" or "junky usefulness" as near as one can make out. The gymnasium was said to represent "German ideality," whereas modernism was identified with the "petty practicality of the French [*wälsche Anstelligkeit*]." The "realists," it was hinted, were motivated by a coarse concern with worldly gain and advantage. "Idealism" was the very "principle" of the gymnasium, the principle of the realschulen being "usefulness in the vulgar sense" and "profitableness for everyday life." In the 1850's, a particularly determined classicist warned of the danger to throne and altar from "the exclusive direction of the mind toward the concrete . . . that utilitarianism which proceeds from materialism and ends in materialism." By the 1870's and 1880's, the stiffening competition for places in the civil service and in the free professions had further aggravated existing antagonisms, and the conflict between classicism and modernism in secondary education had assumed the character of a class war. The nonclassical schools were still primarily the preserves of the lower middle class. On the other hand, it was eminently clear by now that gymnasium cultivation was an upper-class trait. Influential associations of professional men and civil servants absolutely refused to admit that graduates of modern secondary schools might be qualified to enter their vocations. Paulsen traced such attitudes to "the socially aristocratic tendency of the age." A particularly violent critic of modernism in secondary education claimed that the realschulen were able to assert themselves only when a "few dubious theoreticians" attracted the support of "a part of the burgher class and of a seeming liberalism which revels in utopias" and when "this whole intellectual demimonde set out to destroy the aristocracy of intelligence."[31]

As of about 1885, the segmentation of the educational system probably had more to do with German social stratification than any other factor. Even at that time, the vast majority of German children went to school for only eight years and spent all those years at the primary schools, the so-called *Volksschulen*.[32] There they were taught reading, writing, arithmetic, and religion under a regime of the most rigorous discipline. They were destined to be useful as producers, as soldiers, and as docile subjects. They were prepared exclusively for "the practical duties of everyday life."[33] It was not expected that they would try to get a higher education. Some of them went to six-year teachers' preparatory institutes or seminars in order to become elementary teachers themselves. Others, not many, entered vocational schools. Occasionally a few primary school students transferred to one of the less exclusive secondary schools; but almost none of them ever reached a gymnasium or a university. Even their teachers came from the preparatory institutes and not from the regular secondary schools and universities, so that there was practically no contact at all between the elementary and the higher levels of the educational system. Primary school teachers were generally the offspring of small farmers, laborers, petty tradesmen, and shopkeepers. As late as the 1920's, they were painfully aware of unwritten laws which forbade them to move in the social circles frequented by secondary school faculty.[34]

The cost of advanced education around 1885 fell between 4000 and 8000 marks, which meant something in comparison to the average primary teacher's yearly salary of 1500 marks.[35] Still, the financial barriers between elementary and secondary education were probably less important than the social and cultural ones. The secondary schools enrolled their pupils at the age of nine or ten. In a few German states, it was theoretically possible to move from the third or fourth grade of an elementary school to a gymnasium. In reality, special preparatory schools (*Vorschulen*) supplied many of the candidates for admission to the gymnasium. It was nearly impossible to transfer from the higher classes of a primary school to a secondary school. Thus parents and teachers had to make essentially permanent educational plans for very young children, and this without the help of even moderately objective tests of aptitude. Inevitably, a "cultivated" family background often became the actual measure of the capacity for learning. If a merchant did decide to give his son a higher education, he might well be inclined to begin with a realschule. Even if the boy then showed unusual promise, success was not assured. For at this point, he encountered a second set of obstacles, which separated the realschulen from the main classical route to the universities.

The three main categories of secondary schools in Germany around 1885 were the gymnasium, the *Realgymnasium,* and the *Oberrealschule.** All three were nine-year institutions for boys, and teachers for all three were educated at the universities.[36] The gymnasium still devoted almost half of its curricular hours to Latin and Greek. The *Oberrealschule* did not teach the ancient languages at all. It spent about one third of its time on French and English, another third on mathematics and the natural sciences, about a sixth on German, and the rest on history, geography, and drawing. The *Realgymnasium,* as its name suggests, was a compromise. Its curriculum, which included Latin, French, and English, stood almost exactly in the middle between the extremes of the gymnasium and the *Oberrealschule.* By keeping its students in class for more than thirty-one hours per week, it still managed to squeeze in an average of nearly six hours of Latin every week for nine years. The *Realgymnasium* therefore had much more prestige and official support than the *Oberrealschule,* its foremost rival among the realschulen. Detailed and rigid curricular prescriptions made it practically impossible to transfer from one type of secondary school to another.

The differences of accreditation that distinguished the gymnasium from the two modern schools were part of a whole complex of official examinations and "privileges" which played an immensely impor-

---

* With each of these nine-year schools, a six-year version was associated, which may be counted with its parent, since the curriculum was similar for the first six years and transfers were possible. The six-year versions were the *Progymnasium, Realprogymnasium,* and *Realschule.*

tant role in the organization of German society.[37] A "privilege" (*Berechtigung*) was a right earned upon the completion of a specified curriculum. As of 1885, six years successfully spent at any secondary school brought the privilege of a shortened military obligation as a one-year volunteer, rather than a routine draftee. Entry into a forestry service or building institute, the right to become a higher official in the postal department or to enter the provincial bureaucracy on a certain rank level: these were privileges reserved for people who could certify a stated minimum education. It was a peculiarity of the system that the states, rather than the schools or universities, administered the most important examinations upon which the assigning of privileges was based. The secondary schools tested and graded their pupils regularly; but a student had only to pass the nine-year curriculum to be admitted to the examination for the *Abitur*. Standards for this examination were set by the state ministries of culture, whose representatives also supervised the actual testing of candidates.

Beginning in 1834, the German universities gave no entrance examinations and did not have the right to select a limited number of candidates from a list of applicants.[38] They did not supervise their students' programs of study, nor did they test or grade class performance. They had to enroll any applicant who had earned the privilege on the basis of the classical *Abitur,* and they seldom accepted people who did not have this all-important certification. Once registered, a student could prepare himself in whatever way he chose for the next step along the road of examinations and privileges. Usually, his first concern was to pass one of the standard state examinations and thus to earn the official "diploma" in his field of study.* As might be expected, admission to the state examination in a given subject was itself a significant privilege. Even matriculation at a university was of little use, from a practical or professional point of

---

* There were several types of state examinations of roughly equivalent level. Only the tests initially established for future secondary teachers were actually called *Staatsexamen*. Only the degree earned in the *Diplomprüfung* (on subjects not tested in the *Staatsexamen*, mostly technical fields) was actually called *Diplom*. Ignoring the complexities of the system, which were especially great in the fields of law and administration, I am using the terms state examination and diploma in a very general sense.

view, unless it was coupled with the right to take a set of government tests. That right was commonly reserved for those who had already earned the classical *Abitur*, who had been registered at a university for a minimum of three to five years, and who had signed up and paid fees for certain practically obligatory courses in their subject area. There were two purely academic degrees: the doctorate and the *venia legendi*. With the latter and higher of these two degrees, a man was qualified (*habilitiert*) to begin lecturing at a university, and both degrees were conferred by the competent university faculties alone. While students in most fields did tend to work for their diplomas before deciding whether or not to go on to the doctorate, there was no formal relationship at all between the academic degrees and the state examinations. The examinations were established and administered by whatever ministry was concerned with the qualification to be tested, although the competent university faculties were certainly consulted.

Every regulation that was introduced to confer a privilege or to set standards for a state examination inevitably had a certain effect upon the curriculum and the organization of German higher education. This was true to some extent even for the universities, where the standing of a given discipline in the pattern of course offerings could be changed by altered requirements for a government test. It made a difference whether or not future administrators in a certain branch of the service were asked to know some economics. It also mattered how the rudiments of the subject were defined for the purposes of the state examination. In secondary education, of course, the impact of the privilege system was even more immediate. Here the classical ideal was thoroughly entrenched as an official dogma. After 1870, graduates of the *Realgymnasium* were admitted to the state examinations for secondary school teachers of modern languages, mathematics, and natural sciences; but until 1886, even this concession was hedged about with the further provision that they could teach these subjects only at modern schools. Practically all other state examinations and privileges were reserved for gymnasium students. Even for positions in the lower ranks of the civil service, for which a state certificate was not required, the classical

Abitur was commonly preferred. In 1878, graduates of the *Oberreal-schule* who went on to study construction and machine building at the technical institutes had been admitted to the state examinations and positions in these subjects. In 1886, however, this privilege was taken away from them again, because state officials in the field of construction and machine building protested that the status of their calling would be lowered by the admission of graduates from completely nonclassical schools.[39]

Thus private and public concerns, social and institutional realities, came together to define a distinctive elite. The whole system of official tests and privileges was an outgrowth of the examinations for civil servants and secondary teachers which had originally been introduced during the crucial decades around 1800. The history of German higher education during the nineteenth century was intimately connected with the evolution of the German bureaucracy. At the same time, one must remember that a student's certified training as a public forester or building inspector could be useful to him even when looking for employment outside the civil service. Governments needed not only trained lawyers, but also health officials, postal clerks, chemistry teachers, railroad engineers, and other white-collar specialists. Besides, the states were naturally interested in maintaining standards in such fields as pharmacy and medicine. As a result, there was hardly an area or discipline in which some sort of state examination was not eventually devised. In an economic environment in which opportunities for the "self-made man" without formal training were relatively limited, the diploma offered a certain security. The free and learned professions absorbed much of the available middle-class talent. A species of private officials grew up side by side with the regular civil service. One is tempted to speak of a social fusion in which the administrative and professional classes drew together. The officials contributed aristocratic and bureaucratic values; but it was the academic ideology of "cultivation" that provided the most important bond between the various elements of the alliance. In the words of Max Weber, "differences of education are one of the strongest . . . social barriers, especially in Germany, where almost all privileged positions inside and outside the civil service are tied to qualifications involving not only specialized knowledge but also 'general cultivation' and where the whole school and university system has been put into the service of this [ideal of] general cultivation."[40] Paulsen agreed:

> The academically educated constitute a kind of intellectual and spiritual aristocracy in Germany . . . They form something like an official nobility, as indeed they all participate in the government and administration of the state . . . Together, they make up a homogeneous segment of society; they simply recognize each other as social equals on the basis of their academic cultivation . . . Conversely, anyone in Germany who has no academic education lacks something which wealth and high birth cannot fully replace. The merchant, the banker, the rich manufacturer or even the great landowner, no matter how well he stands in other respects, will occasionally be harmed by his lack of academic training. As a consequence, the acquisition of a university education has become a sort of social necessity with us, or at least the acquisition of the *Abitur*, the potential right of academic citizenship.[41]

Against this background, it is possible to appreciate the importance of the universities in German society around 1885. Their influence and the esteem in which they were held stemmed from their close connection with the bureaucracies, from their active participation in the system of state examinations and privileges, and from their traditional role as guardians of pure learning. Following the pattern established around 1800, the universities were financed and administered by the various ministries of culture, although curators sometimes acted as the governments' representatives on the campuses, and officially appointed university judges handled important legal matters at some institutions.[42] The three main academic ranks were those of the full professor (*ordentlicher Professor, Ordinarius*), the associate professor (*ausserordentlicher Professor, Extraordinarius*), and the instructor (*Privatdozent*).* Associate and

---

* Some less important distinctions made in faculty ranks include that between the *planmässiger* or *etatsmässiger* and the *ausserplanmässiger, nichtetatsmässiger*, or

full professors, like most secondary school teachers, were salaried government officials. As such, they were subject to prosecution for bearing unworthy of their position in private as well as in public life, the pertinent legal sources for Prussia being the General Code and the Disciplinary Law of 1852.[43] Full professors were the equals of councilors of state, fourth or even third class; university rectors ranked with councilors of state, second class; associate professors and many secondary school teachers were grouped with councilors of state, fifth class.[44] Instructors were not officials and did not receive regular salaries. In theory at least, their position entailed no more than a certain scholarly accreditation and the right to give "private" lectures in return for fees paid by their students.[45] During the course of the nineteenth century, instructors' places were more and more exclusively reserved for postdoctoral candidates who earned the *venia legendi* on the basis of a second dissertation.

The universities had the statutory right to manage their own purely academic affairs; but only full professors participated in the exercise of this partial autonomy. From among themselves, the professors at each institution elected a rector and a senate every year. Neither had anything like the powers of an American college president or faculty; but the rector did function as a general representative and spokesman for the university, and the senate ruled in matters of academic discipline. A somewhat more important role was filled by the traditional four faculties of philosophy (for arts and sciences), theology, law, and medicine. Each of these elected a dean to a more or less secretarial position for a one-year term. The faculties were responsible for providing appropriate combinations of lectures in their fields; they helped the governments in making up

---

persönlicher Professor. The former held a position for which a salary was officially set aside in the ministry's regular budget. An advanced instructor was sometimes nominally promoted to associate professor without being made a state official and without drawing a regular or permanent salary. In Prussia, he was then generally called a *Titularprofessor* or a *nichtbeamteter* (sometimes *unbesoldeter*) *ausserordentlicher Professor*; in southern Germany, the term *nichtetatsmässiger ausserordentlicher Professor* was used. A man thus betitled really played the role of an instructor, so that it is best to call him that. An unsalaried *Honorarprofessor* had a rank above that of the *Extraordinarius* but a position, in other respects, like that of the *Privatdozent*. He was often a specially appointed elderly authority on a minor field of study, and he sometimes did only part-time teaching.

the various state examinations; they gave the two purely academic degrees; and they looked after the careers of their instructors. Above all, the faculties had the initiative in the field of academic appointments. Whenever a faculty felt that it could not teach all the subjects under its jurisdiction with its regular staff, it could ask the ministry to create a new position, to which the government might then appoint a professor of its own choice. On the other hand, if an already established position had simply to be filled again, the faculty involved could suggest three scholars, in order of preference, as candidates for the vacancy. The ministry was pledged to consider these proposals; but it could also overrule them. Of 1355 men appointed to German faculties of theology, law, and medicine between 1817 and 1900, no less than 322 were placed against or without the faculties' recommendations.[46] Since up to three proposals were ignored in each of these cases, one may gather that the governments' prerogatives even in this department were by no means formalities only. The organs of academic self-government were relatively weak, especially in the executive department, and traditional invocations of the freedom of learning did nothing to change that.[47]

The income of a German university professor was derived from two sources.[48] He had a basic salary from the ministry. In addition, students paid fees when enrolling in his "private" lectures or after passing important qualifying examinations with him. During the nineteenth century, as enrollment increased and the distinction between private and unremunerated public lectures lost much of its original meaning, men who "privately" taught basic courses in popular fields could earn huge amounts from students' fees. As a result, regular salaries declined in relative importance, and differences between the incomes of professors became disturbingly large. Toward the end of the century, instructors generally survived on some 1500 marks per year, unless they were independently wealthy. Associate professors and higher ranking secondary teachers earned somewhere around 5000 marks, which was apparently a satisfactory income. Full professors had anywhere from 6000 to over 40,000 marks, the average in Prussia around 1900 being 12,000 marks. These figures acquire some meaning in comparison to the salary of

Prussian elementary teachers, which was around 1500 marks per year. If that was a subsistence income, then the full professors were quite wealthy, and those popular professors who earned 40,000 marks and more were to be numbered among the very rich. In any case, it was apparently not absurd in those days to compare the financial position of German academics with that of successful lawyers, doctors, and businessmen.

The unusually prominent place of the professor in German society was underlined in other ways as well. The vague sense of "nearness to the throne" still meant a great deal. In the system of carefully related public ranks, the top of the academic hierarchy came rather close to the equivalent of the ministerial level in the regular bureaucracy. Especially distinguished—and loyal—professors were often honored with even higher personal titles. They were made *Geheimräte,* if they were not actually ennobled. Even gymnasium teachers of the 1840's married the offspring of "the most highly regarded families from within the civil service, the daughters of generals, of councilors of state, of government presidents and directors."[49] Marrying an academic had its advantages. The proud wife of an impoverished instructor was still a *Frau Doktor,* a *gnädige Frau.* The evidence suggests that these things mattered. Indeed, the attitude of the highly educated toward the newly wealthy who tried to "climb" into academic circles was reminiscent of the relationship between aristocrats and bourgeois financiers in eighteenth-century France.[50]

In democratic and highly industrialized societies, a university degree or position competes with several other measures of social value and esteem, the most important among them being political or economic in origin. In Germany before 1890, by contrast, academic values bore the stamp of public and official recognition. The nonentrepreneurial upper middle class, the mandarin aristocracy of cultivation, had become the functional ruling class of the nation. University professors, the mandarin intellectuals, spoke for this distinctive elite and represented its values. The academics necessarily held an unusually eminent place in their nation, as long as higher education was an important factor in German social stratification. Until late in the nineteenth century, that condition was met.

In 1885, when the population of Germany stood near 47 million and around 7.5 million children were attending the primary schools, there were only about 238,000 students enrolled in all the German secondary schools. Roughly 128,000 of these were studying at a gymnasium.[51] Attendance had reached 27,000 at the universities, a mere 2500 at the technical institutes, and 1900 at the academies of forestry, mining, veterinary science, and agriculture.[52] For every 10,000 inhabitants, there were only about 50 secondary school students. The ratio of elementary to secondary pupils was more than 30 to 1.

Some 133,000 secondary school pupils were studying in Prussia. Among these, about 84,000 were at a gymnasium, 25,000 at a *Realgymnasium,* 5000 at an *Oberrealschule,* and another 19,000 at even less highly accredited realschulen. Of the Prussian students who passed their *Abitur* in 1885, as many as 3567 received the cherished certificate from the gymnasium, 574 from a *Realgymnasium,* and 32 from an *Oberrealschule.* Among the graduates who went on to a university, 2963 came from a gymnasium, 184 from a *Realgymnasium,* and none from an *Oberrealschule.* For every 10,000 inhabitants of Prussia, 30 students went to a gymnasium, and less than 1.5 received an *Abitur.* Over 85 percent of the *Abitur* certificates went to gymnasium students; 83 percent of the classical graduates went on to a university. Some 85 percent of students at Prussian universities between 1887 and 1890 came from a gymnasium; less than 7 percent had the *Abitur* from a modern secondary school; about 8 percent were enrolled without an *Abitur,* under special provisions and with severely limited privileges.[53]

Given the organizational barriers which separated the gymnasium from the rest of the schools, one begins to appreciate how minute a proportion of the German population had access to the traditional learning and to the official privileges which were its reward. But it is not enough to say that the German educational system was undemocratic or that it provided insufficient opportunities for talent from the lower classes. The obstacles to a vertical integration of society were perhaps less significant in some respects than the lines which separated industrial and commercial from professional and bureaucratic elements within the upper as well as within the middle and lower middle classes. The rigid compartmentalization of the school system, the anachronistic predominance of the gymnasium, and the close identification between higher education and the bureaucracy tended to maintain such a division at all social levels. In all likelihood, many of those students who left the realschulen before graduation found positions in business. But even among the 1026 Prussian secondary school graduates in 1885 who did *not* plan to attend a university, only 18 percent chose professions in agriculture, commerce, or industry.[54] Almost all the rest opted for military careers or for various positions within the civil service. As might be expected, the modern direction in secondary education received much of its support from the nonacademic classes. While nearly 22 percent of Prussian gymnasium graduates between 1875 and 1899 had fathers with university educations, the corresponding figure was only 7 percent for the *Realgymnasien* and a mere 4 percent for the *Oberrealschulen*.[55]

Statistics on the family background of German university students suggest that the elite of the highly educated recruited its successors to a remarkable extent from among its own offspring. Over half of Württemberg gymnasium graduates enrolled at the University of Tübingen between 1873 and 1877 had fathers who were educated at a university.[56] For students of Protestant theology, the corresponding figure was as high as 60 percent, while only 2 percent of Catholic theologians at Tübingen had academic fathers. The special prestige of the Protestant pastor and some of the social and political differences between Protestantism and Catholicism in Germany are reflected in these ratios. The role of the bureaucracy within the educated elite is described by the fact that nearly 40 percent of pupils at Bavarian gymnasiums and Latin schools between 1869 and 1871 were sons of officials. As the century progressed, new groups did increase their representation at the institutions of higher learning. The percentage of academically trained fathers of students at the University of Halle, which had been above 55 percent from 1761 to 1778, fell to just over 33 percent by 1877-1881. But this was still a significant figure, since university enrollment itself was increasing. It was a minute fraction of the population, after all, that still supplied a third of its own replacements, despite the expanding total demand for academic certification.

Less than two in a thousand students at Prussian universities from 1887 to 1890 were the sons of workers, occasional laborers and servants.[57] Around 11 percent were sons of high officials, judges, and lawyers with full academic educations; university professors; academically trained secondary school teachers; and higher army officers. Some 12 percent of students' fathers were clergymen, theologians, doctors, and apothecaries. Almost a quarter were middle and lower state officials and teachers without university educations. About 5 percent were rentiers and innkeepers; another 2 percent were owners of large estates, and roughly 13 percent were independent farmers. Slightly less than a third of the fathers were vaguely described as "merchants" and "industrialists." Under these two labels, statisticians lumped the whole productive sector of the middle and lower middle classes.

Among fathers of students at the University of Leipzig, the representation of higher officials, jurists, professors, gymnasium teachers, clergymen, and doctors was almost 46 percent in 1859-1864 and still 31 percent in 1879-1884.[58] Entrepreneurs and wholesale merchants moved from about 2 percent in the early 1860's to just above 5 percent in the early 1880's, while other merchants and innkeepers increased their share from about 11 percent to just under 20 percent during the same period. Primary teachers and lower officials made up another important segment of some 16 percent around 1860 and 12 percent around 1880. The configuration was even more one-sided in the case of the academic profession itself; for among those who were qualified (habilitiert) to teach at German universities between 1860 and 1889, some 65 percent were the sons of higher officials, professors, military officers, and academically trained professionals.[59] Less than 6 percent of fathers in this sample were owners, managers, or leading employees, in industry, commerce, transport, finance, and insurance.

The statisticians who compiled these figures long displayed the characteristic prejudices of the mandarin elite. Until the end of the nineteenth century, they tended to collect all types and levels of commercial and industrial occupations under one or two vague headings. They were acutely aware of the status differences which separated doctors from veterinarians, and pharmacists from undertakers. At the same time, they saw no essential difference between bank directors and grocers, or between steel manufacturers and provincial tanners. In a way, their categories are as interesting as the numbers they compiled. Both reveal the depth of the gulf which divided the old academic from the new productive groups. The noneconomic lower middle class, the petty officials and school teachers, were much better represented at the universities than the modern "bourgeoisie." This circumstance is surely pertinent to a discussion of German academic opinion after 1890, particularly since so much of that opinion was concerned with the impact of economic change upon the traditional organization of German society.

THE ADVENT OF THE MACHINE AND OF "THE MASSES," 1890–1918

Between 1870 and 1914, Germany was transformed into a highly industrialized nation. An economic boom began sometime before 1870, and the unification did much to strengthen it. Thereafter, the rate of economic growth increased ever more rapidly, reaching a peak during the years from 1890 to 1915. The whole development was unprecedented in its speed and thoroughness. The population of the German states jumped from about 42.5 million in 1875 to some 68 million in 1915.[60] In 1871, about 64 percent of Germans lived in communities of less than 2000 inhabitants. The figure decreased slowly until 1890; but then it dropped to 40 percent by 1910. Meantime, the proportion of Germans employed in agriculture and forestry decreased from over 42 percent in 1882 to 34 percent in 1907. Factories and mines sprang up where farms had been. The German machine industry employed 356,000 workers in 1882, about

1,120,000 in 1907. In steel production, Germany started behind France and way behind England in 1860. By 1910, the Germans made more pig iron and more steel than England and France together. In the space of a few decades, Germany was transformed from a relatively backward and predominantly agricultural nation into one of the greatest industrial powers in the world.

It was a peculiarity of the German experience that large-scale production followed almost immediately upon the beginning of industrial expansion. By the 1890's, great cartels controlled the mushrooming factories, and a tremendous concentration of economic power lay in the hands of a few giant enterprises. During the 1870's, various associations of entrepreneurs were formed to agitate for tariff protection. The heavy industrialists founded a powerful league in 1876, and the consumption goods industries were similarly organized in 1895. During the 1890's, large groups of employers united to combat strikes more effectively, and the Agrarian League of 1893 brought together the landed magnates of northeastern Germany. The workers in turn combined for mutual protection. Their unions had nearly one million members by 1900, more than two million by 1910, and practically all of them belonged to the Association of Free Unions which was affiliated with the Social Democratic Party.

It was particularly difficult in Germany at that time to keep these economic power blocs from controlling the political life of the nation. The government system was ill suited to protect the interests of the consumer. There was no tradition of antitrust legislation and little resistance to high tariff policies. On the contrary, some of the huge financial establishments had a semiofficial character from the beginning, and little was done to achieve a clear separation of economic and political power. Moreover, the constitutional position of the Reichstag and Bismarck's political habits encouraged a fairly narrow conception of material self-interest among the political parties. The Reichstag was not strong enough to develop constructive procedures, since the ministry was not responsible to it. The chancellor did have to draw together a majority of votes on any issue, however, so that political factions were in an ideal position to bargain for petty concessions. The Social Democratic Party, which held 110 seats and was the strongest single party in the Reichstag by 1912, openly subordinated political activity to economic objectives. The industrialists and rye barons acted upon similar principles in practice. The Agrarian League and the manufacturers' corporations were deeply involved in the support of various political parties. Industrialization was so abrupt and the dislocations it occasioned were so noticeable that economic and social rivalries became unusually prominent in the political life of the nation.

This whole process was particularly disturbing, of course, to those elements of the population that stood outside the new industrial sector of the economy. The old burgher class of artisans and small shopkeepers was threatened by the political as well as by the economic might which could now be organized against it. The traditional noneconomic upper middle class of officials, professional men, and academics was even more seriously affected, because it had a great deal more to lose. During much of the nineteenth century, it had played a predominant role in the political, social, and cultural life of the nation, and its leadership was now in effect being challenged. That this group was politically very powerful before 1870 and that it lost much of its influence during the late nineteenth century: both these circumstances are equally important, and both may be statistically illustrated.

Among the 830 deputies at the Frankfurt Assembly of 1848, at least 550 were graduates of universities.[61] Almost 20 percent of the representatives were professors, scholars, or secondary teachers; another 35 percent were administrative or judicial officials; nearly 17 percent were lawyers; 13 percent were theologians and clergymen, municipal officials, doctors, military officers, and writers. Little more than 5 percent of the deputies were landowners and farmers, and the whole world of industry, commerce, crafts, and transportation was directly represented by less than 7 percent.

In his study of Rhenish entrepreneurs from 1834 to 1879, Friedrich Zunkel emphasizes the social and attitudinal differences between a small but growing industrial elite and the *Bildungsbürgertum*, the educated middle class. Until late in the nineteenth century, many leading businessmen purposely kept their sons away from the gymnasiums and universities. They saw a connection between the academics and the bureaucrats, and they did not always trust officials. A gradual change in their outlook apparently began sometime between 1850 and 1870. More and more of them permitted their offspring to seek even humanistic higher educations. They drew closer both to the aristocracy and to the educated elite. They identified more closely with the monarchy and its honors, and they now began to enter politics in larger numbers. During the years from 1849 to 1878, nevertheless, the proportion of entrepreneurs in the Prussian lower house and the German Reichstag moved between the limits of 4 and 9 percent, whereas the corresponding numbers for the British House of Commons from 1832 to 1865 fell between 15 and 30 percent.[62]

In short, German entrepreneurs long left the political arena to the educated middle class. The latter never after 1849 achieved the overwhelming preponderance it had enjoyed in the Frankfurt Assembly. But as late as 1881, more than 6 percent of German Reichstag deputies were still academics and teachers; 23 percent were administrative and judicial officials, nearly 15 percent were lawyers, theologians, municipal officials, and doctors; and less than 13 percent were industrialists, merchants, and tradesmen.[63] Even among the Reichstag deputies of the various liberal parties between 1867 and 1884, Lenore O'Boyle found only about 19 percent businessmen, as against 9 percent academics and 22 percent administrative and judicial officials.[64]

In the Reichstag of 1887, 23 percent of the deputies were officials of various kinds; but the tide had certainly turned by then.[65] For the first time, businessmen, together with artisans, employees, and workers, accounted for 19 percent of the deputies. They were joined by "private officials," a category which certainly included many representatives of industry and commerce; this group made up almost 2 percent of the total. In the Reichstag of 1912, only 12 percent were merchants, industrialists, and tradesmen; but another 4 percent were artisans, employees, and workers, and 12 percent were "private officials." Journalists and publicists, who had accounted for only 3 percent of the Reichstag in 1887, increased their share to 14 percent by 1912. The representation of academics and teachers, by contrast, moved within the limits of 3 and 6 percent after 1887, while the officials fell to between 12 and 14 percent. This sudden decrease resulted partly from the recent exclusion of central government officials from the Reichstag. The new political configuration differed radically not only from the pattern of 1848 but also from that of the 1870's and early 1880's.

A government bill placed before the Prussian House of Deputies in 1910 proposed some slight reforms in the undemocratic electoral system of that state, among them one which would grant special privileges to those it labeled "bearers of culture" (*Kulturträger*).[66] Ordinary citizens would continue to be divided into three voting classes according to income, the wealthiest individuals in any district, those who paid one third of the taxes, being assigned one third of the votes for that district. Members of the educated elite, however, were to be ranked one voting class above that for which their wealth alone would qualify them. A *Kulturträger* was defined as a man who, having completed a minimum of three years of study at a university, had passed the state examinations in his field, or one who had well served the state as an official or as an army officer. Here was a truly ingenious attempt to obtain some reliable votes and to shore up the leadership of the learned in an increasingly hostile environment. The government was eventually forced to withdraw the proposal, and it is doubtful in any case whether it could have fulfilled all the expectations of its sponsors.

After all, the changes that were tending to transform the character of German politics were not only a matter of electoral representation. The nature of the political process itself was being altered. The old cultivated elite had used a characteristic style of political rhetoric to defend its preponderant influence and its unique interests. It had drawn upon the timeless, universal, and immeasurable ideals of political legality, national greatness, and cultural creativity to make its points. Its "idealistic" politics had long avoided the need for an overt weighing of conflicting interests, an open competition between concrete quantities of economic or electoral power, and an explicit method of bargaining and compromise in the making of major decisions. The sudden advent of large-scale industrialization changed all this, as newly organized blocs of socio-economic interests took over the arena of electoral politics to fight undisguised battles for quantitative influence. In one sense, therefore, it was simply the relatively abrupt arrival of modern politics in Germany that threatened the position of the old ruling groups.

In the nonelective sectors of government, the academic classes were a little more successful in maintaining their position. But even here, the new productive elites began to make their competition felt during the closing decades of the century. According to Karl Demeter, only 49 percent of Prussian officer cadets taking the ensigns' examinations in 1867 were nobles.[67] The German officer corps was apparently not quite as exclusively aristocratic as has sometimes been thought. It had to draw upon recruits from the upper middle classes, and the real key to its character lay in its explicit preference for the noneconomic elements within that segment of society. Among the fathers of the officer cadets passing through the examinations in 1867, 33 percent were military officers; 20 percent were landowners; 26 percent were senior officials; 7 percent were clergymen and teachers; 6 percent were minor officials; and only 5 percent were merchants and manufacturers. By 1912–13, this pattern had changed only to the degree that around 15 percent of officers were now the offspring of merchants and industrialists. Higher officials, academics, doctors, and clergymen still accounted for about 40 percent of the corps, while landowners and officers declined in representation. In the meantime, a full secondary education had actually increased in importance as a criterion of entry into the higher levels of the military profession. Thirty-five percent of officer cadets had the *Abitur* in 1890; 65 percent of them held graduate certificates in 1912, the large majority coming from a gymnasium. These figures are extremely interesting. They emphasize once again that a classical higher education was something like a substitute for nobility of birth. They also show that the competition between old and new elites for influence in the nonelective sector of public life took the form, had to take the form, of a struggle for entry into the upper layers of the educational system.

As a matter of fact, demands for changes in the organization of German education became increasingly insistent during the 1880's and after.[68] The critics of existing arrangements were not all of one mind. The claims of cultural nationalism, even volkish (*völkisch*) enthusiasms, were intermingled with socially progressive ideas in the writings of many educators. Nevertheless, there was an element or wing within the reform movement that may properly be described as democratic in its tendencies. Many of its sponsors were primary and secondary school teachers, rather than university professors, and some of them had been educated in the primary schools. It was their contention that the German educational system was too rigidly compartmentalized, too old-fashioned in its teaching methods, and too unrealistic in its curricular emphasis. They urged that the preparatory schools be abolished altogether. According to their proposals, all children were to begin their education by spending four or even six years in a common "basic school" (*Grundschule*). After that, middle and higher schools were to be interrelated in such a way that a student would not find it impossible to transfer from one type of institution to another. By loosening curricular prescriptions, by introducing a significant proportion of electives, and by accommodating several different course programs within the same institution, something approximating a single secondary school was to be created. The ideal of the "integral school" (*Einheitsschule*) suggested that students should not be shunted off into specialized institutions any sooner than absolutely necessary. Though diversification was acceptable an even desirable, it was to take place within the framework of a single unit as long as possible. When a branching off became unavoidable, after nine years of common schooling perhaps, the upper schools were still to emphasize flexibility and diversity in their programs. More genuine attention to each student's own inclinations and the advancement of the naturally talented were to be achieved in this way.

To round out the reformers' plans, the curriculum of the middle and upper schools was to be at least partially adjusted to modern economic and social conditions. Educators were to enrich the intellectual and aesthetic life of men who lived in an age of technology, rather than to insist that personal cultivation was possible only in an esoteric context. For this purpose, not only vocational schools but also other branches of the integral school were to experiment with "working instruction," letting the students engage in a concrete problem, perhaps even a manual task, in the classroom. German, modern languages, and modern history were to be assigned a more important place in the curriculum of all schools, and "civic instruction" (*Staatsbürgerkunde, staatsbürgerliche Erziehung*) was to prepare the younger generation to cope with the duties of a citizen in an increasingly fluid society. Various types of student self-government in the secondary schools were to serve a similar purpose. Primary school teachers, who were to advance beyond their traditional role of drill sergeants, were to receive a full higher education, perhaps even a course of scholarly training at the universities. Teachers' preparatory schools and seminars were to be abolished. Altogether, the reformers envisioned a rather thorough reorganization of German education. Their programs constituted a serious challenge to those aspects of the traditional school system that permitted the assigning of Germans to separate castes according to the manner and content of their learning.

Most of the modernists' proposals did not actually materialize before the Weimar period; but the realschulen did succeed in considerably improving their accreditation around the turn of the century.[69] Curiously enough, they received the support of one of the most unpredictable forces of the Wilhelmian period, that of Emperor William II himself. He called a conference on higher education in 1890, at which he proceeded to express his royal displeasure with several aspects of gymnasium education.[70] He had gone to one of the classical schools himself, and perhaps he felt that it had come dangerously close to repressing the creative potential of his own personality. In any case, he demanded that class hours and homework be reduced. He wanted to see more time assigned to gymnastics and sports. He also thought that teachers were too concerned with imparting information and not determined enough to instill a proper moral and patriotic orientation in their charges. Henceforth, teachers were clearly meant to devote more of their energy to the war against the Social Democrats. The German language and German history were to take a larger place in the curriculum, while somewhat less time was to be spent on Latin and Greek. The final results of the conference owed much to the fact that the ministry had invited many enemies and few defenders of the *Realgymnasium* to participate in the deliberations. It was decided that the old gymnasium would teach less Latin and Greek, and more modern history, geography, and German. This was thought to make any further concessions to the *Realgymnasium* unnecessary, since it would undoubtedly die out in competition with the modernized gymnasium. The *Oberrealschule* was treated more kindly, since it constituted a less immediate threat to the gymnasium. It was given the right to send its graduates to the university to study mathematics and the natural sciences.

To the Emperor's surprise and displeasure, however, the new arrangement satisfied no one, and the battle of the schools continued. Classical philologists began to recognize that they faced a long war of attrition in which the program of the gymnasium would be bastardized beyond recognition, unless they permitted the other types of schools to be fully accredited, so that the reform movement could be channeled through them and away from the gymnasium itself. Reluctantly and rather ungraciously, they admitted their first real defeat, offering essentially to trade recognition of the modern schools for restoration of the old gymnasium curriculum. Thus, another school conference finally resulted in the royal decree of November 26, 1900, which declared the nonclassical schools the equals of the gymnasium in principle. Since various professional associations had declared themselves unalterably opposed to admitting graduates of modern schools to the state examinations in their fields, the accreditation of the realschulen and the privileges assigned to their students continued to be hedged about with a number of specific restrictions. On the other hand, the Prussian example did encourage other German states to improve the standing of their modern secondary schools, so that by 1908, practically all graduates of any German *Realgymnasium* or *Oberrealschule* had at least the right to enroll at the German university of their choice.[71]

For the universities themselves, the Wilhelmian era was a time of great material prosperity and expansion. Growth was especially vigorous during the years from 1882 to 1908, while Friedrich Althoff was in charge of Prussian higher education.[72] Althoff was an intelligent and relatively unconventional administrator. It was he who engineered the accreditation of the realschulen in 1900. In 1899, also under his administration, the Prussian technical institutes were given the right to confer doctoral degrees. While many university men long continued to regard their new rivals with haughty disdain, the technical institutes grew to an enrollment of 11,000 by 1914.[73]

Althoff's methods were often rather autocratic. He was quite prepared to ignore the faculties' recommendations when filling a vacant teaching post. In his efforts to influence faculty policy, he tended occasionally to exploit the weaker sides of professorial characters, so that he has been accused of making German scholars forget how to act and talk like free men.[74] But such strong language was not generally used about Althoff. A more typical view was that, despite his faults, he often knew better than the professors what was good for a university. Even Paulsen implies that the heavy hand of the ministry may at times have been beneficial to academic vitality.[75] In any case, the cause of learning prospered materially under Althoff. The regular budget item for allocations to the Prussian universities climbed from 5.6 to 12.25 million marks while he was in office, during which time some 60 million marks in extraordinary expenditures also flowed to the universities.[76]

Of course, many professors wondered whether their academic institutions might not be spoiled by worldly success.[77] During the late 1870's, there was an ugly controversy over a number of cases in which plagiarists and other unqualified men had obtained doctoral degrees.[78] A few faculties had given out degrees without seeing the candidates, simply on the basis of dissertations sent in by mail. It appeared that there were agents who sold theses to wealthy clients. It seemed at least suspicious that the arts faculties at the small universities of Halle and Göttingen had conferred a yearly average of 153 doctoral degrees from 1873 to 1875, while the corresponding faculty at the University of Berlin had managed an annual average of only about 14 degrees during the same period. The fact that all full professors of a faculty received special fees for examining candidates, the amounts being generally higher for a man who passed than for one who failed, made the overtones of the discussion especially painful. Even though distressing incidents of this sort did not recur during the 1890's or afterwards, there continued to be some uneasiness over the relationship between academic and market values in the new world of sudden prosperity. Scholars of the old school were afraid that the universities, together with the technical institutes, might be turned into factories for practical research and for the mass production of technicians. Naturally, these fears were aggravated by the startling increase in the enrollment at German universities during the later nineteenth century. In 1870, about 14,000 students were registered at all German universities. In 1880, there were still only 21,000; but after that the figures jumped to 61,000 in 1914 and 72,000 in 1918.[79]

The enrollment boom raised a number of serious problems for the universities, and not all of these were effectively resolved. To begin with, the whole schedule of salaries and fees became more and more irrational as the number of students increased. Basic salaries meant less and less, while fees from "private" lectures and examinations made up an ever more important segment of the average professor's income. From a financial point of view, it began to make a very great difference to every academic whether his field of specialization was popular or not, whether students were attracted to his lectures, whether or not his courses were basic for a certain state examination, whether he himself gave many of these examinations, whether he had to share his area of competence with a colleague, and even whether or not a new academic chair or discipline was likely to take students away from his classes. During the 1890's, a series of angry pamphlets described the startling differences between the incomes of various faculty members in such strong colors that Althoff finally forced through some minor reforms in 1897.[80] His approach was sound in principle, for it tended to reduce the importance of lecture fees, while in effect raising basic salaries. Unfortunately, the adjustment which he brought about was quantitatively insignificant, so that the inequality of earnings in the academic world remained a serious difficulty. Paulsen, although in some respects a defender of the status quo in matters of salaries and fees, felt compelled to admit that this inequality was unparalleled anywhere, that it by no means always reflected the value of services rendered to learning, "that the system has a tendency to reenforce a drive toward money-making in a less than fitting sense, that now and then it misleads people to use their positions as examiners in this sense, and that it also sometimes plays some role in negotiations about necessary reforms in the organization of education or about the filling of a teaching position."[81]

Along with the circumstances suggested by Paulsen, a number of other institutional obstacles prevented the German universities from meeting the growth in enrollment with an adequate expansion of the senior faculty. Partly for fiscal reasons, the ministries tended to hold to the traditional notion that every major subject area should be represented by one full professor at every university. In principle, an expansion of the senior faculty could therefore occur only if the delimitation of subject areas was changed, if an old discipline was divided into two fully accepted specialties, or a new discipline was officially recognized as worthy of representation. In the last case, the government could still decide that the new field was too unimportant to warrant anything more than the appointment of an associate professor. If a full professorship was created, then the question of a separate state examination in the new subject area could easily arise, and that involved further negotiations and readjustments. Thus organizational, traditional, and financial problems combined to prevent the creation of a sufficient number of new professorships.

The universities did manage to increase their teaching staff as a whole. The ratio of students to faculty members of all ranks, which stood at 9 in 1870, did not advance beyond 14 before 1906.[82] The difficulty was that full professors did less and less of the actual teaching, while associate professors and especially instructors became an ever more important segment of the faculty. In 1835, there had been only 294 instructors at all the German universities. By 1870, their number had risen to 378; by 1910, to 1401. The full professorships increased much less rapidly, from 805 in 1870 to 1236 in 1910. Thus the ratio of students to full professors climbed very sharply, moving from 17 to 34 between 1870 and 1906 and continuing to increase thereafter.

Instructors and associate professors had originally been considered apprentices and journeymen of learning. They had not been expected to do much of the actual teaching. As long as they had a reasonable chance of advancement, their poverty could be regarded as an invigorating short-term exercise in asceticism. Although this view of the instructor's situation was expressed by many German professors even in the twentieth century, it really became more and more inappropriate after 1870.[83] By 1907, the average age of German instructors was 32.5 years, that of associate professors was 46 years, and that of full professors was almost 54 years. The average professor at the University of Berlin in 1907 was almost 60 years old.[84] At the University of Freiburg during the nineteenth century, instructors waited an average of nine to ten years before acquiring a salaried teaching post—or before giving up and leaving the university or the teaching profession.[85] These figures indicate at least that the academic pyramid tapered very sharply at the top. There were not enough higher positions to permit a reasonable schedule of advancement for the lower ranking members of the faculty. These men were by no means auxiliary teachers any more. By the end of the nineteenth century, the "apprentices" were doing almost as much of the actual teaching as the masters of the trade, even though the masters generally gave the standard—and remunerative—lectures necessary for examinations. The instructors, especially, made important contributions to the university. They provided at least some personal contact with students. They presented survey courses for nonspecialists, and it was often they who ventured into new, less popular, and more specialized fields.

The inequity of the situation, and the threat it posed to the welfare of the academic community, lay in the fact that neither the financial nor the constitutional position of the junior faculty was appropriately adjusted to the new conditions. Instructors were not given salaries. In 1898, a Prussian decree, the so-called *lex Arons*, applied to instructors a part of the disciplinary legislation covering state officials under the General Code and the Disciplinary Law of 1852. This innovation was specifically designed to permit the prosecution of a young physics instructor named Arons for his membership in the Social Democratic Party.[86] It gave the Prussian government as much control over its instructors as it had always had over its regular professors. It robbed the apprentices of learning of their only traditional advantage, their independence from the state. In return, it gave them neither the financial security nor the legal and social status of regular officials.

At the same time, the junior faculty continued to be totally excluded from the agencies of academic self-government, which therefore gradually ceased to represent the whole university. Associate professors and instructors began to feel the need for some representation of their own. During the first decade of the twentieth century, they formed a nationwide Corporation of Junior Faculty (*Nichtordinarienverbindung*), which was active in drawing up petitions to various faculties or even directly to the ministries of culture.[87] What they asked for, above all, was some degree of influence within the faculties. They achieved no concrete results, at least until after the First World War. But the very fact that the corporation was created and began to function would seem to betray a dangerous rigidity of grouping, a lack of contact between hardening ranks within the academic hierarchy.

This brings up the last and perhaps the most serious effect of the enrollment boom upon German universities before the First World War. When studying the academic life and literature of that period, one cannot avoid the impression that interpersonal relations within the scholarly community were not very satisfactory, whether between students and teachers, between younger and older faculty members, or even between colleagues.[88] There was an unhealthy atmosphere of rank-consciousness, favoritism, and mutual resentment. Literary wars between various schools of thought were often rather fierce.

Discussions involving the boundaries and methods of rival disciplines sometimes led to very unconstructive quarrels. One reads of disquieting examples of personal bias, pettyness, and cliquishness in the judging of candidates for the higher scholarly degrees, especially the *venia legendi*. Situations arose in which even the strongest advocates of academic self-government were inclined to welcome the intervention of the ministry against the prejudices of this or that faculty.

Some of these problems had existed even before the rapid growth of the universities during the later nineteenth century. The German professor had always had rather extensive powers of supervision over younger colleagues and students in his field. His dignity as an official and the traditional exaltation of his cultural and social role had given him a great deal of personal authority. The few full professors who made the faculty's decisions were formally empowered to act as a disciplinary court of first instance for its instructors. Instructors were totally dependent upon the goodwill of those with higher rank. Moreover, the joint responsibility of all the full professors of a faculty in the examination of candidates for the doctorate or the *venia legendi* was not always taken seriously. Since there were no regular course examinations and grades, it was difficult to arrive at several independent opinions concerning the ability of a student. As a result, the judgment of the single professor in any field of study became unusually important for all those who worked "under him" at his university. This arrangement was not without its compensating advantages as long as the universities were small. As the ratio of professors to students and junior colleagues decreased, however, the inherent disadvantages of the system became ever more obvious and more dangerous to the vitality and integrity of the academic community.

In 1916, the Arts Faculty at Freiburg University asked instructor Veit Valentin to give up his *venia legendi* because he had insulted Georg von Below, a professor within the faculty. If Valentin would not voluntarily give up his right to teach at a German university, the faculty planned to withdraw it in a disciplinary action. This was but an intermediate phase in a lengthy affair, in which Valentin's indiscretions were less startling than Below's petty ferocity. The whole controversy arose when Valentin wrote a sharply critical review of a polemical book by the reactionary Pan-Germanist Count Ernst von Reventlow. Below, a Pan-Germanist himself, then sent Valentin an extremely unpleasant letter, in which he cast aspersions on Valentin's honor. Valentin responded by breaking off personal relations with Below, whereupon Below sued for disciplinary action on grounds of having been insulted. A faculty spokesman later explained why the whole interchange could not be regarded as a private affair between two colleagues: "The simple but questionable formula of a schematic collegiality simply fails fully to describe the relationship between the younger instructors and the full professors, particularly those in the same field. If that relationship is to develop in a feasible manner for both sides, then it is desirable and useful, especially for the younger man, that . . . [it be] a friendly protector-protege relationship, which presupposes on one side a good will and understanding help in scholarly and professional matters, and on the other side attachment and trust."[89] This conception of academic authority produced the "Valentin case."

It was as if the German universities were actually experiencing that process of dehumanization which many German professors associated with the advent of the machine age. The deterioration in the whole tone of academic life was much lamented among the leading spokesmen of German higher learning. The tragedy was that a widespread sense of crisis was not accompanied by a sufficiently clear discussion of practicable alternatives. A nostalgic and rigid attachment to the values of the past prevented even the kind of conservative reforms that might have rescued some of those values for the present. Institutional adjustments were neglected in favor of vague complaints about mass education. It became a sort of dogma that the universities' troubles were due primarily to the advance of modernism in secondary education, the lowering of standards in the nonclassical schools, the inroads of technological practicality upon the territory of pure learning, and the appearance of new and uncultivated social groups within the universities. As a matter of fact, there was a grain of truth in the charge that "the masses" were invading the sanctuaries of higher learning; but it will be best to see exactly who and what was involved in this process.

The available statistics for Prussia suggest that enrollment in the secondary schools did not increase much faster than the population after 1885; this important ratio remained relatively stable.[90] On the other hand, the realschulen expanded their student bodies more rapidly than the gymnasiums. As late as 1900, more than 58 percent of Prussian secondary school pupils were attending a gymnasium; by 1914, the corresponding figure had dropped to 43 percent.[91] The monopoly position of the classical curriculum was challenged in another way as well. While larger proportions of students at all types of secondary schools chose to take the *Abitur* and to go on to the universities, there was an especially rapid increase in the number of graduates at the nonclassical schools. As a result, the percentage of university students who had received their secondary schooling at a gymnasium tended to fall. For the Prussian universities, it was 78 percent for the period from 1891 to 1895, but only 67 percent for the years 1905 to 1906.[92] This was certainly a noticeable decline in the fortunes of the classical tradition in German higher education. Since more secondary school pupils graduated and continued their studies, university enrollment increased even more rapidly than the population. In 1890, about fifty million inhabitants of the German states supported roughly 29,000 students at universities and around 4000 at technical institutes. In 1910, sixty-five million Germans sent 51,000 young people to universities and roughly 11,000 to technical institutes.[93]

The accreditation of the realschulen and the increase in enrollment did lead to a change in the social composition of the student body at the universities. In Prussia, the proportion of students whose fathers had been educated at a university fell to 27 percent by 1899–1900 and 24 percent by 1905–06. In the faculties of law, it was 33 percent in 1899–1900 and 29 percent in 1905–06; in the faculties of Protestant theology, it actually climbed from 39 percent in 1899–

1900 to 44 percent in 1905–06.[94] In general, there was a trend away from the old identification between the universities and the traditionally cultivated segment of society, and this is not surprising. Astonishing and significant, however, is the fact that the new financial and entrepreneurial groups did not play a clearly predominant role in this changing of the guards. Among students at the University of Leipzig, for example, the sons of industrialists and wholesale merchants increased from 6 percent between 1884 and 1888–89 to no more than 8 percent between 1904 and 1908–09.[95] The mandarin element of higher officials, jurists, professors, gymnasium teachers, clergymen, and doctors fell from 29 percent to 25 percent during the same period. Landowners and farmers lost slightly in representation, and so, curiously enough, did artisans and workers. There was a small increase from 21 percent to 23 percent for smaller merchants and innkeepers; but relatively the most important gains were made by lower officials and primary school teachers, who moved from 13 to 16 percent.

A more pronounced transformation may be observed in a comparison between university teachers who earned the *venia legendi* between 1860 and 1889 with those who did so between 1890 and 1919. In this case, the figures on fathers' occupations changed from 65 to 52 percent for high officials, professors, officers, and academically educated professionals.[96] While the proportion of landowners and farmers, along with that of workers, remained nearly the same, the new elite of owners, managers, and leading employees in all sectors of the modern business community advanced from 6 to 13 percent. Once again, however, this shift was accompanied by an increase from 7 to 9 percent for lower officials and teachers and a gain from 13 to 18 percent for petty merchants, tradesmen, and artisans.

These numbers do suggest some general trends; but they are also rather difficult to interpret, since the groupings on which they are based are neither totally consistent nor very detailed. For a more precise portrait of the German academic community in transition, one must turn to the following figures on the occupations of fathers of Prussian university students for the academic year 1902–03.[97]

		Percent
1.	Officers, military officials, and military doctors	1.9
2.	High government officials, judges, and lawyers with university educations, including professors of law	6.1
3.	Teachers with university educations, including university professors not in the fields of law, theology, or medicine	4.5
4.	Clergy and theologians, including professors of theology	5.8
5.	Doctors, veterinarians, and apothecaries, including professors of medicine	5.0
6.	Writers, private scholars and teachers, musicians, artists, and actors	0.8
7.	Teachers without university educations, middle and lower officials without academic training, noncommissioned officers	22.6
8.	Rentiers	0.6
9.	Large landowners, lessees of domain lands, stewards on great estates	5.2
10.	Middle and smaller but independent farmers	6.3
11.	Independents (not wage earners) in forestry, hunting, fishing, and commercial gardening	0.4
12.	Entrepreneurs, owners and higher level white-collar employees in manufacturing and transportation, commerce, finance, and publishing; directors and general agents in the field of insurance	9.7
13.	Small but independent merchants and shopkeepers, innkeepers, tradesmen, artisans, and small commercial haulers	26.3
14.	Middle and lower level supervisory and clerical personnel in all sectors; smaller insurance representatives and all other "private officials"	2.7
15.	"Other helpers" in all sectors; occasional laborers and servants; and workers (*Arbeiter*), no field being specified (0.07%)	1.0
16.	Other occupations, or none given	1.0

This information may be summarized in several interesting ways. Adding categories 1, 2, 3, and 7, one arrives at a figure of 35 percent for government and the government-controlled sector of education. This is certainly a very high fraction of the total. Again, one can combine headings 1 through 5 to reach a result of 23 percent for the "noneconomic" upper middle class, the academic elite in the narrow sense of the term. Category 6, for private scholars, writers, and artists, is remarkably low, since it presumably includes free-lance journalists and essayists as well. This supports a general impression that there was a sharp separation between the academic elite and the unofficial, unconnected "intelligentsia." The agrarian sector as a whole accounted for 12 percent of students' fathers, and the large landowners alone made up 5 percent of this total. The lower and working classes, the industrial "masses," still added only insignificant fractions to the university population. The business community was not well represented at all; the figure under category 12 seems surprisingly low, particularly since white-collar employees, the "new middle class," made a very poor showing under category 14 as well. Thus large-scale industry, commerce, finance, and transportation, the most progressive sectors of the economy, had relatively little contact with the universities. The older elements of the middle and lower middle class, the independent artisans and shopkeepers, did somewhat better; but even their 26 percent was almost matched by the 23 percent of the middle and lower officials and teachers. The composition of the academic elite was undoubtedly changing. There was a significant influx of elements from the lower middle class. But on this as on every other level of the social hierarchy, the newcomers stemmed surprisingly often from the older, noneconomic—or at least nonindustrial—sectors of the society.

THE WEIMAR PERIOD

During the troubled years between the two world wars, the economic and social position of the educated elite in Germany was

61

affected above all by the disastrous inflation. Although the inflation reached its worst proportions in 1923, the deterioration of the German currency really began during the First World War. For political as well as technical reasons, the Empire did not sufficiently cover its war expenditures through taxation. Instead, it increased the supply of money from 12.5 to 63.5 billion marks between 1914 and 1918.[98] The Versailles settlement further undermined Germany's financial position, for it imposed a huge burden of reparations upon the already shaky economy of the defeated nation. The political disorders of the Republic's early years made recovery more difficult, and the Franco-German conflict of 1923 finally led to the total collapse of the mark. In July 1914, the American dollar had been worth 4.2 marks. The rate stood at 8.9 marks in January 1919, at 192 marks in January 1922, at 17,972 marks in January 1923, and at 353,412 marks by July 1923.[99] From August 1923 until the currency stabilization on November 15 of that year, the exchange rate soared from around 5 million to 4200 billion marks to the dollar. When the new rentenmark was introduced in November, it was assigned a value of 1000 billion old marks.

The damage done by the inflation may be grouped under three general headings.[100] First, it destroyed money savings, devaluated rents, and enriched borrowers at the expense of creditors. It thus harmed the propertied classes generally, although it favored entrepreneurial or newly wealthy groups against old wealth. Second, since wages and salaries lagged behind the spiraling cost of living, the inflation penalized employees and helped employers. Actually, wage earners and management personnel in the large industrial concerns were relatively well equipped to protect themselves against this trend, whereas public employees, professional people, and white-collar workers in the less dynamic sectors of the economy were its helpless victims. Third, there were losses during routine business transactions. Anyone forced to hold currency or to extend short-term credit during commodity exchanges was bound to suffer losses, unless foreign coin or some other stable standard was involved. In the struggle to avoid such transaction problems, the great producers and wholesalers had a natural advantage over small merchants, shopkeepers, and artisans, so that the latter were most seriously hurt by this aspect of the devaluation.

On the whole then, the inflation spelled economic ruin especially for those social groups who were already at a comparative disadvantage in an age of rapid industrialization. It actually strengthened the new entrepreneurial, managerial, and technical elites, and it did not significantly or permanently hurt industrial labor. Instead, its most devastating effects were concentrated upon the two oldest segments of the traditional middle class: the rentiers, officials, professional men, and academics on the one hand, and the artisans, shopkeepers, and petty clerks on the other. Particularly higher officials and university professors apparently labored under a characteristic dual handicap after about 1921. While their incomes melted away, their status remained high for a long time. Their social position continued to demand an expensive style of life, so that they found it hard not to live beyond their means.[101] This helped to give them the air of a superseded ruling class, and it inevitably increased their dissatisfaction with their modern environment. The inflation simply continued those social changes which had already begun with the industrial boom of the late nineteenth century; but it accelerated them enough to make them a revolution.

In the academic world itself, the collapse of the mark caused serious hardships in a number of ways.[102] Travel for the sake of study was now out of the question, even for full professors. Books and other scholarly materials became luxuries. Research institutes fought to survive and cut their activities to a bare minimum. Individuals and even libraries could not afford to keep the necessary handbooks and learned journals. Especially foreign scholarly sources could not be made available. Printing costs were so high that many a student or instructor could not get his work published. Private help, especially from the United States, did something to alleviate the most pressing needs, and organizations were formed to channel the scarce funds that were available to the most endangered areas within German learning.[103] Still, there was a real threat that German research and scholarship would suffer a permanent setback as a result of the economic dislocation.

The sufferings of impoverished students who tried to maintain themselves at the universities have been poignantly described. Most instructors also lived in misery.[104] Even when their listeners were able to pay for private lectures, the fees they received lagged far behind the cost of food and other necessities. The state was occasionally able to grant a stipend to a worthy instructor; but the large majority of academic apprentices was in desperate straits. At the height of the inflation in 1923, there was a sudden drop of 35 percent in the number of instructors active at the University of Freiburg.[105] Many of those who stayed on were forced to take part-time jobs outside the university during the summers and even during the regular semesters. Even then, they just barely managed to survive.

Though the situation of the full professors was not quite as desperate, they too were affected by the devaluation of lecture fees and the serious gap between their fixed salaries and the cost of living. Comparison with other groups shows them at a marked disadvantage: the incomes of all state employees declined sharply in comparison with the wages of industrial workers; higher officials did relatively worse than lower officials; and even within the upper ranks of the civil service, university professors lost ground against nonacademic administrators whose prewar salaries had matched their own.[106] In 1913 a German higher official earned seven times as much and in 1922 only twice as much as an unskilled laborer. At a time of terrifying material need, while struggling with a hopelessly disorganized fiscal system and faced with the possibility of a real social disaster, the German governments were forced to restrict very severely their expenditures for cultural purposes. In money terms, the total Prussian budget for 1922 was thirty times as large as it had been in 1913, whereas its items related to cultural purposes had only increased by a factor of ten. After the recovery, the various ministries of culture were able gradually to increase their expenditures again; but the Corporation of German Universities (*Verband der deutschen Hochschulen*), which was founded in 1920, continued until 1927 to express a deep dissatisfaction with existing salary regulations.[107]

The inflation did not interrupt the increase in enrollment at the German institutions of higher learning. On the contrary, the number of students registered at universities and technical institutes climbed from 80,000 in the summer semester of 1918 to an unprecedented high of 112,000 in 1923.[108] Though many students had to take assorted jobs in order to survive, they apparently stayed on to get an education. Perhaps many of them actually had no other choice. Permanent jobs were hard to find; money earned was not worth much, and it was better to be hungry at a university than at home. The currency stabilization did cause enrollment at the universities and technical institutes to fall to 90,000 in 1924 and 81,000 in 1925; but after that the number climbed again, reaching 114,000 by 1929. The significance of these statistics lies in the fact that students not only faced hardships while at the universities; they also had slim prospects of adequate employment after completing their preparation. The impoverished and shrunken country could not support a rapidly increasing number of academically trained people in the customary fashion. Experienced men told students to think twice before entering the fierce competition for the few openings in the learned professions.[109] Even in commerce and industry, there was now an overabundance of highly educated applicants for clerical positions, so that employers began to regard learned place-seekers with a certain contempt.[110] And yet the influx of students continued. For the first time, a kind of academic proletariat grew up in Germany.

This proletariat did not recruit itself from the lower classes or even primarily from the newly wealthy. Statistical information on the occupations of students' fathers for 1929 demonstrates the contrary: over 23 percent were high officials, academically educated professionals, officers and high military officials.[111] Another 31 percent were middle and lower officials, including teachers. Only about 37 percent were in any way connected with commerce and industry, and no more than around a fourth of these were either owners and managers of factories and corporations, or high-level employees. A mere 2 percent were factory workers, while 23 percent had been educated at the universities. On the basis of similar figures, the Bavarian Statistical Office concluded that the parts of the population that were "not academically trained and less wealthy" accounted for a slightly smaller percentage of students in 1924–25 than in

1913–14, while the "intellectual upper class" had actually increased its representation at the universities, primarily at the expense of the "financial upper class."[112] In other words, the academic proletariat of the Weimar period consisted mainly of those groups which had already been disadvantaged by industrialization and which were hardest hit by the collapse of the mark.

In the political as well as in the economic field, the Weimar period witnessed a continuation of trends which had begun during the late nineteenth century. Officials still accounted for 24 percent of the Reichstag of 1924, while a further 6 percent of the deputies were teachers or professors.[113] But lawyers, doctors, and clergymen now added only 7 percent to the total representation. Factory owners, directors, and syndics made up no more than 6 percent of the Reichstag; but they were joined by artisans and workers (8 percent) and white-collar employees (6 percent), so that the immediately productive sector as a whole stood at 20 percent. Finally, there was a remarkable increase in the most specifically political element within the Reichstag; 20 percent of the delegates were now party secretaries or representatives of trade unions or cooperatives, while another 13 percent were publicists, editors, and publishers. As Robert Michels points out, there was naturally more social mobility in electoral politics than in any other field. Representatives of the lower classes entered more easily into parliamentary leadership than into either the entrepreneurial or the academic elite.

Moreover, the politics of the Weimar period involved a particularly overt battle between socio-economic interests. The Revolution of 1918 and the fall of the bureaucratic monarchy helped to bring this about. The republican form of government, without a tradition in Germany, was more tolerated than revered. Even among its supporters, there was some tendency to regard it merely as an arena in which all substantive political choices had yet to be contested. The troubles of the German economy inevitably moved to the center of the stage the struggles between industry and agriculture, and between employers and workers. There were relatively undisguised wars between classes, and the main contenders in the field were the new industrial elements of society, not the old burgher and academic groups.

The discomfiture of the mandarin elite was increased by the fact that reorganization of higher education became an important political issue after 1918. It quickly became clear that a majority of the German people deeply resented the compartmentalization of the school system and the whole spirit of caste which had come to predominate in the institutions of higher learning. In their founding programs, the parties of the political left announced their intention to remove outdated social barriers, to create more equal career opportunities for all Germans, and to make the country's educational system a genuinely democratic one.[114] Social Democrats and Democrats favored common schooling for all children in the lower grades, so as to bridge the social chasm between the primary schools and the secondary schools. Both these parties also intended to improve the training and status of elementary teachers. The Social Democrats, of course, made the most far-reaching demands. They called for at least seven years of common schooling; they demanded full university educations for all teachers; and they also sought to abolish religious instruction in the primary schools.[115] The People's Party was more guarded in its pronouncements on education, and the Catholic Center Party naturally wished to protect the influence of the Church upon the lower schools.

The Weimar Constitution, the product of negotiations between Social Democrats, Democrats, and the Center, was inevitably a laborious compromise. It nevertheless gave expression to the widespread liberal interest in a progressive reorganization of the school system.[116] According to Article 10 of the Constitution, the German central government could henceforth "establish principles" for "the educational system, including the universities." Articles 142 to 149 did in fact attempt to lay down such principles: The "freedom of learning" was to be guaranteed. Education was to be protected and supported by the state. The central government was to cooperate with the several states and the communities in establishing public institutions for the education of youth. Teachers at public schools were to be state officials. Education at the primary school and at vocational schools (*Fortbildungsschulen*) was to be free of charge. So-called people's universities (*Volkshochschulen*) were to launch a broad and socially motivated program of adult education. Able children of the poor were to be financially assisted in the acquisition of a higher education. Private preparatory schools were to be abolished altogether. All youngsters were to begin their education in the same institution, the "basic school" (*Grundschule*) of Article 146, Paragraph 1, which was to be open to every child, regardless of his parents' "economic or social position or religious beliefs." An exception to this rule was introduced in Article 146, Paragraph 2: "Within the communities, however, if parents or guardians so petition, primary schools of their confession or worldview are to be established, insofar as an orderly school organization . . . is not negatively influenced by this . . . Further details will be settled by the legislation of the states in accordance with the principles of a national law." Article 143, Paragraph 2, asserted that the training of teachers was "to be regulated in a uniform way for the entire nation in accordance with the principles generally established for higher education." Paragraphs 1 and 3 of Article 148, finally, echoed the demands of reformers for "ethical education," "civics" (*Staatsbürgerkunde*), and "working instruction" (*Arbeitsunterricht*).

Unfortunately, there could be some question as to the legal status of these general prescriptions. They were "principles," according to Article 10; but were they to supersede the existing cultural and educational law of the several states? What were the implications of Article 146, Paragraph 2, which owed its existence to the Center and to the sponsors of confessional schools? Could it be used in practice to protect private preparatory schools as well? It was clear that the central government was to exert a certain influence upon the various state ministries of culture. But what sanctions were to be applied if the states defied these general directives? There was one way to resolve such questions, and that was to pass the inclusive "national law" mentioned in Article 146, Paragraph 2. This paragraph seemed to imply that the projected law was necessary only to "settle further details"; but Article 174 asserted that "the present legal situation" would remain in force until the "national law announced in Article 146, Paragraph 2" was promulgated. What was the "present legal situation"? Were the rest of the Constitution's "principles" a part of it?

There was room for disagreement on these questions, and the national school law (*Reichsschulgesetz*) which was announced in the Constitution became one of the most hotly debated political issues of the Weimar period. In 1920, the Reich Ministry of the Interior sponsored a national school conference in which teachers themselves were to make suggestions for the projected reform of German education. The conference was not as productive as had been hoped; but the radical wing of the primary school teachers did find support to settle the issue of teacher training in its own sense. Since few university professors had been invited, it was possible to pass resolutions to the effect that all grades of teachers were henceforth to be educated at fully accredited secondary schools and then at the universities and technical institutes themselves. Teachers' preparatory institutes and seminars were to be dissolved in stages.[117]

While the central government was thus pressing toward a reorganization of primary and secondary education, Prussia prepared to reform its universities. From 1919 to 1921, the Social Democrat Konrad Haenisch was in charge of the Prussian Ministry of Culture. Carl Heinrich Becker, who stood close to the Democrats in orientation, was secretary for higher education within that ministry. In their programmatic announcements and early degrees, Haenisch and Becker gave a full account of their plans.[118] Above all, they intend to draw the German institutions of higher learning into closer contact with the life of the whole nation. They hoped, of course, that the professors would take a benevolent interest in the problems of the Republic and in the new democratic society generally. They also supported the movement toward a more integral school system, proposing to overcome the isolation of the primary schools, to establish curricular links between primary and secondary schools, and to send at least some of the elementary teachers to the universities. They were convinced that the universities would actually benefit from an involvement in new and popular tasks. Participation in the

projected people's universities was to give the professors an opportunity to translate their cultural traditions for the benefit of a new
sort of general public. Committees made up of prominent businessmen and public figures were to advise the ministry in filling existing
teaching positions and creating new ones.

Within the academic community itself, Haenisch and Becker
hoped to increase the influence of students and lower ranking faculty
members. In a decree dated May 17, 1919, Haenisch declared that
any pedagogical reforms at the universities, any changes in course
offerings, were secondary in importance to a reorganization of academic self-government. Perhaps, he said, the state would eventually
try to bring the training of future officials more into line with "the
changed requirements of a new age." "But before that can happen,
the question has to be considered whether the present organs of
university government can actually still be looked upon as alone
rightfully representative of the whole faculty, or whether it is to be
recommended that a broader basis be created for the discussion of
questions of university pedagogy."[119] Further decrees in 1919 and
1920 brought a more precise definition of Haenisch's plans.[120] While
in any case committed to a thorough revision of the chaotic and
unequal pattern of salaries and fees, he proposed to elevate all associate professors to the rank of full professor as quickly as financially
possible. Naturally, the new full professors were to be admitted to
the deliberations of the academic senates and faculties; further provisions were to assure some representation to instructors as well.
Even the students were to play some sort of role in academic self-
government, though apparently a minor one. A Prussian decree of
September 18, 1920, gave them the right to form students' leagues
(Studentenschaften) at the various universities and even to organize
on a nationwide level.[121] As Haenisch explained in 1921, he wished
to encourage democratic tendencies among the students and to make
them feel some emotional attachment to the new regime. He hoped
that an understanding would develop between workers and students,
"the hands and the head" of a progressive society.[122]

These great expectations were not fully realized. On the national
level and within the various states, in elementary and in higher

education, results fell short of justifying the initial optimism of the liberal ministers and governing parties. The political right gained in strength in the legislatures and elsewhere. Serious financial problems joined foreign policy issues in drawing public attention away from questions concerning education. After 1920, successive drafts of the projected national school law had less and less chance of gaining majority support in the Reichstag.[123] Among the most important obstacles to agreement were the unfortunate religious issue and the inevitable difference of opinion over the central government's financial contribution and supervisory competence. While not opposed to having the national government foot a good part of the bill for education, conservative groups argued that the several states ought to have the exclusive right to manage the schools. As long as Berlin and the rest of the huge northern state of Prussia were in the hands of Social Democrats and Protestants, many rightist politicians, southern particularists, and Catholics were especially interested in a decentralization of authority. As a result, there was no really thorough recodification of German educational legislation during the Weimar period.

Instead of the national school law, the so-called Basic School Law (*Grundschulgesetz*) of April 28, 1920, was passed. Following the constitutional provisions in favor of a basic school, this law established a common four-year course in the primary schools for all German children. It ordered public preparatory schools dissolved by 1924–25, private ones by 1929–30.[124] Minor modifications of the law in 1925 and 1927 slightly improved the legal position of institutions and individuals who sought to evade the new settlement. In Bavaria at least, primary schools remained denominational for the most part. But on the whole, the various states were prepared to enforce the system of basic schools. The Prussian Ministry of Culture was especially firm in dealing with obstructionists. It did a great deal to make the four-year common primary school, the most important innovation of the Weimar period in education, a reality for all of Germany.[125]

The central government essentially left the field of education after the passage of the Basic School Law. A section within the national Ministry of the Interior continued to keep in touch with school reform problems; but its role remained that of a mediator between the governments of the several states.[126] As the initiative passed to the state authorities, developments in Prussia again became particularly important. In 1921, Becker succeeded Haenisch as Prussian Minister of Culture, only to be himself replaced after a brief term of office by Otto Boelitz of the People's Party. Boelitz headed the ministry from 1921 until 1925, at which point Becker took over again until 1930. Since Becker ran the ministry's department for higher education even under Boelitz, he provided an element of continuity and exerted considerable influence.[127] His presence may help to explain the fact that the Prussian Ministry of Culture generally took its obligations to the Weimar Constitution rather seriously. It was more cautious in its reforms than the radical states of Thuringia and Saxony. These two governments sent all their primary school teachers to the universities. They also came closest to realizing the ideal of the integral school, a flexible system of middle and higher schools built upon the four-year basic schools.[128] But while the Prussian approach was less revolutionary, it was also more influential for the rest of Germany.

On September 19, 1919, the Prussian Minister of Culture brought out a regulation allowing certain groups among actual or potential elementary teachers to enroll in Prussian universities on the basis of special examinations and certificates.[129] Bavaria published an analogous decree on June 8, 1920, and the system of substitute graduate tests and certificates was maintained in its essentials until 1930. In 1922, all of the German states except Bavaria agreed to let graduates of a new class of secondary schools enroll in their universities. These so-called complementary schools (*Aufbauschulen*) were to take in especially able students who had completed the seventh year of a primary school and to give them an acceptable secondary education.[130] A second link was thus established between the primary schools and the universities. In 1924, a Prussian instruction enlarged the authority of elementary teachers in the selection of candidates for admission to secondary schools. On October 7 of the same year, Prussia resolved to send all future primary school teachers through the existing secondary schools and to dissolve the teachers preparatory institutes and seminars.[131] Though they were not normally to go to regular universities, primary school teachers were to receive an education on the university level at special pedagogical academies. The Prussian Ministry of Culture published its plans for these new institutions in 1925 and began their establishment in 1926. The state of Baden was proceeding with very much the same kind of arrangements during the same year.[132]

In the meantime, modernism in secondary education was also making further progress. In 1924, the Prussian Ministry of Culture published a famous tract entitled "The Reorganization of the Prussian School System."[133] In it, the three traditional types of secondary schools, the gymnasium, the *Realgymnasium,* and the *Oberrealschule,* appeared in somewhat altered forms. Courses in German were strongly represented in all three types. Latin was somewhat cut back even at the gymnasium. Modern foreign languages, history, and civic instruction were emphasized throughout, especially in some subsidiary variations of the accepted types of schools. The complementary schools were upheld. Moreover, an entirely new kind of secondary school was introduced in the form of the German high school (*Deutsche Oberschule*), which offered no Latin or Greek and yet was not as strong in mathematics and the natural sciences as the *Oberrealschule.* Intended primarily for future elementary teachers, it concentrated more heavily than any of the other schools upon German, geography, and modern history. In April 1925, instructions for the introduction of the new course programs outlined in the tract of 1924 were accepted by the Prussian Ministry of State and were put into effect.[134] In the following month, all the German states, again with the exception of Bavaria, entered an agreement to accept graduates of the new German high school and of all the other types of schools mentioned in the Prussian edict as qualified for study at their universities.[135]

A statistical analysis of the secondary school reforms of the Weimar period makes them seem relatively unimportant at first, especially if one looks exclusively at their impact upon the universities. Even in 1931, less than 5 percent of the total male enrollment at

German universities was made up of students who had prepared themselves at German high schools or complementary schools or who had received special graduate certificates of any kind. At the same time, no more than 3 percent of male university students intended to become elementary teachers.[136] But these figures do not fully describe the range and implications of the reform movement. Once primary school teachers had been charged with the early education of all Germans and with the selection of secondary school candidates, an improvement in their training and status was practically inevitable. The decision to send them to fully accredited secondary schools made them at least potentially eligible for university study. Since they needed background primarily in German, in civics, and in modern history, their admission to the secondary schools also necessarily brought about a further strengthening of the modern direction in higher education. The new school types represented only one aspect of this development. The gymnasium curriculum itself was revised in 1924, and the older realschulen also continued to gain strength during the Weimar period. In 1914, over 40 percent of Prussian secondary school students were enrolled in a gymnasium. By 1922, the gymnasium percentage had already decreased to 35, and there is every indication that it continued to fall thereafter.[137] Around the end of the nineteenth century, gymnasium graduates had been in a large majority at the universities. In 1929–30, they constituted little more than a third of total enrollment at the universities and technical institutes. Besides, the technical institutes in turn were growing much faster than the universities. The universities expanded their student bodies from 72,000 in 1918 to 93,000 in 1929; the technical institutes advanced from an enrollment of 7700 to one of 21,000 during the same interval.[138]

Though some of the developments in secondary education did not directly or appreciably affect the universities, they left their mark on the whole tenor of German education. During the 1920's, a number of progressive and experimental schools pursued new pedagogical and social ideals. A lively interest in residential and communal education had arisen among a few reformers even before the war; but the politically and socially radical strands within this movement really became visible only during the Weimar period. There were important reforms in the field of higher education for women and in the area of the so-called middle schools (*Mittelschulen, Fortbildungsschulen*), vocational and clerical schools for primary school graduates. As Becker told an American audience in 1930, the fact that nonacademic groups were getting a better secondary schooling was one of the most important consequences of the whole reform movement.[139] Beyond that, the old barriers between the different types and levels of schools had been lowered to some extent. While the ideal of selecting secondary school candidates on the basis of ability alone had not been extensively realized, the German educational system as a whole was more variegated, a little more flexible, and therefore probably more democratic than it had ever been.

In the field of higher learning, one of the most important developments of the Weimar period was the creation or expansion of three new urban universities in Frankfurt, Hamburg, and Cologne.[140] The University of Frankfurt officially opened in 1914; Hamburg and Cologne followed in 1919. All three took their peculiar character from their antecedents in certain specialized and more or less practically motivated research institutes. In Frankfurt, the establishment of privately and municipally financed centers for the study of medicine and the physical sciences during the nineteenth century had been followed in 1901 by the creation of an academy for social and commercial sciences. The financial sponsors of this institution, among them the merchant and philanthropist Robert Merton, felt that existing universities did not provide future businessmen with enough thorough and up-to-date training in the economic and social problems of an industrial age. In Hamburg, there had long been a special interest in scientific and medical questions connected with tropical exploration, colonial ventures, and international trade. Hamburg merchants also desired and supported a system of public lectures and scholarly institutes in the social and political sciences and in humanistic subjects as well. In 1908, a colonial institute was organized, and the plan soon arose to combine this center with the public lecture system in a full-fledged university. With the support of the city and the help of such men as Max Warburg, this object was reached by 1919. Similarly in Cologne, private and municipal generosity and interest had led to the creation of a commercial institute (*Handelshochschule*) in 1901, an academy for practical medicine in 1904, an organization for advanced public education in law and politics in 1906, an academy (*Hochschule*) for municipal and social administration in 1912, and a research institute for social sciences in 1918. The last of these organizations, which quickly acquired a reputation in the new fields of sociology, social psychology, and social policy, was the real seed of the new university.

Thus it was demonstrated in Frankfurt, in Hamburg, and in Cologne that genuine scholarship could take its impetus from some of the more acute problems of the contemporary scene. At these three modern universities, the academic world was brought closer to the current life of the nation, as Haenisch and Becker had suggested. Elsewhere, however, the reformers' plans in the field of higher learning met with little success. The adult education movement centering in the concept of the people's universities made some progress; but it found little or no official backing from the older universities.[141] Private funds, political parties, municipalities, and religious groups provided most of the necessary financial and organizational support. The students' leagues thoroughly disappointed the reformers who had helped to create them. The leagues showed little interest in curricular or institutional innovations at the universities.[142] Instead, they developed an enthusiasm for gymnastics and worked for the dissemination of Pan-German, volkish, and racist ideologies. The idea of consulting nonacademic experts in problems of faculty staffing was forgotten very soon, and the announced revision of the lecture fee system failed to materialize. The inflation devaluated fees in any case. The states might have profited from the general recalculation of salaries after the currency stablization to reorganize the whole pattern of academic remunerations; but they apparently lacked the necessary funds.[143] Financial difficulties also played a part in frustrating Haenisch's plan to raise all associate professors to the rank of full professor. There were a number of promotions, but the initial objective could not be achieved. The proportion of full professors among faculty members at the universities of Berlin, Heidelberg, and Munich was 24 pecent in 1913–14 and 26 percent in 1930.[144] Thus the trend toward a quantitative preponderance of lower ranking and nonvoting faculty was checked but not decisively reversed.

At the same time, Haenisch's project of increasing the influence of the instructors within the organs of university self-government was only partially realized. Though needy instructors were occasionally provided with assistantships, fellowships, or short-term teaching assignments, they were not given regular salaries.[145] The honorific titles that various states bestowed upon them caused a certain amount of confusion but did not actually improve their position within the universities or vis-à-vis the governments.* Although a series of new university statutes were actually promulgated in several German states during the Weimar period, they did not add a great deal to the existing legal situation.[146] They generally provided for such new academic assemblies as the "greater faculty" (weitere Fakultät), the "greater senate," and the plenum or Vollversammlung, in which many or all associate professors and instructors were given seats. But these enlarged bodies were assigned only consultative functions. Representatives of the associate professors and even a few instructors' delegates were granted the right to participate in the election of the rector and in deliberations of the regular senate and faculties. Once again, however, these inovations were so restricted in scope as to be nearly insignificant.

And yet, despite the limitations of actual reforms, the academic community of the Weimar period continually expressed alarm at the threat of changes in German education. The newly founded Corporation of German Universities violently opposed every innovation which was proposed or actually carried out by individual

---

* Haenisch orginally intended to promote all planmässige Extraordinarien to the rank of ordentlicher Professor. Worthy instructors could then be given the title of ausserordentlicher Professor, it being tacitly understood that they were nichtplanmässig. Since this project was only partially carried out and since some planmässig Extraordinarien were made persönliche Ordinarien in the absence of planmässige Ordinariate for them, the results were rather confusing. I have counted all de facto Privatdozenten as instructors throughout.

reformers, political parties, or ministries. It urged a reduction of the basic school term to three years, so that students could have the indispensable nine-year secondary schooling and still finish their preparation for university study in twelve years. "Bad laws," said the corporation's spokesmen, "can be changed."[147] The thought of having to train primary school teachers made them indignant. They fought the special examinations and substitute graduate certificates; they attacked the newly introduced German high schools and complementary schools; they remonstrated against the reformers' emphasis upon German, civics, and modern history; and they even sought to reverse the growth of the already accepted realschulen. Again and again, they announced their preference for the old form of the gymnasium and insisted that a full course of training in the ancient languages was by far the best preparation, if not actually a prerequisite, for university study.[148] In 1932, the corporation demanded that all German secondary schools remain strictly scholarly institutions. It opposed any integration of elementary and higher education and specifically denounced curricular programs designed to lead from the higher classes of the primary schools to the universities.[149]

The learned opponents of reform apparently saw their resistance to the authorities as a gallant defense of academic standards against a misguided democratic tolerance for laxness and mediocrity. This view was not totally unjustified. The universities, it must be remembered, were forced to accept any student who passed through an accredited secondary school or examination. Thus the professors had every right to be heard on the subject of standards in secondary education. The trouble was that as a group they did not offer positive proposals. Refusing to admit that there was anything wrong with the old school system, they took an uncompromising and often purposely disdainful stance. Above all, they failed to disentangle the problem of academic standards from the whole complex of social prejudices that had grown up around the ideal of classical "cultivation." Instead, they condemned the school reform movement as but one of many interrelated aberrations of a disrespectful age, and they did not hesitate to parade their elitist convictions.

[The corporation] regards with grave concern the ever greater expansion of the circle of those admitted to the universities. [This expansion results in the admission of students] whose preparation in general and whose language training in particular is not sufficient . . . for the demands of an orderly course of study . . . This deterioration is caused as much by the whole orientation of our time as by certain pedagogical aims and methods.

Larger strata of the population [are pressing into the secondary schools, so that standards there have to be lowered.] Thus one often succeeds only through an artificial and wearisome process of forced breeding [*Höherzüchtung*] in making the cultural values [*Bildungsgüter*] of the secondary school accessible to a kind of public which comes from its home environment [*von Hause aus*] wihout any sort of deeper intellectual and spiritual [*geistige*] needs.[150]

In this vocabulary, with this conception of culture, no reasoned discussion of modern alternatives was possible.

The suggestion that the universities themselves might be reorganized was also categorically rejected by the majority of the academic community. In 1922, the corporation was forced to report that organizations of junior faculty were supporting some of the innovations proposed by the Prussian Ministry of Culture. With this exception, most academics opposed any thorough alteration of the status quo.[151] Once again, the tone of the corporation's pronouncements was intentionally arrogant. In turning down the Prussian plan of consulting nonacademic experts in general questions of staffing and curriculum, the corporation made the counterproposal that special boards of university professors be organized to "back the ministries of culture against subjective and unwarranted influences which the parliamentary parties . . . might try to assert."[152] On another occasion, a speaker at a corporation convention suggested that those who were urging a reform of the universities for "egotistical reasons" were revolutionaries "who begin by tearing down the foundations [of university organization] before being clear in their own minds whether they wish to replace this ancient monument with a trade union hall or a free-thinker's temple." The convention apparently approved of this sentiment, for it eventually included the almost habitual slam against "leveling" in its resolutions.[153]

The more formal arguments of conservative academics naturally included a defense of the universities' autonomy and the "freedom of learning." Also, there was the characteristic contention that institutional questions were unimportant in any case, while a sorely needed inner reorientation could not be legislated. The irony of the situation was that those who had been least anxious to keep the bureaucratic monarchy from influencing the universities before 1918 now posed as heroic champions of academic freedom against a liberal and almost overly permissive regime.[154] The tragedy was that the language of "idealism" and of "cultivation," the traditional emphasis upon moral questions and abstract cultural values, was gradually channeled into an automatic defense against any form of institutional or social change. Most German academics were no longer willing to consider any compromises with the modern age. They refused even to distinguish between the several aspects of twentieth-century life which seemed to threaten them. As we shall see, they hated the Republic; they feared the new party politics, and they were horrified at the social transformations associated with industrialization and inflation. Similarly, and more or less automatically, they categorized the efforts of educational reformers as aspects and symptoms of a more general movement in which the masses intended to capture the institutions of higher learning, to disrupt their internal organization, to tear down their standards of excellence, to make them instruments of social leveling, and to force them to abandon their own learned traditions in favor of a narrowly practical type of modern education.

2

THE MANDARIN TRADITION
IN RETROSPECT

To recognize that the elite of the highly educated played an important role in modern German society is to arrive at a new point of view upon German intellectual history as well. The "mandarin" type of the introduction applies to the "cultivated" classes in general; but it was meant to refer more particularly to the university professors. They, after all, were the most important members of the group. The whole complex of institutional, social, and cultural patterns which insured the mandarins' influence had its center at the universities. No one could speak with more authority for the elite as a whole than the men of learning, the "mandarin intellectuals." For their views upon contemporary cultural and political questions, most cultivated Germans naturally looked to the professors, particularly to the social scientists and humanists. It therefore seems worth trying to see German academic opinion as a "mandarin ideology" and the German cultural heritage generally as the "mandarin tradition."

After about 1890, it appeared to many mandarin intellectuals that their influence in German social and cultural life was threatened. In response to this challenge, they tried to restate exactly what they stood for. Since their traditional values were evidently under attack, it seemed wise to examine them all once again. Some German academics undertook this task in a mixture of rebelliousness and despair. The more clear-sighted among them did it because they hoped that the fundaments of their heritage might yet be saved at the expense of its less important accretions. In any case, the joint product of these efforts was a kind of retrospective self-analysis, a complete account of the mandarins' intellectual history by their own hand.

An autobiography, particularly one that emphasizes ancestors, is likely to have peculiar weaknesses. Even when factually accurate, it tends to make up in piety what it lacks in distance from its subject. Not all the German academic histories of the mandarin tradition suffered equally from this weakness. Some were done in a critical spirit; but most neglected the social implications of the ideas they described. This is where later analysts have had to adjust the balance. Since the 1930's, many of these younger commentators have been German expatriate scholars. Some of them were originally taught or influenced by the more critical wing of an older German academic generation. Thus the works of Hans Gerth and Hans Rosenberg, of Koppel S. Pinson, Hajo Holborn, Leonard Krieger, and W. H. Bruford are sequels and occasionally also correctives to the writings of Otto Hintze and Max Weber, of Ernst Troeltsch, Friedrich Meinecke, and Eduard Spranger. If one reads these two generations of authors, adding some titles by Wilhelm Windelband and Karl Jaspers, by Norbert Elias and Wilhelm Roessler, one arrives at a single, internally consistent view of the mandarin heritage.[1] This view is not an uncritical one by any means; but it remains something like an analysis "from the inside." Its language and the position from which it looks back to the sources of modern German thought are still to some degree those of the 1890's and 1920's. For the purposes of the present essay, this is indeed an advantage.

RATIONALITY AND CULTURE

The West European Enlightenment, to begin stating this retrospective view, was never fully assimilated east of the Rhine. There was a German Enlightenment, the *Aufklärung;* but it differed in several important respects from its Anglo-French counterpart. The rationalism of Thomasius and of Wolff was not tempered by the empirical element which predominated in England. Leibniz, particularly as popularized by Wolff, was not an empiricist. Those of his works which were available and popular before the nineteenth century dealt primarily with his attempt to discover a rational world order. With Lessing and many other eighteenth-century German writers, he shared a continuing positive interest in religious questions. Quite generally, the German *Aufklärer* were not so much critics as modernizers of Protestant Christianity. They sought above all to rescue the spiritual and moral implications of the Christian religion by grounding them safely outside the threatened frameworks of the orthodox creeds.

Lessing saw the history of religion as an account of man's spiritual education. The analogy is significant, for the concern with education was a general characteristic of the German Enlightenment. In *Was ist Aufklärung,* Kant used the metaphor of individual growth and maturity to describe the intellectual achievements and ambitions of his time. The tradition of the *Bildungsroman* from *Agathon* to *Wilhelm Meister* is another case in point, as is the one-sided German preference for Rousseau's pedagogical writings. Historians need not attempt to "see through" these overt predilections to a "bourgeois" philosophy of social and political progress. Education was an immediate and burning issue in eighteenth-century Germany, because it was directly related to the confrontation between the burgher, the emerging mandarin, and the unenlightened aristocrat. This confrontation expressed itself in personal and moral terms. The burgher defined a certain group of virtues as distinctive characteristics of his own class, in the moral weeklies of the early eighteenth century, for example. Since he also saw education primarily in ethical terms, particularly if he was influenced by Pietism, his own sense of place and of worth was directly related to his idea of education. The mandarin, of course, identified with the ideal of rational Enlightenment. He asserted himself by insisting upon the spiritual relevance of free intellectual endeavor. Thus education assumed an immense importance in the self-consciousness of burghers and mandarins alike, and the personal and moral implications of learning came to seem far more important than its practical uses.

The divergence between German and Anglo-French thought during the eighteenth century should not be exaggerated. West of the Rhine too, the mandarin segment of society—and the issue of education—were probably more significant than has generally been realized. The peculiarity of the German social situation was only a matter of degree, and so was the consequent difference in intellectual orientations. Nevertheless, some distinctions must be made, if only because German university professors have often made them.

As a matter of fact, there was something rather odd about the image of eighteenth-century thought in German academic writings of the nineteenth and early twentieth centuries. Generally, the Enlightenment appeared in an unfavorable light, and yet it was never very precisely described. Kant was not criticized, though he named the *Aufklärung*. Lessing too was safe from reproach, Thomasius and Wolff perhaps less so. In any case, there was always the suggestion, whether explicit or not, that the Enlightenment had been a West European phenomenon. On the other hand, some of the mainstreams of the German intellectual tradition were almost invariably portrayed as reactions against the Enlightenment, presumably against its Anglo-French version. The reader was thus left to wonder how so many German thinkers came to fight a dragon who had so shadowy a form and lived so far away. The problem was made no easier by the fact that such perfectly good *Aufklärer* as Kant and Herder also inspired intellectual movements which were supposedly directed against the Enlightenment.

This paradox would seem to warn us against stereotyped views of the eighteenth century on both sides of the Rhine. It also suggests that we might look more carefully at the German critique of the Enlightenment. What was its purpose? Whom or what did it mean to oppose?

In part, the answer lies in the field of social theory. There was something about the Anglo-French political tradition that disturbed the German mandarins. It irritated them less around 1800 than during the following thirteen decades, particularly between 1890 and 1933. The antithesis deepened over the years; the dragon only gradually found its shape. Its supposed existence before 1800 was perhaps as much a matter of retrospective inference as of fact.

Other aspects of the West European Enlightenment that provoked criticism in Germany over the years were certain implications of Anglo-French rationalism and empiricism. Again, this point must not be overstated. Kant was a rationalist, and so were the philosophers of German Idealism. It is true that Lockean empiricism made few converts in Germany even before it met with Kant's critique. On the other hand, the mandarin objection to the Enlightenment was not based on specific philosophical arguments alone. Especially after 1890, many German scholars expressed or implied the very general view that the Anglo-French Enlightenment was "shallow" in some way. In suggesting this, they did not mean to criticize the sense of rational *Aufklärung* which was exemplified in Kant's famous essay. Their main quarrel was with something else. What they really disliked was a vaguely "utilitarian" tendency, a vulgar attitude in the West European tradition toward all knowledge. They felt that many French and English intellectuals from the seventeenth century on associated science and learning almost exclusively with the idea of practical manipulation, of rational technique and environmental control. This, in the mandarins' opinion, was a truly dangerous heresy and a rather stupid one as well. This was the main enemy, the real dragon in eighteenth-century thought. It revealed its full malignancy only during the later nineteenth century; but it was certainly born before 1800. Above all, it did not always live in foreign lands. At the University of Halle during the eighteenth century, the fallacious search for immediately useful knowledge had threatened the mandarins at home. The error had been substantially corrected at Jena and at Berlin. Still, the danger of a relapse was always there, and it kept increasing as the nineteenth century wore on. In the battle against this danger the German image of the West European Enlightenment was created.

The mandarins' own ideal of learning, developed as the direct antithesis of practical knowledge, was expressed in the words *Bildung* (cultivation) and *Kultur*. Both terms first became current in Germany during the cultural revival of the later eighteenth century. Even then, they long remained the exclusive property of the learned classes.[2] In this case, the evolution of an idea was inseparably tied to the history of a few words. A kind of semantic conquest established the leadership of the mandarins, and the newly introduced vocabulary revealed the full extent of the elite's claim to a special authority.

The fifteenth edition of *Der grosse Brockhaus,* a standard encyclopedia published between 1928 and 1935, supplied the following definition of *Bildung.* "The fundamental concept of pedogagy since Pestalozzi, *Bildung* means forming the soul by means of the cultural environment. *Bildung* requires: (a) an individuality which, as the unique starting point, is to be developed into a formed or value-saturated personality; (b) a certain universality, meaning richness of mind and person, which is attained through the empathetic understanding and experiencing [*Verstehen und Erleben*] of the objective cultural values; (c) totality, meaning inner unity and firmness of character." The passage begins by describing a process, the "forming of the soul," and ends by characterizing a condition, namely "richness of mind and person" and "inner unity." As a process, cultivation was clearly related to education; but it implied an unusually comprehensive view of that activity. In 1923, the philosopher Karl Jaspers distinguished between education (*Erziehung*) and instruction (*Unterricht*), saying that instruction only implied the imparting of information and the training of skills, whereas education involved the "forming of the personality in accordance with an ideal of *Bildung,* with ethical norms . . . Education is the inclusive, the whole." Apparently using the terms *Erziehung* and *Bildung* almost interchangeably, he concluded that *Bildung* entailed "more than knowledge" and that it was "related to the whole empirical existence of the individual."[3]

The word *Bildung,* as it evolved during the late eighteenth century, contained the single most important tenet of the mandarin tradition. Just to define the term, one has to posit a highly distinctive model of the learning process. Clearly, much more is involved than the transmitting of information and the development of analytical capabilities. Cultivation reflects and originates in religious and neohumanist conceptions of "inner growth" and integral self-development.[4] The starting point is a unique individual. The materials which are "experienced" in the course of learning are "objective cultural values." The terminology here is Idealist or neo-Idealist; but the essential point can be stated more simply. It is epitomized in the neohumanist's relationship to his classical sources. He does not only come to know them. Rather, the moral and aesthetic examples contained in the classical sources affect him deeply and totally. The whole personality is involved in the act of cognition. If the materials to be learned are properly selected, their contemplation can lead to wisdom and virtue. They can attract, elevate, and transform the learner. He can thus acquire an indelible quality, also called *Bildung,* which is a potential rival to the characteristics of the aristocrat.

The German word *Kultur* was adapted from Cicero's *cultura animi* by Samuel Pufendorf and by Gottfried von Herder. Until late in the eighteenth century, it remained very closely related to the concept of *Bildung.*[5] It had the meaning of "personal culture"; it referred to the cultivation of the mind and spirit. Then gradually, it was used in German learned circles in its more general sense to epitomize all of man's civilized achievements in society. In France, this second step was not taken. *Culture* there remained principally *culture de l'esprit,* while *civilisation,* introduced by the physiocrat Marquis de Mirabeau, came to stand for the totality of man's social and intellectual creations and arrangements.

As soon as *civilisation* and *Kultur* were established, respectively, in France and in Germany, a fascinating chain of associations led German intellectuals to see an antithesis between the two concepts. In eighteenth-century Germany, the worldly manners of the aristocracy were adapted from French models. Where there was something like social polish at the petty German courts, it was quite frankly imported from France. The same was true for a long time of literary and artistic fashions and of sexual mores in the aristocratic world as well. To the German burgher, French habits were frivolous or downright evil. Much of his emerging consciousness of class—and of nation—took the form of moral indignation, which was directed against Frenchified courtiers and nobles. The mandarin's position was somewhat more complex. He too distinguished himself from the aristocratic world, which he could only regard as intellectually and emotionally superficial. He did not often encounter well-educated courtiers, and when he did, he generally found men who could imitate French forms without being able to think for themselves. The mandarin might even have admired their bearing and their "accomplishments"; but he was bound to feel a certain dichotomy between their approach to intellectual matters and his own.

At the core, these antitheses are embarrassingly simple; but they can be elaborated. Norbert Elias has succeeded in outlining the intricate pattern of associations that grew up around the contrast between sophisticated social forms, skilled manners, and worldly knowledge on the one hand, and genuine spirituality or cultivated wisdom on the other.[6] In 1784, Kant explicitly distinguished between civilization and culture, identifying civilization with good manners and social niceties, culture with art, learning, and morality. He thought his age was civilized almost to excess, without being truly cultured.[7] Kant did not openly blame the French for this condition; but others among his countrymen were soon to take this further step. By the time of Napoleon at any rate, culture was German and civilization was French.

Elias was interested in the curious fact that an intra-German social distinction was here transformed into a lasting stereotype about the difference between two countries. The French continued to identify with an internationally conceived mission of civilization. The Germans, finding it difficult and yet desirable to define themselves as a nation, tended to see uniquely German characteristics in their preference of culture over civilization. That such a preference did indeed persist in German academic circles will become clear in later chapters. Why it did is a more difficult problem.

Once a certain viewpoint is built into a language, it can certainly outlast the conditions in which it originated for a certain length of time. But it is hard to believe that a semantic survival of this kind would not eventually fade away or be totally altered, unless it continued to be nourished by a social reality. In the case of the antithesis between culture and civilization, that reality was the existence of the educated elite. The verbal contrast remained meaningful, because it reflected the mandarins' interested preference for a particular conception of knowledge.

Here, once again, is an illustration from *Der grosse Brockhaus*:

> *Kultur* . . . ; in particular the ennoblement [*Veredelung*] of man through the development of his ethical, artistic, and intellectual powers; also the result of the activity of such cultivated men, a characteristic, personal style of life; the products of such activity (cultural objects and values). Thus *Kultur* is the forming and perfecting of the world around us and within us . . . Especially in the German theory of culture, it is distinguished from civilization, and this with quite definite evaluative intentions. According to this distinction, civilization is to culture as the external is to the internal, the artificially constructed to the naturally developed, the mechanical to the organic, "means" to "ends" (Spengler).

The entry continues to the effect that the distinction in question is contested, along with Oswald Spengler's use of it in his theory of decadence. Nevertheless, the paragraph concludes by upholding the separation of culture from civilization, adding only that the two can exist side by side and that culture is the more inclusive term.

These formulations may seem more suggestive than clear; but they did have a meaning. *Zivilisation* was identified with the "outward" signs of a limited sort of education. At first, it referred primarily to questions of social form. It suggested superficial polish; but it also implied a generally practical and worldly sort of knowledge. With time, the term civilization was quite naturally expanded to cover all the results of "outward" progress in economics, technology, and social organization, while *Kultur* always continued to stand for the "inner" condition and achievements of cultivated men. "Civilization" evoked the tangible amenities of earthly existence; "culture" suggested spiritual concerns. In short, culture reflected cultivation, whereas civilization was "merely" a product of man's factual, rational, and technical training. In this sense, "culture" was the more inclusive term, and it made sense to argue about the historical relationship between civilization and culture.

It would be wrong to overstate the whole issue at this point. The German academics themselves did not explore all the implications of the antithesis until late in the nineteenth century, when the pressure to do so became overwhelming. Nor would it be fair to suggest that the ideals of cultivation and culture were bound to clash with the demands of reason. Around 1800, such a conflict was no more than a faint possibility, a potentiality in the logical sense. Reason was popular insofar as it implied the general ideal of moral and intellectual enlightenment. Nevertheless, an incipient bias against the practical and technical side of rationality was already established in the language of the emerging elite.

IDEALISM AND THE HISTORICAL TRADITION

The most important formal elements in the mandarins' scholarly heritage were the Kantian critique, the theories of Idealism, and the German historical tradition. Not every German philosophy professor of the nineteenth century was a neo-Kantian. But among those who were not, a considerable number moved "beyond Kant" into some form of Idealism. Besides, the Kantian critique was so generally taught as a point of departure for all philosophical thinking that it influenced many scholars who were not professional philosophers themselves. On some level of theoretical coherence, Kant's position thus affected almost every aspect of German learning, and so did the Idealist scheme and the Rankean line in historiography.

Stated briefly and a bit crudely, the Kantian criticism is directed against a simple common-sense view of experience.[8] According to this view, our knowledge is based upon trustworthy perceptions of the external world. We see the objects around us; we observe their movements. We need only add up the "things" we discover in this way to arrive at an ever more complete awareness of reality. In a more sophisticated version of this theory, the fact that we have sensations may be fully explained in terms of physical and physiological causes, while our ideas in turn may be described as the consequences of our sensations. An object reflects light to our retina, heat stimulates certain of our nerve ends, and so forth. The messages received in this manner are conducted to the brain, where they combine to form impressions or complex experiences, coherent images which are fully determined and therefore totally representative of the objects that caused them. In any case, our knowledge is itself in some sense a part of that natural order of objects and movements which it reflects and comprehends. For that reason, there is nothing particularly problematic about it.

The Kantian philosopher disagrees with all variants of this common-sense view, and his criticism is based upon logical considerations. He admits that we do have sensations; but he wonders how we are to prove that these are related to external objects in any way. He points out that we have no experience of an object. Rather, we have many different sensations at different times, and we tend to group these around constructed references: the objects. How can we do that? What accounts for the apparent coherence and objectivity of our experience? Where do we get our sense of time and space, without which we could not organize our perceptions? Of course we do not experience cause at all. We seem to observe repeated sequences, and even these are not raw sensations. We cannot begin by assuming a causal relationship between objects and sensations, between sensations and ideas, and then pretend to "discover" cause in turn through our impressions alone. In short, it is logically impossible to treat our perceptions as ordinary effects of external reality. We are faced with an unbridgeable gap between experience and the thing in itself. This, roughly, is what Ernst Cassirer has called the problem of terminism. Any Kantian would be especially anxious to emphasize that it is a logical problem, not an ordinary question of fact and certainly not a metaphysical issue. There is nothing wrong, he would say, with our continued pursuit of empirical investigations, as long as we observe two rules. First, we must admit that certain a priori elements, certain categories of a logical character, must necessarily be present in our experience, giving it its organized, objective quality. Secondly, we must resist the temptation to equate our ideas with things, and relationships between ideas with relationships between objects. In short, we must not fall back into the common-sense views that provoked the Kantian criticism.

To be even casually acquainted with these epistemological problems is to be perpetually on guard against the more simple-minded philosophical exploitations of the empiricist tradition. The German academic community as a whole was well armed against the implicit metaphysics of certain nineteenth-century scientisms. Indeed, as we shall see a little later, a generalized suspicion of the common-sense fallacy led some German intellectuals to distrust empirical research in general. Their own heritage in philosophy was not limited to the Kantian criticism; it also encompassed the speculative theories of German Idealism, for which that criticism was but a point of departure.

To begin thinking in Idealist terms, one elaborates in a certain way upon the contrast between the common-sense model of experience and its Kantian counterpart. In the common-sense model, the notion of verification seems to involve a comparison between what we think and what is really so in the "external world." In the Kantian model, this procedure is in some sense reduced to a purely "internal" operation. Impressions and ideas are compared with each other, not with physical objects or events. Truth is not correspondence between idea and object. It lies, rather, in the proper ordering of our sensations and concepts, in the formal or logical rules according to which they are grouped and interrelated. The German Idealists did not hold that reality is an illusion or a well-made dream. In one way or another, they all continued to work with some analogue of the discarded comparison between thought and thing. They distinguished between those contents or elements of consciousness which seem to represent an independent or objective world and those which do not. Their procedure here was much too complex to be summarized in a few paragraphs, and their technical solutions differed in any case. The point to be made is that they transformed the discredited confrontation between objective reality and subjective impression into a sort of dialectical relationship *within* consciousness.

Seeking a metaphysical guarantee for the correspondence between our ideas and the world of the thing in itself, some Idealists also postulated an abstract mind or spirit. The Kantian categories and all the norms of right thinking which insure the order and certainty of our experience cannot be regarded as empirical, psychological properties of this or that individual mind. They are necessary axioms of all knowledge, and it is therefore tempting to attribute them to something like a transcendental consciousness. The transcendental consciousness can be conceived as a purely logical construct; but it can also acquire a quasi-religious meaning. In this sense, German Idealism tended to move from the metaphysics of the common-sense fallacy to those of an absolute Ego or universal spirit.

There was clearly a certain affinity between the theories of the Idealists and the philosophical Protestantism of the German Enlightenment. Schleiermacher was influenced as much by Pietism as by Idealism, and one can well imagine a learned pastor taking inspiration from the new philosophy. But there were other, more important links between the speculations of a Fichte, Schleiermacher, Schelling, or Hegel and the whole cultural and social context of their time. Even the greatest formal theoreticians of Idealism were by no means forbiddingly technical thinkers only. Their vocabulary was not as unfamiliar to their audiences as it is to us. In a way, they were popular essayists, eloquent spokesmen for a creed which could appeal to the layman as well as to the professional metaphysician. To recognize this, as later German academic generations certainly did, one has only to read a few passages in Wilhelm Windelband's *History of Philosophy*. Windelband was one of the most eminent academic neo-Kantians of the late nineteenth century, not an enthusiastic dilettante, and yet his ostensibly descriptive pages seem continually to trumpet the moral and cultural lessons of Idealism.

> Experience is an activity of consciousness directed toward objects; it can therefore be derived only from things or from the consciousness. In the one case the explanation is dogmatic, in the other Idealistic. Dogmatism regards consciousness as a product of things; it traces the activities of intelligence back . . . to the mechanical necessity of the causal relations; if consistently thought, therefore, it cannot end otherwise than fatalistically and materialistically. Idealism, on the contrary, sees in things a product of consciousness, of a free function determined only by itself; it is the system of freedom and of action. These two modes of explanation, each of which is consistent in itself, are . . . irreconcilable . . . If one will not fall a victim to sceptical despair, he must choose between the two. This choice, since both [alternatives] present themselves logically as equally consistent systems, will primarily depend "on what sort of a man one is."[9]

Windelband attributes his concluding quote in the above paragraph to Fichte, the fiery theoretician of the creative Ego and the created Non-Ego. Drawing the inevitable moral, Windelband then goes on to say that ethical considerations alone would recommend a choice of Idealism over dogmatism. This view was quite common among German academics from the eighteenth to the twentieth century. The fifteenth edition of *Der Grosse Brockhaus* defines *Idealismus* as "a philosophical *Weltanschauung* which, in various forms, has dominated Western thought since Plato." The writer of the encyclopedia entry then lists eight types of theoretical Idealism and goes on to remark that "in the practical-ethical sense, *Idealismus* is the belief in the validity of ethical ideas and ideals and the inner readiness to work and even to make sacrifices for their realization."

Since all German nouns are capitalized, it is not possible to make a distinction in writing between Idealism and idealism. This may help to explain how the "practical-ethical sense" of the term became intermingled with its technical meaning. But there were other reasons as well. Even Windelband describes the essence of Idealism by saying simply that it "sees in things a product of consciousness." This proposition, like Fichte's reference to a creative Ego, could easily be rephrased to suggest something like mind fathering matter. The German word *Geist,* which would have to be used in this connection, meant not only "mind" but also "spirit" or "soul." In the formal works of some Idealists, *Geist* stood for the collective thought of mankind and sometimes even for a transcendental consciousness which guaranteed the concurrence of appearance and reality. These conceptions, together with phrases identifying being with being-in-consciousness, were bound to engender more popular teleological images of geist encompassing or creating or "realizing itself" in the world.

In all this, Platonic notions played an important though not always explicit role. When describing the German ideal of learning, the educator Eduard Spranger wrote of studying "the undiscoverable divine whole in the discoverable particulars."[10] In a similar connection, the classical philologist Werner Jaeger introduced the following definition. "Geist is in a certain way all that is. It is the eye which takes in everything real; but in the mirror of nature and of history, geist knows itself, cleansed of the obscurities of its particular and accidental temporal existence. Time may change the content and paths of learning; but no age will come, we hope, which will have lost the awareness that in this ultimate intellectual and spiritual goal lies our dignity as human beings."[11]

Spranger and Jaeger were looking back to the days of the great German Idealists from the perspective of the 1920's; but there is no reason to think that they misinterpreted the intentions of their ancestors. Idealism was a creed as well as a philosophy from the very beginning. Apart from the famous theoreticians of the tradition, there were many minor Idealists around 1800 who helped to propagate and to broaden the moral implications of the system. Close personal and intellectual bonds linked the great artists and poets of the German classical age to the philosophers. Humboldt, the neo-humanist, and Schiller, the dramatist, were as much a part of the Idealist movement as Fichte and Hegel. For all these men, the new philosophy was an expression of strong personal convictions. It reflected their conception of learning, their ideals of cultivation and culture. Windelband recognized this when he described the "aesthetic-philosophical system of education"[12] with its emphasis upon "pure" knowledge and self-cultivation as the true child of Idealist principles. Wilhelm Roessler has made the same point in writing about the "spiritualization" (*Vergeistigung*) of the world by the intellectual elite of those days.[13] That mind and idea do move and should move the world, that "it is the spirit which builds the body for itself," to use Schiller's famous phrase:[14] that was the cultural "message" of Idealism.

Schelling and the *Naturphilosophie* of the early nineteenth century applied Idealistic conceptions to the study of nature; but the new philosophy exerted an even more profound and permanent influence in the humanistic and historical studies. The language of Idealism was particularly suited to the methods and problems of these fields. Here more than in any other area of intellectual concern, it was to provoke new insights and to retain a certain vitality until well into the twentieth century. The very word *Geisteswissenschaft*, which has played a central role in the German classification of the disciplines since the early nineteenth century, seems to imply an Idealistic approach to the humanistic disciplines for which it stands. In its antecedents, the word can be followed back to John Stuart Mill or even to the influence of Descartes before him. In Germany, Max Weber has traced it to Hermann von Helmholtz, the famous psycho-physicist of the mid-nineteenth century.[15] The work of Hegel helped to bring it into general use, and the neo-

Idealist Wilhelm Dilthey finally gave it a clear and systematic definition during the 1880's.

Dilthey used the term "objective geist" to describe the whole range of man's past cultural achievements that are accessible to us in the form of literature, conventions of language, works of art, codes of law, and other documents or remnants of whatever kind.[16] Whenever one or several men create some outward sign or imprint of their private thoughts and feelings, a bit of "subjective geist" is externalized or "objectified." It remains in the world of geist; it does not become a part of nature. Nevertheless, it does come to be as much an element of our "objective" environment as any stone or tree. Obviously, there are many different disciplines which study the "objectifications" of man's consciousness. In a way, most of our thinking is a kind of interaction between our own "subjective" mind and the products of other minds which confront us everywhere. In Dilthey's scheme, this whole confrontation, the investigation of geist in its external signs, falls under the heading of the *Geisteswissenschaften,* the cultural and historical disciplines.

In his terminology, Dilthey was partly indebted to Hegel and to other leading Idealists of the early nineteenth century. In his views on the methods of the cultural and historical disciplines, he drew upon an even richer and more variegated heritage. This was the German historical tradition.

From the late eighteenth to the early twentieth century, German historians were deeply influenced by the philosophical and literary movements in which the mandarin creed expressed itself. From Humboldt and from Hegel, they absorbed some of the Idealistic conceptions which Dilthey later sought to clarify in his redefinition of the humanistic disciplines. Herder and the German Romantic theorists of the early nineteenth century also helped to shape a tradition which was perhaps most memorably exemplified in the work of Leopold von Ranke (1795–1886). Ranke was the great dean and teacher of German historians during most of the nineteenth century. When the younger practitioners of his discipline tried to restate the fundaments of their methodological inheritance after

1890, they naturally gave a prominent place to his thought. They also recognized, however, that Ranke in turn had assimilated ideas which dated back to the German cultural revival of the late eighteenth and early nineteenth century.

Like other aspects of the mandarin heritage, the German historical tradition was developed at least partly in conscious reaction against certain intellectual tendencies in the West European Enlightenment.[17] As German scholars saw it, the historian's greatest sin was to treat the past as a collection of examples to be used to glorify man, progress, and the present, to construct general maxims of statecraft, or to chart the advances of science and reason. In criticizing these practices, the German historians did not intend to forbid all generalization in history. It was only the wrongly used, the "unhistorical" generalization that they attacked. When Ranke made his famous remark about just finding out "how it actually was," he certainly did not mean to urge a complete suspension of interpretive judgment until all the evidence was in and the whole story could be told correctly once and for all. No German historian ever took such a position. Ranke was simply trying to avoid an overly present-minded and unimaginative treatment of the past. He wanted to be "historical," to describe bygone epochs, institutions, and individuals as much as possible "in their own terms," rather than to judge the Renaissance Papacy by Luther's standards and the Middle Ages by our own. This was the ideal of past-mindedness, the central theme of the German historical tradition.

At the risk of being somewhat too explicit and schematic, we may further analyze this ideal in terms of two basic constituents: the principles of empathy and individuality. The principle of empathy implies the attempt to "put oneself in the place of" historic individuals. In treating a medieval ruler, for example, historians try to uncover the emotions and ideas that made him act as he did. They do not trace his behavior to his ignorance and fanaticism, or describe him as the unconscious agent of large and anonymous forces, or impose anachronistic standards upon his time. They emphasize conscious intentions and feelings, rather than statistical regularities or timeless laws of behavior. At the same time, historians should begin by regarding the ruler in question as a unique character, not as a member of an unhistorically abstracted class, such as that of all princes at all times. This is the principle of individuality, and it can be applied to all kinds of subjects. In dealing with groups, historians who accept the principle prefer such categories as "the mind of the Renaissance" to such timeless concepts as "the religious mind" or "the economic man." An idea, an epoch, a nation: all these may be pictured as "individualities," if it is their uniqueness and undivided "concreteness" which is to be emphasized. In being past-minded, the scholar never abstracts from the historical context which he seeks to understand, as it were, "from within." He treats the culture and the whole "spirit" of a given epoch as a unique and self-contained complex of values and ideas.

A whole school of theoretical questions—and answers—grew up around these conceptions. The principle of empathy called attention to the differences of method which distinguish history from the natural sciences. Historical relationships, unlike the laws of mechanics, are based in part upon human intentions. In that sense, they have meaning. The historian's evidence is located in Dilthey's world of "objective geist." To understand a man or an age of the past is to reconstruct a historic individuality out of the surviving "objectifications" of its spirit. Since such reconstruction involves the retracing of meaningful patterns of thought and behavior, historical explanation depends upon the element of meaning. Admittedly, the statement that the historian seeks meaning in his sources, or refers to meanings in his explanations, is not identical with the metaphysical assertion that the historical process as a whole is meaningful. On the other hand, this distinction was not always made by German historians and philosophers before Dilthey. Here again, the Idealist tradition asserted itself. Even before Hegel, the whole thrust of that philosophy encouraged optimistic popular conceptions about geist as a transcendent cause in the evolution of civilization. In this way, the principle of empathy, elevated above the status of an explanatory device, became a substantive philosophy of history.

The principle of individuality probably owed more to German Romanticism and to its antecedents than to the Idealistic systems.

In a lecture in 1923 on "Natural Law and Humanity in World Politics," Ernst Troeltsch discussed the origins of the principle and its role in German political thought. He began by describing French and Anglo-American political traditions in terms of two basic conceptions: the secularized version of Stoic and Christian natural law and the democratic-progressive ideal of "humanity." Particularly in times of stress, Troeltsch argued, these two axioms could be combined into a highly coherent system, an outwardly homogeneous and distinctly Western point of view. In international affairs, this point of view led to pacifism, to cosmopolitanism, and to the idea of a worldwide league of democratic peoples.

Turning to German political theory, Troeltsch said that the tradition of the Lutheran state church had emphasized the conservative and authoritarian implications of Christian natural law. Above all, the German Romantic reaction against the French Revolution had been a revolt against "universal egalitarian morality," against the "whole mathematical-mechanistic West European scientific spirit," and against "the barren abstraction of a universal and equal humanity." The chief product of German Romanticism, according to Troeltsch, was a "new positive, ethical, and historical principle," namely the "concept of individuality."

> Of decisive importance is the mystical-metaphysical sense of this concept of individuality as in each case a particular concretion of the divine spirit in unique persons and in suprapersonal communal organizations. The basic constituents of reality are not similar material and social atoms and universal laws . . . but differing unique personalities and individualizing formative forces . . . This results . . . in a different idea of community: The state and the society are not created from the individual by way of contract and pragmatic [zweckrationale] construction, but from the suprapersonal spiritual forces which emanate from the most important and creative individuals, the volk spirit [Volksgeist] or the religious aesthetic idea. A quite different idea of humanity also results [from this basic conception]: not the ultimate union of fundamentally equal

human beings in a rationally organized total humanity, but the fullness of contending national spirits, which unfold their highest spiritual powers in this contest . . . [Further, this approach leads to a conception of historical development as a progression] of qualitatively different cultures, in which the leading nation at a given time hands the torch to its successor and in which all [cultures] together in mutual complementation represent the totality of life.[18]

At bottom, as Troeltsch suggests, the principle of individuality was a certain conception of the relationship between a group or generality and its constituent elements. The issue may be clarified through the following analogy. The members of an orchestra play different parts, each of them following a score which is suited to the unique qualities of his instrument. The music produced in this way is not made up of identical components. Indeed, its quality and even more certainly its "meaning" cannot be described as a mere conjunction of its several parts. From an evaluative point of view also, the symphony as a whole is not just a sum of scores. No single member of the orchestra can be dispensed with. The total performance depends upon the simultaneous realization of different objectives by many participants, each of whom strives for a kind of limited perfection in performing his own part to the best of his ability.

Undoubtedly, this symphonic analogy could be stated in a more concise and matter-of-fact manner. A touch of expansive enthusiasm may be appropriate for our purposes, however, since the mandarins' own use of the analogy was often both enthusiastic and expansive. On one level, the symphonic imagery could be employed to criticize the idea of knowledge as a mere sum of fundamentally similar facts. Again, the principle of individuality could be regarded as a description of methods actually used by historians in trying to understand a medieval ruler, for example. But as Troeltsch pointed out, the Romantic concept of individuality implied more than a methodological preference; it encompassed assertions about the "basic constituents of reality." The notion of individuality, linked with the symphonic analogy, acquired a "mystical-metaphysical sense," a speculative dimension. In the German historical tradition, this dimension engendered an unusually insistent emphasis upon great "historic" individuals; a tendency to treat cultures, states, and epochs as personalized "wholes"; and the conviction that each of these totalities embodied its own unique spirit.

These predilections in turn raised certain technical difficulties, which demanded further methodological adjustments. How was it possible, for example, to describe continuing movements or trends in history, without falling into the error of applying unhistorical categories or generalizations to the past? Clearly, there was an incentive to solve this problem by picturing historical change as an "immanent" process of "unfolding tendencies." Organic analogies were bound to be attractive in this connection, and the language of Hegel and of Idealism was available as well. It offered the possibility of tracing the dynamic element in history to the realm of mind, making historical conflict and change an analogue of logical contradiction and treating the actual facts and conditions of the past as individualized emanations or concretions of geist.

THE IDEA OF THE UNIVERSITY AND OF LEARNING

To see the German Idealistic and historical traditions as functional parts of a mandarin ideology, one has only to read some of the literature in which German academics after 1890 described their idea of the university and of learning. The word *Wissenschaft* naturally came up very often in that literature, and it must therefore be defined at the outset.

The German *Wissenschaft* is not the equivalent of the English "science," for the latter implies certain methodological commitments.[19] In German usage, any organized body of information is referred to as *eine Wissenschaft*, with the indefinite article. At the same time, all formal knowledge, and the collective activity of scholars in obtaining, interpreting, and ordering it, may be rendered

Wissenschaft or, more commonly, *die Wissenschaft*, with the definite article. Thus *die Wissenschaft* must be translated as "scholarship" or "learning," rarely as "science," and *eine Wissenschaft* simply means a "discipline." In English, it is possible to argue about whether sociology or history is "a science." In German, history is *eine Wissenschaft* by definition, and to ask whether sociology is *eine Wissenschaft* is to wonder about its status as a distinct and clearly circumscribed discipline, not about its more or less "scientific" methods. To call a certain historical investigation *wissenschaftlich* is to praise it for its sound scholarship and perhaps for its past-mindedness. In English, the word "scientific" is sometimes used in a similar sense; but more often, it implies the use of methods analogous to those of the natural sciences.

The German historian was not only certain that his field of work was a discipline; he also knew that it was a *Geisteswissenschaft*, a humanistic discipline, by definition. This gave him a starting advantage in any argument against an advocate of "scientific" methods in history. He had only to call his opponent's approach *naturwissenschaftlich* (appropriate to the natural sciences) or *positivistisch* (positivist) to shift the burden of proof to the challenger. In this way, the German language itself came to favor certain conceptions of knowledge and of learning. As Windelband observed, the Greek *philosophia* "means exactly that which we describe with the German word *Wissenschaft* and which . . . fortunately includes much more than the English and French *science*."[20] Why fortunately? Evidently because the German academics preferred to find in learning itself a dimension of philosophical contemplation and wisdom.

The word *Geisteswissenschaft* almost inevitably evoked the principle of empathy and its ramifications in the Idealistic language of geist. There was universal agreement among German scholars after 1890 that the modern German idea of the university and of learning was irrevocably tied to its intellectual origins in German Idealism and neohumanism.[21] The university as conceived by Humboldt, Schleiermacher, and Fichte, the arguments against the practicality of Halle, and even the actual organization of Berlin University were thought to define the German ideal of higher education for all future ages. The decades around 1800 came to seem a period of primitive purity. In those times, to follow Eduard Spranger's retrospective account, "the occupation with wissenschaftlich ideas in the sense of Kant, Fichte, Schelling, Hegel appeared *the* path toward the perfection of the personality, and the fully and richly unfolded humanistic personality also seemed the best guarantee of a free, conscientious, and intellectually alert citizenry."[22] According to Carl Becker, the universities then had the standing of national sanctuaries. Inspired by German Idealist philosophy and dedicated to a Faustian search for "pure" truth, they were carefully protected against premature demands for practical results. Like "fortresses of the grail," they were meant to have a spiritually ennobling rather than a narrowly utilitarian influence upon the disciples of learning and upon the nation as a whole.[23]

Again and again, the mandarins expressed their interest in the moral impact of learning, its effect upon the whole person. Whether through Platonic metaphors or through the language of Idealism, they invariably described the act of knowing as a complete personal involvement of the knower with the known. The principle of empathy was helpful in this connection, for it could be thought to imply a more than merely conceptual link between the student of the humanistic disciplines and his sources. After all, there were meanings and values embodied in those sources, not just facts. According to the *Brockhaus* definition, cultivation meant "forming of the soul by means of the cultural environment," through the "empathetic understanding [*Verstehen und Erleben*] of objective cultural values." Some of the words used in this definition will concern us again in a later chapter. The point just now is the mandarins' axiomatic concern with the personal relevance of learning.

After 1890, this concern was sometimes expressed in the proposition that wissenschaft could or should lead to a weltanschauung. "Weltanschauung" is usually translated as "world view" or "integral conception of the world," but the term came to imply even more than that. When the academic theologian Reinhold Seeberg spoke of the need for weltanschauung through scholarship, he was not just referring to a complete and systematic understanding of reality, or to a metaphysical as distinct from a "merely" epistemological emphasis in philosophy. He was also recommending an emotionally active stance toward the world, a personal "synthesis" of observations and value judgments, in which the individual's purposes were related to his understanding of the universe. Seeberg explicitly distinguished between "merely empirical knowledge of single parts of the world" and weltanschauung. "Weltanschauung is the spiritual [geistig] man's right of citizenship in the world of geist and therefore the justification of his dominion over the sensible world. It enables man, even without detailed specialized information, to understand the meaning and value of the several areas of human endeavor. It alone makes man a man in the full sense of the word, for it is the proof of his spirituality [Geistigkeit] or of his godlikeness." As might be expected, Seeberg defined cultivation as "the personal attainment of a weltanschauung."[24]

When German academics of the 1890's or of the 1920's talked about the functions of a university, they generally began by insisting upon the need for a combination of research and teaching. They made a sharp distinction between a school and an institution of higher learning, which, they said, should be dedicated to the active pursuit of research. University students were expected to participate in this pursuit to some degree, and even lectures were primarily to report upon recent scholarly work and to provide stepping stones for new advances.[25] Of course it was clear long before 1890 that this ideal could not be fully realized. Much professional training had always been done; some survey lectures were necessary; and the state examinations had a good deal of influence upon the curriculum. The philosopher Karl Jaspers, like many of his colleagues, was prepared to admit that the preparation of occupational specialists was in fact an unavoidable part of the university's duties. He even recognized the tremendous social importance of academic certificates as outward criteria of cultivation. These things seemed to him secondary to the main purposes of the university; but he could accept them as necessary adjustments to reality.[26]

Jaspers was not particularly interested in "general education" (Allgemeinbildung). That is to say, he did not strongly advocate more courses in physics for nonphysicists or in literature for natural scientists. In this respect, too, he shared the views of most of his colleagues. As we shall see, the mandarins complained a good deal about the dangers of "specialization" after 1890. In doing so, however, they were not referring primarily to the fact that experts in different disciplines knew less and less about each other's fields. Most of the professors took a lukewarm, indifferent, or actually hostile attitude toward the idea of interdisciplinary lectures or programs of study. What really worried them was not the isolation of the disciplines *from each other,* but the growing separation, within all disciplines, between scholarship and a certain kind of philosophy. Jaspers expressed this idea in the following way.

> Vitality in wissenschaft exists only in relation to a whole. Every single discipline is such a whole and has to that extent a philosophical character, and the individual discipline exists in relation to the whole of *wissenschaftlich* knowledge as such. Therefore it is the object of the university to instill in its pupil the idea of the whole of knowledge [*Erkennen*]. In this sense, every man who is moved by learning is "philosophical" . . . [Professional training] is devoid of geist and makes men inhumane in their occupations, if it is not directed toward the whole . . . [It is possible to make up for deficiencies of information.] But if this fundament . . . the orientation toward totalities or ideas, is missing, then everything else is hopeless.

In short, Jaspers did not particularly object to the student's concentration upon his own professional preparation, as long as that preparation was sufficiently "philosophical." All learning is "philosophical, insofar as it does not forget the end for the means, does not become submerged in . . . technique and mere details, and does not lose the idea . . . In the idea of universitas, in the philosophical totality, lies the spiritual [geistig] aspect of scholarship."[27]

Thus it was an axiom of mandarin doctrine that the university must be dedicated to the search for a "total," philosophical verity. This quest was not to be abandoned for the sake of immediately practical results; learning was not to be separated from philosophy. If and only if these rules were observed, the theory continued, then academic training might be expected to produce cultivation. This point was made by the educator Theodor Litt, who argued in favor of close ties between wissenschaft and philosophy in order to achieve the kind of cultivation that affected the "totality of man's nature." Seeberg took a very similar line when he suggested that the university did not fulfill its proper function unless its search for scholarly truth was accompanied and motivated by the striving for weltanschauung. Jaspers apparently meant to take a more complex and guarded position, for he did not believe that learning must invariably lead to weltanschauung. Nevertheless, it is hard to escape the impression that his argument about "wholeness" in learning was but a slightly subtler variant of Litt's and Seeberg's point. At bottom, Jaspers was just as convinced as most of his colleagues that the combination of research and teaching at the universities should and would have the kind of total effect upon the student that was always associated with the word cultivation. Indeed, he expressly listed cultivation as a function of the university.[28]

The more one studies the notion of cultivation, the more one is struck by its importance and by its many implications. Just consider what the philosopher and sociologist Georg Simmel had to say on the subject. "Every kind of learning, virtuosity, refinement in a man cannot cause us to attribute true cultivation [*Kultiviertheit*] to him, if these things function . . . only as superadditions which come to his personality from an area [*Wertgebiet*] external to it and ultimately remain external to it. In such a case, a man may have cultivated attributes [*Kultiviertheiten*], but he is not cultivated; cultivation comes about only if the contents absorbed out of the suprapersonal realm seem, as through a secret harmony, to unfold only that in the soul which exists within it as its own instinctual tendency and as the inner prefiguration of its subjective perfection."[29] Simmel's "suprapersonal realm" was the neo-Idealists' world of "objective geist." Apart from that technicality, the paragraph strongly recalls the Pietist and neohumanist ideal of unique self-development. The whole metaphor of tendencies "unfolding" according to an "inner prefiguration" also suggests the principle of individuality and its own circle of related images.

As a matter of fact, it is impossible to imagine the mandarin creed without the concept of individuality or without the symphonic analogy to which that concept was attached. Once cultivation was described as having a total effect upon the whole personality, the cultivated man almost had to be conceived as a unique work of art. That made a problem of the relationship between individual cultivation and national culture. Cultivated men were not alike, and culture, unlike civilization, was held to be more than a sum of more or less similar achievements. On the other hand, there was an incentive to see the nation's spirit, the *Volksgeist,* as "emanating from the most important and creative individuals." This could be done most easily by picturing national culture as a symphonic product of unique constituent elements. No German intellectual consciously developed all of these considerations; but the principle of individuality and the symphonic analogy did in fact play a very important technical role in the structure of the mandarin argument. As an idea, the analogy may be traced to the theological antecedents of Pietism, to Leibniz and his harmony of monads, or even further into the past. Its origins therefore do not depend upon the mandarin hypothesis. That hypothesis does help to account, however, for the perpetuation, the amazingly frequent reappearance, of certain themes and images in modern German academic literature. The principle of individuality was one such theme. The symphonic analogy became a sort of mental habit with many German scholars, and that may have been due in part to its role in the ideology of cultivation.

The quote from Simmel also raises a question about aptitude for learning. Since "every kind of learning, virtuosity, refinement in a man" was not considered cultivation, unless it unfolded the "inner prefiguration" of his soul's "subjective perfection," there was bound to be some difficulty in determining who was capable of being cultivated. If one thinks of education as a process in which a body of information and certain methods of analysis are communicated, one can arrive, at least in principle, at a means for evaluating a student's receptivity. It is possible to assess his native mental prowess, within certain limits, and to find out how much he already knows. Much more difficult problems arise, however, if one considers learning a transfer of cultural and spiritual values. If the pupil's whole personality has to be judged as a potential vehicle for the "unfolding" of these values, it becomes quite impossible to make even moderately objective decisions about his aptitude.

This was a serious problem in the mandarin philosophy of cultivation, for it tended to leave the selection of candidates for higher learning to chance—and to the social prejudices of the cultured elite itself. Until far into the twentieth century, German academics stubbornly resisted the idea that a student's potential ability might be tested. Jaspers actually distinguished between four classes of aptitudes relevant to academic work. In the first of these, he included the ability to learn, memory, and a variety of other functions which Americans would associate with the notion of the intelligence quotient. While granting that these qualities might eventually be measured more or less accurately, he considered them far less important for successful scholarship than three other categories of ability: "intelligence as such" (die eigentliche Intelligenz), "intellectual and spiritual sensitivity" (Geistigkeit), and "creativity, genius" (das Schöpferische, Geniale).[30] These things, he said, could never be statistically assessed. Following Plato, he declared it his ideal that the nation's greatest minds should be its leaders. But since this theoretical objective could never be perfectly realized in practice, he thought it best to leave the selection of university students, the nation's future leaders, to normal sociological processes, rather than to the rationalistic techniques of willfull examiners. He reminded his readers that the masses had always been known to have a low intelligence, and he stressed the importance of family background, feeling that a student's receptivity would be poor unless he came from the tradition of a "cultured family."

An even more important aspect of the German academic heritage was the ideal of "pure" and impractical learning. As Spranger pointed out, this conception was originally developed in conscious reaction against the emphasis on useful knowledge which had predominated at Halle and at other German universities during the eighteenth century. At that time, cameralist governments came close to turning the institutions of higher learning into mere training schools for loyal and orthodox pastors, clerks, and domain administrators.[31] The neohumanists and Idealists succeeded in averting this danger, and their indictment of narrow-minded practicality became a permanent part of the mandarin doctrine. In Spranger's opinion, it helped to protect German learning from that petty view of the relationship between theory and practice which eventually led Western scholars into the errors of positivism.

Jaspers stated the ideal of impracticality in its mildest and most coherent form. He admitted that absolute truth might never be attained; but he nevertheless insisted that it be pursued for its own sake: "Wissenschaft comes into being when, first, rational work frees itself from the mere service of life purposes . . . so that knowledge becomes a goal for its own sake, and when, secondly, the rational does not remain in isolated fragments . . . when everything rational is systematically to become a whole through being internally related."[32] It should be noticed that even Jaspers' position is more extreme than it seems at first. His formulation completely severs the ties between scholarship and all "life purposes," and it makes truth itself a kind of speculative totality. It thus evokes an image of learning that has little to do with the common-sense notion of asking questions and seeking evidence. Indeed, there is very little of the tactile or operational in Jaspers' definition of learning; it does not suggest touching, seeing, or doing something. In that sense, his argument represents an elitist philosophy of leisure; it is aristocratic, other-worldly, contemplative.

The classicist Werner Jaeger stated the same point even more strongly: "Wissenschaft and empiricism [*Empirie*], the latter word taken in the antique sense of practical experience, are two fundamentally different things, and wissenschaft has no place where *Empirie* is required, for theory kills the instinct."[33] As it happened, Jaeger used this distinction during the Weimar period to argue that elementary teachers should be excluded from the universities.

He placed their profession in the realm of practical experience, for which he left no room at the regular institutions of higher learning. To him as to many of his colleagues, wissenschaft meant abstraction, theory.

This equation in turn affected the way in which German scholars thought about the "freedom of learning." There was general agreement after 1890 that this freedom was firmly anchored in the German scholarly tradition. Humboldt, Schleiermacher, and the other intellectual founders of the modern German university had been deeply concerned with it, and their programmatic writings on the subject had been accepted in principle by German government officials as well as by the professors themselves. In the United States today, no one would think of launching an explicit theoretical attack upon academic freedom, even if he intended to limit or to undermine that liberty in practice. Just so it was with the freedom of learning in Germany during the later nineteenth century and thereafter. It was guaranteed—in theory—so that its range and import alone were open to dispute.

This is where the notion of impracticality made a difference, for it affected the ideal of free learning in its very meaning. Humboldt and his colleagues were offended by the official protection of religious orthodoxy. They demanded that the authorities cease their petty censorship of books and lectures, enforcing no restrictions upon the liberty of speech from the lectern. At the same time, they were anxious to challenge the governments' manifest attempts to gain immediately practical advantages from their financial support of higher education. The reformers objected to the predominance of the professional faculties over the faculty of philosophy, and they hoped to reverse this situation. They were the apostles of German Idealism, and they saw wissenschaft in the light of their philosophical systems. They thought that learning should be "pure" or "free" in the sense that no utilitarian considerations should dictate its concerns. As a result, the German ideal of academic freedom, which they defined, was always at least partly informed by the conviction that geist must not be asked to descend from the realm of theory in order to involve itself in practice.

In 1896, the economist Adolph Wagner delivered an academic address to celebrate the founding of Berlin University some nine decades earlier. In reviewing the circumstances under which the university was established, he reported a characteristic incident. Wilhelm von Humboldt had originally suggested that the university be made financially independent through a permanent grant of domain properties. The official then in charge of education within the Prussian Ministry of the Interior had urged the king to reject this proposal. His reasons were quoted as follows. "However exalted the heads may be, the stomachs will always maintain their rights against them . . . He who rules the latter will always be able to deal with the former."[34] Wagner recalled that Humboldt's plan was subsequently discarded and went on to say that the domain holdings would in fact have been insufficient to support the expansion of the university during the nineteenth century. Beyond that, he did not express any real sympathy for Humboldt's objectives or any regret at his failure. Indeed, Wagner appeared to be genuinely convinced that the state had always given and would always continue to give unstinting and disinterested support to pure learning.

This optimism seems a bit curious, particularly since the German universities were not institutionally well protected against bureaucratic interference. The rights of academic self-government were neither extensive nor secure, and the states had ample means of suppressing unorthodox opinions in the scholarly world. Nevertheless, there was relatively little concern over these matters—before 1918. A degree of official influence upon the institutions and upon the whole outward organization of learning simply did not disturb most German professors. The general view was that a certain practical dependence upon the state did not interfere with the ideal autonomy of the universities.[35] To maintain this position, it was necessary to say, in effect, that the worldly setting in which the search for truth takes place is not capable of seriously distorting the results of that search. This proposition in turn could only be based upon an idealistic conception of "pure" learning. If one admits that partisan views can affect scholarship because there is a close relationship between theoretical and practical concerns, one has to seek academic freedom either in financial and organizational autonomy or in the principled tolerance of diversity. Jaspers had a certain sympathy for the latter alternative, and so did some of the more thoughtful among his colleagues.[36] But for many German professors, the ideal of impracticality served as the chief guarantee of "free" learning, as a kind of substitute for institutional safeguards of academic independence.

All this is not to say that the German mandarins saw no relationship between the work of the universities and the everyday life of German society. On the contrary, they had an amazing faith in the power of the written word. They rejected the notion that learning should produce immediately useful results of a technical sort, and they certainly had no "positivist" conception of social engineering. On a more "ideal" plane, however, they firmly believed that learning was relevant to life. Indeed, the broad definition of the academic experience in terms of cultivation and weltanschauung tended to make the universities responsible for the moral condition of their nation. It was all too easy to picture the collective achievements of geist as a kind of spiritual fluid which could be absorbed by the body of German society, once it had been distilled from pure truth within the academic "fortresses of the grail." Higher education acquired a tremendous moral and spiritual significance in this scheme, and the intellectual leaders of the cultivated elite filled the role of intermediaries between the eternal and temporal realms. But they could perform this function and hold their place only as long as no one lost faith in their Idealistic weltanschauung.

SOCIAL AND POLITICAL IMPLICATIONS

Modern West European political theory has developed around two major concepts: natural law and the social contract. Both of these ideas have been interpreted as limitations upon the absolute power of the state. Both have tended to strengthen the individual's right of resistance against bad or tyrannical government. Natural law has provided independent standards of judgment to be used against a despot, and the idea of the social contract has tended to suggest that political institutions ought to be examined from the point of view of their usefulness to society and to its members.

In Germany, the mainstream of political thought has taken a different direction. During the course of the nineteenth century and especially after 1890, the difference between German and Anglo-French social theory increased, attracting more and more general notice. But the divergence really began during the seventeenth and eighteenth centuries, as Leonard Krieger has shown. From Pufendorf to Thomasius, Wolff, and Kant, German thinkers restated the conceptions of natural law and the social contract in such a way as to minimize their antiabsolutist implications. They adopted characteristic "patterns of reconciliation" which allowed the state to appear the guardian of valued liberties, rather than their potential enemy.[37]

Several lines of argument led to this result. The individual was made to transfer many of his rights to society in an initial compact, so that a subsequent absorption of society into the state gave the state an unusually extensive set of powers. Natural law lost its status as an independent source of social norms. Positive law was redefined as an offshoot or an ally of eternal ethical principles. The idealized state became a moral agent, an educational institution, and the freedom from external restraint was transformed into the "inner freedom" of the ethically self-directed individual.

One of the products of these intellectual developments was the German ideal of the "legal state," the *Rechtsstaat*.[38] The term itself did not come into use until the early nineteenth century; but the whole conception dates back to Thomasius, to Wolff, and especially to Kant. Briefly stated, the ideal of the legal state requires that government proceed on the basis of fixed and rational principles, that these by publicly and clearly stated, and that they conform to the timeless requirements of ethics. The two crucial elements in this definition are the attribution of moral purposes to the state and the call for legality. The call for legality could be interpreted in a "liberal" sense; it could be turned into the demand for a political constitution. But this did not really happen in Germany until the early nineteenth century. Before that, the theoretical antecedents of the legal state implied no more than a revulsion against unsystematic and arbitrary government. Even when writing about a "republic," Kant was referring to a future concordance of the positive and the moral law, to a time when an ethically mature people would freely obey precepts which it acknowledged to be its own. This position could be described as "virtually" but not actually constitutional.

For these reasons, it is easiest to understand the theoretical demand for legality in eighteenth-century Germany as an expression of the bureaucratic drive for rationality and predictability in government. As such, it paralleled the actual work of legal codification and reform which culminated in the General Code of 1794. The demand for legality was directed against the purely personal government of eighteenth-century princelings who still regarded their territories and subjects as their private property. It reflected the burgher's search for a certain security in private life, and it justified the official's view of his calling. What it did not do, it was not meant to do: it did not limit the scope of bureaucratic, systematic absolutism, and it did not imply any sort of popular participation in government.

Along with the concept of the legal state, the ideal of the *Kulturstaat,* the "cultural state," has played an important role in modern German political theory.[39] Once again, the word itself did not come into use until the nineteenth century; but the ideas associated with it originated before 1800. The German neohumanists and Idealists of the later eighteenth century judged all human affairs in the light of one great objective. The ideal of cultivation was their ultimate value, and they were naturally inclined to subordinate other concerns and issues to the overriding claims of culture. When applied to politics, this approach led to the ideal of the cultural state.

The cultural approach to government, if one may call it that, did not necessarily imply a favorable view of the cameralist state of the eighteenth century. At least one of the great founders of the mandarin tradition, Wilhelm von Humboldt, nearly developed an incorrigible aversion to paternalistic government, because he was afraid that it might prove a hindrance to cultivation. Indeed, Humboldt probably wrote as rigorous a defense of political individualism upon cultural grounds as any laisser-faire theorist ever did for economic reasons.[40] If there was such a thing as "mandarin liberalism" in Germany, Humboldt was its chief founder and model. What might have happened if the cultivated elite in Germany had really gone into concerted opposition to absolutism at the threshhold of the nineteenth century?

We do not know, because they did nothing of the kind. Instead, they made a characteristic arrangement with their rulers, and it is this bargain which was subsequently idealized in the concept of the cultural state. The terms of the settlement were that the bureaucratic monarchy would give unstinting support to learning, without demanding immediately practical returns, and without exercising too strict a control over the world of learning and of geist. In other respects also, the state would acknowledge and serve the demands of culture. It would become a vehicle, a worldly agent or form for the preservation and dissemination of spiritual values. Indeed, it would seek its legitimacy in this function, and it would be rewarded by finding it there. The state would earn the support of the learned elite, who would serve it not only as trained officials but also as theoretical sponsors and defenders.

Of course, there is no single document which describes the symbiotic relationship between the mandarins and their rulers in these businesslike terms. No contracts were signed. Nevertheless, there is a variety of evidence that the bargain was actually sealed. We have already examined the legal and institutional arrangements which were made during the decades around 1800 and which established the character of German social organization for many years thereafter. The intellectual founders of the mandarin tradition helped to organize this system and described its purposes. Wilhelm von Humboldt himself abandoned his earlier defense of an extreme cultural individualism to make plans for the new Prussian university at Berlin. Together with the other great reformers of that time, he created the somewhat ambiguous ideology of "free" and "pure" learning, which permitted the subsequent accommodation of German scholarship to the realities of bureaucratic absolutism. All this was part of a tacit, incompletely conscious understanding.

On a more theoretical level, the doctrine of the cultural state was implicit in the writings of Fichte and of other prominent intellectuals during the period around 1800. In *Weltbürgertum und Nationalstaat* and elsewhere, the historian Friedrich Meinecke has described the gradual emergence of a German sense of nationality during the later eighteenth and early nineteenth centuries.[41] The peculiar character of this process was partly due to the absence of a unified German state. The nation had to be defined in purely cultural terms, because there was no opportunity to develop an institutional or constitutional sense of statehood. At the same time, the new nationalism was almost exclusively a creation of the educated classes, and this should help to explain the form it took. The cultural arguments of the neohumanists and Idealists were transferred from the cosmopolitan context of the eighteenth century to the new framework of the cultural nation. Sometimes the Romantic *Volk,* the people, played a mediating role in this translation; but this was not always or necessarily the case. The important point is that the nation and, through it, the state were defined as creatures and as agents of the mandarins' cultural ideals.

The principle of individuality and the symphonic analogy were immensely helpful as techniques of argument in the building up of nationalist theory. As Troeltsch suggested, they served to establish satisfying images of the relationships between personal cultivation and national culture, between the individual and the volk, between the nation and humanity. Certain characteristics of the Rankean historical tradition were born in this context. Henceforth, German historians tended to treat states as individualities, symphonically conceived "wholes," embodiments of unique national spirits. The emphasis was generally upon the contention of these individualities on the international plane. During most of the nineteenth century, Rankean history was chiefly military and diplomatic. Particularly social history did not fit into the mandarins' scheme of reality, since it would have challenged the rather one-sided identification of the national "whole" with the cultural mission of its intellectual leaders.

In any case, international conflicts were supposed to reflect struggles between different cultural unities, and this underlying assumption gave meaning and poignancy to the story of states and their battles. Many a German schoolboy has grown up with the impression that it was Fichte who defeated Napoleon.

In a popular history of the German Wars of Liberation, Friedrich Meinecke described the Prussian Reform Period in terms of a "marriage between the state and the world of the mind and spirit." "The German world of the intellect and spirit [der deutsche Geist] approached the state in genuine and unforced sympathy. Springs were activated which have fertilized all of German life, far beyond the immediate goal of German liberation. What had been achieved before then, when the German spirit sought and desired only itself, may reach higher into the sphere of the eternal; but when the spirit descended to the state, it secured not only its own and the state's threatened existence, but also a whole sum of inner values, a source of energy and happiness for later generations."[42] A fertile image, one might call that, and one which strongly suggests the theory of the cultural state. On one level, the paragraph can be read as a social and institutional history of the bargain between the mandarins and their rulers. At the same time, Meinecke meant to refer to the intellectual history of the period around 1800, when German thinkers became theoretically more concerned and more favorably disposed toward the state. In some sense, they developed a more worldly orientation. Meinecke was not uncritical in his attitude toward some of the nineteenth-century consequences of this marriage. He knew that German thought had lost something in its descent. But he also understood the immense importance of the accommodation for the subsequent evolution of German society and culture, and he saw that both partners benefited from the arrangement.

What really happened in Germany around 1800 can be described in several ways. One can stress the fact that the theories of German Idealism and Romanticism supplied German absolutism and nationalism with a certain moral self-confidence. Western liberals have often been preoccupied with this aspect of the problem. The

German historians Ernst Troeltsch and Friedrich Meinecke felt that a unique idea of freedom was set down in the writings of the German Idealists and Romantics.[43] They traced this conception to the emphasis upon mystical "submission" (*Hingabe*) and "inward-ness" (*Innerlichkeit*) in the German religious heritage. When secularized, these traditions engendered an ideal of voluntary submission to the community and a simultaneous concern for the "inner freedom" of the cultivated personality. The adaptation of religious images to the field of politics took place within the confines of the petty court society of the seventeenth and eighteenth centuries, which tended in any case to inhibit the outward expressions of individuality. As a result, German Idealists and Romantics treated the state as that "whole" which even the ruler was pledged to serve. Only the claims of individual culture and of its representatives survived to give a positive meaning to the German idea of freedom.

This is but one of several possible approaches to a single phenomenon. It may not matter very much whether one finds the antecedents of German political theory in Pietism or in the German Enlightenment, in Idealism or in Romanticism, whether one reads religious thinkers, pedagogues, poets, officials, or philosophers. One is likely to find the same group of closely related themes again and again. The mandarins' whole situation created certain basic concerns. These were formed on what Karl Mannheim calls a pre-theoretical level. They were attitudes, not theories; and they manifested themselves in a characteristic set of mental habits and semantic preferences. A language was born which could be applied to various fields of thought. Hajo Holborn has remarked that the very vocabulary of German political theory seemed to take on a unique character during the decades around 1800.[44] As the German and the Anglo-French traditions began to diverge, it became progressively more difficult to restate the terminology of one in the words of the other. In Germany, the mandarins' language set the parameters of political discussion for the whole nineteenth century. That was the real import of the marriage between geist and the state.

The distinctive quality of German social and political thought after 1800 was not so much a matter of this or that specific doctrine as one of general tone. No single proposition was generally held which could be identified as the basic impetus for the divergence between the German and the West European traditions. Even the ideas of the legal and the cultural state were never precisely enough formulated to be assigned such a role. They were not formally related in any case. They could be logically separated, and they also differed to some extent in their social and chronological origins. The notion of legality was older and more purely bureaucratic in its historical antecedents than the conception of the cultural state. The latter was based on the ideology of cultivation and culture, which arose at a relatively late stage in the maturation of the educated elite. It could develop only when even civil servants had graduated from the status of the expert to the self-confidence of the intellectual aristocrat.

Nevertheless, nineteenth-century German political speculation was internally consistent in some way. On a vague and informal level, there was a striking unity of outlook. But to account for this homogeneity, one has to look for a unifying element on the pre-theoretical level. One has to find an ideological explanation for the fact that in practice the theory of the legal state became inextricably intertwined with that of the cultural state. The best way to do this is to point to the processes of social fusion which created a more or less coherent elite.

The common element in all mandarin political theorizing was a characteristically "idealistic" and "apolitical" approach. During the Weimar period, the philosopher Heinrich Rickert cited Fichte's *Closed Commercial State* as a model of "idealistic" politics.[45] He pointed out that Fichte's argument was divided into three separate parts. The first was a theoretical characterization of the ideal state, the second a factual description of the imperfect conditions prevailing at his own time, the third a concluding outline of the path which was to lead from reality to perfection. Rickert felt that if a systematic discipline, a wissenschaft dealing with political affairs was possible at all, it had to take the logical form of Fichte's scheme. He also suggested that the second and third steps in Fichte's method were methodologically simple and relatively unimportant. In other words, the postulation of a theoretical norm for the state was the main purpose of formal argument about politics.

This is precisely the sense in which German academic discussions of social and political affairs tended to be idealistic. The emphasis was always upon the ultimate purposes of government. In the tradition of the legal and cultural state, these theoretical objectives were generally stated in moral and spiritual terms. The analysis of political realities was neglected, and relatively little attention was paid to questions of political technique. These matters were generally felt to be trivial. Indeed, the suggestion was that the details of everyday politics were ethically as well as intellectually beneath the notice of the cultivated man. In this sense and in this sense only, the German intellectual was and considered himself apolitical: he had an aversion for the practical aspects of the political process. In part, his attitude was a defensive one. He had relatively little experience in the field of actual political negotiation. But his distrust of "interest politics" was also a reflection of his own interested preferences. He correctly assumed that he would be threatened in his elevated role if the pragmatic politics of group competition and numerical compromise were allowed to move to the front of the stage.

All this is not to say that all German academics were alike in their political opinions. They shared certain assumptions and used the same basic vocabulary. Still, there was room for a fairly wide range of specific positions within the general framework of mandarin politics. As a matter of fact, the underlying tension between the outlook of the administrative official and that of the cultivated man never totally disappeared from the German intellectual scene. While some members of the educated elite adopted a predominantly legalistic and bureaucratic point of view, there were others who followed Humboldt's lead in emphasizing purely cultural objectives. Again, the Idealistic language of the cultural state could be used to arrive at different conclusions. Two examples from the writings of German university professors of the early twentieth century will help to illustrate this point.

In one of the many retrospective accounts of the mandarin creed, Eduard Spranger discussed the political theories of the German classical age. Characteristically enough, he looked to the period around 1800 as a model for his own times. The chief lesson he drew from the writings of the great Idealists was that of a "transcendental nexus [*überpersönlicher Lebenszusammenhang*] stemming from the divine" which "legitimates the state and which the individual must voluntarily accept and assimilate, if he wishes to raise himself to a higher level of spiritual life."[46] Here, the tradition is used almost exclusively to glorify the state and to preach submission.

A rather different attitude emerges from Ernst Troeltsch's account of the "German idea of freedom." Like Spranger, Troeltsch reviewed the theoretical foundations of the German intellectual heritage with the hope of enlightening his contemporaries. But when he summarized the German ideal of the state, he departed markedly from Spranger's emphasis. He described a mandarin utopia in terms of "the organized unity of the people on the basis of a duty-bound and yet critical submission of the individual to the whole, supplemented and corrected by the independence and individuality of free intellectual and spiritual cultivation [*freie geistige Bildung*]."[47] The plea for submission to the whole is repeated in this sentence; but it is softened by the recommendation of a critical stance. Beyond that, the whole tone is changed by the "correction" introduced in favor of free intellectual and spiritual cultivation. While this is in no sense a conventionally liberal or democratic position, it does limit the competence of the state at least in the mandarins' own realm of cultivation.

Thus it was possible to formulate a variety of specific viewpoints in the language of mandarin politics. Besides, that language actually changed with time. Cultivation, civilization, the legal state, and other terms of a similar importance actually altered their meaning to some extent between 1800 and 1900. The telescopic approach of the present chapter should not be allowed to obscure this fact. The antithesis between culture and civilization, for example, acquired additional significance with the impact of technological change during the later nineteenth century. In a similar way, the ideal of classical cultivation itself was affected by the system of state examinations and privileges which grew up around it. As the gymnasium became an officially favored institution, it inevitably lost some of the qualities which the neohumanists of the late eighteenth century had meant to give it. As the realschulen increased their enrollment and the classicists continued to exclude their rivals from the universities and from the government tests, gymnasium cultivation automatically became socially defensive and snobbish.

The mandarin ideology had always been elitist in character. It represented the special claims of the highly educated, and it was based, from the beginning, upon an idealization of pure and impractical learning. But it was capable of amplification in two rather different directions. On the one hand, it could be exploited to prove that uneducated aristocrats should not be allowed to monopolize the administrative offices and that government should be the servant, not the master, of geist. On the other hand, the mandarin ideology could equally well be directed against all those who had "merely practical" educations, as well as against "merely utilitarian" approaches in education, in industry, and in politics. The idea that true cultivation transforms the whole personality of the learner could be used to challenge birth and tradition as criteria of social stratification. It could also serve to rationalize the prerogatives of a new aristocracy of cultivation.

From the eighteenth to the twentieth century, the mandarins always used both versions of their argument to some extent. But their emphasis changed. While they played the part of insurgents against an alliance of absolute princes and landed nobles, they stressed what might be called the aggressive version of their theory. They gradually veered away from this line, however, as they found themselves advancing toward the favored position which they had begun by demanding. Subtly and slowly, the balance shifted. The mandarins' ties to the rest of the middle class were loosened, and their obligation to the status quo increased. A moment arrived at which their leadership was threatened more from below than from above, and from that point on, they gave an ever greater emphasis to the defensive and vaguely conservative side of their philosophy. By around 1890, at any rate, many German academics had come to assume the stance of Platonic philosopher-statesmen preparing to meet the onslaught of the mechanics. The words they used to defend themselves were not so different from those which their ancestors had created for different purposes a century earlier. The meanings of these terms had been transformed, however, because the realities of the social situation had changed.

The same general pattern may be observed in the evolution of mandarin political theory. Around 1800, the ideal of the legal and cultural state still had decidedly progressive implications. The demand for predictability in government was an attack upon unrestrained absolutism. In launching it, the German intellectuals of the time were speaking not only for themselves, but for the whole burgher class from which they came. When they attempted to redefine the objectives of the state in cultural terms, they were proceeding more specifically in their own behalf. But even this aspect of their program was certainly not consciously undemocratic in its original form. It was stated in universal terms; it implied no sense of caste.

During the 1830's and 1840's, the educated classes in Germany led the reform movement which culminated in the Revolution of 1848.[48] They felt that their rulers had broken the tacit agreement which had been reached before 1812 and which was based upon the model of the legal and cultural state. In the period of reaction after 1815, a number of German princes tried to reassert the principles as well as the practices of purely personal and arbitrary rule. The civic security of private citizens was threatened by the irrational exercise of power, and all but the most doctrinaire conservatives were forced to admit that order had somehow to be imposed upon a group of unenlightened despots who refused to consider themselves the servants of their states.

Nothing did more to discredit the system of petty principalities which still existed in Germany in 1848 than the princes' continual interference in cultural affairs. Such meddling reached ludicrous proportions after 1819.[49] The rulers felt it necessary to combat the intellectual sense of nationality which had arisen as an integral part of the mandarins' program around 1800. The result was that the transmutation of cultural into political nationalism was accelerated and that the call for unification became a liberal demand.[50] Reactionary ministers introduced galling though ineffectual censorship regulations, and those whose views appeared in any way progressive or nationalistic were persecuted as demagogues. We can imagine how educated Germans felt when the reprinting of Fichte's *Addresses* was prohibited in Prussia in 1824.[51] The Prussian Ministry of Culture, whose birth had inspired high hopes among the reforming Idealists, was now made the instrument of obscurantism. Particularly in the 1840's, the ministry put pressure on schools and teachers to inculcate in their charges an orthodox piety and an unquestioning respect for authority. It particularly distrusted the realschulen; but it also attacked classical studies for their heathen content, and it admonished the universities to concentrate more exclusively upon their principal task of producing loyal and useful civil servants. Such views might have been acceptable to German academics in the days of cameralism and of Halle's ascendancy. Since the neohumanists and Idealists had defined the freedom of learning in an antiutilitarian sense, however, no ministry could hope to reimpose so menial a role upon the universities.

No wonder then that liberal bureaucrats, professional men, and university professors played so important a part in the reform movement of the 1830's and 1840's. *Bildungsliberalismus,* the liberalism of the educated classes, was perhaps the most important ingredient in the general sentiment that eventually led to the Revolution. This circumstance might help to explain some of the peculiarities of German political thought on the eve of 1848. In social questions, the mandarins had no great sympathy either for the specific class objectives of the emerging entrepreneurial bourgeoisie or for the radical demands of artisans and workers. They also had little in common with the aristocratic and agrarian conservatives. Their interest in economic questions was limited to a fairly vague longing for social harmony. Nationalism was an important and integral part of their program, not a tragically irrelevant rival of liberalism. In domestic affairs, the mandarins were preoccupied with the need for constitutional reform. Government by law was more important to them than government by consent. They were generally less interested in democratic ideas, in voting rights, and ministerial government, than in constitutional and legal guarantees of civic rights. The experience of reaction had convinced them that constitutions were necessary, because there was no other way of protecting the legal state against the whims of recalcitrant princes. Finally, it was characteristic of mandarin liberalism that all its tenets were closely related to the issue of cultural liberty. To educated Germans of the 1830's and 1840's, the freedoms of thought, learning, and expression were at least as important as the specifically political freedoms. The offenses of reactionary rulers against the rights of geist probably did more to cause the Revolution of 1848 than has sometimes been realized.

In other words, the German mandarins of the early nineteenth century were liberal; but their zeal for social and political reform had its characteristic limitations. The experiences of 1848 and 1849, particularly the appearance of popular and democratic pressures, could only serve to strengthen these reservations. The result was that the cultivated elite began to assume a more defensive position. Heinrich Heffter has described the mood of educated Germans during the 1850's and 1860's in the following terms.

> Against the plutocratic as well as the democratic tendencies of modern economic conditions, mandarin liberalism [*Bildungsliberalismus*] represented the views of an older . . . social group, namely the prestigious leadership [*Honoratiorentum*] of the higher middle class. This group often expressed a strong aversion to the bourgeoisie proper . . . criticizing . . . its materialistic mentality and its interest politics. But all democratic movements were rejected as well. [The adherents of mandarin liberalism] felt themselves to be the intellectual aristocracy [*Geistesaristokratie*] of the nation and in any case a part of the upper class. The moderate liberalism of the educated burgher segment moved . . . further to the right. The experiences of the unsuccessful revolution spurred the reaction against radicalism and, despite all opposition against a reactionary government

system, increased the inclination to compromise with the monarchic-bureaucratic powers.[52]

This inclination to compromise continued to grow during the 1870's and 1880's. Bismarck exploited it. Somehow, changing social realities forced the mandarins, or most of them, toward an ever more unquestioning support of the existing regime. Before the end of the century, the German academic community as a whole had fallen into the role of a vaguely conservative and decidedly official establishment.

3

POLITICS AND SOCIAL THEORY, 1890–1918

ORTHODOXY AND MODERNISM: BASIC CONCERNS

In 1896, the German philosopher Eduard von Hartmann published a savage little essay to warn his countrymen of the "danger of democracy."[1] In France, he said, successive waves of mob arrogance had swept away the aristocracy of birth, the aristocracy of money, and finally the aristocracy of education. In Germany, these three elites were still in existence, and there was little danger that they would jointly constitute a closed caste, precisely because not one but three criteria of selection were operating side by side. Since 1870, the German masses had nevertheless launched an attack upon all differences between men, and the political parties had begun to flatter the mob in their unprincipled race for votes. Since the masses were invariably swayed only by the crudest emotions, they would never be content with the achievement of equality before the law. Their ideal was that of a totally leveled society, of anarchy in fact. Unless the three elites could learn to stand together against this threat, the liberal legal state was bound to be destroyed. The Caesarism of a great demagogue would then become the lesser of two evils, the only alternative to the outright rule of the mob. Throughout the essay, Hartmann was especially anxious to show that democracy constituted a danger to German culture. The "herd," he said, wanted above all to pull the "culture-bearing minority" down to its own level, to destroy the "culture-serving restraints and inequalities of a natural social organization."

At least until 1918, few of Hartmann's colleagues adopted the violent tone of his antidemocratic polemics. Nevertheless, a good number of them actually agreed with him in principle, and most of them accepted his view of "the masses." By 1890 at any rate, the majority of German professors and scholars approved the traditional stratification of German society, tolerated the illiberal aspects of the existing political regime, and shared in the fear and hostility with which the ruling classes met the Social Democratic movement. As Hartmann's article suggests, many members of the cultivated elite were prepared to side with the junkers and Conservatives against any initiatives toward parliamentary or social reform. Beyond that, they often affected a general disdain for the "materialism" and the vulgarity of the emerging industrial society.

Hartmann's arguments were perhaps exceptionally aggressive in their tone. In their substance, however, they typify what I propose to call the "orthodox" position in the spectrum of mandarin political opinion after 1890. The term orthodox is helpful in several respects. It avoids the problems of definition which arise when one tries to decide what is truly conservative. It eliminates the danger of inappropriately extending Anglo-American standards to the German context. Also, it rightly suggests that the orthodox made up a majority and represented a more or less official attitude within the German academic community. Their position was really rather simple, and not surprising. If one regards the mandarin heritage as the ideology of an educated elite, one has no difficulty in understanding the views of a Hartmann. Faced with the threats of the mass age, many German intellectuals had only to exploit the antidemocratic implications of their tradition to arrive at fairly predictable arguments. In this sense too, the opinions exemplified by Hartmann's essay are well described as orthodox: they were doctrinaire, single-minded, and logically uncomplicated; they followed obvious lines of reasoning to inevitable conclusions. As a matter of fact, it was generally the less articulate, politically unsophisticated, and intellectually less distinguished members of the German academic community who made up the rank and file of the orthodox majority.

Some of the greatest German scholars, and especially the well-known social scientists, developed more complex arguments and took a more balanced attitude about the problems of their time. They recognized, above all, that the processes of industrialization and democratization could not be totally reversed. They were realistic enough to suspect that at least some of the disturbing aspects of modern civilization were so intimately linked with the necessities and even the advantages of socio-economic change that a wholesale condemnation of the new age was both irresponsible and pointless. The members of this relatively progressive minority may appropriately be called "modernists" or "accommodationists," because they were prepared to resign themselves to those facets of modern social life that seemed to them inevitable. Their whole approach to the political and cultural affairs of their nation was colored by the conviction that only a partial accommodation to modern needs and conditions would enable the mandarins and their values to retain a certain influence even in the twentieth century.

A 1912 article by the historian Friedrich Meinecke provides the best introduction to the modernist position.

> Unquestionably, there is something "democratic" in the demand that the de facto preferment of the nobility in the diplomatic corps, in the administration, and in the armed ser-

vices cease at last, that the rights of the Reichstag be expanded and the Prussian electoral law broadened . . . But it is always overlooked that the "democratic" demand represents only one side of the great pushing and shoving from below . . . The core of what we face today is something else, something quite instinctive and elemental . . . It is the drive toward an adjustment of the political and social organism to the tremendous changes of economic life and the huge increase of population which we have experienced in the last three or four decades.[2]

The attempt to "hold the new life back by force," Meinecke argued, would result "either in revolutionary explosions or in spiritual or material decay." A wise transformation of "outdated political and cultural institutions," on the other hand, would help to preserve "the good and vital aspects of the old conditions."

Meinecke was neither a convinced democrat nor a friend of government through parliamentary interest bargaining. He was therefore pleased to notice that a "new aristocracy" was being formed in Germany. The masses, he felt, were not in a position to govern themselves. In politics as well as in economic life, they had to place their confidence in talented leaders, so that the "temporary dictatorship of trust" (temporäre Vertrauensdiktatur) was in effect the classic form of modern government. "Parliaments can become useful means to an end, if they make possible the rise of significant talents to power; and for this reason, not because parliamentary rule as such is our ideal, we consider the extension of parliamentary rights a demand worth discussing." Thus it was Meinecke's belief and hope that democracy could be organized to provide its own cure; for the new popular leaders, if given a chance, would simultaneously express and direct the vague aspirations of the people. "The supposedly leveling and shallow mass existence of our time begins to develop an antidote out of its own substance, to transcend and to correct itself."[3]

Meinecke was not the only modernist who was interested in the "temporary dictatorship of trust" as a mode of government for the twentieth century. Max Weber's political ideas were developing in a similar direction toward the end of the Wilhelmian period.[4] It should be emphasized that neither Weber nor Meinecke envisioned anything approximating a totalitarian regime. Their models were American and English; their respect for civic rights cannot be questioned, and their plans were always constructed within the framework of a parliamentary system. Meinecke thought of union leaders, party tribunes, and even socially progressive entrepreneurs when he wrote of the new aristocracy. Weber was interested in any arrangement that might have put a vigorous, responsible, and intelligent statesman in charge of German foreign policy after Bismarck's departure. Both men were convinced that the Reichstag could serve as a training ground for political talent, if the path to the highest ministerial offices were opened to its leaders.

As Meinecke said, it was the alternative of stagnation or revolution which the accommodationist wanted to avoid. They hoped to guide the social and political forces that had been released by the industrial revolution, to take the sting out of democracy, to wean the Social Democratic workers from the radicalism and internationalism of Marxist orthodoxy, and to inculcate in the masses a certain minimum of respect for the cultural traditions and national ideals of the mandarin heritage. But they knew that their scheme had little chance of success, unless timely concessions were made. The haughty intransigence of the Prussian junkers and agrarian Conservatives seemed to them at once shortsighted and egotistical. Such leading modernists as Max Weber, Friedrich Meinecke, Ferdinand Tönnies, Lujo Bretano, and Ignaz Jastrow devoted much of their political writing to an attack upon the overrepresentation of rural areas in the Prussian legislature and in the German political system as a whole, upon the tax and tariff privileges of the agrarian magnates, and upon the junkers' predominance in various branches of the government. It particularly annoyed the reformers that the Conservative Party habitually used patriotic phrases to justify repressive policies, while never losing sight of its agrarian clients' own particular interests. "The aristocracy which dominates in Prussia," said Meinecke, "boasts of its willingness to make sacrifices in the national interest. In the future, it will have to prove it by making concessions to the justified demands of urban and industrial Germany."[5]

Convinced that the policies of the Conservatives would "tear us apart instead of uniting us," the modernists sought support for their own program from the middle-class National Liberal and Progressive parties. Meinecke hoped to convert the National Liberals into a "true party of the middle," a party of national reconciliation and social peace. "Only the liberal idea in its modern form, cleansed of the dogmatism of earlier times, filled with an understanding for the demands of the state and of realpolitik, but also with the spirit of social harmony and a sense of national community, can become the binding agent that ties might and the masses together again and gives the state the inner strength to protect the nation's vital future interests."[6] It is not surprising that Meinecke often felt frustrated in his aims, for the National Liberal Party was at least partly the political representative of the industrialists. It was therefore deeply involved in the competition of economic interest groups which played an increasingly important role in German politics after 1890. The mandarins had no part and wanted no part in these struggles. "We do not want to shrink down to being the Conservatives' middle-class auxiliary corps and an appendix of the heavy industrialists of Westphalia," Meinecke begged;[7] but the National Liberals continued to oppose social reforms and to provoke the Social Democrats.

Thus the mandarin reformers were never completely at home in the bourgeois liberal camp. They were always trying to transform the liberal parties, to direct their attention away from entrepreneurial interest politics, to guide them toward moderate social reform, and to interest them in progressive cultural and educational programs. The ordinary channels of Wilhelmian politics could never really satisfy the accommodationists, who were therefore strongly attracted to the Harnack-Naumann wing of the Protestant-Social Congress and to Friedrich Naumann's own short-lived National Social Union. Some of the names which come to mind in this connection are those of Troeltsch, Meinecke, Max and Alfred Weber, Brentano, Gerhart von Schulze-Gävernitz, and Adolf Harnack himself. These men wanted social reform without Marxism. They shared

Naumann's belief that genuine concessions at home would align the democratic movement behind a strong national foreign policy. In any case, such plans as these were more genuinely compatible with their basic objectives than the programs of any of the existing parties.

In a way, it would be perfectly reasonable to describe the accommodationists as "enlightened conservatives." On the other hand, it would then be difficult to find many liberals among the German professors. The main point to be made about mandarin politics is precisely that it fell outside the framework of the conventional party system. If one visualizes a spectrum of opinion ranging from Hartmann on the right to Meinecke in the left center and beyond him to the Weber brothers and a few younger social scientists, one has to move very close to the extreme left of the scale to encounter any criticisms of mandarin political theory in its fundamental assumptions.

These assumptions were rooted in the traditional model of the legal and cultural state. They suggested that it was desirable and possible to keep the political process free of the new economic class interests. With very few exceptions, all the German academics dreamed of a state or of a political party which would create social harmony out of conflict, which would be guided by cultural and ethical objectives and by the ideal of German greatness in world affairs. Since the elite was rapidly losing its influence upon the new electoral politics, it had only two basic alternatives. It could stand against democracy, or it could try to convert the masses, the businessmen, and their parties to an "idealistic" politics. The first choice led into the arms of the junkers, who knew how to benefit from the elevated and patriotic rhetoric of mandarin orthodoxy. The other option involved Naumann's experiment and other similar movements. In either case, the mandarin intellectual typically rationalized his recommendations by criticizing the interest politics, the narrow utilitarianism, and the political immorality of the day. In 1901, the modernist philosopher and pedagogue Friedrich Paulsen stated this argument in the following terms. "The party system hinders the forces which would otherwise unite in communally useful activity.

... [It] has a tendency to wreak havoc in public life, to destroy right and justice, and to ruin individual characters."[8]

It should be added at once that the mandarins' charges against the politics of their day were not entirely unfounded. Bismarck's system and his tactics did not encourage political responsibility, and the behavior of the parties in the Reichstag was not always a model of enlightened principle. Nevertheless, there were serious weaknesses and dangers in the idealistic argument as well. To begin with, it was rather vague. It could be used, and misused, for or against almost any group. The orthodox directed it mainly against the Social Democrats. Even Hartmann professed to speak in defense of legality and cultural values, and yet he might have known that he was only helping to rationalize a junker regime which was anything but ideal in its motives. This was obvious to Meinecke and to other modernists; but who was to decide where moral earnest ended and obscurantist hypocrisy began?

Another difficulty was that the elevated discourse of mandarin politics could lead straight into the realm of illusion. Some German academics became so obsessed with the need for an ethical rejuvenation of political life that they developed a kind of polemical indifference to the specific questions of political technique and organization. As the modernist Leopold von Wiese put it, relatively mildly, during the First World War, "all the observations which I can make concerning political problems lead me again and again to the realization: the spirit is more important than the organizational form."[9] If one stands sufficiently far "above" the political process, as many mandarin intellectuals thought they did, one begins to believe that all interests of whatever kind, all organization, and all negotiation can be totally eliminated from politics. If this position is taken to its logical extreme, it begins to prevent one from seeing the facts; it becomes irresponsible and therefore dangerous.

As a matter of fact, the yearning for an escape from interest politics helped to lead many educated Germans into the pseudoidealistic world of anti-Semitism and aggressive nationalism.

It can be statistically demonstrated that anti-Semitic sentiments were widely current in the German academic community of the late nineteenth century. Figures on the percentage of Jews among the students and teachers at German secondary schools and universities throw much light upon the situation of the Jewish intellectual. The German Jews were relatively more concentrated in the urban centers than the non-Jewish population. Also, they were strongly represented in commerce and industry.[10] For these reasons and probably also because of their own cultural traditions, they sent proportionately many more of their children into the institutions of higher learning than the Protestants and Catholics.[11] The existing prejudices against them effectively barred these students from many of the official careers that attracted their non-Jewish colleagues. As a result, Jewish talent flowed into the most genuinely "free" professions of medicine and private law, into journalism, and into the literary and artistic occupations.[12] Within the academic world, the position of the instructor offered a perfect opportunity for the young Jewish intellectual, again because it lay outside the framework of official careers. In 1909–10, almost 12 percent of the instructors at German universities were of the Jewish religion, and another 7 percent were Jewish converts to Christianity (*Getaufte*).[13] This was at a time when Jews made up somewhere around 1 percent of the German population.

One suspects that Jewish instructors were unusually able men, since they had to earn the *venia legendi* from prejudiced examiners. Even after passing that hurdle, they found it extraordinarily difficult to advance into the official academic ranks of associate and full professor. The difficulty was that the non-Jewish full professors had to recommend Jewish instructors for advancement, and here biases became visible.[14] In 1909–10, less than 3 percent of full professors at German universities were of the Jewish religion, and another 4 percent were converts.[15] Protestants and Catholics held over 93 percent of the full professorships, although they supplied less than 81 percent of the instructors. At the biggest and most prestigious of the German universities, in Berlin, there was not a single Jewish full professor in 1909–10. Georg Simmel, one of the most brilliant and productive German sociologists and philosophers of those days, was finally given a full professorship at Strassburg in 1914, four years before he died at the age of 60.* Ernst Cassirer, probably the leading philosopher on the critical wing of the Neo-Kantian school, and like Simmel a Jew, needed Dilthey's special support to earn the *venia legendi* and got his professorship at the struggling and progressive new urban University of Hamburg in 1919, when he was 45 years old. Many other examples could be cited to make the same point.

P. G. J. Pulzer has shown how political anti-Semitism welled up in Germany in the late 1870's and 1880's. George Mosse has treated the spread of volkish and anti-Semitic attitudes at the German secondary schools and universities during the same period and afterwards. Fritz Stern has vividly described the connection between anti-Semitism and the psychology of "antimodernity" among the second-rate literati of cultural disenchantment.[16] In general, my research can only support conclusions which have thus been well established.

I have only one additional suggestion to make: one should perhaps distinguish between three different types of German anti-Semites. The first is the artisan or shopkeeper who is threatened by modern economic developments and projects his resentments toward the "Jewish capitalist." This displaced burgher is strictly a consumer of anti-Semitic ideas. He requires leadership; he becomes a political tool; and he thrives on the crudest intellectual simplifications. He makes his appearance in times of economic and political crisis, when he is most desperate and his manipulators have the greatest need of his services: after 1878, after 1922–23, and in the early 1930's.

Then there is the enthusiast of the volkish ideology. He is half intellectual, half misfit; he scoffs at the conventions of "bourgeois" life. He is often self-taught, or young, or incompletely educated, a social and intellectual "climber." He brews his eclectic theories primarily from the literature of German Romanticism, and he feels

---

* Simmel's parents converted to Protestantism. He was not a formally religious man, and I do not know what he considered himself. The point is that his German contemporaries considered him of Jewish background. Some of them also held that his early works were too "negative," or "merely critical," a characteristic charge in that context.

that his emotional identification with the mythical volk makes him somehow "democratic." He is a university student, a former member of the youth movement, a pamphleteer, or a "radical" primary teacher. He transmits ideas. In a sense, he even creates them; but he owes more of his fundamental assumptions to his intellectual and social superiors than he is prepared to admit. He thrives in an atmosphere of intellectual and cultural crisis; but he does not alone produce that condition. For this, he depends to a large extent upon the mandarin intelligentsia.

The third type of anti-Semite is a member of the academic establishment. He is intellectually and socially respectable, even conventional. He has a rather snobbish dislike for the "radical," rabble-rousing anti-Semite, although he may occasionally feel a certain paternal fondness for the "idealism" of the volkish student. He develops his ideas within the framework of mandarin political orthodoxy. When he undertakes, within that context, to build a flimsy theoretical bridge between the symbol of the Jew and the shortcomings of modern interest politics and "materialism" generally, he moves the whole weight of the mandarin political tradition into the anti-Semitic camp.

These comments are meant to suggest that the relationship between antimodernity and anti-Semitism can be discovered in the writings of orthodox German academics as well as in the pamphlets of a Julius Langbehn. The only difference was that the mandarin version originated in a slightly different intellectual and social context. Relevant examples were certainly much more abundant in the 1920's than in the 1890's. At the German universities of the Weimar period, in a time of economic as well as intellectual crisis, the three types of anti-Semitism interacted and reinforced each other. Before 1918, full and public statements of the anti-Semitic creed by German academics were relatively rare. But Heinrich von Treitschke's lectures and publications already fit the general pattern in the late 1870's. The economist Adolph Wagner lent his considerable prestige to Adolf Stöcker's Christian-Social Party, which eventually made anti-Semitism an important part of its program. Beyond that, a mild form of anti-Semitism was widespread on all sides of the mandarin political spectrum, as the above figures on Jewish instructors and professors sufficiently indicate. The whole phenomenon will become clearer in later chapters. But there is reason to suspect even now that the mandarins' dream of a politics "above" socio-economic classes and interests could lead some of them, along with many of their readers and students, into the murky waters of anti-Semitic thought.

A much more obvious chain of associations led from the German professors' revulsion against interest politics to their enthusiastic defense of the "national cause." Modernists and orthodox alike were totally and often quite uncritically committed on this issue. They missed no opportunity to preach German greatness, always with the hope that patriotic sentiment would "overcome" the petty egotism of the parties. Here was a field of concern in which the mandarin intellectual could still play the role of the spiritual leader, directing the attention of Germans away from their material demands, demonstrating the ideal priority of the "whole" over the short-range interests of its members. It was too tempting a prospect. The orthodox were generally the most aggressive militarists, and they also enjoyed using nationalism as a weapon against Social Democracy. Some of them had come to identify quite thoroughly with the Prussian bureaucracy and officer corps. In that sense, they were simply spokesmen for the junkers. Even the less aggressive nationalism of the modernists certainly served interests which were more specific than the claims of the "whole." But this is not the complete story; for many of them apparently believed quite honestly that the defense of the national cause was a duty of political idealism.

Thus during the years around 1900, the German university professors, along with other segments of the administrative and professional classes, made up the predominant element within the membership of the Pan-German League.[17] The same groups also played a very important role in the agitation for an expanded navy.[18] After 1906, as the danger of antagonizing England became more and more obvious, a few of the modernists began to caution against an unrealistically aggressive naval program. This was the origin of a disagreement which was seriously to divide the German academic

community after 1915. The division did not become very pronounced before 1914, however. Until then, and particularly from
1897 to 1906, every segment of the mandarin political spectrum was
very well represented among the *Flottenprofessoren,* the academic
propagandists of naval expansion.[19]

In arguing their case, these men did touch upon the economic
and commercial advantages of sea power. But they also placed a
great deal of emphasis upon cultural and moral considerations. They
assigned a worldwide mission to German intellectual and cultural
traditions, feeling that a counterweight to the English was needed
in this field. They argued that German colonial activity should not
and would not be governed by the objectives of the capitalists alone.
The German personality, they hoped, would be enriched and broadened by the experience of international activity. Above all, the patriotic cause of German world power would overcome the "petty
fragmentation of the parties" and the "conflicts of economic interests"
within Germany.[20]

At least the modernists among the academic propagandists for
naval expansion were consistent enough to realize that social reform
at home was absolutely necessary, if the masses were to be won over
to the national cause. This was Naumann's program and that of the
Protestant Social Union, which supported the naval agitation in a
resolution of 1900. The accommodationist intellectuals certainly did
not mean to be mere spokesmen for the capitalists. In 1899, many
university professors were so genuinely shocked at the influence of
entrepreneurial interests upon the German Naval League that they
formed their own Independent Naval Union (*Freie Vereinigung für
Flottenvorträge*) to carry on the work in a more genuinely "idealistic" atmosphere. "In the days before 1870, we had a high common
goal, upon which all our energies were concentrated. In the same
way, the best among our people wish even now that great unifying
tasks will arise for our nation in the future as well, so that national
enthusiasm, wide horizons, and ethical demands upon our energies
will keep our nation strong and fresh."[21] This was the language of
mandarin nationalism in its purest form.

Of course, this terminology was not without its practical applications. Even the modernists occasionally employed it in the arena of party conflict itself. Thus in 1907, a group of academic leaders organized a huge meeting to publicize their support of a strong colonial policy and to criticize the Catholic Center Party and the Social Democrats, who had refused to extend credits for the maintenance of colonial troops. The issue had been precipitated by serious malpractices in the German colonial administration; but the enraged patriots managed to forget that. The Reichstag had been dissolved, and new elections were coming up. The public demonstration, which had been instigated by such eminent scholars as Gustav Schmoller, Hans Delbrück, Dietrich Schäfer, Max Sering, and Ignaz Jastrow, was clearly intended to affect the voting. And yet Delbrück, the first representative of the academic community to address the gathering, wasted only two opening sentences before turning to that well-tried theme "the fragmentation of the parties." Actually Delbrück was less addicted to this argument than most of his colleagues. He went on to say that parties did fulfill an important function in modern political life. Still, he could not suppress the urge to draw the usual moral from the politically mixed composition of the gathering. Many had come, he said, who usually withdrew from the faction-ridden politics of the age, and members of many different parties were present as well. "That is our proof that we are standing up for a demand which reaches beyond all party life, which is of a genuinely national nature."[22] In short, there is no simple formula to separate hypocrisy from "subjectively honest" intentions in the world of mandarin nationalism. The emotional need for an escape into "idealism," the mandarins' most characteristic contribution to German politics, was too prevalent over the whole spectrum of academic opinion.

That spectrum, it should be added, had very definite limits, as did the freedom and diversity of thought within it. This was demonstrated in the "Arons case" of 1893–1900, in the "Spahn case" of 1901, and in the experiences of Robert Michels after the turn of the century. Before 1918, there were no Social Democrats among the officially appointed full and associate professors at German universities. The Arons case arose in Prussia over a young physics instruc-

tor at Berlin who was publicly active as a Social Democrat.[23] Leo
Arons apparently kept his politics out of the classroom, and there
was never any question about his competence as a scientist. Nevertheless, the state was determined to withdraw his *venia legendi*. By
law, any disciplinary action against him had to be heard in the first
instance by his own faculty. Under pressure, the members of the
faculty of philosophy at Berlin agreed to give him a warning and to
urge him to restrict his political activities in the future. They
refused to go further than that. Under the leadership of Gustav
Schmoller and of a few prominent modernists, they energetically
defended the traditional independence of the German academic in
general and that of the instructor in particular. They also argued
that links between the academic world and the Social Democrats
might help to bring the Social Democrats around to a more cooperative attitude. But the government would not relent. The new "lex
Arons" of 1898 subjected Prussian instructors to the Disciplinary
Law of 1852, which made it possible to overrule the Berlin faculty
and to withdraw Arons' instructorship in a higher court. This was
a very far-reaching attack upon the statutory liberties of the German
university. Nevertheless, the German academic community as a
whole accepted the "lex Arons" without much further protest.

The Spahn case elicited a somewhat more lively response.[24] In
1901, Althoff announced the creation of a new Catholic professorship in history at the University of Strassburg. Spahn was to be the
first appointment to this position. Althoff's plan originated as part
of a complex set of negotiations between Prussia, the Papacy, and
the German Center Party; but this was not generally known at the
time. Lujo Brentano and Theodor Mommsen, two of the more
outspoken members of the modernist camp, organized a protest in
the name of academic objectivity and freedom. Other scholars joined
in, and a public debate ensued. The case caused more of a stir than
the action against Arons, although it was still only a very small segment of the academic community that participated. Those who did
speak up were generally anxious to direct their critical remarks at
the Catholics, rather than at the Prussian authorities. Apparently,
the mandarins found it easier and more natural to protect the ab-

stract purity of learning against the "special interests" of a confessional group than to fight for the scholarly liberty of a political sectarian.

The traditional ideal of impracticality in scholarship favored this somewhat one-sided interpretation. It also helped German scholars to believe that the freedom of learning was secure in Wilhelmian Germany. The manifest discrimination against Jews and Social Democrats did little to shake their confidence, because many of them shared the attitudes which permitted these practices. Max Weber pointed this out in a 1908 letter to the *Frankfurter Zeitung*.[25] He described the recent experiences of his student Robert Michels. Michels was a Social Democrat and a man who preferred not to have his children baptized. He quickly found out that he could never hope to earn the *venia legendi* at any German university. He therefore sought and obtained an academic position in Italy. Some of the German professors with whom Michels corresponded about his situation seemed to think it quite in order that his religious and political views would "make him impossible" in Germany. It was this attitude that angered Weber. In 1908, when an academic convention was scheduled to treat "the freedom of learning" with particular reference to the danger of Catholic clerical influence, Weber exploded. In his open letter, he declared himself unable to "behave as if we possessed a 'freedom of teaching' which somebody could still take away from us." He urged that the continual references to the autonomy of scholarship be dropped "in the interests of taste and also of truth." "In Germany," he concluded, "the freedom of learning exists only within the limits of officially accepted political and religious views." Perhaps he put it harshly; but in the essentials, he was right.

ECONOMICS AND SOCIAL POLICY

The distinctive qualities of mandarin social thought revealed themselves with particular clarity in the economic doctrines of German academics. More specifically, there were two intellectual traits which distinguished German contributions to economic theory during most of the nineteenth century and especially during the period from 1890 to the First World War. The first was a persistent preference for historical methods of economic analysis; the second was a characteristic set of assumptions concerning the objectives of all economic activity. Both predilections were deeply rooted in the traditions of the mandarin ideology; both had far-reaching consequences in the realm of social action; and both were to come under attack around the turn of the century.

The historical emphasis in German economics was almost as old as the German historical tradition itself.[26] Adam Müller and Friedrich List, the historical jurist F. K. von Savigny, and even Hegel and Ranke may be counted among its precursors during the early nineteenth century. The so-called historical school of economics itself was commonly divided into an "older" and a "younger" branch. The older branch dated back to the 1840's in the works of Wilhelm Roscher, Bruno Hildebrand, and Karl Knies; the younger branch was founded by Gustav Schmoller during the 1870's.

Schmoller and his followers objected to the timeless abstractions and rules of English classical theory. They thought it wrong to deduce propositions about the economy of any country at any time from a few axiomatic assumptions concerning the behavior of the economic man or the conditions of the free market. They felt that the economic life of a nation could be understood only in the context of the institutions, social patterns, and cultural attitudes in which it had developed. Since these environmental conditions and the nature of economic activity itself were subject to change over time, study of them required the techniques of the historian, rather than those of the natural scientist. Thus, according to the German school, economics was to be an inductive discipline. Its generalizations were to be based upon close and initially unsystematic observation of actual conditions of production and exchange in various countries and periods. The economist was to survey all the aspects of man's socio-economic life, taking all kinds of motives into account, instead of isolating one special type of behavior in the manner of the classical school. In this sense, the procedure was to be more purely "empirical" than that of the English economists.

Of course, there was room for certain differences of emphasis within this general scheme. It was possible to use elements of classical doctrine in an otherwise historical survey of modern economic life. "Historical" or "developmental" laws could be formulated to take the place of the "ahistorical" generalizations of classical theory. The traditional language of past-mindedness, the principle of individuality, the "organic" conception of development, and the Romantic notion of the volk spirit: all these tools were available to the historical economist, who had the further choice of either using them or simply expounding upon them from time to time. Joseph Schumpeter has pointed out that the animus against theory could leave the ordinary economist without any sort of formal training, so that he ended by collecting information for this or that historical monograph in the ad hoc manner of the layman. Undoubtedly, this was true only of the less distinguished members of the school. Schumpeter himself repeatedly expressed respect for the scholarship of such men as Gustav Schmoller and Georg Friedrich Knapp, the historian of Austro-German agrarian organization. It is possible to describe Max Weber and Werner Sombart as late disciples of the historical school, and their work is considered interesting even today.

One of the principal errors of English classical theory and especially of its popularizations, according to many German economists, was the idea that the "natural" or "iron" laws of economics would make government interference in the economy useless or actually harmful. The average mandarin had a very sharp eye for the logical weaknesses of the laisser-faire doctrine. He refused to believe that the theories of the Manchester school were based upon objective observations of economic necessities. Instead, he saw these theories as parts of a peculiar utilitarian ethic of entrepreneurial individualism. From his point of view, the normative preferences implied in the laisser-faire creed were thoroughly objectionable. They enshrined the accumulation of wealth by selected individuals as the ultimate goal of mankind. They subordinated social and political concerns to the requirements of industry and commerce, and they gave no place at all to the intellectual and cultural, the "nonpro-ductive," aspects of human endeavor.

All this was heresy to the mandarins, not because they agreed with the Marxist critique of capitalism, but because they refused to regard economic activity as anything but a means to higher ends. Their viewpoint was neither that of the entrepreneur nor that of the worker. To them, the whole productive sector of industry and commerce was just one of several parts of society's machinery, and a relatively subordinate one at that. This accounts for their methodo-logical emphasis upon the noneconomic context of economic life. It also helps to explain why they would not allow "the economic man" to impose his preferences upon the rest of the nation. In any conflict between the prerequisites of material productivity and the general objectives of the legal and cultural state, the mandarins inevitably gave preference to the latter. In this as in every other argument about priorities, the cultivated elite came back again and again to the classical themes of its own tradition: the claims of the "whole" upon its constituents, the requirements of social harmony and of morality, of national greatness and of cultural creativity. They could see no point in material prosperity, if it interfered with these objectives, if it did not create the preconditions for the fullest possible self-development of the individual and of the cultural nation.

These views inspired the Social Policy Association (*Verein für Sozialpolitik*), the most important organization of German econo-mists and social scientists during the later nineteenth and early twentieth century.[27] Founded in 1872 under the leadership of Gustav Schmoller, Adolph Wagner, and Lujo Brentano, the Social Policy Association was intended not only to encourage scholarly and tech-nical discussions of contemporary economic and social problems but also to exert a guiding influence upon the government and public opinion.[28] Generally speaking, the members of the association showed a preference for the methods of the historical school. They were opposed to the laisser-faire scheme. They also proposed to examine questions of economic policy from an ethical point of view, looking toward social reform. The word *Sozialpolitik* itself implied such an approach, for it suggested positive action to ease social problems on the basis of a social or communal orientation, not an individualistic one. Particularly the followers of Schmoller and of Brentano were sometimes identified with an "ethical direction" (*ethische* or *sozialethische Richtung*) in economics. They normally used with approval such terms as social and community and the interest of the whole. The terms utilitarianism, materialism, and particular interests (*Sonderinteressen*) almost always had negative connotations for them.[29] Most of them were modernists who wished to soften the clashes of industrial interest groups, to overcome Marxist "materialism" as well as entrepreneurial "egotism." In pursuit of these ends, almost all of them moved toward "a new recognition of the justification for state interference in economic life," to use Brentano's formulation.[30] It was this aspect of their program that earned them the pejorative and quite misleading title of *Kathedersozialisten*, Socialists of the Chair or (better) of the Lectern.

The measures recommended by the Socialists of the Lectern at various times included social insurance schemes, factory inspection laws, state ownership of railroads, progressive tax measures, minimum wage regulations, limited public works programs, and collective bargaining arrangements. Among these, the proposals on taxes and public works and, more especially, the arguments in favor of labor union rights were really the most radical. The other objectives of the program, which could easily be adapted to existing social and political conditions, had been fully or partially achieved by the bureaucratic monarchy before 1890.

There was an important difference between subgroups within the Social Policy Association. Though really a divergence of emphasis more than one of principle, it had important political consequences. Proponents of an active social policy could base their recommendations upon either of two ultimate objectives: the welfare of the national "whole" or the personal development of the individual. The choice between these two alternatives entailed a further decision about the nature and scope of government interference in the social process. Wagner, Schmoller, and Brentano, the three most prominent early members of the association, did not fully agree in their attitudes on these issues.

Wagner differed from Schmoller even in his methodological views. He approved of the emphasis upon the institutional context of economic activity; but he was not particularly interested in historical modes of analysis as such. Somewhat more abstract in his theoretical approach than Schmoller, he was considered a "state socialist." He recommended nationalization of the major service industries, particularly those that seemed close to operating under monopolistic conditions, as in the fields of transportation, communication, banking, insurance, power, and utilities. He was influenced less by Marx than by various non-Marxian socialists and by the surviving traditions of Prussian cameralism, of which he spoke with great warmth. He was a fervent propagandist of the "national cause," a strong advocate of colonial expansion. The unions did not interest him, whereas Stöcker's Christian-Social experiment benefited from his active support. He actually left the Social Policy Association in 1879. It was characteristic of him that he eventually devoted much of his energy to the campaign in favor of high agricultural tariffs. He helped to develop many of the nationalistic, autarchic and anti-modernistic arguments which were used by agrarian interests to recommend the forced preservation of rural Germany (the *Agrarstaat*) against the supposedly overrapid growth of the industrial sector (the *Industriestaat*).[31] Along with Max Sering, an advocate of agrarian colonization, Wagner repeatedly found himself allied with the Conservatives.

Schmoller too was deeply impressed with the traditions of the German bureaucracy. Almost more of a historian than an economist, he did much original research on the evolution of the Prussian administration. Like Wagner, he was especially partial to the nationalistic argument in favor of social reform. He sought domestic social unity as a prerequisite for a strong foreign policy. Less systematic than Wagner in his approach to questions of economic policy, he was more interested in social insurance schemes than in nationalizations. He believed that a paternalistic government could carry out conservative social reforms by limiting the more destructive consequences of the war between labor and management. He was convinced that the cause of moderate social programs had always been most naturally and successfully championed by the Prussian monarchs and their officials, "the appointed representatives of the idea of the state, the only neutral elements in the social class war."[32] This bureaucratic version of the mandarin creed was his most characteristic tenet, and he knew that it separated him to some degree from his colleague Brentano.[33]

Among the three prominent older members of the Social Policy Association, Lujo Brentano was most committed to the ideal of "enabling everyone to unfold his traits and capabilities freely."[34] In his view, this was the principal objective of an ethically oriented social policy. Brentano may not have been a great economic theorist or a subtle logician; but he exerted considerable influence, both inside and outside the classroom, as an enthusiastic prophet of social reform. He was a free trader and an advocate of international cooperation. He defended commerce and the modern industrial state against the propagandists of economic autarchy and the agrarian state. In this and other respects, he was a much more genuine modernist than Wagner or Schmoller. A Naumann supporter and an inveterate foe of the great landowners, he gamely entered a prolonged battle against the raising of grain tariffs. He even recovered a certain respect for the classical economists in the process, particularly in the field of international trade. Although he occasionally resorted to the principle of the supremacy of the "whole," he was primarily interested in clearing the legal ground for the growth of labor unions.[35]

When Schmoller supported the expansion of collective bargaining rights, he thought chiefly of driving a wedge between the trade unions and the Social Democratic Party. He wanted to win the workers over to the existing regime, to increase the influence of the government in the settlement of industrial disputes, and to convert the unions into harmless auxiliaries of bureaucratic social policy. Brentano understood and even shared this point of view to some extent. It is not clear that his plans for the unions and for a new system of bargaining procedures would have given labor the institutional independence it really wanted. Nevertheless, there was a real difference of attitude between Brentano and Schmoller, partly because Brentano had been deeply impressed by his study of the English trade union movement. Unlike many of his colleagues, he felt that the workers were entitled in principle to play an active role in the determination of their own future. As a moralist and as an individualist, he hoped that a relatively autonomous and self-confident labor movement would enhance the self-respect and integrity of the individual worker. He was one of the few mandarins who could imagine that Humboldt's ideal of personal self-development might in some way be relevant to social strata other than his own.

Among the younger members of the Social Policy Association, such men as Heinrich Herkner, Otto von Zwiedineck-Südenhorst, Gerhart von Schulze-Gävernitz, and Arthur Salz took positions somewhere between those of Schmoller and Brentano. Wagner had a much smaller following, and there were no outright Marxists or Social Democrats among German academic economists before 1918. In other words, there was a good deal of agreement among the advocates of social reform, at least until around 1900. The average Socialist of the Lectern stood somewhere near the middle of the accommodationist range in the spectrum of mandarin political opinion.

In 1894, the modernist Ignaz Jastrow published a pamphlet under the characteristic title "Social-Liberal."[36] He argued that the liberal parties had done poorly in recent elections in Prussia and elsewhere because they had paid too little attention to the need for constructive social policies. He then proceeded to demonstrate that liberal principles, properly understood, could provide an excellent theoretical basis for such programs as the removal of social barriers between various branches of the school system, the raising of primary teachers' salaries, the development of an improved system of vocational education and the protection of apprentices' rights, the extension of local self-government and the reduction of the landowners' juridical and administrative privileges in rural districts, the protection of the smaller independent farmers and rural laborers against the junkers in Prussia, the revision of the outmoded and blatantly inequitable tax system, and the development of effective policies in the fields of poor relief and public health. These recommendations were fairly typical of the modernists' approach.

The members of the Social Policy Association did not intend to suggest that economic decisions should always be governed by non-economic objectives. They only meant to apply certain correctives to the existing system of production and distribution, and they believed that the criteria upon which they selected these adjustments were as objective as such assumptions could ever be. The Socialists of the Lectern were not particularly revered by the Social Democratic workers, and they also had to defend themselves against continual and vehement attacks from pamphleteers and political spokesmen of the entrepreneurial faction. They tended to view this unpopularity with both sides in the industrial conflict as a consequence and a sign of their genuine impartiality. Standing "above" the quarrels of competing interest groups and fortified against Manchesterism and Marxism alike by their logical commitment to historical techniques, they saw no reason to doubt that their own standards of social policy were relatively immune from the errors of bias and would therefore prove more or less permanent.

The first serious challenge to the traditions of the Social Policy Association came from the Austrian economists C. Menger, E. von Böhm-Bawerk, and F. von Wieser. These men were among the pioneers of those innovations in economic analysis that centered upon the concept of marginal utility and of the marginal technique more generally. Even the layman can appreciate the great importance of these ideas for the subsequent development of modern economics. They cleared the ground for a general departure from the notion of the inherent value of an economic good, since they based their analysis of prices directly upon the quantitative ratios at which any two commodities are actually exchanged. They thus focused attention upon market relationships which might or might not be expressed in monetary terms. One could say that the marginal method prepared the ground for modern equilibrium analysis, for the emphasis upon exchange functions, and for the use of mathematical models of such functions. One of the leading advocates of all these modern techniques in the German-speaking countries after 1912 was Joseph Schumpeter. He taught in Germany during much of the Weimar period; but his early academic background was Austrian. Undoubtedly, he was interested in the ideas of contemporary Italian and Anglo-American theorists; but he was also influenced by the work of Böhm-Bawerk. In any case, the members of the older Austrian school certainly contributed to the renewed emphasis upon analytical abstraction. In a sense, their ideas were sophistications of classical doctrines, and they were bound to clash with the pointedly antitheoretical orientation of the German historical school.

The famous "methods controversy" (*Methodenstreit*) broke out in 1883, when Menger wrote a commentary on the techniques of economic analysis in which he criticized Schmoller and his followers rather sharply. Schmoller answered in an uncomplimentary review of the book, and the contest began. Apparently, very few German economists sided completely with the Austrians. It was a real battle of the schools. Schmoller's defenders saw themselves primarily as historians. The Austrians stressed the need for theoretical analysis and defined economics as a social science. Anyone who has witnessed analogous confrontations will understand that the emotional temperature of the discussion was rather high. Yet the leading secondary accounts agree that in principle, each side admitted the other's right of existence from the beginning. In a 1910 lecture, Schumpeter took the part of the social scientists, without failing in his charity toward the historians.[37] In fact, he felt even then that the methodological feud might well be dropped in favor of whatever substantive work the contending parties liked to do. The issue might well have been settled in this way by about 1900, perhaps slightly to the advantage of the theorists, if it had not become entangled with a much more serious controversy, which broke out just after the turn of the century.

This second conflict concerned the role of value judgments in economic theory, and it jeopardized the traditional assumptions of the Socialists of the Lectern in this area. In all likelihood, the realities of contemporary politics helped to undermine some of the old assumptions. Particularly between 1894 and 1900, reactionary representatives of the entrepreneurial faction acquired considerable influence within the government. The result was a public campaign against academic "socialists," some of whom suddenly found their scholarly freedoms rather limited in practice. The lesson was obvious. The increasing visibility of economic class differences made it more and more difficult to treat the mandarins' noneconomic ideals as universally accepted objectives of all social policy. Obviously, no single set of social programs and goals would satisfy landowners, entrepreneurs, and workers. The contest among the mass parties suggested that the ultimate policy decisions would have to be made in the arena of electoral politics. Indeed, the German academic economists themselves found it impossible to preserve that broad political consensus which had been a real though unacknowledged basis of their agreement in the field of social policy. Increasingly after 1900, some of the younger members of the association began to break away from the patterns established by their elders.

Werner Sombart was one of the rebels. His views are not easy to describe, because they changed quite thoroughly at several points between 1890 and 1933. Sombart began his career as one of the strongest academic supporters of the German labor movement. By 1900, he had begun to move away from his earlier sympathy with the objectives of the Social Democratic Party; but he was still praising the trade unions for effecting a more equitable distribution of profits and for encouraging entrepreneurs to devise more efficient methods of production.[38] In achieving these results, he argued, labor was actually helping to ensure the economic and social viability of the capitalist system. He urged trade union leaders to face up to this consequence of their policies, to disavow the revolutionary politics of Marxist Social Democracy, and frankly to cooperate with progressive industrialists in building a socially harmonious and technically efficient system of production. Apparently, the Marxist leaders had already begun to distrust his corporative analogies; but at the turn of the century he was still described as a social revolutionary in the bourgeois press. In any case, he was speaking as a social radical when he attacked the traditional ideals of social policy in 1897.[39] His argument was that the economist should base his recommendations only upon values that were indigenous to his own field of study. Instead of accepting ethical prescriptions devised by philosophers, he should hold to the principle of productivity. On this basis, the economist might well show a certain partiality in favor of the most productive groups within society, meaning the technicians, the managers, and certainly also the industrial workers.

Sombart's remarks could be interpreted as a criticism of traditional social policy from the standpoint of labor; the case for the industrialists was stated by Ludwig Bernhard in 1912.[40] Bernhard claimed, in effect, that government insurance and factory legislation had provided the workers with vast opportunities for malingering, that discipline in the factories was disintegrating, and that even the best managers found it difficult to maintain a decent level of productivity in the face of the mounting costs, bureaucratic entanglements, and inefficiences occasioned by official paternalism. After 1912, Schumpeter too assigned an important place to the creative entrepreneur in his theory of economic dynamics. He particularly emphasized the innovating and risk-bearing function, so that his arguments could be construed in a promanagerial or antipaternal sense by a man of Bernhard's convictions. Actually, Schumpeter himself managed to stay clear of the theoretical discussion of objectives in social policy, eventually joining those economists who urged a rigorous logical distinction between wissenschaft and value judgment.

In any case, both Bernhard's and Schumpeter's positions were quite as radical in their departure from the mandarin tradition as Sombart's leftist sympathies around 1900. Bernhard's thoroughly unsentimental pursuit of productive efficiency and Schumpeter's glorification of the entrepreneur as an "economic man" had little to do with the conventional language of academic morality. The mandarin form of the proentrepreneurial argument, as expressed by Adolf Weber among others, typically contained at least a few pious remarks about the businessman's duty to the national community. It was therefore all the more decisive for the future of the ethical direction in German economics that even Adolf Weber began to move away from the pattern set by Schmoller and Brentano.

In a 1909 essay, Weber argued that economists should henceforth try harder to avoid policy recommendations based upon pure value judgments, even at the cost of abandoning the old emphasis on social reform. He also urged a new look at the valid aspects of English classical theory, apparently at least partly for the sake of its laisser-faire implications. In all social questions, he said, the economists of the future must be even more strenuously neutral than they have been up to now. This will help them to increase "the authority of true wissenschaft." Supported by this authority, they may then proceed to the "economic education of the nation," showing that wages can only be raised through increased productivity and "that there is no real conflict between capital and labor."[41]

While Adolf Weber thus objected to the ethical direction in German economics on the basis of a mandarin form of neo-Manchesterism, a few members of the academic community began to revise their own attitudes toward social policy upon a rather different set of grounds. The motives of this group are most easily understood in connection with Max Weber's and Werner Sombart's characterizations of modern capitalism.

Schumpeter grouped Sombart and Weber, along with Arthur Spiethoff, under the heading of the "youngest historical school."[42] He did not mean to imply anything like a consistent identity of views between Roscher or Schmoller and these scholars of the youngest generation. Specifically in questions of method, the older and even the younger historical schools did not always meet with Weber's approval. Still, as compared with Ricardo or Böhm-Bawerk, Weber and Sombart did indeed make their most important and characteristic contributions as historians or sociologists of capitalism. They described institutions, industrial and commercial practices, technological and behavioral patterns; they were interested in the evolution of these arrangements, and they invariably emphasized the "style" or "spirit" of a given economic system, epoch, or stage of development.

Max Weber's *Protestant Ethic* began to appear in the *Archiv* in 1904 and immediately exerted a tremendous influence upon contemporaries.[43] It must have been startling indeed to be shown a connection between a set of religious beliefs and a mode of business behavior, and the implications for the sociology of religion were clearly fascinating. But it seems to me that the essay's greatest impact derived from its major premise: that there was such a thing as a spirit of capitalism, a set of quite amazing intellectual preferences and attitudes which, far from being natural or inevitable accompaniments of all economic activity, required a wholly independent explanation. For Max Weber, one of the most important characteristics of modern capitalism was the thorough and impersonal rationality of its organization, the abstractness and complexity of the means-ends calculations upon which it was based. Indeed, Weber saw this kind of abstract rationality in every aspect of modern life: in religion and in learning, in government and in administrative organization, in technology and in economic enterprise. In his work on the methods of the social sciences, he accordingly gave an important place to the category of behavior that is rational with respect to a stated end (*zweckrational*). The phenomenon of bureaucratic rationalization and "routinization" interested and concerned him immensely, whether it appeared in government, in business, or in union organization.

Between 1902 and 1914, Werner Sombart developed ideas which partially resembled Weber's.[44] In trying to distinguish between various phases in the history of capitalism, particularly between "early capitalism" and "high capitalism," Sombart emphasized the highly abstract character of modern business calculations and objectives. In the early stage of capitalist development, he said, there was still a fairly direct connection between man's immediate needs and his economic behavior. The producer had some sense of personal relation or obligation to the consumer. The concept of a fair return for a given amount of effort still played a certain role in wage and price setting, and men worked no more than necessary to maintain themselves at a standard of living that was considered appropriate to their relatively fixed station in life. In high capitalism, by contrast, all economic relationships became impersonal. The firm, which replaced the individual as the principal agent of economic activity, engaged labor at the lowest possible wage to produce whatever could be sold in the market at the greatest attainable profit. Advertising was used to create demand, and cutthroat competition was no longer considered unethical. Each participant in the game of business was simply expected to maximize his gains and to accumulate as much capital as possible; and all this in a situation in which wealth was no longer sought primarily for the comforts it could command. In short, what had formerly been means now became abstract ends. Man with his needs and desires was no longer "the measure of all things."[45] In this whole transformation, to continue with Sombart, the Jews played a major role. Standing outside the traditional estate system which still enveloped early capitalist society, they were able to develop all those practices and conceptions which were eventually to characterize the era of high capitalism. They, more than Weber's Protestant sectarians, were the first really modern men of business.

Sombart's analysis could be interpreted as an emotional indictment of modernity, though perhaps he did not mean it to be read in that way. His attitude was undergoing a rapid transformation around 1910; but it is not easy to say exactly when he first began to change his mind. The most obviously loaded phrase in his description of modern capitalism, the one about man's displacement as "the measure of all things," was written in 1913. On the other hand, his comments on the Jews, which appeared in 1910, were put in a fairly neutral tone, perhaps even with some suggestion of that ideal of social progress and technological efficiency that Sombart had adopted around the turn of the century.

From a Marxist point of view, Weber's and Sombart's accounts of capitalism were somewhat evasive. Weber argued that the separation of the worker from the means of production is only one aspect of modern social rationalization. He pointed out that the modern civil servant does not own the tools of his trade or possess the political power which he represents. He is separated from the means of administration, just as the soldier is separated from the means of violence. In every phase of modern life, Weber saw division of labor, specialization of tasks, complexity of organization. He regarded the phenomenon of bureaucratization as the most general, striking, and problematic aspect of modern social reality. He thus directed attention away from the economic contradictions and social injustices of the capitalist system. He made that system a part, rather than the essential cause, of the modern dilemma. This shift of emphasis implied a predominant concern with the cultural shortcomings of modernity, and in that sense, it conformed to the mandarins' traditional hierarchy of values. Particularly Sombart's portrait of high capitalism was saturated with the cultivated man's horror of commerce. Perhaps such horror was justified; but it was also ambiguous. It could inspire a great variety of reactions, as Sombart himself was amply to demonstrate in his subsequent career.

All this is not to say, however, that Weber's analysis was fully in tune with the views of most German academics. On the contrary, it diverged rather sharply from the mandarin tradition in social policy as well. It should be remembered that the German academic heritage simultaneously suggested two rather different objections to modern capitalism. On the one hand, there was the charge that the factory system and economic rationalization in general posed a threat to the individual spirit in search of self-expression. On the other hand, there was a widespread fear of the socially disjunctive forces released by industrialization. Those who were most afraid of social conflict tended to seek harmony and order through bureaucratic social reform. Those who were concerned primarily with the spiritual dangers inherent in industrial organization faced more difficult problems. Would government-sponsored social policy alter the spirit of capitalism? Was the cameralist approach really less of a threat to individual vitality than unrestrained capitalism? Which aspects of industrial organization could be changed and which were unavoidable? Weber's work raised these questions, and so, more indirectly, did Sombart's. In effect, Weber's analysis made it more difficult for his audience to confound the spiritual and the social dangers inherent in capitalism and thus to arrive at a thoughtlessly unqualified rejection of industrial civilization itself. Weber himself tended to speak of rationalization and bureaucratization as more or less unpleasant inevitabilities. His tone was that of the heroic pessimist, the man who faces facts; but it was also characteristic of him that he would not tolerate the obscurantist illusion of a total escape from modernity.

The trouble with much of the traditional social policy was that it came to imply this illusion. Wagner, Schmoller, and their followers seemed to identify industrialism quite simply with the reign of mammon. They acted as if government restraints on entrepreneurs would suffice to cure all the evils of modern social life. Since their predominant concern was for order and cohesion, their policy recommendations ran increasingly into the reactionary channels of the agrarian state and of cameralist paternalism. In the meantime, the national argument, the supposed claim of "the whole" upon its members, was being used more and more openly to suppress, not to justify, social and parliamentary reform.

It was this antimodernistic trend in German social policy which began to alienate some of the younger accommodationists after the turn of the century. They were forced to re-examine their own positions. In this context, such men as Bernhard and Schumpeter moved toward an unusually frank acceptance of the entrepreneurial function. Schumpeter now began to see the national agitation of the anti-industrial cliques as the most serious contemporary danger to social progress and international cooperation.[46]

Until about 1910, Sombart too stood for productivity and for the rights of the producing classes. Max Weber recognized capitalism as an aspect of rationalization. But above all, he came to realize that the cameralist line in social policy implied a degree of bureaucratization that posed a far more serious threat to the vitality of modern social life than capitalism itself. He saw, as did his student Robert Michels, how the phenomenon of bureaucratization transformed even the radical politics of labor organizations. By 1918, he was ready to describe socialism itself as the ideology of an intelligentsia in search of bureaucratic places.[47] In the face of these developments, he became more and more committed to the pluralistic class politics of overt parliamentary bargaining as an alternative to hypocrisy and stagnation.

Alfred Weber shared some of his brother's concerns. In several articles between 1910 and 1913, he questioned the emphasis upon cameralistic state action and upon the ethic of government service in modern German social theory and practice.[48] He noted that even some of the labor leaders were beginning to play the role of industrial officials. Company unions were growing behind the flimsy ideological screen of the corporate community. On all social levels, men were being forced to submerge their private identities in the service of huge organizational machines. The original objective of social policy, to assure a minimum of security in the face of a totally uncontrolled and often brutal form of capitalism, was now fulfilled. The difficulty was that especially in Germany, too little of this progress had been achieved through the independent action of the workers' own associations, so that the cost in subservience to the state had run too high. Weber feared the cultural consequences of the general regimentation and advised individuals to protect the privacy of their personal life against their employers and their government alike. Beyond that, he wanted to encourage union development and collective bargaining, while cutting back the state's paternalistic role in social policy.

In 1912, the young sociologist Leopold von Wiese arrived at similar demands in a somewhat different way. He made a distinction between political, economic, and cultural socialism, confronting this triad with its opposite, namely political, economic, and cultural individualism. He approved cultural individualism, while he rejected its economic counterpart. "An analysis of the relationship between security (socialism) and freedom (individualism) shows that cultural individualism can go hand in hand with economic socialism, so that the social policy of the future must sponsor the expansion of political and moral freedom too, although the idea of freedom requires an inner renewal in the process."[49] Wiese's use of the term socialism in this passage was characteristically vague. It meant economic integration and social policy on a national level; but it did not imply outright nationalization or Marxist revolution. The "inner renewal" of freedom was just the traditional tempering of individualism with moral responsibility. The most significant and unusual element in Wiese's argument was the suggestion that political and cultural freedom was to be a positive goal of social policy in the future.

One can read the remarks of Alfred Weber and Leopold von Wiese as radically stated defenses of Brentano's orientation against Wagner's in a gradually sharpening debate. As a matter of fact, Brentano himself warned against an overly general use of ethical arguments in social policy as early as 1901. He specifically accused "economically reactionary tendencies" of having misused such arguments to defend their own special interest, and he went on to say that "all efforts to influence social life can be successful and just only insofar as they do not run counter to the actual nature of things or to the requirements of a natural (progressive) development."[50] Coming from a leader of the ethical direction in German economics, this was a remarkable qualification. It indicated that the whole basis of mandarin social policy was now in question. At the 1905 meeting of the Social Policy Association, Friedrich Naumann explicitly challenged the dogma that the state, now in the hands of reactionary landlords and bourgeois, could be regarded as a champion of social policy. Schmoller, the chairman of the association, accused Naumann of demogogic class politics in return. This so angered Max Weber and a few others of his persuasion that a split in the association was barely avoided. The traditional notion of a more or less universally accepted set of policy objectives was clearly disintegrating, along with the political consensus that had made it possible.

There was only one way to escape from this dilemma, and that was to banish all value judgments from the wissenschaft of economics. Characteristically it was the modernist segment of the academic community that began to urge this solution after 1900. During the first decade of the twentieth century, Max Weber brought out several of his famous studies in the methodology of the social sciences. In part, these were addressed to the conflict between the historical and the theoretical economists, which was still not entirely resolved. At the same time, Weber's attempt to draw a line between wissenschaft and value judgment was clearly intended as an intervention in the debate over the future of social reform. Weber did not mean to say that economists should never discuss policy questions at all. But he did ask that they concentrate on the clarification of relevant factual and logical relationships. Above all, he insisted that normative judgments be methodically factored out of the discussion wherever possible, so that they could be clearly stated and made the subject of conscious reflection and critical analysis in their turn.

At the Vienna meeting of the Social Policy Association in 1909, Weber restated the case against the intermingling of ethics and economics, and Sombart, still speaking as a social radical, supported Weber's arguments in the sharpest possible terms. The result "almost amounted to a row," according to Schumpeter.[51] Of course, the issue continued to trouble German economists and social scientists for many years after 1909. Weber was by no means able to convince all of his colleagues. In the years between 1909 and 1914, various champions of social policy came forward to defend their own views. Herkner continued to insist that some social objectives were so reasonable and so generally acceptable that the economist could fairly assume them. Brentano moved rather close to Weber's position, without ever fully understanding it. He thought that people should be more objective, and he knew what that meant, because it was so perfectly clear to him that the pamphleteers who attacked him were not. He could not doubt that any unprejudiced observer of the German social scene would have to favor the further development of trade union initiative. Salz reviewed the arguments of all the contending parties, only to settle on the will to create a true "community" as the only possible basis of social policy.[52] In this way, the traditions of the association lingered on; but the serenity and the unity of an earlier day were never quite recaptured.

SOCIOLOGY: TÖNNIES, SIMMEL, AND MAX WEBER

Modern German sociology was a true child of mandarin modernism; it cannot be understood apart from this ancestry. It reflected the mandarins' characteristically pessimistic attitude toward modern social conditions. It dealt with the destructive effects of capitalism

upon precapitalist forms of social organization. It traced the disturbing results of this process in political and cultural life, and it raised
some troubling questions about relations between men in modern
society.

Indeed, German sociology echoed anxieties and concerns which
had been thematic in the social and political theories of Romantic
conservatism. But it differed from these older philosophies in several
important respects. It indulged no dreams of the soil. It was not
agrarian or feudal in orientation, because it had no social connection
with the landed aristocracy. It had no roots in the capitalist middle
class either. If anything, the German sociologists were intellectually
obligated to Marx; but they did not always fully acknowledge that
debt, and they felt no commitment to proletarian socialism. They
were mandarins, and they spoke for themselves.

A sense of resignation was typical of all accommodationist social
theory. The modernists, unlike their orthodox colleagues, realized
that there was no total escape from modernity. They proposed to
face facts, to accept some facets of modern life as inevitable or even
desirable, while seeking to temper its more accidental and less toler-
able aspects. This attitude led them to control their emotional response to their new environment, to uphold a heroic ideal of rational
clarification in the face of tragedy. They preferred analysis to hypocrisy and destructive despair: they became scientific.

This was the spirit in which the discipline of sociology was created, which distinguished it from the more sentimental and more
reactionary critiques of modernity. It was this spirit, too, which
dictated some of the methods of the new science. The social bond
had to be conceptually isolated as an object of cognition, so that
modern social problems could be studies in their "essence," that is,
in isolation—or abstraction—from both Marxist and Romantic
critiques of modern conditions. Sociology had to be separated from
the philosophy of history, so that its analytical and critical character
might be preserved. It is not surprising that the sociologists quickly
became involved in a controversy with representatives of more traditional types of social theory, who were generally orthodox in their
political views. Institutional as well as theoretical issues played a role

in this debate, since the sociologists were proposing to carve a new specialty out of the established pattern of academic subjects, examinations, and positions. Though the findings and the descriptive terms of the new discipline were extensively popularized for use in political polemics, the scope and methods of sociology continued to be hotly contested from the 1890's to the 1920's and even thereafter.

If one disregards indirect antecedents and developments in related fields, one may say that Ferdinand Tönnies was the father of modern German sociology.[53] It was Tönnies who in 1909 founded the German Society for Sociology (*Deutsche Gesellschaft für Soziologie*), to which most of the leading German sponsors of the new discipline belonged at one time or another. Tönnies' pioneering study of *Community and Society* (*Gemeinschaft und Gesellschaft*), which appeared in 1887, set all the important themes not only for his own subsequent writings but also for the work of his colleagues and successors between 1890 and 1933. Thus practically everything which can be said of German sociology during the period we are studying must be established in a description of Tönnies' famous antithesis.[54]

For Tönnies, two contrary conceptions of law, two types of association, and even two different styles of thought arose from a fundamental dichotomy between two forms of the will: *Wesenwille* and *Kürwille*. The German word *Wesen* refers to the "essence" or "nature" of something, so that the compound *Wesenwille* might well be translated as "the natural will" or "the essential will." One must picture a situation in which the description of a man's will with respect to some question is in fact equivalent to a characterization of that man's personality: this will expresses his nature; he is that will. There was always some suggestion of the primitive, unreflected drive in Tönnies' natural will, and yet he did not mean to confine the term to the level of the purely instinctual and irrational. He included habits and even a certain class of intellectual commitments among the ordinary sources of natural will. Once again, one must imagine a type of conviction which is so essential to a man's character that it cannot be separated from it. Such a conviction would most probably have an evaluative content. It would be closely related to the man's primary goals. It might be based in part upon conscious deliberations; but it would certainly owe very little to the kind of technical thinking that is completely independent of the thinker's character.

Küren means "to choose," and the compound *Willkür,* which Tönnies very often used in place of *Kürwille,* suggests an arbitrary willfulness. More specifically, Tönnies associated *Kürwille* with what Max Weber later called *zweckrational* behavior, meaning action which is rational with respect to a given end. An act of *Kürwille,* or rational will, in Tönnies' scheme, is very much a calculated act. It presupposes a logical distinction between means and ends and a series of mental operations in which possible choices are located in a hierarchy of means-ends relations. In describing a specific instance of rational will, one refers to a particular place in such a system; one does not have to characterize the individual chooser. In this sense, rational will may appear relatively arbitrary with respect to the personality in question. Tönnies came back again and again to the aspect of calculation, the exclusively mental, even artificial, basis of rational will. Indeed, his whole description of the two forms of will hinged upon the role of conscious reflection in determining behavior. In the case of natural will, thinking is closely related to the whole personality and to its primary goals, whereas rational will proceeds upon more or less "impersonal," emotionally and morally neutral modes of analysis. In short, the mandarin distinction between knowledge as wisdom and knowledge as "mere technique" was implicitly contained in the antithesis between natural will and rational will.

All human relationships and groupings, according to Tönnies, may be classified with respect to the quality of the will which creates them and holds them together. The members of a community are united in and through their natural will; the partners of a society come together to achieve some specific object of rational will. The adjectives *gemeinschaftlich* (communal) and *gesellschaftlich* (societal), when applied to a given "social entity" *(soziale Wesenheit),* describe the character of the associative bond which is involved. Among social entities of a predominantly communal type, Tönnies included the basic family relationships, such as that between mother and child or that between siblings, as well as friendships, clans, neighborly relations, village communities, small town corporations, guilds, and religious associations. On the other hand, the temporary agreement between the partners in an exchange, in most modern business associations, and in interest groups would fall into the category of societal entities.

Tönnies often used organic analogies to describe communal associations, and he liked to picture societal relationships as mechanical ones. He did this quite deliberately, for it seemed to him that the language of "nature," "growth," and "development" was peculiarly suited to the subject matter of community and of natural will, whereas society and rational will were more appropriately described in the vocabulary of mechanistic rationalism and conceptualism. This aspect of Tönnies' theory is particulary difficult to state; but as I understand him, he meant to suggest that the traditional distinction between "Romantic" and "rationalist" modes of social analysis was not so much a logical as a psychological and social one. From his point of view, each of the two divergent intellectual traditions legitimately expressed one side of the permanent antithesis between the two great forms of the will and of association, and he extended this argument to the field of political and legal theory as well. The fictions of the social contract and of natural law, it seemed to him, were excellent typical descriptions of societal legality, whereas communal law was genuinely and necessarily a product of organic evolution, of custom and tradition. In the preface to *Community and Society*, Tönnies acknowledged his indebtedness to Sir Henry Maine, whose work in legal history had led him to distinguish between "status" and "contract," and to Otto Gierke, the historian of German corporate law (*Genossenschaftsrecht*). These men had clearly made a deep impression upon him; but he was also a careful student of Hobbes and a relatively enthusiastic reader of Comte and of Spencer. In this, he stood out among his colleagues. Unlike many of those who later adopted his distinction between community and society, he was in no obvious or simple sense an enemy of natural law or an advocate of organic and corporative conceptions.

True, the antithesis between community and society quickly became a very popular device in the orthodox argument against modern society, and this is not hard to explain. Tönnies himself regarded the gradual replacement of communal with societal social bonds as the great tragedy of history. In relating the rise of natural law to the fall of Rome and in tracing the acid effects of industrialization upon community, he did not hide his revulsion against developments which nevertheless seemed to him inevitable. He helped to revive the distinction between culture and civilization, which subsequently inspired many a polemic against technology and liberal society.[55] His treatment of classes as societal entities and of estates as their communal counterparts was also destined to find many imitators on the political right.

It is all the more remarkable that Tönnies himself was never attracted to any of the reactionary arguments which others derived from his theory. He simply could not believe that the language of mandarin orthodoxy could restore the realities of community. He repeatedly warned against the illusion that "a dead ethic or religion can be brought back to life through any sort of compulsion or instruction."[56] In this respect, he was influenced by Marx. There was no doubt in his mind that capitalism was the main force behind the movement from community to society, from primitive communism to modern socialism. Agriculture, the small town guild, communal legal traditions, and even the family itself had to be sacrificed, so that there might be worldwide markets, rational patterns of social organization, mass production, and an army of uprooted workers to be exploited in the factories. Of this, he had no doubt, and he could not abide "idealistic" phrases designed to disguise these realities.

Altogether, Tönnies' views were more unusual and more complex than those of his readers, so that he was often misunderstood. In a short autobiographical sketch and elsewhere, he made every effort to explain his position and to separate himself from his politically orthodox interpreters.[57] He defended urban and industrial Germany against the reactionary ruralists. He did not believe in social revolution; but he was very actively interested in the labor unions and cooperatives. He regarded these associations as the most promising communal elements in modern social life. He did not feel that the decline of modern culture could actually be reversed. He called himself a pessimist; but this did not stop him from advocating radical measures in the field of social policy. He acquired the reputation of being a "socialist," which hurt his academic career. His sympathetic study of the Hamburg dock strike of 1896 antagonized Althoff, the powerful director of higher education in the Prussian Ministry of Culture. In letters to his friend Friedrich Paulsen, Tönnies expressed his contempt for the class politics of the National Liberals, the dishonest "patriotism" of the Conservatives, and the servility of the German academic community.[58] He was very much an outsider. He became an instructor in economics and political science (*Staatswissenschaften*) at Kiel when he was 26, advanced to associate professor at the age of 54, and did not receive an official teaching assignment in sociology itself until he was 65, in 1920.

Tönnies' most abiding commitment was to the ideal of rational clarification. He included modern wissenschaft among the creations of rational will; but he nevertheless stressed his own loyalty to "the rigorously wissenschaftlich manner of thinking, which rejects all belief in spirits and spooks." During the 1920's, in the face of popular attacks upon individualism, he announced his "full personal sympathy" with the "freeing of thought from the bonds of superstition and delusion" and with "all movements of liberation against feudalism and serfdom." He admitted that many of the romantic and conservative ideals of social reintegration that he now opposed had originally been rooted in community. The difficulty was that they had long since become "intellectually and spiritually empty," "fundamentally untrue and hypocritical," so that "a vital individualism and the [forms of] society" were now in fact the only alternatives to "force and tyranny."[59] Tönnies never abandoned his conviction that the whole course of modern culture was profoundly tragic; but he resisted the temptation to escape from pessimism into what seemed to him obscurantist illusion.

His methodological program, too, was rather more complex than it might at first appear.[60] He did not regard the "social entities" (*Wesenheiten*) of which he wrote as empirical realities. He thought of them, rather, as "pure" or "essential" ideas. He knew that all existing groups and associations were actually mixtures of communal and societal elements, and it did not disturb him that his treatment of the various social linkages was based upon no systematic observation. He distinguished between "theoretical," "applied," and "empirical" sociology. Theoretical sociology was to uncover such pure social entities as those of community and society. Applied sociology was to use these ideas in the study of particular historical cultures and circumstances. Empirical sociology or "sociography" was to survey present social conditions, perhaps with the aid of statistics. Tönnies explicitly identified applied sociology with the philosophy of history.[61] While the historian emphasizes the individual fact or circumstance, he said, the sociologist tries to find large regularities in the evolution of society. Since the trend from community to society naturally seemed to him the most important of these regularities, he probably saw the applied sociology of the future essentially as an elaboration of his own theory. In this respect, he may be compared to Comte. On the other hand, it was theoretical sociology which primarily interested him, and in this field, his methodological position may be considered original. His emphasis here, as we said, was upon isolating the social and psychological forces that bind men together. He tended to divide human motives into "social" and "egotistical" ones, and it was his predominant concern with the sources of social cohesion that defined the focus and the whole tone of his work.

Indeed, something very similar can be said of most of the leading German sociologists of this period, who were certainly influenced by Tönnies. Typically, they took a rather skeptical view of modern social and cultural conditions, while carefully avoiding reactionary conclusions. They were fascinated with the apparent change in the quality of interpersonal bonds, and they saw the modern "social question" as an outgrowth of this transformation. They generally used the word "social" to imply a "positive" sense of the "socially binding." They were clearly disturbed at the estrangement of men in modern society. As mandarins, they were disposed to regard this phenomenon as a spiritual problem. They respected Marx; but they could not accept his "materialist" account of alienation as a change in the relationship between producer and production. Like Max Weber, they tended to see the dilemmas of capitalism as aspects of a larger set of problems. Their fundamental concern was the apparent conflict between *all* forms of modern social rationalization and the ideals described in Tönnies' natural or essential will. In the final analysis, these ideals were based upon the model of the cultivated man, whose rationality is self-expression, whose knowledge is wisdom, and whose ideas are inextricably linked with his primary goals and with his whole character. Where such men communicated, and all men shared, such "essential," morally and emotionally meaningful ideas, the mandarins might have said, there was community.

The greatness of Tönnies and of other distinguished German sociologists of his day lay in the fact that they would not abandon all rationality, or even all "calculation," for the sake of community and "culture." They opted for wissenschaft in a consciously gratuitous choice. It was their essential will to do so. The only other way to explain their behavior is to refer again to the extraordinary subtlety of the accommodationist response to modernity. This was partly a result of the plain recognition that tears would not bring back community, but there was something more to it as well. When orthodox popularizers of Tönnies talked about community, they generally proposed to "overcome" the divisive aspects of modern economic and political life by extending the competence of the state. The real object of their moralistic slogans was the escape from the pluralistic to the paternalistically integrated nation. The cameralist bureaucracy was the true source of community in their plan, which would have perpetuated the existing stratification of German society. The capitalist would have been transformed, in their ideal, into a servant of "the whole," into the state official's colleague. The worker would have become a dutiful soldier, and the bureaucratic version of the mandarin ideology would have sanctified this one-sided solution of "the social problem."

Tönnies and others of his persuasion regarded such schemes as enormous fallacies, and this for several reasons. They saw the state as the chief enemy, not as a potential source, of community. To them, the bureaucracy was by far the most dangerous form of rationalization in modern life, because it stifled individual creativity. In a way, they were just as interested in cultural and social vitality as in communal coherence. They sought forms of association that were free and spontaneous, not officially dictated and bureaucratically patterned. They had more in common with Brentano than with Schmoller and Wagner. They represented the Humboldtian side of the tension between intellectuals and bureaucrats which never entirely disappeared from mandarin consciousness.

The most unusual aspect of Tönnies' theory, in the context of orthodox mandarin opinion, was his suggestion that the workers' associations were the most promising elements of community in modern social life. Tönnies could not have arrived at this conclusion if he had not conceptually separated the abstract social entities from the empirical evidence available about various historic societies. His methodological choices were thus of great importance for the political implications of his results. The contrast between community and society would necessarily have led to a conservative line of thought if the concept of community had been no more than a generalization upon social facts in the past. The accommodationist program called for a selective translation of mandarin values to the modern setting. In sociology, this objective required an unprejudiced examination of associative forms, an analysis which was inspired but not unduly controlled by the historians' and the poets' accounts of past felicities. In this respect also, Tönnies established a pattern which was to reappear in the work of several of the leading German sociologists of the late nineteenth and early twentieth centuries. These men's whole conception of the new discipline reflected their determination to isolate "the social tie" or "the interpersonal realm" as a timely field of analysis—and of abstraction.

Thus, during the two decades after 1894, Georg Simmel developed his "formal" sociology of human "interaction" (*Wechselwirkung*).[62] He distinguished between the "form" and the "material content" of social relationships. His point was that such phenomena as superordination and subordination, such structures as that of the voluntary association and such characteristic patterns of social life as polite sociability, group conflict and differentiation may be described and analyzed in a purely formal way, that is to say, without reference to the particular purposes and concerns of the relationships. Voluntary associations may be constituted and maintained for various reasons, and different sorts of people may join them; but it remains possible to study them strictly as voluntary associations. The phenomena of social domination and subordination may play a role in economic enterprise, in politics, or in religious affairs; but the sociologist can look beyond these differences of content in order to focus upon the formal patterns involved. Of course, social forms do not appear separated from their contents in reality; but every discipline legitimately and necessarily abstracts from the totality of experience in its concepts. Thus sociologists must undoubtedly work with empirical materials which are already being studied by historians, economists, psychologists, and others; but they have a uniquely constructed object of cognition in the forms of social interaction.

On the basis of these arguments, Simmel moved even further away than Tönnies from the old conception of sociology as philosophy of history. He did feel that the emphasis upon forms of interaction in all fields of human endeavor might cause sociologists to discover certain limited "historical laws" which would not emerge from a more conventional study of political, economic, or cultural affairs. But he cautioned against the tendency to regard such laws as permanent philosophical truths about the whole course or direction of man's cultural evolution. Simmel appreciated and occasionally drew upon the work of Marx and of Tönnies; but he tended to redefine these men's theories in the light of his own methodology. He thus established pure or formal sociology as an independent and specialized discipline. Whether he also gave it a truly empirical character is a somewhat more difficult question.

In an essay on social psychology published in 1908, Simmel argued against the tendency to attribute a single will or psyche to a collectivity.[63] He recognized that the participants in a mass meeting, for example, do appear to act in some manner as a crowd. But he thought it necessary to treat such phenomena as the products of many specific "interpersonal influences." He admitted the usefulness of statistical and typological generalizations about whole groups. But in these cases too, he believed it possible in principle to find more thorough explanations in the actual relationships between men. He defined "society" itself as an aggregate of interactions, not as a sum of individuals; but this choice reflected a dynamic rather than a wholistic conception of group life. Thus it was characteristic of Simmel that he did not try to draw a very sharp line between individual and social psychology. He simply emphasized the sociologist's interest in social interaction and interpersonal influences. He was apparently prepared to accept whatever helpful suggestions any sort of psychololgy could offer in this field.

This is not to say that Simmel actually relied upon specific discoveries of contemporary psychologists. In practice, his "psychology" was really a product of common sense, a matter of personal though often brilliant insight. Since he also failed to undertake any systematically empirical studies of group behavior or opinion, his pure sociology came in fact to resemble Tönnies' theoretical approach. Indeed, this was a general characteristic of German sociology during our period. It was thought that certain persistent forms of social relation could be isolated, and that neither experimental psychology nor what Tönnies called sociography were required for this purpose. Analogies taken from geometry were often used to imply that the social patterns in question could be understood, perhaps "phenomenologically," as patterns, in their essential nature or "inner logic." It might be remarked that these ideas did not prove entirely fruitless and that they are by no means easy to challenge. Beyond that, our present concern is only to observe that Simmel and Tönnies had a good deal in common. In practice, Simmel differed from Tönnies primarily in the greater variety of his interests. Instead of grouping his arguments around a single theme, he was content to write several substantively unconnected essays on various forms of social interaction. Among these, those on the philosophy of money and on the sociology of superordination and subordination were certainly the most interesting.

Simmel's view of the role of money in modern society was conditioned not only by his own interpretation of Marx, but also by the general conception of capitalism current in the mandarin community during this period. The main points of his argument may be stated as follows. The use of money increases the freedom of partners in many kinds of social relations. Contracts and exchanges are depersonalized, as compensations in kind become unnecessary, while traditional and moral notions of obligation are translated into the precise and limited terms of a financial equation. Men do not need to live next to each other to engage in trade. They can choose their residences and their partners more freely. Ownership itself becomes an abstraction, so that people do not even have to know each other while jointly owning some property. Any individual can join a voluntary association, simply by way of a money contribution, without tying his whole person to the group. A highly flexible and variegated system of social interactions thus becomes possible, one in which personal attachments need not play a role. A new style of life and of thought arises, in which the habit of precise calculation becomes ever more prevalent. Group life is "rationalized." A relatively free but also a more or less "atomized" society is created.

In discussing the phenomenon of superordination and subordination, Simmel began by saying that sociology could deal only with situations in which there were truly mutual relations (*Wechselbeziehungen*) between persons. A case in which an inferior was regarded exclusively as an object by his superior would thus fall outside the scope of the new discipline. Simmel hastened to point out, however, that such situations were much rarer than was commonly thought, that subjects generally had some range of choice even under the most extreme despotism, and that practically all leaders were influenced by their followers to some degree.

In going on to describe the relationship between inferior and superior in more detail, Simmel drew upon a variety of examples and anecdotes from history and from everyday experience. He wrote as if to elucidate meanings, not to supply evidence in support of generalizations. Occasionally, the theories of Montesquieu, Hobbes, or Machiavelli appeared to stand behind this or that part of his argument. He saw the traditional connection between despotism and leveling, and he stressed the particularly impersonal character of mass rule. As a mandarin, he was especially interested in intellectual leadership and in subordination to an "ideal" authority, an "objective" principle, a religious belief, or a law considered binding upon rulers and ruled alike. In a kind of geometry of social interaction, he portrayed people as entering into an association or relationship more or less completely, like circles that may overlap to a greater or lesser extent. In this way, he thought it possible to imagine an equality of "weight" in the contributions of the several partners to an association, in which the leader commits more of his personality than those he leads. This suggested that one of the main problems of sociopolitical cohesion was that of finding the proper levels of entry for the participants, a small degree of commitment being most harmless and stable in the case of such large associations as the modern national state. Apparently, Simmel did not agree with those of his colleagues who would increase the individual's emotional investment in the state by trying to replace the loosely societal structure of modern political life with more communal forms. In any case, he thought it characteristic of modern man that he was involved in many relationships and groups, although invariably on a relatively tangential level. In this respect also, it seemed to him that social life had become at once freer and less personally integrated than it had been in the past.

Many of these ideas have a familar ring. The discussion of subordination reflects the mandarins' concern over the changing style of politics in modern times. The whole treatment of association and of money reminds one of Tönnies. Simmel's originality lay in the subtlety of his distinctions and in the brilliant insights he communicated through many vivid examples. Beyond that, his methodological views exerted a profound influence upon the subsequent development of German sociology. He became the acknowledged father of the "formal" direction within the new discipline. Leopold von Wiese and other German sociologists of the 1920's owed much to Simmel's distinction between the forms and the contents of social patterns.

The other great German sociologist of the prewar period, of course, was Max Weber. His work on the methodology of the social sciences helped to clarify some of the terms and analytical categories used by Tönnies, Simmel, and their followers. Weber's *Protestant Ethic* and his studies in the sociology of religion provoked much fruitful discussion, which cut across the boundaries of established disciplines. But the three most interesting aspects of Weber's thought, in the perspective of this chapter, are his analyses of class and status, legitimacy, and bureaucracy.

The modern concept of class was rather unpopular in the German academic community during this period. It implied social stratification by economic criteria, that is to say, by wealth or in accordance with a man's objective place and rank in the capitalist system of production. For obvious reasons, the mandarins disliked this scheme. They did not want to see society organized on a class basis, and they therefore distrusted the notion of class even as a descriptive device. They had a point, of course. Particularly in the German context, noneconomic criteria of social stratification were simply too obvious to be ignored. They were less important than they once had been; but they still mattered, especially to the mandarins.

A number of German academics between 1890 and 1930 participated in an extensive critique of the class concept. Some of them worked with the traditional "estate," using it as an occupational category. Estatist theories were particularly popular in orthodox circles during the Weimar period; but they also appeared earlier and in less reactionary settings.[64] Max Weber's contribution to the discussion was a careful definition of status in terms of "style of life" and "social honor," which separated legitimate additions to a purely economic view of stratification from the obscurantist moralizing that was so often attached to estatist theory. Above all, Weber recognized that much of the social and intellectual tension in his own environment stemmed from a sudden and probably temporary disequilibrium between economically founded claims to social standing and older status considerations. "When the bases of the acquisition and distribution of goods are relatively stable, stratification by status is favored. Every technological repercussion and economic transformation threatens stratification by status and pushes the class situation into the foreground. Epochs and countries in which the naked class situation is of predominant significance are regularly the periods of technical and economic transformations. And every slowing down of the shifting of economic stratifications leads, in due course, to the growth of status structures and makes for a resuscitation of the important role of social honor."[65]

In his work on the character of political authority and legitimacy, Weber introduced the concept of "charisma." He characterized charisma as an attributed gift of grace in the leader which justifies his demand for obedience. Typically, according to Weber, charismatic authority is personal and relatively unstructured. It can be transmitted to a successor through family inheritance or through magical signs and ceremonies. In the process of being thus perpetuated, however, it is necessarily institutionalized or "routinized" to some extent. It is supplemented and eventually replaced by "traditional," "legal," and "rational" types of dominion. The charismatic warrior chief, to simplify by way of example, begins a line of kings, whose sacred claims to obedience become more and more a matter of tradition. As their rule is modernized, tradition is transformed into law, and law comes to acquire the character and the authority of reason. Weber pointed out, of course, that essentially all historic governments have been based upon mixtures of the several types of legitimacy. Moreover, Weber felt that new injections of the charismatic element could occur at various points in the evolution of a political system. This, indeed, is the most fascinating aspect of the whole argument. One has the impression that Weber's charisma was the initiating force in the machinery of the political process. It stood for the original source of renovation and vitality in history. The institutional apparatus, which was designed to channel and to perpetuate it, also reduced its substance, so that new infusions were necessary from time to time. In that sense, Weber's charisma resembled Tönnies' natural will. Both were spiritual energies derived from intense interpersonal commitments. Both created social cohesion and vitality, and both seemed in dangerously short supply in the modern age.

Weber was particularly interested in bureaucracy as an aspect of rationalization in politics. He regarded the bureaucratization of Wilhelmian social and political life with deep misgivings, which is why he hoped for the emergence of energetic political leaders within the framework of a reformed parliamentary system. In his study of the Chinese literati and in his general discussion of political authority, he drew a pointedly unsentimental portrait of the modern official, of his ideology and his education.

The actual social position of the official is normally highest where, as in old civilized countries, the following conditions prevail: a strong demand for administration by trained experts; a strong and stable social differentiation . . . The possession of educational certificates . . . is usually linked with qualification for office. Naturally, such certificates or patents enhance the "status element" in the social position of the official.

Only with the bureaucratization of the state and of law in general can one see a definite possibility of separating sharply and conceptually an "objective" legal order from the "subjective rights" of the individual which it guarantees; of separating "public" law from "private" law.

Educational institutions on the European continent, especially the institutions of higher learning . . . are dominated and influenced by the need for the kind of "education" that produced a system of special examinations and the trained expertness that is increasingly indispensable for modern bureaucracy.

Social prestige based upon the advantages of special education and training as such is by no means specific to bureaucracy. On the contrary! But educational prestige in other structures of domination rests upon substantially different foundations. Expressed in slogan-like fashion, the "cultivated man," rather than the "specialist," has been the end sought by education and has formed the basis of social esteem in such various systems as the feudal, theocratic, and patrimonial structures of dominion . . . Behind all the present discussions of the foundations of the educational system, the struggle of the "specialist type of man" against the older type of "cultivated man" is hidden at some decisive point . . . This fight intrudes into all intimate cultural questions.

For twelve centuries social rank in China has been determined more by qualification for office than by wealth. This qualification, in turn, has been determined by education, and especially by examinations. China has made literary education the yardstick of social prestige in the most exclusive fashion, far more exclusively than did Europe during the period of the humanists, or than Germany has done.

The examination of China tested whether or not the candidate's mind was thoroughly steeped in literature and whether or not he possessed the *ways of thought* suitable to a cultured man and resulting from cultivation in literature. These qualifications held far more specifically with China than with the German humanist *Gymnasium* . . . As far as one may judge from the assignments given to the pupils of the lower grades in China, they were rather similar to the essay topics assigned to the top grades of a German *Gymnasium*.

The dualism of the *shen* and *kwei,* of good and evil spirits, of heavenly *yang* substance as over against earthly *yin* substance, . . . [suggested that the task of education was] the unfolding of the *yang* substance in the soul of man. For the man in whom *yang* substance has completely gained the upper hand . . . also has power over the spirits; that is, according to the ancient notion, he has magical powers.[66]

It should be noticed that Weber saw two possibilities at once: that of a conflict between the bureaucratic and the "cultivated" ideal of education, and that of a partial fusion between the two. He knew that a conflict was possible, because he stood with those modernists who had come to distrust the cameralist side of the mandarin tradition. In every other respect, Weber's paragraphs could be read as a statement of the mandarin hypothesis, even though some of them were intended to refer primarily to conditions in China.

Max Weber and a few other leading social scientists in the modernist camp hold a special place in the intellectual history of the mandarin community. They apparently shared some of the emotions with which the majority of their colleagues viewed the social transformations of their time. But their intellectual response to these changes far surpassed the orthodox norm in subtlety, critical control, and precision. Though never without a certain pessimism, they put their ambivalence at the service of analysis. They became at least partly conscious of their own situation.

THE WORLD WAR: HARMONY AND DISHARMONY

Early in August of 1914, the war finally came. One imagines that at least a few educated Germans had private moments of horror at the slaughter which was about to commence. In public, however, German academics of all political persuasions spoke almost exclusively of their optimism and enthusiasm. Indeed, they greeted the war with a sense of relief. Party differences and class antagonisms seemed to evaporate at the call of national duty. Social Democrats marched singing to the front in the company of their betters, and the mandarin intellectuals rejoiced at the apparent rebirth of "idealism" in Germany. They celebrated the death of politics, the triumph of ultimate, apolitical objectives over short-range interests, and the resurgence of those moral and irrational sources of social cohesion that had been threatened by the "materialistic" calculation of Wilhelmian modernity.

On August 2, the day after the German mobilization order, the modernist Ernst Troeltsch spoke at a public rally. Early in his address, he hinted that "criminal elements" might try to attack property and order, now that the army had been moved from the German cities to the front. This is the only overt reference to fear of social disturbance that I have been able to discover in the academic literature of the years 1914–1916. The surprising patriotism of the Social Democrats dispersed such apprehensions before the fighting had actually begun, so that Troeltsch could proceed to marvel at the national strength and unity "which has after all been only etched and not really dissolved by the luxuriant and disjunctive life of the great urban centers."[67]

Temporarily freed from their anxiety over the politically and socially centrifugal tendencies of the mass and machine age, the German university professors sang hymns of praise to the "voluntary submission of all individuals and social groups to this army."[68] They were almost grateful that the outbreak of the war had given them the chance to experience the national enthusiasm of those heady weeks in August.

> In these great weeks, [the war] has already presented us with a stirring portrayal of the one-sidedness of merely economic drives, with a new inculcation of the spiritual and the communal.

> The first victory we won, even before the victories on the battlefield, was the victory over ourselves . . . A higher life seemed to reveal itself to us. Each of us . . . lived for the whole [*das Ganze*], and the whole lived in all of us. Our own ego with its personal interests was dissolved in the great historic being of the nation. The fatherland calls! the parties disappear . . . Thus a moral elevation of the people preceded the war; the whole nation was gripped by the truth and reality of a suprapersonal, spiritual power.

> When we celebrate this war on a future day of remembrance, that day will be the feast of the mobilization. The feast of the second of August . . . That is when our new spirit was born: the spirit of the tightest integration of all economic and all political powers into a new whole . . . The new German state! the ideas of 1914![69]

That last phrase, "the ideas of 1914," was never forgotten after the economist Johann Plenge introduced it in the paragraph cited above. Rudolf Kjellen, a Swedish Germanophile, quickly picked it up and used it to entitle a pamphlet which became famous in Germany.

Kjellen's pamphlet preached the mission of German culture during and after the war and combined a whole series of mandarin slogans into a "world-historical perspective."[70]

How the printers must have labored in those years to cope with the immense volume of literature that flowed from the universities to the public. It is hard to imagine how so many essays were published without financial contributions from the authors; but there were untold numbers of unpublished speeches as well. Considering it "the duty of the intellectuals to encourage, to strengthen and to vitalize the . . . people," Rudolph Eucken managed to give thirty-six public addresses within the space of one year.[71] Such heroes of the lectern as Dietrich Schäfer, Gustav Roethe, and Reinhold Seeberg probably did as well or better.

The German academic community as a whole was convinced that Russia, France, and England bore more responsibility for the outbreak of the war than Germany.[72] This needs no elaborate explanation, particularly since the Allied view of Germany as the sole aggressor was also a creature of bias. What does require further analysis is the German contribution to the "cultural war" which accompanied the physical conflict. German scholars tended to feel, with Ernst Troeltsch, that the Allied powers were chiefly to blame for the outbreak of this battle of ideologies. They were annoyed and shocked at the lack of sympathy for the German cause among the neutrals, which they traced to the technical efficiency of Allied propaganda agencies. Troeltsch argued that democracies could not fight an aggressive war without disguising it as a defense against an overwhelming moral threat.[73] Since Cromwell, he said, the English had developed an especially pronounced talent for this sort of hypocrisy; they habitually identified their side of a conflict with justice, charity, and the rights of the oppressed. The French achieved an analogous effect with their arguments about the future of reason and humanity.

German academics were particularly indignant at those English publicists who made a distinction between German culture and Prussian militarism, suggesting that militarism had come to predominate over culture. In a public announcement dated October

23, 1914, many German professors of all political leanings and from various universities protested against this suggestion: "In the German army, there is no other spirit than in the German people, for both are one, and we too belong to it."[74] After all, the mandarins were not disposed to regard the "ideas of 1914" as a purely military phenomenon. "Indeed, it is precisely the deepest forces of our culture, of our spirit and of our history which sustain this war and give it its soul."[75] As these phrases suggest, the German academics' contribution to the "cultural war" were not at all purely defensive. The mission they assigned to the German nation was just as universally conceived as the Allied campaign for democracy, progress, and peace.

One of the most unrestrained of the German patriotic outbursts was written early in 1915 by Werner Sombart, who formally abjured his former politics in a preface. His pamphlet described the war as a confrontation between the respective world views of "traders and heroes." The "traders," of course, were the English; the "heroes" were German.

> Trader and hero: they constitute the two great opposites, the two poles, as it were, of all human orientation . . . The trader approaches life with the question: what can you give me . . . The hero approaches life with the question: what can I give you? He wants to give things away, to spend himself, to make sacrifices—without a return . . . The trader speaks only of "rights," the hero only of his duties.

> [The trader] regards the whole existence of man on earth as a sum of commercial transactions which everyone makes as favorably as possible for himself, whether with fate or God (the trader's spirit molds religions in its own image too), or with his fellow men individually or as a group (which is to say with the state). The profit which is expected to result for the life of each individual is as much well-being as possible . . . Within this conception of life, material values will thus be given an important place . . . Economic and especially commercial activity will achieve honor and respect. Consequently, economic interest will . . . gradually subordinate the other

aspects of life. Once the representatives of the economy have the upper hand in the country, they will easily transfer the attitudes of their profession to all sectors of life . . . until the trader's world view and practical commercialism finally join together in an inseparable unity, as is the case in England today.[76]

Sombart thought it possible to show that English philosophy and learning were dominated by the "trader's spirit." Bacon held useful inventions to be the principal goal of science. Spencer was more interested in the increase of technical comforts than in the deepening of man's understanding. English ethical theories have been focused "not on life per se, on supraindividual life as such, but on 'this or that [individual] life'." The happiness of the greatest number of individuals is the highest goal of human endeavor, according to the "animalistic" (*hundsgemein*) ideal of the utilitarians; and what is this happiness but "comfort with respectability: apple pie and Sunday service, peaceableness and football, money-making and leisure for some hobby." The English virtues are those that enable traders to live at peace with each other, purely negative, consisting of things not done and natural drives not satisfied: "moderation, frugality, industry, honesty, justice, restraint in all kinds of things, modesty, patience, and so on."[77]

Sombart had nothing but scorn for English conceptions of freedom and the state. Both, he said, were based strictly upon the trader's desire to be left at peace with his transactions. Hence the persistence of contractual notions in English political theory; hence that characteristic "fear of the state." According to Sombart, even war is a purely commercial enterprise in the eyes of English statesmen. Like More's Utopians, they save their own men and try to bribe others to fight for them. They calculate; they weigh their gains against their losses. They never fight a hopeless battle, and money is their favorite weapon. They understand so little of the real meaning of heroism that they confuse battles with sports events. Take them prisoner after a bloody engagement, and they will offer to shake hands on the match; because sport, the companion of comfort, is the only form of cultural endeavor that their petty souls can comprehend.

Sombart's tale of the traders was something of a masterpiece in its own category. Its fulminant tone and the undisciplined breadth of its associations was seldom if ever matched by its competitors in the field of polemics. Its theory about British sports was almost certainly original, too. Many of its stereotypes, however, appear to have been common property in academic circles. One finds them again and again in the literature of the "cultural war," although generally in a less inclusive and flamboyant form and sometimes more subtly stated. The psychologist and philosopher Wilhelm Wundt, for example, brought out a little treatise on "the nations and their philosophies" almost simultaneously with Sombart's tract.[78] Once again, the emphasis was upon the shallowness of British ethical theories and the simplicity of common-sense realism in English epistemology since Locke. Such terms as "egotistic utilitarianism," "materialism," "positivism," and "pragmatism" played a disconcertingly large role in Wundt's characterization of the Anglo-Saxon mind; "materialism" and "positivism" performed analogous services in his description of the French.

It is interesting that the mandarins were apparently more anxious to discredit the social and political achievements of England than those of France. Toward the French, they often displayed a certain amused condescension, while their heaviest polemical weapons were directed against the English. In part, this may have been a reflection of the military situation. England was the bigger threat. She had been the great maritime and colonial rival since the turn of the century, and the emotions of that conflict were not forgotten. But the roots of the antagonism lay deeper still. Above all, England was the prime example of a highly industrialized and politically advanced nation. English society was what German society would soon be, unless the mandarins could prevent it. That is why Sombart and Wundt reacted with such fury against Spencer's cheerful proclamations about the natural relationship between individual liberty and industrial development.[79]

The German academics meant to show that English conceptions

of freedom had little to do with the personal and cultural individualism of the German tradition.[80] English liberty, they felt, involved a lack of restraint upon the acquisitive instincts, a sense of opposition to the state, and the purely theoretical right to participate in political negotiations. Beyond that, neither English nor French society really tolerated any kind of diversity. The force of public opinion stifled all genuine individuality, especially in the cultural field, so that a shallow common ground alone remained. Worst of all, the economic interest groups who had de facto control over the political system were also the chief agents of public opinion. Amid the dreary homogeneity of a leveled society, their commercial mentality ruled over the nation's intellectual and spiritual life.

It was during the cultural war that the historians Troeltsch and Meinecke tried to define "the German idea of freedom." In doing so, they drew upon the conventional image of England to a considerable extent, and yet their analysis of the German heritage was not wholly uncritical. Indeed, they contributed substantially to the mandarin self-analysis which is discussed above, in Chapter Two. Being modernists, they were prepared to admit that certain aspects of the English system could profitably be applied to Germany. They sought minor adjustments, technical changes which would not affect the fundaments of German culture. At the same time, they meant to protect the German idea of freedom against the mixture of egotism and delusion which they detected in English and French political traditions. They also suggested that the world would benefit from a German victory, because the Germans would regard other nations as autonomous "individualities," allowing them to follow their own paths, rather than seeking to dominate them in the name of some intolerantly universal ideal of "progress" or "humanity."[81]

The mandarins rejected egalitarianism and parliamentarianism primarily upon cultural grounds. They habitually identified these political ideals with the "commercialism" and the "shallowness" of "Western," that is, English, French, and American, mass society. They became addicted to a kind of ideological geography, in which technical progress, along with spiritual decay, appeared to increase to the west, while an apparently inseparable mixture of economic backwardness and cultural profundity was associated with the easterly portion of the map. Needless to say, Germany was located very near the middle of this scale. To a modernist of Alfred Weber's stamp, the problem of his nation's future therefore presented itself as a choice between its eastern and its western face.[82] On the one hand, England could be regarded as the major enemy, while a natural alliance with Russia and the Western Slavs would strengthen the eastern aspects of the German orientation. On the other hand, Germany might seek to re-establish closer ties with England, permit some minor adjustments of its political system to the Western model, and find an outlet for its energies as a guardian and translator of Western traditions toward the east. Though he vacillated, Alfred Weber ultimately leaned toward the pro-Western choice. He also supported such modernists as Troeltsch and Meinecke in their demand for minor adjustments of the German political system. Most of the orthodox academics, however, devoted all their polemical energies to the anti-Western position.

The most important point to be made about the German intellectuals' attack upon the West is that it was produced for domestic consumption. It was directed against a devil who lived in Germany, chiefly in the factories, political assemblies, and big urban centers. In this respect, the German position in the cultural war was very closely related to "the ideas of 1914." Everything that had disturbed the mandarins in the social and cultural life of their country since 1870 was introduced into the caricature of England. Everything they had sought to preserve or to re-create became a part of the "spirit of 1914." The purpose of both maneuvers was to erect permanent symbols of the mandarins' own values and, if possible, to perpetuate the national consensus embodied in the "ideas of 1914" beyond the period of the war itself. Thus Sombart's characterization of the English trader functioned primarily as a foil for his praise of the German hero. "The virtues of the hero are the opposite of the trader's: they are all positive . . . Sacrifice, faithfulness, openness, respect, courage, religiosity, willingness to obey, charity. They are the warrior's virtues, virtues which fully unfold only in and through war."[83] As one might expect, the hero thought little about economics, was more interested in ideas and cultural values than in material advantages, and believed in the submission of his personal interests to the spiritual community within which he arose.

Sombart's conclusions, too, were predictable. English commercialism and utilitarianism, he said, had made frightening progress in the economic and political life of prewar Germany, making it a "life without ideals." The philosophy of comfort had begun to make converts, until "the miracle occurred," until the "ancient German hero's spirit" burst forth again in 1914. Occasionally, there were indications that the revival was not yet consummated. "It hurt me to read in the report of a German warrior from the front to a Berlin newspaper: how the writer spoke with a certain respect of the safety razors which, he said, one found quite generally among the English soldiers, even in the trenches. That is sad: to pay attention to the removal of the stubble . . . amid such great events. Rather, every safety razor in the trenches seems to me an ugly symbol of the hollow English peddler's culture."[84] Still, it was Sombart's hope that the lessons of the war would carry over into peacetime to provide a cure for the creeping sickness of Wilhelmian materialism. Indeed, this was the avowed purpose of his little tract, which was dedicated to the young heroes at the front. It was to show them "the direction in which the enemy of the German nature will have to be sought forever in the future."[85]

Sombart magnified the irrational undercurrents which he detected in his environment. But he did not invent the emotions that he exaggerated; for his colleagues felt them too. It was during the First World War that Tönnies' concept of community was converted into a popular slogan. In the mandarins' exhortations, the call for community was coupled with the demand for a future "socialism," in which the spirit of wartime integration would be preserved. Even a modernist of Meinecke's persuasion could regard the conflict as a corrective to the dangerously superficial and materialistic tendencies of prewar society and politics. Heinrich Herkner hoped for a more national and communal spirit among German workers and entrepreneurs as a result of the war experience. Johann Plenge announced the death of "English freedom," saying that "this all too individualistic conception of freedom cannot maintain the state." Rudolf Eucken saw the "world-historical importance of the German spirit" in its ability to achieve technical and organizational marvels without falling prey to spiritual shallowness. The Neo-Kantian philosopher Paul Natorp rejoiced at the death of the purely "external" civilization, the luxury, the material squabbles, and the heedless egotism of the recent German past, and dreamt of a "true" socialism of the future, in which neither egalitarianism nor the race for unearned income would play a role. Wundt joined Sombart in his castigation of "comfort" and hoped that party conflicts and socialist radicalism would be much reduced after the victory. Alois Riehl, finally, stated the arguments of the German cultural war, the "ideas of 1914," and the whole mandarin creed in these three sentences: "We want to defeat England, not to imitate her. Her example has shown all too clearly where it leads, when a state follows commercial and industrial goals exclusively." "The belief in the reality of the intellectual and spiritual [geistige] world, in the life of the whole which transcends the existence of the individual, this belief, which awoke in all of us during the early days of August, must never more die out."[86]

Yet despite everything that was said in its behalf, the "spirit of 1914" did not outlast the war. The social and political differences it was intended to "overcome" were only temporarily submerged in the enthusiasm of the August days. Before the war was one year old, they came to the surface again, and they steadily increased in intensity between 1915 and 1918. Two issues in particular were responsible for the reappearance of the old antagonisms: the question of German war aims and the problem of internal political reforms. In both of these areas, the modernists advocated a policy of moderation and compromise, only to be thoroughly ignored by the orthodox. The orthodox were at least partly to blame for the resulting failure of national unity, which was accompanied for the first time by really serious and heated disagreements among the mandarins themselves.

The war aims controversy was begun by the German industrialists, the Pan-German League, and the agrarians during the winter of 1914–15.[87] Afraid that the government under Chancellor Bethmann-Hollweg would be satisfied with moderate territorial acquisitions especially in the west, the ultra-annexationists launched a ruthless propaganda campaign in favor of a more aggressive program. On July 8, 1915, the so-called Intellectuals' Petition (*Intellektuelleneingabe*) supported the ultras' demands.[88] Organized by Professors Reinhold Seeberg and Dietrich Schäfer, it was signed by 1347 higher officials and judges, teachers, theologians, lawyers, professional men, writers, and academics. Among these signers, 352 university professors formed by far the largest single professional contingent. Under the continued leadership of Seeberg and Schäfer, the whole group of mandarin petitioners subsequently formed the Independent Commission for a German Peace (*Unabhängiger Ausschuss für einen deutschen Frieden*) in order to maintain their efforts in behalf of extensive annexations.

On July 9, 1915, the day after the Intellectuals' Petition had been handed to the government, a group of mandarin intellectuals around Professors Hans Delbrück and Adolf von Harnack submitted a counterpetition which urged more moderate war aims and tried to protect Bethmann-Hollweg against the annexationists' effort to tie his hands.[89] This second proposal bore only 141 signatures, 80 of them those of university professors.

From the time of these two petitions until the end of the war, the German academic community was divided into two groups of unequal size over the question of war aims. The large majority retained its ties with the Independent Commission and supported the ultra-annexationist program sponsored by the Pan-German League, by the army leadership, and, after the Reichstag peace resolution of July 1917, by the so-called Fatherland Party (*Vaterlandspartei*). The academic majority joined the agitation in favor of unlimited submarine warfare, always prepared to launch an attack against any sign of moderation on the part of the civilian authorities. Urging a "victorious peace" (*Siegfrieden*), it demanded extensive territorial acquisitions in Belgium, Poland, and western Russia, along with military "safeguards" in eastern France and an enlarged colonial empire taken chiefly from the English. It pictured Germany as the future leader of a huge Central European power bloc, equivalent in wealth and influence to the United States and Russia.

The minority was in sympathy with Bethmann-Hollweg and later with Richard von Kühlmann, the foremost representative of a more realistic war aims diplomacy in the Foreign Office. The academic advocates of a negotiated peace (*Verständigungsfrieden*) were by no means opposed to a significant extension of German power. They differed from the extremists only in the relative moderation of their demands. They were not internationalists on principle; nor did they reject the forceful aggrandizement of their country's influence upon moral grounds. They simply recognized that there were practical limits to German expansion, and they tried very hard to make this clear to their countrymen. They argued that Germany could not simultaneously face the permanent hostility of England and the United States, a desperately revanchist France, a thwarted Russia, and a whole cluster of national irredentisms on her eastern border. There would have to be a diplomatic effort after the war, they said, and it was insane to destroy in advance every possibility of a stable and favorable power combination. A choice would have to be made between an eastern and a western drive, and the eastern choice was not only less dangerous but also more fruitful in the long run. Moreover, it was possible to create a political sphere of influence and a field for economic and cultural penetration in Central Europe without resorting to more than a certain minimum of overt annexation. On the basis of these arguments, the moderates opposed the full incorporation of all Poland, warned against extensive territorial acquisitions in Belgium, and tried above all to keep a certain flexibility in the German diplomatic offensive.

It will not come as a surprise that most of the modernists stood on the moderate side in the war aims controversy, while the orthodox generally followed the ultra-annexationist line. Some of the leading literary advocates of the "victorious peace," signers of the majority petition, or members of the Independent Commission were Reinhold Seeberg, Dietrich Schäfer, Georg von Below, Gustav Roethe, Eduard Meyer, and Ulrich von Wilamowitz-Moellendorff, all representatives of orthodox principles. Aligned with the moderate minority were such well-known modernist academics as Hans Delbrück, Adolph von Harnack, Max and Alfred Weber, Ernst

Troeltsch, Friedrich Meinecke, Gerhart von Schulze-Gävernitz, Heinrich Herkner, Paul Östreich, Lujo Brentano, Ernst Tönnies, and Leopold von Wiese. As Klaus Schwabe has remarked, most of the Socialists of the Lectern from Schmoller to Brentano were in favor of a negotiated peace.

What exactly was the relationship between the traditional views of the mandarin modernists and their relatively restrained approach in the war aims debate? Three answers to this question seem possible, although all of them involve a certain amount of conjecture. The first has to do with the fact that the modernists generally had a little more respect for the political and social achievements of the western democracies than their orthodox colleagues. This caused them to choose the western solution of Alfred Weber's problem in ideological geography. They preferred to seek German expansion toward the east and to keep open the possibility of a future alliance in the west, which is why they were especially opposed to extensive annexations in Belgium and France. They also had a much more realistic view of English and American resources and strengths than the fanatical antimodernists. Particularly in the debate over the introduction of unlimited submarine warfare, this ideological difference played an important role, for it resulted in strikingly divergent attitudes toward the possibility of American entry into the war.[90]

Although the German Social Democrats had taken up arms in 1914, many of them found it difficult to shed their internationalist principles altogether. In any case, they liked to think of their nation's role in the war as a purely defensive one, and every ultra-annexationist tract was therefore a serious attack upon their integrity and their morale. This simple equation provided a second link between modernist political theories and the moderate position on annexation. Agrarian conservatives, right-wing industrialists, and orthodox mandarins tended to use the war aims agitation as a weapon not only against the Marxist left but also against those middle-class and Catholic political elements that joined the Social Democrats in the peace resolution of 1917. The leading modernists were horrified at this irresponsible resuscitation of the class war from the right. They could not help but recognize that moderation in the war aims question was absolutely necessary for the maintenance of the temporary social peace at home. If the German people "were forced to recognize that the war was growing beyond the bounds of a healthy national self-assertion and becoming a war of conquest, the moral cement which now holds it together would begin to crumble."[91]

For modernists and orthodox alike, the issue of annexations was intimately associated with more traditional questions of social policy. Especially during the later years of the war, the modernists became more and more convinced that a revision of the Prussian electoral system and a minor extension of Reichstag prerogatives could no longer be postponed. Their arguments in favor of these reforms were not significantly different from what they had been before 1914. But their relief at the loyalty of the masses in 1914 and their anxiety over the maintenance of popular morale led them to state their demands more urgently than ever before. They were shocked to discover that political leaders who sympathized with these views could not assert themselves against rightist intrigue and intransigence. They became ever more deeply aware of the degree to which German policy was controlled by shortsighted and blustering generals, cold-blooded industrialists, and unreconstructed junkers. As their reform proposals went unheeded and as the social divisions within the nation grew ever more serious toward the end of the war, they also felt an increasing contempt for the political rationalizations and nationalist phrases of their orthodox colleagues.

When the Fatherland Party was formed in 1917, primarily in opposition to the Reichstag peace resolution, it naturally attracted the ultra-annexationists from the educated classes as well as other right-wing elements. Under the leadership of Ernst Troeltsch, the modernists helped to organize the Popular League for Freedom and Fatherland (*Volksbund für Freiheit und Vaterland*), a political union designed to consolidate moderate and reformist resistance to the coalition of the annexationists. The following are extracts from an address delivered by Friedrich Meinecke at a founding rally of the Popular League.

Our hearts are just as hot as [those of the gentlemen of the Fatherland Party]; our fists are quite as tight and hard for the battle as theirs; but our heads are cooler and clearer! What is it that separates us from them? The Fatherland Party says it is pursuing no internal political goals . . . It only wants a peace which really safeguards our future. It defends itself especially fervently against the suspicion that it misuses the word "patriotic" in order to revive the . . . class war.

Let us begin quite mildly with a criticism of this curious program. True, there is probably a not inconsiderable number of adherents of the new party who think this way . . . We must reproach these credulous ones with being thoroughly deceived or at least completely indifferent about the domestic political effects of their actions. They fulminate against the present Reichstag majority [of the Social Democratic, Center, and Progressive parties]: they want to break it up. That would have immeasurable political consequences. And are we to believe that the cleverer operators and instigators within the movement do not know that—and do not ultimately desire it with all their hearts? After all, we are moving toward a reform of the Prussian electoral system, and if the Reichstag majority were to disintegrate, the electoral reform would run aground as well . . . Is it purely an accident of the situation that above all the conservative and industrial opponents of a thorough electoral reform are so full of loving care for the Fatherland party? We are not that easily fooled. Domestic and international questions . . . are intimately connected . . . The policy of conquest and force . . . must eventually result in a repression of the nation's desire for political freedom, in the establishment of a despotic militarism.[92]

Meinecke had been a modernist critic of German nationalist excesses even before 1914; but he had always retained a certain sympathy for the patriotic ideology of the right-wing National Liberals and Conservatives. It was only during the wartime controversy with his orthodox colleagues that his accommodationist theories took on a certain critical sharpness. He was moving toward the political left, actually associating himself with an alliance of Progressives and Social Democrats, rather than merely seeking to convert the National Liberals.[93] This gradual shift of emphasis was painful for him, for he was deeply attached to the cultural context in which right-wing nationalism was conceived. But his "head was cool and clear"; he was a realist, and he knew that moderate war aims and internal reforms were necessary in order to avoid a social and national disaster. Reluctantly he took the consequences of his insights. He cut a few more of those ties that had bound him to the emotional world of the orthodox mandarins, and he prepared to wage a harsher and more determined battle against attitudes that he understood only too well.

Meinecke was not the only modernist who moved toward the political left during the First World War. At least a slight shift of emphasis seems to have been quite common. Ernst Troeltsch was more of a social rebel than Meinecke. He eventually became a bitter critic of the ruling classes' elitist pretensions. Hans Delbrück was the most rigorous and consistent opponent of the annexationist movement among the modernists. In his case, the absurdity of the ultras and the irresponsibility of the military leaders was the primary cause of a growing dissatisfaction with the existing regime. Leopold von Wiese was disturbed especially by the heedless enthusiasm with which the concept of community, the notion of a vaguely unmaterialistic "socialism," and the slogans about a "new idealism" were used to bolster the orthodox arguments against "egotism" and "individualism." He hastened to admit that Manchesterism was indeed to be rejected. He thought it possible to create a new liberalism in which the contradiction between "state socialism" and "individualistic liberalism" would somehow be reconciled. He even joined in the usual condemnations of "the democratic orientation rooted in envy," "the feud against the unusual and the original." Still, he tried to stem the tide of communal rhetoric; he pointed out that the individual personality was still the ultimate unit of social and cultural value, and he tried to preserve the basic civil liberties against the new "socialism." He also came forward with a fairly direct attack on the mystical aspects of the officially sanctioned enthusiasm. He found the "new idealism" depressingly humorless, at once vague and frighteningly dogmatic, exaggerated, impractical, and somewhat ridiculous. He even criticized it on aesthetic grounds. Let us not forget the lighter side of life, he said, the graceful, the polite, and the well formed. Let us not despise all elegance along with the clear and well-lighted streets of our cities.[94]

That brings us to the last of the three links between moderation and modernism. This one is at once the most difficult to describe and the most important, for it points up a very fundamental difference between modernist and orthodox reactions to the war. To state it briefly, there was a certain similarity of mood and tone which connected the moderate position in the war aims controversy to the modernist system, while a similar affinity of style allows us to group the arguments of the annexationists with the more general attitudes of the orthodox mandarins. It is simply impossible to overlook the growing emphasis upon "cold reason" and "hard facts" in the political writings of the modernists and in the moderate proclamations of the years 1915–1918. The sense of facing up to a distinctly unpleasant reality had always been characteristic of the accommodationist position. The modernists were not enthusiastic democrats; they were not fond of the industrial age, and they did not anticipate the mass culture of the future with great optimism. They simply resigned themselves to what they considered inevitable, and their main argument against the orthodox position was that a rebellion against the unavoidable would very probably be much worse than useless.

The moderate position on war aims reflected a similar sense of sober realism and painful self-restraint. While the ultras hypnotized themselves and others with their superpatriotic emotionalism, the moderates spoke for realpolitik and a responsibly calculated foreign policy. They knew that the men of the Fatherland Party would not hesitate to criticize them for their supposed lack of patriotism. The Pan-Germanist Professor Georg von Below, for example, was always ready to launch slanderous attacks upon modernists and moderates.[95]

Since the moderates were in the minority and since their own arguments often did violence to their emotions, they tended to be almost apologetic in their approach. Witness Meinecke's defense of the Popular League against the Fatherland Party: "Our hearts are just as hot as theirs; our fists are quite as tight and hard for the battle; but our heads are cooler and clearer!" Why did he think it necessary to talk about his heart? And why did Wiese spend so much time apologizing for his individualism and distinguishing it from egotism before moving on to criticize the emotional exaggerations and the mystical tendencies of the "new idealism"?

There was only one modernist who never excused himself for disagreeing with the majority of his colleagues, and that was Max Weber.[96] He was a fervent patriot himself. Indeed, it is hard to discover anything that was holier to him than the unrestrained egotism of his own nation, unless it was that absolute intellectual honesty which he refused to sacrifice to his own emotional needs or to those of anyone else. He had nothing but contempt for the superpatriotic and xenophobic hysteria which set in after 1914. When exhibited by industrialists and junkers, he considered it pure hypocrisy; when he detected it among his colleagues, he thought it undisciplined, womanish, and in any case repulsive. His ethic was one of self-restraint. He thought it the intellectual's duty manfully to face unpleasant realities, and when he suspected other scholars of deviations from this norm, he scornfully consigned them to the category of the volatile "literati."

What sources within Germany originated the misleading and confusing intermingling of these two questions: that of a realistic peace on the basis of negotiation on the one hand and that of a liberal reorganization on the other? It was the babbling and scribbling of the literati which first connected them. Ever since the beginning of the war, they have sought to falsify our national battle for existence into a struggle for the presently existing, supposedly specifically "German," purely bureaucratic political structure . . . The vast majority of the nation, however, denies that our brothers at the front are to have shed their blood for nothing better then such literati's products and the uncontrolled rule of the bureaucracy which they sanctify.

For this plain fact of universal bureaucratization really stands behind the so-called "ideas of 1914" too, behind that which the literati euphemistically call the "socialism of the future," behind the slogan of "organization," the "communal economy" and more generally behind all similar phrases of the present.

The impression that the shameful . . . and slanderous agitation of . . . the so-called Fatherland Party has made upon the workers can easily be imagined. After all, every worker knows . . . in whose interests these people are working.

Anyone who talks about foreign policy has the duty of exercising moral self-discipline and a sense of proportion.

[Before opting for unlimited submarine warfare in the face of American protests, it is to be demanded] (1) that no step of any kind is undertaken . . . before all *calculations* upon which the decisions are founded have been made with an absolute maximum of caution, (2) that all those individuals who vouch for the accuracy of each one of these *calculations* are quite clearly designated as responsible in the official documents, along with the assumptions and methods of their *calculations*. For if even a single factor in these *calculations* is wrong, then the greatest bravery of the troops cannot prevent [a disaster].[97]

The anger in these paragraphs was directed against all those who protected their own interests or revealed their prejudices and fears by joining in the national hysteria of the war years. It was the failure of these people to calculate, to weigh the consequences of their actions, that alienated Weber and caused him to challenge the mandarin ideology of 1914 in its very foundations. The harshness with which he attacked the ultra-annexationists and the opponents of internal reform was symptomatic of a growing antagonism between modernist and orthodox mandarins. By the end of the war, this enmity was almost as pronounced as the larger social division between the mass of the German people and the defenders of an unreconstructed caste system. As the military situation became ever more hopeless after 1916, the modernists' appeal to sanity became more insistent. The ultras, however, moved progressively further away from reality, as if searching for more ponderous psychic counterweights to the disheartening experience of defeat and to the threat of social revolution. As a result, the World War fatefully strengthened that curious system of contrasting associations: the antithesis between the willful enthusiasm and unreason of the orthodox mandarins and the reluctant realism and disciplined caution of the modernists.

4

THE POLITICAL CONFLICT AT
ITS HEIGHT, 1918–1933

The Revolution of 1918–19 proved that the rhetoric of the cultural war had failed to convert the German people. They still demanded social and political reform. The lower classes allowed themselves to be led by the Social Democratic Party; but their anger was directed less against capitalism than against the bureaucratic monarchy and its traditional ruling castes. Apparently, they sensed that the universities and the gymnasiums were important parts of the old social and political system; for they showed almost as much resentment toward the institutions of higher learning as they did toward the officer corps. The demand for educational reform was a significant element in their quest for a more democratic society.

The academic community as a whole did everything in its power to resist the new regime. The orthodox majority of professors, the former ultra-annexationists, sympathized with the German National People's Party, which also represented the old agrarian Conservatives, Pan-Germanists, right-wing bureaucrats, and army officers. The men of the National People's Party have sometimes been called monarchists, and this label is useful insofar as it implies nothing more concrete than a certain nostalgia for the past and a deep hostility toward the new regime and toward the liberal parties. Among the liberal parties, the German Democratic Party was the main organ of academic republicanism. Indeed, such leading modernists and wartime moderates as Max and Alfred Weber, Ernst Troeltsch, and Friedrich Meinecke were among the most prominent early sponsors of that party, which eventually united almost all those intellectuals who had formerly been interested in Friedrich Naumann's projects or in the Brentano wing of the Social Policy Association.

The other parties were decidedly less popular among German academics. Some Catholic scholars may have supported the Center, and a few academic spokesmen of entrepreneurial interests may have been associated with the right wing of the German People's Party.* Especially in Bavaria, the left wing of the People's Party attracted a few modernists, including Moritz Julius Bonn, a rather harsh critic of the German industrialists after 1918.[1] Some orthodox members of the faculty at Munich University probably favored the vague monarchism and separatism of the Bavarian People's Party. Social Democratic university professors continued to be rarities even after 1918. As far as I know, there were only four prominent scholars who had obvious sympathies or affiliations with any of the Marxist parties: the philosopher Ernst von Aster, the sociologist Karl Mannheim, the economist Emil Lederer, and the jurist-politician Gustav Radbruch.[2] In other words, one may reasonably describe the political life of the German academic community during the Weimar period in terms of two major groupings: an accommodationist minority of republicans associated for the most part with the Demo-

---

* For example, I would associate Adolf Weber and Hermann Schumacher with the determinedly entrepreneurial wing of the German People's Party; but this is a guess.

crats, and an orthodox majority of monarchists in sympathy primarily with the Nationalists.

THE MODERNISTS AND THE POLITICS OF ACCOMMODATION

The views of academic republicans may most easily be described as logical extensions of prewar modernism.[3] The intellectual founding fathers of the German Democratic Party believed that the Republic was the natural form of government in a highly industrialized society and a political necessity for Germany after 1918. The Republic alone seemed to them capable of bridging the social differences within the strife-torn nation, of attracting enough popular support to maintain order and to assert the authority of the state against the threat of "bolshevism." The old regime had lost control of the masses; it was futile to seek its restoration. Germany needed a government that could reunite the country, if only to check separatist tendencies in the Rhineland and in Bavaria, to prevent further losses of territory, and to undertake the long diplomatic struggle for a revision of the Versailles settlement. Popular leaders had to be found who could steer a steady course between the extremes of senseless reaction and anarchy, revive national sentiments among the lower classes, and alleviate the class antagonisms that had produced the Revolution of 1918. Since there was no realistic alternative to the Republic, it was wise to accept the inevitable. A rejection of the Republic by the old elites could only result in a further drift toward leftist radicalism and disorder. An accommodating approach toward the new regime, on the other hand, might well provide opportunities to influence it from within, to guide it into properly moderate paths, and to make it as responsive as possible to the cultural and political traditions of the mandarin caste. At a special convention in 1926 in Weimar, 64 German university professors signed an appeal to all those of their colleagues who were prepared to work constructively for the common good "within the framework of the existing democratic-republican political order." Among the signatures to this resolution, one finds the names Gerhard Anschütz, Ernst von Aster, Brentano, Jonas Cohn, Delbrück, von Harnack, Willy

Hellpach, Heinrich Herkner, Wolfgang Köhler, Lederer, Meinecke, Mommsen, Radbruch, Franz Schnabel, Ludwig Sinzheimer, Tönnies, Alfred Weber, and Werner Weisbach.[4]

It must be emphasized that most modernists were not democrats at heart. Almost all of them would have preferred a moderate parliamentary monarchy to the Republic. Their position was self-consciously practical and realistic. Their assent to the new regime was an almost purely intellectual matter, the consequence of their realization that it was the only remaining road to stability.

> That democracy basically does not suit us and that (especially in Germany, incidentally) it has the shortcomings of mediocrity and pettiness . . . unfortunately cannot be denied. Neither can it be denied, on the other hand, that we do not have anything better.
>
> We became Democrats, because we made clear to ourselves that there was no other way to preserve the popular unity and at the same time those aristocratic values of our history that were capable of living on.
>
> Today the republic is the form of government which least divides us.[5]

Meinecke once called himself and those who agreed with him *Vernunftrepublikaner,* republicans through reason, not republicans at heart.[6] He compared the leading modernists of the First World War and of the immediate postwar era to the French *politiques* of the Religious Wars.[7] What he meant to say is that he and his like-minded colleagues felt it their duty to preserve order and the authority of the new state against the excesses of warring creeds. They thought of themselves as occupying a sane middle ground between the emotional extremes of orthodox antirepublicanism and revolutionary socialism. They became the spokesmen of a matter-of-fact politics of reason and moderation.

In the field of foreign policy, the modernists were forced to combat the fanatical nationalism which was current among so many of their compatriots. The war had left a legacy of hate, and the Versailles settlement a mood of desperation. The former ultra-annexationists found it easy to identify the Republic with defeat. Affecting the pose of superpatriots, they delighted in counseling an aggressive foreign policy, although it was perfectly clear that the new regime was of necessity committed to a cautious diplomacy and a gradual and peaceful revision of the peace settlement. The new government's long-range objectives required a partial dampening of the passions that had arisen during the war. Once again, the modernists undertook the difficult and thankless task of counseling restraint. The historian Hans Delbrück, for example, devoted a good deal of his energy to a sort of private war on two fronts.[8] On the one hand, he attempted to combat the growth of General Ludendorff's reputation as a national hero, the continued self-righteousness of the former ultra-annexationists, and the vicious legend that the civilian left had stabbed a victorious German army in the back in 1918. On the other hand, he was equally determined in his polemics against pacifist and Marxist attempts to assign all of the responsibility for the World War to Germany. In retrospect, Delbrück's position seems reasonable enough; but in its own time, most Germans must have found it half-hearted and emotionally unsatisfying.

It was characteristic of the republican academics that they were relatively tolerant in their attitude toward the Social Democratic Party. They always remembered with gratitude that the moderate leaders of the working class had done everything in their power to control the Revolution of 1918, to prevent radical experiments, and to guide the masses toward the parliamentary republic. Partly for that reason, the leading accommodationists were less addicted to conventional moralisms about Marxist and lower-class "materialism" than the orthodox polemicists.

When such men as Max Weber, Moritz Julius Bonn, and Joseph Schumpeter discussed the problem of socialism, they generally kept their arguments on a matter-of-fact plane.[9] They tried to show that the existing economic system was not in fact producing the rapid increase of economic misery that Marxists had predicted. They pointed out that the workers had managed to improve their lot to some degree without recourse to revolution, and they refused in any case to admit that the final crisis of capitalism was in sight.

They recognized that a process of concentration and cartelization had greatly reduced the number of independent firms, especially in heavy industry, and they also granted that the industrial proletariat had increased considerably in recent years. But beyond that, they raised a whole series of difficult questions concerning the prospects for socialism. Had not the class of white-collar employees grown even more rapidly than the manual labor force, and was it not utterly unreasonable to expect this new army of clerks to cooperate with the conventional proletariat? Was it possible to dispense with the services of private entrepreneurs in all sectors of the economy, or should they be tolerated at least in small or new enterprises, where risks were still great and flexibility essential? If the government did decide to socialize some of the great monopolies, the presently most dangerous and yet potentially most profitable parts of the economy, would the workers really benefit from what might easily become an unprecedented concentration of power against them? Had not the experience of wartime "socialism" suggested that an intermingling of public and private control over certain industries could only increase the economic strength and the political influence of the great industrialists? And if the entire economy was fully socialized, how were managerial decisions going to be made in practice? In a situation in which a huge and still growing hierarchy of functionaries had already begun to take the place of the old-fashioned factory-owner, would not the "public ownership of the means of production" simply result in an ever more thorough bureaucratization of the economy? Would such a process increase either the individual worker's standard of living or his influence upon the decision-making process in his industry?

A present-day socialist might consider these questions unfairly posed, irrelevant, and unoriginal. They did amount to a defense of the status quo against genuine social revolution. Bonn was prepared to accept the nationalization of the great steel and coal combines because he feared their political influence and their monopolistic practices, but the accommodationists as a group opposed any far-reaching innovations. Even our modern socialist would recognize, however, that the arguments of Weber, Bonn, and Schumpeter were considerably more sophisticated than the antimaterialist rhetoric of most of their colleagues. In their own day, these challenges to Marxist doctrine were also fairly new. A moderate socialist of the 1920's, a man of von Aster's persuasion, took them seriously and even accepted some of the observations upon which they were based.[10]

All this is but to emphasize the fact that the leading modernists hoped to draw socialist theoreticians into a debate in which both groups divested themselves of the conventional slogans with which they were normally armed. We are not now trying to decide whether the accommodationists' view of their own role was accurate. What concerns us is that they thought themselves relatively free of class resentment and ideological bias. They proposed to launch an unideological or even anti-ideological attack upon doctrinaire Marxism and thus to clear the ground for a "realistic" and immediately practical social policy, one which would reduce class antagonisms and secure the stability of the new regime.

In pursuit of these objectives, the modernists occasionally became quite critical of their own class as well. Meinecke had a certain emotional sympathy for the orthodox position; but he had also come to recognize its irresponsibility: "All generations within the academic world, down to the level of the students, produce those emotional politicians who only complain continually about the shortcomings of the parliamentary republic and never make clear to themselves that it was created by an iron necessity of politics."[11] Troeltsch had this to say about the political motives of the mandarin caste:

> The academic class . . . has become more and more conservative, monarchistic, and nationalistic . . . Patriotic . . . indignation at the fate of Germany partly accounts for this. But [the patriotic incentive for opposition to the Republic] . . . gains its force only in conjunction with another, a more important, motive. This other element . . . is the class war against the danger of a proletarization of society, against the threat of educational reforms which would destroy higher cultivation,

eliminate the leading position of the academic occupational groups [*Stände*], and make the primary teacher the spiritual and political ruler of Germany.

The universities . . . cannot accept the idea . . . that a modern revolution in the great industrial states introduces the manual laborers into the ranks of the ruling classes and necessitates an intellectual and emotional adjustment to their interests and to their manner of thinking.[12]

The phrasing suggests that Troeltsch himself was a little disturbed at what he characteristically identified as the rule of the elementary teacher. Still, he did not hesitate to describe the orthodox position as a rationalization of class resentment, a tool in the class war from the right. Even for an accommodationist, this was a remarkable departure from the "idealistic" conventions of mandarin politics.

Of course, there were varying shades of opinion within the modernist camp. Troeltsch was more thoroughly disenchanted with the monarchists than Meinecke, while a few of the younger social scientists were even more radically critical than Troeltsch. But these were differences of emphasis only. In general, the accommodationists all sought to moderate the political controversies of the Weimar period by challenging the class content of doctrinal positions at both ends of the political spectrum. They meant to disarm the contending parties, to debunk their slogans, and thus to make them all republicans through reason. The typical modernist made a distinction between realistic, "objective" politics on the one hand, and what Vossler called "metaphysical, speculative, romantic, fanatical, abstract, nationalistic, and mystical politics" on the other. He identified realistic politics with republicanism and a moderate social program, fanatical politics with the realm of myths, "nationalistic and imperialistic myths . . . or socialist myths about salvation through class war."[13]

Along with this distinction and parallel to it, the modernists sometimes introduced or implied a second antithesis, which was also designed to defend the Republic, particularly against its enemies on the right. As an example, consider the following argument from a speech by Gerhard Anschütz. "If we want to continue to . . . [regard] the state as a sovereign power which predominates over all particular interests in the interest of the community, then such a power can today be based only upon the whole of the people, upon its assent to the state, upon the national solidarity of all forces within it."[14] This was the old emphasis upon the sovereign power as a guardian of communal against particular interests. It derived from the traditional ideal of the state as an independent agency, one which could fulfill "objective" (*sachlich*) political requirements, without being hampered by the "subjective" (*unsachlich*) and "egotistical" demands of various interest groups within the nation. The remarkable thing about the modernists after 1918 is that they used this characteristic scheme to *defend* the Republic. They actually transferred their notion of an autonomous sovereign power from the bureaucratic monarchy to the new regime. In the new situation, they said, a moderate parliamentary democracy was in fact the only form of government that could be made strong enough, partly through its popular roots, to rise above the ever more violent clash of economic class interests.

One can increase one's understanding and even one's sympathy for this whole conception by trying to visualize the context in which it was applied. From the modernists' point of view, it was after all quite clear what kind of foreign policy would best meet the "objective" demands of Germany's postwar position. Such "subjective" pressures upon the government as the nationalist agitation on the right could do nothing but harm. Again, one can imagine the modernists' consternation at the economic chaos, the radical uprisings, counterrevolutionary attempts, and separatist movements which repeatedly threatened the unity of the Reich and shook the Republic to its foundations, especially between 1918 and 1924. It was in analyzing these crises that such accommodationists as Alfred Weber and Moritz Julius Bonn made extensive use of the notion of an "independent state."[15] Particularly under the influence of the inflation, they argued that modern industrial capitalism had created such concentrations of economic power in the hands of the producing elites that the goverment was scarcely able to protect itself against their influence and their obstructionist tactics. The interests of consumers and the welfare of the community as a whole were therefore always in danger of being ignored. The centrifugal forces released by modern socio-economic developments, the intense conflicts of mutually irreconcilable ideologies, were threatening to tear Germany apart, unless something could be done to bolster the tottering authority of the central government and to safeguard its role as a genuinely sovereign power, an agent capable of positive action in the name of the whole nation.

The accommodationists thought they knew what had to be done to stave off disaster. The economy had to be put in some sort of order as quickly as possible; extensive socialist experiments could only prolong the misery of the population. At the same time, a reasonably progressive social program, based upon the theories of the Social Policy Association, was an absolute necessity. Anything that might improve the workers' lot and increase their sense of identification with their work was obviously worth trying. Above all, revolutionary disorders and separatist movements had to be kept in check, government had once again to become orderly and consistent, and the civil rights of the individual had to be protected against political extremists and fanatics.

Because the modernists held these things to be self-evident and because they were frightened by the obstructionist tactics of the radical right and left, they came to look upon the Republic as the only possible embodiment of the independent "legal state" in the new environment. This may help to account for their persistent interest in a strong presidency at the head of the Republic.[16] They hoped that a directly elected popular leader would be able to check the excesses of interest politics, to represent the nation as a whole against particular egotisms, and thus to lead the people out of the chaos of the class war. They identified the president with the notion of an "objective" approach, especially in foreign affairs and in social policy. Especially after 1929, when a new economic crisis led to a rapid growth of the Communist and National Socialist parties and greatly increased the threat of social and political disorder, many accommodationists sought salvation in proposals designed to strengthen the presidential prerogative. Some of them also advanced other vague schemes for a more "conservative," "indirect," or "qualitative" democracy.[17] Sometimes, they actually came rather close to the more blatantly antiparliamentary "reform" proposals of their orthodox colleagues. Still, their purpose was and always had been to safeguard private civil rights and a moderate social and political program against hopeless reaction or total revolution. The tradition of the "legal state" made them believe that a restriction of the democratic principle might, in an extreme situation, be the best means to these ends.

This brings us to the most important and interesting aspect of the modernist platform, the part which I propose to call the "theory of form and content." Like all the rest of the accommodationist program for the Weimar Republic, it was intended at once to legitimize the new regime and to make it conform to the modernists' ideal of government. It was also designed to deal with the problem of cultural continuity in the new environment. It caused much disagreement between republican and antirepublican academics, and it was to have far-reaching implications in the field of education. The following passages from Hermann Oncken, Friedrich Meinecke, Ernst Troeltsch, and Alfred Weber will introduce this aspect of the modernist scheme.

> Again, [as in Prussia after 1806], the task is neither to sacrifice the past—that would be treason—nor to wish to conserve it— that would be futile romanticism. Rather, the task is to gather up all moral forces of the past in the forms that are necessary for our reconstruction today.

> Let us trust that all truly vital values of our past are capable of flowing into new [political] forms, if only those who have hitherto guarded [these values] will help to achieve this.

> After all, political and social patterns of organization [*Gestaltungen*] are in reality only questions of the form and technical make-up of life, prerequisites of an organizational and material kind for the life of the mind and spirit.

> The manner in which the intellectual and spiritual [*das*

Geistige] is connected with the political is decisive, not the political form.[18]

This fascinating distinction between political forms and their cultural content played an extraordinarily important role in modernist theory, for it permitted a technical adjustment of "organizational patterns" to the requirements of the new age, while simultaneously setting the stage for an argument in favor of continuity in the cultural field.

The modernists were deeply distressed at the apparent discontinuity in German history in the year 1918. They came back to that issue again and again in their writings. Meinecke spoke of the enormous difficulties occasioned by the "revolutionary break with our past" and of the need to "bridge the huge split which has appeared in our nation as a result of the World War and the Revolution." The gulf between past and present was all the more dangerous because it coincided with the social chasm between the mandarin caste and the rest of the German people. As Meinecke knew, "the gash which separates the German people today corresponds approximately to that which separates the social segments trained in the primary schools from those with an academic education." The Revolution had revealed a deep popular resentment of mandarin traditions. There was a real danger that the new society would totally reject the values of the German past and those who had "hitherto guarded" them. Meinecke addressed one of his passionate speeches in behalf of national reconciliation to the "ancient, original culture-bearing segment [Kulturschicht] of the nation, which must not die [untergehen], because it is indispensable for the maintenance of the first prerequisite of culture, namely tradition."[19] Unless the "tear" in the nation, the "rent" in history, could yet be mended, the future would indeed be an age of reckless leveling and cultural shallowness. The mandarins' whole value system was at stake.

This is not to say that the modernists were motivated exclusively by a desire to preserve their own traditions. On the contrary, they were genuinely anxious to convert the most dangerous enemies of the Republic and to strengthen the new regime. One must remember that according to the theory of the cultural state, government derives its legitimacy primarily from the moral and cultural values that flourish under its disinterested protection. A state that is either hostile or indifferent to these values has no profound claims upon popular allegiance, no real justification for its use of force, and no solid roots against fluctuations in its material fortunes. Thus, unless the modernists could "win the universities for the new state,"[20] the state would inevitably suffer from the instability occasioned by its lack of cultural "content." It would have no defenses against the ever more violent fluctuations of the class war. It would be the helpless tool of purely material interest groups, and its decline would necessarily lead to anarchy.

What the modernist sought, then, was a real union of mandarin traditions and political democracy, a union which would benefit both partners equally. The new society would avoid all forms of political domination by a narrow ruling caste (*Herrentum*), while still providing a framework in which a natural aristocracy based on culture and capability, intellect and spirit, could make its salutary influence felt.[21] Social exclusiveness, which had unfortunately become characteristic of German "cultivation," would have to be dropped. The educated elite of the nation would have to pledge its loyalty to the new society, demanding only that the just prerogatives of learning and of talent be acknowledged. The new state would be a "conservative democracy," protected by stable cultural traditions against radical excesses, against "shallowness," against the tyranny of a prejudiced majority and the vacillations of pure interest politics. "Intellectual and spiritual aristocracy is by no means incompatible with political democracy . . . The values of our spiritual aristocracy . . . have to be carried into the political democracy, in order to refine it and to protect it against degeneration."[22]

These are the terms in which the theory of form and content was conceived. The modernists always regarded democracy as a technical necessity of modern times, not as an ideal in itself. They wanted to face unpleasant facts, and one of these was the death of the bureaucratic monarchy. Unless mandarin cultural values and the whole tradition of the cultural state could be dissociated from an outmoded social and political framework and transferred to the Republic, the learned elite would be condemned to impotence and the new regime to "shallowness," rootlessness, and instability.

As one might expect, the theory of form and content profoundly affected the accommodationists' conception of education and their whole attitude toward the German cultural heritage. That heritage had to be translated into a language appropriate to the modern context. Radically incompatible elements had to be weeded out and inessential parts sacrificed to permit concentration on the most vital and enduring ones. The leading academic republicans turned especially to the late eighteenth and early nineteenth centuries in their search for models and heroes appropriate to the new situation. Meinecke and Troeltsch, along with those who felt as they did, emphasized the great German Idealists, particularly Humboldt and Kant himself. They preferred the decades before 1848 to the years that followed upon the collapse of the mid-century revolution.[23] They argued that the early ideals of the mandarin tradition had been subtly corrupted during the later nineteenth century, that something narrow, vulgar, and class-conscious had crept in to debase an originally universal and libertarian conception of spiritual nobility. With Hans Delbrück, they resented and fought against the orthodox glorification of Bismarck.[24] They castigated the crude nationalism and the cultural hypocrisy of the Wilhelmian period. To cite the Neo-Kantian modernist Ernst Cassirer, they tried to show "that the idea of the republican constitution as such is by no means a foreign . . . intruder within the German intellectual tradition as a whole, that it grew up, rather, from the very soil of that tradition, nourished by its very own energies, the energies of Idealist philosophy."[25] This desire to unite a purified version of the German heritage to the new society was the basic motive in all the accommodationists said and did.

THE ORTHODOX REVOLT

While the modernists made themselves the spokesmen of "cold reason," the orthodox chose the role of despairing patriots and moralists in an age of total corruption. Their emotions and their arguments were simpler and less ambivalent than those of the accommodationists. They simply continued to exploit the antidemocratic and antimodernistic implications of the mandarin tradition to the fullest possible extent. They argued that the foreign and domestic enemies of the old Germany had combined to destroy it, and that materialistic and unpatriotic elements within the German population had successfully completed a long campaign of subversion in the Revolution of 1918. Especially during the early years of the Weimar period, the orthodox expressed their horror at the recent history of their country in truly extravagant terms. "Shrouded in a sinister mist, the future confronts us, like an abysmal chaos which threatens to devour . . . not only our own people, but all of European culture." "Will there be rivers to wash away our present shame? A wish for insensitivity, which almost lets the living envy the dead, is widely prevalent." Such unrestrained exhibitions of pessimism were at least partly motivated by a desire to embarrass the new regime. An undifferentiated condemnation of present realities could serve as the basis for a characteristically "apolitical" attack upon the Republic. "We smashed the old 'paternalistic state,' and from the fragments we have gained, not respect for personality, but the rule of the street and of the self-seeking instincts." "Everything which is independent, unique, national . . . everything which is specifically German is to be eradicated and replaced with the dreadful monotony of colorless homogeneity and dead numbers."[26]

As these phrases suggest, the orthodox mandarins utterly repudiated the modernist distinction between political forms and their cultural content. As far as the orthodox were concerned, the Republic was not just a piece of political machinery, a purely technical device, a vessel capable of holding whatever was poured into it. On the contrary, it was inevitably imbued with certain principles of its own, and it could not be dissociated from the forces that had created it. It was the culmination and the embodiment of national decadence. It was based upon the notion of equality, "the daughter of envy and of covetousness"; it was a democracy, "a victim of demagogues and babblers, saturated with the lowness of vulgar instincts, with the passion of the envious, of outcasts, and of the disinherited." And by the same token, the ideal of popular sovereignty was totally incompatible with that of the legal state; for popular sovereignty inevitably subordinated the state to the unprincipled "mandate of individual citizens."[27] With these arguments, the orthodox attacked the very foundation of the accommodationist position.

Needless to say, the former ultra-annexationists went much further than the former moderates in trying to refute the charge of German war guilt. They did not hesitate to clear their own nation of all responsibility for the failure of diplomacy in 1914. They continued, moreover, to defend the German recourse to unlimited submarine warfare and their own agitation against a negotiated peace.[28] Many of them actually argued that Germany had lost the war because the civilian leaders had encouraged defeatist sentiments by adhering to an insufficiently inclusive war aims program. This charge was coupled, of course, with the more general theory that Social Democrats and other "unpatriotic" elements had undermined the nation's morale and betrayed the Germany army. The Republic and its supporters, in other words, were really responsible for the harsh provisions of the Versailles settlement, and any foreign policy based upon diplomatic acceptance of that settlement was practically treasonous. Willfully ignoring the realities of the international situation, such Pan-Germanists as Willy Andreas were soon voicing truly fantastic demands for renewed territorial expansion.[29]

In this climate of opinion, the German universities became strongholds of right-wing opposition to the new regime. The antirepublican hysteria of professors and students continually led to incidents. Whenever a lecturer expressed anything resembling pacifist or Marxist views, there was a student riot against him, particularly if he was Jewish.[30] Liberal governments occasionally tried to protect the victims of these campaigns; but the university faculties generally favored the side of the students. In any case, they did little to defend their unorthodox colleagues. Friedrich Wilhelm Foerster, an internationally minded pedagogue and Christian moral philosopher escaped these pressures by fleeing to Switzerland. In 1920, some socialist students at Munich were mistreated in the presence of the rector for protesting the acquittal of Count Arco, Kurt Eisner's murderer. Max Weber, who spoke out against this incident, became the target of right-wing abuse in his turn. Under the threat of violence, the philosopher Theodor Lessing was forced to withdraw from the Technical Institute of Hanover, because the nationalists claimed that he had insulted Hindenburg. Günther Dehn, a theologian at Heidelberg, received little support from his faculty in a similar incident, which began with the charge that he had slandered the army. The "cases" of Georg Nicolai, Hans Nawiasky, and Ernst Cohn fit into the same general pattern.

Some of the orthodox academics went to remarkable lengths to demonstrate their contempt for the Republic. The physicist Philipp Lenard, who eventually became a National Socialist theoretician of "Germanic physics" and "Nordic research," used to fly the Imperial flag at his institute.[31] He also refused to observe the holiday in commemoration of the murdered Walter Rathenau. The silliest among the antirepublican dignitaries liked to describe the colors of Weimar as black, red, and yellow,* rather than black, red, and gold.[32] Of course, holidays are no more than symbols; yet a republican statesman might well have felt uneasy when in 1923 the Corporation of German Universities announced that "now as always, all German universities will hold fast to January 18, Founding Day of the Empire, as a day of patriotic memories and spiritual elevation, in order, at the same time, to give expression to the unity of the German universities."[33] The birth of the Republic was not celebrated. In fact, the regular academic festivities and speeches which henceforth regularly graced January 18 were often deliberate insults to the new regime. In one Founding Day address, Baron Marschall von Bieberstein of Freiburg University accused the "usurper" President Ebert of "high treason."[34] Bieberstein received a warning from the ministry for his performance; but he was not afraid to publish his speech a few years later. The rector who had asked him to speak in the first placed used to refer to the Republic as the "rabble state" (*encanaillierter Staat*). In 1922, when the government proceeded against the propaganda activities of right-wing extremist groups by intro-

---

* Yellow stood for envy and for the Jews.

ducing the Law for the Protection of the Republic, various ministries of culture actually thought it necessary to issue special decrees applying the law to the universities.[35]

In 1925, the so-called Gumbel Case erupted at Heidelberg. Emil Gumbel, an instructor, had ventured the following remark about the soldiers who had been killed during the war: "I do not actually mean to say that they fell on the field of dishonor; yet they lost their lives in a dreadful way."[36] The resulting furor was overwhelming. Gumbel made a public apology, with the result that a formal charge of treason against him was dropped. The ministry had temporarily suspended him from his teaching post. His faculty at Heidelberg, although it did not actually withdraw his *venia legendi*, resolved by "all votes against one" that it "considered Dr. Gumbel's membership in the faculty thoroughly displeasing." The academic commission that had investigated the case declared that Gumbel's political activities showed an "utter lack of objectivity" and not the "least influence of wissenschaftlich qualities." It thought him "slick," since he was able to "shift the objective picture of things and to remodel it in the direction desired by him." After all, he had been so lacking in "tact," "reserve," "quiet matter-of-factness and intellectual dignity" as to introduce a "French-speaking Frenchman" into the proceedings.[37] In 1931, when the Baden ministry quietly promoted Gumbel to the purely titular rank of an "irregular associate professor," his transgression was by no means forgotten. The rabidly nationalistic and anti-Semitic German Students' League sent a letter of protest against his promotion to the Corporation of German Universities. The Corporation sympathized with the students a little too openly, so that a few modernist professors felt it necessary to write a sharply critical letter to the Corporation's executive committee in their turn.[38] Among the signatures to this last comment upon the whole affair, one finds those of Aster, Karl Barth, Albert Einstein, Hajo Holborn, Emil Lederer, Radbruch, and Tönnies.

It is worth remarking that we do not know the name of a single academic who was definitely on the nationalist side in the Gumbel controversy. This circumstance reflects some general characteristics of the available evidence. The members of the accommodationist minority were repeatedly forced to take a public stand as individuals, because they opposed the mainstream of academic opinion. On the other hand, those who agreed with the Corporation's attitude in the Gumbel affair did not need to take the extraordinary step of writing—and signing—a letter of protest. A few representatives of the orthodox position acquired some degree of political renown. These were the leaders: the Germanist Gustav Roethe, the Protestant theologian Reinhold Seeberg, the historians Dietrich Schäfer and Georg von Below, and the classical philologist Ulrich von Wilamowitz-Moellendorff. But the large mass of antirepublican professors are not personally known to us. Perhaps they were intellectually less distinguished than the modernists. On the other hand, there can be no doubt that the general consensus of the mandarin leadership was antirepublican in the orthodox vein. Meinecke sadly reported a provincial rule of thumb according to which "one can be with the People's Party up to the level of the secondary teacher; but above that one may and can be only German National."[39] The orthodox were not all as articulate as the more prominent modernists; but in the Gumbel controversy and in many similar cases, they had the force of numbers on their side.

To justify its proceedings against Gumbel, the faculty at Heidelberg charged that he had "deeply offended national sentiment": "He has slapped the face of the idea of national dignity, an idea which the university has to represent."[40] This was the final step in the elevation of the "national cause." The orthodox were now prepared to include it quite formally among the objectives of German learning. They considered it the intellectual's duty to feud against the errors of foreign states, particularly in the war guilt question.[41] They believed, as Hans Rothfels did, that this kind of service to the nation allowed them to become genuinely engaged in the "whole of German history and of German life," without involving them in the narrow interest politics of the parliamentary parties.[42] They absolutely refused to admit that their supposedly apolitical nationalism was quite as factional, divisive, and "utilitarian" in practice as the Social Democratic demand for reform.

As these attitudes spread, "freedom of learning" became an ever more one-sided concept. The mandarin intellectuals had always been afraid that scholarship might be pressed into the service of limited practical objectives, whether they were those of cameralist princes, religious denominations, powerful businessmen, or representatives of "particular" socio-political interests. The influence of such "utilitarian" pressure groups seemed dangerous, because it could undermine the ideal purity of learning. Moralistic arguments in support of the nation, the "general interest," and the legal and cultural state, on the other hand, appeared to be much less serious threats to the abstract liberty of scholarship. Before 1918, this distinction allowed orthodox academics to tolerate extensive control of the universities by the Wilhelmian bureaucracy. During the Weimar period, the situation was reversed. The orthodox now claimed that the republican authorities were the tools of "particular interests." Opponents of the new regime therefore began to champion freedom of learning as a defense against "utilitarian" reforms of the educational system. This did not prevent them from simultaneously identifying the objectives of scholarship with the national cause. There had been no fear of coercion from an all-powerful state as long as it was run by an "apolitical" and "objective" bureaucracy which acted for the "whole nation" and was otherwise committed to preserve the purity of learning. Government pressure did not become an issue until the "interest politics" of Weimar aroused the patriotic opposition. The commentator upon this subject in the semi-official *Das akademische Deutschland* made that very clear.[43] He and his orthodox colleagues were alarmed only when they faced the "subjective" (*unsachlich*) present-mindedness of modern political parties. They saw no reason to protect Gumbel's academic freedom against his nationalistic critics. To speak for the nation, they insisted, was not to take sides in the quarrels of party politicians and religious denominations. Only those who tried to enforce such a taking of sides, those who sought to exert pressure in favor of the new "party state," for example, were guilty of an offense against the freedom of learning.

Much of orthodox political theory was based upon the repetition of a few conventional slogans. There was much lamenting of "individualism," in which that term was used almost interchangeably with "egotism." The educator Aloys Fischer even spoke of an "individualism of the fourth estate," linking it with "materialistic and utilitarian tendencies." In tracing the roots of the German decline from greatness, Max Sering complained of "that barren rationalism which, born out of the British commercial state and the French Revolution . . . denies respect for the work of ancestors, brings material interests into predominance . . . and kills the joy in work through a hastening for profit and through class hatred." Gustav Roethe focused more directly upon the Social Democrats and their radical critique of social and cultural conventions: "If Social Democracy describes as cant and lies [einen Zopf, eine Lüge] everything that is holy to Germans, if it ridicules . . . all that inspired and guided our fathers and ourselves . . . if it robs the people of its belief in God, in kingship, fatherland, family, in the right to inherit honestly acquired property . . . what remains to a human being intellectually and spiritually so impoverished and denuded but a wild pursuit of sensual pleasures! That is where we have finally arrived, thanks to the materialistic world view of Social Democracy."[44]

In trying to make sense of these outbursts, one notices two related themes which run through them all. The first of these might be called the motif of commercialism, the second that of social and intellectual decomposition. We have already remarked upon the mandarins' unusually intense reaction against the social consequences of industrialization. It expressed itself in their caricature of English society during the war, in their polemics against the politics of economic interest, and in their persistent allusions to a vaguely defined materialism. The term materialism was not really intended to describe any sort of formal position in philosophy; nor was its range of application restricted to the historical materialism of the Marxists or to that nineteenth-century preference for explanatory schemes adopted from the physical sciences which has been called materialistic by its critics. On the contrary, the word was used most often to condemn what Sering called the "predominance" of "material interests," meaning the supposedly augmented role of economic and other this-worldly considerations in the motivation of various individuals and social groups. Of course, it was primarily "the masses" who were said to be guilty of this kind of materialism.

When the orthodox did use the word materialism to describe Marxist principles or other formal theories, they tended to assume a causal relationship between these doctrines and the vulgar materialism that was their main concern. This is important, for it illustrates a fundamental ambiguity in their whole scheme. They never really distinguished between the fact of industrialization and the attitudinal changes with which they themselves identified it. They linked commerce with commercialism, machines with mechanistic conceptions, and the new economic organization with rationalism and utilitarianism. This confusion permitted them to trace everything disturbing in their modern environment to two different sorts of causes at once: to materialist or utilitarian theoreticians on the one hand, and to factories and parliamentary democracy on the other. They were not forced to decide which of the things they disliked might be unavoidable consequences of modern economic development and which might be eradicated by a concerted polemical attack. They could behave as if "materialist" philosophers had really caused millions of people to become gradually more covetous than they had been before the offending books were published, and as if an Idealist revival could now radically reverse this process. With Georg Steinhausen, they could describe materialism as a very general sign of decadence, linking it with the interest politics of the hated political left, the absence of "national" sentiments among the masses, and the widespread lack of respect for intellectual and spiritual leadership in general and for university professors in particular.[45]

Indeed, the intellectual's vice of attributing an exaggerated importance to the written word was particularly highly developed among the German mandarins. It certainly played an important role in the orthodox variations upon the concept of disintegration. When using such words as disintegration (*Zersetzung*) or decomposition (*Dekomposition*), men of Georg von Below's convictions intended to describe not only the loosening of "natural," irrational, or ethical bonds between men in an industrial society, but also those purely intellectual techniques which presumably helped to destroy the traditional sources of social cohesion by subjecting them to the acids of critical analysis. Thus von Below accused the Social Democrats of "describing as cant and lies everything that is holy to Germans" and Sering castigated "that barren rationalism which . . . brings the material interests into predominance." The historian Karl Alexander von Müller may be credited with the following sentence: "We are surrounded on all sides by the destructive and the low-mindedly iconoclastic [*das Zerschwätzende*], the arbitrary and the formless, the leveling and mechanizing of this machine age, the methodical dissolution [*Zersetzung*] of everything that is healthy and noble, the ridiculing of everything strong and serious, the dishonoring of everything godly, which lifts men up in that they serve it."[46] As a companion to "disintegration" the noun *das Zerschwätzende* is quite appropriate. It comes from *schwätzen*, to blabber, and the prefix *zer* implies dissolution or disintegration. To *zerschwätzen* something is to talk about it in a destructive way or to apply so many flat or even disrespectful words to it that it finally falls apart. Naturally, noble feelings and moral values are particularly vulnerable to the acids of *das Zerschwätzende*, and the grouping of that acid with other evils of the mass age tends to identify it with such things as party propaganda and the debunking of venerable institutions and traditions by "materialistic" theoreticians.

Von Müller developed the imagery associated with the words *zersetzen* and *zerschwätzen* in a series of essays on nineteenth-century German history. He wrote of the growth of factories and big cities, of the decline of rural Germany, of the race for profits, of the growth of an uprooted proletariat, and of the modern tendency to rationalize interpersonal relations in purely economic or utilitarian terms. He linked these things with the arrival of opportunist mass parties and newspapers and with the appearance of a literature of social and political radicalism. He described what he considered the increasing predominance of criticism over constructive thought, the decline of poetry and the birth of the journal; and he indulged in the usual complaints about the noisy shallowness of the age. He even suggested that the lack of great national leaders during the war was a consequence of the general degeneration, and both the notion of disintegration and the word itself came up again and again to lend an air of consistency to his loose associations. He did not hesitate to describe the "forms of the Western states" as "decomposed by the unlimited absolutism of barren party rule."[47] Von Below liked to group various social groups, religious denominations, and political parties among the "elements" or "parties" of "national decomposition." One could, he said, "count a good two thirds of the German population as members of these parties of national decomposition."[48] To him that was the strongest possible argument against democracy.

In an emotional environment of this type, Oswald Spengler's *Decline of the West* was nothing more than a particularly thorough exploitation of a common theme. German professional historians apparently disapproved of Spengler's scholarly methods; but some of his conclusions were fairly warmly received, at least among the orthodox. The historian Eduard Meyer expressed his view of the matter in the following terms. "Spengler has brilliantly described precisely these elements of inner disintegration [*Zersetzung*] in the sections [of his *Decline of the West*] devoted to criticism of presently dominant points of view, in the chapters on the state and on politics, on democracy and parliamentary government with its ugly party machinations, on the all-powerful press, on the nature of the metropolis, on economic life, money, and machines. I thoroughly share his damning judgment, and I look perhaps even more pessimistically toward the future of our people than he does."[49] Georg von Below was even more imaginative in his use of Spengler's theories. "The West will decline," he said, "when there are no more servants, when serving is considered dishonoring, when all social stratification is replaced by a society which is atomized for the sake of social climbing."[50] As far as I know, the problem of running a really cultivated household in the twentieth century has never again received such serious attention from social philosophers.

It is impossible to be very precise in describing these orthodox fulminations, since their authors themselves rather thrived on vagueness. They were perfectly content to blur any possible distinctions between various kinds of disintegration. They were at once the victims and the exploiters of an integral mood, an undifferentiated emotional reaction against the modern age.

During the Weimar period, the long-established connections between mandarin antimodernity and anti-Semitism became ever more overt. Many of the orthodox professors were quite explicit in ranking the Jews among the elements of national decomposition. "As the classical party of national decomposition, the Jews gained an influence upon the proletariat." "From Moses Hess to Landauer, Toller, and Eisner, it has been the Jewish fashion to acquire influence by indulging and arousing the instincts of the proletariat and to make unpatriotic politics with this influence." "W. Sombart's statement that educated persons with a Christian-German background adhere to Marxism only if they have some defect, whereas Jews with an academic education normally speak for it in large groups cannot, in the main, be denied." Agreeing with Below, the author of these passages, Michael Doeberl thought it significant that Marx was Jewish, suggesting that this should help to account for his characteristically "aggressive [*rücksichtslos*] logic and acid [*zersetzend*] criticism." Müller associated "the first noisy outbursts of a new radical literature" during the early nineteenth century with "the first appearance of the liberated Jews in literature": "The faiths intermingle; the Israelites are emancipated. Then iron and coal begin their victory procession."[51] For Müller and for some of his colleagues, the Jews were somehow similar both to the intellectual acids of decomposition and to the economic facts represented by iron and coal.

The orthodox meant to preach a total revolt against modernity. They therefore refused to admit that the break in German history at 1918, the gulf between the old national leadership and the rest of the people, could possibly be bridged, unless a spiritual revolution could yet transform the attitudes of the masses. In fact, the antirepublican professors did their best not only to exaggerate the gap that separated Weimar Germany from its prerevolutionary antecedents but also to make those antecedents look more homogeneous than they had actually been. In contrast to the modernists, they tried to obscure the differences between the Germany of Goethe and that of Bismarck or William II. They described the bureaucratic monarchy of the 1890's and those loyal to it as the legitimate heirs of the great German Idealists, for they intended to consolidate the whole weight of the past on the other side of the great divide of 1918, to unite the whole German tradition against the new society. Thus the historian Erich Marcks called Bismarck's time the "brightest height in the ups and downs of Germany's fate" and the events of 1918 a "monstrous fall from the brightest height to the darkest depth." Gustav Roethe attempted to demonstrate that ever since the eighteenth century, German poets and thinkers had been unanimous in condemning democracy and the notion of equality, in despising the masses, and in glorifying the creative individual and leader alone: "If even the individual must subject himself to the state, the worst crime is a conspiracy of the masses against the state."[52]

In this orthodox restatement of the mandarin heritage, the ideology of the legal and cultural state, like the conventional emphasis upon the "whole," acquired an exclusively illiberal meaning. Thus Walther Lotz challenged the very idea that "all state activity must necessarily and always be to the advantage of the governed."[53] Reinhold Seeberg, a Protestant theologian and onetime rector of Berlin University, developed a capsule history of German culture in which he pictured Idealism and religion as joint defenses against the allied forces of the Enlightenment, individualism, and materialism. He associated Idealism with patriotism, with the Prussian sense of duty to the "whole," with an organic conception of the nation and with the ideal of a strong state, one which could transcend the this-worldly interests of the individual. Seeberg's little secular sermon ended in an ode to the black, white, and red colors of the German Empire, which were also those of the nationalist opposition to the Weimar Republic. "May Idealism and religion be your banner, along with the good conscience of duty fulfilled. *Black* and serious may the eternal will, to which our wills are obligated, shine into your life! *White* and pure may your heart and conscience remain in the fulfillment of duty! *Red* and joyful may the inclination toward the ideal shine in you! Students, do honor to the colors of the old German Empire, which was founded fifty-four years ago today! In this sense of Idealism and religion, now and forever more: *Deutschland über alles in der Welt!*"[54]

For the Republic, of course, the constant attacks of a disaffected intelligentsia constituted a genuine danger. It was not so much that the antirepublican professors had any concrete plans to alter the existing form of government. Most of them knew that a restoration of the monarchy was not possible. Some of them speculated about the possibility of dismembering Social Democratic Prussia.[55] Michael Doeberl was a Bavarian federalist.[56] Others would have liked to see the creation of an upper house within the legislature, some agency not elected by universal suffrage yet powerful enough to check the Reichstag. The two possible candidates for this position were the existing Federal Council, the Reichsrat, which represented the various German states, and the Preliminary Economic Council (*vorläufiger Reichswirtschaftsrat*), a purely advisory commission which had been created in 1920 to bring together the spokesmen of various professions and industries.[57] It is questionable whether any of these proposals ever had any real chance of implementation. Recommendations to "transcend the party state," to regulate the activities of the parties, and to replace the "purely individualistic suffrage" and the "atomistic-individualistic conception of the state" would have been hard to convert into legislation.[58] Indeed, one sometimes wonders whether even their sponsors took such projects very seriously.

No, the real threat to the new regime came precisely from the vaguest and most shapeless aspects of the orthodox rebellion. It was the total irresponsibility of the antirepublican literature, the constant harping upon the immorality and degeneracy of existing conditions, that was most dangerous to political stability. Above all, there was this conclusion to be drawn from the orthodox polemics: that the social and political life of the Weimar period was so hopelessly corrupt that only a violent emotional wrench, a "spiritual revolution," could possibly save the nation. "Despite everything that is now being announced in the streets, it is and remains . . . the spirit which creates the body for itself." "More important than the inanimate structure . . . is the inner renewal for the outward reorganization . . . the spirit, the truly social spirit which rises above class and party interests and above poisonous materialism." "We are . . . bitterly in need of a spiritual revival . . . And we are in need of a leader . . . the great all-conquering popular hero . . . When Jesus Christ was crucified . . . his followers also felt only the dark at first, the night which seemed to descend around them."[59] This was the mandarin animus against the "merely technical" in politics, now carried to a hysterical extreme. The "idealistic" elevation of "the spirit" became pure escapism as it was channeled into the call for a savior.

The orthodox academics disarmed themselves in advance against whatever antimodernistic revolution the future would bring. Carl Neumann spoke of Germany's ripening for a great epic. Müller and Below made their extravagant pleas for a leader to rescue the nation from defeat, materialism, and decay,[60] and Gustav Roethe wrote this poem for an academic audience:

> Let not Bismarck die within you!
> Don't give it up, the banner attained!
> Will yourself, German land!
> Will yourself, master misfortune!
> Bismarck was dead, is no longer dead!
> In your soul, which awakes,
> He arises for you, returns and lives![61]

And all these things were said to a younger generation of academic "idealists," for whom the vilification of present conditions came to be coupled with messianic expectations of a vague and yet violent character. Thus the orthodox caricature of the mandarin tradition was a revolt against reality, in which the borderline between pessimism and nihilism was obscured.

THE SOCIAL SCIENCES IN THE TWENTIES

German social scientists during the 1920's did their scholarly work in an atmosphere of extraordinary tension and instability. The academic community was politically more divided than ever before;

the very foundations of the mandarin tradition appeared to be in question. To write about government, economics, or society was necessarily to enter into the heated debate concerning contemporary political alternatives. The prevailing sense of crisis was so profound that even methods of analysis in the social sciences, not just the research results, acquired an immediate political relevance. It became increasingly easy to discover a man's party preferences in his methodological program for his discipline. The substantive quality of German learning did not benefit from these conditions.

The debate over the future of sociology may serve as an example. In an earlier chapter, we discussed some of the pamphlets in which Konrad Haenisch and Carl Becker announced the plans of the Prussian Ministry of Culture for the reform of German education. In 1919, Becker inserted a plea for sociology into one of these tracts.[62] He argued that there was a need for interdepartmental programs of study at the universities. These new courses were to counteract the excessive compartmentalization and specialization of German learning and to bring research to bear particularly upon the acute problems of modern social and economic life. Becker meant to make scholarship more responsive and more pertinent to contemporary concerns, to bridge the gap between the academic world and the rest of society. He also saw a need for intellectual "synthesis," for a drawing together of disjointed and overly esoteric research results into meaningful general theories. He sponsored a "sociological" approach in the interdisciplinary courses he proposed because he believed that sociology was particularly productive of the kind of synthesis he had in mind. In all probability, Tönnies' *Community and Society* was Becker's chief model of "synthetic" sociology. In any case, his wording suggested that he was thinking of a vaguely universalist, "socially" motivated, and decidedly present-minded discipline, which would indeed be ideally suited to the task of modernist synthesis.

Of course, Becker's proposal encountered violent opposition from the orthodox, who felt that it sounded rather socialistic. The German philologist Friedrich von der Leyen polemicized against it by picturing the universities overrun by the masses and enslaved by socially radical theoreticians and speculators.[63] Von Below, a master in the art of the vague but ominous hint, wanted to know how Becker could possibly accuse German professors of being insufficiently involved in current political affairs, unless of course he was really complaining about their opposition to the Socialist Republic.[64] Moreover, Below simply did not see the need for any sort of sociology in Germany. He assumed that the champions of the new discipline would propose to investigate two sets of relationships: those between men and those between the individual and his material and cultural milieu. But had not the German Romantics shown the way toward a satisfactory treatment of these problems, particularly in the concept of the "volk spirit" (*Volksgeist*)? What was the point of falling back into the discredited positivism and naturalism of Western sociology? During the Enlightenment, Below argued, the autonomy and independence of individual human reason had been overestimated. In Germany, however, the balance had been righted by Romantic environmentalism and traditionalism. German learning had indeed become somewhat too unconcernedly empiricist and specialized from about 1860 to 1880. It had lost touch with its own philosophical heritage. But that was no reason to insult the universities, as Becker had done, by suggesting that the task of synthesis ought now to fall to the materialistic positivism with which the French and English had tried, unsuccessfully, to imitate the techniques of the German Romantics. Surely, Becker's presumption could only be traced to his own Marxist leanings. In the face of such renegade critics, German learning would know how to preserve, or rather to revive, its own great traditions.

The exchange between Becker and Below prompted two leading German sociologists to clarify their own views on the subject under discussion. One of these was Tönnies; the other was Leopold von Wiese. In 1919, Wiese founded the Research Institute for Social Studies at Cologne, which helped to pave the way for the opening of the new urban University of Cologne about a year later. With the help of Alfred Vierkandt, Wiese eventually succeeded in making the so-called Cologne school one of the most important and productive traditions within modern German sociology.

As might be expected, both Tönnies and Wiese repudiated Below's militant neo-Romanticism.[65] They made it perfectly clear that their sympathies were generally on Becker's side. Nevertheless, they would not agree with Becker's assertion that sociology was pure synthesis. Tönnies thought that the new discipline might lead to "synthetic" insights in a few special areas of concern; but this did not seem to him its main function. Wiese refused even more emphatically to see sociology as a sub-category of philosophy or as a positivist theory of history. Instead, he now began to outline his own plans for an independent and specialized discipline of "formal sociology." In 1921, he wrote several programmatic articles for the new journal of the Cologne school, and his first systematic work was published in 1924.[66] It is hard to say just how much the debate between Becker and Below influenced Wiese; but there can be no question that he was subsequently very careful to avoid the conception of sociology as pure synthesis.

"Until 1900," according to Wiese, "sociology was almost always a bit of intellectual history, metaphysics, ethics, or politics, or a bit of cosmology, biology, or psychology . . . The emergence from these limitations and the achievement of an autonomous way of posing fundamental questions is the decisive, gradually advancing process which alone makes sociology a real discipline." In describing the questions and procedures that helped to make sociology thus independent of an older tradition, Wiese did not hesitate to use language which was generally disliked as positivist. He spoke of "dissolving the whole into its elements" and of "achieving a result by putting these elements together again." In defense of his preference for an "isolating" conceptualization, he was not afraid to challenge a then fashionable emphasis upon the intuitive understanding of phenomenal "wholes."[67] At the same time, his own method was by no means strictly empirical in the ordinary sense of that term. On the contrary, he made it his task to construct a highly elaborate and abstract system of social structures and processes, in which immediate observation played no more of a role than it did in Simmel's work. Like Simmel, Wiese distinguished between the forms and the content of patterns and processes in the "interpersonal realm." His very definition of sociology was based upon the assumption that the relationships (*Beziehungen,* hence *Beziehungslehre* or *Beziehungssoziologie*) between men could be described quite apart from the objectives involved.

The most important concept in Wiese's system was that of "social distance." Again, as in Simmel's case, one has to use geometric analogies to understand these ideas. Wiese thought it possible to order various types of social relations in quantitative terms, as if measuring the lengths of the pertinent connecting lines between individuals. He distinguished between social configurations (*Gebilde*) and social processes. Under the heading of configurations, he treated a variety of groupings and relationships that could be regarded as relatively permanent, and of course it was the nature and the closeness of the interpersonal links that primarily interested him. In his theory of social processes, the predominant concern with social bonding was even more obvious; for he described processes essentially as changes in a set of social distances. Accordingly, he distinguished between "processes of drawing together" (*Prozesse des Zueinander*) and "processes of drawing apart" (*Prozesse des Auseinander*). He managed to classify such characteristic phenomena as competition, imitation, "approach and adjustment," assimilation, and cooperation according to the degree of association or dissociation which they entailed or represented. Throughout, his tone suggested a positive valuation of "drawing together" and an anxious care for the preservation of social cohesion. In this respect, his approach reflected the typically ambivalent attitude of mandarin modernists toward the dissociative aspects of modern social life.

Nevertheless, there was at least one German sociologist who felt that Wiese's system was morally too neutral, too unengaged and irrelevant. Hans Freyer scoffed at the "formalism" of the Cologne school.[68] Wiese, we have said, did very little empirical work. His systematic expositions were in fact catalogues of typological categories and abstractions, and rather long and complicated catalogues at that. It seems, however, that Freyer's charge of formalism was directed not so much at these characteristics of Wiese's theory as at his failure to condemn the "societal" and liberal aspects of nineteenth-century civilization. Freyer was an activist of the nationalist right and a disciple of Spengler. He thought it the duty of sociologists to see social patterns in their historical context, to identify the patterns as either healthy or decadent, to prepare the "positive" bases of reconstruction in a predominantly "negative" age.

Another right-wing critic of modernist sociology was the Austrian economist and sociologist Othmar Spann. His objection to all of modern social theory, particularly to the work of Tönnies and of Weber, was that it was based on a "naturalistic" and "individualistic" approach.[69] Modern social theory stressed men's natural interests as motives of association, and it conceived all groups and classes in "nominalist" fashion as sums of individuals. It thus made the Marxists' view of social organization a foregone conclusion, according to Spann. Spann's "universalist" philosophy of socioeconomic life was meant to correct this awful situation once and for all. Drawing on Romantic and corporative traditions, Spann proposed to demonstrate the moral and logical priority of the national and communal "whole" over its members. He tried to show that it was the nature of a true social group to "put itself in the service of spiritual concerns" (dem Geiste zu dienen). He therefore condemned the "individualistic" and "naturalistic" concept of class, urging that it be replaced with the "universalist" category of "the estate" (der Stand).

Apparently, Spann was not alone in feeling that the methods of German sociologists required revision. By 1923, Werner Sombart, too, was ready to make a polemical distinction between German and Western sociology, between the "noological" and the "naturalistic" approach.[70] German sociology, he argued, should regard itself as a humanistic discipline, avoiding the limitations associated with the idea of social "science" and doing justice to the intellectual and spiritual sources of social cohesion.

One has the impression that the flood of programmatic pamphlets that discussed the future of German sociology during the Weimar period did very little to increase the quantity or quality of substantive work in the field. Facile slogans and crude stereotypes came to play too large a role in the scholarly literature. Too many intellectuals insisted on behaving as if German learning was in imminent danger of being corrupted by the crudest sort of positivism, even though there was not the slightest evidence of such a possibility. A rhetorical blow struck against "naturalism" and other mythical villains came to seem a guarantee of future creativity in scholarship, while present achievements often took the form of conventional generalities about the supremacy of "the whole" or the importance of geist. Efforts to revitalize the German learned tradition were sometimes so desperate, so willful and strained, that the results could only be caricatures. Too many academic controversies of the day degenerated into fruitless name-calling.

This was true to some extent in the field of economics and social policy as well. There was probably less agreement among German economists during the 1920's than ever before. The conflict between theorists and historians, the bearing of marginal analysis upon the problems of value and price, the relevance of mathematical models, the relationship of economics to the humanistic disciplines, and the role of value judgments in social policy: all these issues became entangled with each other and with the deepening differences between various segments of the academic community. Altogether, the result was a bewildering panorama of opinions, particularly since the nervous instability of the intellectual climate encouraged the polemical use of fashionable antitheses. There were those who resisted these pressures. Joseph Schumpeter and Emil Lederer continued to experiment with the new marginal and equilibrium analysis. Lederer was interested in price movements and monetary policy.[71] As much a Keynesian as a Marxist, he began seriously to investigate the possibility of economic planning. The layman cannot judge the theoretical results of such efforts; but he can guess that they were based upon substantive work of a certain caliber. Conversely, he has reason to doubt the usefulness of popular polemics in which too many German economists of the day accused each other of "individualism," of imitating the natural sciences, of overemphasizing "technical-materialistic" factors, or of favoring mechanistic analogies.[72]

While such phrases were being produced, the language of "community" triumphed in the field of social policy. The theoretical debate over the ethical direction in German economics was really over. Nothing substantively new was said on this subject after the war; but the slogans survived. In an increasingly hopeless assault upon contemporary realities, some of the leading experts in the field continued to preach the "supraeconomic," cultural, or spiritual objectives of social policy and the need for a sense of community between entrepreneurs and workers. Götz Briefs and Otto von Zwiedineck-Südenhorst tended to use these arguments as much against business as against labor.[73] Briefs lamented the fact that "none of the mighty economic combines has ever *publicly and axiomatically* recognized the interest of the state and of the people as its standard of behavior."[74] More commonly, the tacit assumption was that the workers' lack of "communal spirit" stood as the main obstacle to a solution of the social problem. Arthur Salz warned against distrusting the industrialists merely because they were powerful. He tried to show that it would be easier to convert a few business leaders than to keep a democratically elected government from misusing its powers against them. Such pro-entrepreneurial spokesmen as Adolf Weber, Hermann Schumacher, and Robert Liefmann more or less took it for granted that the capitalists would learn to think of themselves as stewards for the whole community.[75] In Weber's mind, this certainly alleviated the need for legislative measures in support of social policy. Widespread doubts about the usefulness of such measures, together with the generally uneasy intellectual climate, led to the conviction that there was a "crisis of social policy" during the 1920's.[76]

In the meantime, Werner Sombart's views continued to be transformed during the 1920's and early 1930's. On the one hand, he now began to feel that economics ought to be more thoroughly identified with the methods of the humanistic disciplines. On the other hand, he once again changed his position on the future of capitalism.[77] The era of "high capitalism," he said, was now essentially over. The increasing complexity of economic organization, the decline of the individual enterpreneur as the predominant agent of industrial enterprise and the spreading rationalization and bureaucratization: all these phenomena indicated the opening of a new age of "late capitalism." To meet the demands of the new condition, Sombart proposed a planned economy, making it quite clear that what he had in mind was neither Marxist nor socialist. In discussing the objectives of future planners, he stressed the arguments for economic autarchy and for a reversal of the existing drift away from agriculture and the healthy rural environment. He was clearly moving toward the ideal of a corporative society, in which public and private officials would presumably fulfill particularly important functions. As he said before a congress of civil servants in 1928:

> the bureaucratization [*Verbeamtung*] of the world . . . may be a blessing, if we imbue it with the proper spirit, that is, if the ideal content which is undoubtedly contained in the [notion of the official's calling] is not lost in the process . . . the thought that officialdom means service to the fatherland, service to the community. This thought is destined to preserve mankind from a danger which is much greater than [that of] bureaucratization, and that is the danger of succumbing to mammonism, to the profit devil, to material interest mongering . . . Bureaucratization . . . is nothing but a return to the natural, divinely willed condition of human society: the subjection of the economy to the higher and highest purposes of the community, to culture and to the salvation of the human soul.[78]

Thus Sombart ultimately transformed his cultural critique of capitalism into a call for bureaucratic control. By 1934, he was moving toward a "German socialism" which seemed to echo some of the slogans of National Socialist ideology.

Wolfgang Hock has described some of the German literature of the late 1920's and early 1930's which expressed a peculiar form of anticapitalism.[79] Ferdinand Fried's *Das Ende des Kapitalismus* (1930) was among the most striking and influential of these tracts. The views expressed in this literature had nothing in common with Social Democratic or other left-wing critiques of capitalism. The arguments used were typically moralistic; there was a pronounced note of nostalgic escapism; corporative and neo-Romantic analogies played an important role; and the spiritual and communal "overcoming" of modernity was portrayed in the vague terms which always characterized this brand of "idealism." In all likelihood, the victims of industrialization among the old middle classes made up the audience for these ideological morality plays. But it would not be difficult to trace some of the assumptions of the new "anticapitalism" to the mandarins' own socio-economic theories and attitudes.

As the traditional philosophy of the "cultivated" was matched against the difficult problems of modern industrial society, it began to give rise to neurotic excesses of various kinds. These extremes, which appeared primarily on the political right, were matched by a simultaneous rise of radical disaffection on the left wing of the German academic community. Beginning during the First World War and increasingly during the 1920's, a few of the most determined modernists began to criticize the very axioms of the mandarin creed. They were so totally disenchanted with the main line of mandarin orthodoxy that they came to see it primarily as ideology, as rationalization. Instead of merely arguing against commonly held notions, they began to debunk or to unmask them, to treat them primarily as defenses of social privilege. Max Weber's attack upon the "literati" who produced the "ideas of 1914" was based on this type of criticism. On one occasion, Weber explicitly traced the antiparliamentary rhetoric of the learned to "fear for the prestige of their own segment of society: that of the diploma holders."[80] Tönnies' polemic against the obscurantist exploitation of "communal" ideals was another case in point, and so was Leopold von Wiese's critique of wartime harangues against "individualism."

Among the younger social scientists, such men as Ernst von Aster, Moritz Julius Bonn, Emil Lederer, Franz Oppenheimer, and Karl Mannheim used the method of radical debunking, or thought about it, especially during the tense years of the Weimar period. Aster, Lederer, and Mannheim were strongly influenced by Marxism. Bonn once expressed his distrust of the grandiloquent phrases used to argue for German colonial expansion before the war.[81] He demanded a rigorous examination of alternatives in terms of the specific interests of all social groups and an end to the rhetoric about the national "whole." Lederer was thoroughly skeptical of the "communal" illusion as early as 1914.[82] He saw it as a glorification of the herd instincts and as a true example of cultural leveling. He did not believe that it contributed anything at all toward a genuine solution of contemporary social problems. During the later Weimar period, Lederer began to watch with particular anxiety the fate of the new proletariat of subordinate white-collar employees. He suspected as early as 1929 that their resentments and their susceptibility to socially romantic myths might be used to preserve capitalism through fascist terror. The sociologist Franz Oppenheimer proposed to treat modern capitalism as an aberrant development, the effect of a preindustrial ruling caste's monopoly in land.[83] He polemicized against the Marxists on the basis of this theory; but he also developed his own "law of socio-psychological determination," according to which men consider everything wise and just that serves their group.

One of the most unusual of the radical critics was the "nominalist" philosopher and moderate Social Democrat Ernst von Aster. He expressed himself with particular sharpness about the "snobbery of cultivation" and the "merciless moralizing" which too often took the place of political analysis in the 1920's.[84] During the Wilhelmian period, he said, the academic and adminstrative elites and the rest of the old ruling class had simply identified the interests of the state with their own. On that basis, they had then divided the nation into two parts: "a national, loyal, 'good' one; and an oppositional, disloyal, antinational, 'bad' one, which was to be fought to the death." According to the "patriotic-religious ragout" which had become official doctrine, a lack of "national" feeling was the greatest of *moral* failings. Especially since the defeat of 1918, the jingoism of the political right had evolved into a kind of exhibitionist cult, an escape from the unheroic necessities of the moment.[85]

Between 1929 and 1931, Aster saw the rhetoric of the nationalists developing into a veritable mythology, a new "metaphysics" of reaction. It seemed to him that the vagueness of many of the new concepts (*Volk* and *Reich,* for example) was designed to train declassed burghers to react on a purely emotional level to whatever "magic potions" were applied to their resentments. The ground was thus prepared for an unprecedented tyranny over men's minds, in which the individual would count for nothing. It shocked Aster that men who thought Marxism utopian could pretend to believe in the entrepreneurs' voluntary submission to "the community." The whole theory of community, he said, was the most extreme example of a utopia, "a backward-looking, romantic utopia!"[86] He felt that modern society was actually moving away from community, toward a loosening of social ties, and he approved of this trend. In any case, he was convinced that a true community of millions could never be created. Those who talked as if it could be, as if the interests of the volk could be separated from the interests of its members, were simply paving the way for minority rule by terror.

One is struck by the extraordinary differences of approach and tone which separated the arguments of the radical critics from the traditional patterns of mandarin thought. Instinctively, one begins to look for unique personal experiences which may have led them into unorthodox paths. Evidence to this effect is not hard to find. Tönnies, Wiese, and some of the other modernists among the sociologists had unusual backgrounds. An early and atypically serious interest in Hobbes may have helped to make Tönnies a "positivist" in social questions. Wiese was decisively influenced by Spencer; Aster, Lederer, and Mannheim, by Marx. During their younger years, both Tönnies and Wiese spent a good deal of time outside the academic world, in travel and in social work.[87] Tönnies was the son of a Frisian farmer. It has been suggested that his conception of community was nourished in the region of his birth. He entered rather late and reluctantly into the academic world.

The young Wiese rebelled against the military career that had been planned for him. After fighting his way into and through the gymnasium with some distaste, he wavered between a learned and a literary vocation, read Herbert Spencer and August Bebel with enthusiasm, worked as a secretary and statistician for a philanthropic industrialist, became interested in the cooperative and trade union movement, and took a grant to travel around the world, before permanently settling down to an academic career. Under the Empire, he was never blessed with much in the way of official support, so that he moved around among the less distinguished universities, technical institutes, and academies until 1919. His political views were always unorthodox. Although disillusioned with socialism, he leaned toward the left wing of the Social Policy Association, opposing official paternalism and favoring the independent development of the unions instead. He was one of the leading sponsors of the people's university movement after 1918,[88] and he also figured among the warmest supporters of the Republic within the academic community. Success came to him at Cologne after 1920; but he was never to join any of the traditionally most prestigious university faculties.

Thus the radical was typically an outsider in some way. Very often, he had contacts in the world of the nonacademic, unofficial, and unconnected intelligentsia, with artists, journalists, and writers. At the same time, one cannot help but notice the relatively large proportion of Jews among the critics of mandarin orthodoxy. Jewish intellectuals were very prominent among the innovators in various disciplines, as well as among the authors of progressive social and political doctrines. Robert Michels has remarked upon the relatively large number of Jews among the intellectual supporters of the socialist movement.[89] In part, these facts may reflect certain characteristics of the Jews' own cultural heritage, along with their international dispersion. But the more immediate effects of anti-Semitism upon the Jewish intellectual should not be overlooked. We know that anti-Semitic sentiments were almost universal at the German universities. Even those unusual academics who, following the example of Lujo Brentano and Karl Vossler, took a public stand against the excesses of the anti-Semites during the Weimar period, did not disguise their own more moderate predisposition against the Jews.[90] In any case, Jewish instructors found their progress through the academic ranks hampered by their colleagues, and they often faced less tangible social barriers as well. According to Sigmund Freud, experiences of this kind tended to encourage "a certain independence of judgment" in many Jewish intellectuals.[91]

Friedrich Meinecke reported the following story during the Weimar period.

A colleague who has been able to follow the movements within the academic youth of Berlin more precisely than anyone else has told me: Of the 10,000 students, about 9,400 sit quietly in the lecture halls, seminars, and institutes, intent only upon their studies and examinations. About 600 are in high spirits, and of these, 400 are hypernationalistic and anti-Semitic; the remaining 200 divide themselves among Communists, Social Democrats, and Democrats and are mostly Jews. Anti-Semitism has played a role in the nationalistic student movement for more than forty years; this has driven the Jewish elements even more toward leftist radicalism, which in turn has offered new points of attack for a *naive and uncritical national feeling*. This vicious circle is well known and apparently continues to operate unchanged.[92]

The impressions upon which this account was based may well have been somewhat one-sided, and one wonders whether the "vicious circle" was ever truly circular. Still, there was a grain of truth in Meinecke's remarks. Anti-Semitism produced outsiders among Jewish intellectuals, and the status of the outsider, no matter how it is attained, often makes for radicalism as well as for creativity.

These considerations may help to explain the presence of a few disaffected critics within the mandarin community; but they cannot completely account for the phenomenon of radicalism in Germany. It has always struck me as particularly interesting that so many of the great debunking analysts of modern culture have been German or Austrian, not English or French. Golo Mann has argued that there were always two totally different and unrelated groups of intellectuals in Germany: the highly respected, official establishment of the university professors, and a volatile, "bohemian," and almost indiscriminately acid minority of radicals.[93] The problem is still to account for the peculiarly sharp antagonism between the critic and the conventional academic. Could it be that the language of "idealism" had something to do with all this?

Whether in politics or in the affairs of learning itself, the mandarins were committed to a particularly "elevated" level of discourse.

Their whole tradition forbade them to recognize any limitations upon the autonomy and potency of pure geist. Economic and social questions had to be treated as subordinate, "merely practical," and it was almost immoral to talk about worldly interests. Offenders against these standards were quickly and easily condemned as "materialists" or "positivists." The result was that mild criticisms of conventional notions were very hard to express. To challenge the orthodox at all, the critic almost had to make a leap into a new vocabulary, one in which interests could be considered, groups were sums of people, and the rule of the spirit was an ideal, not a reality.

In other words, the orthodox mandarins always had a certain tendency toward "merciless moralizing." The more they felt threatened, the more thoroughly this tendency possessed them. They became arrogant and humorless, until their moralistic rhetoric was practically impenetrable. Faced with their self-assurance, the would-be challenger was forced into the technique of radical debunking. Aster's fury and Weber's irony were in part the result of frustration. Thinking of Marx and of Bertolt Brecht, of Nietzsche and of Freud, one begins to suspect that idealism has always produced its own enemies. The peculiarity of the Weimar period was only a matter of degree. An "unmasking" type of criticism was becoming more prevalent on the left wing of the academic community, just as a dangerous caricature of communal idealism was making its appearance on the right. The old social philosophy of the cultivated elite was beginning to disintegrate.

THE CRISIS OF MANDARIN POLITICS

The division between the accommodationists and the orthodox deepened considerably during the 1920's. At the same time, a broad range of common assumptions continued to unite all but the most radically disaffected members of the mandarin community. The distinction between modernists and orthodox has its uses; but it should not obscure the underlying similarities in the situation and outlook of all cultivated Germans during the Weimar period.

Thus even relatively progressive intellectuals observed the political and social life of those years with considerable anxiety. Lujo Brentano was shocked at the intensity of the party conflicts that troubled the young republic. "It is," he said, "as if victims of a shipwreck were wrestling with each other on a cliff in order to drag each other into the abyss."[94] Especially between 1918 and 1925, a feeling of moral horror was widespread among academics of all political leanings. "A frightening decay of any feeling of standing together, of all naturally rooted moral sentiments reveals itself wherever one goes, a neglect, almost a hatred for all spiritual and moral values, which used to be unknown among us." "In the life of the political parties as well as in occupational organizations and economic leagues, public questions are presently treated primarily in an egotistic and materialistic sense. The health of our conditions urgently demands that this whole orientation be ethicized."[95] The point is that very few German professors could wholly escape the feeling that the violent factional clashes of the day were signs of a moral failure. Even the modernists found it difficult to identify themselves thoroughly with any of the warring social groups. Too many of the issues that were being contested seemed to them unworthy and destructive in the first place, so that they often gave way to the old mandarin habit of standing "above" politics. They condemned the whole conflict, not just the parties engaged in it; and because the new parliamentary organization revealed the depth and bitterness of group antagonisms more clearly than the bureaucratic monarchy, they could never entirely free themselves from the notion that the Republic itself was somehow to blame for the disheartening aspects of the new politics.

Republican as well as antirepublican academics looked upon the mass and machine age with deep misgivings. Alfred Weber still hoped that Germany might eventually combine Western technological progress and parliamentary democracy with an overriding commitment to nonutilitarian cultural values, which he associated with the unspoiled East.[96] At the same time, he had serious doubts about the unity and vitality of the Western cultural community. Industrial development had led to commercial rivalry and then to war. It now seemed that the end product of Spencer's "progress" was anything but desirable. "Nothing is more problematic today," said Weber, "than . . . the nature and reality of the intellectual and spiritual fundament of Europe."[97] One has the impression that these anxieties were emotionally more natural to him than his reluctant acceptance of technology and democracy.

Although the modernists were not as fond of the imagery of social "dissolution" and "disintegration" as their orthodox colleagues, they did use these terms on occasion. Alfred Vierkandt described a nineteenth-century process of social disintegration in which an "atomistic" individualism gradually dissolved the communal bonds left over from earlier forms of social organization. Even Ernst Troeltsch once permitted himself a vague reference to "the age of the press and of journalism which vulgarly debunks [zerschwätzen], prematurely reveals, and rapidly uses up everything."[98] This kind of generalization about the cultural implications of democracy was a widespread malady of the time. It certainly affected the orthodox more seriously than the accommodationists; but its germs were everywhere.

This is why the ideal of "community" achieved such prominence all along the spectrum of mandarin opinion. The *Brockhaus* definition of the term suggests the grounds for its popularity: "Community, a group of human beings who feel united in being and in action through common thinking, feeling, and willing . . . The community is considered naturally and organically grown. A jointly binding orientation [Gesinnung] rules in it, and not the battle over interests." As might be expected, the term was often given an even more general meaning than this. The historian Gerhard Ritter connected the word with the conventional formulation of the "national" ideal by urging "selfless submission [Hingabe] to the fatherland, which stands above the parties, to the national community which includes us all." Vierkandt traced the new interest in a self-conscious ethic of community to the exhaustion of formerly natural and unconscious resources of communal sentiment during the eighteenth and nineteenth centuries.[99]

According to the *Brockhaus* definition, a community was something "naturally and organically grown," presumably a product of a definite set of circumstances, not simply the result of an ethical choice by one or several individuals. At the same time, the definition made moral and cultural values seem the most important bonds between the members of a community. Most of the mandarins, of course, were primarily concerned with this second aspect of the problem. They regretted the loss of that traditional consensus with which they had always been identified. The consistent difference between modernists and orthodox lay in the fact that only the modernists kept both parts of the definition in mind. They suspected that some of the ancient forms of community could not possibly be restored in the new environment, least of all on the basis of a "spiritual revolution," which is to say by words alone. In a sense, they were more resigned, more genuinely pessimistic than their orthodox colleagues. Still, the disappearance of the ancient forms of community and the search for more or less updated substitutes was one of the most persistent concerns of all the mandarins' social theories.

To a very large degree, one is dealing with unexpressed moods and fears in all this, even when one turns to particular words or concepts as characteristic vehicles of emotion. The German university professors felt themselves involved in a genuine tragedy. They were oppressed by the sense that their own ideals were threatened with extinction, along with their whole manner of life. The accommodationists felt this even more strongly than the orthodox, precisely because they tried to shed all reactionary illusions. The best description of this psychological problem and of the whole emotional context of mandarin politics was written by Friedrich Meinecke. In his "Conversation in the Fall of 1919," he reported an imaginary exchange of ideas between "Reinhold," representing Meinecke himself, and his former friend "Eberhard," an orthodox opponent of the Republic.[100] In one of the most revealing sections of this fictional dialogue, Eberhard attacks Reinhold's position as follows. "You with your leanings toward the Germany of Goethe, with your aristocratic and humanistic ideal of cultivation should rightly stand with us in a common . . . front against the rule of the vulgar masses, against the dictatorship of the primary school teacher and of half-cultivation, the threatening outlines of which are already discernible against the murky cloudbank of modern democratic culture." Reinhold answers that he would choose to live during the *Biedermeier* period of the early nineteenth century, if that choice were open to him; but he adds that "such romantic needs are justified only for one's personal inner life . . . I am not enthusiastic about democracy; but it is unavoidable." "*Eberhard*: But it will destroy the most characteristic aspects of what you love and value." "*Reinhold*: That may be so; it is even quite certain that the particular intellectual and spiritual world in which we both feel well is destined to disappear. If only while it blossomed, it blossomed as vigorously and beautifully as possible." Eberhard is not convinced. He accuses Reinhold of a certain lack of integrity in accommodating the "spirit of the times." Would it not be more honorable, he asks, to choose a "manly end" (*charaktervollen Untergang*)? Reinhold admits that he has often wondered about that himself. He eventually reaffirms his determination to cooperate with the new regime in order to guide it from within whenever possible. But he makes it quite clear that he finds the choice a sad and agonizing one to make.

Throughout the Weimar period, it was often said in academic circles that a crisis was in progress. No one felt the need to define the exact nature of this crisis, to ask where it came from or what it involved. "Sometimes, the present situation is represented as a crisis of the . . . economic system only, sometimes as one of politics and of the idea of the state, or as a crisis of the social order. At other times, it is conceived more deeply and inclusively as a crisis of the entire intellectual and spiritual culture, as a crisis of the religious consciousness . . . of the West."[101] In any case, the crisis existed, if only by virtue of the fact that almost every educated German believed in its reality. Obviously, it had a great deal to do with general cultural questions; but it also pertained to political and social affairs.

Ernst Robert Curtius once traced the "European cultural crisis" of this period to the change in the economic and social position of the nonentrepreneurial middle class.[102] That still did not define the problem; but it did help to identify the basic anxiety that caused men to speak of a crisis. At bottom, the mandarins were afraid that there had been a decisive reversal of priorities. Geist and its representatives had lost control of society. The new politics and economics had become emancipated from the influence of the cultured sage and of his values. Fundamental decisions were now being made upon a new set of criteria, by way of a series of numerical calculations, which often seemed automatic and mechanical. In turn, events in the newly autonomous realms of social behavior were apparently capable of exerting a tyrannical influence upon the world of thought, as if geist had become the creature of its body.

Nothing did more to lodge this somber view in the minds of educated Germans than the inflation of the early twenties. Here was a truly shattering experience. While a few capitalists prospered, the demonic machinery of a derailed monetary system practically demolished German learning. The vulnerability of scholarship was suddenly revealed with frightening clarity, even while the mandarins were made conscious of their unpopularity with the newly influential masses. It now appeared that the governing classes in Germany were made up of several rather different groups. There was an economic, a political, and a learned elite, and the relative fortunes of these three social segments were obviously capable of very rapid and drastic change. The mandarins were forced into a heightened awareness of modern social realities. Alfred Weber and Robert Michels developed some of the sociological insights that suggested themselves, while the professorial elite as a whole began to evolve a new and painful sense of self.[103] In the academic literature dealing with the inflation, references were made to the "old," "learned," or "cultivated" middle class, the *Ideellenschicht,* the "bearers of old cultural traditions, of a profound and thorough education, of an integral world view and of high social and moral standards." There was fearful talk of leveling and "mechanical equalization," of the proletarization of German learning, and the "dismantling of our culture." The mandarins were not accustomed to a situation in which "the scholarly writer does not earn as much with a printed line as the street sweeper earns with two whisks of the broom."[104] "A social revolution has swept across the land of poets and thinkers," said Mortiz Julius Bonn in 1923, "which has made poetry and thinking a superfluous luxury." "A peculiar pattern of life has arisen," Rudolf

Eucken generalized, "which seeks salvation in economic well-being, thereby denying the autonomy and independent value of matters of the mind and spirit [*Geistigkeit*]."[105]

In a lecture on the "plight of the intellectuals" (*geistige Arbeiter*) in 1923, Alfred Weber seriously questioned whether "the continuity of intellectual and spiritual life [*des Geistigen*], a highest good of the nation," could be saved at all. Every civilization, he said, had entrusted the "spiritual and intellectual sphere" to a group of guardians: "A culture-bearing and cultivated social segment has always existed as something special. It would be a terrible pseudo-democratic mistake to believe that it did not now exist or that it could be dispensed with." In modern European countries, Weber said, this elite has been composed of "writers and journalists, artists and scholars, higher officials and theologians and . . . [to a lesser degree] of doctors and lawyers." It has been a "rentier intelligentsia," economically dependent, directly or indirectly, upon unearned income. Though threatened in a "capitalist-mechanistic society," it has been "almost the only reasonably independent island outside of the antitheses of classes and interests, an asylum for the more-than-economic ideas which remain." The danger, as Weber saw it in 1923, was that this group would now become an "adjunct of the economy," that it would fall into the "domain of the great industrial magnates," if it did not disappear altogether. Modern developments were urgently raising the question of "the relationship of the intellectual and spiritual to the economic." Unless a hitherto lukewarm state was prepared to fight for "the primacy of the intellectual and spiritual over the economic," Weber feared a general decline of Western culture and the arrival of a new dark age.[106]

In the realm of politics too, the mandarins feared a radical change in the whole relationship between geist and reality. The historian Hermann Oncken expressed a widespread conviction that the new parliamentary democracy had failed to produce the creative personalities Germany needed. Oncken saw creative statesmanship as an art, a product of genius. His question was whether "the fertile womb of the intellectual and spiritual Germany" would continue to supply the gifted leadership without which the new political system could not survive.[107] Gerhard Ritter voiced the conventional lament that "the technical, organizational" had "achieved such a predominance over the individual that the intellectual and spiritual content of our present party battles is inversely proportional to their noise." He went on to complain that "the idea of the fatherland" was being "drowned in the strife of material interests," that the German people's "soul" was being forgotten in the "many efforts to care for its material needs."[108] The phrasing was orthodox; but the underlying assumption was prevalent over the whole range of the mandarin spectrum: the old elites found it hard to accept the "impersonal" machinery, the language of interest bargaining and compromise— and the change in personnel— which seemed inevitably associated with the new mass politics.

Friedrich Meinecke saw the growing estrangement between geist and politics reflected in the outlook of German social scientists.[109] During the early nineteenth century, he said, German historians favored an idealistic approach to government. They were content to spend most of their energy on philosophical speculations about the nature of the "true" or "good" state. They simply trusted that their theoretical decisions would become effective in the world of practice. Around mid-century, a generation ranging from Friedrich Dahlmann to Heinrich von Treitschke sacrificed some part of the earlier ideality in exchange for more realistic and historical analysis. After the establishment of the Empire by Bismarck, a third generation of scholars moved even further from the postulation of what ought to be to the observation of what was. The early Socialists of the Lectern brought a certain ethical bent to their work on the new social problems. But even Schmoller himself was primarily a historian; and for the historian, this was an age of specialized and detached recounting of facts. With Max Weber, finally, the intellectual's self-negation in the morally neutral description of an ever more disheartening reality reached truly painful proportions. Meinecke felt that Weber's approach might actually be unavoidable in the new environment. Apparently, the old cultural ideals were becoming ever more irrelevant to the new politics, so that the modern intellectual was forced into an analytical detachment which was bound to produce a conflict between his reason and his emotions.

No one knew exactly how and why the division between Geist and politics had come about. Alfred Weber spoke of a "curse" which "seems to separate the world of the mind and spirit [*das Geistige*] from politics, to degrade politics, insofar as it is to be practically effective, to the level of businesslike flexibility, foxy cleverness, and a mutual taking advantage of each other."[110] Like Meinecke and in accordance with modernist doctrine on this question, Weber dated the divorce of intellect from politics from 1870, not from the Revolution of 1918. He also left room for the typically accommodationist hope that the intellectual aristocracy might yet be wedded to political democracy. But this was the faith of desperation, and there were few who shared it.

For many German academics, the disillusionment with the new politics led rather quickly to a passionate revulsion against all aspects of a vaguely defined modernity. A kind of self-pity turned often to hysteria and sometimes to hate. The instinctive dislike of factories and big cities could reach neurotic proportions. Even the normally moderate accommodationist Paul Natorp was so incensed at the "so-called 'culture' of our urban and industrial age" and at the "desert of stone which calls itself Berlin" that he seriously urged a total demolition of factories and big cities for the sake of the nation's social and emotional health: "Do not the very stones cry out? Tear down! Tear down!"[111] From this sort of passion, a rather short path led to the violence of orthodox attacks upon "the masses."

As the masses plod along the daily treadmill of their lives like slaves or automatons, soullessly, thoughtlessly, and mechanically, . . . all events in nature and in society appear shallowly mechanized to their technicized and routinized manner of thinking: Everything, they believe . . . is as mediocre and average as the mass products of the factory; everything is the same and can be distinguished only by number. There are, they think, no differences between races, peoples, and states, no ranks of talent and achievement, no superiority of one over the other; and where living standards are still different in fact, they seek—envious of nobility of birth, education, and culture—to create a fully equal plane.[112]

After reading paragraphs of this type from the pens of German university professors, one ceases to wonder at the degree to which German students of the Weimar period sided with the right-wing opposition to the Republic. During the 1920's antirepublican, chauvinist, Pan-German, and volkish sentiments became ever more pronounced among the students, while socialist or liberal ideas made very few converts.[113] Indeed, the students were soon in conflict with republican authorities. The immediate issue was whether Austrian anti-Semitic student corporations could be affiliated with the national German Students' League (*Deutsche Studentenschaft*), while "non-Aryan" but German-speaking Austrians were excluded. This question led to schisms within the German student organization. It also embarrassed the German governments to such an extent that they were forced to legislate the membership criteria to be used by the officially recognized students' leagues in their jurisdictions. Baden did this in 1925, Prussia between 1925 and 1927.[114] When the students refused to conform to the Prussian ministry's membership regulations, the national Students' League was denied official recognition in Prussia. Rival student formations of a more liberal cast never achieved large memberships. The whole idea of a nationally recognized representation of students thus collapsed, while right-wing extremism made further progress among the younger academic generations. The most remarkable aspect of the whole controversy was that university professors generally sided with the Pan-Germanist and racist elements among the students. Some of them professed to believe that the Students' League had really arisen primarily as a reaction against the "dislike and enmity shown to the whole academic world by the newly arisen powers [*neu emporkommende Gewalten*]."[115] The Corporation of German Universities accordingly expressed its sympathy and support for the national league during its conflict with the Prussian authorities.[116] Two years later, an academic spokesman described the Pan-German movement among the students as a hopeful sign of a possible future link between the German people and the German intelligentsia. He thought it unfortunate that this fine attempt to transcend narrow political parties and interests had been forced into opposition by unwarranted attacks from leftist parties and governments.[117]

In 1929, the National Socialists began a concerted drive for control of the German student organizations. They sought to wrest power from right-wing nationalist and volkish elements, and they achieved a victory by 1931.[118] Thus the Third Reich triumphed among the students two years before it captured the rest of the nation. This circumstance, like the poor showing of the republican parties among younger voters generally, must affect any considered judgment of German academic politics during the Weimar period. This is not to suggest an identity of views between orthodox academics, volkish enthusiasts and National Socialists. The students were younger, more activist, vaguely more "revolutionary" or "democratic," and certainly more muddle-headed than their professors. There was a class difference too. The old middle and lower middle classes, the chief consumers of fascist propaganda, were relatively well represented among the students, while the faculty identified more exclusively with the cultivated elite. In principle, the mandarins had as little love for rabble-rousing demagogues as they did for the parliamentarians and party leaders of democratic liberalism. Everything they said about geist and politics, they said as intellectuals, as spokesmen for the minority of the highly learned, not as representatives of industrial or agrarian interests and certainly not as conscious propagandists for the mass politics of National Socialism. To overlook that fact would be to misunderstand the whole purpose and tendency of the mandarin ideology.

Still, when all allowances have been made for subtle differences of intention, for varying levels of intellectual vulgarity, and for nuances of opinion based on differences of class and status, there remains a residual similarity between the views of professors and students at German universities. The "idealism" of the chauvinist and volkish movements accompanied the idealism of the mandarins like a slightly

distorted echo; the antimodernity of geist was shadowed by the antimodernity of the volk.[119] To insist that there was no connection between the two would be to say that teachers do not influence their
pupils. The mandarins would have been the last to accept such a
judgment.

The German professors certainly failed as educators, and the irony
is that they consistently displayed an immense faith in the efficacy
of cultivation. Their critiques of modern politics almost invariably
ended in a resolution to increase the moral impact of learning upon
public life. They called on education to strengthen the spiritual
sources of social cohesion which seemed to them their country's only
hope. "Materialism" and "utilitarianism" had torn the social fabric
of the nation; the traditions of idealistic learning would mend it
again, primarily by restoring geist to its proper place in German life.
"If youth should discover that all forms are secondary . . . that the
desired renewal of society must take place in the souls and attitudes
of men . . . then there might be a chance to transcend the present
. . . social warfare and to prepare the renewal of society . . . through
a reform of education." "A thoroughly changed type of education
must work . . . to create the irrational fundaments and forces of
communal life."[120]

This was the link between the crisis of mandarin politics and the
crises of "culture" and of wissenschaft, which were also much discussed in the German academic community between 1890 and 1932.
These larger crises grew out of the general conviction that geist had
become divorced from the new realities and that mandarin cultural
values were in danger of being ignored. The orthodox proposed to
solve this problem through a "spiritual revolution"; the accommodationists wanted to achieve some sort of compromise between modernity and tradition. There had to be a re-engagement of learning;
the only question was what form this re-engagement was to take.

5

THE ORIGINS OF THE CULTURAL CRISIS, 1890–1920

THE PROBLEM OF CULTURAL DECADENCE

Sometime around 1890, German academics began to express misgivings about the current condition of German learning and of German cultural life more generally. They spoke of a decline in the vitality of their intellectual traditions, a loss of meaning and relevance. They wondered whether they themselves were partly to blame for the shallowness of the age, the apparent separation of geist from politics, and the violence of the new social conflicts. They began to suspect that the universities had been neglecting their proper function of spiritual leadership, that mandarin culture had been forsaken by its guardians as well as by the rest of German society. These doubts continued to trouble the German academic community from the 1890's to the 1930's, reaching their greatest intensity during the early years of the Weimar period. By the 1920's, no German professor doubted that a profound "crisis of culture" was at hand.

It is very difficult to define or to describe this crisis. The historian can only try to understand what the mandarins themselves said and wrote on the subject, and much of that lacks clarity. Of course, there were the standard complaints about the decline of idealism and the rise of positivism and popular materialism. Georg Simmel spoke of the "mammonism" which was noticeable especially in the big cities. The modernist Theobald Ziegler emphasized the tremendous psychological impact of technological achievements. He was disturbed by a new "realism," which was often expressed in a particularly noisy and aggressive fashion in Wilhelmian Germany. The new realism led too easily to the blind worship of power and success, and it was accompanied by an exceedingly superficial identification of knowledge with practical results.[1]

The root of the trouble, of course, lay deeper. Somehow, the mandarins felt, there had been a decline in intellectual creativity. Outward progress had been accompanied by an inner helplessness and lack of vitality. The psychologist William Stern argued that only a firm and integral weltanschauung could have given his countrymen the strength to master the new technology without losing their humanity.[2] The search for weltanschauung had been neglected during the nineteenth century, and the result was the painful shallowness, the lack of direction, and the anxiety of *fin de siècle* civilization. The popular philosopher Rudolf Eucken lamented "a sinking of life into the profane, the secular, the vulgar. And all that amidst remarkable progress at the periphery of life, amidst an amazing virtuosity in technical achievements . . . We find ourselves involved in a serious intellectual and spiritual crisis, which we are unable to master."[3] Eucken described a cult of work in which the soul was neglected, a pursuit of superficial pleasure which revealed men's inner uncertainty. Modern Germans, he said, were careful research workers but not independent thinkers, conscientious officials but not creative

statesmen, "capable workers but shallow men."[4] They had forgotten
how to distinguish fundamental values from trivial ones; they had
lost touch with that "invisible world" which could give life some
meaning. They were confused; they felt powerless and aimless. Because they lacked the inner concentration necessary to unify and to
direct their experiences and strivings, they had become the victims
of mean instincts and the slaves of their own machines.

Some of these problems, said Eucken, were timeless ones; but they
had been aggravated by industrial technology and by the appearance
of the "social question." People no longer understood the meaning
of their work, even though they made a fetish of it. "Work emancipated itself from man; it formed huge complexes, which increasingly
generated their own forces and followed their own laws. Thus there
arose a sharp conflict between work and soul." "The centrifugal tendencies predominate over the centripetal ones, and all those evils
appear which are brought about by man's being overcome by his
work . . . No fixed goals guide our striving, no simple ideas stand
out from the chaos and raise us above its turmoils and doubts." Of
course, the World War and the Revolution of 1918 made matters
worse. "We thought we had a rich heritage of culture, and now all
our traditions are shaken, and the inherited fundaments of our manner of life are tottering."[5]

In the field of higher education itself, German professors found a
whole series of developments which seemed to them symptoms or
aspects of the general decadence. To begin with, they felt that too
many students were graduating from secondary schools and going on
to the universities, many of them neither talented nor well enough
prepared to profit from the academic experience. Karl Jaspers
charged that all standards had been sacrificed in an effort to accom-
modate a mass of mediocre minds. The philologist Hermann Paul
said that there was too much rote learning, too much thoughtless
cramming for examinations even in the secondary schools. The
Abitur had become primarily a test of memory. When the students
arrived at the university, they were neither trained nor inclined to
do independent work. They signed up for the required lectures without actually attending them. After a traditional period of dissipation,

they repeated the senseless cramming, this time to pass the state examinations and thus to move into the secure positions which had been the real object of their labors from the beginning. Theobald Ziegler seconded Paul's gloomy report and went on to complain that social snobbery and job-hunting were the main causes of the enrollment boom in the secondary schools. Karl Weinhold thought that the students had lost that youthful idealism which had formerly caused them to study philosophy and the classics purely for their own sake. Werner Jaeger, finally, felt that the former eminence of German learning had been based upon the dedicated humanism of a small elite. The attempt to extend the traditional education to ever larger numbers, he argued, was bound to have unfortunate consequences: "Higher education [*Bildung*] has become an article of mass consumption, cheap and bad . . . The mass as such is uncritical and fanatic."[6]

The main conclusion to be drawn from these observations, according to the mandarins, was that German learning had entered what might be described as a second Halle era. A vulgar practicality predominated over the "free" search for ideal truths.[7] Outwardly, the universities had never been more prosperous. Seminars and research institutes were growing, and the careful work of German scientists, philologists, and historians was internationally renowned. But almost no one was really satisfied with these achievements. Instead there was general agreement that in scholarship as in other fields, specialization had led to a neglect of essentials. Erich Marcks saw "the same change" at the University of Heidelberg "which our life in general and the learning of these decades in particular shows us everywhere: division of labor . . . victories of realism, the achievements broader and more sure, the average more even and probably also higher than formerly." But he wondered what had become of "the old universalism, the tendency toward the inclusive, the relevance of the individual discipline . . . to the vital problems of the fatherland and of the age, the connectedness of learned work with the . . . personal life of the individual."[8]

Again and again, the mandarins lamented the predominance of specialization and "positivism" in wissenschaft. Apparently these terms were intended to describe a considerable range of sins. The educationist Eduard Spranger dated the positivist wave from about 1840 and spoke of the transformation of "the metaphysical totality of learning [*metaphysiche Gesamtwissenschaft*]" into a "sum of specialized disciplines." He observed a growing differentiation between wissenschaft and occupational training and an equally serious rift between learning and weltanschauung. Jaspers took note of the same phenomenon. German academics felt a sense of guilt, he wrote, because they had failed as "bearers of tradition" in losing sight of "the conceptual world of metaphysics." "The university is impoverished," he said, "when there is only philology and no more philosophy; only technical practice, no more theory; endless facts and no ideas." Meinecke described a kind of "positivism" in German philology in the 1880's, which entailed much detailed work on safe texts and a lack of attention for more difficult and unexplored fields. He also objected to the type of analysis which reminded him of a rose being plucked apart: "Now the leaves will go on lying there, and they will not grow back together again." The philosopher Max Scheler, finally, scoffed at the "one-sided occupationalism" of his contemporaries and at a specialization "which has systematically given up all agreement in questions of purpose as distinct from all questions of technique." He felt that German higher education was no longer producing "men of mind [*geistige Personen*], who affect the whole of the nation's life as models and leaders." The university, he said, had degenerated into a professional school.[9]

Those who asserted that there had been a decline in the nation's intellectual and cultural life often went on to announce that a revival was already under way. This was quite natural, since the widespread criticism of specialization and of positivism could itself be interpreted as the beginning of a vaguely antipositivist revitalization movement. Thus Eucken was convinced as early as 1904 that "the age of specialization . . . fortunately lies behind us." In 1921, he concluded that the cultural crisis, which had been aggravated by war and revolution, "must lead either to a destruction or to an elevation of man's state," and in the same year he wrote the following retrospective description of the 1890's. "At that time there was a reversal in literary life: thoughtless [geistlos] and superficial positivism had played out its role; a stronger tendency of the age toward the subjective [Wendung zum Subjekt] was apparent."[10] Meinecke's memoirs contain a similar passage: "In all of Germany, something new could be felt around 1890, not only politically but also culturally . . . a new and deeper longing for the genuine and true but also a new awareness of the problematical fragmentation [zerrissene Problematik] of modern life awoke and tried to dive down again from its civilized surface into the now eerie, now tempting depths."[11]

The moods expressed in these passages were prevalent outside the German academic community as well. Indeed, the cultural malaise of the fin de siècle was an international phenomenon, or at least a European one. Intellectuals in France and elsewhere agonized over the problem of decadence, and perhaps their fears were not altogether different from those of their German colleagues.[12] But the general anxiety was certainly most intense in Germany. Above all, the Germans went further than anyone else in tracing the cultural problems of the day to the shortcomings of higher education and to the decline of learning itself. The revulsion against positivism and against the Enlightenment was most pronounced in Germany, where neither positivism nor the Enlightenment had ever been popular. Finally, it was especially characteristic of the German cultural critics that all their concerns were focused upon the newly problematical relationship between individual cultivation and modern civilization. Both Burckhardt and Nietzsche addressed themselves to this problem. Nietzsche was particularly critical of German higher education.[13] He disliked the official role which the universities had come to play, their subservience to the bureaucracy and their excessive nationalism. He also felt that learning was being corrupted by the influx of bourgeois mediocrity in search of secure careers. He was convinced that only a small elite was capable of humanistic cultivation in its original sense, and he could not abide the philistine thoughtlessness which made the new specialist in "objective" wissenschaft a caricature of the cultivated man. Paul de Lagarde and Julius Langbehn, popular pamphleteers of cultural despair, fulminated against the sterility of the routinized gymnasium curriculum. The whole youth movement was in part a revolt against the stifling authoritarianism of the schools. Reformers of all shades of opinion contrasted the mechanical and conventional quality of Wilhelmian higher education with the ideals of Pestalozzi and Humboldt.[14]

There was thus a great deal of cultural criticism, and much of it dealt with the problems of pedagogy and learning. The difficulty is and was that most of this criticism was so very ambiguous. One can evoke its objections in summary fashion by using such terms as philistine, bourgeois, sterile, mechanical, and modern civilization. These words were then and are now so loaded as to make precise definitions and arguments seem unnecessary. But how exactly did this sterility come about, and what did it consist of? Who were the philistines, and what was bourgeois? Did machines make men's minds mechanical? What were the attributes and causes of "modern civilization"? Above all, what was to be done to improve the situation?

The German cultural critics varied widely in their answers to these questions, if and when they bothered to raise them at all. And yet there was something like a single theory of decadence, which transcended very important individual differences of opinion. The very vagueness of the vocabulary in which the general disenchantment was expressed could serve to produce the appearance of agreement. Terms may become fashionable because they permit their users to regard each other as allies before having fully understood one another. "Crisis" and "civilization" are good examples, and so is "alienation." A recent study of speeches at German gymnasiums during the Wilhelmian period demonstrates how thoroughly the phrases and attitudes of university professors were absorbed by the mass of cultivated Germans.[15] It is the pervasiveness of these moods which suggests a single theory of decadence. The logical obscurities of that theory were not accidental. Like the confusions inherent in the "idealistic" attack upon politics, they reflect the actual ambiguities in the situation and ideology of the mandarin caste.

More specifically, there were three series of questions which could be raised about the German academics' account of cultural decline and revitalization, one on which they achieved a vague agreement, a second which divided them along predictable lines, and a third with which they never dealt conclusively at all. The first series concerns chronology: when did the decline end and the revival begin? In this field, a consensus was reached, although not a very precise one. Most academics agreed that the curve of cultural vitality had reached its lowest point sometime between 1850 and 1890, and that the upturn had begun around 1880 or 1890. Beyond that, they used the word crisis to imply a simultaneous presence or intersection of decline and revival, a crucial period of decision. The frequency of their references to such a crisis made it appear that the agony of decision persisted and even grew in intensity from the 1890's to the end of the Weimar period.

The second group of questions involved the assigning of various intellectual movements either to the decline or to the revival. Were the Social Democrats and their ideas the chief obstacles in the path of the revitalization movement, or was the place-seeking and the social callousness of the "cultivated" an even more serious handicap? Were the nationalist, Pan-German, and volkish movements of the Wilhelmian period a part of the revival or just another sign of political vulgarity and spiritual shallowness? Were Henrik Ibsen, August Strindberg, Emile Zola, and Gerhart Hauptmann the leaders of "a great war of liberation" against "bourgeois dullness, prudery, and hypocrisy," as Werner Weisbach thought;[16] or was "naturalism" a companion of that positivism which most mandarins abhorred? Was the "spirit of 1914" a possible source of salvation in the cultural field as well as in politics, or was the supposed community of the war years simply another disheartening example of intellectual conformity and mass fanaticism? To quote from a 1919 essay by Ernst Troeltsch,

> was that which the World War brought to the surface really the German spirit? Is there such a thing in the first place, or has it not been totally broken down and derailed by modern capitalist-industrialist developments? What are the educational tasks and goals which grow out of the collapse? To what extent can we proceed on the basis of the criticisms and warnings which awoke among us long before the war? . . . [These questions]

seem to us like a crisis which has sprung from our own inner development, like a settling of accounts with the Bismarckian age and a return to traditions which were interspersed or at least mixed with wholly new or foreign elements.[17]

In a sense, Troeltsch answered his own questions, and his phrasing clearly implied the modernist attitude toward the World War and toward post-1870 Germany in general. Indeed, something very similar can be said about all the questions in this group: most university professors answered them along fairly conventional and therefore predictable lines. The orthodox favored the nationalist movements and did not object to the Wilhelmian period as a whole. The accommodationists looked farther back. As one moves toward the radical modernist end of the opinion spectrum, one finds an increasing suspicion of Nietzsche and, more especially, of his simplifiers and distorters. But one has to travel pretty far in that direction before encountering the identification of Hauptmann with the revival.

This brings up a third group of questions, the most difficult and the most important of the three. What were the causes of cultural decadence, and in what way was it related to technological change? How did the supposed decline look from the point of view of the individual intellectual, and what did it mean to him? What was the nature of "culture," and what exactly was involved in its stagnation? Why and how had the German elite lost the ability to "affect the whole of the nation's life as models and leaders"? These questions were very difficult to answer, partly because they demanded a distinction between the purely intellectual aspects of the postulated decline and its socio-economic roots or correlates. Nothing like a thorough and generally accepted solution of these problems was ever achieved on either of the two wings of the academic community. But there were some outstanding individual efforts, which demonstrated the range of possible approaches. Four specific examples come to mind.

In an essay published in 1911, Werner Sombart proposed to investigate the relationship between "technology and culture."[18] He urged that the dogmatic controversy over Marx's theories on this subject be superseded by genuinely empirical investigations, and he presented a smattering of evidence to show that certain technological advances had clearly affected cultural developments, at least in the sense that they had created new possibilities and provided new tools. From this sensible base, he then moved toward a much more general discussion of modern culture and technology. His prize examples dealt with contemporary music.[19] He thought it impossible to imagine that Mozart's or Beethoven's works could have been composed in the twentieth-century environment. No, he said, our own age can only produce a "loveless" kind of music, which is itself no more than just technique. Among the lower classes, a shallow and internationalized type of street music, which is made "mechanically," has replaced the folk song, which grew "organically." The victorious two-step or "Yankee Doodle," so typical of the technological spirit of America, has made the dance machinelike. The wealth produced by technological progress provides support for an unprecedentedly large number of musicians, many of them of low quality. Modern communications facilities inevitably produce an international, rather than indigenous, style, along with a general leveling of tastes. The producers of modern musical entertainment naturally act on capitalist principles, and they have a wealth of technology at their command. We cannot imagine Haydn played in a huge and brilliantly lit auditorium, since his works were written for intimate gatherings in small candlelit rooms. Modern man, in his haste, is continually exposed to artificially harsh and violent sensations. Only a noisy and sensational type of music can reach him. Finally, the gramophone, along with big entertainment halls and popular dance bands, has provided the technological basis for the democratization of musical styles, and modern music is mass music.

The young sociologist Leopold von Wiese was primarily concerned with the place of the creative individual in modern society. In 1917 he described the intellectuals of his time as men resigned to loneliness and powerlessness in the face of anonymous social forces beyond their control. "With a certain melancholy, they sense themselves to be fragments, which can never achieve a satisfying unity."[20] In the "communal" literature of the World War, they revealed their loneliness and their longing to escape from their isolation. Liberated for good or ill from the naive certainties and social bonds of the Middle Ages, they must endure what their own learning has taught them: that they are tiny and helpless fragments vis-à-vis the evolutionary chain, the increasingly complex and yet unsatisfying accumulation of knowledge, and the ever more inexorable logic of impersonal processes in economic and social life.

In a lecture delivered on April 7, 1918, Wiese discussed the relationship between "the writer and the state." He described modern intellectuals as the antagonists and then the successors of the ancient priestly caste. Early allies of the secular state against the tyranny of an organized church, the intellectuals soon discovered that concentrated political power is even more dangerous to their independence than institutionalized religion. The democratization of society does not reduce this threat. On the contrary, it increases the demand for the writer's services in the molding of public opinion. The true intellectual, however, will resist these pressures; for the social and economic categories of organized public life seem to him meaningless abstractions.

> Certainly I am an aristocrat, but I am a democrat and a socialist at the same time, only of a wholly different kind than that which corresponds to your political systems.

> Sometimes even poets are highly political. But when? During wars of liberation and popular revolution, in countries with a young culture, in newly created states, where everything is still in the stage of hopeful germination, not yet dissected through laborious division of labor and technical routine; among nations in which poets and scholars, statesmen and party leaders, teachers and political deputies are united in the person of the writer, who arises . . . from among the peasant population. As soon as the social rigidification begins, as soon as politics becomes a business or a specialized occupation, the poets are silent, either stepping aside or fighting against the leviathan.[21]

From the turn of the century to his death in 1918, Georg Simmel brought out a whole series of essays under such titles as "Personal and Objective [*sachliche*] Culture," "The Concept and Tragedy of Culture," "The Crisis of Culture," and "The Conflict of Modern Culture."[22] He invariably began his argument by positing the neo-Idealist distinction between "subjective geist" or "subjective culture" on the one hand, and "objective geist" or "objective culture" on the other. He identified subjective culture with the notion of individual cultivation, the purely personal harmony of knowledge, feeling, and aspiration in the fully developed individual. His subjective geist stood for the creative mind and spirit of the individual or, in summation, of whole groups of intellectuals or of mankind in general. Objective geist or objective culture, by contrast, implied the products of subjective geist, the forms in which it expressed itself, the fruit of man's mental and physical labors.

Given these distinctions, which can be traced to Fichte and to Hegel, one can almost anticipate what Simmel had to say about the crisis of modern culture. The unity of subjective geist leads to the diversity of objective geist. Objective geist can never do full justice to the richness of an individual's immediate experience. Yet as the realm of objective culture continues to grow, its complexities increasingly defy the individual's comprehension. There is an estrangement too, a sense of tension and conflict. In a way, objective culture freezes or ossifies the dynamic forces which create it, and the elements of objective culture acquire their own inner logic and necessity. Man feels oppressed by theories, laws, and conditions he has created; they are not as fluid and changeable as his spirit; he does not recognize them as his creatures; they confront him as alien and objective necessities, limitations upon his subjective preferences. Subjective culture implies freedom of self-expression and a complete and integrated understanding of the world; the growth of objective culture appears to make both self-expression and understanding more difficult. Books formerly written, factories already built, economic relationships newly discovered, and laws once made become strangers to subjective geist and obstacles to its creativity. Language as an aspect of objective geist becomes ever more complex. Subjective verbal culture, the personal mastery of words, cannot keep step.

Thus harmonious individual cultivation becomes ever more difficult; the accumulations of the past oppress the present; complexity does not return to oneness; means overwhelm ends; and sensitive souls acquire an instinctive hatred of objects—and of libraries. Modern specialization and division of labor creates an ever greater gap between the subjective geist of the individual producer or consumer and the objective reality of goods produced, so that technological progress deepens the "conflict of modern culture." In short, Simmel's theory of the crisis turned the mandarin conception of self-cultivation into an elaborate allegory of spiritual alienation and impotence.

Late in 1918, Alfred Weber wrote an article in which he asked why the "intellectual and spiritual leaders" were less influential in Germany in his own day than they had been in the early nineteenth century.[23] He decided that part of the answer lay in the fact that modern intellectuals discussed specific questions and undertook partial analyses of fairly technical problems, without being able to provide integral solutions or to deal with the important issues of life as totalities. He traced this self-restriction of modern scholars to the general structure of modern existence, making the usual references to mechanization, specializaton, fragmentation, and the like. It puzzled him, however, that during the war, the French and English had apparently responded more enthusiastically to their ideological leaders than the Germans. How was that to be explained? The fault, he said, lay only partly with Germany's practical men of affairs and their lack of interest in questions of principle. The deeper source of the difficulty, ironically enough, was the greater profundity of the German mind: Weber argued that the Germans had felt the problematical aspects of modern civilization more deeply than other peoples.

To make this clear, he drew on a distinction which had already had a considerable career in German social and cultural philosophy. In 1887, it had reappeared in Ferdinand Tönnies' *Community and Society,* and thereafter it had played an important role in the writings of Julius Langbehn and especially in Oswald Spengler's doctrines. This was the differentiation between culture and civilization.

Spengler had managed to apply most of the current criticisms of modernity to "civilization," which he described as an end product in the decline of true culture. Without commenting extensively upon this theory, Weber thought it characteristic of the German intellectuals that they had confronted the Western sense of civilization with their own ideal of culture. In this way, they had expressed their profound uneasiness over some of the conditions and implications of modern mass existence, whether in politics or in the cultural field. Unfortunately, to continue with Weber, they had not been able to supplement their valid criticisms of Western practices and traditions with clear proposals for workable alternatives. As a result, their partial analyses had only produced uneasiness and confusion. At bottom, German intellectuals had not really solved the problem posed by the dichotomy of civilization and culture, and their failure in this respect had reduced their influence upon the German people.

Sombart, Simmel, Wiese, and Alfred Weber were unusually talented individuals. Simmel, Wiese, and Weber stood with the radical modernists, the most creative segment of the mandarin community. Sombart was rapidly changing his position around 1911; but even after 1914, he was separated from the rank and file of the orthodox majority by his extraordinary mental agility. Nevertheless, none of these four men really succeeded in dispelling some of the confusions which were generally characteristic of the mandarins' arguments in this area. Of the four, Simmel was certainly most coherent and systematic in stating his case. He described the estrangement between mind and its creatures; but he did not ask himself how this eternal dilemma of the sorcerer's apprentice had become particularly acute in recent times. He seemed to identify intellectual specialization with the technological division of labor, and he thus implied two very important connections, which he nonetheless failed to explore. One of these related the socio-enonomic facts of modernity to its intellectual causes or attributes; the other linked the intellectual's private problems of creativity and certainty to the cultural situation of modern society in general.

Like Simmel and Weber, Wiese saw the problem of the contemporary intellectual partly as one of thwarted creativity. But he also drew upon the conventional model of social disintegration to suggest that the productive poet needed roots. The alienation of the intellectual from his community was thus conceptually merged with his theoretical disengagement, his inability to make "integral" assertions about the fundamental problems of the spirit. What did Wiese's poet really regret: a failure of creativity, a loss of certainty, or a decline of his spiritual influence?

Sombart made an explicit attempt to analyze the relationship between technological and cultural change; but he achieved most of his effect by way of a rather shoddy analogy between machines and mechanical dancing. His evocative images begin to seem unconvincing as soon as one seriously wonders how electric light interferes with Haydn, and whether Haydn's contemporaries shared Sombart's reverence for Haydn—or for candlelight. If Sombart meant to say that average moderns prefer bowling to poetry, one could hardly quarrel with him. But his failure seriously to consider the attitudes and the social makeup of Mozart's audiences stamps him a bad sociologist, while the offense he publicly takes at the "low" culture of others identifies him as a mandarin.

The fact is that Sombart and many of his colleagues wrote with the unconscious arrogance of men who had until recently been thoroughly accustomed to setting the cultural standards of their nation. They behaved as if "the masses" were truly preventing them from privately listening to Haydn, from cultivating their own "subjective geist." In a curious way, the whole theory of cultural decadence was a projection of the intellectual's personal fears and doubts upon the rest of society. The feeling was that individual cultivation had become more difficult than formerly. This led to a vague dissatisfaction of the spirit. The mandarin intellectual lamented a sense of intellectual impotence. He did not know whether it was creativity or certainty he sought. He suspected that there was some relationship between his spiritual malaise and his changed relationship to society, as indeed there was. But instead of honestly exploring the complexities of the relationship, he gravitated toward primitive analogies between "community" and moral certainty, "society" and spiritual doubt. The tension between knowledge and cultivation became an antithesis between rational analysis and emotional commitment, while both were transformed into general characteristics of modern social life. Even the division of labor was treated as a secondary analogue of intellectual specialization, and the Marxist alienation of worker from product as an almost incidental extension of the estrangement between geist and its offspring.

The mandarins insisted upon a purely "idealistic" view of modern dilemmas. Even when they discussed factory work and its "meaning," they would not abandon the abstract language of cultivation. They never broke the pattern which allowed many of them to seek the ultimate solution of modern cultural problems in a spiritual revival, a reactivation of their own moral leadership. As a result, their complaints seemed almost irrelevant to the needs of ordinary men. The whole literature of decadence had a curiously self-centered air. It appeared an uncontrolled projection, a primarily personal escape from the psychological tensions of modern intellectual life. Wiese apparently understood the workings of this egocentricity; for he saw the wartime literature of community as the intellectuals' self-revelation and self-pity.

Alfred Weber got to the heart of the problem when he lamented the reduced impact of the German intellectuals upon their nation. His whole argument was based upon the traditional distinction between knowledge as wisdom and knowledge as merely technical analysis. Without this antithesis, the theory of cultural decadence would have to remain an enigma. The point is that the mandarins were never content to cultivate their own gardens. They thought of themselves as a priestly caste, and they meant to legislate ultimate values to a peasant population. That was their model; it has to be assumed, if any of their *fin de siècle* anxieties are to be understood. All of the logical flaws in their account of cultural decline seem to correct themselves, once this is clear. Technological change accelerated the dissolution of wisdom, because it made the achievement of intellectual "totality" more difficult. Intellectual specialization and the growth of "objective geist" had the same effect. The Yankee Doodle resembled a machine, because both seemed to evade the dictates of the sage. All modern developments seemed to strive in the same direction: the decline of Idealism and the entry of "the masses" into higher education, positivism and the threat to academic standards, realism in foreign policy and realism as an intellectual and literary orientation, popular materialism and scientific materialism.[24]

All these changes were summarily described in the antithesis between culture and civilization, the parallel in the cultural field to the socio-political distinction between community and society. The word crisis helped to cement the various emotional associations upon which the theory of decadence was based. It also expressed the mandarins' sense that a crucial decision had soon to be made. The consensus was that many university professors had themselves been temporarily seduced by narrowly practical conceptions of learning, by the immediately accessible advantages of routine specialization. The question was whether some sort of culture could yet be revived in the twentieth century and what direction the existing revitalization movement was to take. As may be imagined, modernist and orthodox academics differed in their answers to this question.

THE MODERNIST INITIATIVE

The accommodationists proposed to meet the problems of cultural decadence in three ways. They favored certain institutional reforms of the educational system; they wanted to adjust mandarin pedagogical theories to the requirements of the mass and machine age; and they tried to create a synthetic cultural ideal which would reflect their own traditions and yet be appropriate to the twentieth century.

One of the most prominent champions of accommodationist principles in education, curiously enough, was a man who began his career as a primary school teacher and did not become a university professor until he was sixty-six or sixty-seven years old in 1921. Georg Kerschensteiner taught in a primary school and at a gymnasium before he was made a School Inspector (*Schulrat*) in Munich in 1895.[25] In this capacity, he devoted most of his energies to a re-organization of the Munich vocational schools. His work in this sorely neglected field brought him a good deal of recognition and enabled him to play an active political role on the left wing of the liberal parties in Bavaria. In 1910, he visited the United States, where he read and was deeply impressed with John Dewey's *How We Think*. When his own theoretical writings began to appear after 1899, however, they were patently less influenced by Dewey than by contemporary neo-Idealism and by Kerschensteiner's practical experiences as a pedagogical reformer.[26] Indeed, one could describe his work as a mixture of common-sense proposals and neo-Idealist terminology, in which the theoretical element thickened progressively as the self-taught author's indebtedness to German academic philosophy increased.

Kerschensteiner's version of the cultural state doctrine was unusually democratic: "As soon as the state is or wishes to become a legal and cultural state, that is to say the most complete form of community we know . . . it must organize its educational institutions according to the principle of equal rights for all. The ideal and unquestionable right of the individual in respect to his education is to be educated according to his educability."[27] If this ideal was to be approached, there had to be some way of assessing a child's aptitudes and inclinations, and Kerschensteiner hoped that a new "descriptive" or "synthetic" psychology would provide the tools for such an undertaking.[28] He was less interested in intelligence tests than in the classification of youngsters according to certain personality types. Future teachers, for example, were to show an especially strong interest in individuals, rather than in theories. They were to be of exceptionally good character, "socially" motivated, and capable of that "sympathy" which "feels the pulse of life in the smallest as in the greatest things."[29] Above all, the distinction between the theoretically and the practically inclined was to play a characteristically large role in this typology. No wonder that Kerschensteiner found the old "analytical" psychology of little use!

His most important deviation from mandarin orthodoxy lay in his theory of cultivation, for he refused to admit that the classical gymnasium alone gave its students a "general education" (*Allgemeinbildung*), while all other schools could impart only unimportant technical skills. He doubted that Latin was necessarily the best vehicle for the training of young minds and characters, and he had even less sympathy for the fanatical advocates of a purely "German" curriculum. Anyone is cultivated, he said, who has achieved a certain unity of outlook, who is thoroughly trained and thoughtfully involved in his own sphere of activity: "Only an individual who finds himself through his work can, in the course of his development, become what one calls a truly cultivated man."[30]

Kerschensteiner's ideal educational system was richly and frankly variegated according to the abilities, the inclinations, and the chosen professions of the students. At the same time, there were to be no social barriers between the several branches of what came to be called the "differentiated Integral School" (*differenzierte Einheitsschule*).[31] All children were to go to a common basic school for four years. The branching off of distinctive curricular programs was to be deferred as long as possible. Transfers from one school type to another were to be made relatively easy, and a certain elective variety was to be available within every wing of the system. There was to be a nine-year gymnasium, divided after three years into two departments, one for languages and history and one for mathematics and the natural sciences. Both were to be further differentiated after another three years, the language branch being split into one segment for modern languages and one for Latin and Greek. Most important, the educational opportunities for primary school pupils were to be improved. Even those young people who had begun work as apprentices after graduating from primary school at the age of fourteen were to be freed from their obligations to their masters for several afternoons each week and given some advanced vocational training.

The vocational school program, of course, was Kerschensteiner's special interest, and it was originally in this field that he developed the concept of "working instruction" (*Arbeitsunterricht*). He argued that the course of training for the young apprentices should be neither too general nor too theoretical. He wanted to engage their attention and to appeal to their practical bent by building the learning process upon their active participation in work projects chosen in accordance with their own interests. He believed that they would benefit from the experience of cooperation; he advocated student self-government within certain limits; and he urged teachers to consider themselves members of a little working community. He was highly critical in any case of the passive and routine character of German classroom instruction. The drilling of teacher candidates in their future subjects was an especially painful example to him. As a result, he gradually enlarged his concept of "working instruction" to cover all forms of student participation in the teaching process. Working instruction came to mean something like "active" or "autonomous" learning, the opposite of authoritarian inculcation of information and of passive receptivity on the part of the student. The earlier association of manual labor with the term working instruction became less and less prominent. In exchange for it, Kerschensteiner adopted the neo-Idealist theory of objective and subjective geist. He began to write of the need for an active "experiencing" (*Erleben*) of the values inherent in the available "cultural goods" (*Kulturgüter*), so that the "potential energy" of these objectifications could be turned into the "kinetic energy" of cultivation.[32] He acknowledged his debt to Simmel.

Finally, to give his system a certain unity and to point up its social implications, Kerschensteiner generalized upon the ideal of "civic education" (*staatsbürgerliche Erziehung*). What he had in mind went considerably beyond the imparting of basic political information to young people who left the primary schools with little knowledge of their own society. He defined civic education broadly enough to include everything that would make students valuable citizens, including even their vocational skills. But his main concern was with a kind of moral education. While his pupils were engaged in their cooperative projects, he wanted to teach them certain attitudes toward their work, to overcome or to enlighten their naive "egotism," to make them realize "the dependence of the particular economic and social interests of . . . [their] professions upon the overall interests of their fellow citizens and of their fatherland."[33]

He believed that a fully developed personality would inevitably be a good citizen too, and it is clear that he considered "social orientation" (*soziale Gesinnung*) a necessary attribute of good patriots and of all good men. He expected to strengthen this quality in his students neither by lecturing them nor by having them read ethical or nationalistic tracts. Once again, he proposed to rely primarily upon the practical experience of the working community. "How extensively we are able to stimulate [the student's] interest beyond his occupational field depends upon how thoroughly we succeed in integrating his general intellectual training with his vocational interests, in making him see his own purposes and aims as substantial constituents of [society's purposes]."[34]

The state had the duty to educate everyone to be a good citizen. Kerschensteiner himself thought that his views might well be summarized in that way. His whole scheme was clearly designed to alleviate what the mandarins called "the social problem," and he was by no means the only modernist pedagogue who was motivated by this consideration. There was a very general initiative toward a reform of primary and secondary education which began even before 1890 and culminated during the early Weimar period.[35] Kerschensteiner was only one of several leaders of this movement; but unlike some of its more radical members, he was respected in university circles, and he expressed most of the movement's major objectives. At bottom, all the proposed innovations were designed to increase the educational opportunities for talented youngsters from the lower classes and to break down the caste system based upon the old monopoly position of the gymnasium. The reformers were convinced that the established distinction beween exclusively classical cultivation and "merely" practical training was outdated and socially harmful. They proposed to apply to all students the ideal of educating the whole man, insisting that total cultivation was to be achieved within the framework of a student's vocational training, rather than through an esoteric curriculum alone. The gymnasium itself, they said, had placed a one-sided emphasis upon the intellect. They wanted to affect their students' wills, not just their minds, and that is why they emphasized such things as "active" learning, "working instruction," civic education, student self-government, and the practical community of pupils and teachers. Above all, they were convinced that the requirements of the modern productive system could not simply be ignored. People had to be trained for the work they would actually have to perform, even if that meant an increased curricular emphasis upon "realistic" subjects and modern languages. There was only one way to "humanize" the machine age, and that was to accept the need for mechanics and to give some thought to their education.

Most of the reforming pedagogues were primary and secondary school teachers, rather than university professors, but the reformers did find a certain amount of theoretical support from the leading accommodationists within the academic community. The famous pathologist Rudolf Virchow, a consistently radical modernist, was quite indifferent to the arguments of the gymnasium enthusiasts.[36] He thought it a little odd that Latin rather than Greek had been chosen as the main vehicle of "humanist" education. But these accidents happened, and there was a time when Latin had a certain usefulness as an academic language and a professional preparation for lawyers and theologians. Now, however, it had become little more than an excuse for the wrong kind of teaching and learning. Virchow did not care very much what subjects were taught in the secondary schools, as long as students arrived at the university with the ability to observe and to think for themselves, and with their natural enthusiasm for learning still intact. He thought mathematics and the natural sciences excellent vehicles for the training of young minds, and he saw no reason to prefer the dead to the living languages. Beyond that, he simply seconded the demand of every German educational reformer for more active and autonomous learning and an end to the senseless drilling in the secondary schools.

Hermann Paul and Wilhelm von Christ wanted to introduce more seminars and small discussion groups at the universities themselves, to have some of the large and routine lecture series published in handbook form, and to give the students more opportunity to write essays and research papers of their own. Theobald Ziegler recommended general and especially philosophical lectures for nonspecialists. He also pointed out that a really profound study of any particular discipline was likely to reveal the interconnectedness of all knowledge and to provide its own cure for the narrowness usually associated with overspecialization. Alfred Weber added a word in favor of improved educational opportunities for children from poorer families, for he felt that the nation's fund of talent was not being fully exploited.[37]

The educator Rudolf Lehmann, finally, restated the modernist position on education in a 1908 article, which opened with the following proposition: "The progress of a people rests upon the general dissemination of its cultural goods. What is initially only the property of a ruling class, a privileged minority, becomes, through schooling, the general property of all the 'cultivated' members of the people." Lehmann acknowledged that it was not easy to combine breadth with depth in education and that only a very talented teacher could raise his pupils above the broad average in knowledge and understanding. The state, he said, was chiefly interested in an even spread of basic skills, whereas a learned minority strove for the "highest unfolding of the intellectual and spiritual powers of man." This could lead to friction and had in fact caused a good deal of social resentment, for the routinization of "cultivation" in the classical gymnasium had become increasingly inappropriate for a changing society. "The division between the people and the cultivated, the general sickness in the social body of European nations since the days of humanism, sharpened into an unnatural separation of the relatively few classically cultivated from the large majority not only of the lower classes but also of the productive bourgeoisie." The rivalry between the gymnasium and the modern secondary schools assumed the character of a class war: "In reality, the ruling class fought consciously or unconsciously for the exclusiveness of its education and thereby of its position in cultural life vis-à-vis the masses."[38] A democratic movement in education reached even the primary schools, and there were demands for improvements in teacher training and for the establishment of popular academies and university extension programs.

Lehmann argued that these pressures were inevitable and, on the whole, justifiable. He also felt that the heated controversy over what subjects were to be emphasized in the secondary schools was rather pointless. "Whether a people places more emphasis upon the forming of the character [*Charakterbildung*] or upon intellectual training, upon physical or only upon mental education—this matters more than the question: Greek or English? In short, it is more the spirit than the subject matter upon which the unity of the school system and of education generally rests." The study of the classics and of history should certainly not be neglected, Lehmann continued, and the aesthetic cultural ideals of the gymnasium deserved a continuing place in the German educational system. "On the other hand, there rises the inexorable necessity of modern life, which sternly demands an insight into the . . . laws of nature and of the social order . . . [How else can one hope to understand modern life], not to mention acquiring, somehow and somewhere, a formative influence upon it?"[39]

The modernist initiative achieved its greatest force and coherence during the early Weimar period. Immediately after the Revolution of 1918, the reformers found their proposals emphatically seconded by the victorious political left. It seemed for a short time as if innovations even more radical than their own might actually be enforced by the new governments. In Prussia, Haenisch and Becker planned to reorganize not only the primary and secondary schools but also the university faculties themselves. Attacks upon the existing academic system came from all sides; occasionally, even some of the younger professors chimed in. Thus Kurt Wolzendorff argued that "the aim of any reform of the universities is apparent from a critical recognition of what the situation has been up to now: a system of self-government made up of estates and guilds had closed itself off against new blood from below . . . The task is therefore to break up the old system and to allow a truly free play of forces to develop by organizing a form of self-government regulated by the general interest."[40] Haenisch, Becker, and Wolzendorff meant to bridge the gap which had come to separate the universities and the learned elite from the rest of the people.[41] They invoked the memory of 1848, for they wanted the academic community to become once again as actively involved in the life of the nation and as responsive to the aspirations of all Germans as it had been in the days of the Frankfurt Parliament. Leopold von Wiese was interested in the new people's universities and popular academies, because he felt that they would establish ties between workers and intellectuals. For the same reason, he wanted to work through active discussion groups and small "working communities," which would affect attitudes and hearts as well as minds, especially if the subject matter was not too esoteric. "All popular education [*Volksbildung*] must stem from the true needs of simple human beings. In this sense everything that is not true to reality, all mysticism, and all overly enthusiastic ideology is to be rejected. A down-to-earth quality [*Erdverbundenheit*], the connection with the nonacademic life of human beings, must be maintained. No dualistic principle, no split between the interior and exterior [form of experience] must be allowed to arise. . . Popular education must produce the strength for a new community which stands above class differences."[42]

At the National School Conference of 1920, Paul Natorp used the term *genossenschaftlich* (cooperative, communal, comradely) to describe a plan for "communal education as the basis for the reconstruction of the nation and of humanity."[43] In some respects, his organizational scheme was a fairly conventional variation upon the model of the differentiated integral school, for he advocated a common kindergarten, a six-year basic school, and a good deal of elective diversification within the various institutions of secondary education. He also supported the people's universities. He urged a balance between manual and intellectual training; he warned against over-emphasizing humanist scholarship at the expense of modern and technical subjects; and he made the inevitable remarks about the necessity of forming the student's whole character in the context of the working community.

More noteworthy than these standard examples of modernist pedagogy was Natorp's recommendation that German education, along with the nation's economic and political life, be reorganized around small, socially mixed, and preferably semirural "communities." The purpose of this scheme, according to its author, was to cure the inner sickness of German culture and society by reintegrating mental and spiritual activity with materially productive work, from which it had unhappily been divorced. Natorp believed that both partners in the re-established union would benefit. Work would recover some meaning, and intellectual activity, even language itself, would draw vital nourishment from its roots in the concrete realities of productive work and communal life. There would be no education without cooperative labor for the common maintenance, and the gulf between intellectual and manual workers would simply disappear. In each social unit, the individual would have ample opportunity to develop his particular capabilities through education and experience, and those who were destined for intellectual leadership would easily distinguish themselves among their comrades. The close and personal intermingling of a continually renewed aristocracy of natural talent with the other members of the productive group would benefit leaders and followers alike. No longer would a large and unhappy majority of proletarians be left without guidance or support. They would naturally follow the advice of their most talented fellows and deputies, who in turn would understand the group life in which they participated. The political and cultural problems of the nation would be resolved in a federally organized "community of productive work," a pyramid of working cooperatives, within which the dangerous anonymity of modern social life would cease to be a problem.

Natorp was something of a visionary and a religious mystic, but when he described his mandarin utopia, he was only giving exaggerated expression to what many of his colleagues also felt. Indeed, there was always an element of illusion and wishful thinking in modernist theory, and sometimes a bit of obscurantism as well. Thus Jonas Cohn, who considered a "social orientation" (*soziale Gesinnung*) the goal of popular education, gave this account of his objectives. "Social orientation must be a permanent attribute of the soul . . . directed . . . toward the inclusive totality [*das Ganze*] of the community . . . so mighty that it procures precedence for this inclusive totality over one's own advantage, over the advantage of other single individuals as well as of subordinate communities." "If a social organization of the economy is to become fruitful, then work must find its honor in the circumstance that it is a service to the totality." "As soon and insofar as the economy is run for the benefit of the totality, a strike is a crime."[44]

In a similar vein, Alfred Vierkandt advocated "social pedagogy" (*Sozialpädagogik*) in order to "ethicize" modern politics. He thought it necessary to cultivate an "occupational ethic," "because of the great power of occupational organizations and because of the dangers of an egotistical misuse of power . . . because of the coldness and indifference with which large segments of the population today face their work and because of the inner impoverishment which is connected with this."[45]

Nevertheless, it would be wrong to believe that the accommodationists were primarily interested in forging weapons against the unions and the Social Democrats. Most of them, and that includes Vierkandt himself, preached the spirit of community to all classes and declared themselves anxious to remove every form of caste privilege and sentiment from the universities and from the educational system as a whole. Meinecke once argued that the class antagonisms which troubled his country could be traced to a certain narrowness in the cultural ideology of the old ruling elites.[46] Formerly, he said, German Idealism had not been a class philosophy. Its greatest early representatives had been men of large and liberal views. Even in the 1870's, its socially ameliorative tendencies had come to expression in Schmoller's and Brentano's notion of social policy. In the meantime, however, "fully and harmonically developed human beings" had become rarities among upper-class Germans. Instead, one encountered only "occupational men, specialists, and functionaries," and "all the complaints that we have only civilization, but little true culture, are based on this fact." Of course, Meinecke also reproached the proletariat for its sins against idealism. But the modernists' conception of the social crisis certainly covered a good deal more than the rise of the working class movement. Vierkandt spoke of using civic and even moral instruction to overcome the social and cultural "dissolution" of the nineteenth century, and he proposed to accomplish this by guiding the students toward a "consciousness of values" and an integral weltanschauung.[47]

This brings up the most difficult and the most important aspect of the modernists' initiative, which was their effort to solve the problem of cultural decadence by devising and disseminating a new set of cultural ideals. When the accommodationists emphasized the training of the student's whole character and orientation, they were partly motivated by a desire to counteract the overly scholarly, passive, and perhaps esoteric nature of secondary school education, especially in the gymnasium. Vierkandt, for example, came back again and again to the idea that the young people—and their mentors—should be actively and deeply interested in their contemporary environment, and that their studies should bear some relation to it.[48] He talked about a balance between the active and the contemplative life; but he clearly had something else in mind as well. He said that teachers had too often been no more than second-rate scholars, and he urged that special chairs for pedagogy be established within the faculties of philosophy at all universities.[49] The purpose of these new professorships, however, was not to be the study of educational psychology, of the learning process, or of teaching methods. Instead, attention was to be directed to the relationship between education and "culture," meaning cultural norms above all. Moreover, the chair for pedagogy was to be assigned the place that the philosophers had held during the early nineteenth century; it was to be considered the center and heart of the arts faculty. Presumably, university life would then be strongly influenced by the official representative of the ties between learning and culture. The search for values and for weltanschauung could begin, and that would certainly help to involve the academic community once again in the life of the nation.

Max Scheler said the same thing even more bluntly. He charged that ever since the later nineteenth century, the universities had fulfilled only a part of their proper function.[50] They had concentrated on the routine transmission of an inherited body of knowledge, on the advanced vocational training of civil servants and professional men, and on the continuation of methodical research in highly specialized disciplines. In the meantime, they had neglected their duty of making knowledge and cultural traditions accessible to all classes of the population; they had turned out specialists and technicians rather than well-rounded human beings; the professors had not been personal models to their charges. Above all, German learning had failed to draw any cultural values from its increasing fund of accumulated information. The task of "synthesis" (*Synthese*), of combining the scattered results of compartmentalized research into a meaningful whole, had been left to enterprising publishers, who were willing to paste heterogeneous elements together, or to a few talented but not always responsible laymen such as Nietzsche and Houston Stewart Chamberlain. Thus the universities were partly to blame for the unsatisfactory state of German cultural life. Scheler proposed to remedy the situation by creating two new types of academic institutions at the side of the old universities. The people's universities were to take over the job of disseminating knowledge in a meaningful way, and a new group of academies were to be staffed with leading intellectuals from various disciplines who were especially suited for the task of "synthesis." Scheler actually demanded that research professors as well as students be asked to attend some of the lectures at the new academies, which were to be attached to existing universities. In that way, learning might again become meaningful for the present, and the nation would no longer be left without cultural guidance.

It should be noticed that the concept of synthesis bore no close logical relationship to the rest of the modernist system. Thus the only ties between the ideas of working instruction and synthesis lay in the new emphasis upon pedagogy and the common ideal of forming the student's whole character. For this reason, one can account for the notion of synthesis only in terms of the mandarins' traditional commitment to morally meaningful knowledge, knowledge which could create spiritual nobility through an integral cultivation of the personality. In any case, the accommodationists certainly succeeded in creating the impression that synthesis was a necessary part of their reforming initiative, the part, moreover, which was most likely to solve the problem of cultural decadence. Becker gave his official sanction to the idea that the new pedagogy and the increased effort at synthesis would repair the damage done by the excesses of specialization at the universities.[51] Finally, even Konrad Haenisch, a Minister of Culture and a Social Democrat, supported the synthesis movement and described it as an integral part of his program:

> But if . . . out of the new academic generation, the great personal leaders are to arise whom the German people, having suffered for decades from the plight of mechanism and materialism, need more sorely in these most difficult times in our history than ever before, if our suffering people's recovery is to come from the inside, out of the German spirit and the German soul, from German art and German learning, if in our spiritual life not only the intellectual but also the irrational is to receive its due, then the barriers will have to be broken which presently separate the universities and the people . . . Then our universities, which have given us largely hardworking officials and excellent specialists during the last decade, will have to return once again to the great synthesis, to the harmonious development of whole characters.[52]

THE ORTHODOX RESPONSE

The idea of selectively accommodating modern realities in order to maintain some influence upon them was utterly foreign to the orthodox. In their view, mandarin cultural traditions had already been diluted far too much in a series of compromises with modernity, and the general decadence of the age was the inevitable consequence of this process. There could be no cultural revival unless the old values were restored in all their purity. Moved by these convictions, the majority of German university professors put up a stiff resistance against everything the accommodationists proposed. At least until 1920, the orthodox were generally on the defensive. The modernists were the first to attack the status quo before the First World War; and for a short time after 1918, the tide of social and political change favored the reformers and intimidated their opponents.

The orthodox were especially anxious to prevent permanent institutional innovations in German education. Two examples may suffice to indicate how they tried to block the modernist initiative in this field. In an essay published in 1912, the educator Aloys Fischer subjected the concept of working instruction to a close and critical analysis.[53] He began by rejecting the emphasis upon manual activity and upon "realistic" subjects which was originally implied in this term. Next, he modified the ideal of "active" learning, which was also included in the meaning of working instruction, by saying that there was a good deal of need for passive absorption of information in the primary and secondary schools. The suggestion that students should cooperate in common work projects also seemed to him exaggerated, since he did not wish to see attention diverted from the pupil as an individual. He urged a compromise between the "socialistic" and the "individualistic" tendencies in education. And he was prepared to accept student self-government only if it did not interfere with the authority of the classroom teacher.

Especially in the context in which Fischer's essay was written, it clearly implied that German pedagogy was not in need of reform. A man of Kerschensteiner's convictions might well have disapproved of it on that account; but he could not claim that Fischer's arguments were meaningless. There were a few orthodox zealots, however, whose anxiety to thwart the modernist initiative led them to write actual nonsense.

The following passages are taken from a 1919 article by the philosopher Ferdinand Jakob Schmidt.

> The object of the educational process is not primarily the training of the individual mind, but the highest, essentially equal fixation of the human beings' orientation: the intellectual and spiritual formation of the personality toward ethical freedom.

> The basis of the national educational organization is the school system with its various types of schools, created for the individual occupational capabilities under the presupposition that their organization is social. Their organization is social only if in all of them the equality of the education of the stu-

dent's orientation is made the highest fixative principle, and it is organically subdivided only if each of these groups of schools is assured the independence of being able unmolestedly to combine its own appropriate task of instruction with the fulfillment of the unified, social-humanistic educational objective.[54]

One has to read these paragraphs several times in order to get a hint of their real meaning. Schmidt showed a remarkable predilection for such words as social, equal, and unified (*einheitlich*), and it was probably no accident that *einheitlich* was reminiscent of the reformers' integral school (*Einheitsschule*). The phrase about the independence of the various school types, one eventually discovers, meant that the gymnasium and its preparatory schools should not be tampered with. The common basic school was an unfortunate aberration, in Schmidt's opinion, because the organic unity of the educational system could never be achieved through a "mechanical chaining together" of essentially differing educational tasks. Finally, according to Schmidt's notion of equality, it would be unfair to the old primary school to let its brightest students transfer to secondary schools at some point during their career, for that would impoverish the primary schools and create serious class differences "in accordance with the most one-sided class principle there is, namely the principle of intellectualism."[55] Ferdinand Jakob Schmidt was a professor at a reputable German university. It is frighteningly likely that, in some way, he believed what he wrote.

The orthodox knew, of course, that the reforming pedagogues were at least partly motivated by social and political considerations. Gustav Cohn traced the attacks upon the classical gymnasium to the "democratic-radical tendencies" of the age. Eduard Spranger thought it possible to relate the various currents within the reform movement to the "most fundamental sociological structural principles" of nineteenth- and twentieth-century society, namely, liberty, equality, fraternity. According to Spranger, the principle of liberty in education called for the highest possible self-development of the individual. In a sense, it was an aristocratic ideal, and it was embodied in its purest form in the German educational system of the early nineteenth century. The notion of equality, on the other hand, called for "the organizational creation of equal conditions of competition." It was a "mere mantle for the will to power and for the individualism of classes"; it led to democracy and to socialism. In Germany, the notion of equality had become an ever more serious threat to liberty since the middle of the nineteenth century. After 1918, it had finally produced the demand for a common basic school and for such modernistic innovations as the German high school, which was designed to perpetuate the undesirable "spirit of Weimar."[56]

Spranger objected to the reformers' attempt "to achieve through rational organization what can truly arise only out of the organic life of the mind and spirit." Fortunately, he said, the spirit of fraternity, a movement of the heart and an enemy of organizational rationalism, was alive in the German youth movement. Unconcerned with outward equality, the young people accepted natural gradations of ability and authority. They cultivated the idea of leadership (*Führergedanke*), "an aristocratic motive on a communal basis." Thus there was hope that the conflict between individualistic liberty and socially oriented equality would eventually be resolved on a higher plane and that the German school system would yet become a true community. "True fraternity . . . [is] a total relationship from man to man, which involves the whole nature and not merely the interests of human beings." "The sense of these unique sociological forms cannot be experienced by everyone who approaches them only from the conceptual side, least of all by those who think in democratic categories . . . Ancient German spirit is here coming to life again." "Education today must irrevocably be the cultivation of individuality, an elevation toward personality. But the individualities will then not stand side by side in a foreign and unrelated way, but they will be connected through a tie of understanding."[57] This kind of "total" integration of political and educational theories made the discussion between modernists and orthodox neither clearer nor less heated.

One of the strongest orthodox arguments against the reforms was that they would result in a general lowering of standards in higher education. Such defenders of the gymnasium as Eduard Meyer thought of the old classical curriculum as a tough intellectual regime for a small elite of students.[58] In his view, the clamor against the gymnasium, the enrollment boom, and the new emphasis upon modern subjects were all based upon the mistaken idea that almost anyone should be able to get the *Abitur*. Meyer was afraid that ever new social groups would demand entry into the higher schools, the universities, and the learned professions. German learning would be progressively diluted and eventually ruined, unless the ministries of culture found the strength to keep second-rate students in the lower schools. Already, the old curriculum was being softened, and there was too much talk about physical education and other trivialities.

In 1920, Friedrich von der Leyen struck a similar note in response to one of Becker's essays. He did not like the proposal that boards of nonacademic experts might advise the ministry in making appointments. The idea of allowing students to participate in the discussion of academic reforms seemed to him foolish, although he wished to see the old fencing corps preserved. He also objected to the people's universities, though he could imagine that private associations might wish to teach the workers some local geography, history, and folklore (*Heimatkunde, Heimatgeschichte*), once the class resentment fostered by the political left was overcome. What really infuriated him, however, was Becker's suggestion that new groups of secondary school students and future elementary teachers be allowed to enroll at the universities, that general lectures for nonspecialists be introduced, and that prominent individuals from public life be given special appointments from time to time. Von der Leyen was vehement. "If the gates were now opened to everyone, if everyone lectured to everyone about everything, then standards would totally disappear ... In return, socialism would have achieved its goals; unbearable presumption, the twin of an incomplete education, would grace the new institutions of learning. Every creative thought would be drowned, extraordinary achievement banished, and an army of bureaucratic mediocrities would preside over the teaching function and force itself into the best positions."[59]

It would not be so very difficult to sympathize with the anxiety over standards if that anxiety had not been so persistently confounded with class prejudices and social resentments. As it was, German higher learning had become an upper-class preserve, and the *Abitur* controversy therefore really was a kind of class struggle. Unfortunately, the mandarins never managed to extricate themselves from this dilemma. On the contrary, the orthodox majority did everything in its power to block the only available escape route, which would have had to begin at a search for more or less objective ways of testing a student's capabilities. Here is what Spranger had to say on that subject. "I see a final symptom of the connection between democracy and rationalism in the growth of technical methods by which the intellectual characteristics are to be tested and in accordance with which the choice of schooling is to be organizationally regulated . . . For individuality is here ultimately looked upon as something measurable and numerically describable, not as a structural principle of the soul." Spranger insisted that there was only one true measure of the capacity for learning, and that was the integral activity of the scholar. "Even if all elementary processes are there: their working together in a total intellectual achievement is not yet proven . . . For the human mind is not put together out of atoms of primitive acts; but [it is] an organic unity, in which interest and inner depth [*Innerlichkeit*], far-seeing combination and fortunate intuition often play a driving role."[60] Spranger admitted that it might be possible to discuss certain subordinate capabilities in isolation; but that seemed to him "destructive analysis, not creative synthesis." He was in favor, he said, of encouraging talented youngsters from the lower classes. He certainly did not want the new monied aristocracy to capture German learning. On the other hand, he refused to believe that a "soul" could be "technically treated." Therefore he approved of the existing *Abitur* examinations, which were partly oral and partly written and applied only to graduates of accredited secondary schools. Above all, he wanted to rely on the overall judgment of individual examiners, to have "the technical eliminated from the whole procedure as far as possible . . . for individuality can only be grasped through vital intuition."[61]

In fairness to Spranger's argument, it should be admitted that educators find it very difficult even today to arrive at a reasonably accurate prediction of a student's performance. The techniques used to that end are generally quite complex and seldom "purely mechanical" in Spranger's sense. On the other hand, the orthodox mandarins' total rejection of aptitude testing was clearly based upon their inclusive definition of learning as a spiritually ennobling process. Above all, there was always the suggestion that a cultivated background was an adequate criterion of academic potential.

In 1919, the famous classical philologist Ulrich von Wilamowitz-Moellendorff tried to show what beneficial lessons could be derived from a study of ancient Greek culture and particularly of Plato's *Republic*.[62] He emphasized five such morals for his own time. First, he said, the philosophers and not the uneducated masses should rule, since democracy bred demagogues and led to tyranny. Second, there was a vast difference between higher learning, conceived as the philosophical training of an elite, and the teaching of practical and vocational skills. Third, it was wrong to think that educators could easily determine who was capable of higher learning. Fourth, it was well known, certainly to Plato, that the intellectual and spiritual qualities of a future philosopher were inherited, like other traits, so that it was not entirely foolish to select candidates for higher learning on the basis of heredity. Fifth, it had been Plato's only error to underestimate the need for a national spirit of community.

Another orthodox argument against the modernist program was based upon the traditional demand that "pure" learning should not be subjected to utilitarian considerations of any kind. Spranger used a slightly expanded version of this doctrine to show that there was a great difference between the universities, technical institutes, and pedagogical academies, and that primary teachers should not be sent to the universities.[63]

Wilhelm Kahl, in 1909, distinguished between two broad tendencies which, he said, had been present in the university reform movement ever since 1848. One was the "external," organizational, "realistic" direction, the other the "internal," idealistic one. The organizational alternative involved such egalitarian demands as that for the extension of faculty voting rights to assistant professors, which Kahl indignantly repudiated. "The universities will submit even to far-reaching state supervision, gladly and to their own gain, as long as it is exercised in the spirit of their freedom of learning. They would unitedly resist a self-dissolution, hatched in their own ranks, through attempts at unhistorical reforms of the foundations of their constitution."[64] But the most dangerous thing about the organizational reform proposals, according to Kahl, was that they would divert attention from the need for an "inner" renewal of German learning, an idealistic revival which would help to overcome the cultural problems of the age.

Kahl, Wilamowitz, Spranger, and their orthodox colleagues were apparently opposed only to institutional, egalitarian, or "utilitarian" changes in German education and learning. Kahl did not rule out an inner revitalization; Wilamowitz was prepared to draw a certain kind of practical moral from the results of classical scholarship; and Spranger wished to bring a spirit of "fraternity" into the schools and universities. Thus the orthodox agreed with the modernists in two respects at least: both groups sought to increase the influence of mandarin learning upon the life of the nation, and both believed that the problem of cultural decadence might be solved in this way. The orthodox desired changes only in the content and meaning of learning, whereas the modernists wanted to begin with institutional reforms. The orthodox tried to reactivate the axioms of the mandarin ideology and to give them as antimodernistic an emphasis as possible. They thought of the revitalization as a restoration, whereas the accommodationists envisioned an adjustment to modern realities. Nevertheless, there was a certain similarity between the programs of the contending factions. The modernists also hoped to gain new cultural values from learning, which is why they talked about the need for synthesis. What Kahl and Wilamowitz had in mind could as easily be described as a re-engagement of learning as could some of Becker's objectives, and this despite the orthodox insistence on the purity of learning.

For a small group of violent cultural nationalists, many of them German philologists, the road to spiritual recovery through higher education began with a greatly increased emphasis upon all things German and capable of inspiring patriotism. These extreme nationalists did not represent the mainstream of orthodox opinion, which was classically oriented. For that reason, they sometimes found themselves unwillingly allied with the modernist pedagogues, from whom they differed violently in their politics. They tended to regard the old academic curriculum as too old-fashioned and too passive on the national question. In a way, they represented the threat to mandarin tradition from the growing radical right in German politics. They stood closer to the volkish movements than any other segment of the academic community. They also had a friend in William II, whose erratic support of the nonclassical schools against the gymnasium was based primarily upon his interest in the national cause. As a matter of fact, there was always a nationalist and volkish fringe element in the educational reform movement of the Wilhelmian period, particularly among primary school teachers.[65] Within the universities, however, explicitly volkish opinions were relatively rare, and the extreme nationalists themselves were a minority.

Several articles by Friedrich von der Leyen and Carl Neumann[66] may serve as examples of the extreme nationalist point of view. In 1906 and 1908, von der Leyen indulged in the usual complaint that specialization and a lack of meaningful teaching at the secondary schools and universities had contributed to the "emptiness and barrenness" of Germany's "intellectual and moral life." He urged academic lecturers to spend less time on scholarly detail. Instead, he said, professors ought to give students the feeling of direct contact with the vital and total meaning of their sources, to help them interpret their reading, not just to memorize the material in their handbooks. He also suggested an increased emphasis upon modern German literature, and he thought that national political affairs might occasionally be discussed in the classroom. He wanted to see good teachers and not only scholars at the universities. He did not hesitate to support the modernist arguments in favor of extending faculty rights to the younger professors.

Leyen's primary concern, however, was the cause of Germanic studies. He felt that the German intelligentsia had always lacked and now sorely needed a thorough acquaintance with its own national heritage. By 1920, he had dropped many of those proposals which had earlier brought him uncomfortably close to the modernists. In an article published during that year, he actually launched a very sharp attack upon Becker's conception of synthesis. Only his zest for "national" education was quite unchanged. After the usual preliminaries about the irrelevance of merely technical approaches to academic reform, he proposed the establishment of a special university for Germanic studies, which was to be exclusively devoted to the strengthening of the "national self-consciousness and the national will." As for the rest of the universities, they too were to make a choice, once and for all, between two basic world views, "the national and the international"; for it was their wavering between these two principles which had caused them to fail in their task of national leadership during the war. One should have thought that the academic "spirit of 1914" would have seemed a sufficient and proper sort of intellectual engagement even to Leyen; but apparently, he did not see it that way. Under the circumstances, it is difficult to interpret his repeated assertion that he did not wish to encourage a narrow and fanatical nationalism. Carl Neumann made a similar disclaimer; and yet he wrote of "implanting a feeling of respect for the eternal preconditions of German life and being." Both Germanists clearly thought of their educational program as a weapon against what Neumann called "internationalism and bolshevism," "pacifist egotism," and "unhistorical invidualism." When accompanied by such phrases, the finer distinctions between different degrees of national passion come to seem irrelevant.

National education was to the extreme nationalists what civic education was to the modernists. In both cases, political motives had an immediate influence upon an educational ideal. It must be emphasized, however, that there were some individuals within the orthodox camp who related their pedagogical views only indirectly and perhaps unconsciously to their political attitudes. These were the single-minded humanists, and one of them was Werner Jaeger. In a lecture delivered in 1920, Jaeger identified Greek culture with the ideal of "forming body and soul according to their own inherent law." As a conception of education, this seemed to him very different from practically or socially motivated theories: "It would be to overlook the profound difference between a mere means and a self-contained pure value . . . if one were to expect a useful effect from every bit of knowledge . . . With this conception of the relationship of pure values to the problem of man's education and to the concept of culture itself, humanism stands or falls; for it is after all nothing but the way to [an understanding of] man which the Greeks have shown."[67]

Jaeger went on to criticize two suggestions that had recently been made by a fellow-classicist. One was that gymnasium teachers might take a more historical approach to the Greek and Latin sources, working partly with excerpted selections and spending more time on the later authors, who had some influence on more recent times. The other proposal was to de-emphasize language study and close reading in favor of a broader interpretation of various works, perhaps even on the basis of translations. Jaeger disapproved of both recommendations, the first because he was less interested in literary history than in "strengthening the youths' feeling for the great and beautiful through pure, undivided impressions," the second because he could not imagine a distinction between the "form" and the "content" of Greek literature. He accordingly declared himself in favor of the old grammatical drill in the lower grades, of translation, memorization, and verse-making exercises. He agreed that students should be made to understand the total meaning of their sources; but he insisted that general interpretation should go hand in hand with the analysis of language.

Though less anxious than most of his colleagues to identify modernism with democracy and socialism, Jaeger advanced the usual arguments against "realism" in education. Since his views represent a special case, one of the milder varieties of orthodoxy, it may be worth quoting a few of his remarks at length.

Realistic education remains essentially intellectual and wissenschaftlich. It is the typical expression of modern culture with its predominance of civilization, of occupational specialization and division of labor . . . [Humanism] is and remains a supra-scientific goal, because wissenschaft, especially so-called exact wissenschaft, is not the whole man.

We [gymnasium supporters] do not wish to support the leveling and the turning away of valuable spiritual forces from civilization, which threatens everywhere; but we all want to help to loosen up the rigid mechanism and to imbue it with a breath of pure humanity. In return, we ought to be given the right to develop our idea freely. The structure of the gymnasium [must not be dictated by the purely organizational arguments in favor of easy transitions between different types of schools.]

We hope for the rebirth [of the gymnasium] out of the spirit of genuine humanism, so that this force . . . may once again shine out upon the whole spiritual life of the German people. We hope that [the gymnasium will form] leaders among our youths who are trained to be neither scholars and bookworms, nor technicians and specialists, nor literateurs and aesthetes, but who are educated in the qualities of confidence and sureness in everything they do . . . [They are to be capable] of thinking and judging clearly, of recognizing the general in the particular and the present in the past, of striving for just and unselfish goals to which a whole people can look up in communal unity. They are to have faith in the power of the mind and spirit.[68]

To call these passages apolitical is to use an elusive term in a relative sense, and the one advantage of doing so is that it allows one to speak the mandarins' own language. In 1916, Eduard Spranger distinguished between the humanistic and the political ideal in German education.[69] He said that the old Humboldtian emphasis upon individual self-development through classical studies had come into conflict with a more politically and socially oriented tendency in education, which since the latter part of the nineteenth century had found its historical justification in the necessities of national and international politics. As might be expected, Spranger was able to "overcome" the differences between the two movements with a few remarks about the role of the ethical community; and in so doing, he found himself once again in the mainstream of orthodox opinion. As a description of his colleagues' views, his account was quite sensible; for most of the antimodernists actually combined the nationalism of the Germanists with Jaeger's humanism.

Thus Eduard Meyer attacked the Germanists for failing to understand the importance of classical studies, while simultaneously approving of their political views. Albert Rehm, although a vigorous defender of the gymnasium, found the Germanists much more congenial than those he called the utilitarians and the unhistorical ones. Eduard Norden took a very similar position. Meyer recommended ancient history for reasons reminiscent of Wilamowitz's morals upon Plato's *Republic*. Rehm considered the study of antiquity a good counterweight to the shallowness of modern life and to the "civic and sociological" approach of the modernists. Norden praised the discipline and manliness of the Romans and their sense of duty to the national community, while Rehm and Gustav Roethe pointed to the lessons to be drawn from Greek history. For Norden, Tacitus was an essential source of German national consciousness and pride. Roethe turned to the Greeks for help against "the socialistic and materialistic barbarism . . . from which all the triumphs of technology cannot save us." The classical curriculum alone, he felt, could produce individuals capable of standing above the clamor of the herd, so that the gymnasium would always be the training ground for the nation's "intellectual general staff."[70] Beyond that, there was general agreement among the orthodox that a new "idealism" was to make itself felt in German education and learning.

Idealism, humanism, and nationalism: perhaps there was no logical reason why these three should have been connected. If not, then the association had social and psychological causes. In any case, most orthodox mandarins had this triad in mind when they discussed the problem of cultural decadence and the possibility of a revitalization through education. Their objectives were different from those of the modernists; but they were just as interested as their rivals in a re-engagement of scholarship. In some way, they sought to make learning more influential; they wanted it to yield certain socially and culturally effective energies; they hoped for a richer harvest of ideology. In this undertaking, they were bound to clash with the accommodationists, who had their own purposes in seeking a renewal of wissenschaft. The competition between the two groups could only heighten the inevitable strain upon the traditional methods of scholarship and research; it could only produce what it did produce: a crisis of German learning.

THE INVOLVEMENT OF LEARNING

About 1920, German academics began to speak of an existing crisis of learning (*Krise der Wissenschaft*). The word crisis, of course, had been used a good deal since the 1890's. There had been repeated references to a social and cultural crisis, and the demand for a reexamination of scholarly methods and purposes had always been included in the discussion of cultural decadence. Thus the crisis of learning did not appear unexpectedly upon the Weimar scene. It was not given a name until relatively late, perhaps because the mandarins became truly desperate about their situation only during the 1920's. In substance, though, the crisis of learning arose well before it was formally labeled. It really originated around 1890, when German university professors first began to feel that scholarship had lost some of its former influence and vitality. From that moment on, there was a growing revulsion against "positivism" and "psychologism" in learning, and it was this revulsion that eventually became the crisis of learning. To understand the crisis, one must therefore begin by asking how the mandarins defined such terms as materialism, positivism, and psychologism.

When German academic philosophers of the early twentieth century looked back upon the evolution of their discipline since about 1800, they found much to deplore.[71] They thoroughly idealized the classical age of German speculative philosophy from Kant to Fichte, of course; but they were already less enthusiastic in treating Hegel and the natural philosophy (*Naturphilosophie*) of the early nineteenth century. Hegel, along with almost every other German philosopher who wrote before 1840, did acquire some new disciples after 1890. Besides, the language of synthesis and of objective geist may have been informally and indirectly derived from Fichte and Hegel. Nevertheless, there was a broad consensus that Hegel and the philosophers of nature had been a little too willfully speculative and that their excesses had helped to discredit systematic philosophy for several decades. Beginning about 1840, the theory ran, the doctrines of German Idealism and the whole standing of formal philosophy as a discipline came under attack. Disenchanted with theoretical speculation, men placed their faith in immediate empirical observation. A new realism thus made its appearance, which in turn fathered the errors of materialism, positivism, and psychologism.

In describing these aberrations, mandarin historians of philosophy generally drew upon the Kantian or neo-Kantian critique of the common-sense fallacy.[72] They were quick to point out that the philosophically unsophisticated empiricist, the naive realist, tends unconsciously to make certain metaphysical assumptions about the existence of the external world and the relationship between objects and ideas. He becomes a materialist, from the neo-Kantian point of view, if he begins to believe that all physical bodies, events, and ideas are members of a single continuous system of moving particles. In another sense, a Kantian might also call someone a materialist for holding that objects are the physical or physiological causes of ideas.

The error of psychologism, in the view of the German neo-Kantians, was the tendency to regard the a priori elements in our thinking as empirical properties of the mind or of the cognitive functions. In opposing this fallacy, the disciples of Kant repeated that no amount of empirical investigation of perception and thinking could remove the purely logical discontinuity between experience and the "thing in itself."

In the common-sense scheme, man's knowledge may be pictured as the product of a primarily quantitative process of growth. Little chunks of experience are gradually stacked together. These chunks are called facts, and it is not always clear in ordinary usage whether the word fact refers to a certain kind of sentence, to an idea, or to something which is "discovered" in the world around us. In the common-sense view, this ambiguity is perfectly acceptable, since it reflects the close and necessary relationship between the experience and the thing in itself. In any case, man accumulates facts, filling out his "areas of ignorance," and moving the "frontier of knowledge" along. His theories, to round out the scheme, are simply conjunctions of facts. They too are "discovered," and there is no need for philosophical speculation of any kind. This, to the neo-Kantian critic, is positivism.

In all probability, none of the three fallacious isms was ever formally developed by any philosopher, certainly not in the crude forms epitomized above. Especially in Germany, where empiricist philosophies never thoroughly took root, self-confessed materialists or positivists were very rare indeed.[73] It is therefore rather difficult to discover the villains against whom these pejorative labels were directed. Apparently, psychologism was thought to have predominated during the decades between 1850 and 1890. The term referred more or less vaguely to Hermann von Helmholtz, Hermann Lotze, Wilhelm Wundt, and their followers. These men were heirs of the physiological and psychophysical tradition in German psychology, a tradition which dated back to the 1830's and 1840's in the work of E. H. Weber, S. Müller, and G. Fechner. Lotze and Wundt were philosophers as well as psychologists, by no means limited in their interests to the field of psychophysics. Until well into the twentieth century, psychologists held professorships of philosophy at German universities. This probably helped to delay the clear separation of psychology from philosophy, and it may also have increased the philosophers' dislike of psychologism. In any case, such men as Lotze were indeed accused of believing that further knowledge about the physiology and psychology of sensation could obviate the need for a logical and philosophical analysis of these issues. Moreover, it was considered one of the dangers of psychologism that the logical subject of epistemology, the conscious "I," might come to be regarded as a mere construct, a hypostatized bundle of psychic structures and events. Wundt in particular seems to have thought it unnecessary to posit a soul as the integral carrier of psychic activity.

The charge of materialism was sometimes directed against Ludwig

Feuerbach and the young Hegelian radicals of the 1830's and 1840's, although it was never demonstrated that these men adhered to any formally materialistic metaphysics. That left certain popularizers of a "scientific" world view, among whom Ludwig Büchner (*Kraft und Stoff*, 1855) and Ernst Haeckel (*Welträtsel*, 1899) were mentioned most frequently; and of course it also left Marx and Engels. But while Marxism has traditionally been equated with historical materialism, that doctrine does not necessarily imply a materialistic ontology. As for positivism, the label was meant to refer primarily to Comte, particularly when it was used to discuss methods in the social studies and humanities. The notion that it is possible to "discover laws" in history, the theory of stages in the evolution of society, the belief in progress: all these were broadly positivist in the mandarins' view. On the other hand, there is simply no evidence that Comte was ever taken very seriously in Germany, except as a foil for anti-positivist polemics.

Thus our mandarin accounts of nineteenth-century positivism, materialism, and psychologism are quite incomprehensible, unless one recognizes that these pejorative terms were used in a relatively vague and indirect sense. It is probably true that roughly from 1850 to 1880, German scholars were comparatively unconcerned with philosophical or methodological questions. They did much successful empirical work in various disciplines; and in the process, they began to drift away from the Idealistic traditions of the early nineteenth century. On the whole, this process was more unconscious than deliberate. But it led men to act as if materialistic or positivistic conceptions of knowledge were acceptable to them. They were too busy to state their positions formally. They simply created the impression that they had temporarily forgotten the Kantian criticism, that they were allowing themselves to slide from an unstudied empiricism or realism toward the unconscious metaphysical assumptions of the common-sense heresy. It was this intellectual tendency which came under attack beginning around 1890. The mandarin intellectuals now sought a revival of Idealism in wissenschaft, and they began by criticizing their immediate predecessors. They were disturbed not so much by any systematic development of anti-Idealistic philosophies as by an unpremeditated neglect of Idealism and of speculative philosophy in general. Influenced by the neo-Kantian movement, they leveled the charges of materialism and positivism at anyone who acted as if he had forgotten the Kantian criticism. "Materialism" thus came to describe the more or less unconscious assumption that ideas have material causes, while "positivism" referred to the additive view of knowledge and to a vaguely scientific distrust of philosophical speculation.

Naturally enough, the charges of positivism and materialism were applied most easily to men of an experimental and technological bent. That is why the two terms were so often used in conjunction. A technician or scholar who was content to do only specialized research might well be suspected of positivist leanings, especially if he felt that value judgments should be kept out of learning and that wissenschaft could not yield weltanschauung. In an age of great technological progress, even an inordinate respect for the natural sciences could be regarded as positivist in tendency. Such eminent historians of philosophy as Wilhelm Windelband actually intermingled their critique of materialistic metaphysics with their repudiation of popular materialism. In this way, the technical attack upon the philosophical exploitations of the common-sense fallacy merged with the more general revulsion against the mass and machine age.[74]

It should also be remembered that such words as positivism were very often used in conjunction with the term Idealism, "positivism" to identify a discredited tendency in learning, "Idealism" to suggest the simultaneous presence of an alternative. Particularly in the humanistic disciplines, the antithesis between Idealist and positivist methods became a veritable obsession with German scholars. To understand the attack upon positivism, one therefore has to elaborate from an Idealist point of view upon the neo-Kantian critique of common-sense experience. The naive empiricist among historians sees himself as a passive collector of historical "facts." Some of his facts describe the thoughts of historic personages; others portray the material realities of some epoch in the past. Historical explanation,

for the naive empiricist, is the discovery of causal connections between facts, particularly between facts which describe realities and
facts which describe thoughts.

The Idealist repudiates two "positivist" assumptions which, he
says, are implied in the naive empiricist's scheme. The first assumption is the common-sense epistemology itself, the whole idea that
"external facts" somehow enter the mind and there, "inside," more
or less automatically add up to form generalizations and explanations.
The Idealist stresses the active role of consciousness in explanation;
he sees facts and, more especially, causal connections as products, not
discoveries, of geist. The second assumption challenged by the Idealist is that we can distinguish between facts about thoughts and facts
about realities. The Idealist points out, on the contrary, that the
realities of the past are not accessible to us at all, except insofar as
certain "facts" were selected and described by men who found them
significant in terms of their own ideas. The notion of causal relations
between the facts of the past, especially between facts about realities
and facts about thoughts, is therefore a very clumsy positivist simplification.

Apparently, every German academic who was even vaguely aware
of these objections to positivism considered himself an Idealist. Neo-
Hegelians conceived the relationship between ideas and realities in
history as a dialectical process within man's consciousness. The metaphor of geist "realizing" itself in history once again became popular.
The whole idea of understanding the "subjective geist" of an epoch
through its "objectifications" was associated with Idealism and identified as a reaction against the narrowness of positivism in the social
studies and humanities. In every discipline and field of study, the
antithesis between Idealism and positivism was used to distinguish
a profound, vaguely humanistic, and value-oriented approach from
a more superficial one. Finally, the general enthusiasm for Idealism
undoubtedly owed something to the popular sense of the word
idealism.

In 1904, in an essay on "positivism and Idealism in linguistics,"
the philologist Karl Vossler repudiated a kind of narrow empiricism
which, he said, exhausted itself in detailed analyses of verbal "ma-

terial" (*Stoff*), while ignoring all logical connections between words, along with the meaning, the intellectual and spiritual content, of living language. In 1905, the philosopher Alois Riehl defined Idealism (or idealism) more popularly as "the creation of a higher, purer, more spiritual reality, the continual battle against everything low outside and within us . . . the elevation of the soul . . . toward the noble, the high, the great." Friedrich Meinecke struck a more cautious note. He observed in his memoirs that the number of philologists and historians at German universities had sunk particularly low around the end of the nineteenth century, after which it climbed rapidly enough to make the decade before the First World War a golden age in these fields. "Around the turn of the century," he said, "a new Idealism began to stir": "Idealism is a large and loose concept. If I dare to speak of an Idealism of those years . . . what I primarily have in mind is an increased interest in the phenomena of intellectual and spiritual life . . . People were fed up with the mere matter-of-fact empiricism and positivism with which the facts of historical life had often been treated."[75] Thus the war between positivism and Idealism was a very uneven affair. To some extent, the positivist was a mythical villain, created as a foil for the revival in learning. His heresy lay not so much in what he propounded as in what he neglected to think and to say. His sins were vaguely defined and great in number, because there were many roads which led away from Idealism.

Meinecke believed that there was a new "interest in the phenomena of intellectual and spiritual life" around the end of the nineteenth century. He particularly mentioned a change in the approach to "the facts of historical life." As a matter of fact, there was a shift of emphasis in German historiography sometime around 1890, which was ultimately to have a profound effect upon the crisis of learning.[76] Beginning in 1883, the famous methods controversy (*Methodenstreit*) agitated German economists. The contest divided the defenders of the old historical tradition in economics from the advocates of a more systematic approach. The questions at issue thus inevitably provoked a fresh interest in problems of historical method. In the meantime, the concerns of practicing historians had been changing as well. Ranke himself had emphasized political and institutional history. He had focused his investigations upon the state and especially upon foreign policy. Under the influence of Bismarck's achievement, some of Ranke's students had carried this emphasis even further, until the so-called "primacy of foreign policy" had become a veritable dogma. It was only around 1880 that a change began to take place in this respect. The foreign policy theory was never actually challenged; but a number of prominent scholars began to move from political and institutional to intellectual, cultural, and social history. Kuno Fischer and Eduard Zeller had an influence in this direction. Burckhardt was read with increasing interest. Around 1870, Wilhelm Dilthey's studies in intellectual history began to appear and to gain a growing number of admirers. By the time of his death in 1911, Dilthey had become one of the foremost German historians and philosophers of his time, even though some of his works were yet to be published. Among the younger men, Friedrich Meinecke was perhaps the most eminent representative of the new intellectual and cultural history. His *Weltbürgertum und Nationalstaat,* which appeared in 1908, was a subtle portrait of the conflict between cosmopolitan and nationalist tendencies in modern German thought. Meinecke treated ideas as evolving historical individualities; the results he achieved with this method were widely and justly respected.

From about 1890 on, social and cultural problems acquired a new importance in the mandarins' thinking, and this may help to account for the new direction in German historiography. The connection became quite clear during the Lamprecht controversy, which began in 1893.[77] Karl Lamprecht believed that a new and rigorous method would enable him to arrive at a universal cultural history of mankind. He proposed to use the discoveries of modern anthropology, psychology, and sociology and to build his "sociopsychological" approach upon the fundamental laws of human behavior. He was particularly interested in basic interpersonal relationships, such as family structures, and he believed in comparative techniques.

Lamprecht divided world history into a few major "cultural epochs" (*Kulturzeitalter*), the latest of which was the "subjectivist" age. This was subdivided into two phases: the first began during the later eighteenth century, and the transition to the second took place sometime between 1850 and 1880. Cutting across the cultural epochs, and most markedly since the Renaissance, Lamprecht detected a single continuous development which was basic to almost everything else. This was the process of "psychic differentiation," in which men became gradually more conscious of themselves as individuals, more differentiated from each other, and less completely immersed in the emotional and intellectual life of their clan or group. From the "symbolic" epoch, men thus moved through the "typical" and "conventional" ages, to the modern era of individualism and subjectivism. At the borderline between any two cultural eras, and apparently also between the first and second phases of the subjectivist era, Lamprecht observed certain characteristic transition phenomena. These included the intrusion of radically new stimuli from the material environment, the "dissociation" of old patterns of thought and behavior, and the gradual emergence of a new "dominant" or "synthesis."[78] For the decades between 1850 and 1880, he naturally cited urbanization, the technological explosion, and the general "politization." He tried to evoke the psychological pressures of modernity, and he saw such cultural movements as naturalism, impressionism, and expressionism as outgrowths of the "social psyche" resulting from such pressures. In glancing at some of Lamprecht's work on earlier ages, one is struck by the rather turbulent mixture of anthropological information, imaginative portraiture, and embarrassingly superfluous rhetoric about psychosocial laws and the like.

Apparently, Lamprecht was convinced that his method was particularly appropriate to his own time. As long as men were less differentiated, he said, historians could achieve some results by using individual psychology in the study of representative individuals. Now, however, this approach was no longer fruitful. Standing at the opening of a new phase within the subjectivist epoch, Lamprecht noted that Marxism in social theory, naturalism in ethics, and agnosticism in religion were outdated, although the entrepreneurial groups continued to think in purely economic terms. His own method, which was "oriented toward dynamic and psychogenetic and therefore optimistic-idealistic goals," seemed to him capable of providing the basis for a new weltanschauung and of successfully "confronting the exclusively economic goals of the social segments that have grown up out of economic enterprise."[79]

In view of all this, one is at least initially surprised to discover that Lamprecht was widely criticized for his positivist leanings. He believed that it was possible to interpret history in terms of certain fundamental laws of behavior, and this was held against him. He also gave prominence to environmental stimuli as factors in the transition from one age to another, and that caused even Meinecke to suspect him of "economic materialism."[80] Georg von Below, who launched the general attack on Lamprecht in 1893, made even more far-reaching accusations. He used every device in the arsenal of anti-positivist polemics, associating cultural history with Enlightenment rationalism and pragmatism, with narrow empiricism and cosmopolitanism, with English historical positivism, and with the general decline of German historiography during the 1860's and 1870's. He also pointed out that the democrats and the masses were particularly interested in cultural history, whereas right-thinking men continued to emphasize the state, the nation, and the kind of collective concepts which had been originated by the German Romantics.

Below's comments did not terminate the Lamprecht debate. Indeed, the whole caliber of the discussion increased considerably when such scholars as Otto Hintze and Friedrich Meinecke entered it in the years after 1893. Even without following these developments any further, however, one may conclude that the Lamprecht controversy helped to make German historians acutely self-conscious about their methods during the late 1890's and thereafter. In history as in other disciplines, the widespread sense of social and cultural crisis produced a reorientation in the methods and purposes of learning. Thus from 1890 on, the substantive concerns of German scholarship were inextricably intertwined with the mandarins' passionate interest in a revival of "Idealism."

6

FROM THE REVIVAL TO THE
CRISIS OF LEARNING, 1890–1920

THE BACKGROUND IN PHILOSOPHY
AND PSYCHOLOGY

When decribing the revival in German philosophy during the later
nineteenth century, the mandarins of the 1920's generally gave
qualified praise to the neo-Kantian tradition. More specifically,
they distinguished between two major strands within that movement: a primarily critical wing and a more constructively Idealistic
tendency.* The critical wing was identified chiefly with the Marburg

---

* Two fairly prominent neo-Kantians, Alois Riehl (1844–1924) and Richard Hönigswald (1875–1947), are hard to assign to either of the major wings. In addition, Leonard
Nelson was often held to represent a third genre of neo-Kantianism. He seems to have
made few converts during the period surveyed here. Cassirer considered him a thinly
disguised common-sense philosopher.

school of neo-Kantianism, the Idealistic branch with the Baden or Southwest German school, which was founded by Wilhelm Windelband and Heinrich Rickert around 1890.

Hermann Cohen (1842-1918) was considered the father of the Marburg school. Probably its most important representative during the Weimar period was Ernst Cassirer. In addition, Paul Natorp was sometimes identified with this group, although his mature concerns would seem to place him closer to the Baden wing. In any case, the Marburg school was but the most important branch of a broader tradition of neo-Kantian thought which dated back almost to the middle of the nineteenth century. The Kant of this tradition was the critical Kant, the destroyer of all metaphysical speculation whether materialistic or Idealistic in character. Cohen was apparently interested particularly in the problems and methods of the natural sciences. He regarded mathematics and mechanics as the principal models of scientific knowledge. He was primarily an epistemologist, and this was true of Cassirer as well. Cassirer did much valuable work as a historian of philosophy. But he also proved a highly effective critic of the common-sense fallacy, and his own substantive work was an undogmatic treatment of knowledge as a construction in "symbolic forms."[1]

Even their detractors recognized that Cohen and his followers performed great services to philosophy in a relatively hostile climate. Their restatement of the Kantian criticism helped to check unsophisticated exploitations of the common-sense fallacy at a decisive moment in the history of German thought. While an untutored empiricism and "scientism" threatened to dominate the intellectual scene, they managed to show that the problems of cognition continued to demand logical and philosophical analysis. In that sense, the Marburg school helped to reverse the incipient trend toward positivism and materialism in nineteenth-century thought.

Nonetheless, German philosophers of the 1920's were almost unanimous in treating the Marburg tradition itself as a part of the general decline of philosophy during the decades before 1900. Because Cohen and his followers were "merely" logicians and epistemologists and because they emphasized the natural sciences, they were quite frequently accused of positivist tendencies, or "logicism" (*Logizismus*), or of a "merely critical" approach. The revival in philosophy, it was commonly held, did not begin until 1890, when men once again took a substantive interest in ethics and metaphysics. Criticism of the Marburg variety had been useful, especially before 1890. After that, it was no longer needed. Windelband stated the charges against Cohen and against all other empirically oriented neo-Kantians in the following way.

> This agnostic neo-Kantianism of the eighth and ninth decade of the nineteenth century had a decided bias toward positivism, because it neglected the rational element in [Kant's] critical philosophy. The empiricist epistemology which was read into Kant tended increasingly to replace philosophical criticism with a psychological and causal analysis [of experience]; and because it confused Kantian a priority with psychic priority, it ended by leaning again toward David Hume on the one hand and toward Auguste Comte on the other. But the result of this empiricism . . . was nothing but the complete dissolution of philosophy into epistemology. This had never truly been Kant's own intention: He always saw his "critical task" . . . as a prelude to "doctrinal" work. The epistemology which partly called itself by his name, however, was basically nothing but the conscious abandonment of all wissenschaftlich weltanschauung. And in this abdication, in this empiricism, a certain naive materialism probably also played a confused and unconscious role.[2]

The passage indicates how hard it was to escape the mandarins' charge of "materialism."

The proponents of a revival in German philosophy simply refused to be satisfied with a "merely critical" approach to the excesses of nineteenth-century scientism. That is why some of the most brilliant nineteenth-century critics of common-sense metaphysics received very little attention in mandarin histories of philosophy. They failed to contribute to the "doctrinal" task of Idealistic reconstruction, and that was enough to condemn them. Their work was described in the most cursory fashion, and the usual terms of disapproval were directed against them. Jules Henri Poincaré and Ernst Mach were either ignored or disliked as "empirio-criticists," positivists, or "conventionalists," since they could be considered enemies of speculative philosophy.[3] Their treatment of the "I" as a bundle of sensations and their preference for the notion of function over that of cause was generally reported with disapproval. They were said to regard all but pure observation statements as more or less efficient conventions, and for this reason, they were sometimes grouped with the pragmatists. The pragmatists in turn were said to hold that all man's theoretical constructions are ultimately tested only in terms of the practical considerations of survival and adjustment. William James was occasionally mentioned in this connection. The theory was, however, that Nietzsche and Hans Vaihinger (1852–1933) had independently established the pragmatic view in Germany. Vaihinger's "philosophy of the *as if*," described by him in an autobiographical sketch, did in fact meet the mandarins' own definition of pragmatism, although its creator also liked to call it "positivist idealism."[4]

Even Nietzsche, incidentally, made a rather poor showing in the standard handbooks of German academic philosophy. The general view was that he had forcefully reasserted the rights of the cultivated personality against the leveling tendencies of the mass age. In an artistically exaggerated form, he had also spoken up against the replacement of aesthetic values by a philistine practicality. On the other hand, he had not significantly improved upon the substantive work of the great German Idealists, whose disciple he was.[5] This was the line taken by the neo-Kantian Alois Riehl among others. The Nietzsche revival which apparently took place on a popular level, in certain political and literary circles, and among young people, had no marked repercussions in the German academic world.

In 1929, the members of the Vienna Circle (*Wiener Kreis, Verein Ernst Mach*) published what was clearly meant to be the first in a series of manifestos. Their tone was that of exasperated outsiders, men who were fed up with the "growth of metaphysical and theologizing tendencies" in the philosophy of the German academic establishment. They criticized all the major schools within that establishment in rather virulent terms. They announced that all hitherto so-called philosophical problems were the product of semantic confusion and logical tautology. As such, they could be analyzed out of existence. A new kind of philosophy would henceforth address itself directly to the specialists in the various disciplines, helping them in the clarification of their methods and tasks. The members of the circle also expressed their sympathy with the progressive social and political movements of their time. They noted a "curious unanimity" among themselves in an area of concern which had not, after all, brought them together. Why should agreement in philosophy be accompanied by a political consensus? Rudolf Carnap suspected that "those who hold on to the past in the social field also cultivate . . . [outdated] positions in metaphysics and theology."[6]

There is much to be said for this hunch. The evidence suggests that the range of philosophical positions from Carnap to Cassirer entailed a certain maverick status, which often expressed itself in politics as well. Even the Baden neo-Kantians were more often modernists than their colleagues among the outright metaphysicians. Carnap and his friends were clearly reacting against an established tradition, just as the average mandarin philosopher reacted against the real or imagined sins of the "positivist" age. It was this confrontation of self-conscious reactions and counterreactions, together with the exceedingly broad application of descriptive isms, which allowed philosophical discussions to merge with social conflicts.

One cannot avoid being startled by the intensely programmatic character of so much that was written by German philosophers between 1890 and 1920. One encounters manifestos, demands, and plans, and one has the impression that intentions were sometimes confused with achievements. In ethics, a critical analysis of utilitarianism was almost always a prelude to the call for absolute values.[7] Theodor Lipps proposed a reconstruction of philosophy through an investigation of pure consciousness. He described the "I" as the "thing in itself," which could be directly experienced in a new and decidedly un-"mechanistic" psychology. "In the individual I," he said, "philosophy finds that supra-individual I which is reason. Thereby philosophy is given the real which transcends the individual consciousness, the real as such . . . At the same time, this is the only manner in which we are capable of immediately grasping the 'thing in itself.' " Moritz Geiger called for an autonomous metaphysics which would stand above the empirical disciplines and deal wtih questions of ultimate being. Julius Ebbinghaus expected "progress in metaphysics," because "the realization is dawning that something must be able to be judged necessarily true . . . if man is not to sink into an abyss."[8] He traced the new awareness of these needs to the catastrophic experience of the First World War. Others proposed to construct a science of philosophical "totality" or to create a "philosophy of identity" which could overcome the dualism between matter and geist in favor of geist.[9] As symptoms of the general "crisis," these programs are certainly of interest. Beyond that it is hard to say how much influence they had on the actual development of German philosophy after 1890.

By far the most important factor in that development was another branch of the neo-Kantian movement. The Baden or Southwest German neo-Kantians were widely esteemed, especially for their work in the "philosophy of culture."[10] Windelband and Rickert, along with such younger men as Jonas Cohn and Paul Natorp, were more interested than Cohen or Cassirer in Kant's ethics. Their critique of utilitarian ethics was based upon the Kantian categorical imperative: we may not know what is good, but we do know that ethical axioms have certain formal characteristics; they are not deduced from other, practical considerations; they are universal in the sense that one would recommend them to anyone. This is an a priori "category" of ethical reflection. It does not immediately give us a set of detailed prescriptions; but it does establish the basic rules for a logic of morals. It tells us something about the form of ethical statements, if not about their content.

In epistemology, the Baden neo-Kantians naturally began with the traditional attack upon the common-sense fallacy. They stressed the a priori element in our thinking and rejected psychological or more generally "genetic" approaches to this problem. They denied the reality of the thing in itself and the objectivity of sensations as ordinarily conceived. One might say that they regarded the external world as a creation of consciousness, or that they defined "being" as "being-in-consciousness." Admittedly, these phrases are awkward; but they are meant to suggest that the Southwest German school was consciously moving toward a post-Kantian Idealism. "To understand Kant," said Windelband, "is to go beyond him."[11] Rickert worked with a "consciousness as such," not only with individual consciousness. Windelband and especially Cohn were Fichteans as much as Kantians. Indeed, all the members of the group referred to themselves most often as Idealists. In their terminology, the common-sense fallacy was based upon "naive realism."

Their veneration for the work of the great German Idealists may help to explain their own preponderant interest in cultural questions. In the Idealist tradition, even the natural universe is in some sense the creation of geist. But in a much more direct and significant way, it is the world of history and of culture in which geist expresses or realizes itself. Just as a work of art or a "cultivated" personality is the creation of an individual mind and spirit, so all man's achievements are collectively the product of geist. Not only man's knowledge but also his valuations are a part of culture, and in that sense, the philosophy of culture is at least partly a philosophy of valuations.

According to Rickert, the epistemologically real or objective is that which follows the norms of right thinking. The a priori elements in our thought may themselves be described as necessary logical norms. They are to man's knowledge what the formal rules of ethics are to his specific valuations. Knowledge is in the realm of theoretical reason; moral judgments are in the realm of practical reason; and in both spheres, there are norms of right thinking to guide us. The commitment to truth is itself a valuation; and in this sense too, Idealist philosophy is the philosophy of norms and valuations (*Wertphilosophie, Philosophie der Wertungen*).

On the basis of these views, the members of the Baden school developed their philosophies of culture. They asked questions about the relationships between the norms of different "spheres," the logical rules and presuppositions of the several areas or types of knowledge. Could all the various aspects of man's cultural achievement be comprehended in the same way? Should one approach the investigation of history and of cultural affairs generally with the methods used in the study of nature? What is the relationship between the historical investigation of cultural valuations and the substantive acceptance of values? What is the relevance of psychology, of history, and of logic to philosophy? In the Idealist scheme, these questions acquired a new importance. The Baden neo-Kantians felt that they had the tools to make the required distinctions and decisions. In close cooperation with Wilhelm Dilthey and Georg Simmel, Windelband and Rickert began a series of investigations into these problems during the 1890's. The terms *Geisteswissenschaft* (humanistic disciplines) and *Kulturwissenschaft* (cultural disciplines) served as focal points for these discussions, which soon spread from philosophy to the other disciplines. In this way, the theories of the Baden school acquired an immense importance for the methodological controversies of the 1920's and thus for the "crisis of learning."

One of the fields in which the new theory of the humanistic disciplines was eventually to have a considerable influence was that of psychology. Here again, an antithesis began to develop around the turn of the century between positivistic and Idealistic alternatives. As of about 1890, German academic psychology was still dominated by Wilhelm Wundt.[12] It was he who transformed the physiological and psychophysical work of Fechner and Helmholtz into an autonomous science of psychology. At Leipzig in 1879, Wundt opened the first laboratory of experimental psychology in the world. As head of the so-called Leipzig school, he presided over an astonishingly extensive and variegated series of research projects on the physiology of the sense organs, reaction time, psychophysics, and word association. In the field of theory, he apparently thought it unnecessary to attribute the multiplicity of psychic functions to an hypostatized "soul." He also adhered to some version of psychophysical parallelism, the theory that conscious events run parallel to physiological processes, without there being any conventionally causal determination of one by the other. At least, these things were often said of Wundt by younger men who were anxious to demolish his position.

Among Wundt's most interesting and influential theses was that of "apperception" and "creative synthesis," which was loosely adapted from Kant. In apperception, Wundt argued, such elements of experience as sensations, images, and feelings are organized into a coherent whole. The stimulation of the sense organs is followed by perception, in which elementary impressions enter consciousness. After that, the act of apperception transforms the unstructured sum of elementary impressions into an organized, coherent experience to which our attention is directed, and this experience in turn forms the basis for volition and reaction. After 1880, Wundt became more and more interested in philosophical questions and in the cultural and social studies. His famous "folk psychology" or "psychology of peoples" (*Völkerpsychologie*) was an analysis of various cultures in terms of the basic psychological orientations implied in their languages.

On a slightly lower level of prominence than Wundt's, four younger men were commonly regarded as leaders in German psychology around 1890. These were Hermann Ebbinghaus, Carl Stumpf, Georg Elias Müller, and Oswald Külpe. Ebbinghaus was probably more famous outside than inside Germany for his sophisticated statistical studies of rote learning and forgetting. He worked with nonsense syllables and used himself as a subject. Apparently, he thought in terms of associative linkages between materials which are simultaneously present in consciousness. Stumpf, the leader of the "Berlin school," devoted his energies to the field of learning and "tone psychology" (*Tonpsychologie*). He was interested in the impressions of consonance and dissonance which are generated by different pitch combinations. He also remarked upon the fact that these impressions are not ordinary summations of the sensations caused by different notes. Rather, the quality of dissonance appears to be attached to a given note constellation as a whole. It is likely that his reflections upon this subject eventually had some influence upon the younger gestalt psychologists, of whom Stumpf spoke with a certain parental benevolence.[13] G. E. Müller appears to have been influenced by Wundt and by Ebbinghaus. As head of the "Göttingen school," he worked chiefly in the field of word learning and association. In 1923, he chided the gestalt psychologists for failing to remark that the most compelling parts of their argument had long ago been presented in his own "theory of complexes."[14]

313

Külpe, who was more than eleven years younger than any of the four men we have mentioned so far, founded the so-called Würzburg school of "thought psychology" (*Denkpsychologie*). He and his followers were less interested in sensation and memory than in active problem solving. They felt the difficulty of describing this process in terms of elementary associations, and they stressed the importance of volitional and attitudinal states in the achievement of intellectual tasks. While Wundt, Ebbinghaus, Stumpf, and Müller represented the status quo in German psychology around 1890, Külpe's thought psychology could be chronologically and logically grouped with the new movements of the period between 1890 and 1932, which were generally described as reactions against the condition of German psychology before 1890.

Once again, one faces the difficult problem of decline and revival. In psychology as in every other discipline, many German scholars of the 1890's and 1920's assumed the role of revolutionary innovators. Intent upon the much-discussed need for an intellectual and spiritual renaissance, they found it hard to be fair to their predecessors. They chose to make war upon associationist and positivist tendencies in psychology, and they began by exaggerating the importance—and the intellectual simplicity—of these tendencies in the "old psychology." Following a familiar pattern, they described the period between 1850 and 1890 as one of decadence and sterility.[15] Experimental psychology, the argument ran, was born in the shadow of the natural sciences. It was therefore infected with "naturalistic" errors from the very beginning. It took physiology as its model; it made the associationist scheme an epitome of all mental processes; it adopted the theory of parallelism. It tried to "dissolve" the notion of an integral soul, and it favored an atomistic and mechanistic analysis of consciousness in terms of primitive and logically isolated units of sensation. It was Lockean, simple-mindedly empirical, and positivistic.

Yet in describing the works of Wundt, Ebbinghaus, Stumpf, and Müller, such non-German accounts as Gardner Murphy's certainly do not create the impression of a thoughtless positivism.[16] On the contrary, Müller, Stumpf, and particularly Wundt opened up some of the antiassociationist arguments which were later used against them. Ebbinghaus apparently felt that the experimental science of psychology should be completely independent of philosophy, and this was bound to be held against him. Wundt, however, took the opposite position. In an essay published in 1913, he argued that the field of psychology extended considerably beyond the area in which laboratory techniques could be applied.[17] He mentioned thought psychology and his own folk psychology as examples of nonexperimental developments, and he pointed to the problem of parallelism in order to demonstrate that psychology could not and should not be separated from philosophy. It was characteristic of the whole position of his discipline at this time that he quickly became involved in the issue of academic staffing and examining. The difficulty, as he saw it, was that present holders of academic chairs in philosophy did not welcome psychologists as competitors for their professorships. The question of required lectures and examination subjects, with its implications for the private fee system, led to further rivalries and complications. Wundt urged the establishment of special chairs in philosophy for psychologists beside the existing professorships of philosophy. He did not support those of his fellow psychologists who sought refuge in separate chairs and examinations for their discipline. He tried to overcome the philosophers' objections to his own proposals, because he wished to preserve the working connection between philosophy and psychology. He was certainly not inclined to exaggerate the similarities between psychology and the natural sciences.

Nevertheless, Wundt did not always fare much better than Ebbinghaus in the highly colored accounts of the revival in psychology which became current after 1890. Careful distinctions became unfashionable and intellectual debts were forgotten as psychology too became involved in the "crisis of learning."

THE RENEWAL OF THE HUMANISTIC DISCIPLINES

The most important and distinguished contributions to the revival in German learning after 1880 dealt with the methods and objectives of the humanistic disciplines, the *Geisteswissenschaften*.[18] A number of simultaneous developments in the scholarship of the day provoked a new interest in this field. The methods controversy in economics and social policy, the Lamprecht debate, the new emphasis upon social and intellectual history, the birth of sociology, and the "cultural philosophy" of the Baden neo-Kantians: all these seemed to demand a re-examination of the German historical tradition and of the humanistic disciplines more generally. The result was a methodological debate which cut across disciplinary lines, influencing every field of knowledge outside the natural sciences. It affected the very language of scholarly discourse in the social studies and humanities. It created some of the most striking terms and concepts that played a role in the literature of cultural decadence and revival. Indeed, the label *Geisteswissenschaft* itself acquired a new and more formal meaning in this context. Of course the movement had its antecedents. Like other aspects of the mandarin tradition, it can be traced to the work of the German Idealists and Romantics around 1800. But the so-called neo-Idealists of the 1880's and 1890's made explicit what had often been merely assumed in the theory and practice of their predecessors. This helps to account for the impact of their thought abroad as well as at home.

In 1883, Wilhelm Dilthey published his famous introduction to the humanistic disciplines. In 1892, Georg Simmel followed with an important essay on the problems of the philosophy of history. The year 1894 saw the appearance of Dilthey's work on descriptive and analytical psychology and Wilhelm Windelband's rectoral address on history and natural science, which Meinecke called a "declaration of war against positivism." Heinrich Rickert's discussion of scientific conceptualization and its limitations was published in 1896. In 1910, a year before his death, Dilthey brought out his Berlin Academy treatise on the construction of the historical world in the humanistic disciplines. Finally, Max Weber wrote a number of methodological tracts between 1903 and 1919.[19]

It will not be possible to settle specific questions of intellectual precedence among these men. Dilthey's essay of 1883 was essentially a critical history of the humanistic disciplines. Though he introduced some of his most important methodological concepts in 1894, he did not publish a systematic statement of his own philosophy until 1910. Thus Dilthey's ideas developed to some extent concurrently with the work of Simmel and of the Baden neo-Kantians Windelband and Rickert. Still, it is probably fair to attribute a large share of originality to Dilthey. At least by implication, he anticipated many of the intellectual concerns of the 1890's in his introductory essay of 1883. He made a more elaborate attempt than anyone else to define the unique character and methods of the humanistic disciplines. Above all, it was Dilthey who focused the whole discussion of historical method upon the concepts of *erleben* and *verstehen*.

The German word *erleben* may be translated as "to experience." *Leben* means life; the *Erlebnis*, the act of *Erleben*, has the sense of a "vital experience," something one "lives through," in which one is deeply involved. Dilthey often used the term *Erlebnis* to describe an artistic experience, a moment of acute awareness in which the artist's emotions and intuitive faculties as well as his intellect participate. The impressions received during such a moment are not all associated with stimuli from the external environment. My experience of a beautiful morning is conditioned as much by my mood as by the brightness of the sun. Reflection upon my experience may cause me to distinguish between "external" and "internal" sources of my overall impression, between conditions actually present in my environment and memories evoked by the scene, or between intellectual and emotional components in my response. But these distinctions are not contained in the experience itself; they neglect its integral character. A vital experience as defined by Dilthey takes place on a preconceptual level; it lies in the undifferentiated, unanalyzed continuum of naive consciousness, of "life."

When we try to describe our vital experiences, we do generally separate what we perceive from what we feel, what is present from what is past, what is "inside" us and what is external or objective. We thus transform the vital experience into the raw materials of what we ordinarily call knowledge; we prepare the ground for the conceptual apparatus of scientific empiricism. Sometimes, though, we voluntarily or involuntarily give more direct expression to our vital experience; we convey a mood through exclamations, gestures, or facial expressions. The poet responds to a vital experience without fully submitting to the conventions of ordinary empirical description. He uses language evocatively; he selects phrases for their sounds and rhythms, not just for their dictionary meanings. A poem may thus reflect the character of a vital experience more directly than explicitly. Indeed, the poet himself may not become fully aware of the connection between his experience and its artistic expression. This is what Dilthey had in mind when he chose the word *Ausdruck* to describe the "direct expression" of vital human experience.

In their everyday meaning, the German words *verstehen* and *das Verstehen* would translate simply as "to understand" and "the understanding." In Dilthey's use of these terms, however, they were intended to designate a technique, a way of knowing, which was absolutely basic to all the humanistic disciplines. When I see a man who waves his fists, contorts his face in a certain way, and takes several steps toward me, I understand that he is threatening me. I do not arrive at this conclusion through an extended series of inferences, and I do not regard his actions as accidental or involuntary. Instantly, I know that he has something in mind; I grasp what he means, and I convey my own intention by running away. An observer of this scene would say that I fled because the man threatened me. But this statement would be based upon the observer's understanding; the word "because" which it contains would not be identical with the "because" that might appear in a physicist's explanation of an event in mechanics. The point is that when we understand certain gestures, we grasp their meaning; and the same applies to words, to whole essays, and indeed to everything which is the external expression of a human thought, experience, or intention.

To develop this point, Dilthey elaborated the neo-Idealist terminology which we have already encountered in Simmel's adaptation. Dilthey described all products of man's mental and spiritual activity as "objective geist," sometimes as the "world of geist" or the "intellectual [*geistig*] world." His use of the word objective in this connection was to indicate that in a language, a law code, or a written poem, a complex of initially subjective processes have been externalized, fixed in a material or objective form. Together, all existing objectifications of geist make up the intellectual world, the realm which is studied in the humanistic disciplines. "Understanding," in these terms, is the process by which we grasp the meanings expressed in the objectifications of the intellectual world.

To see how Dilthey conceived the method of understanding, one has to begin by picturing a three-step sequence in which a vital experience leads to a direct expression, perhaps a poem, which in turn evokes a vital experience in the reader of the poem. Dilthey described the last step in this sequence as "re-experiencing" (*Nacherleben*). He argued that all understanding in the humanistic disciplines is ultimately based upon this element of re-experiencing. On the other hand, Dilthey certainly did not mean to say that our knowledge of the intellectual world is simply a matter of intuitive empathy. His method of understanding (*Verstehen*) was a much more formal and empirically controlled procedure than the word empathy would suggest. He did not see anything mysterious in the fact that certain meanings become associated with appropriate gestures. We understand a language because we have learned to use it ourselves. Indeed, we may often misinterpret both gestures and words. In this respect, the humanistic disciplines have all the shortcomings of other empirical disciplines. The historian no less than the physicist must defend his account of a subject. He must not be willful in his interpretation. He must deal with all the relevant evidence, and he must satisfy our desire for an internally connected and consistent story. The only question is what sort of internal connections we look for in the humanistic disciplines.

In answering this question, Dilthey often referred to the notion of "stucture" (*Struktur*). The Pythagorean Theorem is certainly a part of objective geist. In understanding it, we do not explain it in terms of the laws of nature. In a way, we reproduce it in our minds; and yet we do not empathize with Pythagoras personally. The theorem has a "structure," an "objective" meaning, and it is this we "understand." If we turn to a poem, a legal code, or the ground plan of a factory, the situation changes slightly; but there is still a sense in which our understanding differs at once from ordinary psychological insight and from our knowledge of events in nature.

When studying a bit of objectified geist, we find that it is patterned in a certain way; its parts are meaningfully related to each other. The character of the relationships involved may differ. The structure of a poem may reflect aesthetic conventions to which the poet explicitly subscribed. The preamble of a constitution may state objectives to which the remaining provisions are related as means are to ends. Ultimately, our understanding of such patterns is based upon our self-knowledge. Moreover, there may be an element of direct expression (*Ausdruck*) in every objectification of geist. To that extent, our understanding does depend in part upon our own experiencing and re-experiencing. Dilthey's whole emphasis, however, was upon the "objective" structures, the explicit and logical patterns he found in the intellectual world. He thought it possible to understand the structure of a poem without claiming to have relived the poet's vital experience. It would also be quite consistent with his scheme to say that we can learn even about ourselves—by applying the technique of understanding to our old letters, for example.

Of course, Dilthey knew that there was a difference between the Pythagorean Theorem and a metaphysical system as objects of understanding. He put metaphysical systems in the same class with imaginative literature. In his view, a metaphysical construction, like a poem, was at least partly the expression of a certain weltanschauung and could be understood as such. Even in this case, understanding was not based on ordinary empathy alone. Instead, Dilthey thought it possible to describe all world views as composites of three basic orientations, which were associated with the human faculties of thought, will, and feeling. He emphasized that none of the three fundamental stances toward the world ever appeared in pure form and that the mixtures which did occur were unconsciously, not consciously, chosen.

This is the most obscure part of Dilthey's work, and it is also the area in which he came closest to neo-Kantian conceptions. In a way, we have been misrepresenting him in talking as if meanings were discoverable constituents of the intellectual world. In fact he argued that meaning was a necessary presupposition, something like an a priori category of understanding. In addition to the a priori elements in all thought, he posited special categories for the humanistic disciplines. Among these, meaning was the most important, although Dilthey apparently felt that it could be broken down further to account for the various aspects and assumptions of understanding. Dilthey hoped to settle some of these questions in a formal critique of historical reason, but this project was never completed. It would probably have drawn extensively upon his notion of a "descriptive and analytical psychology."

Dilthey was perfectly consistent in rejecting the interpretation of unconscious motives as a task for the humanistic disciplines. The technique of understanding, as he described it, could deal only with the manifest content of the intellectual world. It could not possibly help to decide whether medieval monks were masochists. It *could* approach the organization and the timetable of a Benedictine monastery, and it could grasp how these patterns were related to certain stated convictions and intentions. This is important, because it helps to account for Dilthey's views on psychology. He felt that ordinary psychology, "explaining [*erklärende*] psychology" in his terminology, was of little use in the humanistic disciplines. On the other hand, he considered it possible and necessary to develop a descriptive psychology of consciousness which could tackle some of the problems raised by the technique of understanding. Our sense of time, our present awareness of the past, would be a subject of study for such a psychology, as would the typological structure of man's weltanschauungen. All the categories of knowing and understanding could be uncovered in this type of analysis, rather than being assumed upon purely logical grounds. In a way, Dilthey's psychology was meant to be a basic geography of the intellectual world. The manifest content of that world, in his scheme, must necessarily reflect the organization of our minds. Ultimately, understanding is possible only because there is a special relationship between geist and its creations.

On this general point, Simmel, Windelband, and Rickert were in essential agreement with Dilthey. Simmel adopted the terminology of objective and subjective geist, as well as the concept of understanding. At the same time, he differed from Dilthey in several important ways. He distinguished between propositions and persons as objects of understanding. In the case of propositions, he shared Dilthey's emphasis upon manifest meanings. In the case of persons, however, he saw the act of understanding in more ordinary terms as a kind of psychological insight. Among other things, this meant that one important type of understanding could be applied to unconscious motives as well. The rather formidable wall which Dilthey erected between a self-contained world of pure geist and the rest of reality was thus breached at a decisive point.

Simmel was particularly anxious to show that the technique of understanding could not yield miraculous results. He warned against picturing a sort of telepathic communication between souls. He tried to show how easily we may err in our interpretations of other minds and how quickly we change our psychological models to adjust to any newly discovered bit of information. He did believe that a few men had a genius for understanding the motives and feelings of others, and he wondered whether some sort of racial memory was at work in these cases. But on a more ordinary level, he went so far as to recommend to historians the study of social psychology, since he felt that the averaged reactions of large groups and crowds were more primitive and therefore easier to understand than the more idiosyncratic thoughts and responses of individuals. Evidently, Simmel did not agree with Dilthey's views on the new psychology.

In a sense, the whole theory of understanding grew out of the old principle of empathy in the German historical tradition. Dilthey focused his investigations almost exclusively upon this problem, and Simmel developed his own theory on the subject. Windelband and Rickert were somewhat less concerned with the problem of empathy. They used the doctrine of understanding primarily in order to emphasize the profound difference they saw between the methods of the natural sciences and those of the social studies and humanities. They also shared Dilthey's conviction that ordinary psychology was of little use in the humanistic disciplines. But beyond that, they were primarily interested in the principle of individuality, differing in this respect from Dilthey.

Dilthey did see a difference between an explanation in which the particular case is made an instance of a general rule, and a description based on understanding in which a single complex of meanings is grasped. He freely admitted that the historian sometimes uses the systematizations of other disciplines to connect the events he relates. He was also prepared to treat particular world views as composites of more basic elements. Nevertheless, he believed that the object of our understanding is always a kind of individuality, a unique meaning. In that sense, one could call Dilthey an individualist. He insisted that ethical choices be regarded as purely individual matters, expressions of particular personalities. He was always suspicious of overly general concepts in the humanistic disciplines, and he particularly disliked people who talked too carelessly about the feelings of large groups and classes, as if these were anything but collections of individuals. If this strikes us as inconsistent with the rest of Dilthey's views, we need only remember that the objects of the intellectual world were his primary sources. He could permit statements about the organization of a whole society or the objectives of a certain association, as long as these were based upon the manifest content of available documents. In his system, it was perfectly legitimate to discuss the meaning of the Prussian General Code. On the other hand, it was both dangerous and unnecessary to move from there to any general conclusions about the motives and desires of eighteenth-century Prussians.

Simmel's contribution to the individuality problem was an attack upon the notion of historical laws. Like Dilthey, Simmel believed that historians may use explanations taken from other disciplines. At the same time, he pointed out how difficult it would be to arrive at a full analysis of the relationship between two historical conditions: A and B. To demonstrate this, he proposed to describe A and B more precisely in terms of their constituent elements $a, b, c \ldots n$ and $a', b', c' \ldots n'$. Strictly speaking, the assertion that B is the consequence of A would involve identities or "real" causal connections between all the elements $a, b, c \ldots n$ and their respective counterparts a′, b′, c′ . . . n′. Under the concept of real causal connections, Simmel pictured something like primitive interactions between atoms or other elementary constituents of reality. He hastened to say that even in the natural sciences, we have no way of knowing whether our analysis has penetrated down to this level, so that the whole notion of real causal chains becomes a hypothetical analogy. Nevertheless, he thought it worth pointing out that unlike the natural scientist, the historian knows full well that he has not achieved anything approximating an analysis in terms of sequences which may even presently be taken to be elementary. He also knows that any system of conditions which he may try to isolate for study is open to influences from without, so that all his explanations must have a casual and provisional character.

Simmel did not regard this as a particularly disheartening state of affairs. Even the most tentative approximation of reality seemed to him valuable, as long as its status was not misjudged. He even had a kind word for the metaphysical speculations which invariably accompanied the supposed discovery of a general cause in history. These seemed to him to answer men's need for self-expression, and he had no objection to that. In short, he did his part to challenge the ordinary conception of historical laws; but he did not think it necessary to develop a philosophical defense of the individuality principle.

That task was taken up by Windelband. Working with an antithesis that had already been stated by Dilthey, Windelband distinguished between a "nomothetic" and an "idiographic" approach to experience. In the nomothetic method, he said, we explain particular objects and events by ordering them under general rules. We classify them; we treat them as subordinate instances; and we abstract as much as possible from those of their characteristics which fall outside the scope of our generalizations. In the idiographic method, on the other hand, we are interested in the unique quality of the item in question. We try to give a complete account of it; we seek to grasp its gestalt in all its concreteness (*Anschaulichkeit*). As Windelband saw it, the idiographic technique was especially suited to the fields of biography and history. It almost had to imply some sort of personal understanding, although groups of men, whole nations, or complexes of meaning could apparently be treated as individualities. Windelband thought that the idiographic method could be applied in the study of nature as well; but he did not develop this point in any detail. He did suggest that in psychology, nomothetic techniques were often applied to the realm of consciousness. It was this circumstance more than anything else which caused him to feel that the traditional line between the natural sciences and the humanistic disciplines (*Geisteswissenschaften*) did not coincide with the border between nomothetic "generalizing sciences" (*Gesetzeswissenschaften*) and idiographic or "historical" disciplines (*Geschichtswissenschaften*). In any case, he said, the epistemologists of the past had failed to realize the importance of the idiographic approach. They had allowed the nomothetic method to be taken as the epitome of all knowledge, and it was time to rectify that error.

As may be imagined, the idiographic theory made it especially difficult for the historian to decide how to choose his subjects and how to vary the emphasis in the various sections of his story. In Dilthey's system, the whole problem of historical selection could not become too serious, since one had only to reproduce what the men of the past considered important in their own intellectual world. For Simmel, the question became more complicated, since unexpressed motives had to be taken into account, and since the world of geist was not so clearly isolated from the sphere of reality in which crops fail. Simmel certainly saw the difficulty; but he was content to have historians experiment with any explanation which could even partially clarify any aspect of the past. In Windelband's scheme, however, the very sharpness of the contrast between the two methods appeared to demand a more definitive theory of idiographic selection. In nomothetic knowledge, the relationships between instances and general rules were held to provide adequate criteria for the necessary choices of subject matter; but the search for generalizations was explicitly excluded from the idiographic realm, and it seemed only natural to ask what was to take its place.

Windelband suggested that it was the intrinsic importance or value of a given object of idiographic investigation which led the historian to isolate it for treatment; but he did not explore the matter in any detail. This is where Rickert made his most important contribution to the whole discussion. He began by distinguishing between a "formal" and a "material" approach in the classification of the disciplines; the formal approach was concerned with methods, the material approach with subject matter. Rickert was essentially prepared to accept Windelband's scheme as the most basic formal antithesis. But on the material level, he objected to the traditional distinction between nature and geist. He pointed out that many psychologists considered themselves natural scientists and that man could be treated either as a part of a nature or as a unique phenomenon. Surely it was his role as the creator of culture which set him apart and made him a special subject for study.

After the usual remarks upon the uselessness of the old individual and social psychology for the historian, Rickert proposed that the "material" division of knowledge be based on the difference between nature and culture, not nature and geist. He tried to show that the word culture inevitably implied human valuations and purposes which were more than mere by-products of primitive needs or personal whims. This, he said, is what the Marxists had failed to understand. Assigning the realm of culture to the cultural disciplines (*Kulturwissenschaften*), he went on to argue that the "formal" line between nomothetic and idiographic methods ran parallel to the "material" distinction between the natural sciences and the cultural disciplines. The natural sciences were principally, though not exclusively, "generalizing sciences"; in the cultural disciplines the predominant emphasis was upon the historical or "individualizing" approach.

As a neo-Kantian, Rickert warned against the common-sense notion that our knowledge is a passive mirror image of reality (*Abbildung*). He pointed out that any sort of description involves an active transformation (*Umbildung*) of experience, a conceptualization. In this process, we isolate what appear to us the essential (*wesentlich*) aspects of any object or event; we construct our own objects of cognition. In the "real" world, there is no essential difference between nature and geist. There is only one kind of being.

It is the quality of our interest which causes us to distinguish between the natural and the cultural; we want to know different things about these two realms.

With this as a background, Rickert felt able to solve the problem of idiographic selection. In the cultural disciplines, he said, we hold essential that which embodies or relates to man's conscious objectives and valuations. Our method is generally idiographic, because a cultural object interests us precisely in its individuality and uniqueness. The relationships we do uncover might be described as teleological in character, because they reflect purposes. Where we deal with the general at all, it is the evaluative meaning of the word general that we have in mind. Indeed, it is each historian's sense of the generality and importance of certain values which guides him in his choice of subject matter and emphasis. This poses a difficulty, for it would seem to make idiographic selection entirely dependent upon changing personal preferences. A universally valid cultural discipline, a generally accepted scheme of selection, would have to be based upon an inclusive system of objective and timeless cultural norms. Of course we do not presently have such absolute standards, Rickert argued, but we should not rule out further progress in that direction. Maintaining a close working partnership between the empirical cultural disciplines and Idealist philosophy, we might be able to approach "the suprahistorical within the historical," to create a culturally founded weltanschauung.[20] This prospect was the main point of Rickert's reflections.

Windelband and Rickert developed their systems in a purely theoretical framework. In this, they differed from Max Weber, the last contributor to the discussion of methods in the humanistic disciplines. Weber formed his own views in a series of confrontations with the doctrines of others. His essays therefore interest us not only as criticisms but also as histories of the controversies that he treats. From Weber we learn that Wilhelm Roscher and Karl Knies, the fathers of the historical tradition in German economics, worked extensively with the principle of individuality. As early as 1853, we find, Knies regarded the historical approach as a totally unique form of investigation, one which was not fully described in the existing distinction between natural sciences and humanistic disciplines. Again, Weber's writings show us the great breadth of the movement toward a new philosophy of the cultural and historical studies which began after 1880. Wundt's "creative synthesis," we discover, was thought to exemplify the mind's ability to combine sense impressions or ideas into new combinations which were culturally more valuable than the sum of their constituents. The suggestion was that this type of "creation" took place only in the realm of geist, which therefore had to be investigated in special ways. That men are motivated by ethical considerations, that they have free will, and that their behavior is irrational in the sense of incalculable: all these propositions were held to describe the characteristic dignity of human life and to reveal the need for unusual methods in its study. In numerous variations upon the theory of understanding, such philosophers and psychologists as Theodor Lipps and Hugo Münsterberg sought to show that our knowledge of other psyches is a more primitive function of our immediate consciousness than the formal abstraction of scientific analysis.[21]

Weber directed his criticism against such outgrowths of the methodological debate. He did not doubt that particularly Simmel and Rickert had made some important discoveries about the nature of explanatory techniques in history and in related disciplines. He only sought to separate these from their unwarranted speculative extensions. Although he often drew upon the theories of the Baden neo-Kantians, he was not a trained philosopher. On the other hand, he had a great zest for examples, a certain contempt for transparently hasty arguments in favor of free will and the like, the willingness to rest his case at least partly on descriptions of the historians' de facto procedures, the patience to make numerous distinctions, and the determination to define some sort of a boundary between wissenschaft and value judgment.

To begin with, Weber had no serious objections to Simmel's views on the role of interpretation in the humanistic disciplines. He believed that we do often explain human actions and expressions by referring to their meanings. He liked Simmel's distinction between motives and statements as objects of understanding, although he did not propose to regard understanding as a simple extension of self-knowledge. He noted that one did not have to be Caesar to interpret Caesar's behavior, nor a madman to see some meaningful or coherent elements in the acts of a schizophrenic. Dilthey's insulation of the intellectual world did not appeal to him. Like Simmel, Weber regarded understanding as a type of causal explanation, and this made him impatient with careless remarks about teleology in history and with the notion that understanding affords us special insights into a realm of incalculability and freedom. On the one hand, as he pointed out, we can never achieve a full description or causal determination of any event, whether material or mental; on the other hand, an explanation based on understanding certainly increases our sense of the calculability or predictability of the behavioral pattern we have understood. It is therefore inappropriate to entangle the discussion of interpretation in the humanistic disciplines with an overly philosophical treatment of the individuality principle and of the free will problem.

With Rickert and against Münsterberg and others, Weber argued that all knowing must involve conceptualization and that the postulation of two radically contrasting modes of being or consciousness is unnecessary and indefensible. He pointed out that the particular is no more accessible without "abstract" concepts than the rule. He was highly critical of the often unacknowledged tendency to solve this problem by picturing the concrete historical individuality as the emanation of an idea. More clearly and insistently than Rickert, he traced the qualitative differences between types of explanation to the diversity of our interests. Once the questionable notion of a fully "determined" event is discarded, it becomes possible to observe that our sense of satisfaction with an answer depends to a large extent upon the nature of the question asked. When explaining a particular development, we may indeed use available causal rules; but we do not seek to establish any new ones. Nor do we attempt the impossible task of uncovering all the "real" or elementary connections involved in the process. We are satisfied to find an "adequate," not a necessary, relationship between two circumstances, and we do not proceed to erect this relationship into a general law. Essentially, that is the extent of the difference between idiographic and nomothetic knowledge.

If we were interested in the grounds of a man's behavior, Weber continued, we would not be fully satisfied even if we could discover that in identical circumstances all other men had acted in precisely the same way. This is where understanding becomes relevant, because we are looking for information about the man's feelings and thoughts. We want to find an adequate cause of his behavior, and the laws available to us from systematic psychology or from other generalizing disciplines may not help. In that case, we either treat the man's actions as rational with respect to his purposes (*zweckrational*), or we introduce a bit of psychological insight. Psychological insight, the most primitive form of understanding, is based upon experience; but it is not generally stated in the form of rules. In order to show what would happen if we did try to make laws out of our understanding techniques, Weber quoted from the German humorist Wilhelm Busch: "He who is pleased when someone suffers, usually is disliked by the others."[22] Here, as Weber said, we have a fine example of a "rule of adequate causation" which is derived from understanding. Typically, it could help historians to trace Anglo-German tension after the Boer War to the German attitude during that conflict. In order to see why it should not be stated as a general law, we need only imagine a history book with an appended catalog of all the Wilhelm Busch "rules" which were implied in it. The resulting list of little sayings and ditties, apart from causing some embarrassment, would be appallingly long and quite devoid of any information which was not already contained in the text. Apparently, Weber introduced the quote from Busch not only to expose the fallacy of a fully lawful (*gesetzmässig*) history, but also to take away some of the glamor which was threatening to attach itself to the process of understanding.

Weber certainly respected Rickert, and he borrowed a great deal from him; but he avoided the formalities of Rickert's theory of idiographic selection and his complex speculations on the subject of the cultural disciplines. Weber generally preferred to maintain the old distinction between the natural sciences and the humanistic disciplines, and he was more circumspect than Rickert in delimiting the role of value judgments in historical selection. Weber began by admitting that historians work with a concept of cultural relevancy in choosing subjects for study. They do not investigate events that have had no bearing upon some set of cultural purposes and values. They consider things important depending upon the directness of their relationship to more or less central aspects of man's cultural life. Weber used the term "value-related" (*wertbezogen*) to characterize the relevant, and he argued that any selection on this basis must involve a judgment, since the concept of culture itself implies a valuation.* At the same time, he tried to distinguish between judging something to be value-related and actually valuing it. He also pointed out that however we select what we intend to study, even if our incentives are purely personal preferences, the validity of our discoveries is logically independent of the motives that influenced the choice of subject matter. In other words, the selection problem does not provide a bridge on which we can move from observation to value judgment: the study of culture does not lead to a science of what is culturally relevant; nor do we require "objective" decisions on the relevancy issue in order to write accurate histories.

The logical separation between *Wert* (value) and wissenschaft was Weber's objective in another area as well. As we know, the technique of understanding was held to be applicable to conscious convictions and choices as well as to less explicit motives in others. It was therefore easy to picture understanding as an immediate grasping of ethical judgments and cultural values. Moreover, it was possible to imagine that the understander had fully to re-experience what he understood, so that only a saint could really interpret the feelings and actions of another saint. In the face of such generally unacknowledged misconceptions, Weber once again emphasized the logical

---

* This is how Weber cleared up the problem of Wundt's "creative synthesis": An architect builds a house of stones. Culturally, something new appears, although in the morally and emotionally neutral terms of a causal equation, the process is no more creative than the formation of a crystal.

difference between the validation of an account and the description of its psychological origins in some hunch, intuition, or affinity. Beyond that, he did a great deal to clarify the whole problem of understanding when he introduced his well-known concept of the ideal type.

According to Weber's definition, the "ideal type" is a pure construct, a hypothetical model, an "idea." The "free market economy" is an ideal type, as is the mandarin concept of the present essay. Weber believed that most of the abstractions and general terms used in social and cultural studies were ideal types, and he suggested such examples as feudalism, imperialism, the religious sect, early Christianity, and the handicraft system. He thought it important to stress that we do not discover concepts of this kind in any body of evidence. They are neither averages nor ordinary hypotheses, though they may lead us to the latter. If, having constructed a type of capitalism, we notice that it does not fit a group of facts about a certain country at a given time, we do not therefore discard our type as worthless. On the contrary, we may find divergences from a type quite as interesting as close correspondences to it. Moreover, we can imagine several different models of mercantilism, for example, and we do not doubt that each of them could have a perfectly legitimate use as an interpretive device. How are we to account for this impression?

The easiest way to describe Weber's views on this question is to refer again to the theory of understanding. Precisely those aspects of a historical situation which lend themselves to an interpretation through understanding may be epitomized in an ideal type. Thus we can build a model of behavior which is rational with respect to certain purposes, and we do not require any empirical evidence to do this. The internal consistency of a certain weltanschauung, the way in which given psychological needs adequately cause certain kinds of responses, the relationship between different parts of a meaningful pattern, the structured quality of certain developments: all these may be hypothetically treated as if they were logically coherent systems, and as such, they need have no exact counterparts in reality. Indeed, our whole sense of understanding in the social and cultural studies stems from the fact that consciously or unconsciously, we order much of our material with reference to ideal models of this kind.

Once this is clear, the real point of Weber's theory is not hard to uncover. On the one hand, the ideal type is clearly distinguished from the concept of nomothetic laws in history. It does away with the "positivist" notion that generalizations about cultural developments are induced from the material of the past. On the other hand, it also undercuts the tendency to picture understanding as an immediate or intuitive grasping of motives and values. It takes some of the mystery out of the problem of empathy, and it further clarifies the process of idiographic selection. Weber never tired of emphasizing that while our judgments of cultural relevancy influence our choice of ideal types, they do not or should not enter into the purely empirical investigation in which we essentially compare our evidence to our models.

In a way, the ideal type and the theory of understanding were particularly appropriate to the work Weber was doing on the *Protestant Ethic*. This is what Schumpeter meant when he included Weber in the "youngest historical school" of German economics. On the other hand, Weber's position could also provide the logical basis for a reconciliation between the theorists and the historians among economists. Even the controversy in social policy might have been resolved through Weber's clear separation of scholarship and value judgment. In sociology, Weber's distinctions were particularly relevant to the problem of "formal" analysis. If one applies his description of understanding and his concept of the ideal type to the writings of Tönnies, Simmel, and von Wiese, one immediately achieves a new clarity of understanding. Tönnies' social entities (*soziale Wesenheiten*) were types; his forms of the will were categories of understanding. Simmel wrote as if to elucidate the inner logic or meaning of social structures and relationships; it became Weber's task to demonstrate the usefulness—and the limitations—of this procedure. The disadvantages of von Wiese's formalism lay in his failure to compare his typological system to a body of evidence, not in the supposedly positivist nature of his logical analysis. In an essay published in 1913, Weber explicitly extended his methodological arguments to the problems of sociology.[23] He used the notion of purposeful (*zweckrational*) behavior to clarify some of Tönnies' theories, and he described *Gemeinschaftshandeln* (acting communally) and *Gesellschaftshandeln* (acting societally) as two typical categories of social behavior.

Finally, Weber spoke to the new interest in history. Much of his argument was developed in a commentary upon Roscher and Knies; but his remarks were certainly relevant to more recent exploitations of the German historical tradition as well. On the one hand, Weber challenged the idea that the historian can avoid any form of "isolating" conceptualization, that he can describe all the aspects of a given situation. On the other hand, he disposed of a whole cluster of speculative notions which were based upon the principles of empathy and individuality. He asked the social scientists not to compare their explanations to the laws of mechanics or to the "real" causal relationships between elementary constituents of reality. But he also demanded that the historians drop their misconceptions about historical intuition, about teleology and "freedom" in history. In sum, his thought could not be adequately described in the popular slogans about positivism and idealism. It was much too clear for that. Unfortunately, too few of his contemporaries understood what he wrote.

LEARNING AND LIFE: THE PROBLEM
OF VALUES

The innovations in philosophy and in the humanistic disciplines after 1890 were certainly not motivated by technical and logical considerations alone. The search for an idealistic weltanschauung was an important element in the scholarly revival from the start. The work of the Baden neo-Kantians was meant to provide the basis for a restoration of Fichtean Idealism. Windelband, Rickert, and their followers consistently emphasized the philosopher's role as a discoverer of norms and valuations. Rickert's cultural philosophy resurrected the old model of geist realized in the universe of culture. Since Rickert treated values as the main foundations of that universe, his philosophy of culture could appear to promise the "discovery" of permanent moral truths. Thus historical observation and speculative philosophy tended to flow together in the theories of the Baden neo-Kantians.

It is often the simple implication of a complex argument that gains a wider audience. Neither the Baden school nor the new theorists of understanding asserted that they had actually established the grounds for an idealistic weltanschauung. But Windelband and Rickert certainly let it be known that they were well on the way to this goal. Their readers might have taken their objectives for achievements. In a similar way, the doctrine of understanding and the whole emphasis upon the uniqueness of methods in the humanistic disciplines lent itself to a number of popular interpretations. The mandarins had always preferred to see the act of knowing as a kind of total relationship between the knower and his subject. There was a great temptation to adapt the theory of understanding to this inclusive view of cognition, especially in the climate of the cultural crisis. Dilthey gave no comfort to the seekers of ethical certainties. He refused to regard a given weltanschauung as anything more than a purely personal choice, although one that reflected certain psychological predilections and historical conditions. He also felt that there were no timeless and "objective" values. He could find nothing but the actual choices made by individuals in their respective historical settings. Far from being troubled by that situation, he welcomed it as a mark of man's freedom. Simmel and Weber certainly did what they could to check idealistic exploitations of the methodological discussion. But this was less true of Windelband and of Rickert. In developing their theories of idiographic selection, these men came perilously close to identifying the significant with the permanently valuable. They thus suggested a continuous interrelationship between the empathetic understanding of historic valuations and the unearthing of timeless norms in the philosophy of culture. Rickert began by defining the criteria of idiographic selection in terms of "value-relatedness"; but he ended by promising to find "the suprahistorical in the historical." Such phrases did not help in preventing the confusions which provoked Weber's commentary.

Thus the revival in learning was accompanied by a profound yearning for the restoration of an idealistic weltanschauung. Emotional needs influenced the technical discussion of methodological alternatives. The mandarins wanted to re-create a condition in which wissenschaft could be said to affect the whole person, the whole nation, and all the concerns of "life." They sought spiritual power, not just spiritual comfort. Positivism and specialization, they felt, had reduced the efficacy of learning by restricting it to the realm of passive observation and mere technique. Geist had abandoned its kingdom, which had now to be recovered.

Sentiments of this sort have appeared in other times and places. The circumstances of social history do not suffice to account for them. But their intensity among German academics after 1890 certainly had something to do with the impact of modernity upon the mandarin tradition. Indeed, the revulsion against "merely technical" knowledge affected educated Germans outside the universities as well. The mood was so intense that it almost escaped the professors' control. In the form of popular "life philosophy," it threatened the very foundations of traditional learning.

Vulgar *Lebensphilosophie*, philosophy of life, is rather hard to describe.[24] I believe the term itself was first used by Dilthey's students and editors to describe and to entitle the master's later works. Though Dilthey apparently approved the label before he died in 1911, it did not come into general use until the 1920's. As more and more fragments of Dilthey's projected critique of historical reason were edited and published by his pupils during the Weimar period, he gradually acquired public renown as a philosopher of life. His thought influenced Martin Heidegger's philosophy of existence and possibly Edmund Husserl's phenomenology as well. In the meantime, a process of vulgarization and diffusion had begun even before 1920 to transform Dilthey's complexities into a popular philosophy.

As early as 1920, Heinrich Rickert wrote a critique of "life philosophy," in which he described his subject matter as a broad and fashionable movement, not as the work of one man. Between 1929 and 1932, Ludwig Klages, a private scholar, published three volumes on "geist as the enemy of the soul"; but vulgar philosophy of life certainly did not originate with Klages. In short, the doctrines of the movement cannot be safely attributed to anyone in particular, and yet they clearly achieved a certain influence. Indeed, popular life philosophy had much in common with some of the volkish, anti-Semitic, and neo-conservative literature of anti-modernity. Both originated on the fringes of the academic world or outside it; both exaggerated attitudes which were present among the mandarin intellectuals themselves; and both threatened to outbid the professors for the attention of the half-educated and the young.

In a very general sense, life philosophy was the doctrine that life in its immediacy is man's primary reality. This idea could be interpreted in a variety of ways. It could be treated as a metaphysical truth, in which case freedom, creativity, "wholeness" in experience, and the like appeared as the most general characteristics of reality. Klages apparently held some such theories. He also enlarged upon such terms as experiencing, understanding, Einfühlung (empathy), and Anschauung (viewing, intuiting) to suggest a whole battery of more than "merely conceptual" ways of knowing the immediate reality of life. Dilthey's "immediate experience" took on the character of a mystical device in the philosophy of life. In pedagogy, experiencing could acquire the sense of active learning, almost of "acting out" a sequence of events and reactions. In a more general usage, the act of experiencing involved the knower's imagination and emotion as well as his intellect. Like "empathy" and "viewing," the concept of experiencing (Erleben) thus suggested that the undivided impressions of naive experience are less misleading, in many ways, than the material which reaches us through the filter of analytical abstraction and scientific classification.

In a further variety of life philosophy, all conceptual knowledge and geist itself were portrayed as hindrances or "enemies" of life. Again it was Klages who eventually carried this notion to an extreme. But Windelband and Rickert, the foremost critics of life philosophy, also suspected Nietzsche, Bergson, Simmel, and Eucken of holding this view, at least in a modified form. Simmel did see an antithesis between subjective geist, which was always in creative flux, and the products of this geist, which tended to acquire an objective reality, following fixed laws of their own and restricting the freedom of the creator. On the other hand, Simmel also pointed out that conceptualization was unavoidable, so that nothing could be achieved without a continuing interaction between formative creativity and created form.* Eucken talked about a conflict between life and knowledge; but he managed to "overcome" it by elevating life itself to a higher plane of meaning. This was regarded as an idealistic solution of the problem.[25]

A final variant of life philosophy was the notion that life could be made the ultimate criterion of truth and of morals. Social Darwinists and moralists of the will to power were accused of this fallacy, which was sometimes called biologism. Interestingly enough, Rickert and Windelband also considered American and German pragmatism a part of life philosophy. In their opinion, James, Bergson, Nietzsche, and Hans Vaihinger could be grouped together, because they all tended to believe that our generalizations are selected primarily on the basis of their usefulness in the service of life. Even Dilthey was sometimes accused of this view, because, among other things, he had treated weltanschauungen primarily as symptoms of psychological needs and historical conditions. In response, the neo-Kantian critics of life philosophy went to great lengths to show that the truth of any proposition must be independent not only of its utility, but also of its historical and psychological origins. In fairness to the American pragmatists, Windelband distinguished the "usefulness" of a concept in the organization of evidence from the more immediate "practicality" of a proposition which suits our prejudices or adds to our comfort. As a "pragmatic" criterion, prac-

---

* Primarily during the last decade before his death in 1918, under the influence of Dilthey and of Bergson, Simmel developed a philosophy of culture in which the concept of "life" played an important role. He used his (initially sociological?) distinction between "form" and "content" in a (vaguely) neo-Kantian sense to separate mental or logical categories or activities (forms) from the subjects, "things," or ideas (contents) which are thought or contemplated.

ticality was clearly the more absurd and despicable of the two; but even heuristic usefulness failed to convince Windelband. In his opinion, some philosophically acceptable analogue of the correspondence between our statements and a posited reality was necessary to the very idea of truth.

All this does not seem very interesting at first, particularly since the doctrines associated with vulgar life philosophy are so hard to attribute to any systematic representatives. On the other hand, the critique of life philosophy does throw some light upon the mandarins' view of their opponents. Dilthey tried to uncover the emotional and historical sources of ethical and metaphysical convictions, precisely because he did not believe that any absolute truths could be obtained in these fields. It was this skepticism, this ejection of moral choice and weltanschauung from the realm of wissenchaftlich knowledge, which made him suspect to his more conventional colleagues. The pragmatists and "conventionalists" posed an even greater threat to the mandarin system, and so did the popular prophets of "life." It is certainly startling to find Bergson, Klages, Dilthey, James, and sometimes even Mach and Poincaré grouped together under the same general heading. But to the mandarins, this equation made sense. They had to insist that an idealistic weltanschauung could be logically founded upon an idealistic wissenschaft. They could not tolerate the separation of learning from life. It did not matter to them whether the divorce proceedings were initiated by a wissenschaft grown modest and skeptical through positivism, or by an irrationalism grown arrogant in its defense of life. They had to maintain that their wisdom was both well-founded and inaccessible to the man in the street. They did not want to be replaced by mere analysts and technicians; but they had equally little desire to abdicate to the vital urges of self-made anti-intellectuals, political activists, and literary dabblers in biologism. They were prepared to go rather far in their own flirtations with understanding, experiencing, and the like. Rickert and Windelband publicly sympathized with certain aspects of popular life philosophy. They regarded it as a misguided form of idealism, an untutored but fundamentally justified reaction against the old "intellectualism." They meant to make every possible concession to life, as long as they did not have to abandon the fortress of wissenschaft.

One of the main difficulties with this program around 1920 was the so-called problem of *Historismus,* another one of those complicated issues involving the relationship between scholarly observation and value judgment. The German word *Historismus* is not fully equivalent to the English "historical relativism." When a British or American historian talks about the problem of historical relativism, he is generally concerned with the sources of systematic bias in our accounts of the past. He observes that antagonists in a war tend to disagree about its origins long after it is over. This suggests that personal interests and allegiances often or always influence a historian's point of view and that the ideal of objectivity may have to be revised accordingly. In other words, historical relativism appears primarily in the role of an obstacle to historical certainty; this is not so in the case of historism. In a way, *Historismus* might most appropriately be translated as "the historical approach" or even as "past-mindedness" in the Rankean sense. In historism, all statements and value judgments are treated historically, as parts of an ever changing development. Nothing appears fixed and permanent; everything flows. Our own truths and ethics are as conditional a part of our epoch as the Spanish inquisitor's were of his. This is the *problem* of historism, the difficulty inherent in the historical approach to ideas. Clearly, there is a certain similarity between this problem and that of historical relativism. A mandarin philosopher might say that historism implies or leads to a kind of relativism. But whereas the British or American historical relativist talks mainly about the apparent impossibility of an objective account of the past, the problem of historism deals primarily with the difficulty of rescuing timeless truths and values from the flux of history.

It is really not surprising that the dilemma of historism became particularly acute in Germany just before 1920. The Lamprecht controversy and the new interest in social and cultural history stimulated a re-examination of the German historical tradition. The apparent threat to the mandarin heritage as a whole had the same effect.

During the war, there was an incentive to contrast English and French scholarly methods with those of German learning, and the general anxiety of the cultural crisis helped to focus attention upon the problem of values. After the turn of the century, the word historism (*Historismus*) began to appear in German academic histories of philosophy. Like "positivism" and "materialism," it was meant to identify an obstacle to the revival of Idealism. The critics used "historism" to castigate the tendency to treat values and ideas as "merely historical," as strictly ephemeral products of a certain environment. During the decades before 1890, they argued, too many philosophers had become simply historians of past philosophies. This too was historism.

Finally, the work of Dilthey and his successors greatly aggravated the problem of historism. There was some irony in that circumstance. The whole theory of understanding was meant to deepen the relationship between the historical observer and his subject. The principle of empathy had always implied the discovery of meanings—and values—in the cultural process. If anything, the revival in the humanistic disciplines had strengthened this aspect of the German historical tradition. But of necessity, it had also reinforced the principle of individuality, the sense that all objectifications of geist are unique in their setting. Dilthey frankly treated weltanschauungen as products of specific historical and psychological contexts. Rickert and Windelband tried to bridge the gap between "the historical" and "the suprahistorical"; but their solution was obviously strained. The dilemma of historism was not resolved.

No man did more to explore the concept of historism and to make it an issue during the crisis of learning than Max Weber's friend Ernst Troeltsch. Mainly between 1918 and 1922, Troeltsch published a number of essays and one longer study on this subject.[26] Typically, he used the word historism to describe nothing less than the historical approach to man's experience, which he then identified essentially with the German historical tradition. He traced that tradition to the great German Idealists and Romantics. As might be expected, he saw a decline in German historiography during the decades after 1848. Positivism and Darwinism, he said, had come to aggravate an indigenous tendency to overspecialize, while the task of "synthesis" and the fight against "naturalism" had been left to such dilettantes as Paul de Lagarde. Troeltsch gave credit to Dilthey and to the Baden neo-Kantians for the renewal of the humanistic disciplines after 1890; but he also regarded the revival as a natural extension of the German historical tradition itself.

Troeltsch began his reflections upon the German intellectual heritage in the context of the cultural war. He consistently emphasized the contrast between German historiography on the one hand and English and French traditions on the other. In English and French positivism and naturalism, he wrote, historical reality is conceived as a composite of fundamentally similar constituent units, which combine and recombine in various ways. Change, in this scheme, is "causal-genetic." The elements interact like balls on a billiard table, and no really new factors are ever added to the system. Each constellation generates its successor. The analogy from mechanics suggests determinism. The historian observes the process "from the outside," as it were. His object is always to analyze a given configuration down to its basic constituents, which may then be recombined in accordance with inductively established laws of interaction. The positivist suspects that association psychology will eventually come up with a kind of atomic theory of mental life. At bottom, he sees history as applied sociology.

The German historian, by contrast, works primarily with the category of "individual totality." He treats persons, periods, and especially states as unique and meaningful "syntheses." Following neo-Idealist theories, he knows that the past lives in his own consciousness. This encourages him to replace the abstractly analytical procedure of the French and English sociologist with an emphasis upon immediate empathy and "sympathetic understanding." He prefers the psychology of the higher mental functions to psycho-physicism and associationism. With Wundt, he believes that there is "creative synthesis" in the world of geist. Cultural values, which are born of the creative tension between the individual and his community, enter the historian's system as something entirely new, as products of man's spiritual freedom. The true historian does not try to force the material of the past into a naturalistic causal chain. Rather, he wants to understand the meanings and values of other epochs. In selecting his evidence, he works with the concept of the essential (*das Wesentliche*), not with historical laws. He emphasizes those aspects of a bygone era which the men of that age themselves considered most important. Finally, he describes historical development as the unfolding of tendencies, ideas, and values which are inherent in the very structure of a given period. In this as in all his work, he is guided by the ideal of past-mindedness, of "historical tact."

Having described the historical approach in these familiar terms, Troeltsch went on to consider the substantive philosophy of history. By way of introducing this part of his subject, he drew upon the old distinction between the formal, that is to say, epistemological or methodological, and the material or substantive analysis of philosophical problems. This dichotomy was often mentioned in the discussion of the revival in philosophy. The theory was that a substantive interest in ethics and a substantive consideration of metaphysical issues would have to supersede the overly formalistic tendency of critical neo-Kantianism, if any further progress was to be made. Windelband himself applied this antithesis to the field of history as early as 1916.[27] His argument was that the new interest in questions of method was helpful only as a preparation for a substantive philosophy of history, which in turn would eventually contribute to an integral theory of norms (*Wertwissenschaft*) and to a neo-Idealist metaphysic of the intellectual world. Troeltsch adopted this thesis, as he moved from a formal description of historism to a consideration of its most important substantive implications.

What Troeltsch meant when he wrote of the *problem* of historism and how he proposed to solve that problem may be epitomized in the following sequence of arguments: The true historian sees every idea and every aspect of cultural life in a historical context. The more thoroughly he commits himself to the ideal of past-mindedness and the more deeply he appreciates the sense in which every age has its own unique spirit, the more he must come to doubt the possibility of eternal truths and cultural norms. The whole intellectual world reveals itself to him as a world of historical individualities. He cannot step outside this realm, as the positivist does, to abstract timeless laws of social interaction. He knows that no religious conviction, no weltanschauung, no ethical standard can be exempted from the rule of historicity. An extreme cultural and moral relativism seems the only possible conclusion. This is the bane of historism.

While one cannot evade this dilemma by positing an unhistorical absolute, Troeltsch argued, it may nevertheless be possible to discover an antidote against unlimited skepticism in the structure of the historical method itself. After all, our study of the past is never entirely passive. We can only "understand" those motives and ideas which we ourselves have shared to some extent. When we select, we do so with respect to our own sense of cultural value, so that an element of judgment and will is contained in our historical perspectives from the very beginning. Moreover, there is an intimate relationship between our conception of the past and our values and aims for the present and the future. Indeed, what we are and hope to be is never anything more than an extension of our historical knowledge. Our own cultural values are at one and the same time the products of the past and the criteria used in its understanding. This is only to say again that our consciousness is the real field of historical investigation. When we study meaningful relationships in history, we are also uncovering the dimensions and potentialities of our own minds. With every act of historical judgment, we tend to describe our own place in the structure of the intellectual world. Our final choice of a position is an active synthesis, an act of self-definition, in which our perspectives upon the past are merged with our sense of identity and with our desires for the future.

On the basis of these considerations, Troeltsch recommended that philosophers of history concern themselves with the problem of "cultural synthesis." He believed that on some higher plane, the problem of historism and the very antithesis between historism and naturalism might eventually be resolved. He also hinted at an ultimate conception of the intellectual world as the symphonic whole of man's potentialities. In the meantime, he saw the material philosophy of history as an intermediary between empirical history and ethics, an intermediary which would save the historian from thoughtless overspecialization, the moral philosopher from formalism. He admitted that the choice of an appropriate cultural synthesis for one's own time fell outside the province of ordinary historical investigation. On the other hand, he thought it necessary to re-establish some contact between the empirical disciplines and the realm of philosophical reflection in which such issues could properly be considered.

Here Troeltsch's methodological convictions flowed together with his social, political, and pedagogical concerns. He was convinced that the moral challenges of the World War, the Revolution of 1918, the growing "Americanization" of German society, and the dangerous enthusiasms of the volkish movement had helped to make the problem of historism a vital issue. "The present-day crisis of historism," he said, "is a profound inner crisis of our time. It is not just a problem of wissenschaft, but a practical problem of life."[28] Troeltsch's attitude was based on the modernist theory of form and content. He was afraid that the break in the continuity of German history at 1918 might precipitate a state of total chaos. Beginning in 1916 and more particularly between 1918 and 1921, he made a conscious effort to construct a composite cultural ideal, a synthesis, which would be appropriate to the modern environment and still preserve the best and most vital aspects of older German traditions.[29] He would not admit that an ethical renewal could be based upon the socialist ideology or upon bourgeois democratic conceptions alone. Even the school reform movement struck him as superficial, as long as it did not embody a new and consistent set of values.

Troeltsch was genuinely frightened by the moral and intellectual climate of Germany in 1919 and 1920. Among the educated classes, he noticed the signs of a "new spirit"; but what did it really involve?

> Here we meet a hatred of all historical inheritance, of wissenschaft and of discipline . . . of every commitment to necessary and valid truths . . . We meet anarchism . . . It destroys [every tradition] and believes that freedom and creativity will then come of themselves. That is the spirit of nihilism . . . In feverish dreams, one seeks the freedom and health of barbarism . . . [But if there really is to be] a saving "new spirit," then it can-

not be that of anarchism and nihilism, nor that of pacifist democracy or of proletarian socialism: Rather, it must be a spirit of faith, which . . . finds ideas appropriate to the new situation out of the treasure of the old.[30]

Troeltsch despised and feared the volkish enthusiasts and extreme nationalists who seemed to profit from the intellectual confusions of the day. Many of the prophets who opposed the Republic in the name of a great idea, he knew, were throwing up an ideological smoke screen around more concrete objectives.[31]

On the other hand, it was impossible to deny that a genuine "intellectual and spiritual revolution" was under way. It manifested itself particularly in the youth movement and in the world of learning itself:

> It is the revulsion against drill and discipline, against the ideology of success and power, against the excess and the superficiality of the knowledge which is stuffed into us by the schools, against intellectualism and literary self-importance, against the big metropolis and the unnatural, against materialism and skepticism, against the rule of money and prestige, against specialization and bossism, against the suffocating mass of tradition and the evolutionary concept of historism . . . Furthermore, a profound intellectual revolution undoubtedly lies in the changes within scholarship which are today still little noticed. The need for synthesis, system, weltanschauung, organization, and value judgment is extraordinary. The mathematization and mechanization of all European philosophy since Galileo and Descartes . . . is meeting with growing skepticism . . . In the cultural and historical disciplines, people are defending themselves against the tyranny of the evolutionary concept, against mere summations and critical assertions.[32]

Apparently, Troeltsch was impressed with this "intellectual revolution," and yet he could not entirely trust it. He worried about its "nihilist" tendencies. He warned against discarding the "critical and exact methods, the rigor of thought and of research" which had been established by many generations of scholars. But he also felt the need for a "new immediacy and inwardness, for a new intellectual and spiritual aristocracy, which counterbalances the rationalism and the leveling tendencies of democracy . . . [and the] spiritual barrenness of Marxism . . . with a more organically synthetic mentality."[33] In short, Troeltsch wanted to make use of the spiritual revolution, without allowing it to get out of control. Surrounded on all sides by the dangers of "nihilism," excessive nationalism, and Marxism, he wanted the new movements in learning to culminate in a conscious reconstruction of German culture. For political reasons, he also sought to disseminate the "contents" of the German heritage more thoroughly among all classes of the population. He assumed that this type of cultural "extension" would naturally produce a "synthesis" and that it would be possible "to form clear and strong traditions again."[34]

It is remarkable how consciously Troeltsch pursued his project. Cultural synthesis as an escape from historism became cultural synthesis as a deliberate reconstruction of German national consciousness. A philosophical dilemma turned into a pedagogical experiment. "The question about education," said Troeltsch, "concerns the contents and goals of intellectual and spiritual life itself, considered from the point of view of the conscious and intentional forming of the individual and of society as a whole by means of the intellectual and spiritual content." In an essay published in 1919, he explained that the word cultivation (*Bildung*) could properly be applied neither to the naive passing on of a single, homogeneous tradition, nor to a situation in which a generally accepted authority was able to dictate the substance of learning. In his view, cultivation was always self-conscious; it "presupposes a plurality of historical traditions, therefore complexity and a problematic nature, and finally a process of conscious selection and unification." Thus he could legitimately propose to construct an ideal of "German cultivation" by "drawing upon the fullness of historical life," while simultaneously undertaking a systematic "concentration and simplification."[35]

For this purpose, Troeltsch described his nation's heritage in terms of three main components: the culture of classical antiquity (includ-

347

ing its humanist offshoots), Christianity, and the "Nordic-Germanic world of the Middle Ages." Since the Renaissance, he said, the historical forces of the Enlightenment, of modern statecraft, of rationalism, technology, and democracy had been superimposed upon the original triad. But he regarded these later developments as practical necessities rather than cultural ideals. He scolded those "professors, rentiers, and writers" who believed that one could "simply ignore or do away with the whole technical-capitalist basis" of modern civilization.[36] He had no sympathy for the "estatist idylls" of "conservative romanticists"; nor did he believe that the old single-minded humanism was appropriate any longer: "The old simplicity and unity is not possible and would strike us as unbearably narrow, if it suddenly overtook us, before the memory of the rich life of recent centuries had disappeared. No complaint can help there. In fact, complaining in itself is treason against ourselves, is dangerous weakness, as long as we still have any faith at all in the future. We can only simplify by creating order and system, by bringing out dominant values and themes, which guide and therefore unify the whole complex."[37] This was modernist theory at its persuasive best, and yet Troeltsch did not include any post-Renaissance developments among the "dominant values" of German cultivation. Of course he regarded the German classical era itself as a great age of synthesis, in which the three main ingredients of German culture were combined in a harmonious way. But he was clearly less impressed with the rest of the nineteenth century. Above all, he rejected all those achievements of scholarship which, while useful as information, had no direct spiritual meaning for the individual. Thus it was still the spiritual impact of learning, its normative function and its relevance to life, which motivated Troeltsch's cultural synthesis.

This brings us back to the pedagogical initiative of the early Weimar period; for Troeltsch was not alone in his desire to use the innovations in learning to revitalize German higher education. As Rudolf Lehmann said in 1921: "The hope in the coming generation has always been most strongly nourished by . . . despair about the present. From the disheartening present, we seek the vision of a glorious future . . . and again education represents the only power which can guarantee such a future."[38] Lehmann's conclusion was that a number of new academic chairs for pedagogy ought to be established at the German universities. These new professorships were to be devoted to the study of all those contemporary movements in philosophy, psychology, and the humanistic disciplines which could relate education to the cultural needs and aspirations of the age. Lehmann wrote that his objectives could be realized only

> if pedagogy finds its ultimate justification in an integral view of the world and of life [*Welt- und Lebensanschauung*] . . . Here is the link that connects pedagogy with philosophy . . . : There is a transition from practical pedagogy to the philosophy of education; the tasks of pedagogy as derived from the temporal, from the needs of the present, culminate in supratemporal and suprahistorical values. This path corresponds not only to the ascent from the singular to the general which every discipline . . . must undertake, but also to the deepest spiritual urge of our time. For this urge is toward a synthesis which draws together what is and what ought to be and which promises suffering humanity a substitute for lost faith and shattered hopes.[39]

Alfred Vierkandt took an even grander view of the new "social pedagogy" which he advocated. He called the existing methods of instruction positivistic and even capitalistic, because he felt that they consisted of a heaping up of individual pieces of information.[40] He wanted students to experience (*erleben*) the total meaning of the literature which they read, to empathize with its ideal content, to understand and perhaps to absorb the values embodied in it, rather than having to concentrate exclusively upon philological formalities. In that way, the pupils' ethical sense would be trained, not only their critical faculties. The positivist notion that value judgments were purely subjective and could not be taught, said Vierkandt, was no longer accepted. In all the disciplines, a new idealism was making itself felt:

Just as . . . our philosophy today is attempting to develop a theory of culture in the direction of facts as well as of values and norms, so our education must create a cultural consciousness and a will to culture . . . It must create conscious ethical convictions, conscious sympathy for duties and values . . . It must have among its objectives a conscious . . . weltanschauung of an idealistic nature, as it has come to life, especially since the turn of the century, in our literature and philosophy, in our reform movements, and especially in our youth.

We are generally experiencing today a full rejection of positivism; we are experiencing a new need for unity, a synthetic tendency in all the world of learning—a type of thinking which primarily emphasizes the . . . concepts of value, purpose, and goal, rather than that of causality.[41]

Much the same point was made by Theodor Litt, who urged his students and colleagues to follow the innovations in learning with particular care.[42] He was convinced that such men as Dilthey, Simmel, Eucken, Troeltsch, Windelband, Spranger, Natorp, and Rickert had already begun to create a philosophy capable of dealing with cultural values, not just with material objects. Paul Natorp, whom Litt mentioned, wrote the plan for communal education that was discussed in an earlier chapter. During the first two decades of this century and especially during the early Weimar period, he published a series of essays on the philosophy of education. Such concepts as social pedagogy, social idealism, synthesis, community and weltanschauung figured very prominently in his writings. Trained in the cultural philosophy of the Baden neo-Kantians, he was moving toward a Protestant mysticism in which the objectives of personal salvation and social renewal were intimately associated. The extraordinary breadth and obscurity of his associations alone would suffice to link his work with the crisis of mandarin learning.

In a brief but suggestive essay on the cultural life of the Weimar period, Werner Richter has argued that an age of rigid specialization and positivism in German learning came to an end only with the

First World War.[43] In his view, the reaction against one-sided intellectualism in pedagogy, together with Becker's call for synthesis, helped to turn the tide during the early years of the Republic. In other words, "the great countermovement against positivism and historism" really gathered momentum only during the 1920's.

There are some things to be said against this view. The antipositivist polemics of the 1920's cannot be taken to prove that positivism was ever a very considerable force in German intellectual life. Also, there is much evidence that the idealistic revival really began long before the start of the Weimar period. Richter is quite right, however, in emphasizing the abrupt acceleration of the revitalization movement in 1919 and 1920. German university professors now became much more self-conscious about their program than ever before. They began explicitly to relate methodological questions to their political and pedagogical objectives. The shocks of war and revolution undoubtedly made a difference. In any case, the crisis of learning was now on everyone's mind.

Richter also implies that the synthesis movement was begun by the modernists and not by their orthodox colleagues. Becker and Troeltsch, not Below or Jaeger, issued the important proclamations of 1919 and 1920. This is a point worth stressing, because the accommodationists soon lost control of the drive they launched. The orthodox too were anxious to increase the impact of learning on life. Particularly the younger members of the antirepublican camp and the extreme nationalists quickly appropriated the language of crisis to their own uses. It could become a dangerous weapon in orthodox hands. Meinecke may have suspected this as early as 1916, when he scolded particularly the nationalists for demanding premature synthesis. Troeltsch himself was skeptical about certain aspects of the spiritual revolution. He clearly sensed the possibility of a right-wing revolt against reason. Until about 1920, the accommodationists were generally in control of the synthesis movement; but the orthodox refused to leave the field to their rivals. Instead, there now ensued an intense competition between the two wings of the mandarin establishment, as each side tried to put its own stamp on the revolution in learning.

THE GREAT DEBATE, 1919–1921

In 1919, Max Weber delivered his famous lecture on "Wissenschaft as a Vocation."[44] He was speaking before an audience of students interested in academic careers. He warned them that advancement within the profession was very slow and that the best minds did not always receive the recognition they deserved. With this as a background, he then took up some of the methodological and philosophical questions which were agitating the academic community. His remarks on these subjects were so uncompromisingly critical of contemporary fashions as to provoke an immediate response. Weber died in 1920; but this did not end the debate he had begun. Throughout the Weimar period and especially between 1919 and 1921, his speech remained one of the central issues in the "crisis of learning."

Weber did not hesitate to challenge the general outcry against specialization. Under modern conditions, he said, it was impossible to make a genuine contribution to knowledge without doing detailed research in a narrow field of study. "Inspiration" (*Eingabe*) was neither more nor less important in scholarship than in any other endeavor; but it could be expected to come only as a result of hard work. Brilliant hunches were quite useless in any case, unless someone was able methodically to exploit and to substantiate them. Weber was clearly thinking of the relationship between the positing of a type and its use in empirical work. He was shocked at the prevalent "cult" of intuition and immediate "experiencing" (*Erleben*). He was tired of hearing that the scholar had to be a personality. He admitted that the artist might hope to create something of permanent value. But the scholar had no such hope. All of the scholar's contributions were bound to be superseded sooner or later. To do research was simply to participate in that "process of intellectualization" which had been making gradual headway against magical interpretations of reality for thousands of years. This process was apparently endless, and its consequences were not always pleasant. Technological progress brought certain practical advantages; but it did not necessarily increase the individual's knowledge of conditions around him. Few contemporaries could describe the mechanics of a streetcar, though they had to use it every day. Modern man was accustomed to feel that in principle, he could learn to comprehend almost anything which puzzled him, that the necessary explanations were available. But he also knew that in practice, he could master only a minute fraction of the knowledge accumulated by his species. Unlike his early ancestors, he died before he had exhausted the potential range of his experience. The progress of civilization had made his individual death a contradiction.

Weber went on to describe the great expectations which had motivated scholars of earlier ages. The Greeks believed that the proper handling of conceptual tools, the isolation of pure ideas, could lead to an understanding of true "being." Observation and experiment during the Renaissance were supposed to produce a restored appreciation of nature, along with true art, its imitation. The philosophers of the seventeenth and eighteenth centuries, finally, dreamed of charting the universe with their laws in order to discover its meaning and its Creator. Unfortunately, the progress of learning had not achieved any of these extravagant objectives. One by one, they had been dropped. Indeed, modern intellectuals had come to fear that knowledge was actually a hindrance to true art, true nature, or true happiness. Disillusioned, many had developed an interest in the irrational; but that could only result in a further extension of the rationalizing process into a hitherto scarcely charted region. The growth of wissenschaft was apparently inescapable, and yet it could not be justified in terms of any ultimate objective:

> What is . . . the sense of learning as a vocation, since all these earlier illusions, "way to true being," "way to true art," "way to true nature," "way to true God," "way to true happiness," have sunk out of reach. Tolstoi gave the simplest answer when he said: "[Learning] is senseless, because it does not answer the question which alone is important for us: What shall we do? How shall we live?" The fact that scholarship yields no answer to these questions is simply indisputable. It only remains to be seen in what sense it yields "no" answer and if, to those

who pose the question correctly, it does not offer something after all.[45]

Weber now proceeded to distinguish between two sorts of problems: one which wissenschaft could and one which it could not solve. Every discipline, he said, had to work with certain assumptions or stipulations (*Voraussetzungen*), the adequacy of which it could not itself establish. It had to assume that the information it sought was worth knowing. The natural scientist could not prove that his generalizations were of interest or that the universe he discussed was admirable. The humanistic disciplines could try to describe and to explain the cultures of the past and present; but they could not decide the merits of this or that aesthetic ideal or the value and purpose of cultural activity itself.

Weber was highly critical of colleagues who preached political and personal creeds from the lectern. He thought it possible to talk about the characteristics of various forms of government without telling students how to vote. "Simple intellectual integrity," he said, demanded a clear distinction between wissenschaft and value judgment: "It is certainly possible that the individual can only incompletely succeed in excluding his subjective sympathies . . . [But] that proves nothing, for other, purely factual errors are also possible; and still they do not prove anything against the duty: to search for truth."[46] Experience, Weber said, would lead to polytheism, as James Mill had once remarked. A plurality of competing value systems was as much a fact of modern life as the diversity of national cultures. The scholar could describe these systems; he could analyze their logical and psychological bases and their whole internal structure. But he could not save anyone from the stern duty of a personal choice. That is why students were wrong to regard their professors as spiritual mentors and all-around coaches in the business of living. Academics were often particularly ill-suited for the task of political and cultural leadership in any case. Those who did have natural gifts in that direction could always exercise them outside the classroom, where their audiences were not captive and their pronouncements not unfairly protected against criticism.

What services could wissenschaft provide? It could produce technical tools for the execution of many projects. It could supply methods of analysis for anyone who meant to investigate some problem for himself. More important, it could cause people to recognize "unpleasant facts" and to achieve a certain clarity about their actions and objectives. It could uncover limited functional interrelationships, suggest how any stipulated end might be achieved, and predict the effect of a given action with some degree of accuracy. It could even identify the basic value system from which a particular decision might be derived, and it could assess the internal consistency of any postulated hierarchy of purpose. "For you arrive of necessity at these or those internally meaningful consequences, if you remain true to yourself . . . Thus, if we understand our business, we can . . . force the individual, or at least help him, to give himself an account of the ultimate sense of his own actions. This does not seem to me to be a small matter, even for the purely personal life. Here too I am tempted to say of a teacher who succeeds in this: he serves 'ethical' powers: the duty to create clarity and a sense of responsibility."[47]

Weber knew that to justify learning in these terms was once again to make a personal decision without benefit of scientific "proof." He told his students that he had chosen his own road. Others were free to make the "sacrifice of the intellect" which was necessary to return to an ethical or metaphysical absolutism. All he asked was that such people give up the absurdly "antiquarian" idea that one could create a new religion simply because it would be nice to have one. The process of intellectualization had gone so far that the old epics, the old monumental art, and the old communal faiths were no longer possible. "Prophecy from the lectern" (*Kathederprophetie*) could never bring them back; it could only create ephemeral and fanatical sects of the most dangerous sort.

Weber's friend Karl Jaspers once said of him that "honest observation, free from illusion" was his "incentive toward intensive value-judging."[48] Properly interpreted, the remark is quite justified. Weber's emotions were very much in evidence during his address. He obviously spoke with restrained passion, not coldly or indifferently. It was characteristic of him that he adopted a pointedly severe tone toward his audience. His whole attitude was that of a man who asks himself and others for self-discipline in the face of tragic realities. He had the ability, perhaps even the inclination, to suffer from his own insights. He thought of intellectual integrity as a duty. He found it quite natural to swim against the tide of popular opinion. He was not just calling for scholarly precision. He abhorred what must have struck him as a general lack of self-restraint, a mounting wave of escapism and hysteria, within the academic community. His "process of intellectualization" was so broadly defined that it almost paralleled the prevalent concept of civilization. He was apparently able to sense the deep-seated fears which this process inspired in many of his contemporaries. He himself did not accept it lightheartedly; but he could see no acceptable alternative to it. Thus his lecture not only challenged the search for weltanschauung through learning; it also touched upon the sensitive issue of mandarin anti-modernity itself.

Jaspers' observation had another meaning as well. Among German academics of his time, Weber was something of a political activist. He avoided the idealistic retreat, the apolitical stance. He expressed himself frequently and forcefully about contemporary social and cultural questions. The point is that he did these things without violating his own rules of academic behavior in any way. When he urged the separation of wissenschaft and value judgment in social policy, for example, he actually meant to clear the ground for more progressive policies. He appeared to limit the competence of scholarship; but he left it three important functions: the facing of "facts," the weighing of consequences, and the assessment of internal consistency in the setting of objectives. In practice, this program did very little to contract the scope of scientific and scholarly discourse, whether in politics, in ethics, or in any other field. All it excluded was the search for ultimate values in the cultural philosophy of the German Idealists. Nor was Weber a positivist, properly speaking. In the atmosphere of the spiritual revolution, his methodological recommendations could sound vaguely cautious and old-fashioned. In reality, he effectively included the cruder exploitations of the common-sense fallacy among the illusions of a former age.

Unfortunately, most of Weber's contemporaries failed to understand him. They saw only that he had broken with the mandarin tradition, that he demoted the scholar from the role of the sage to that of the analyst and technician. From their point of view, Weber's lecture represented the abdication of learning as the counselor of life.

The most violent reaction to Weber's lecture actually came from outside the academic community. Ernst Krieck had begun his career as an elementary teacher and a polemicist in the cause of his profession.[49] He was an extreme nationalist, a man who considered the universities too old-fashioned and too lukewarm in their patriotism. It would be unfair to compare him to any group of professors, if only because he exceeded all ordinary measures in fanaticism and just plain intellectual vulgarity. His pamphlet on *Die Revolution der Wissenschaft* (the revolution of learning), published in 1920, began with a series of right-wing clichés, many of which were loosely adapted from orthodox polemics. Germany, he announced, had lost the sense of its greatness. There were no compelling ideas to guide it, and so it fell prey to the degenerative forces of democracy and Marxism. The great traditions had been forgotten; society was dissolving into its atoms; the nation had lost its soul; a cultural crisis was at hand. Since there was no communal spirit, individuals felt powerless and isolated; a hopeless fatalism prevailed; literature was barren and art without style. A religious revival might be of some help; but it could not take place within the established churches, which had become totally decadent. An esoteric spirituality would be equally useless, since it could not produce that spirit of national solidarity which was so sorely needed. Only a common national religion could bring about a sense of moral unity and renewed purpose, elevating the state above the level of a utilitarian machine.

There was no room for uprooted intellectuals in Krieck's new society. He proposed to dismantle the whole academic establishment, unless it could justify its existence by contributing to the spiritual life of the nation. The pose of objectivity, the refusal to make value judgments, seemed to him a weakness and a vice. German scholarship, he said, had become a senseless mechanism, which sought only to perpetuate itself. Overly specialized and esoteric, it was a kind of sinecure for a tired clique of scholars. Accordingly, its methods were hopelessly sterile. Historism had become fatal to the social sciences, for it prevented knowledge about the past from influencing the present. A barren rationalism had spread from the natural sciences even to the humanities. When economists declared that they would refrain from making value judgments, they handed the future of their country to party politicians. In philosophy, the freedom of the will was consistently de-emphasized, as if to urge Germans to resign themselves to national impotence.

On the basis of these arguments, Krieck called for a revolution in learning. His proposals followed a predictable line. The passive stance of objectivity must be dropped. There must be an effort to combine pieces of information into total perspectives. While looking into the nation's past, historians must discover its character and therefore its future. He called for a greater emphasis upon the fundamental truths of life and the spirit. Like all truths, these were necessarily relative to a certain point of view. Of course, it was the duty of scholars to rise above narrow class and party doctrines; but beyond that, scholarship must recover its roots in the national community. Only in that way could it be saved at once from partisan perspectives and from a sterile eclecticism. Krieck did not ask that learning be popularized by the universities themselves. Even a certain kind of specialization was acceptable to him, as long as every discipline kept in touch with the realm of philosophy and weltanschauung, and with the spiritual needs of the whole community.

Krieck's demands were seconded, though in a slightly different way, in Erich von Kahler's essay *Der Beruf der Wissenschaft* (The calling of learning). This was written in 1920 explicitly as an attack upon Weber's position. Kahler argued that in placing severe limitations upon the ability of wissenschaft to answer the fundamental questions of life, Weber had in effect proclaimed the bankruptcy of his type of scholarship. Once upon a time, Kahler said, learning had been an integral part of man's existence in this world, ultimately linked with his religion and his cultural values, a source of spiritual strength and satisfaction. Now however, it was completely isolated, relevant only to its own special problems, fenced in by arbitrary and unrealistic standards and procedural schemes. In the meantime, the immense suffering of the World War and the subsequent social disintegration had convinced especially the Germans that life itself would henceforth have to be recognized as the ultimate value. For this reason, it was no longer appropriate to dissect life with innumerable restrictive concepts, moving further and further away from immediate reality. In the same way, the social organism could no longer be divided by the egotistical doctrines of the parties. An appreciation of the natural totality of life and of the original and organic whole of society would once again have to be cultivated. The teacher could no longer afford to be a party man in the afternoon, while working to dissect life with his concepts in the morning. He must always be the same whole man, an integral personality, and therefore also a leader of men.

Kahler did not think that anyone could gain a direct view of absolute truth. Instead, he said, the individual's perspective upon that truth was determined by his position in history and in the nation. Nevertheless, there was one and only one possible view of truth for any nation at a given time. Just as the general manifested itself in the particular, the eternal in the temporal, so the absolute became concrete in the specific tasks which it set for nations at various points in their history. The arguments about historism and the whole discussion concerning value judgments were therefore quite irrelevant. The new learning would recognize absolute truth in its manifestations, so that knowledge would once again be immediately valuable for "life." It would reveal not only what was, but also what should be and what had to be done. A direct relationship would once again exist between the individual and the eternal.

Kahler was a private scholar and philosopher, not a university professor.[50] His association with the circle of aesthetes around the poet Stefan George may help to account for his visionary approach to knowledge. Some of his remarks are very difficult to reproduce. He used the language of a seer, spoke of "viewing" (*Schauen*) and "in-

359

spiration" (*Eingebung*), and delighted in imagery about the eternal flux of life, about arch-being and the like. The following paragraphs exemplify his style.

> Toward such a knowing, which will see together with its law the living in its seed, in its unity and singularity, [toward this] only he can help and teach us who has brought himself together as a human being, in whom thinking and feeling, knowing and acting, are not conceptually differentiated and ignorant of each other, in whom the teacher and the leader have not become separated.

> [The new knowing] will have to be knowing in the unique ancient mystical meaning, which expresses the one unmistakable ability to touch one's own fate, and not an accumulation of just so many technical pieces of information.[51]

This was the prophetic language of life philosophy. Its knowledge was that of an inspired sect. Its insights were difficult to communicate. Its value depended upon qualities in the knower which in turn were scarcely teachable.

Krieck and Kahler represented the extreme limits of the methodological radicalism which became fashionable during the crisis of learning. Of course, there were differences between them. Kahler was an aesthete, Krieck a political agitator. Both sought to make scholarship serve present needs as they understood them. In this respect, they actually resembled some of the modernists. It was in their specific aims that they distinguished themselves. Krieck demanded support for his national myth; Kahler contemplated a more esoteric "vision." The modernists wanted the universities to study contemporary problems and to take an interest in the new pedagogy. But they did not prescribe particular ideologies or methodologies. They were relatively restrained in their attacks upon the old scholarship; and they did not ask professors to become propagandists or prophets, even in the cause of the Republic. Krieck and Kahler, by contrast, rejected all limits upon the efficacy of a new kind of knowledge. Although for different reasons, they envisioned what really would have been a total revolution in learning.

Most German academics, having repudiated the "utilitarianism" of the modernists, were not prepared to give their unqualified support to Krieck's or Kahler's type of engagement. Some of the orthodox eventually moved rather far away from Max Weber's position; but Krieck's violence and Kahler's frankness were too much for them. They desired a gradual transformation of traditional learning within its ancient institutional framework, not an explicit and public reversal of standards. Kahler's language probably shocked them more than his arguments: "We are tired of being fed philosophies of life morning, noon, and night . . . We are tired of always having someone shout in our face about the shame of the time and our guilt . . . We want to work quietly and piously."[52]

Arthur Salz, the author of this exclamation, probably stood somewhere near the center of the mandarin spectrum in his views. Late in 1920, he wrote an essay "in favor of wissenschaft, against the educated among those who despise it." The title, borrowed from Schleiermacher, was chosen with care. Salz intended to present a partial defense of Weber against Kahler, while totally ignoring Krieck. His argument was that the ancient ideal of learning should not be challenged at a time when so many values were under attack. He suggested that the present imperfections of German scholarship might all be considered temporary effects of postwar social and political dislocations. He counseled patience, since excessive criticism might aggravate the degeneration of the national community. The German universities had been leaders of the nation once. Perhaps they would return to the role of greatness again in the very near future.

Salz did warn against what he considered the excesses of Kahler's position. He pointed out that the new learning would be difficult to communicate and could never attain the universal validity of the old scholarship. Intuition, after all, had definite limits of application. Wissenschaft had the task of describing and therefore conceptualizing crude experience. Constructs, though always imperfect, could not be avoided. At the same time, Salz expressed a good deal of sympathy for Kahler's intentions. He seconded his objections to excessively "cold" concepts and schematizations. He denounced the utilitarianism and rationalism, the "leveling" and despiritualizing tendencies, of Western science. He pointed with pride to the fact that the Germans had always retained a greater respect for intuitive perception than English and French scholars. The atomization and mechanization of the universe was indeed regrettable; but not all directions within the old learning were equally guilty of such aberrations. Scholarly techniques, Salz added, reflected the moral and intellectual climate of an age. A new spirit was even now in the making, and one could hope that it would transform German learning from within. Salz detected a general movement toward "synthesis." He anticipated a new phase in the history of the German universities, one which would create more direct methods of "grasping the spiritual." Max Weber's description of learning seemed to him too modest. In reality, he thought, truly outstanding scholars should be spiritual leaders, as the German Idealists had been. He agreed with Kahler's requirement that learning should have "the guidance of life as a goal, intuition as the method, and universality of scope." He demanded only that the development of the new engagement be allowed to take place within the institutions and traditions of the old wissenschaft.

Salz's most interesting contribution to the great debate was his statement and resolution of a characteristic dilemma. On the one hand, he said, learning should be directed more toward eternal truths than toward contemporary practices. He praised the German scholarly tradition for consistently seeking to augment man's ethical stature, rather than his material comfort alone. On the other hand, there was a sense in which learning gained vitality from its involvement with the present. Salz was certain that the universities should participate in the deeper cultural currents of the time, in the contemporary initiative toward a spiritual renewal, for example. Thus a certain kind of present-mindedness was acceptable; but it had to be distinguished from ordinary utilitarianism and reconciled to the ideal of theoretical purity. Salz solved this problem to his own satisfaction by adopting a highly suggestive simile. He described the "sanctum of learning" as a temple which opened out in all directions. The flame of wissenschaft, a spiritual flame, had to be protected against pollution from considerations of earthly practicality. With its purity assured, however, it could shed an all the more brightly ennobling light upon its environment. It could exert a salutary influence upon the times, without being debased in the process.

In short, Salz's arguments amounted to a very partial refutation of Kahler's remarks. Troeltsch pointed this out in a short review of the whole exchange.[53] Troeltsch himself was still not quite sure how to evaluate the intellectual and spiritual revolution. He insisted that it was not related to the social and political upheaval of 1918. He traced it primarily to a search for new dogmas among the younger academic generations. He described it as a somewhat fanciful rebellion against the intellectualism of the old education, against "Wilhelmian militarism," but also against modern parliamentary democracy. At the same time, Troeltsch continued to feel that the style of learning itself was changing. He referred particularly to Edmund Husserl's phenomenology, which seemed to permit its disciples to "view" (*schauen* or *erschauen*) the "essence" (*Wesen*) of ideas and experiences. To describe what he considered a complete revolution in learning, Troeltsch enumerated a whole series of contemporary innovations: "the freedom from positivistic causalism and determinism; the overcoming of neo-Kantian formalism . . . [in favor of material philosophies of culture]; the movement toward an immediate experiencing [*Erlebensunmittelbarkeit*] of not analyzable but understandable [*zu verstehenden*] cultural tendencies . . . and the visions of a new phenomenological Platonism which views and validates norms and essential interrelationships [*Wesensgesetze*]."[54]

Troeltsch reported these developments without strenuously objecting to them. Still, the spiritual revolution as a whole clearly worried him a good deal. His solution was to urge that the new intellectual techniques be strictly confined to the realm of speculative philosophy. He proposed a three-fold distinction between "the positive, more or less exact disciplines," "philosophy which seeks total understanding," and "the practical and personal life." He did not admire the "young gentlemen" who meant to "take these three in one jump," thereby intruding their purely private emotions and mystical urges into the work of scholarship. In philosophy, he said, he did not share Weber's skepticism; but in the field of learning, he entirely agreed with him. Troeltsch's real criticism of Salz was that he had failed to draw a clear enough line between philosophy and the exact disciplines.

Troeltsch's cautious response to Salz was to prove typical of the modernist position after 1921. Somehow, the accommodationists were forced into a defensive stance toward the crisis of learning. They were deeply interested in the new methods of the humanistic disciplines, most of which had actually originated in the modernist camp. The question was how far these techniques should be extended in the search for new philosophical certainties. Troeltsch and other modernists began to realize that the intellectual revolution could become dangerous, unless it was contained within specified limits. No one fully embraced Weber's position; but many tried to approximate the spirit of scholarly caution and precision which came to be considered Weber's legacy. Of course, the modernist withdrawal toward methodological caution was partial and gradual. Troeltsch was somewhat ambivalent in his attitude, and that was true of others also. Moreover, the line between the two mandarin camps was not too clearly drawn on this whole issue. There was a difference between the generations too. The younger men were more easily attracted to the "new spirit" than their older colleagues. On the orthodox side of the spectrum, the radical nationalists felt particularly "revolutionary." Still, it is generally fair to say that the initiative in the revitalization of learning really passed from the modernists to the orthodox after 1921. From that time on, the spokesmen of political accommodation and social progress often took a vaguely old-fashioned attitude toward scholarship, while the antimodernists continued to advocate a kind of methodological radicalism. As Troeltsch suspected, the orthodox line was foreshadowed in Salz's argument. Rejecting "utilitarian" present-mindedness, the mandarin majority sought a purely spiritual engagement. To this end, they tried to enlarge the various antipositivist techniques in philosophy and in the humanistic disciplines. Of course they thought of their program as a reactivation of the great neohumanist and Idealist traditions of mandarin learning.

In the fall of 1921, Eduard Spranger outlined the new orthodoxy.

Lecturing on "the present state of the humanistic disciplines and the school," he began by discussing the critical condition of German education: "Full of faith . . . the young generation is awaiting an inner rebirth . . . Today more than ever before, the young adult . . . lives through the fullness of his intellectual and spiritual faculties . . . [There is] a drive toward wholeness . . . [and] a religious yearning: a groping back from artificial and mechanical circumstances to the eternal spring of the metaphysical."[55] To demonstrate that learning could once again satisfy these needs, Spranger briefly presented a potpourri of the latest neo-Idealist and neo-Kantian techniques. A reference to "objective geist" took him back to Hegel as well: "In the humanistic disciplines, it is the historically conditioned geist which comes to know itself."[56] Invariably, Spranger's adaptations of the new scholarly methods yielded more in the way of direct "experience" than the originals for which they stood. Weber's ideal type became ideal in the normative sense:

> At the head of economic studies, we place the economic, at the head of political studies, the political standard of value . . . What deviates from these we judge, within the respective discipline, to be invalid [wertwidrig]; and we thereby criticize not only the chosen means but often enough the failure to posit the proper norm itself . . . In a methodically related fashion, we also establish total ethical norms for given cultural situations on the basis of our empathetic understanding, in relation to which we criticize the epoch's ethical will itself, not merely its technical means for the achievement of its purposes. We dare to designate whole epochs as ages of disintegration.[57]

Understanding also acquired much new meaning. "We call understanding the interpretation of intellectual and spiritual manifestations by tracing them back to meaningful interrelationships . . . value-relationships . . . The a priori of understanding . . . lies in the awareness of structure. This awareness comprehends the complex of related meanings, as they operate in the individual, in the objective culture, and between the two."[58] These passages are almost impossible to translate. They were meant to imply the full integration of the individual geist into a well-charted system of "structurally" related meanings.

Under the circumstances, Spranger's partial "agreement" with Weber cannot be taken very seriously. "Every teacher of the humanistic disciplines ought to realize that his task entails not only the representation of his own . . . value judgments, but the penetration of the possible fundamental points of view as such [Grundstandpunkte überhaupt] . . . The only question is whether this is the last word."[59] Naturally, it was not. Spranger was working on a new psychology of the humanistic disciplines "which can really penetrate the intellectual and spiritual being of men and of cultures."[60] This gave him the basic anatomy of geist itself and allowed him to chart the "structure" of culture in general. He thus arrived at a conception of philosophy as a science of values (Wertwissenschaft), as the discipline dealing with the normative relationships uncovered in the humanistic disciplines.

Spranger believed in "objectivity." He felt that German learning should be influenced neither by the crude interests of party men nor by the immediately practical demands of life. He rejected the "pragmatism" of Krieck and Kahler. But he firmly believed in the reintegration of learning and weltanschauung. In conclusion, he came back to the idea of cultivation as an experiencing of "formed values." As might be expected, he particularly recommended the traditional sources of classical humanism as agents of cultivation. "Not the origins in time are to be looked for—these are frequently dark and distorted—but the intellectual and spiritual arch-phenomena [Urphänomene] out of which a certain genre of experience breaks forth with metaphysical passion. Not its supposed simplicity, not its priority in time, make antique literature the appropriate school of understanding, but the genuineness, the purity, and depth from which the creations of its geist emanate."[61]

On this note, the great debate ended. Spranger really won it. In the years that followed, the crisis of German learning deepened, and instead of merely organizational reforms, it came to involve synthesis, experiencing, "wholeness," and the movement from wissenschaft to weltanschauung.

7

THE CRISIS OF LEARNING
AT ITS HEIGHT, 1920-1933

DEVELOPMENTS IN PHILOSOPHY
AND PSYCHOLOGY

The cultural philosophy of the Baden neo-Kantians continued to be an important force in German academic philosophy during the 1920's. In 1924, Rickert tried to show how the doctrines of this school might be used to resolve the intellectual issues of the day. He began by posing a question. "Could it be that the manner in which modern man conceives the mutual relationships between Greek learning, the Roman state, and the Christian religion corresponds to the manner in which Kant related theoretical research, practical life, and religious faith to each other?"[1] The answer was yes, of course, and Rickert proceeded to demonstrate the importance of this tripartite relationship for the philosophy of history. Western man, he said, was distinguished by his rationalism. Unlike the Oriental, he demanded rational explanations for all events in his environment. He organized his own activities in patterns of rationally related means and ends. European capitalism and European learning were but the most striking products of this bent.

Because of the one-sidedness of the Western emphasis upon calculation and reason, there were bound to be periodic waves of irrational reaction. Scholarship was itself necessarily rational in character. It therefore tended to underestimate or to ignore the irrational aspects of life. Rickert sternly disapproved of irrationalist and intuitionist tendencies in learning itself; but he did insist that a rational philosophy of culture must be able to comprehend the irrational to some degree.

> The philosophy which was still in fashion toward the end of the last century did in fact show a far-reaching lack of comprehension for anything not related to reason. After all, it proposed to turn even the humanistic disciplines into sciences [*Gesetzeswissenschaft*], and it recommended that the historian undertake studies in the psychological laboratory! One must not be surprised that now the pendulum is once again swinging far toward the opposite side . . . Thus the example of the present . . . shows especially clearly what the task of a universal and all-sided philosophy is. If it does not equally avoid a one-sided rationalism and a one-sided antirationalism, then the turmoils which are prevalent today will always return.[2]

With this as an introduction, Rickert returned to the central theme of the tripartite relationship between Greek wissenschaft, the Roman state, and the Christian religion. Drawing on Dilthey and on Max Weber, he expanded his original triad through a number of historical and "philosophical" equations. He thus arrived at the following parallels.

> Greeks: Romans: Orientals
> wissenschaft: state: religion
> thinking: will: feeling

Rickert actually spoke of a tripartite division of the soul, although he hastened to admit that the Greeks were not without will or feeling. In the philosophy of history, he said, we are interested in the "objective content of cultural goods," not in ordinary psychology. The Greeks introduced the distinctive element of rationalism into Western culture. They placed the ethic of truth, the norms of learning and of the theoretical realm, above all other values, including those of the religious sphere. In this, they were exaggerating; they fell into the error of "intellectualism." It was not until the Middle Ages that European man achieved a "synthesis" of the values of the three realms.

This medieval synthesis had to break up, however, since it took place under the stifling authority of the Roman Catholic hierarchy. If there was to be any further progress, then the three forces had to free themselves from external restrictions and to unfold themselves in full autonomy. "We understand that, at least initially, everything had to be directed toward a further differentiation of the overall culture, if the tendencies of the Renaissance and the Reformation were to unfold themselves. Wissenschaft, state, and religion needed freedom or independence, and not only from the church, but also from each other . . . [In short,] modern culture is dominated by forces which contend with each other, and thus modern cultural consciousness has, in Hegel's terms, the character of 'fragmentation.' "[3]

In this connection, Rickert came back to Max Weber's essay on learning as a vocation. He scoffed at some of the more hysterical critics of that essay and remarked that Weber had only stated the conflicts between scholarship and the other spheres of life in the sharpest possible terms. Weber may have been guilty of some exaggeration, Rickert said, but he was certainly right to point out the limitations of learning. Ideally, a philosophy of culture should do justice to all aspects of life; but in practice, modern wissenschaft was itself a party in the tripartite conflict. It was intellectualistic in the Greek sense, and there lay the difficulty: "a full appreciation of the atheoretical cultural life in the sense of the Roman tradition and the Christian religion cannot be reached from the Greek point of view. The establishment of the theoretical value as the highest of all values is incompatible with a truly inclusive philosophy of modern . . . culture."[4] According to Rickert, this dilemma accounted for the various shortcomings of eighteenth-century learning and philosophy. In fact, it accounted for the poverty of all non-Kantian philosophy, whether it was conceived before or after Kant. Only Kant had managed the "critical overcoming of intellectualism" and produced a "critical theory of the atheoretical."[5] This was his great achievement. He had separated the three spheres from each other and shown that each of them worked with its own norms in complete autonomy. Thus religion could never interfere with scholarship again, and of course the reverse was true as well. It was precisely this tripartite division that had allowed Kant to do justice to the three spheres, each on its own terms. For this reason, Kant was the great "philosopher of modern culture."

In the last chapter of his essay, Rickert broached the "problem of ultimate unity." On the highest level of reflection, he said, the three realms could after all be brought together in a final synthesis. Kant had made a start in that direction in his own system; but he had not fully freed himself from the "moralistic-rationalistic" tendencies of his own day. Fichte, however, had taken a further step. He had shown that in the last analysis, the value of wissenschaft could itself be considered a part of the practical sphere, since the theoretical realm could not produce any normative judgments at all. Rickert admitted that Fichte's solution might not be the final answer; but he thought that it pointed in the right direction. The great general philosophy of valuations was yet to be constructed. In it, the Baden neo-Kantians saw their ultimate aim.

In many ways, Rickert's formulations were ideally suited to the intellectual and emotional climate of the 1920's. They responded to the contemporary glorification of life, without openly sacrificing the integrity of scholarship. Nicely assigning everyone to his place under the neo-Kantian umbrella, they also promised the ultimate resolution of all conflicts in a revival of Fichtean Idealism. This was a statesmanlike defense of the mandarin tradition under difficult circumstances. As might be expected, however, it failed to convince a large part of its audience. As the revival of learning moved forward, the neo-Kantian creed was swept aside.

The latest innovations in philosophy assumed various names; but they were often grouped under the general heading of "critical realism."[6] Perhaps the most representative of the new realists were Hans Driesch, Max Frischeisen-Köhler, Traugott Konstantin Oesterreich, and Erich Becher. Most of these men were themselves strongly influenced by the neo-Kantian tradition. But it did not fully satisfy them.

Their objections followed a well-established pattern. They simply subjected all neo-Kantians to the condemnation which had originally been directed only against the Marburg school. Kant's modern successors, they said, had allowed his philosophy to degenerate into a series of purely formal statements. Methodological precepts had taken the place of metaphysics, since the neo-Kantians denied the possibility of any substantive knowledge of external reality. In principle, Windelband, Rickert, and their followers could make no statements at all about the "content" of our experience, just as they could not arrive at any specific ethical prescriptions. In this sense, their philosophy was an empty formalism. The Kantian critique of the common-sense fallacy was justified, of course; but it had not succeeded in exterminating the purely mechanistic view of nature which was prevalent in the sciences. No real progress could be made against these misconceptions, unless philosophers could once again make statements about Being, unless a new metaphysics could be consciously constructed to replace the unconscious metaphysics of the naturalistic age.

The new realists drew upon those nineteenth-century German philosophers who had developed some interest in metaphysics, in nature philosophy (*Naturphilosophie*), or in any other substantive theory of reality. Alois Riehl represented that direction within neo-Kantianism which was most congenial to the realists. Even such psychologically oriented philosophers as Hermann Lotze were sometimes mentioned. This is not to say that the new realists condoned the heresies of psychologism and materialism. That was their dilemma: they wanted to reconstruct some sort of epistemological realism, without falling into any of the errors associated with the common-sense scheme. It was bound to be a difficult undertaking. Becher opted for a modified version of the causal approach, treating sense impressions as complete images of external objects and as their effects. He also postulated the trustworthiness of memory and an orderly universe. He avoided the danger of materialism in part by making "qualities as such" (*Beschaffenheiten an sich*) the external counterparts of anything that might be predicated of internal impressions, including the primary qualities of extension and motion as well as such secondary qualities as color.[7] This broke the mechanistic causal chain between object and sensation. Becher was convinced in any case that there were spiritual as well as mechanistic types of causality.

Almost all the critical realists gave credit to Edmund Husserl and his phenomenology for helping them in the construction of their new epistemology. Unfortunately, I do not really understand Husserl's work.[8] So far as I can make out, he proposed to treat what we would ordinarily call qualities, or impressions, or attributes of objects as if they were purely logical entities. If we ignore the question whether anything at all is green "in reality," we might still be able to make certain statements about green-ness. Of course, this is just an example of a technique that might be expanded in various directions. The knowledge it could bring would in some ways resemble mathematics or geometry, because it would be totally independent of reality and of observation in the ordinary sense. Husserl used the term *Wesen* to describe these disembodied qualities, and it is probably fair to translate *Wesen* as "essence."

Whatever Husserl may have had in mind, there is no question that some of his followers interpreted him along the lines of the above description. In any case, they made rather liberal use of the vocabulary thus acquired. Max Scheler celebrated the birth of a new "objective idealism" and described the "essences of all areas of being" as the unique subject matter of philosophy.[9] He was apparently prepared to regard even ethical values as immediately accessible essences. The direct "viewing" of essence (*Schau, Wesenschau*) and of "pure meanings" became something of a fashion, in which the mandarins' predilection for a purely contemplative knowledge found full expression. It might be remarked that Tönnies had used the word *Wesen* in his concepts of *Wesenwille* (natural or essential will) and *soziale Wesenheit* (social entity). He had suggested that it was possible to discuss "pure" social entities, regardless of whether they could ever be empirically observed in their pure form. Analogous ideas were very common among German sociologists and humanists. The sense of understanding the structure or inner logic of a historical phenomenon could also be conceived as the viewing of a pure meaning or essence. Husserl himself actually used the word structure in discussing his method. At least on a vague level, the language of phenomenology was thus very much attuned to certain characteristics of the mandarin tradition, not to speak of its popularization in vulgar life philosophy. Of course, there were more and less irresponsible users of the new terminology. Werner Jaeger, among others, urged "modesty" about "man's ability to penetrate the inner [meaning] of things."[10] Even Driesch and Becher placed certain limitations upon the field in which the viewing of essences could properly be applied.[11] Nevertheless, they made the phenomenological method a very important part of their nonmechanistic epistemology.

The critical realists and such allied thinkers as William Stern and Scheler were anxious, above all, to establish the basis for a new metaphysics. In this, they apparently succeeded to their own satisfaction. As a prominent realist put it, the rebirth of German philosophy culminated sometime after 1900 in the "public resurrection" of metaphysics.[12] Many different groups participated in this revival. Clemens Bäumker and other Catholic philosophers were occasionally grouped with the critical realists because of their interest in Aristotelian and scholastic metaphysics. In psychology, the integral "I" was rescued. Stern developed a "personalistic" philosophy in which not only individuals but also groups and abstractions appeared as "personal wholes." The old doctrine of psycho-physical parallelism, the notion that psychic and physical processes run parallel without interacting, was discredited and replaced with more spiritualistic hypotheses. There were new defenses of free will and new forms of theism. Driesch, Oesterreich, and others interested themselves in parapsychology, the discipline dealing with occult phenomena.[13]

Altogether, the new metaphysical movement amounted to a broad and highly self-conscious attack on all mechanistic views of reality and causation. Especially Driesch and Becher developed "neovitalistic" and "psychovitalistic" theories expressly for this purpose. Driesch had begun his career as a biologist. Certain experiments on the sea urchin (*Seeigel*) convinced him that it was necessary to postulate an entelechy, a nonmechanical life plan or force, to account for the growth of a mature specimen even from a segmented embryo. Becher was inclined to regard electrical charges as "spiritual" (*seelisch*) in some sense, and this led him to propose a "psychic" (*psychistische*) conception even of the universe of "dead" matter. Beyond that, he saw special reasons to treat living organisms in terms of nonmechanistic or vitalistic types of causality. He was impressed with the evidence for purposiveness not only in the development of the individual organism, but also in the symbiotic relationships among different species. He concluded that living nature had the quality of soul on an even higher level than ordinary matter, and that a supraindividual soul, a God, had to exist. He described the discovery of soul in nature as a "psychological" one, and he felt that the approach of the humanistic disciplines should supplement that of the natural sciences even in the study of subhuman life.[14] This is how the critical realists achieved the rout of mechanism.

Of course, Driesch's work with the sea urchin may well have been a brilliant experiment. Even entelechy as a biological term may have been quite appropriate in its original context. It was the rapid transformation of an experimental hypothesis into metaphysics which reflected the mood of the crisis. There was a conscious search for an antimechanistic philosophy, an overwhelming predisposition to exploit all available evidence in this direction. It is this predisposition which seems to call for an explanation in terms of ideology.

Something very similar may be said of the German psychologists of the 1920's, or about many of them at any rate. They were all very conscious enemies of the old associationist psychology; but they were not all equally inclined to speculate. The gestalt psychology of Max

Wertheimer and Wolfgang Köhler clearly outranked some of the other movements of the time in the quality of its observations and analysis.

The word *Gestalt* literally means configuration or form. In 1890, Christian von Ehrenfels introduced the label "gestalt qualities" to describe those attributes of an experience which cannot be traced to its constituent sensations. It was an occasional remark by Ernst Mach that aroused Ehrenfels' interest in this problem. Between 1911 and 1917, G. E. Müller developed his own "theory of complexes" to explain that experiences often have a quality of "being together," which defies analysis into elements. He imagined some total process within the nervous system which corresponded to the "wholeness" of a perceived complex and accounted for the relatedness of the parts of that complex.[15] As late as 1923, Müller claimed that the younger gestalt psychologists had added very little to his own early work. Nevertheless, Wertheimer and Köhler generally dated the birth of gestalt psychology from 1912, when Wertheimer published a paper on apparent movement in the perception of stroboscopically interrupted light stimuli. In fact, Wertheimer, Köhler, and their followers undertook a much more thorough and far-reaching revision of the old association hypothesis than anything suggested by such precursors as Ehrenfels, Carl Stumpf, and Müller.[16] In trying to understand gestalt psychology, one must therefore begin by considering those models of perception and thinking that Wertheimer and Köhler hoped to challenge. One must try to see the "atomistic," "mosaic," or "machine" theory of consciousness as they saw it. Köhler's *Gestalt Psychology* is particularly helpful for this purpose, since it was written as a criticism of American introspectionism and behaviorism as of 1928.

According to the theory which the gestalt psychologists intended to invalidate, perception may be described as a conjunction of elementary sensations, each of which reports a simple object in our environment by way of impacts upon our sense organs. These specific stimuli are then conducted along appropriate nerve strands to a particular location in the brain. Assuming an external reality which causes these impressions, we regard our experience as a patterned sum or mosaic of primitive sensation atoms. According to this theory, the physiological processes which correspond to perceptions are made up of many individual impulses along insulated conductors. Even our actions are triggered by such isolated units of electrical energy, which order the appropriate muscles to move. When we learn, we train our minds to associate particular elements of experience or reaction. Physiologically, this involves an increase in the conductivity of certain nerve paths. In this way, one associative sequence becomes more likely than another, and learning takes the form of habituation.

Wertheimer and Köhler believed that this mechanistic model of experience played a decisive role, though an often unacknowledged one, in the thinking of associationists and behaviorists. The gestalt psychologists also suspected that for many adherents of a scientific world view, reality itself was a mosaic of simple facts, so that the atomistic approach was often coupled with the metaphysics of the common-sense fallacy. Köhler observed, for example, that the American introspectionists would admit only very specialized reports of a subject's experience. In their view, a man never actually saw a book or a tree; he "really" had much more primitive sensations, to which he then attributed learned meanings. The trained introspectionist was always anxious to exclude these meanings from his reports. Köhler wondered where this scientist proposed to find his elementary sensations and what proof he had for his theory of superimposed meaning. The behaviorist, according to Köhler, was even more dogmatic. He refused to consider anything but "objective" observations, and he exiled all "direct experience" from the realm of psychology. In his battle against the introspectionist, he was inclined to call everything subjective which was not a part of the "external" world of physics. His stimulus-response scheme actually assumed the atomistic model of sensation and reaction, although he would never admit this. Finally, the behaviorist fully agreed with the American introspectionist in the matter of insight and understanding. In our ordinary experience, Köhler argued, we associate feelings with objects. We say: this picture is pleasing. We do not say: I see this picture, *and* I have this cluster of subjective experiences which may or may not be related to my looking at the picture. We also "see" a man's embarrassment. We do not have many isolated sensations from which we then construct a theory about the man's "inner state." In both these cases, to continue with Köhler, the atomistic psychologist would utterly dispense with our naive view. He would insist upon practicing his art of reduction, trying to separate meanings and inferences from the presumed raw materials of experience. This would seem to him the only really scientific procedure.

We do not know whether the gestalt psychologists painted a fair portrait of their opponents. They probably exaggerated a bit. Nevertheless, their own views can only be described as reactions against this type of psychological atomism. Wertheimer and Köhler occasionally used rather suggestive language to contrast the mechanistic approach with their own. To the old association psychology, they applied such words as dead, dry, meaningless, empty, static, and fragmented (*stückhaft*); to gestalt psychology, such terms as inner structure, dynamic interrelationship, totality, and wholistic (*ganzheitlich*).[17] At the same time, they always treated their own theories as hypotheses for specific and preferably experimental investigations. They repeatedly warned against vitalism, against teleological conceptions, and against reliance upon intuition. They did not approve of casual generalizations about "wholes," meanings, and "feeling states," and they particularly disliked speculative judgments in favor of an idealistic and humanistic (*geisteswissenschaftlich*) psychology. Here is what Wertheimer had to say about the rule of "wholeness": "There are situations in which what happens in the whole is not derived from the nature of the several parts or from the way in which they are put together, but where . . . *that which happens to a part of this whole is determined by the inner structural laws of this whole.* [This rule] did not only emerge from [research] work; it is also posited only *for the sake* of [further] work."[18]

Probably the most interesting studies undertaken by the gestalt psychologists had to do with the properties of what they called the visual field. The following are some of their findings in this area. A pigeon will recognize and remember a cup containing food in terms of its place in a pattern of several cups. A cat can be trained to respond to the lighter of two shades of gray, even if both are light-ened or darkened between trials. A number of optical illusions can be created, apparently because of man's tendency to organize his perceptions. Subjects can be conscious of seeing two entirely different shapes in a certain arrangement of lines; but they cannot see both at once.

On the basis of this kind of evidence, Wertheimer and Köhler argued that our visual experience generally takes the form of *Gestalten*, of organized wholes, and that the mosaic hypothesis is untenable. They suggested that the physiological processes upon which sensation is based must themselves be dynamic interrelationships and groupings, rather than sums of isolated units. They admitted that in one manner of speaking, visual organization takes place inside, not outside ourselves. But they also insisted that in another sense, the gestalt quality of our visual field is as objective a part of external reality as any isolated sensation unit. It was this consideration which led Wertheimer and Köhler to advocate a new approach to a whole cluster of traditional problems. Thus they proposed to trace our understanding of others to the perception of certain behavioral gestalten, which we automatically and directly define as anger or embarrassment. They also hoped to show that our attitudes can become parts of our visual field. We organize that field around ourselves, and we seem actually to see groupings and tensions in our experience of a social gathering. Köhler discovered gestalt properties in physics. Wertheimer coined the term "productive thinking" to describe gestalt insights which lead from known syllogisms to new discoveries.[19] An example would be our "seeing" a circle as a polygon with an infinite number of sides. In short, the gestalt psychologists thought it possible to apply their techniques and hypotheses in many different fields.

Kurt Lewin's "experimental psychology of the will" was closely related to the work of the gestalt school. In 1929, he reported a series of investigations which seemed to invalidate the association hypothesis, at least in its primitive form.[20] He described his efforts to ascertain how strong an associative link or habit would have to be before it became hard to discard even in an act of will. He quickly found that the question was badly put. No matter how thoroughly he trained a man to open a doorlatch in a certain direction, he needed only to tell him to take the opposite approach with a differently constructed door in order to produce an immediately correct response. The habit asserted itself only when the habituated subject was told to perform some extraneous task, which incidentally required passage through the door in question. This suggested that such factors as intention (*Vornahme*) and need (*Bedürfnis*) played a much greater role in problem solving than habit, so that the association scheme was relevant only under very special circumstances. In Lewin's view, this discovery cleared the way for a more general shift of emphasis in favor of "dynamic and wholistic conceptions." Subsequently, Lewin discovered that the "saturation" of a subject, the condition in which further repetition of a task becomes more and more inefficient, could be overcome by presenting the same chore as an incident in a larger assignment. This and other experimental results encouraged him to posit "dynamic" concepts, to think of psychic vectors, tensions, and fields.

It is not difficult to write intelligibly about the work of Wertheimer, Köhler, and Lewin. These men operated with a minimum of slogans and obscurities. It is possible to describe their arguments, because they themselves wrote with some clarity and precision. That is less true in the case of German thought psychology (*Denkpsychologie*) during the 1920's. Begun by Oswald Külpe, the school of thought psychology proposed to study the "higher" functions of consciousness. E. R. Jaensch and Richard Hönigswald were the most active adherents of the school during the Weimar period. Jaensch investigated eidetic images, especially in children. He was also interested in memory images generally, and he worked on the processes involved in the comparison of successively presented visual objects.[21] In this area, he observed certain dynamic "transition phenomena," such as the "growth" of a line which is shown first in a shorter, then in a longer form.

Jaensch was clearly dissatisfied with the old association psychology. Hönigswald intended to describe the higher mental processes without any reference to physiological or associationist models.[22] He talked about analyzing the "principles" of our conscious thinking and about achieving "knowledge of our knowledge." As he saw it, his new humanistic (*geisteswissenschaftlich*) and pointedly antimaterialistic psychology of thought was closely related to philosophy. Indeed, it is not easy to see how he proposed to distinguish his own work from that of epistemologists and logicians. He was clearly influenced by the neo-Kantian tradition, and he sometimes sounded as if he intended a "psychological" elaboration of the Kantian criticism. It is not surprising that he felt the need to defend himself against the possible charge of psychologism. His argument was that only the old atomizing type of psychology could be guilty of this fallacy.

There may have been some connection between thought psychology and the work of Husserl's followers. But a more obvious tie linked thought psychology to the "humanistic [*geisteswissenschaftlich*] psychology" of the Weimar period. Humanistic psychology took its inspiration from Dilthey. Karl Jaspers and Eduard Spranger were interested in a system of psychic types, each of which would be associated with a certain weltanschauung. Spranger went particularly far in linking his "structural" psychology with his philosophy of understanding and objective geist.[23] It seemed to Spranger that every individual could be described as a particular combination of such ideal types as the theoretical, the economic, the aesthetic, the social man, the religious man, or the man of power. The problem of psychology, he said, was to select "types whose inner structure appears meaningful, lawful, and therefore accessible to understanding." "The structure of a personality depends upon the direction and the gradation of its evaluative dispositions. A certain direction of value-judging, and thus also of experiencing and striving, is always ranked highest."[24] As these phrases suggest, Spranger sought access to the "integral totality" of a subject's cognitive and volitional dispositions. The objectifications or expressions of a man's personality were to provide the raw material for investigation, and the goal was to penetrate the structure of meanings within which he lived. Apparently, Spranger also thought it possible to apply the concept of structure to "supraindividual cultural forms," to the problem of generation change, and to various internally consistent fields of knowledge and endeavor.

On one occasion, he talked about the "structure of politics," observing that some modernists who lectured at the so-called Hochschule für Politik had a very poor understanding of it.[25]

William Stern did a number of studies in the field of child psychology, linguistic learning, and intelligence testing. However, his main objective eventually became the construction of his "personalistic" psychology and philosophy.[26] For him, the undivided totality of the person, a purposive "whole," was the basic starting point of all science and philosophy. All the contrasts between atomistic and wholistic, mechanistic and teleological conceptions, he thought, were contained in the antithesis between the personalistic and the impersonalistic point of view. At the focal point of the integral person, the outward environment "converged" and interacted with inner dispositions. A "teleo-mechanical parallelism" resolved the dialectic tension between person and object: "In every case, it is the person which stands at the end point of these [recent anti-atomistic] movements, the person in its living, meaningful, profound, meta-psychophysical wholeness."[27]

With that celebration of the whole man, we have reached a point beyond which it is really impossible to translate or to paraphrase an argument. Most of Stern's theoretical work can only be regarded as speculative elaboration of existing conceptions in German psychology and philosophy. The same must be said of Felix Krueger's "developmental psychology."[28] Krueger adopted some of the theories of the gestalt school; but he also proposed to extend wholistic methods to social and cultural studies. He accordingly became involved in organic theories of development and in the terminology of understanding. The "cultural whole" (*Kulturganzes*) was an important concept in his system, and he stressed the need to understand psychological processes in their appropriate social and cultural environment.

In the cases of Spranger, Stern, and Krueger, it is practically impossible to distinguish revivalist intentions from intellectual or scholarly achievements. One can discover that these men meant to "overcome" the "mechanistic" psychology of former days. They wanted a more spiritual and philosophical psychology. They insisted on comprehending the whole man and the whole culture. One can see all that. But then one flounders among the slogans. One wonders whether the work of some German psychologists of this period was anything more than an ideological reaction against a loosely constructed conception of positivist fallacies. It is the exclusively programmatic aspect of much that was written which leads to this impression.

In 1921, Mathias Meier wrote a typical attack upon "the empiricist disintegration [*Zersetzung*] of the concept of [the soul as] substance":[29]

> It is with reference to Locke and Hume [and their "skeptical-sensualistic views"] that we must understand the viewpoint of modern psychology, which . . . is based upon epistemological positivism and metaphysical nominalism . . . For Hume, the soul is but a passive organ of impressions . . . no more than a sum of psychic acts.
>
> The various tendencies and viewpoints which I have outlined are more or less closely connected with the naturalistic conception and fragmentation of the soul . . . The progressive mechanization of the soul, too, is implied in this. But today, neovitalism directs itself sharply against biological mechanism.
>
> The Germans need [Romanticism]. They will not let themselves be Americanized and made a "people without music." Particularly in philosophy, a tremendous movement has begun to get away from the dry conceptual world and to found a philosophy of life.
>
> Despite all positivism, criticism, skepticism, and agnosticism, the need for a metaphysically founded weltanschauung was felt ever more strongly . . . A psychology which is free of metaphysics is hardly possible after all . . . Not unmetaphysical but antimetaphysical is what psychology has become. It will have to free itself from that tendency. The experiences of the war have taught us to see farther, and the distrust of metaphysics . . . has lessened. The psychology with a soul is finding ever more adherents.[30]

Meier did not fully support the neo-Romantic revival and the philosophy of life, although he valued these tendencies as "contributions toward a renaissance of Idealism." Nor did he approve of the new interest in the unconscious, which was commonly associated with spiritualist experiments. "While undoubtedly of great value in its antimaterialistic effect," he said, "the fashionable spiritualist and occultist movement of our time contains the danger that it will ultimately lead to a pseudo-Idealism and pseudomysticism."[31] The problem, for Meier, was to guide these energies into the proper channels, to re-create a "metaphysically founded weltanschauung" and a "psychology with a soul."

Meier was correct, by the way, in saying that a new interest in the unconscious was characteristic of his time. But one should add that it was in no way related to Freudian psychoanalysis. I have encountered only one favorable comment upon Freud's work in the academic literature of this period, and that was written by the radical critic Ernst von Aster.[32] He tried to relate Freud's theories to the positions of various other contemporary schools, particularly insofar as they implied departures from the old psychophysical and associationist models. He also undertook a touching defense of Freud against the charge that he was reducing man to the animal level, ignoring his character as an intellectual and spiritual being. To fend off this type of attack, Aster glorified the process in which men draw energy from the "mother earth" of the instinctual realm in order to expend it in the higher world of the mind and spirit. The effort, alas, was in vain. Freud continued unpopular, and Aster's hunch as to the reasons why may not have been entirely wrong. Of the three explicit critics of Freud I have encountered, one suggested that he had "failed to break away from rationalism and materialism," a second simply asserted that "the Freudian school consisted mostly of dilettantes," and the third complained about the supposedly exaggerated importance which Freud attributed to eroticism.[33]

The man who made the last of these three accusations, Alois Wenzel, was one of those German psychologists who worked with a non-Freudian conception of the unconscious. His reference was to those phases of thought and perception which do not reach the level of awareness and coherence. He argued that these aspects of psychic life could not be analyzed in mechanistic terms and that they had ultimately to be traced to a soul. From there, he moved rather quickly into the vitalist and spiritualist theories which were so popular with the new realists in philosophy. Oesterreich and Driesch, two leaders of the new realism, also worked a good deal with the notion of the unconscious; in their case, this was associated with an interest in parapsychology.[34] Both Driesch and Oesterreich felt that their research would invalidate the old psychophysical parallelism, re-establish the concept of a substantial soul, and suggest the metaphysical assumption of a fundamentally psychic or vital reality. Thus the purposes of the new psychology merged with those of the revival in philosophy.

THE SYNTHESIS MOVEMENT

In examining the German academic pamphlet literature of the Weimar period, one is struck, above all, by a frantic sense of engagement. Addresses at German universities were traditionally designed to relate the specialized concerns of the speakers to the moral, philosophical, and political problems of the day; but the determination to derive salutary lessons from scholarship had never been quite as pronounced as it was during the 1920's. After 1921, the professors tried harder than ever to show that they were not mere specialists and that their work had elevating implications. Thus an astronomer felt compelled to move in a page and a half from spiral nebulae to the "historical right of existence of the German Empire."[35] Academic speeches bore such titles as "The intellectual crisis of penal law," "Early Christianity and culture," and "Hygiene, civilization, and culture."[36] Books were written on "Morphological idealism" and on the "Metaphysics of community."[37] A professor of forestry devoted a lecture to the problems of socialization in forestry. He observed that a stand of trees was "sociologically" comparable to a "living community."[38] A colleague, while rector of Munich University, dealt with the "importance of the forest and of forestry for culture through the changing ages." He pointed out that the trees of a forest "stand together for the protection of the whole against the destructive storm," that they shield "mother earth" from the parching sun and "the mechanical force of the rain."[39]

The theory of cultural decadence was still very much in fashion. Almost habitually, men continued to lament a loss of soul and of conviction, the growth of relativism and determinism, the isolation of the creative individual. They talked about the tyranny of the natural sciences, about the impoverishment of man's will through a one-sided emphasis upon the intellect, about a general sense of impotence and pessimism. After years of "spiritual renewal," they still saw their own time as a no-man's-land between decline and revival. They tried to describe the available alternatives in the contrasting images of dryness and vitality, intellect and emotion, powerlessness and creativity.[40] The theme of crisis was now a ritual and an obsession. Social and political anxieties interacted with cultural and intellectual concerns. There was a crisis in politics, a crisis of social policy, a cultural crisis, and, of course, a crisis of learning. All the methodological innovations of recent years began to intermingle. Every field of study was affected. After announcing the crisis in their discipline, speakers tended to follow immediately with an attack upon the overspecialization and positivism of the nineteenth century. An argument in favor of new methods and concepts generally completed the pattern of these crisis proclamations.

In an address on "the crisis in medicine," the rector of Munich University for 1928 told his audience that the German medical profession had never been more harshly criticized than at the time of his speaking. He listed the charges: the dependence of the body upon the soul had been forgotten; an excessive concern with technical details and specialized research had cut all human ties between doctors and patients; organs and symptoms alone were treated, never the sick individual as a whole; physicians had sacrificed their "integral perception [Anschauung], their intuition, and their whole artistry to . . . the mistaken notion that medicine is a natural science." Oswald Bumke himself found these accusations somewhat exaggerated; but he agreed that one could speak of a crisis in medicine.

The attack upon materialism and mechanism had begun during the second half of the nineteenth century, he said, "and yet the materialistic floodtide is only now ebbing away." Man was still treated as a "reflex machine," which made it impossible "empathetically to understand" (*mitfühlend zu verstehen*) his complaints. Bumke thought that a movement "which strives for large perspectives, for synthesis, and for a unified image of the world"[41] was just beginning to replace older, more specialized approaches in medicine. He warned against careless research methods; but he agreed that some compromise had to be achieved between detailed analysis and a more intuitive awareness of problems and human beings as integral wholes.

Friedrich Schürr said essentially the same thing in an account of the crisis in linguistics. He began with the usual complaint that his discipline had been corrupted by thoughtless specialists and would-be natural scientists during the nineteenth century. The search for immediately observable regularities, especially for phonetic laws (*Lautgesetze*), had become purely mechanical. No one had paid attention to subtle changes in the meaning of words, to the relationship between a language and its culture, or to the causes of semantic developments. In linguistics as in other humanistic disciplines, Schürr argued, the natural scientist's conception of law could not comprehend "true reality" "in its wholeness." A thorough re-examination of scholarly methods therefore became necessary.

> In our field, too, Idealism strives for the whole [*das Ganze*], toward general and ultimate causes. Here too its characteristic is the effort to get beyond conceptual thought to the viewing [*Anschauung*] of true reality. This is the same trend which reveals itself in today's philosophy as a striving for metaphysics.

> The goal of the linguist can no longer be the establishment of generally valid relationships (so-called "laws"). Rather, the general toward which he must strive is the large interrelationships of a historical nature. To grasp these interrelationships, he has but one research . . . method: intuition. Everywhere in scholarship today the tendency is toward the grasping of the large interrelationships; the need for synthesis exists every-

where; but this is only the sign and expression of the fact that intuition is everywhere stirring as a principle of life. An understandable and highly necessary reaction against the exclusive domination of the intellect, which . . . subjected everything to analysis, dissected, circumscribed, mechanized, and thereby killed it. The interminable chaos of the individual results of research demands summation and organization, demands the vital breath of intuition. Synthesis: that is creation; analysis, death.[42]

Synthesis, the whole, understanding, viewing: the slogans were always the same. Biologists and physicians meant to study the whole organism;[43] pedagogues and psychologists, the whole man. In sociology and in economics, it was the whole community. In every discipline, scholars made war upon individualism, naturalism, mechanism, and the like. The new methods of the humanistic disciplines spread like wildfire, along with intuitive and phenomenological approaches. In a history of contemporary economic thought published in 1927, Paul Mombert wrote of a crisis in that discipline, of the transition from an age of analysis to one of synthesis, of an increasing interest in philosophical questions, a growing emphasis upon instinctive and intuitive methods and upon man rather than the material environment.[44]

Werner Sombart was one of the more enthusiastic champions of the new trends in learning. In 1923, he made a distinction between German and "Western," French and English, sociology. The Western variant was "naturalistic." It searched for laws and tried to trace social processes to the basic facts of the old psychology. It tended to find its causal explanations in man's animal nature. German sociology was humanistic. It was interested in meanings; it recognized man's geist as a social force.[45]

In 1930, while preparing to change his politics once more, Sombart summarized his latest position on the methodological controversies in economics. He distinguished between three basic types of economic thinking: the evaluating, the ordering, and the understanding (*verstehend*) approaches.[46] While admitting that most economists actually combined the three methods in various proportions, he cited St. Thomas Aquinas', Vilfredo Pareto's, and his own systems, respectively, as relatively pure examples of "evaluating," "ordering," and "understanding" economics. In evaluating economics, he said, norms are the main object of study, since the "right" economic system is sought. Elements of weltanschauung necessarily enter into this process, so that it becomes possible to group all evaluative doctrines under a few fundamental attitudes toward reality. One of these is the "harmonistic" orientation, which places man in the center of the universe and bases its judgments upon utilitarian and hedonistic considerations. Most French and English economists, according to Sombart, have been harmonists in their valuations.

In his characterization of "ordering economics," Sombart made use of all the traditional arguments about the "isolating" method of the natural sciences, the insistence upon analysis in terms of elements, the search for mechanical laws, "quantification," and "mathematization." He associated the emergence of the natural sciences and of the ordering approach with the "dissolution [*Zersetzung*] of European culture," with secularization, urbanization, the growth of a technological conception of knowledge, the phenomenon of individualism and the disappearance of the traditional community, the death of metaphysics and the predominance of means over ends in modern life.[47] He wrote with much pathos about the "coldness" of naturalistic knowledge, which can never penetrate to the essence (*Wesen*) of reality. Of course, he made the usual remarks about the unfortunate extension of naturalistic analysis to the realm of geist.

That set the stage for his account of understanding economics, in which all the new theories in the humanistic disciplines were profusely intermingled. Sombart worked with such things as "gestalt ideas" and "normative ideas." He used the maximal definition of understanding as a "grasping of meanings" (*Sinnerfassen*), a "knowing of essences" (*Wesenserkenntnis*). He excluded determinism from the realm of culture; he believed it possible to comprehend the "essential [*wesensmässig*] style of an epoch," and he insisted that many of the concepts or ideas with which he operated were more than mere fictions or working ideas. His position on the conflict between theorists and historians and on the question of social policy was a slightly garbled adaptation of Weber's line, in which "meaningful relationships" (*Sinngesetzmässigkeiten*) played an important role. Finally, after suggesting the possibility of an integral doctrine of the economy as a "whole," Sombart took a concluding bow to the neo-Idealist conception of a self-contained intellectual world and to the "impracticality" of all truly scholarly work in this realm.

Compared to such enthusiasts as Sombart, German historians of the 1920's showed remarkable restraint in their attitude toward the new learning. In Otto Hintze and especially in Felix Rachfahl, the old Rankean tradition of political and institutional history lived on.[48] Both men emphasized the state as the essential focus of historical analysis, and both seemed determined to continue the fight against Karl Lamprecht's type of cultural history. Apparently, their relatively "old-fashioned" stand on this issue helped to immunize them against some of the methodological excesses of more recent movements. Hintze criticized Troeltsch for confusing historism as a method with historism as a weltanschauung, and Rachfahl wanted to keep empirical history free of speculative encumbrances. He did not succeed in developing his own position without indebting himself to Rickert and his followers; but he certainly tried to dissociate himself from the more extreme exploitations of understanding. He was one of those politically orthodox members of the older generation who could not bring themselves to appreciate the revolutionary insights of younger colleagues from either political camp. At most, one can imagine him approving of the kind of argument in which Erich Rothacker defended the concept of the "volk spirit" as a unique individuality, associating it with the idea of organic development and tracing the whole scheme to Ranke himself.[49]

The most important disciple of Lamprecht after his death in 1915 was probably Kurt Breysig. Breysig distinguished between descriptive, classifying (*ordnende*), and interpretive (*deutende*) history; of course he devoted his own energies to the last of the three.[50] In so doing, he discovered that epochs in which the "I-factor" predominates tend to alternate with periods of devotion to the community. He also found that the human faculties of imagination, feeling, will, and reason had each been the "dominant" of an age. He thought it the unfortunate peculiarity of the modern period that all four dominants were now involved in a very unharmonious struggle for dominance. Breysig was also interested in the problem of the changing generations in history.

Friedrich Meinecke, a much more distinguished cultural historian than either Lamprecht or Breysig, was influenced by Windelband, by Rickert, and by his friend Ernst Troeltsch. In an essay published in 1927, he described three types of causality in history: the mechanical, the biological-morphological, and the spiritual-ethical.[51] Among these, he said, the last-mentioned has justly received a great deal of emphasis in recent years. In studying the values of the past, we select our material for its intrinsic cultural importance, not for its influence in some other type of causal scheme. We investigate man in his highest achievements; we enter the realm of freedom. Naturally, young people are especially anxious to experience and to re-create the great values of our heritage. For this reason, they take a particular interest in the spiritual-ethical approach and in cultural history. They are perfectly justified in doing so. But they must not neglect the other kinds of causality, which play a role in the more earthly aspects of man's historical existence, in his political history above all. Again, there is nothing wrong with choosing one's subjects on the basis of one's own values. Indeed, we have no other basis for selection in the spiritual-ethical realm. Only our personal involvement can allow us to bring this aspect of the past to life. At the same time, it is not good to jump too quickly from observation to value judgment. Here again, youth must learn the art of tact and balance.

Meinecke's strictures remind us that there were those who tried to resist the temptations of the crisis. Scholarly caution occasionally asserted itself, and not just among historians. The philologist Karl Vossler, a moderate accomodationist in politics, took an exceptionally firm stand. He went so far as to reject the whole idea of general education (*allgemeine Bildung*) at the university, calling it a sham and a deception. Less sophisticated and more old-fashioned in his views than Weber, he nevertheless seconded Weber's objections to the sermon from the lectern. "The character and the will are only indirectly trained at the university, only through the exercise of the mind, of judgment, of the critical faculties, and of comprehending reason. The independence and responsibility of thought remains our . . . most important goal. Moral sermons, moral indignations, exhortations, enthusiasms from the lectern or in the seminars therefore have the air of little powder- or rouge-pots in an army barrack . . . With us, one works with one's head; one does not sing and one does not pray."[52]

Karl Jaspers, too, was a relatively critical observer of the revival in learning. "The university is not . . . the place for the activities of prophets and apostles," he said. He refused to make an exception to this rule even for "apolitical" champions of the "national idea."[53] It also seemed to him that there were too many premature programs for a reconciliation between learning and weltanschauung, too many offenses against the ordinary standards of critical scholarship and reasoning. Nonetheless, he could not help regretting the growing division between the natural sciences and the humanistic disciplines, between the specialized disciplines and philosophy, between learning and the "whole of life." "Today, a philosophical weltanschauung is longed for again, and the fragmentation of the disciplines . . . is not felt to be the ultimate and necessary condition." "The sharp separation of factual knowledge and value judgment, appropriate and ethically stimulating as it is in the field of detailed scholarly research, is yet felt to be something which cannot be the last word . . . Thus . . . the idea of the university . . . is urging us on from an epoch of splintering and dissolution toward a new gestalt, the creation of which is the joint task of today's teachers and students."[54]

There was clearly a considerable difference between Jaspers' ambivalent attitude and Weber's sharply defined position. No one really recaptured Weber's clarity after 1920. The most unequivocal attacks upon the whole "spiritual revolution" came from such radical critics as Wiese, Lederer, Tönnies, and Aster. Wiese cautioned against the new "enthusiasts," against "speculative construction," and against the excesses of Idealism as early as 1921. In the same year, Lederer criticized the recourse to experiencing and to "integral viewing" (*Gesamtschau*) in a particularly "dithyrambic" treatise in economics. Tönnies refused to "go along with the transition from theoretical opinion to 'cultural synthesis,' which Troeltsch finds indispensable."[55] Apparently, the radicals were coming to feel ever more completely disenchanted, bitter, and suspicious. They smelled obscurantism and hypocrisy. Tönnies scoffed at the growing "belief in spirits and spooks," while Aster traced the whole revival to "the metaphysics of nationalism." But these men stood far outside the mainstream of academic opinion.

Most professors supported the synthesis movement. Some reservations were expressed, but rarely in the vigorous terms used by Weber, by Tönnies, or even by Vossler. During the 1920's, a number of well-known scholars tried to define the German "idea of the university" and of learning. They wrote those retrospective accounts of the mandarin heritage which were discussed in Chapter Two. But these efforts invariably culminated in a celebration of the contemporary "renewal." This was inevitable, since almost everyone agreed on the need for a reintegration of scholarship, cultivation, and weltanschauung. Theodor Litt praised the new methods in the humanistic disciplines as means to that end. Spranger traced the whole crisis to the democratization of education, the separation of scholarship from occupational training, and the even more serious breach between learning and weltanschauung.[56]

Werner Jaeger described the way in which the particular acquired a philosophical dignity in the new methodology. He was convinced by the notion of teleological explanation and by the emphasis upon structural insights. He applauded the new bonds between scholarship and cultural philosophy. "Here is the point," he said, "from which factual learning may find the path to the knowing of values, if not to value judgments."[57]

The orthodox Reinhold Seeberg alleged that synthesis itself was a positivist notion, since it suggested that scattered facts had only to be recombined. But this was not enough for him. He sought a new emphasis upon metaphysics. He was pleased to note, he said, that the German volk was unhappy with the whole spirit of Weimar. That explained the general yearning for a new weltanschauung. Well then, the professors would formulate it, the students would "experience it within themselves," and the whole nation would be "swept along" by the new spirit.[58] Were Meinecke's reservations and Jaspers' half-hearted warnings enough to stop all that?

One has the impression that they were not. Emotions were running too high, and criticism was all too easily discredited as positivist. The revival was surrounded by a cloud of suggestive slogans and fashionable terms. Most of these had fairly respectable antecedents. Their origins lay deep in the mandarins' traditional theory of knowledge. Often, it was a distinguished and conscientious scholar who reintroduced these terms and concepts after 1890. But then they were swept into the crisis. They acquired ever larger and vaguer meanings. They interacted and even merged with each other, until each became just another emotional phrase in the litany of the "spiritual renewal." Arguments and ideas which had once been stated with a modicum of precision were transformed into automatic associations. This happened to many concepts and terms. It certainly happened to "wholeness" and "synthesis," the words most often used between 1920 and 1933 to summarize the goals of the crisis.

In the fifteenth edition of *Der Grosse Brockhaus*, the following paragraph appeared under the heading "whole, wholeness" (*Ganz, Ganzheit*).

> in philosophy, the term for the substantive and meaningful coherence, completeness . . . integrity and . . . autonomy of objects of whatever kind . . . Wholeness can really be grasped and demonstrated only intuitively [*anschaulich*] and can barely be defined; the structure of a whole [*ganzheitlich*] object does not consist of isolated parts, is not a sum of parts (additive); rather, it consists of members which are meaningfully interrelated moments of this whole, which form a unity. The concept whole is contrasted to the concepts sum, aggregate, mechanism, machine, and it has therefore become a basic concept in biology, psychology, in the humanistic disciplines, and in philosophy.

Of course, the "whole" was one of the central categories of Romantic philosophy, just as "synthesis" might be considered a popularization of the Hegelian dialectic. In that sense, the crisis of the 1920's could be described as a neo-Romantic and neo-Hegelian revival. There certainly was a new interest in the classics of the German philosophical tradition after 1890.

Nevertheless, one cannot account for the crisis of learning in terms of its theoretical antecedents alone. The academic literature of the 1920's reflected visions, unconscious semantic preferences, and mental habits, not just factual propositions or formal arguments. One can imagine a clearly stated idea being passed along from one generation of scholars to another and thus consciously perpetuated for many years. The problem of transmission becomes more difficult, however, when incoherent notions and emotional predilections are primarily involved. In such cases, one may trace the longevity of popular conceptions at least partly to their persistent usefulness as ideological tools. Of course, the explanation in terms of ideology must "work." One must be able to show that the ideas in question actually fulfilled important functions in the rationalizations of a specified group. But this can easily be done in the case of the German elite and its search for "wholeness" and "synthesis."

Consider the mandarins' determination to train the students' whole character and their emphasis upon the whole nation. Think also of their preference for "whole" insights, for morally profitable experiences, rather than "merely" analytical techniques. These three conceptions were, after all, among the most important tenets of the mandarin creed. We have repeatedly traced their relevance to the social and cultural pretensions of the German elite. Notice, finally, that the argument upon wholeness was easily transferred from one field to another, from philosophy and the humanistic disciplines to pedagogy, and from there to politics. It was used so widely and indiscriminately during the Weimar period that one may fairly describe it as an unconscious mental habit. As a matter of fact, it was very closely related to three other customary patterns of argument which appeared again and again in the literature of synthesis and which certainly had ideological implications. These were: the technique of negative definition, the technique of the higher third, and the symphonic habit.

The technique of negative definition was used, for example, in the *Brockhaus* article on the whole and wholeness. The whole was there defined primarily in terms of what it was not: "it does not consist of isolated parts, is not a sum of parts . . . [It] is contrasted to the concepts sum, aggregate, mechanism, machine." In the same way, Idealism was often described exclusively in terms of its hypothetical opposite, positivism. Synthesis itself was generally identified as the contrary of the supposed overspecialization and materialism of the nineteenth century. In all these cases, the mandarins were primarily reacting against a former condition, whether real or imagined. They were more precise in specifying what they wanted to overcome than in stating alternatives. They were clearly opposed to shallow utilitarianism and barren rationalism; it was more difficult to describe what they proposed instead.

The technique of the higher third was based upon that of negative definition. It involved the rejection of two clearly stated alternatives in favor of a third choice which, without being conceived as a compromise, was held to unite the advantages of the two excluded possibilities on a vaguely "higher" plane of resolution. This method of argument was applied to all kinds of subject matter. In Spranger's essay on the "sociological structural principles" of education, for example, the supposed conflict between individualistic liberty and socialistic equality was "overcome" through "fraternity."[59] As might be imagined, the resolution in terms of fraternity was much less precisely defined than the discarded elements of liberty and equality. This was characteristic of almost every argument in which the technique was applied. Synthesis in terms of the higher third offered an escape from some of the most painful dilemmas in which the mandarins found themselves.

As an example, consider the following definition of geist by Karl Jaspers.

> What geist is cannot be said in a simple formula. It can only be circumscribed as a synthesis of opposites. Every single [characteristic] which is predicated about it, when taken by itself, is not yet geist, but always only in connection with the other. One power of geist is the wanting-to-become-clear [*Klar-*

werdenwollen], but only in connection with an opposite, the wanting-to-become-whole [*Ganzwerdenwollen*].

> It always wants clarity and never reaches its end; it always wants wholeness and is never complete . . . The beginning and the end of geist are dark. If we call the dark fullness the mystical, then geist originates in the mystical and always returns again to the mystical, not because it seeks it . . . but because, in a manner of speaking, it always dives down again with the newly won clarity and seeks new energies.[60]

Geist, Jaspers continued, is always striving to differentiate and to divide up its material for purposes of analysis. At the same time, it always seeks relatedness and integrated perspectives. It wants to transcend national boundaries, without losing its national roots. It requires interchange with others, without thereby becoming shallow and popularized. It needs tradition, without lapsing into static inflexibility. It must remain at once individualistic and universal, subjective and objective: "The intellectual and spiritual [*geistig*] self is always [developing by means of] a synthesis of the subjective self with the objectively whole and general . . . [It is a double error to believe] that geist is the objective, generally valid, or that it is the subjective, existential."[61] These sentences seem terribly obscure, unless one reads them as an account of the crisis. After all, that crisis originated precisely because the old unity of knowledge and wisdom had disintegrated. Objective geist had become alienated from subjective geist. Geist now appeared divided into two parts, one of them striving toward clarification, analysis, and "dissolution," the other toward a future synthesis. If geist was still to be regarded as a single agent, it could only be described in the language of the higher third.

The symphonic analogy, like the concept of wholeness, certainly did not originate in the 1920's. One might almost say that it was always implied in the German intellectual tradition. But it acquired a new popularity—and the status of a habit—during the crisis of learning. It almost always came into play when a German academic of this period discussed the relationship between an individual and the group to which he belonged. It helped to reconcile the principle of individuality with the notion of wholeness, the ideal of nationality with that of humanity. Particularly since the days of the "cultural war," the mandarins liked to picture the cultural and political uniqueness of nations as an asset to a symphonically conceived international community.[62] It was during and shortly after the World War that the historians Troeltsch and Meinecke really "discovered" the principle of individuality and the symphonic analogy in the works of the German Romantics. In 1923, Troeltsch contrasted these aspects of the German heritage with "the whole mathematical-mechanistic West European scientific spirit," its "universal egalitarian morality" and "the barren abstraction of a universal and equal humanity."[63] Interestingly enough, Troeltsch was no longer fully satisfied with the German tradition either. As a modernist, he felt that it had been corrupted during the Bismarckian age. The notion of individuality, he said, had too often been interpreted in a narrowly nationalistic sense. As a counterweight to this tendency, he was prepared to recommend a partial acceptance of English and French conceptions. He closed his lecture by advocating a "cultural synthesis" which would somehow combine the valid aspects of both the West European and the German traditions.

As Troeltsch's essay suggests, the mandarins continued to contrast their own cultural values with those of their enemies in the First World War. The only change that took place in this field during the 1920's was a shift of emphasis from the English to the French comparison. Of course, the international situation had altered since 1914. Whereas England had been Germany's most dangerous enemy before 1918, the threat during the interwar period came chiefly from France. In addition, the mandarins' own domestic concerns had changed between 1914 and 1920. In 1914, German academics had been anxious, above all, to castigate utilitarianism and interest politics. In 1920, their main social and political problem was that of democracy and leveling, an issue most easily treated through a confrontation of France and Germany. Moreover, the German cultural crisis had deepened during the early years of the Weimar period. Methodological questions were now more important than political alternatives. The very axioms of the mandarin ideology were being discussed and defended. Thus the antithesis between French "rationalism" and German "inwardness" was moved to the center of the stage. The German way of life was still identified as the nonutilitarian, the heroic way; but above all, it was now presented as the spiritual antithesis of French "civilization." It is not difficult to imagine how this contrast was described, either on a fairly sophisticated level by a moderate of Karl Vossler's stature, or in the crudest possible terms by an extreme nationalist and racist.[64]

Inevitably, synthetic techniques and conceptions played an important role in the literature devoted to the Franco-German comparison. Thus Ernst Robert Curtius argued that the European cultural crisis had affected not only Germany, but also her neighbor across the Rhine. This seemed to him a good sign, for it suggested a certain flexibility in the competing cultural standards. "There is a Celtic France which awakes again today and which expresses itself in a movement . . . [toward] spiritual renewal and national synthesis . . . [The French genius] will not let itself be subordinated to Latin civilization. The French spirit, no less than the German, is a synthesis of differing elements and therefore capable of renewal. If this synthesis finds a form which enlarges the self-consciousness of the French spirit, then the foolish idea of 'Germanism' [the French caricature of Germany in terms of the "northern fogs"] will die out."[65] Since German intellectuals, too, were moving toward "synthetic and universal cultural studies," Curtius hoped for a more fruitful exchange between the two cultures. Narrow provincialism would be overcome, and it would then be possible even in France "to accept an idea of Europe which is not based upon the hegemony of one national culture but upon the organic and equal cooperation of all European cultures . . . In France, too, the idea of a European intellectual and spiritual community in the sense of a polyphonous harmony has a tradition."[66]

In a series of articles on "poetry and civilization," Fritz Strich employed both the Franco-German antithesis and a group of synthetic techniques to describe the "Faustian man." Based upon an analysis of Goethe's life and of his *Faust,* Strich's Faustian man was intended as an archetype of the German character. The key to that character, according to Strich, was the conflict between Faust's "dark urge" and "infinite yearning" on the one hand, and his search for aesthetic and ethical order on the other. "The German man has this tragic fate, that his intellectual and spiritual demands are directed against his own nature, that a Faustian man will and must conquer Helena."[67] Strich's Faust, his Goethe, and his German man were all suspended between urge and form, East and West, classicism and romanticism: "Russia was able to build its culture upon the irrational soul, France its civilization upon the rational mind . . . The German, however, has always been the very tension between the antitheses." It was clear to Faust and to Goethe, according to Strich, that they had to seek form not in eighteenth-century France but in classical Greece. France "has dissipated the beautiful, sculptured form in which the antique logos was embodied. Instead, [France] has made the abstract, rational spirit alone the general and dominant principle. Thus form became reason, law became rule, and culture became civilization." "Goethe's Storm and Stress was a revolt of the Faustian spirit against Western, French civilization, a revolt of passion against reason, of individuality against society, and of freedom against the rule." Goethe's "viewing [*Anschauen*] itself was a thinking, his thinking a viewing. The methods of West European scholarship—observation, analysis, abstraction—were not his. It was the intuitive . . . and synthetic power in him that made him wholly one with the world in being."[68] In short, Strich's Faustian man was himself a kind of cultural synthesis; but the French and therefore vaguely positivistic dimension was the least important constituent in his makeup.

In a sense then, the synthesis movement was in part a painful exercise in self-definition. Threatened in their social and cultural position, the mandarins made a desperate attempt to rescue the fundaments of their ideology. Many of their tenets were hard to reconcile with those modern realities and attitudes which they represented as peculiarily English or French. They became aware of a whole series of disturbing antitheses, and it was partly their effort to overcome these tensions that led them into the path of synthesis. In a way, their agony was a creative one, for they were forced to delve ever more deeply into their own past and consciousness, to state the axioms of their faith, to describe their most fundamental allegiances. In trying to identify the German character or spirit, they were clearly searching for permanent cultural commitments, and the difficulty of that task in their new situation was reflected in the increasingly tortured style of their writings.

In a famous lecture at Munich University in 1927, the poet Hugo von Hofmannsthal tried to account for the "atmosphere of intellectual and spiritual disquiet and uncertainty in which we live." He compared his own age to the period around the end of the eighteenth century, when German intellectuals rebelled against the French Enlightenment. The difference he saw was that his contemporaries were more serious and less dreamy than the Romantics had been.

> For it is not freedom which they seek, but commitment [Bindung]. . . They want to tie themselves down to necessity, but to the highest necessity, to that which stands above all creeds and is the locus of all thinkable creeds. Never was a German struggle for freedom more fervent and therefore more unyielding than this . . . striving for true authority [Zwang] and this denying oneself to insufficiently authoritative authority . . . For wholeness . . . that soul and mind and the whole spirit should become one, that is at stake today.

> [The new seeker knows] that it is impossible to live without believing in wholeness, that there is no life in a halfhearted belief, that it is impossible to flee from life, as Romanticism supposed: that life becomes livable only through valid commitments . . . All bisections into which mind had divided life are to be overcome in mind and to be transmuted into intellectual and spiritual unity . . . For climbing from synthesis to synthesis, laden with a truly religious responsibility . . . a search

thus undertaken . . . must arrive at this highest step: that geist becomes life and life geist, in other words: to the political realization of the world of geist and to the intellectual realization of the political, to the formation of a true nation.

The process of which I speak is nothing but a conservative revolution of an extent never before known in European history.[69]

Hofmannsthal was an Austrian and not a university professor. But in his ideas, he stood closer to the mandarins than many non-academic writers of his time. When he introduced the notion of a conservative revolution, he was not primarily interested in the party politics of the right. Rather, he was trying to describe that yearning for moral certainties which was generally expressed in the characteristic slogans about the need for synthesis.

It should now be clear that these slogans had more than one meaning. The word synthesis was popular precisely because it seemed to cover all the methodological and substantive objectives which were combined in the crisis of culture and of learning. More particularly, the term was used in four ways. First, "synthesis" occasionally meant nothing more complicated than summary or generalization, the opposite of overspecialization or purely monographic writing. We sometimes use the word in that way today, as did the modernist Carl Becker in his repeated remarks about the value of sociology. Apparently, Seeberg and Spranger also had this first meaning in mind when they identified synthesis with a positivist context, in which discrete research results occasionally had to be added together. A second application of the term made it the converse of analysis in the vague and far-reaching sense of intuition, viewing, wholeness, and the like. Schürr's program for a new linguistics was clearly synthetic in this manner.

The third and fourth meanings of synthesis, unlike the first two, established a connection between purely methodological alternatives and substantive cultural choices. When Troeltsch spoke of a cultural synthesis of West European and German traditions, for example, he envisioned a situation in which Germans would actually change their society, their values and allegiances, not just their manner of studying and describing such realities. Identifying Troeltsch's cultural synthesis as a third variation of that term, one can distinguish it from a fourth. Notice that Troeltsch was clearly recommending an accommodation or compromise between existing cultural traditions. The same cannot be said of Hofmannsthal. He too was searching for a new allegiance as well as for a new method; but he made no attempt to describe the endpoint of his ascent "from synthesis to synthesis." Thus the fourth meaning of the word synthesis was even more purely escapist than the third. In extraordinarily vague terms, it implied a reversal of that process of social and cultural "disintegration" which had troubled the mandarins ever since 1890. In its fourth variation, "synthesis" was intended to describe a path toward a yet undefined set of social and cultural values and conditions.

In making these distinctions, one actually runs the risk of misrepresentation; for the mandarins themselves made no effort to clarify the discussion in this way. Indeed, that is the most important point to be made about the term synthesis: it meant several things at once. The crisis of learning was like a semantic disease. The German language itself was affected by the passions of the day. Words became emotional stimuli. They trailed ever larger clouds of implicit meanings. Audiences were trained to respond to an expanding circle of vaguely antimodernist and antipositivist allusions. "Synthesis" evoked the "whole" and all it represented. It suggested the symphonic analogy. It triggered the habitual and mutually related patterns of negative definition and the higher third. The escape it promised was an "overcoming."

The mandarins never really identified the causes of cultural decadence. They could not decide whether technology and democracy or positivism and materialism were to blame. The same obscurity infected their calls for synthesis. Sometimes, synthesis meant a new way of studying cultural matters. Sometimes, it implied a new set of values, a new cultural or even social and political reality. Often, it suggested all of these at once. The elite saw its modern environment as a dilemma. It also sensed that its intellectual traditions were being torn in a series of painful contradictions. Weber's position had been clear and consistent; but it involved the abandonment of the mandarin claim to wisdom. The choice of Klages, of Kahler, and of life philosophy was another possibility; but it meant the end of scholarship. Jaspers and Spranger, each in his own way, wished to hold the middle ground between these unpleasant alternatives. In the process, they quickly became entangled in antithetical thinking and in synthesis. On a purely abstract plane, these problems might not have seemed so difficult. When joined by the practical and emotional overtones of the crisis, they were insoluble.

It should also be noticed that major groups or factions within the German academic community differed in their ideas of synthesis. Distinctions can be made, even though the differences were often no more than gentle shadings of emphasis. In part, it was a matter of chronology. In 1919 and 1920, synthesis originated as an accommodationist concept. Becker used the term to ask for a present-minded, sociological summing up of scholarly perspectives. Troeltsch worked on his balanced adjustment of German cultural traditions to modern needs. The higher third had little part in these efforts. By the middle of the decade, however, there had been a change. Attacks upon analysis in terms of intuition became more frequent, while the technique of negative definition played an increasingly central role in the literature of the crisis. As this shift became more and more pronounced, several sections of the academic community began to retreat from the movement. The modernists stuck to their less inclusive definition of synthesis, if they did not actually abandon the term. Even some of the older members of the orthodox camp preferred to seek their way from scholarship to weltanschauung without the help of the methodological revolution. Feeble and often contradictory reservations were expressed, as the synthesis movement fell into the hands of the most unstable elements within the mandarin community. Thus by the end of the decade, synthesis was almost purely an escapist device, a herald of spiritual renewal and an ally of the conservative revolution.

THE NEW PEDAGOGY

By 1921, the high point of the modernist initiative in primary and secondary education had been passed. Although a small part of the reformers' program was actually carried out during the early 1920's, the tide had already turned against radical innovation. It was certainly clear by 1925 that little further progress would be made. Accordingly, one finds little emphasis upon the possibility of institutional change in the pedagogical literature of the 1920's.

This is not to say that the modernists were entirely silent after 1921. Carl Becker continued to speak for a more flexible and socially progressive school system and for an improvement in the status and training of teachers.[70] In 1923, a group of educators attended a government-sponsored conference on civic education and resolved to support programs of citizenship training in the "spirit of the Weimar constitution."[71] Willy Hellpach pursued the cause of moderate reform in Baden and speculated about the underlying source of the humanist-modernist controversy in secondary education: "Economics and technology occupy the field . . . the acquisitive threatens the 'cultivated' society. It is a crisis of Western culture . . . Those threatened and displaced defend themselves characteristically with a word . . . They identify themselves as culture, the new as mere 'civilization.' "[72] But Hellpach's bluntness and Becker's persistence were really exceptional. On the whole, there were few defenders of modernist reform during this period. One has the impression that resurgent orthodoxy held the field, and that the arguments of the traditionalists had been accepted by the majority of German academics.

Most of these arguments were no longer new. There was the defense of private and denominational primary schools upon religious grounds.[73] From Aloys Fischer in 1922, there was the suggestion that no permanent innovations be accepted until the country had once again achieved "settled conditions, as we had them before the war." Spranger added a few conventional remarks about the dangers of "psychotechnical" measures of individual ability and about other symptoms of cultural "Americanization." Jaeger continued to defend the classical gymnasium upon purely humanist grounds.[74] Roethe, Spranger, and Rehm restated the more popular argument that the study of Greek and Roman antiquity could serve as a source of German national consciousness and an antidote against the materialism, the utilitarian rationalism, and the leveling tendencies of the time.[75] Rehm spoke of the need for "total opposition to an age which . . . is about to make the servants of the state, including the university teachers, mere 'functionaries of society.' " The only opponents of the classical gymnasium who seemed to Rehm worthy of consideration were the fanatical defenders of a purely national culture. To them, Rehm praised the patriotic virtues of Romans and Greeks and their "great doctrine of the state, in which, through which, and for which all citizens live."[76] To complete this train of thought, E. Schwartz wrote that no cultural recovery could be expected until Germany had become a great power again, until "next to the lecture room and the laboratory, the military drilling field and the training ship will [again] care for the complete education of youth." "To want to banish this somber thought through organization and socialization, through showy reforms of secondary schools and universities, or yet through silly phrases about a clear path for the talented, is childish self-deception."[77]

In 1925, the faculty of philosophy at the University of Berlin declared itself opposed to any "pedagogization" (*Pädagogisierung*) of the universities for the sake of future secondary teachers.[78] The authors of the memorandum warned against a divorce between research and teaching and preferred to regard gymnasium teachers as potential scholars. They emphatically rejected the idea of attaching practice schools to the universities. Of course, they said, it was desirable to impart a "deepened total cultural consciousness" to future teachers. But it was possible, in their opinion, to achieve this objective within the existing system of departments and subjects. After all, there was already a movement toward a more integral understanding of texts in philology, and a new "higher psychology of understanding" was being developed. In philosophy, they added, the trend was away from a purely logical and epistemological emphasis and toward a substantive philosophy of culture. The Berlin faculty did not approve of the label "sociology" for any of the new developments. But it did consider them promising signs of a broadly cultural concern within the existing academic fields and therefore reasonable alternatives to special courses in education for future teachers.

The most interesting part of this argument was the suggestion that certain new directions in German learning could actually take the place of institutional adjustments in favor of secondary school teachers. Even a kind of specialization was apparently no longer regarded as an evil in itself, as long as a "deepened total cultural consciousness" was achieved within the existing disciplines. A more philosophical pedagogy, too, appeared desirable, though not one that was sociologically oriented. To us, these distinctions may appear obscure; but to the orthodox academics of the 1920's, they were both clear and of the utmost importance. In their minds, the true, "inner" direction of the reform movement was clearly separable from the superficial or "merely organizational" path of the most determined modernists. Even a certain type of synthesis could appear unnecessary and superficial in this way, if it achieved no more than the summation of information, if it did not advance the cause of Idealism. The increased emphasis upon pedagogy, finally, was salutary only as long as it did not result in the "pedagogization" of the universities. Departments of education, practice schools, and experimentally oriented educational psychologists had no place within the traditional scheme of mandarin learning. German secondary school teachers had always been the foot soldiers of German learning and idealist cultivation. They were trained in academic philosophy, not in educational psychology. What could be more dangerously superficial than a reversal of these established priorities?

It is the spirit which builds the body for itself. One must never forget how much that sentence meant to the mandarins. Indeed, there is no better motto for the history of German pedagogy after 1921; for what we have said about the memorandum of the Berlin faculty could easily be extended to that whole subject. As the 1920's advanced, there was an important change in the character of the academic literature upon educational questions. Quite apart from the fact that orthodox tracts apparently came to outnumber modernist ones, there was a general shift of emphasis away from the discussion of practical or organizational alternatives. The whole debate became more theoretical. Ideas which had been developed in the synthesis movement began to appear in essays on pedagogy. The crisis in philology was said to complicate the problems of the classical gymnasium. It had to be overcome through some kind of synthesis.[79] Occasionally, a crisis of pedagogy was posited and then prepared for eventual resolution in terms of a reconstructed Idealism.[80] Fundamental questions were asked about the relationship between education and cultural change. Yet it became increasingly clear that all the soul-searching tended to exclude the possibility of far-reaching institutional innovation, rather than preparing the ground for it. Of course, there had always been a close relationship between pedagogy and speculative philosophy in Germany. But after 1921, there appears to have been a whole new process of theoretical abstraction —or sublimation. Since a few accommodationists participated in this process, one cannot treat it as a purely orthodox movement. The modernists themselves had never proposed an exclusively organizational approach to reform; but they had certainly made institutional change a part of their platform. As that part was deemphasized between 1921 and 1933, accommodationist pedagogy was submerged in mandarin pedagogy, theoretical speculation took the place of practical reform, and the renewal of the spirit was once again taken to be more important than the condition of the body.

One can follow this trend in the works of Georg Kerschensteiner and Theodor Litt after 1920. Litt repeatedly emphasized the limitations of reform.[81] He thought it wrong, for example, to exaggerate the student's autonomy in the learning process. He was prepared to admit that teachers ought, within certain limits, to consider the natural inclinations of their pupils. But he also underlined the educator's role as a traditional authority and as a guide. Above all, it worried him that some radicals appeared to treat pedagogy as an independent area of study, and education as an autonomous agent of social and intellectual change. In opposing this view, he emphasized the dependence of pedagogy upon various other disciplines. He also stressed the subordinate role of the teacher as a transmitter of an existing body of knowledge and tradition. It seemed to him that some of the reformers, particularly those who sympathized more or less openly with the Social Democrats, had shown too little respect for the German political heritage. These men wanted to teach civics, he said, as if it could be based upon a purely private ethic, as if a community could be conceived without reference to an established political authority, as if the state itself were evil. Convinced, on the contrary, that the legal and cultural state was a great moral good, that the German tradition was based upon this ideal, and that German pedagogy could not ignore the nation's heritage, Litt inevitably arrived at this conclusion: "There can be no ethicization [*Versittlichung*] of the German idea of the state and of German political reality, unless it grows out of the concrete experiences which made our people realize the nature and dignity of the state, through further development of the ideas in which our great thinkers have expressed the content of these experiences."[82] In other words, Litt did not like to think of an education which was not principally devoted to the perpetuation of the mandarin heritage.

In Kerschensteiner's case, a decreasing enthusiasm for reform was very clearly related to an increasing respect for German Idealist philosophy. This correlation was foreshadowed in Kerschensteiner's work even before 1921; but it became ever more noticeable in his later and more systematic writings.[83] What had once been an emphasis upon active learning, even upon manual training, was gradually turned into a theory of experiencing (*Erleben*), in which the student's autonomy consisted of the "inner" assent with which he absorbed the values contained in the objective culture of his environment. The notion of adjusting instruction to the pupil's own inclinations, too, was softened, though not entirely discarded: Kerschensteiner spoke of developing the "ethically possible" within each student. He also adopted the terminology of wholeness in order to establish a principle of totality: the pupil's learning and orientation were to fuse into an inner unity, his soul was to be "freed of contradiction." The objectives of student self-government were restated, so that the willing submission to natural leaders appeared more central. Civic instruction became an exercise in "inner freedom" and in devotion to the legal and cultural state. "The goal of civic education is the realization of the idea of the ethical community in a national ideal, the ideal of the national cultural and legal state." "Even with talented youngsters, and more especially with the untalented ones, it is one of the most important tasks of civic instruction to let the student feel the insufficiency of his own judgment and to arouse in him the feeling of modesty."[84]

The problem of authority was clearly a central theme in Kerschensteiner's writings after 1921, and it is interesting to see how he dealt with it. As a mandarin, he could accept only one type of authority, namely that of "higher" cultural values and of their "bearers." Again and again, he spoke of the reverence or the feeling of authority which was due to genuine values and to those who bore or embodied them. Like Litt, he sought to re-establish the authority of the classroom teacher. He proposed to do this by awakening the students' respect for the sublime and for its representatives. Once the proper sort of cultural reverence was established, it could serve as the fundamental source of authority in society as a whole, so that the problems of pedagogy were ultimately identical with those of the social order. This was the main point of Kerschensteiner's argument.

The modernist Jonas Cohn arrived at an even broader statement of the issue of authority in education. Like Hofmannsthal in his proclamation of the conservative revolution, Cohn used the words *binden* (to bind, or tie) and *Bindung* (tie, restraint) to suggest the sense of having an allegiance, of being rooted in or committed to an idea, a norm, a locality, or a group. In a series of essays entitled *Befreien und Binden* (To liberate and to bind), he described the crisis of German pedagogy in these terms: "In reality, the crisis of our educational system can only be understood in connection with the general cultural crisis. Our time is a period in which the liberated geist seeks fulfillment, without losing its freedom. But it can only find fulfillment, if it binds itself. Therefore the task of education appears to our times as a combination of liberating and binding."[85] When applied to classroom instruction, this conception led to a slightly modified version of Kerschensteiner's views. Cohn insisted that students were naturally desirous of firm guidance. A loving teacher would therefore begin by using his personal authority to lead his charges toward certain intellectual and moral commitments. As these were established, the pupils would be less and less bound to the person of their mentor, who could gradually begin to treat them as his equals. In a sense, the students would become more "autonomous"; but their autonomy would actually be based upon the ethical and emotional "ties" which they had made their own as a result of the learning process: "The profoundest and ultimate liberation, the awakening of autonomy, takes place by way of the most rigorous binding."[86]

To Cohn, this was more than a nice paradox and certainly more than a casual observation upon discipline in the schools. He was convinced that the central problem of modern existence was contained in the relationship between liberation and binding. His modernist principles caused him to accept that process of intellectual "clarification" in which man's natural and instinctual ties are subjected to rational analysis. Indeed, this is what he meant when he spoke of the liberation of the individual through self-consciousness. The only question was whether the analysis of one's own experiences, motives, and allegiances tended to rob them of their immediacy and force. There was no doubt in Cohn's mind that modern man had weakened his sense of rootedness and that an effort was required to reverse this development. At the same time, he did not wish to give up the advantages of "clarification." Accordingly, he made it the major purpose of his essay to show that it was both possible and necessary to combine intellectual liberty with emotional and moral commitment.

> The crisis of our culture is not a sign of its senility . . . but a result of the very victories of geist . . . Man has become free; he asserts the right to criticize all tradition . . . Just for that reason, there is the danger that his own homeland will become an indifferent place to him, his own life a means to be used up in the wheels of the factory, the world an alien force . . . The firm universe, in which things and men have a fixed meaning, in

which cultural work is meaningfully integrated, has disappeared . . . If there is to be culture which is "modern" at the same time, then man must once again achieve a necessary relationship to his immediate environment, which he shapes and upon which he depends, [and he must achieve this] without narrowing his free perspective . . . without sacrificing the rights and duties of free thought, research, and creation. If geist is the cause of the crisis, then it must also seek within itself the means to its cure.

It is not true that initial clarification hinders the subsequent immediate and unified experience and the ability to act with integral conviction . . . Only a persistent tendency to doubt, which never ceases its probing, a stubborn refusal to go beyond preliminary exercises of the reason . . . is harmful for the freshness of experience and creation.[87]

Perhaps it should be emphasized again that Cohn was very much a modernist. He proposed to "accept the order, functionalism, and cleanliness which is characteristic of everything civilized [*allem Zivilisatorischen*]" and thus to "make it a part of culture." He denied "that factory products are necessarily inexpressive or ugly, as long as they do not try to simulate the charms of handicraft."[88] We may certainly suppose that he was serious and firm in his respect for clarification and for the liberty of analysis.

Nevertheless, there were two highly critical areas of obscurity in Cohn's position, and these could be exploited to reverse the implications of his argument. First, he did not at all succeed in specifying how liberation could be reconciled with binding. The difficulty, of course, lay in his own definitions. Without being very explicit on this point, he implied that man's ways of thinking and knowing were at least partly responsible for his loss of roots. Once this was established, the idea of a conflict between analysis and commitment was very hard to escape, and Cohn's own resolution of that conflict could easily appear an unexplained and more or less gratuitous assertion. This impression could only be strengthened by a second ambiguity in Cohn's argument. What did he mean when he criticized the "persistent tendency to doubt which never ceases its probing" and the "stubborn refusal to go beyond preliminary exercises of the reason"? Presumably, the reference was to that "merely formal" or exclusively logical direction in philosophy which was quite generally in disrepute among the mandarins. Was it this kind of thinking which had endangered the old ties, and if it was, how could it be distinguished from the presumably less dangerous forms of clarification?

To raise these questions is simply to point out that Cohn did not entirely avoid two characteristic notions which shaped the mandarins' whole attitude toward the cultural crisis. The German academics believed, we have said, that social and cultural disintegration was due both to certain socio-economic forces and to purely intellectual changes. The cure of the crisis therefore had to stem at least partly from a reorientation of men's minds and hearts. Moreover, there was always an implied distinction between two different kinds of knowledge or thought: a harmful and vaguely disintegrative type, and a constructive, elevating, and somehow synthetic one. If one combines this theory of two knowledges with the idea that modernity has intellectual as well as substantive causes, one can easily take the step from antimodernity to a species of anti-intellectualism. Of course no mandarin could ever have become an enemy of all geist. That choice was left open for others. But opposition to the supposedly destructive side of reason was possible, apparently, for a good many members of the German elite.

As a matter of fact, much of the pedagogical literature of the 1920's, especially on the orthodox side, was devoted to the search for authority and ties, and the borderline between mandarin revivalism and simple anti-intellectualism was occasionally obscured. Aloys Fischer worried about the decline in patriotic allegiances in an age when "the material values of civilization" threatened to produce an "international solidarity of interest."[89] It seemed to him that feelings and beliefs lost much of their strength, once they were made the object of conscious analysis. He proposed an increased scholastic emphasis upon *Heimatkunde,* the study of local and regional geography, history, and folk culture, in order to re-create the "irrational power of faith." The usual reflections about the growth of individualism and class-consciousness led him to speak of man's "yearning for union with the whole, from which he has been split off through individuation."[90] "The thoroughly individualized man . . . moves toward new ties (*Bindungen*) . . . He yearns for this as for a necessary self-completion." "There is no more persistent and agonizing concern for man, when he remains free, than this: to find something to which he may bow."[91]

It was the chief task of education, according to Fischer, to "create the irrational bases and forces of communal life." The difficulty was that many of the old social and cultural authorities had lost their hold upon youth. A "crisis of the authorities" was "the common basis of the difficulties of our culture as well as of our educational work." Fischer described the German youth movement as the young people's attempt to find an unspoiled focus for their loyalties. He also felt that they were rebelling against those intellectual and scholarly traditions which were generally discredited among the mandarins themselves: naturalistic positivism, utilitarianism, and the like. There was a new emphasis upon geist, as distinct from reason (*Verstand*), a revulsion against the old intellectualism, a trend toward "synthesis, system, toward [the] totality of human existence, and toward a new inclusive weltanschauung": "A revolution of the spirits is taking place."[92] Fischer expressed some concern that the younger generation might reject every form of discipline, losing itself in a new anarchic individualism or a purely private mysticism. But in the end, he hoped to be able to guide the new energies into the proper channels.

Eduard Spranger took a very similar line. He spoke of a tremendous tension "between the world of achievement and the culture of the soul, between realism and romanticism, and, even more specifically, between reality and [the] youth movement . . . Rarely . . . has the polarity between inwardness and the external world been felt more strongly than we feel it." To account for this situation, Spranger produced the usual list of social and intellectual ills, all of which he associated with the age of technology. Of course, he sought the cure in education, more particularly in the classics of the mandarin tradition. "If only in order to understand the true meaning of

413

cultivation, we must re-establish connections with those minds and those souls with whom the separation between the world of things and the world of the soul, between doing and being, between the material and the form of life, was not yet as drastic as it is in our case. That applies to the poets and thinkers whom—probably instinctively for that reason—we call our German classical writers. They had cultivation in the full . . . sense of the word. Therefore they were still masters of life, not its wage laborers."[93]

The point of all this agonizing was to find a way of binding the intellectual and moral energies of youth to some authority, preferably to one which was embodied by the mandarins themselves. If that authority was to be made effective, it had to be rooted in the students' wills and not just in their minds. Education had to produce firm commitments, and teaching methods had to be adjusted to this task. In short, there was a greater incentive than ever before to train the pupil's "whole character" and to make him "experience" the meaning of his sources. There was a great need for a new pedagogy.

It seemed to Theodor Litt, at any rate, that the old pedagogy had too often fallen into one of two serious errors, that of psychologism or that of rationalism (*Logizismus*).[94] Under the first of these categories, Litt castigated the tendency to derive all teaching methods from a quasi-experimental psychology, as if education were a natural science and completely independent of philosophy. This, of course, seemed to him a positivistic or naturalistic fallacy. Rationalism was the contrary inclination to deduce pedagogy from certain eternal principles, as if neither the practical experience of teachers nor the various personalities of the students mattered at all. According to Litt, this was dangerous formalism, the antithesis of mechanistic psychologism, but unsatisfactory in any case. A third variety of pedagogy, said Litt, was influenced by life philosophy, which stressed the immediate totality of the student's character and of the learning experience. But this approach was too closely dependent upon certain temporal accidents; there was not enough connection with the world of permanent ethical or cultural ideals. Litt therefore sought another type of "synthesis" between psychologism and rationalism. The true aim of pedagogy, he said, was to bring the eternal values to the individual in the form that was best adapted to his own character and to his time.

Fischer's philosophy is harder to fathom; but he may have had some sympathy with that life philosophy of which Litt spoke. The idea that the schools should prepare for life and not just for scholarship was certainly a favorite with him. He talked a great deal about "forming the character," about the "element of weltanschauung" in education, and about the "training of the emotions." In comparison with these objectives, the modernists' civic education and working instruction seemed to him of decidedly secondary importance. "Working education" (*Arbeitspädagogik*), he said, was the "pedagogical exponent of an economic and technological age," the product of a widespread shift of emphasis from a "purely idealistic conception of the cultural process to a realistic one." "It is the acceptance of the partial man, of specialization, of the expert and specialized occupational man." Fischer did not approve of this acceptance or "resignation," as he called it. He was a determined enemy of all "utilitarian rationalism" and of every sort of schematization and "desoulment" of life or of man. To this extent, he approved of life philosophy, its emphasis upon experiencing and its yearning for unclassifiable "totality."[95] He only wondered whether it would be possible to institutionalize the incidence of unique experience beyond a certain point.

In the end, Fischer decided that "working pedagogy" and "experience pedagogy" (*Erlebnispädagogik*) were both guilty of certain exaggerations and misstatements. Once stripped of these encumbrances, however, the two movements could be shown to have a core of validity in common. They were both directed against the mechanical drill and the one-sided emphasis upon the intellect which had hitherto been characteristic of the German schools. The two movements deserved praise for "their joint discovery and transcendence [*Überwindung*] of the soulless and positivistic educational approach of a civilizationist epoch which—despite all pessimistic prophecies about the decline of the world—we have surpassed precisely because these [antipositivist] ideas have come alive and are preparing the ground for a new departure." In this way, Fischer felt able to focus

the whole pedagogical discussion upon "the area of emotional cultivation through the experiencing of values in poetry and art, ethics
and law, state and society."[96]

It should be added that Fischer was not an unimportant man in
his field. In 1925, two new pedagogical periodicals were founded in
Germany, and Fischer was an editor of the more prestigious of the
two. It bore the proud title "Education: monthly journal for the
interrelationship of culture and education in learning and life." Its
four editors were Fischer, Litt, H. Nohl, and Spranger. In an introductory outline of the journal's purposes,[97] Fischer placed the usual
emphasis upon the breadth of the antipositivist and antiutilitarian
revival, which he described as "an amalgam of philosophical and
pedagogical ideas, impulses, and projections." It seemed to him impossible that any sphere of thought or action could be isolated from
this movement, and he particularly talked about the need for keeping pedagogy in touch with it. He wrote of the desire to replace
knowledge and cleverness with wisdom and passion in education. He
was emphatic in his demand that pedagogy be regarded as a part of
philosophy, not as a specialized discipline or as a craft. For these
reasons, the new journal was to be devoted to the "interrelationship
of culture and education in learning and in life."

The other periodical, the "Journal for German education," was
to be chiefly concerned with the study and teaching of German history and culture. The editor Ulrich Peters listed one or two modernists among potential contributors. But on the whole, the periodical
was clearly intended to be the organ of the extreme cultural nationalists. In his programmatic introduction, Peters simply announced
that one-sided intellectualism had been overcome and that the methods of understanding and interpretation (*Deutung*) had replaced
"observation and conclusion." The new approach in the Germanic
studies (*Deutschkunde*), which had thus been made possible, could
be described in a few emphatic sentences. Education "by no means
limits itself to the area of information and knowledge, but also en-
compasses the domains of feeling, will, and creation. Today we do
not want to train the intellect only or even primarily; but we wish
to form the whole human being, body and soul." "Intuitive vision

[*geistige Schau*] is the mark of the new style in learning. And its second mark is synthetic vision [*Zusammenschau*]." "Education, in this sense, cannot be free of presupposition; it cannot be free of value judgments or of goals. The presupposition is faith in the vitality of the German people . . . [The goal] is the return of the German soul to itself."[98]

In some respects, these phrases cannot be considered representative of more widespread attitudes, since the extreme nationalists were a particularly unstable group. On the other hand, there were attacks upon "the primacy of the intellect" or "mere intellectuality" from more respectable segments of the orthodox camp as well. Even Becker occasionally used the language of "binding."[99] *Der Grosse Brockhaus* may safely be considered an example of average mandarin opinion, and here is what it had to say on the subject of "intellectualism": "the excessive emphasis upon the thought-out and reasoned as over against the will, practical action, and all [immediate] values of life . . . With the growth of civilization, there is always an increase of intellectualism, which many philosophers of culture consider destructive of vitality . . . For this reason, the pedagogy of the present has made it its goal to prevent the forces of the will and of practical action from being atrophied through intellectualism."

We must conclude that a certain kind of anti-intellectualism was the ultimate result of the whole pedagogical crisis. This is a paradoxical conclusion and an uncomfortable one; but one cannot avoid it. Of course one resists the suggestion that there was any connection between the ideals of a Humboldt and the phrases of a Fischer or a Peters. But the evidence suggests that these apparently so dissimilar sets of notions *were* related, at least as a caricature may be related to its original. We have followed the evolution of mandarin attitudes through various stages: the assumptions about the causes of cultural disintegration, the rejection of "superficial" adjustments to modern realities, the call for an "inward" renewal, the search for a more "synthetic" learning, and the demand for spiritually and not just intellectually effective ties through education. Each item in this list bore some relationship to an older axiom of the mandarin creed, although the fear of modernity and the desire to escape from it invariably gave a new meaning to the original ideal. The doctrine of spiritual ennoblement through learning became the theory of two knowledges. The old dictum about the body and the spirit became an anti-"organizational" tool. As the twentieth-century variants of a preindustrial ideology were combined into a new weltanschauung, a mandarin form of anti-intellectualism began to take shape. Logically, the end products of this process may not have been related to its beginnings. Historically, psychologically, ideologically, they were.

THE SOCIOLOGY OF CULTURE AND OF KNOWLEDGE

Some of the developments in German learning between 1890 and 1933 are interesting in that they actually influenced the course of the crisis. Others fascinate us primarily as indirect reflections of the mandarins' situation. The sociology of culture and of knowledge falls into the latter category. The whole idea of cultural sociology (*Kultursoziologie*) is based upon the mandarins' concern over the relationship between culture and civilization. The sociology of knowledge has been making converts among intellectuals of all countries until the present day; nevertheless, its most important conceptions are deeply rooted in the German intellectual context of the Weimar period. Like cultural sociology, the sociology of knowledge mirrors the methodological as well as the substantive dilemmas of those days. Both theories cannot be fully understood apart from their origins. In return, an understanding of these two movements can add much to one's comprehension of the issues which helped to give them birth.

"Cultural sociology" was the term chosen by Alfred Weber to describe the range of his own concerns.[100] In conscious reaction against Wiese's procedure, Weber hoped to bring sociological conceptions to bear upon the empirical data of history. He did not intend to restore the old confusion between sociology and universal or "philosophical" history. But he did believe that sociologists should call attention to certain continuities of development, certain general characteristics of the social order, which might be overlooked by the "individualizing" historian. It seemed to him particularly important to understand the connection between the creative activity of individuals and the larger context of material and social conditions in which it arose. To deal with this problem and to respond to some of the issues raised by the Marxist theory of history, he introduced a rather casual metaphor and a set of only slightly more rigorous distinctions. The metaphor was of a body of water in which the motion of individual waves may be distinguished from that of larger swells and currents, while an even more general tidal change serves as a substratum for the rest. To Weber, this was more than an image of the relationship between individual creativity and its context; it also suggested that there were different sorts of motions or changes in history.

Weber distinguished between the "societal process" (*Gesellschaftsprozess*), the "process of civilization" (*Zivilisationsprozess*), and the "motion of culture" (*Kulturbewegung*). Under the first of these headings, he included all those aspects of a given historical situation which might be described in a static analysis of economic, geographic, or even sociopolitical givens. Weber was interested in the fact that we regard these things as material realities or necessities. They seem to arise directly out of man's biological needs and out of those properties of the physical world which we cannot alter. They may change; but we do not change them. They are incontrovertible, so that we can only respond to them, take them into account in our behavior. The process of civilization, by contrast, accounts for the appearance of unilinear progress in history. It is based upon man's purely intellectual advances: his scientific discoveries, his technological innovations, and his growing knowledge of himself. Like his brother, Alfred Weber was fascinated with the general intellectualization and rationalization of life. It was this apparently inevitable development which he associated with civilization. Accordingly, he argued that the process of civilization could be checked but never reversed. That seemed to account for the repeated attempts to describe historical change in terms of progress; but it also suggested the limits of such an interpretation. After all, Weber argued, there are some aspects of man's creativity that cannot be listed in a catalog of purely intellectual discoveries and advances. These are the constituent elements of the "cultural movement," which follows its own laws. In literature and in the arts, in religion and in philosophy, it is clearly impossible to picture change as an additive process, a movement in a single direction. In this realm, the soul plays more of a role than the mind. Culture and cultivation are based at least partly upon subjective states, on feelings and experiences which are much harder to perpetuate or even to communicate than the discoveries of science. For this reason, the motion of culture poses special problems for the historian and the sociologist. Its spirit or essence has to be grasped in a unique way, and its independence from the process of civilization has to be kept in mind. According to Weber, the failure to make these distinctions was one of the main causes of theoretical disagreements over the nature of historical change and our knowledge about it.

It would be pointless to pretend that Alfred Weber was an expert in the precise statement of methodological problems. His interests and his skills lay elsewhere. He was a master in the art of evocative writing; he used language to paint subtle portraits and to suggest fine differences of mood. When he took a position on a question of logic, he moved almost instinctively toward a middle position between discredited extremes. The Marxists did not fully convince him, and yet he distrusted the overly "idealistic" attacks upon them. He had a certain sympathy for the idea that sociological synthesis should throw light upon the conditions and needs of the present, and yet he emphatically disapproved of the tendency to prognosticate about the health or decadence of a given culture. He sensed the need for special approaches in the understanding of cultural movement; but he also liked to criticize the enthusiasts of the antipositivist revolt and their immediate "viewing" of essence. He was more successful in describing than in stating his own position.

Partly for this reason, it is best to see Weber's theories primarily as elaborations of his own cultural concerns. He was much more thoroughly committed to the purely cultural aspects of the mandarin heritage than to its political and bureaucratic amplifications in the ideology of the legal state. This preference placed him in the camp of the radical accommodationists and made him a harsh critic of Wilhelmian society. It was the painful vulgarity, the parvenu quality of Wilhelmian success and "realism," that made him aware of the difference between the process of civilization and the movement of culture. He saw that cultivation had become a matter of certificates, a mark of social acceptability, and a guarantee of political reliability. He was frightened by the general subservience to the official ideology, which threatened to confine the dimensions of the German personality to a narrow patriotism and an even narrower conception of bureaucratic service. He was concerned about the growing lack of contact between geist and politics. He wondered how the future bearers of culture were to maintain at least a minimum of material and spiritual independence vis-à-vis the burgeoning apparatus of government and industry. In his sociology of culture, he was only trying to create instruments that would be capable of dealing with some of these problems.

Something similar may be said about the sociology of knowledge. This young social science deals with the relationship between expressed thought and the social context in which it originates. As that definition suggests, there are no very sharp lines of demarcation between the new discipline or subdiscipline and a whole range of less formal approaches to the same general issue. Because the sociologist of knowledge raises some of the oldest and most critical problems of all social theory, he finds his newly chosen field already occupied by intellectual historians, general sociologists, and philosophers of culture. He encounters the Marxist scheme, in which a superstructure of intellectual rationalizations is treated as the function of a substructure of socio-economic realities. He hears various environmentalist doctrines, "scientific" as well as "romantic" ones, and he is also confronted with the arguments of the relativists and historicists. He discovers, finally, that practically every account of past or present cultural life is based upon some more or less explicit sense of the relationship between thought and its "situation."

All these problems are nearly as old as social theory itself. But they became particularly acute for the German academic community of the Weimar period, and this for several reasons. To begin with, the

German intellectuals had been introduced in a particularly abrupt fashion to the language of class conflict in politics. In that language, the arguments of opponents are often attacked in a very distinctive way. Instead of being challenged on factual or logical grounds, they are "debunked" or "unmasked": they are described as rationalizations or defenses of the antagonists' class interests and prejudices. All participants in a debate of this type are trained to consider the opinions of others mere expressions of underlying social resentments. Political theories begin to be understood as strictly "relative" to this or that socio-economic position.

It may be objected that economic class conflicts were no more intense in Germany after 1890 than they had been in other countries at other times. But even if that is true, it misses the point. After all, it is not so much the fact of class conflict as its visibility, its psychological impact, which is at issue. The peculiarities of Bismarck's political system and the unusually abrupt arrival of industrialization caused Germans to be particularly conscious of the new economic "interest politics." The mandarins themselves had been thoroughly accustomed to the language of "idealism" in politics, which caused them to be all the more deeply shocked by the new vocabulary. Most of them expressed their disapproval by unmasking the "egotism" and "materialism" which they detected in the arguments of rival political leaders. They began to preach community. They fell into that "merciless moralizing" which provoked the scorn of a few radical critics. Ernst von Aster debunked the search for community as a "backward-looking utopia" as early as 1929. In short, unmasking techniques were freely used in an increasingly fruitless discussion. It was the violent clash of two political languages, not the economic and political situation alone, which led to this result.

Other trends in German intellectual life between 1890 and 1932 also contributed much to the vocabulary of the new subdiscipline. Obsessed with the problematical relationship between learning and weltanschauung, the German academics liked to examine various styles of thought from a very special point of view. They distinguished between positivist and synthetic knowledge, between merely technical and morally meaningful scholarship, between mere instruction and integral cultivation, between "disintegrating" and wholistic conceptions. In the process, they tried to connect various methodological positions with vaguely defined social and cultural situations. For example, they treated positivism and materialism as inevitable accompaniments of the mass and machine age. The language of understanding itself implied that ideas should be comprehended in their respective contexts. Indeed, the problem of historism arose because it was possible to doubt whether thoughts or judgments could ever be regarded as anything more than symptoms of strictly temporary conditions. Alfred Weber distinguished between the process of civilization and the movement of culture because he felt that the "products" of these two realms of activity were differently related to the temporal substratum of the "societal process." This very general issue has concerned some modern social theorists of all countries. But it presented itself in an especially troubling form to the German academics, because they were traditionally committed to the idea that cultural values could be grasped in a more than purely intellectual way. All these problems reappeared in the works of Max Scheler and Karl Mannheim, the two fathers of the new subdiscipline.

Scheler was a highly unorthodox Catholic thinker, the defender of a new religious metaphysics and an adherent of the phenomenological method in philosophy. His theoretical arguments were often very difficult, if not obscure. It will be neither possible nor necessary to describe them in all their ramifications. In some of his occasional essays, Scheler argued that Germany was in need of a new intellectual elite and a new cultural principle.[101] He was dissatisfied with the emphasis upon "inwardness" (*Innerlichkeit*) which he found running through all of German thought since the later Middle Ages. This tendency, he said, had led to disastrous consequences. While thinkers were encouraged to retreat into a realm of pure fancy, the rulers, the junkers, and Bismarck had been allowed to set the nation's policy in reality. Ever since Luther, the champions of inwardness had been unable to find the proper balance between an abject servility toward their governors and an arrogant intolerance toward the views and traditions of others. Even in their response to foreigners, Germans had always been either too self-deprecating or too aggressive. Particularly during the early years of the Weimar period, Scheler was intensely critical of the state of German culture.[102] He felt that the men of learning had failed in their leadership, because they had fled either into skepticism or into a totally isolated inwardness. The Social Democratic masses had developed a hatred for all things of the mind. Catholic orthodoxy was threatening the freedom of learning. Half-educated fanatics, second-rate mystics, and anti-intellectual sects were claiming to perform the task of synthesis which the old intellectual elite had neglected.

Scheler argued that these troubles and confusions stemmed from a series of misconceptions about the relevance of knowledge to society and to life. His own solution of this very general problem was based upon a distinction between three types of knowing.[103] One of these, the "knowledge of achievement" (*Leistungswissen*) included all those facts and principles that are intended to aid man in his mastery of his natural and social environment. "The knowledge of cultivation" (*Bildungswissen*), by contrast, resulted from that part of man's mental and spiritual activity that took him beyond the animal purpose of practical success and adjustment. Through the knowledge of cultivation, man glorified or deified himself, making his understanding a microcosm of the universe. An individual perspective upon reality, a weltanschauung, was implied in the concept of cultivation. Finally, there was "the knowledge of salvation" (*Erlösungswissen*), in which man approached the ultimate metaphysical or religious questions. The knowledge of salvation was the highest form of knowing, while the knowledge of cultivation fulfilled the role of an intermediary between it and the knowledge of achievement.

In Scheler's mind, these arguments were central to the sociology of knowledge, and this requires an explanation. One must remember that during the 1920's, the term sociology itself was still sometimes used to refer quite generally to the systematic study of society and history. In the same way, the sociology of knowledge could thus be identified as the study of knowing from the point of view of its relevance to society and culture. In any case, Scheler clearly worked with some such definition. His main point was that a purely abstract theory of knowledge was likely to neglect some of the most important questions to be asked about man's intellectual activity. At the same time, he did not approve of anything approximating a Marxist analysis of ideology. He apparently intended to create a discipline which could deal with the most pressing problems of his time, and these were the problems raised by the crisis of mandarin leadership. Scheler argued that the participants in the debate over Max Weber's "Learning as a Vocation" had utterly failed to understand each other, because they had confounded the different types of knowledge.[104] Weber was right, in other words, as long as one realized that his subject was knowledge of achievement and nothing more. For knowledge of cultivation and of salvation, Scheler would not accept Weber's strictures. From them, he expected morally meaningful insights, answers to the important questions of life. Indeed, Scheler traced most of the intellectual dilemmas of the age to the confusion of the three "forms of knowing." The material and social developments of the nineteenth century, he felt, had obscured the natural relationships between these forms and society. In the face of the fanaticism and anti-intellectualism which was threatening to engulf German culture, it was necessary to create a new intellectual elite, one which properly understood the sociology of knowledge.

In the United States and probably elsewhere as well, it is generally Mannheim, rather than Scheler, who is regarded as the originator of the sociology of knowledge. In part, this circumstance may be traced to the forbidding obscurity of Scheler's language; but there are other reasons as well. Scheler's essays were written almost exclusively as responses to the German cultural crisis, whereas Mannheim's writings can be partly understood without this setting. Mannheim was a radical modernist and something of a Marxist. This aspect of his thought has been stressed in the United States, because it is easily assimilated into American vocabulary. In the following brief outline of Mannheim's major writings before 1933, the radical and Marxist elements are not meant to be neglected; for there really was a vast difference between Scheler's and Mannheim's sociologies of knowledge. At the same time, Mannheim did have some intellectual obligations to the unique traditions of the German humanistic diciplines, and these influences upon his thought must be taken into account.[105]

Mannheim's principal thesis, of course, was that all theories and other cultural phenomena must be understood in their social and historical context. The terms in which he stated this axiom of his system were not always as clear as one would have liked. He described ideas as being "bound to a situation" *(situationsgebunden)*, and he emphasized the relationship between knowledge and "existence." His point was that we cannot account for the genesis of an expressed thought without discussing its roots in some "real" conditions of life. Indeed, we cannot even describe an idea without some such reference to its "situation." We can talk about the personal psychology of the individual who originated the proposition in question, and we can examine its factual and logical bases. In almost every case, however, we will find that these traditional tools of intellectual analysis do not suffice to elucidate the meanings which confront us. We need the help of a sociology of knowledge.

To make this clear and to underline the timely quality of his arguments, Mannheim examined the modern problem of ideology. Beginning with the phenomenon of mutual "uncovering" or "unmasking" *(Enthüllung)*, he noted that men often regard their opponents' views as conscious or unconscious lies, as distortions of reality which are occasioned by personal predilections and interests. In order to understand the sociology of knowledge, we have only to exchange this "particular" approach for the "general total conception of ideology": we must accept the fact that our own position is just as open to the debunking type of criticism as that of others, and we must drop the notion that ideological distortion is as superficial and as purely individual a matter as a lie. Instead, we have to realize that a man's total outlook, his unconscious assumptions and the whole organization or "structure" of his thought, may be affected by his situation.

Sometimes, Mannheim wrote as if his concept of the situation were strongly influenced by Marxism. He was a self-conscious social radical, and this affected his terminology. On the most formal and general level, he described an ideology as any situationally conditioned view of reality. In these terms, what he called a utopia was really just a special type of ideology, one in which present conditions are seen and judged in terms of an abstracted future ideal. Mannheim explicitly acknowledged the possibility of a reactionary utopia. Yet he sometimes equated utopia with a progressive and revolutionary mentality, ideology with the kind of conservative obscurantism that intends only to preserve the status quo. All this implied that economic class interests played a role in the "existential determination" of knowledge. As a matter of fact, Mannheim did consider the group origins of an idea an important element in its context. On the other hand, he formally insisted that "by these groups we mean not merely classes, as a dogmatic type of Marxism would have it, but also generations, status groups, sects, occupational groups, schools, etc."[106]

Thus, although Mannheim was undoubtedly influenced by Marx, there were aspects of his sociology of knowledge which reflected other intellectual traditions as well. Particularly in his early essays on the interpretation of weltanschauung and on historism, one encounters many of the problems that had originally been raised in the controversies concerning methods in the humanistic disciplines. It is of the utmost importance, for example, that Mannheim equated the situation of an idea not only with its origins in a social group but also with its place in a specific historical epoch. This raised the old questions of understanding: how could the gap between past and present be bridged in the act of historical interpretation, and how was an idea imbedded in the context of its own time? On the first of these questions, Mannheim took a familiar line. He insisted that the weltanschauung of another age is not "given" us in the same way as the facts of the natural universe. Rather, we seem to have a "pretheoretical" knowledge of these meanings and attitudes. We may try to state this knowledge in a systematic way; but this is clearly an ex post facto attempt at clarification. Nor is our procedure based upon any formal theory of individual psychology. Indeed, we do not yet fully understand our methods. But we do know that the task of interpretation is an "active" one, that our own purposes and values play some role in it.

In discussing the imbeddedness of an idea in its historical context, Mannheim again referred to the pretheoretical foundations of knowledge. He noted that we often recognize certain similarities between the art and the formal philosophy of an age, and yet we do not believe that the artists' works are anything like logical consequences of the philosophers' propositions. Instead, we tend to trace both art and philosophy to less formal, pretheoretical purposes and attitudes which are present in the age or group. It is these informal antecedents of all knowledge and cultural systematization that we regard as the fundamental expressions of the historical situation. Of course, we may write histories of art or of philosophy as if we were dealing with isolated systems, as if the various phases of development within each of these fields were nothing but logical or dialectical consequences of antecedent stages. Mannheim did not deny the heuristic value of this "rational-dialectic" method of analysis, particularly in the area of Alfred Weber's process of civilization. Nevertheless, he continued to feel that in reality, all the cultural "motifs" of an epoch were related to each other and to the context on a sublogical level: "The various 'motifs' condition each other; they are part and function of a totality which is the ultimate substratum, the real subject of integral historical change [Allwandel]."[107] On occasion, Mannheim described the attempt to grasp this historical "totality" as a task of "synthesis."

What happened when Mannheim transferred these ideas to the sociology of knowledge may easily be imagined. He now had a basis for the contention that men's "socio-historical situation" expressed itself in all their explicit theories, because it entered into their thinking on a pretheoretical level. It influenced their epistemology and their whole vocabulary as much as their art. Even their conceptions of systematic knowledge and of truth itself reflected their conditions of life, their attitudes and purposes, so that all knowing necessarily contained an actively ideological element. The sociology of knowledge thus acquired the task of uncovering this circumstance and of drawing the consequences. Of course, Mannheim was very much aware of the possible objections to his arguments. Having experienced the furor over the "problem of historism," he expected to be accused of undermining all truths and values. How could any certainties survive the attack of his "relativism"? Had he not totally ignored the neo-Kantian distinction between the genetic analysis of an idea and the question of its truth or falsity? Was not every possible sense of historical fact or reality dissolved in a chaos of competing illusions?

Mannheim tried to meet these charges in several ways. To begin with, he simply denied having advanced any such proposition as "that facts do not exist."[108] He apparently felt that ideological disagreements would stop short of engulfing precisely those very limited statements which are commonly called facts. He also repeatedly described the assertion that two times two makes four as an unchallenged truth. Moreover, he envisioned the possibility that men of similar outlooks could correct each other's factual errors. Even ideological opponents, he thought, might well be able to refine the terms of their debate to such an extent that disagreements over detailed matters of fact would be eliminated and only the fundamental divergence of interpretation and outlook would remain. Thus, without ever clearly defining a line between the realm of factuality and that of ideology, he implied that ideology encompassed our most fundamental convictions, whereas factuality included only certain mathematical or trivially factual propositions.

By way of a further argument in his own defense. Mannheim accused his potential critics of being themselves ideologically committed to an outdated conception of knowledge. The charge of relativism was meaningless, he said, unless it was contrasted with the unwarranted assumption that there was in fact some absolute standard of truth. The "absolutist" critics of the sociology of knowledge derived their idea of truth primarily from mathematics. Moreover, they were chiefly Idealists. They naturally believed that the formal truths of the neo-Kantian philosophy stood totally outside the temporal sphere of "situational determination" and historical change. In this, they were deceived.

> That in the "idealistic" conception of knowledge knowing is regarded mostly as a purely "theoretical" act in the sense of pure perception, has its origins, in addition to the above-mentioned orientation toward mathematical models, in the fact that in the background of this epistemology there lies the philo-

sophical ideal of the "contemplative life" . . . This great esteem for the contemplatively perceived is not the outcome of the "pure" observation of the act of thinking and knowing, but springs from a hierarchy of values based on a certain [pretheoretical] philosophy of life. The idealistic philosophy, which represents this tradition, insisted that knowledge was pure only when it was purely theoretical. Idealistic philosophy was not upset by the discovery that the type of knowledge represented by pure theory was only a small segment of human knowledge, that in addition there can be knowledge where men, while thinking, are also acting, and finally, that in certain fields, knowledge arises only when and in so far as it itself is action, i.e. when action is permeated by the intention of the mind, in the sense that the concepts and the total apparatus of thought are dominated by and reflect this activist orientation.[109]

In some ways, this preventive attack upon potential critics seems a little unfair, particularly since it assumes that only an idealist would ever be tempted to challenge Mannheim's arguments. Here, Mannheim's own situation appears to have guided his hand. It is remarkable that his description of active knowledge coincided very closely with what the neo-Kantians had in fact condemned under such labels as pragmatism, functionalism, and life philosophy. Clearly, it was criticism primarily from this direction which Mannheim wanted to invalidate. His sociology of knowledge thus came to involve a socially and intellectually radical attack upon the whole mandarin tradition of contemplative knowledge and pure truth. As he saw it, this tradition was itself an ideology in what he now proposed to call the "evaluative" sense of that term: it was a disguised defense of the status quo, an antiprogressive device.

In another, somewhat more conventional plea for the sociology of knowledge, Mannheim suggested the possibility of using the techniques of the new subdiscipline to *cleanse* social theory of ideological elements. In this part of his argument, he addressed himself to men of Max Weber's convictions, men who thought it possible to make a logical distinction between scholarship and value judgment, who wanted to try insofar as possible to approach some sort of objectivity on this basis. To these scholars, Mannheim recommended his methods as purely critical tools. If you want to attain the greatest possible objectivity, he argued in effect, you must be interested in anything I can tell you about the influence of context on various theories. After all, it is only after being aware of such possible sources of error and distortion that you will be able to correct for them to some extent. Undoubtedly, you have more faith than I in your ability to rescue scholarship from ideology. Our disagreement on this issue need not, however, prevent us from jointly desiring the elucidation of any potentially or actually ideological aspects of knowledge.

This part of Mannheim's self-defense was clearly related to his admission of a realm of factuality and to his feeling that even ideological opponents could enlighten each other in a debate. As we noticed earlier, however, he made these theoretical concessions neither clearly nor wholeheartedly. He always returned to the argument that only the most trivial propositions could escape the influence of context, whereas all really important assumptions and theories were utterly inseparable from their roots in a situation. In this connection, he noted that the misguided search for quasi-mathematical truths about society had led German sociologists into the errors of formalism. Precisely because they refused to acknowledge the "active," ideological element in social theory, they had been forced to abandon the ground of unhampered empirical observation. They had retreated into the realm of abstract types, meanings, and "essences." They had turned the originally utopian-progressive ideal of rational explanation into a passive, unrealistic, and ultimately conservative scheme. Thus while recommending sociology of knowledge even to these anti-ideological thinkers, Mannheim simultaneously proceeded to urge upon them a more "dynamic" view of knowledge.

This view, the most interesting product of Mannheim's reflections, was expressed in his theory of "perspectivism" or "relationism," which can be epitomized as follows. "Truth in itself" may be compared to the Kantian "thing in itself." We never actually know it, and yet our observations appear to refer to it. We never see the chair; but we do have visual experiences which we may describe as perspectives of the chair. What we ordinarily mean when we talk about the chair is something like a sum of such perspectives. In an analogous way, every system of "active" knowledge, every ideology, is a perspective upon the truth. We do not consider all observation useless, even though we have abandoned the old metaphysical assumptions about the thing in itself. Similarly, we ought not to despair of knowledge, simply because we are forced to recognize its "relational" character and to dispense with the absolutist notion of truth in itself. When we learn to see a certain social reality from a fresh point of view, we have in fact increased our understanding of it. Moreover, it is in the nature of relational knowledge that every new perspective upon some set of events will seek not only to give an internally consistent account of it, but also to explain why and how older theories approached it from a different viewpoint. In this way, later interpretations subsume earlier ones, and our awareness becomes ever more sophisticated and comprehensive. Relationism is thus neither as fruitless nor as unstable as the absolutists would have us believe. It proceeds through a series of syntheses, each of which is "active" in the sense of being motivated by a set of situationally conditioned preferences. In short, relationism replaces the outdated concept of truth in itself with the more realistic ideal of knowledge as a symphonic product of all possible perspectives.

These arguments are reminiscent of Troeltsch's attempt to solve the problem of historism by means of a culturally relevant synthesis. Whether Mannheim's answers to some very old questions will stand the test of criticism is another matter. They seem particularly vulnerable in two respects. First, it might be argued that the extremely vague concept of situation opens the door to all sorts of redundancies and logical circularities. If everything that influences a man's thought may be described as part of his situation, then it is not terribly surprising that ideologies reflect situations. Second, Mannheim's own arguments may be used to show that his whole theory is true only from his point of view. This is not just an unfair quibble. It implies, rather, that the concept of truth in itself cannot be discarded and that Mannheim himself must have used it. Could he have achieved his initial definition of ideology without reference to something which was being distorted? Does the analogy with the Kantian thing in itself really achieved its object, or did Mannheim simply obscure the problem of historical explanation by entangling it with epistemological and even ontological formulations? Is it possible to restate the undoubtedly useful parts of his theory so clearly as to avoid some of these difficulties?

Another vulnerable point in Mannheim's system is his account of the intelligentsia. In describing relational knowledge, he argued that some perspectives would subsume earlier viewpoints in a synthesis. His own theory of "existential determination" demanded, however, that some particular group be identified with this synthetic function, since no form of knowing could be posited which did not express an actually experienced situation. It was necessary to find a correlate in social reality for the theoretical ability to rise above the limitations of a single perspective. Mannheim found this correlate in the phenomena of social change and mobility. When whole strata move to a new position in the social and political life of their nation, or when individuals migrate from one socio-economic context to another, he argued, new viewpoints are necessarily superimposed upon older ideologies, and people become accustomed to relational thinking. Moreover, there is one group in every society which is particularly well equipped to champion the cause of perspectivism, and that is the intelligentsia. Even on the individual level, the intellectual very often experiences several situations. Typically, he leaves the social context in which he grew up in order to enter his profession. On a collective level, the intelligentsia thus comes to include members from various original "situations." All these members are now committed to a new social role as intellectuals. They have no immediate stake in the struggle between the various economic interest groups. It is their duty to communicate with each other and with the rest of their society. In the debates which ensue among them, the influences of their situations are at once revealed and put in perspective. Unless they succumb to the temptations of absolutism, the intellectuals may thus become the chief agents of relationist synthesis.

Mannheim clearly pictured the intelligentsia as a progressive element in society. He knew that very few of his colleagues shared his radically modernistic outlook. But he apparently hoped to convert some of them to the ideals of "active" knowledge and utopian synthesis. It is all the more remarkable that his sociology of knowledge culminated in so curiously sentimental an ideal of the intellectual elite. Mannheim was undoubtedly one of the most distinguished rebels against mandarin orthodoxy, and yet he ended by dreaming of synthesis and by elevating the intellectuals above the mundane realm of ideology, in which the rest of humanity was presumably immersed. He forgot what he had begun by affirming: that the explanatory techniques of the sociology of knowledge can be applied to all types of groups with equal justification. Subtly and unconsciously, he shifted his ground, assuming that entrepreneurs and workers are somehow more irrevocably and narrowly "interested" than men of mind. He forgot that the very idea of "interested" thought is no more than a typological device of understanding. He was a rebel, even a self-consciously revolutionary thinker. But he was also a mandarin.

CONCLUSION
THE END OF A TRADITION

The right-wing opposition to the Weimar Republic was not internally homogeneous. The spectrum of the "national opposition," which attracted many students, was broader than the range of opinion represented in the volkish associations. The theories of the "conservative revolution" were more abstractly utopion, less anti-Semitic, and generally less violent than the doctrines of radical activists in the volkish and national camps. Mandarin orthodoxy itself was distinguished from the other antirepublican creeds by its devotion to the formal traditions of German learning. The national, volkish and neoconservative movements grew up on the fringes of the academic establishment, not within it. The conservative revolution received some support from younger scholars. The national opposition attracted fraternity students, along with orthodox professors of the old school, men who still dreamed of the Fatherland Party. The volkish forces rapidly increased their influence among the younger nationalists during the 1920's. Still, the invisible barrier between academic and nonacademic critics of the existing regime continued to function until after 1933.

Precisely stated differences of opinion played less of a role in these distinctions than such factors as age, temperament, and social place. The elderly *Geheimrat* voted German National not only because he identified with the traditions of the Wilhelmian age, but also because his status demanded it. The ordinary student in a socially distinguished fencing corps made the same concession in advance to his future standing, unless he had been converted by an "experience" of his roots in the national community. Many a primary teacher was volkish or National Socialist because he resented the *Geheimrat*. The neoconservative intellectual or aesthete was less bound by professional traditions, less disciplined, more imaginative, and more engaged than the orthodox academic. The two men also differed in their ages and in their receptivity to current intellectual fashions. The neoconservative philosopher had no respect for the official culture of the Wilhelmian period, no yearning for the monarchy. He understood some of the modernists' arguments, which caused him to redouble his efforts at synthesis.

These differences of tone and emphasis played a role in the political struggles of the early 1930's, in which the National Socialists triumphed over their rivals among the enemies of the Republic.[1] By 1930, Hitler's followers had gained a foothold in the state government of Thuringia. They promptly created a new professorship at the University of Jena for the "race scientist" F. K. Günther. The move elicited only weak and equivocal protests from academic circles. The dismantling of German scholarship had begun. Between 1929 and 1931, the National Socialists wrested control of the National Student Union from volkish and nationalist elements. Students, like other middle-class youths, were consistently more susceptible to National Socialist propaganda than their elders.[2] By 1930, student elections at many universities returned National Socialist majorities. Brown shirts and swastikas now appeared more and more frequently in German academic buildings. Exploiting an already well-established tradition of "patriotic" protest, National Socialist students engaged in rowdy classroom demonstrations against Jewish, internationalist, or liberal professors. The tactics of the storm troopers were applied to the universities.

Most academics realized at last that this was not the spiritual revolution they had sought. It was too violent and too vulgar. It declared itself the master of geist, not its servant. Faced with a mounting danger to all moral and cultural standards, a few professors began to express their concern. Often without abandoning the apolitical terminology which was their habit, they tried to stem the tide of the new activism. They wrote in defense of historical continuity and tradition, as if they sensed that the minimal restraints of civilization were under attack. Their tone was one of helplessness and pessimism. In 1931, Karl Jaspers warned of a coming abyss of individual nullity and unfreedom.[3] Typically enough, he regarded the mass and machine age as the ultimate source of the approaching disaster. If Western culture survived at all, he felt, it would do so only in the hands of a few isolated aristocrats of the mind. In 1932, Aloys Fischer citicized those of the younger generation who seemed determined to break with their nation's past and with all of Western history, giving themselves up to the pursuit of violent revolution and to the worship of everything primitive.[4] Fischer's tone made it possible to wonder whether he was objecting to the radicals of the right, to those of the left or, most likely, to both. The moderate Ernst Robert Curtius took a similar position in an essay entitled "German geist in danger."[5] Repeating a number of familiar complaints, he saw the German heritage weakened by neglect, by thoughtless specialization, and by the gnawing skepticism of historism. He observed with sorrow that the universities and the old learning were regarded with nothing but hatred and contempt among large segments of the German people. He lamented the spread of a revolutionary mentality, which sought to negate all established truths and values. He cited Mannheim's *Ideology and Utopia* as an example. As others had done before him, Curtius sorted out and reviewed the major strands in the German cultural tradition, wondering what was irrevocably lost and what might yet be salvaged. He wrote as if the discovery of a single certainty might still prevent an otherwise inevitable catastrophe.

One cannot help being moved by these desperate pleas; and yet they also strike one as futile. Of course there was a real difference between the spiritual revival which the mandarins had been preaching and the fanaticism which now threatened to engulf them. The difficulty was that this distinction was hard to describe in the mandarins' own language. The orthodox members of the academic community had done everything in their power to revile the existing social and political regime. Their prescriptions for the future had always been more fervent than precise. What had they said of their own age that could now be useful in its defense? Were not at least some of the young people attracted to National Socialism because they felt that a decadent society had to be utterly destroyed before a new national community could be created? What could an orthodox mandarin say to convince such enthusiasts that theirs was the wrong sort of "idealism"? What arguments, what words were still available to control the murderous fantasies which now took possession of the German people? It would have been useless to speak of simple, gratuitous humanity, because the young had been taught to seek their norms in a wissenschaftlich weltanschauung. Common sense in politics was discredited, along with the merely practical knowledge of positivist learning. Where could an argument against unreason have begun?

Max Weber was dead, and there were not enough Karl Vosslers. The Mannheims and Asters had no chance to be heard. The few academics who did speak up often took a curiously unsystematic and inconclusive line, as if all the decisive arguments had indeed been lost already. In 1931, one German professor expressed his uneasiness at the excessive "politization" of the universities.[6] He granted that students should take an interest in the affairs of the nation; but he objected to the intolerant and vulgar demagogy which was becoming prevalent. He spoke as if the difference between acceptable mandarin politics and the new rightist radicalism was largely a matter of tone and mannerism. In 1932, the Corporation of

German Universities asked students to resist "irresponsible speeches and fraternal strife," to preserve a "sense of responsibility" and "clarity of thought."[7] Apparently, the mandarins were frightened by the new fanaticism; but their warnings often strike one as pitifully inadequate. To the emotional radicalism of the young, they opposed what looked like no more than the habitual caution of a tradition-minded older generation. To the brutality of the emerging political style, they opposed their own sense of intellectual cultivation and good form. The new mentors of German youth could easily neutralize such pleas as too passive and too snobbish. Beyond that, the mandarins themselves had not done enough to safeguard the clarity of thought to which they thus belatedly appealed.

In an article dated 1955, Eduard Spranger describes some of his personal experiences and attitudes during the years 1932 and 1933. At a meeting of the Corporation of German Universities in October 1932, Spranger reports, he argued against a resolution introduced by Theodor Litt. Litt would have censored the National Socialist rowdies among the students. Spranger dissented, because he thought "the national movement among the students still genuine at the core, only undisciplined in its form."[8] The whole story of the mandarin reaction to National Socialism is contained in that sentence. Litt, along with Jaspers, Vossler, and a few others, saw the coming danger a little more clearly than most of their colleagues. Spranger probably represented the outlook of the majority. The orthodox variant of the theory of form and content favored the National Socialists. The form was a bit too "undisciplined"; but the content was "still genuine" in October 1932! No clear and substantive argument against the new fanaticism could be based on such convictions.

The National Socialists easily established their total control of the German universities after 1933. There was little effective resistance.[9] The student "revolution" was temporarily useful as a political weapon; but it was quickly choked off when the job was done. The Führer principle was employed to destroy academic self-government. The freedom of learning and the idea of objectivity in scholarship were officially repudiated. The Third Reich had no use for "impractical" scholarship, classical humanism, or the "apolitical" stance. It also refused to tolerate the presence of an "academic proletariat" at the universities. Enrollment quotas were introduced, and the limitations were made especially stringent for women. The number of students at German universities dropped by almost a third between the academic years 1931–32 and 1934–35. The decline actually began even before the national quota system came into effect. Theoretical subjects, such as philosophy, lost more ground than the preprofessional courses. Meantime, certificates of good character and political reliability were required of applicants for university study. Future teachers and university instructors had to demonstrate their integration into the national community by attending work camps and political retreats. Higher education lost its purely intellectual and scholarly character.

Among the secondary schools, the gymnasium was most subject to official disapproval. Some of the youngest nonclassical institutions flourished as dispensers of a strictly German curriculum and as vehicles of political indoctrination. The primary school and its teachers gained in status and accreditation. Thus the whole educational program of the National Socialists acquired a vaguely "democratic" air. The fact that advancement within the system depended upon political loyalty, rather than family background, helped to create this impression.

There was no security of tenure for German professors in the Third Reich. Anyone could lose his position, as well as his pension, if he displeased the authorities. On the whole, this weapon sufficed to guarantee the universities' submission. Its uses were demonstrated on a grand scale during the early years of the regime. Nearly 1700 faculty members and young scholars lost their places, among them 313 full professors.[10] An estimated 80 percent of these men were dismissed on racial grounds. The rest were suspected of "pacifism" or of left-wing political sympathies. Most of the victims emigrated before 1936, chiefly to England and America. Among the prominent philosophers, social scientists, and humanists who left their country during this period were Ernst von Aster, Moritz Julius Bonn, Ernst Cassirer, Jonas Cohn, Richard Hönigswald, Werner Jaeger, Wolfgang Köhler, Emil Lederer, Kurt Lewin, Robert Liefmann, Karl

Mannheim, Franz Oppenheimer, Joseph Schumpeter, and Max Wertheimer. A good many of the exiles were Jews, and almost all of them were distinguished modernists. Among the younger men, the students of Max Weber and of Meinecke certainly outnumbered those of Rachfahl and Below. The withdrawal of these men from their country weakened a very important and creative sector of the German intellectual community. Correspondingly, it was the modernist wing of the German intelligentsia that introduced the English-speaking world to the methods and problems of mandarin scholarship. American and West European scholars might well have ignored Natorp, Krueger, Scheler, and Spann, had they arrived in the place of Cassirer, Köhler, Mannheim, and Schumpeter. The translation of a learned tradition into a new semantic context is a difficult undertaking; but when it succeeds, it tends to stimulate both the translators and their new public. The character of the German emigration after 1933 helped to make such translation possible and has since exerted a profound influence upon British and American learning.

Quite apart from the moral and personal aspects of the problem, the emigration represented a very serious loss of substance for German learning. It is all the more disturbing that the rest of the academic community did so little to defend old colleagues. A few disciples of learning actually welcomed the fact that intellectual competitors had been removed from the scene. The psychologist Erich Jaensch was pleased that the spokesmen of an "un-German" direction in his discipline, presumably Wertheimer and Köhler, had been purged.[11] Jaensch belonged to a small clique of scholars who publicly celebrated the advent of the Third Reich. Some of these academic spokesmen for National Socialism had been extreme cultural nationalists before 1933. Many of them were relatively young men. Almost all of them had been deeply involved in the methodological confusions of orthodox synthesis. They represented the most unstable products of the spiritual revolution of the 1920's. Prominent among those who at least temporarily deluded themselves about Hitler's regime were Willy Andreas, Hans Freyer, Martin Heidegger, Erich Jaensch, Felix Krueger, Phillip Lenard (the physicist), Karl Alexander von Müller, Julius Petersen, Wilhelm Pinder, Erich Rothacker, Carl Schmitt, Werner Sombart, and Othmar Spann. Some of these men should probably be described as willing collaborators, rather than enthusiastic supporters of National Socialism. Others lost their initial illusions about the regime after a few years. The personal motives in question are not easy to assess in retrospect. In 1935, Müller accepted the editorship of the *Historische Zeitschrift*, after Meinecke had given it up under pressure.[12] Did Müller allow himself to think he could do some good by keeping the journal out of worse hands? All sorts of rationalizations were possible then, and more are possible now.

The National Socialists did not always welcome the early support they received from prominent academics. They had no use for intellectuals who tried to see the Third Reich in terms of their own theories. They instinctively distrusted established professors in any case. They much preferred to work with such pamphleteers as Ernst Krieck and Alfred Bäumler. These two men were promptly appointed to new professorships in 1933. Krieck immediately became rector of Frankfurt University. Bäumler was to represent "political pedagogy" at Berlin. Both appointments were widely regarded as impositions upon the universities.

In 1933, the National Socialist Teachers Association of Saxony presented a collective proclamation of support for National Socialism, which was signed by some 960 faculty members at several German universities.[13] The document was clearly compiled with an eye to quantity. Not many of the signatures were those of prominent professors. Young and relatively unknown scholars accounted for a large proportion of the list. It is hard to say whether they were more enthusiastic, more opportunistic, or just less secure in their academic tenure than their elders. In any case, the document actually represented a relatively poor showing for the National Socialists. It demonstrated what it was meant to disprove: that fully committed supporters of the Third Reich were a small minority within the German academic community.

This was the context in which mandarin scholarship was overrun by National Socialism. The average mandarin felt aloof and vaguely shocked. There was too much violence, he felt, too little respect for the traditions of geist. Yet the "national movement" seemed "genuine at the core"—until it was too late. Personal frailties played a role. There was the fear of losing one's position, the fear of being placed "outside the national community," along with the "discredited professors," the leftists, and Jews.[14] Many a scholar's behavior in the face of these risks contrasted sharply with the otherworldly idealism he had so often preached to others. Gone were the heroic poses which had earlier been taken against the tolerant authorities of "the rabble state." An ambiguous passivity took their place. The freedom and purity of learning were not vigorously defended against this attack from the right. There was little active opposition to the new order, even before it became quite clear that such resistance would lead to imprisonment or worse. When the fiction of the genuine core had to be abandoned, the National Socialist terror had been firmly established. Many German intellectuals now defined their position as one of "inner emigration." They sought a retreat in esoteric scholarship. They finally realized that National Socialism was as much their enemy as any socialist republic could ever have been. The insight brought no profit; for the mandarins' empire was in ruins.

Whether a genuine revival of the mandarin tradition has taken place since 1945 is hard to say; but on the whole I rather doubt it. In 1946, Meinecke called for the establishment of small Goethe societies in all German cities and towns.[15] Meeting in churches whenever possible, members of these cultural communities were to give public readings of the German classics, combined with recitals of the best German music. In this way, Meinecke hoped to reactivate the original sources of the nation's spiritual life in the uncorrupted age of Goethe. For most of Meinecke's countrymen, however, the postwar economic miracle was more absorbing than the possibility of a cultural revival. For years after 1945, most Germans were in a state of ideological exhaustion. They tended to ignore the difficult problems of social, political, and cultural theory. They began by concentrating on the task of physical survival, and many of them did not rest in their pursuit of material security until it had long been replaced by wealth and success. In a very short time, Germany once again became an immensely prosperous industrial nation. Since the National Socialist era was considered an interruption of German history, rather than an integral part of it, German intellectuals tended to treat the men of the Weimar period as their immediate predecessors. In that way, the vocabulary of the cultural crisis was occasionally adapted to the postwar scene. Even today, some educated and half-educated Germans like to discuss the modern world with the melancholy air of former culture bearers. But these residual and superficial attitudes cannot be compared to the genuine emotional agonies of the twenties and the thirties. At bottom, German intellectuals have adjusted to the mass and machine age. Hitler's regime and the postwar economic boom have made a difference. Mandarin culture has become a distant memory, although a cherished one. Of course, the problems and dilemmas of modernity will continue to occupy thoughtful people in Germany and elsewhere. But in all likelihood, the younger generation of German intellectuals will eventually find a fresh terminology to deal with these issues.

To what extent were the German mandarins to blame for the terrible form of their own demise, for the catastrophe of National Socialism? The question is unavoidable. It might as well be raised explicitly.

One obviously inadequate answer would make the German academics directly responsible for what the National Socialists said and did. It would treat Hitler's propaganda as a coherent set of theoretical propositions, propositions seen as logical extensions of earlier tendencies in the German intellectual tradition. This approach flatters the pamphleteers of the Third Reich. It neglects obvious differences of attitude and social position between the professors and the storm troopers. At bottom, it is based on an inappropriate use of the logical sequence in historical explanation.

A somewhat subtler misinterpretation has become current among formerly orthodox mandarins and among other spokemen of a "cultivated" traditionalism. According to this theory, the German elite did its very best to protect the nation's heritage against the forces which finally triumphed in 1933. These were the corrosive forces of the machine age, which had concerned German intellectuals since 1870: there was the popular clamor for a more practical scholarship and the attempt to involve learning in the politics of the mass parties; there was the "democratic" attack upon academic standards, upon the intellectually and spiritually aristocratic ideals of the German universities. All these pressures originated well before the Weimar period, most notably among the parties of the left. The manipulators of popular envy and fanaticism had always done their best to breach the fortress of pure learning. Hitler's hordes simply completed the conquest. Though valiantly defended, German idealism had been weakened by the onslaught of materialism and positivism. Specialization and purely technological thinking had destroyed the link between knowledge and cultivation. Skepticism, relativism, and historism had undermined the philosophical and ethical standards of idealistic learning. Thus the way had been prepared for the likes of Krieck, for half-educated pamphleteers who used the arguments of the relativists to enslave the universities.

This version does have a certain coherence. It is often used by men who would also stress the role of "the masses" in the political crises of the early 1930's. Even Meinecke occasionally came rather close to this interpretation;[16] and a recent publication of the German Federal Republic confidently traces the advent of Hitler to "the pressure of the masses which stood behind him."[17] A new conservative orthodoxy seems to be rising from these foundations.

The Socialist and Communist parties together lost fewer votes to the National Socialists during the 1930's than any of the parties patronized by the middle and upper classes. But that is only the most rudimentary of the arguments against the new orthodoxy. The others have to do with the intellectual and cultural climate in which Hitler rose to power. Who did more to create this climate: such "positivists" as Tönnies, Weber, and Vossler, or such "idealists" as Krueger, Spann—and Spranger? Did even Mannheim and Aster do more damage to the standards of scholarship than those who "overcame" their radical critique? Ernst Krieck used the arguments of historism

in his pamphlets; that is true. But was it not the escape from relativism, rather than relativism itself which became his weapon? Who
nourished the yearning for intellectual and emotional escape?

Hitler did not achieve power because this or that explicit doctrine was commonly held in Germany. The scholarly controversies
of the day contributed only indirectly to the problems of the Weimar Republic. The orthodox mandarins did not actively desire the
triumph of the Third Reich; nor were they to blame for the actual
propositions of National Socialist propaganda. Their responsibility
was more indirect than that, more negative than positive. It was
more a matter of ideological affinities and mental habits than one
of formal theories. But their responsibility was great nonetheless.
They helped to destroy the Republic, without having chosen its
successor. They willfully cultivated an atmosphere in which any
"national" movement could claim to be the "spiritual revival." They
fostered chaos, without regard for the consequences. It may be
foolish to suppose that any group of intellectuals can set the course
of a nation. It may be unfair to blame a thinker for the errors of all
his interpreters. But the mandarins abandoned intellectual responsibility itself. That would be a serious charge against them, even
if the subsequent catastrophe had been avoided.

One cannot condemn the German elite for having disliked the
mass and machine age, which threatened their way of life. It is the
element of hysteria and of nihilism in their reaction which offends.
Abandoning "clarity of thought," they began to respond on a purely
emotional level. They distorted the peculiar assumptions of their
creed; they stretched its very language. Their arguments became
ideological in Mannheim's evaluative sense of that term. They
nourished a whole series of semiconscious illusions which prevented
the rational discussion of political alternatives and discredited every
possible mode of social and cultural adjustment to modernity.

In politics and social theory, the most dangerous of these illusions
was the dream of a total escape from interest politics, the yearning
to transcend the political mechanism in terms of some idealistic absolute. This emotion was coupled with an equally desperate revul-

sion against capitalism and "materialistic" socialism, which is to say, against economic rationality itself. Both of these attitudes implied a refusal to consider practical consequences of social action on a "merely technical" level. They led to the kind of antithetical thinking which defined future choices only negatively, by excluding all intellectually accessible alternatives. The search for community and the ritual elevation of "the whole" eventually signified no more than an uncritical readiness for any adventure. The source of these passions was the hatred of the "class" society, which had overrun the status patterns of an earlier age. This is the area in which mandarin antimodernity began to resemble some of its lowbrow variants. Large segments of the middle and lower middle classes were also victimized by the sudden disequilibrium between class and status elements in German social stratification. On a pretheoretical level, common resentments created ideological affinities.

In cultural questions too, the average mandarin refused to accept a revised estimate of his own role and influence. He mixed self-pity with a certain arrogance. He showed a profound lack of humor about the intellectual's condition. He saw his own dissatisfactions as the spiritual decay of a whole society. His theory of cultural decadence dealt primarily with the psychological obstacles to creativity and with the problem of philosophical certainty. But he instinctively projected these issues upon a kind of metasociological plane. The fear of intellectual positivism and skepticism became entangled with the revulsion against modern social rationalization and diversification. "Merely critical" reason was discredited. The private search for spiritual satisfaction became a public campaign in behalf of moral authority. Knowledge was asked to re-create the irrational sources of social cohesion. In an increasingly uncritical climate, the young were taught a dangerous respect for their own vital urges.

Scholarship itself suffered from the twofold pressure to sustain an elevated impracticality and to achieve an immediate spiritual influence. Cultural meanings had to be not only understood but assimilated. The ever more hectic pursuit of morally profitable insights caused intellectual ambitions to outstrip scholarly achievements.

Programs were celebrated for their own sake, as if they were results.

Men knew which theoretical tendencies had to be overcome and which were to be strengthened. Methods of scholarship were judged on the basis of their usefulness in the idealistic reconstruction. A kind of name-calling invaded academic discussions. This only increased the sense of intellectual uncertainty and instability. There was less and less tolerance for the eternal tension between knowledge achieved and wisdom desired. Synthesis somehow became more than seeing a connection. In a desperate rush, the powers of geist were expanded, so that it might master life and cure the age. The standards of scholarship became less important than this colossal aim of total mastery. The distinction between geist and "mere intellect" became ever more emphatic. Unwittingly, the mandarins prepared the ground for the anti-intellectualism that finally overwhelmed them.

The story told in the foregoing pages should not be read as a defense of simple-minded positivism, of unprincipled politics, or of uncritical practicality and professionalism in learning. If contemporary American intellectuals incline to these vices, it has not been my purpose to excuse them. Every tradition has its giants and its dwarfs. In Germany, the tensions of the 1890's and 1920's were creative as well as destructive. One thinks of Tönnies and Wiese, of Dilthey, Simmel, and Weber, of Wundt and Wertheimer, Troeltsch and Meinecke. It has not been my object to condemn the mandarin tradition. As originally expressed by the great neo-humanists and Idealists, this tradition set forth a noble and compelling view of man. It had its own characteristic biases. But it retained some of its brilliance until far into the crisis of its decline. It was finally destroyed as much by circumstances as by its own failings. The mandarin intellectuals found themselves transported into a social and cultural environment which challenged all their values. They rebelled. While a few courageous individuals sacrificed assumptions which seemed to prevent an unhampered view of the new realities, the escapist element became ever more prominent in the rhetoric of their colleagues. Thus an originally inspiring vision became distorted and corrupted, while irresponsibility took its place. Under immense pressure, intellectual foibles and weaknesses became vices. In that sense, the decline of the German mandarins was not a melodrama but a tragedy.

BIBLIOGRAPHY

NOTES

INDEX

BIBLIOGRAPHY

A full list of pertinent titles would have been unbearably long and not very useful. The selection which follows is intended to serve as an introduction. The index may be used as a guide to additional citations in the notes. My dissertation, "The German Universities and the Crisis of Learning, 1918–1925" (Harvard University, 1960), contains titles for the Weimar period which have been omitted here. The thesis is available through Widener Library, Harvard University.

I

Social and Institutional History of the Universities

These are the most important printed sources. Some secondary works by German experts are also included, especially those which contain statistical information, extracts from primary sources, and immediate observations. A few books by and about the most prominent educational administrators are also listed in this section.

Akademische Vorschriften für die Badischen Universitäten zu Heidelberg und Freiburg, Karlsruhe, 1920.

Alexander, Thomas, and Beryl Parker, *The New Education in the German Republic*, New York: The John Day Co., 1929.

Baumgart, Max, *Grundsätze und Bedingungen zur Erlangung der Doctorwürde bei allen Fakultäten der Universitäten des Deutschen Reichs*, Berlin, 1884.

Becker, Carl H., *Gedanken zur Hochschulreform*, Leipzig, 1919.

—— *Secondary Education and Teacher Training in Germany*, New York: Teachers College, Columbia University, 1931.

—— *Vom Wesen der deutschen Universität*, Leipzig, 1925.

Beier, Adolf, ed., *Die höheren Schulen in Preussen (für die männliche Jugend) und ihre Lehrer*, 3rd ed., Halle, 1909.

Boelitz, Otto, *Der Aufbau des preussischen Bildungswesens nach der Staatsumwälzung*, Leipzig, 1924.

Bornhak, Conrad, *Die Rechtsverhältnisse der Hochschullehrer in Preussen*, Berlin, 1901.

Busch, Alexander, *Die Geschichte des Privatdozenten: Eine soziologische Studie zur grossbetrieblichen Entwicklung der deutschen Universitäten*, H. Plessner, ed., Göttinger Abhandlungen zur Soziologie, 5, Stuttgart, 1959.

Conrad, Johannes, "Einige Ergebnisse der deutschen Universitätsstatistik," *Jahrbücher für Nationalökonomie und Statistik*, new series, 32 (1906): 433–492.

—— *Das Universitätsstudium in Deutschland während der letzten 50 Jahre*, Jena, 1884.

Deutsche Hochschulstatistik, published jointly by the Hochschulverwaltungen of the various German states, beginning with the summer semester of 1928, vols. I–VIII.

Doeberl, Michael, Otto Scheel, et al., *Das akademische Deutschland*, vol. III: *Die deutschen Hochschulen in ihren Beziehungen zur Gegenwartskultur*, Berlin: C. A. Weller, 1930.

Eckardt, Alfred, *Der gegenwärtige Stand der neuen Lehrerbildung in den einzelnen Ländern Deutschlands und in ausserdeutschen Staaten*, Weimar, 1927.

Eulenburg, Franz, *Der "akademische Nachwuchs": Eine Untersuchung über die Lage und die Aufgaben der Extraordinarien und Privatdozenten*, Leipzig, 1908.

—— *Die Entwicklung der Universität Leipzig in den letzten hundert Jahren*, Leipzig, 1909.

Fischer, Aloys, "Die Entwicklung der deutschen Schulgesetzgebung seit 1918," *Pädagogische Kongressblätter*, publ. by Münchener Lehrerverein, with the geschäftsführender Ausschuss des 1. Pädagogischen Kongresses, I (Munich, 1925), 132–187.

Haenisch, Konrad, *Neue Bahnen der Kulturpolitik: Aus der Reformpraxis der deutschen Republik*, Berlin, 1921.

———— *Staat und Hochschule: Ein Beitrag zur nationalen Erziehungsfrage*, Berlin, 1920.

Hellpach, Willy, *Die Wesensgestalt der deutschen Schule*, Leipzig: Quelle and Meyer, 1925.

———— *Wirken in Wirren: Lebenserinnerungen*, 2 vols., Hamburg: C. Wegner, 1948–1949.

Jastrow, I., *Die Stellung der Privatdozenten*, Berlin, 1896.

Königlich Preussisches Statistisches Landesamt, *Preussische Statistik: Amtliches Quellenwerk*, vol. 204: *Statistik der preussischen Landesuniversitäten, Studienjahr Ostern 1905/06*, Berlin, 1908.

Köttgen, Arnold, *Deutsches Universitätsrecht*, Tübingen, 1933.

Landé, Walter, ed., *Aktenstücke zum Reichsvolksschulgesetz*, Leipzig, 1928.

———— *Preussisches Schulrecht: Kommentar* (Sonderausgabe von M. von Brauchitsch, *Verwaltungsgesetze für Preussen*, vol. VI, 1, 2), 2 vols., Berlin: C. Heymanns Verlag, 1933.

———— *Die Schule in der Reichsverfassung: Ein Kommentar*, Berlin: R. Hobbing, 1929.

Lenz, Max, *Geschichte der Königlichen Friedrich-Wilhelms-Universität zu Berlin*, 4 vols., Halle: Buchhandlung des Waisenhauses, 1910–1918.

Lexis, Wilhelm, ed., *Die deutschen Universitäten*, 2 vols., Berlin, 1893.

———— ed., *Die Reform des höheren Schulwesens in Preussen*, Halle, 1902.

———— ed., *Das Unterrichtswesen im Deutschen Reich*, 4 vols., Berlin: A. Asher und Co., 1904.

Mayer, Josef, *Das höhere Unterrichtswesen in Bayern: Vorschriftensammlung*, Munich, 1928.

Minerva: Jahrbuch der gelehrten Welt, various editions for the Weimar period.

Mitteilungen des Verbandes der Deutschen Hochschulen, K. Voigt, ed., published by the Verband der Deutschen Hochschulen, vols. I–XII (1920–1932).

Die Neuordnung des preussischen höheren Schulwesens, Denkschrift des Preussischen Ministeriums für Wissenschaft, Kunst und Volksbildung, Berlin, 1924.

Paulsen, Friedrich, *Die deutschen Universitäten und das Universitätsstudium*, Berlin, 1902.

———— *Geschichte des gelehrten Unterrichts auf den deutschen Schulen und Universitäten vom Ausgang des Mittelalters bis zur Gegenwart*, 3rd ed., suppl. by Rudolf Lehmann, 2 vols., Leipzig: Veit und Co., 1919, Berlin and Leipzig: Vereinigung wissenschaftlicher Verleger, 1921.

Plessner, Helmuth, ed., *Untersuchungen zur Lage der deutschen Hochschullehrer*, vol. III: Christian von Ferber, *Die Entwicklung des Lehrkörpers der* deutschen Universitäten und Hochschulen 1864–1954, Göttingen: Vandenhoeck und Ruprecht, 1956.

Pottag, Alfred, Die Bestimmungen über die Volks- und Mittelschule und über die Ausbildung und die Prüfungen der Lehrer und Lehrerinnen in Preussen, 25th ed., Berlin, 1926.

Die Reichsschulkonferenz in ihren Ergebnissen, published by the Zentralinstitut für Erziehung und Unterricht, Berlin, Leipzig, n.d. (1920).

Richert, Hans, ed., Richtlinien für die Lehrpläne der höheren Schulen Preussens, in Walter Landé and Hans Güldner, eds., Weidmannsche Taschenausgaben von Verfügungen der Preussischen Unterrichtsverwaltung, 19, vol. I, 6th and 7th ed., Berlin, 1927.

Richter, Werner, and Hans Peters, Die Statuten der preussischen Universitäten und Technischen Hochschulen, vol. I: Otto Benecke, ed., Die grundlegenden Erlasse der Staatsregierung, Berlin, 1929, vol. VI: Die Satzung der Universität zu Berlin, 1930, Weidmannsche Taschenausgaben von Verfügungen der preussischen Unterrichtsverwaltung, Hans Güldner and Walter Landé, eds., 61 a, f.

Ruppel, Wilhelm, Über die Berufswahl der Abiturienten Preussens in den Jahren 1875–1899: Eine statistische Studie, Fulda, 1904.

Sachse, Arnold, Friedrich Althoff und sein Werk, Berlin: E. S. Mittler und Sohn, 1928.

Schröder, Otto, Aufnahme und Studium an den Universitäten Deutschlands, 2nd ed., Halle: Buchhandlung des Waisenhauses, 1926.

Die Verhandlungen der Konferenz zur Berathung von Fragen betreffend das höhere Unterrichtswesen in Preussen, nach den Berichten des Deutschen Reichs-Anzeigers und Königl. Preussischen Staatsanzeigers, Berlin, 1891.

Volkmann, Hellmut, Die Deutsche Studentenschaft in ihrer Entwicklung seit 1919, Leipzig: Quelle und Meyer, 1925.

Weber, Alfred, Die Not der geistigen Arbeiter, Munich: Duncker und Humblot, 1923.

Weiss, Konrad, "Bemerkungen zu den bisherigen Verhandlungen über das Reichsschulgesetz," Die Hilfe: Zeitschrift für Politik, Literatur und Kunst, 19 (1923): 340–342.

Wende, Erich, C. H. Becker, Mensch und Politiker: Ein biographischer Beitrag zur Kulturgeschichte der Weimarer Republik, Stuttgart: Deutsche Verlags-Anstalt, 1959.

——— Grundlagen des Preussischen Hochschulrechts, Berlin: Weidmannsche Buchhandlung, 1930.

Zentralblatt für die gesamte Unterrichtsverwaltung in Preussen, Ministerium für Wissenschaft, Kunst und Volksbildung, vols. 61–74 (1919–1932), Berlin, 1919–1932.

II

Secondary Accounts

These are the most useful secondary accounts, especially for the history of the disciplines in Germany. Also included are the best works pertaining to mandarin politics and those general essays which have most decisively influenced my whole interpretation.

Antoni, Carlo, *Vom Historismus zur Soziologie*, trans. Walter Goetz, Stuttgart: K. F. Koehler, n.d. (1950).

Ascher, Abraham, "Professors as Propagandists: The Politics of the Kathedersozialisten," *Journal of Central European Affairs*, 23 (1963): 282–302.

Barnes, Harry Elmer, ed., *An Introduction to the History of Sociology*, Chicago: University of Chicago Press, 1948.

Besson, Waldemar, "Friedrich Meinecke und die Weimarer Republik," *Vierteljahrshefte für Zeitgeschichte*, 7 (1959): 113–129.

Bruford, W. H., *Culture and Society in Classical Weimar, 1775–1806*, Cambridge: University Press, 1962.

Dahrendorf, Ralf, *Gesellschaft und Demokratie in Deutschland*, Munich: R. Piper, 1965.

Elias, Norbert, *Über den Prozess der Zivilisation: Soziogenetische und psychogenetische Untersuchungen*, vol. I: *Wandlungen des Verhaltens in den weltlichen Oberschichten des Abendlandes*, Basel, 1939.

Engel, Josef, "Die deutschen Universitäten und die Geschichtswissenschaft," *Historische Zeitschrift*, 189 (1959): 223–378.

Hartshorne, Edward Yarnall, *The German Universities and National Socialism*, Cambridge, Mass.: Harvard University Press, 1937.

Hock, Wolfgang, *Deutscher Antikapitalismus: Der ideologische Kampf gegen die freie Wirtschaft im Zeichen der grossen Krise*, Frankfurt: F. Knapp, 1960.

Hodges, Herbert Arthur, *Wilhelm Dilthey: An Introduction*, London: Oxford University Press, 1944.

Höfele, Karl Heinrich, "Selbstverständnis und Zeitkritik des deutschen Bürgertums vor dem ersten Weltkrieg," *Zeitschrift für Religions- und Geistesgeschichte*, 8 (1956): 40–56.

Holborn, Hajo, "Der deutsche Idealismus in socialgeschichtlicher Beleuchtung," *Historische Zeitschrift*, 174 (1952): 359–384.

Hughes, H. Stuart, *Consciousness and Society: The Reorientation of European Social Thought, 1890–1930*, New York: Knopf, 1958.

Huszar, George B. de, ed., *The Intellectuals: A Controversial Portrait*, Glencoe: Free Press, 1960.

Iggers, Georg G., "The Dissolution of German Historism," in Richard Herr and

Harold T. Parker, eds., *Ideas in History: Essays Presented to Louis Gottschalk by His Former Students* (Durham, N.C.: Duke University Press, 1965), pp. 288–329.

Kollman, Eric C., "Eine Diagnose der Weimarer Republik: Ernst Troeltschs politische Anschauungen," *Historische Zeitschrift*, 182 (1956): 291–319.

Krieger, Leonard, *The German Idea of Freedom: History of a Political Tradition*, Boston: Beacon Press, 1957.

Lehmann, Rudolf, *Die pädagogische Bewegung der Gegenwart: Ihre Ursprünge und ihr Charakter*, Alfred Werner, ed., Philosophische Reihe, 43, Munich, 1922.

Lilge, Frederic, *The Abuse of Learning: The Failure of the German University*, New York: Macmillan, 1948.

Lindenlaub, Dieter, *Richtungskämpfe im Verein für Sozialpolitik: Wissenschaft und Sozialpolitik im Kaiserreich vornehmlich vom Beginn des "Neuen Kurses" bis zum Ausbruch des Ersten Weltkrieges (1890–1914)*, 2 vols., Beihefte der Vierteljahrschrift für Sozial- und Wirtschaftsgeschichte, 52–53, Wiesbaden: Franz Steiner, 1967.

Lukacs, Georg, "Die deutsche Soziologie vor dem ersten Weltkrieg," *Aufbau: Kulturpolitische Monatsschrift*, II (Berlin, 1946), 476–489.

———— "Die deutsche Soziologie zwischen dem ersten und dem zweiten Weltkrieg," *Aufbau: Kulturpolitische Monatsschrift*, II (Berlin, 1946), 585–600.

Marienfeld, Wolfgang, *Wissenschaft und Schlachtflottenbau in Deutschland, 1897–1906*, suppl. 2 of *Marine Rundschau*, April 1957.

Michels, Robert, *Umschichtungen in den herrschenden Klassen nach dem Kriege*, Stuttgart: W. Kohlhammer, 1934.

Mommsen, Wolfgang J., *Max Weber und die deutsche Politik, 1890–1920*, Tübingen: Mohr, 1959.

Mosse, George L., *The Crisis of German Ideology: Intellectual Origins of the Third Reich*, New York: Grosset and Dunlap, 1964.

Murphy, Gardner, *An Historical Introduction to Modern Psychology*, with a Supplement by Heinrich Klüver, New York: Harcourt, Brace and Co., 1929.

Nolte, Ernst, "Zur Typologie des Verhaltens der Hochschullehrer im Dritten Reich," *Aus Politik und Zeitgeschichte* (Beilage zur Wochenzeitung *Das Parlament*), Nov. 17, 1965.

O'Boyle, Lenore, "Liberal Political Leadership in Germany, 1867–1884," *Journal of Modern History*, 28 (1956): 338–352.

Pinson, Koppel S., *Pietism as a Factor in the Rise of German Nationalism*, New York: Columbia University Press, 1934.

Roessler, Wilhelm, *Die Entstehung des modernen Erziehungswesens in Deutschland*, Stuttgart: W. Kohlhammer Verlag, 1961.

Rosenbaum, L., *Herkunft und Beruf der deutschen Abgeordneten, 1847–1919*, Frankfurt, 1923.

Rosenberg, Hans, *Bureaucracy, Aristocracy and Autocracy: The Prussian Experience, 1660–1815*, Cambridge, Mass: Harvard University Press, 1958.

Rossmann, Kurt, *Wissenschaft, Ethik und Politik: Erörterung des Grundsatzes der Voraussetzungslosigkeit in der Forschung*, Dolf Sternberger, ed., Schriften der Wandlung, 4, Heidelberg: Lambert Schneider, 1949.

Samuel, Richard H., and R. Hinton Thomas, *Education and Society in Modern Germany*, in Karl Mannheim, ed., International Library of Sociology and Social Reconstruction, London: Routledge and Kegan Paul, 1949.

Schieder, Theodor, "Die deutsche Geschichtswissenschaft im Spiegel der Historischen Zeitschrift," *Historische Zeitschrift*, 189 (1959): 1–72.

Schumpeter, Joseph A., *History of Economic Analysis*, E. B. Schumpeter, ed., New York: Oxford University Press, 1954.

Schwabe, Klaus, "Zur politischen Haltung der deutschen Professoren im ersten Weltkrieg," *Historische Zeitschrift*, 193 (1961): 601–634.

Sontheimer, Kurt, *Antidemokratisches Denken in der Weimarer Republik: Die politischen Ideen des deutschen Nationalismus zwischen 1918 und 1933*, Munich: Nymphenburger, 1962.

Stern, Fritz, *The Politics of Cultural Despair: A Study in the Rise of the Germanic Ideology*, Berkeley, Los Angeles: University of California Press, 1961.

Suranyi-Unger, Theo, *Die Entwicklung der theoretischen Volkswirtschaftslehre im ersten Viertel des 20. Jahrhunderts*, Jena: G. Fischer, 1927.

III

Sources on German Academic Opinion

These are the most interesting group proclamations and position papers (other than those listed under I), newly founded journals, academic speech series, handbooks, printed letters, and the like. A few influential proclamations by nonacademics are included as well.

Die Ausbildung der höheren Lehrer an der Universität, Denkschrift der philosophischen Fakultät der Friedrich-Wilhelms-Universität Berlin, Leipzig, 1925.

Bekenntnis der Professoren an den deutschen Universitäten und Hochschulen zu Adolf Hitler und dem nationalsozialistischen Staat, publ. by Nationalsozialistischer Lehrerbund, Dresden, n.d. (1933).

Bergsträsser, Arnold, and Hermann Platz, *Jugendbewegung und Universität: Vorträge auf der Tagung deutscher Hochschullehrer in Weimar, 1927*, Karlsruhe, 1927.

Brentano, Lujo, et al., *Wahlprogramm der vereinigten Liberalen und Demokraten Bayerns*, im Auftrage des Süddeutschen Verbandes nationalsozialer Vereine in seinen Grundzügen erläutert, Munich, n.d. (1904).

Briefwechsel zwischen den Herren Yves Guyot und Daniel Bellet und Herrn Lujo Brentano, publ. by the Kulturbund deutscher Gelehrter und Künstler. Correspondence took place in October 1914.

Erklärung der Hochschullehrer des Deutschen Reiches, Berlin, October 23, 1914.

Fischer, Aloys, Th. Litt, H. Nohl, E. Spranger, eds., *Die Erziehung: Monatsschrift für den Zusammenhang von Kultur und Erziehung in Wissenschaft und Leben*, vol. I, Leipzig, 1925.

Friedrich-Wilhelms-Universität zu Berlin. A series of academic speeches appeared as pamphlets with this heading on the title page. In catalogues, as in the Bayerische Staatsbibliothek, these series are also listed under: Berlin, Universität.

Harnack, Adolf von, Friedrich Meinecke, Max Sering, Ernst Troeltsch, Otto Hintze, *Die deutsche Freiheit: Fünf Vorträge*, Gotha, 1917.

Heidelberger Universitätsreden. This is the serial title for academic speeches at Heidelberg after 1926. Before that, the more informal title "Universität Heidelberg" was generally used at the head of pamphlets.

Hintze, Otto, Friedrich Meinecke, Hermann Oncken, Hermann Schumacher, eds., *Deutschland und der Weltkrieg*, Leipzig, 1915.

Die Idee der deutschen Universität: Die fünf Grundschriften aus der Zeit ihrer Neubegründung durch klassischen Idealismus und romantischen Realismus, Darmstadt: Herman Gentner, 1956.

Jahreshefte der Universität Freiburg i. B. Most academic speeches at Freiburg appeared under this general title during this period. But see also: "Freiburg, Universitätsreden" as a general heading for academic pamphlets.

Kahl, Wilhelm, Friedrich Meinecke, Gustav Radbruch, *Die deutschen Universitäten und der heutige Staat: Referate erstattet auf der Weimarer Tagung deutscher Hochschullehrer am 23. und 24. April 1926*, Recht und Staat in Geschichte und Gegenwart: Eine Sammlung von Vorträgen und Schriften aus dem Gebiet der gesamten Staatswissenschaften, 44, Tübingen, 1926.

Kahler, Erich von, *Der Beruf der Wissenschaft*, Berlin, 1920.

Kjellen, Rudolf, *Die Ideen von 1914: Eine weltgeschichtliche Perspektive*, Zwischen Krieg und Frieden, 29, Leipzig, 1915.

Koellner, Hertha, *Das Schulprogramm der deutschen Sozialdemokratie*, Pädagogisches Magazin, 771, Langensalza, 1920.

Kölner Vierteljahrshefte für Sozialwissenschaften, vol. I (Munich, 1921), pp. 1–93.

Krieck, Ernst, *Die Revolution der Wissenschaft: Ein Kapitel über Volkserziehung*, Jena, 1920.

Lampe, F., and G. H. Franke, eds., *Staatsbürgerliche Erziehung*, publ. for the Zentralinstitut für Erziehung und Unterricht, Breslau, 1924.

Münchener Universitätsreden. Beginning in 1924, academic speeches at Munich appeared in this series. Before that, the title "Universität München" appeared as a general heading for academic pamphlets.

Peters, Ulrich, ed., *Zeitschrift für Deutsche Bildung*, vol. I, Frankfurt, 1925.

Schmoller, Gustav, et al., *Reichstagsauflösung und Kolonialpolitik*, Offizieller stenographischer Bericht über die Versammlung in der Berliner Hochschule für Musik am 8. Januar 1907, publ. by the Kolonialpolitisches Aktionskomité, Berlin, 1907.

Tönnies, Ferdinand, Friedrich Paulsen, *Briefwechsel 1876–1908*, ed. Olaf Klose, E. G. Jacoby, and Irma Fischer, Kiel: Ferdinand Hirt, 1961.

Unabhängiger Ausschuss für einen deutschen Frieden. A series of *Flugblätter* thus catalogued at Bayerische Staatsbibliothek, Munich.

Die Verhandlungen des achtzehnten Evangelisch-sozialen Kongresses abgehalten in Strassburg (Elsass) am 21. bis 23. Mai 1907, nach dem stenographischen Protokoll, Göttingen, 1907.

Vierkandt, Alfred, ed., *Handwörterbuch der Soziologie*, Stuttgart: Ferdinand Enke, 1931.

Wortlaut der sich gegen Annexionen richtenden Delbrückschen Eingabe. Dated Berlin, July 9, 1915. Apparently circulated as a single sheet, probably by the Unabhängiger Ausschuss.

IV

Autobiographical Material

These are the most interesting autobiographies and memoirs. Also included are the various series of *Selbstdarstellungen*. Each of these very valuable series contains a number of short essays (generally 20–70 pp.) by leading scholars about themselves.

Bonn, Moritz Julius, *So macht man Geschichte: Bilanz eines Lebens*, Munich: List, 1953.

Brentano, Lujo, *Mein Leben im Kampf um die soziale Entwicklung Deutschlands*, Jena: Eugen Diederichs, 1931.

Dessoir, Max, *Buch der Erinnerung*, Stuttgart, 1946.

Eucken, Rudolf, *Lebenserinnerungen: Ein Stück deutschen Lebens*, Leipzig: K. F. Koehler, 1921.

Die Geschichtswissenschaft der Gegenwart in Selbstdarstellungen, Sigfrid Steinberg, ed., 2 vols., Leipzig: F. Meiner, 1925–1926.

Meinecke, Friedrich, *Erlebtes, 1862–1901*, Leipzig: Koehler und Amelang, 1941.

——— *Strassburg, Freiburg, Berlin, 1901–1919: Erinnerungen*, Stuttgart: K. F. Koehler, 1949.

Die Pädagogik der Gegenwart in Selbstdarstellungen, Erich Hahn, ed., Leipzig: F. Meiner, 1926.

Die Philosophie der Gegenwart in Selbstdarstellungen, Raymund Schmidt, ed., 7 vols., Leipzig: F. Meiner, 1922–1929.

Die Volkswirtschaftslehre der Gegenwart in Selbstdarstellungen, Felix Meiner, ed., 2 vols., Leipzig: F. Meiner, 1924–1929.

Weisbach, Werner, *"Und Alles ist zerstoben": Erinnerungen aus der Jahrhundertwende*, Vienna: H. Reichner, 1937.

Wilamowitz-Moellendorff, Ulrich von, *Erinnerungen, 1848–1914*, 2nd ed., Leipzig: K. F. Koehler, n.d. (1928).

Wundt, Wilhelm, *Erlebtes und Erkanntes*, Stuttgart: A. Kröner, 1920.

V

Writings by German Academics

On the whole, only the most interesting and important individuals are considered, and the emphasis is upon these men's occasional writings. Some less generally known academics are included because they would be excellent subjects for biographies. Finally, I have listed a few items which seem to me particularly good introductions to widespread opinions or to the history of the disciplines. In citing articles, I have used the abbreviation *Schmollers Jahrbuch* as described in the headnote to the notes.

Anschütz, Gerhard, *Drei Leitgedanken der Weimarer Reichsverfassung: Rede gehalten bei der Jahresfeier der Universität Heidelberg am 22. November 1922*, Recht und Staat in Geschichte und Gegenwart, 22, Tübingen, 1929.

Aster, Ernst von, "Die Krise der bürgerlichen Ideologie," *Die neue Rundschau*, 42 (1931): 1–13.

——— *Marx und die Gegenwart*, Philosophie und Geschichte, 24, Tübingen, 1929.

——— "Metaphysik des Nationalismus," *Die neue Rundschau*, 43 (1932): 40–52.

——— *Die Psychoanalyse*, Berlin: Volksverband der Bücherfreunde, Wegweiser-Verlag, 1930.

——— "Zur Kritik des deutschen Nationalismus," *Die neue Rundschau*, 36 (1925): 1–15.

Becher, Erich, *Der Darwinismus und die soziale Ethik*, Ein Vortrag gehalten zur Hundertjahrfeier von Darwins Geburtstage vor der Philosophischen Vereinigung in Bonn nebst Erweiterungen und Anmerkungen, Leipzig, 1909.

——— *Geisteswissenschaften und Naturwissenschaften: Untersuchungen zur Theorie und Einteilung der Realwissenschaften*, Munich, Leipzig: Duncker und Humblot, 1921.

——— *Grundlagen und Grenzen des Naturerkennens*, Munich, Leipzig: Duncker und Humblot, 1928.

——— "Die Philosophie der Gegenwart," in Erich Becher, ed., *Deutsche Philosophen* (Munich, Leipzig: Duncker und Humblot, 1929), pp. 279–306.

Bernhard, Ludwig, *Akademische Selbstverwaltung in Frankreich und Deutschland: Ein Beitrag zur Universitätsreform*, Berlin, 1930.
—— *Der Staatsgedanke des Faschismus*, Berlin: J. Springer, 1931.
—— *Unerwünschte Folgen der deutschen Sozialpolitik*, Berlin, 1912.
Bonn, Moritz Julius, *Die Auflösung des modernen Staates*, Berlin, 1921.
—— *Die Krisis der europäischen Demokratie*, Munich: Meyer und Jessen, 1925.
—— *Nationale Kolonialpolitik*, Schriften des Socialwissenschaftlichen Vereins der Universität München, 5, Munich, 1910.
—— *Das Schicksal des deutschen Kapitalismus*, 3rd and 5th ed., Berlin, 1930.
—— *Sozialisierung*, Munich: Verlagsabteilung der Deutschen Volkspartei, 1925.
—— "Die wahre Weltrevolution," *Die neue Rundschau*, 34 (1923): 385–394.
Brentano, Lujo, *Ethik und Volkswirtschaft in der Geschichte*, Rede beim Antritt des Rektorats der Ludwig-Maximilians-Universität gehalten am 23. November 1901, Munich, 1901.
—— *Reaktion oder Reform? Gegen die Zuchthausvorlage*, Berlin, 1899.
—— *Die Stellung der Studenten zu den sozialpolitischen Aufgaben der Zeit*, Vortrag gehalten am 15. Januar 1897 zur Eröffnung der Thätigkeit des sozialwissenschaftlichen Vereines von Studierenden an der Universität München, Munich, 1897.
—— *Über Syndikalismus und Lohnminimum: Zwei Vorträge*, Munich, 1913.
—— "Über Werturteile in der Volkswirtschaftslehre," *Archiv für Sozial-Wissenschaft und Sozialpolitik*, 33 (1911): 695–741.
Briefs, Götz, "Gegenwartsfragen des deutschen Wirtschaftslebens," Philipp Witkop, ed., *Deutsches Leben der Gegenwart* (Berlin: Volksverband des Bücherfreunde, Wegweiser Verlag, 1922), pp. 253–304.
—— "Über das Verhältnis des Proletarischen zum Sozialistischen," *Kölner Vierteljahrshefte für Soziologie*, III (1923), 99–109.
—— *Untergang des Abendlandes, Christentum und Sozialismus: Eine Auseinandersetzung mit Oswald Spengler*, Freiburg, 1920.
Cassirer, Ernst, "Der Begriff der symbolischen Form im Aufbau der Geisteswissenschaften," in Fritz Saxl, ed., *Vorträge der Bibliothek Warburg*, 1921–1922 (1923), pp. 11–39.
—— *Die Idee der republikanischen Verfassung: Rede zur Verfassungsfeier am 11. August 1928*, Hamburg, 1929.
—— *Der kritische Idealismus und die Philosophie des "gesunden Menschenverstandes,"* Philosophische Abeiten, Hermann Cohen and Paul Natorp, eds., vol. I, no. 1, Giessen, 1906.
Cohn, Jonas, *Befreien und Binden: Zeitfragen der Erziehung überzeitlich betrachtet*, Leipzig, 1926.

——— *Erziehung zu sozialer Gesinnung*, Pädagogisches Magazin, 742, Langensalza, 1920.

——— *Der Sinn der gegenwärtigen Kultur: Ein philosophischer Versuch*, Leipzig: Felix Meiner, 1914.

Curtius, Ernst Robert, *Deutscher Geist in Gefahr*, Stuttgart: Deutsche Verlagsanstalt, 1932.

——— *Französischer Geist im neuen Europa*, Stuttgart: Deutsche Verlagsanstalt, 1925.

——— "Die Universität als Idee und als Erfahrung," *Die neue Rundschau*, 42 (1932): 145–167.

Delbrück, Hans, *Ludendorffs Selbstporträt*, Berlin, 1922.

——— "Die Marxsche Geschichtsphilosophie," *Preussische Jahrbücher*, 182 (1920): 157–180.

——— "Professor von Below als Vorkämpfer der Vaterlandspartei," *Preussische Jahrbücher*, 172 (1918): 126–129.

——— "Der Stand der Kriegsschuldfrage," *Zeitschrift für Politik*, 8 (1924): 293–319.

——— "Von der Bismarck-Legende," *Historische Zeitschrift*, 133 (1925–26): 69–82.

Dilthey, Wilhelm, *Gesammelte Schriften*, vol. VII: *Der Aufbau der geschichtlichen Welt in den Geisteswissenschaften*, ed. B. Groethuysen, Leipzig: Teubner, 1927.

——— *Pattern and Meaning in History: Thoughts on History and Society*, ed. H. P. Rickman, New York: Harper, 1962.

Driesch, Hans, *Grundprobleme der Psychologie: Ihre Krisis in der Gegenwart*, Leipzig: Emmanuel Reinicke, 1926.

——— "Philosophie und positives Wissen," A. von Gleichen-Russwurm, et al., *Der Leuchter: Weltanschauung und Lebensgestaltung*, book I (Darmstadt: O. Riechl, 1919), pp. 337–366.

Eucken, Rudolf, *Erkennen und Leben*, Leipzig: Quelle und Meyer, 1912.

——— *Die geistigen Forderungen der Gegenwart*, 3rd ed., Berlin, 1918.

——— *Geistige Strömungen der Gegenwart*, 3rd expanded ed. of *Grundbegriffe der Gegenwart*, Leipzig, 1904.

——— *Die weltgeschichtliche Bedeutung des deutschen Geistes*, Ernst Jaeckh, ed., Der Deutsche Krieg, 8, Stuttgart, 1914.

Fischer, Aloys, "Arbeiten und Lernen: Psychologische Betrachtungen zur heutigen Schulreformbewegung," *Das Arbeitsprinzip im naturwissenschaftlichen Unterricht: Zweites Jahrbuch der Pädagogischen Zentrale des Deutschen Lehrervereins* (Leipzig, 1912), pp. 1–61.

——— *Arbeits- und Erlebnispädagogik*, Bücherei der Quelle, 51, Vienna, 1932.

——— *Erziehung als Beruf*, Leipzig, 1922.

———— *Die kulturellen Grundlagen der Erziehung*, Rolf Hoffmann, ed., Die Akademie, 3, Erlangen, 1925.

———— "Psychologisch-ethische Vorfragen der Heimaterziehung," Walther Schönischen, ed., *Handbuch der Heimaterziehung* (Berlin, 1923), pp. 27–105.

———— "Unsere Zeit und die Mission der Pädagogik," *Die Erziehung*, 1 (1925-26): 1–7.

———— "Das Verhältnis der Jugend zu den sozialen Bewegungen und der Begriff der Sozialpädagogik," in Aloys Fischer, ed., *Jugendführer und Jugendprobleme: Festschrift zu Georg Kerschensteiners 70. Geburtstag* (Leipzig, 1924), pp. 209–306.

Frischeisen-Köhler, Max, "Die Philosophie der Gegenwart," in Max Dessoir, ed., *Lehrbuch der Philosophie*, I (1925), 553–627.

Harnack, Adolph, and Hans Delbrück, *Evangelisch-Sozial*, Berlin, 1896.

Hartmann, Eduard von, *Tagesfragen*, Leipzig, 1896.

Herkner, Heinrich, "Der Kampf um das sittliche Werturteil in der National-ökonomie," *Schmollers Jahrbuch*, 36 (Munich, 1912): 515–555.

———— *Krieg und Volkswirtschaft: Rede am 26. Februar 1915*, Deutsche Reden in schwerer Zeit, 19, Berlin, 1915.

———— *Die soziale Reform als Gebot des wirtschaftlichen Fortschrittes*, Leipzig, 1891.

———— "Studien zur Fortbildung des Arbeitsverhältnisses," *Archiv für soziale Gesetzgebung und Statistik*, 4 (1891): 563–599.

Hintze, Otto, "Troeltsch und die Probleme des Historismus," *Historische Zeitschrift*, 135 (1926–27): 188–239.

Hönigswald, Richard, *Die Grundlagen der Denkpsychologie: Studien und Analysen*, 2nd ed., Leipzig, B. G. Teubner, 1925.

———— *Zur Kritik der Machschen Philosophie: Eine erkenntnistheoretische Studie*, Berlin, 1903.

Jaeger, Werner, "Die geistige Gegenwart der Antike," in Werner Jaeger, ed., *Die Antike*, V (1929), 167–186.

———— *Humanismus und Jugendbildung*, Votrag gehalten in der Versammlung der Freunde des humanistischen Gymnasiums in Berlin und der Provinz Brandenburg am 27. November 1920, Berlin, 1921.

———— *Stellung und Aufgaben der Universität in der Gegenwart*, Berlin, 1924.

Jaspers, Karl, *Die Idee der Universität*, Berlin, 1923.

———— *Man in the Modern Age*, trans. Eden and Cedar Paul, London: G. Routledge and Sons, 1933.

———— *Max Weber*, Rede bei der von der Heidelberger Studentenschaft veranstalteten Trauerfeier, Tübingen, 1921.

———— *Philosophie*, vol. I: *Philosophische Weltorientierung*, Berlin: J. Springer, 1932.

Jastrow, I., *"Sozialliberal": Die Aufgaben des Liberalismus in Preussen*, 2nd ed., Berlin, 1894.

Kerschensteiner, Georg, *Autorität und Freiheit als Bildungsgrundsätze*, Paul Östreich, ed., *Entschiedene Schulreform*, 28, Leipzig, 1924.

⸺ *Der Begriff der Arbeitsschule*, 3rd ed., Leipzig, 1917.

⸺ *Der Begriff der staatsbürgerlichen Erziehung*, 5th ed., Leipzig, 1923.

⸺ *Das einheitliche deutsche Schulsystem: Sein Aufbau, seine Erziehungsaufgaben*, 2nd ed., Leipzig, 1922.

⸺ *Die gewerbliche Erziehung der deutschen Jugend*, Fest-Vortrag gehalten aus Anlass der 50 jährigen Jubelfeier des Bayrischen Kunstgewerbe-Vereins im Saale des alten Rathauses zu München am 3. Juli 1901, Darmstadt, 1901.

⸺ "Das öffentliche Unterrichtswesen im Volksstaate," *Die neue Rundschau*, 30 (1919): 1171–1187.

⸺ *Die Seele des Erziehers und das Problem der Lehrerbildung*, Leipzig, 1921.

⸺ *Selbstregierung der Schüler*, Bücherei der Quelle, 10, Vienna, 1925.

⸺ *Staatsbürgerliche Erziehung der deutschen Jugend*, Gekrönte Preisarbeit, Erfurt, 1901.

Köhler, Wolfgang, *Gestalt Psychology*, New York: Liveright, 1929.

Krueger, Felix, *Über Entwicklungspsychologie: Ihre sachliche und geschichtliche Notwendigkeit*, Leipzig: Engelmann, 1915.

Lamprecht, Karl, *Die historische Methode des Herrn von Below: Eine Kritik*, Beigabe zur *Historischen Zeitschrift*, vol. 82, pt. 2, Berlin, 1899.

⸺ *Moderne Geschichtswissenschaft: Fünf Vorträge*, Freiburg, 1905.

⸺ *Zwei Reden zur Hochschulreform*, Berlin, 1910.

Lederer, Emil, *Planwirtschaft*, Tübingen, 1932.

⸺ "Die Umschichtung des Proletariats," *Die neue Rundschau*, 40 (1929): 141–161.

⸺ "Zur Soziologie des Weltkrieges," *Archiv für Sozialwissenschaft und Sozialpolitik*, 39 (1914): 347–384.

Lehmann, Rudolf, "Die Bedeutung der Erziehungswissenschaft für die Gegenwart," *Preussische Jahrbücher*, 183 (1921): 211–217.

⸺ "Kultur und Schule der Gegenwart," *Die neue Rundschau*, 19 (1908): 753–761.

Lewin, Kurt, *Die Entwicklung der experimentellen Willenspsychologie und die Psychotherapie*, Leipzig: S. Hirzel, 1929.

Litt, Theodor, *Berufsstudium und "Allgemeinbildung" auf der Universität*, Leipzig, 1920.

⸺ *"Führen" oder "Wachsenlassen": Eine Erörterung des pädagogischen Grundproblems*, 3rd ed., Leipzig: B. G. Teubner, 1931.

⸺ *Möglichkeiten und Grenzen der Pädagogik: Abhandlungen zur gegen-*

wärtigen Lage von Erziehung und Erziehungstheorie, Leipzig, Berlin: B. G. Teubner, 1926.

—— *Nationale Erziehung und Internationalismus,* Sozialpädagogische Abende im Zentralinstitut für Erziehung und Unterricht, 3, Berlin, 1920.

—— *Die Philosophie der Gegenwart und ihr Einfluss auf das Bildungsideal,* Leipzig: B. G. Teubner, 1925.

—— *Wissenschaft, Bildung, Weltanschauung,* Leipzig: B. G. Teubner, 1928.

Mannheim, Karl, *Essays on Sociology and Social Psychology,* Paul Kecskemeti, ed., New York: Oxford University Press, 1953.

—— *Essays on the Sociology of Knowledge,* Paul Kecskemeti, ed., London: Routledge, 1952.

—— *Die Gegenwartsaufgaben der Soziologie: Ihre Lehrgestalt,* Tübingen, 1932.

—— "Historismus," *Archiv für Sozialwissenschaft und Sozialpolitik,* 52 (1924): 1–60.

—— *Ideology and Utopia: An Introduction to the Sociology of Knowledge,* Louis Wirth and Edward Shils, trans., New York: Harcourt "Harvest," n.d. (1955).

—— "Das Problem einer Soziologie des Wissens," *Archiv für Sozialwissenschaft und Sozialpolitik,* 53 (1925): 577–652.

Marcks, Erich, *Geschichte und Gegenwart: Fünf historisch-politische Reden,* Stuttgart: Deutsche Verlagsanstalt, 1925.

—— *Die Universität Heidelberg im 19. Jahrhundert,* Festrede zur Hundertjahrfeier ihrer Wiederbegründung durch Karl Friedrich gehalten in der Stadthalle am 7. August 1903, Heidelberg, 1903.

—— *Wo stehen wir?,* Der Deutsche Krieg, 19, Stuttgart, 1914.

Meinecke, Friedrich, *Die deutsche Erhebung von 1914: Aufsätze und Vorträge,* 2nd ed., Stuttgart, Berlin: J. G. Cotta, 1914.

—— *Deutsche Kultur und Machtpolitik im englischen Urteil: Rede am 12. April 1915,* Deutsche Reden in schwerer Zeit, 29, Berlin, 1915.

—— "Drei Generationen deutscher Gelehrtenpolitik," *Historische Zeitschrift,* 125 (1922): 248–283.

—— *Die Entstehung des Historismus,* Munich, Berlin: R. Oldenbourg, 1936.

—— *The German Catastrophe,* Cambridge, Mass.: Harvard University Press, 1950.

—— "Kausalitäten und Werte in der Geschichte," *Historische Zeitschrift,* 137 (1927–28): 1–27.

—— *Nach der Revolution: Geschichtliche Betrachtungen über unsere Lage,* Munich, Berlin: R. Oldenbourg, 1919.

—— *Politische Schriften und Reden,* Georg Kotowski, ed. (Friedrich Meinecke, *Werke,* Hans Herzfeld, Carl Hinrichs, Walther Hofer, eds., vol. II), Darmstadt: Siegfried Toeche-Mittler Verlag, 1958.

—— *Weltbürgertum und Nationalstaat: Studien zur Genesis des deutschen Nationalstaates,* Munich, Berlin, 1908.

—— *Das Zeitalter der deutschen Erhebung, 1795–1815,* 3rd ed., Bielefeld, 1924.

—— *Zur Theorie und Philosophie der Geschichte,* ed. Eberhard Kessel (*Werke,* vol. IV), Stuttgart: K. F. Koehler, 1959.

Mombert, Paul, *Geschichte der Nationalökonomie,* K. Diehl, P. Mombert, eds., Grundrisse zum Studium der Nationalökonomie, 2, Jena: Gustav Fischer, 1927.

Natorp, Paul, *Der Deutsche und sein Staat,* Erlangen: Verlag der Philosophischen Akademie, 1924.

—— *Genossenschaftliche Erziehung als Grundlage zum Neubau des Volkstums und des Menschentums,* Berlin: J. Springer, 1920.

—— *Hoffnungen und Gefahren unserer Jugendbewegung,* Tat-Flugschriften, 36, Jena, 1920.

—— *Individuum und Gemeinschaft,* Vortrag gehalten auf der 25. Aarauer Studien-Konferenz am 21. April 1921, Jena, 1921.

—— *Philosophie und Pädagogik: Untersuchungen auf ihrem Grenzgebiet,* Marburg, 1909.

—— *Sozialidealismus: Neue Richtlinien Sozialer Erziehung,* 2nd ed., Berlin: Julius Springer, 1922.

—— *Sozialpädagogik: Theorie der Willenserziehung auf der Grundlage der Gemeinschaft,* 2nd ed., Stuttgart, 1904.

—— *Student und Weltanschauung,* Tat-Flugschriften, 29, Jena, 1918.

—— *Der Tag des Deutschen: Vier Kriegsaufsätze,* Hagen, 1915.

Oesterreich, Traugott Konstantin, "Die philosophischen Strömungen der Gegenwart," in Paul Hinneberg, ed., *Die Kultur der Gegenwart,* pt. I, sec. 6: *Systematische Philosophie,* 3rd ed., Leipzig, 1921, pp. 352–395.

Oncken, Hermann, *Nach Zehn Jahren,* Berlin, 1929.

—— "Politik als Kunst," *Handbuch der Politik,* 3rd ed., vol. I: *Die Grundlagen der Politik* (Berlin, 1920), pp. 8–14.

—— *Unser Reich,* Rede bei der Gedächtnisfeier zur Wiederkehr des Tages der Reichsgründung, veranstaltet von Universität und Stadt Heidelberg am 18. Januar 1921, Heidelberg, 1921.

Oppenheimer, Franz, *Richtungen der neueren deutschen Soziologie,* Drei Vorträge gehalten am 1.–3. Mai 1928 an der University of London, School of Economics, Jena: G. Fischer, 1928.

—— *Die soziale Frage und der Sozialismus: Eine kritische Auseinandersetzung mit der marxistischen Theorie,* Jena: G. Fischer, 1912.

Paulsen, Friedrich, *Parteipolitik und Moral,* Vortrag gehalten in der Gehe-Stiftung zu Dresden am 13. Oktober 1900, Dresden, 1900.

———— *Über die gegenwärtige Lage des höheren Schulwesens in Preussen*, Berlin, 1893.

Rachfahl, Felix, *Preussen und Deutschland in Vergangenheit, Gegenwart und Zukunft*, Recht und Staat in Geschichte und Gegenwart, 13, Tübingen, 1919.

———— *Staat, Gesellschaft, Kultur und Geschichte*, Jena, 1924.

Rickert, Heinrich, *Kant als Philosoph der modernen Kultur: Ein geschichtsphilosophischer Versuch*, Tübingen: J. C. B. Mohr, 1924.

———— *Kulturwissenschaft und Naturwissenschaft*, Leipzig, Tübingen: Mohr, 1899.

———— *Die Philosophie des Lebens: Darstellung und Kritik der philosophischen Modeströmungen unserer Zeit*, Tübingen: J. C. B. Mohr, 1920.

Rothacker, Erich, "Savigny, Grimm, Ranke: Ein Beitrag zur Frage nach dem Zusammenhang der Historischen Schule," *Historische Zeitschrift*, 128 (1923): 415–445.

Rothfels, Hans, *Die Universitäten und der Schuldspruch von Versailles: Zum 28. Juni 1929: Eine ungehaltene akademische Rede*, Königsberger Universitätsreden, 5, Königsberg, 1929.

Salz, Arthur, *Für die Wissenschaft: Gegen die Gebildeten unter ihren Verächtern*, Munich: Drei Masken Verlag, 1921.

———— *Macht und Wirtschaftsgesetz*, ein Beitrag zur Erkenntnis des Wesens der kapitalistischen Wirtschaftsverfassung, Leipzig: B. G. Teubner, 1930.

———— *Die Rechtfertigung der Sozialpolitik: Ein Bekenntnis*, Heidelberg, 1914.

———— "Der Sinn der kapitalistischen Wirtschaftsordnung," *Archiv für Sozialwissenschaft und Sozialpolitik*, 52 (1924): 577–622.

———— *Das Wesen des Imperialismus*, Leipzig, 1931.

Scheler, Max, "Die deutsche Philosophie der Gegenwart," Philipp Witkop, ed., *Deutsches Leben der Gegenwart* (Berlin, 1922), pp. 127–224.

———— *Die Formen des Wissens und die Bildung*, Vortrag gehalten zum zehnjährigen Stiftungsfeste der Lessingsakademie in Berlin, Bonn, 1925.

———— *Philosophische Weltanschauung*, Bonn: F. Cohen, 1929.

———— "Universität und Volkshochschule," in Leopold von Wiese, ed., *Soziologie des Volksbildungswesens: Schriften des Forschungsinstituts für Sozialwissenschaften in Köln*, I (1921), 153–191.

———— "Von zwei deutschen Krankheiten," A. von Gleichen-Russwurm, et al., *Der Leuchter: Weltanschauung und Lebensgestaltung* (Darmstadt, 1919), pp. 161–190.

———— "Weltanschauungslehre, Soziologie und Weltanschauungssetzung," *Kölner Vierteljahrshefte für Sozialwissenschaften*, 2 (1922): 18–33.

———— *Die Wissensformen und die Gesellschaft: Probleme einer Soziologie des Wissens*, Leipzig: Der Neue Geist Verlag, 1926.

Schmoller, Gustav, "Die Entstehung der deutschen Volkswirtschaft und der deutschen Sozialreform," *Schmollers Jahrbuch*, 39 (1915): 1609–1640.

—— "Wechselnde Theorien und feststehende Wahrheiten im Gebiete der Staats- und Socialwissenschaften und die heutige deutsche Volkswirtschaftslehre," *Schmollers Jahrbuch*, 21 (1897): 1387–1408.

—— *Zwanzig Jahre Deutscher Politik, 1897–1917: Aufsätze und Vorträge*, Munich, Leipzig: Duncker und Humblot, 1920.

Schumpeter, Joseph, *Imperialism, Social Classes: Two Essays*, trans. Heinz Norden, New York: Meridian Books, 1955.

—— "Sozialistische Möglichkeiten von heute," *Archiv für Sozialwissenschaft und Sozialpolitik*, 48 (1921): 305–360.

—— *Wie studiert man Sozialwissenschaft?*, 2nd ed., Schriften des Sozialwissenschaftlichen Akademischen Vereins in Czernowitz, 11, Munich, 1915.

Simmel, Georg, "Der Begriff und die Tragödie der Kultur," in Georg Simmel, *Philosophische Kultur: Gesammelte Essais*, Philosophisch-soziologische Bücherei, 27 (Leipzig: W. Klinkhardt, 1911), pp. 245–277.

—— *Der Konflikt der modernen Kultur: Ein Vortrag*, 2nd ed., Munich, Leipzig, 1921.

—— *Der Krieg und die geistigen Entscheidungen: Reden und Aufsätze*, 2nd ed., Munich, 1917.

—— "Persönliche und sachliche Kultur," *Neue Deutsche Rundschau*, 11 (Berlin, 1900): 700–712.

—— "Das Problem der Soziologie," *Schmollers Jahrbuch*, 13 (1894): 1301–1307.

—— *Die Probleme der Geschichtsphilosophie: Eine erkenntnistheoretische Studie*, Leipzig, 1892.

—— "Soziologie der Über- und Unterordnung," *Archiv für Sozialwissenschaft und Sozialpolitik*, 24 (1907): 477–546.

—— "Über das Wesen der Sozial-Psychologie," *Archiv für Sozialwissenschaft und Sozialpolitik*, 26 (Tübingen, 1908): 285–291.

Sombart, Werner, "Der Anteil der Juden am Aufbau der modernen Volkswirtschaft," *Die neue Rundschau*, 21 (1910): 145–173.

—— *Beamtenschaft und Wirtschaft*, Vortrag gehalten auf dem Mitteldeutschen Beamtentag am 11. September 1927, Berlin, 1927.

—— "Der Bourgeois einst und jetzt," *Die neue Rundschau*, 24 (1913): 1481–1509.

—— *Dennoch! Aus Theorie und Geschichte der gewerkschaftlichen Arbeiterbewegung*, Jena, 1910.

—— *Die drei Nationalökonomien: Geschichte und System der Lehre von der Wirtschaft*, Munich: Duncker und Humblot, 1930.

—— *Händler und Helden: Patriotische Besinnungen*, Munich, 1915.

——— "Ideale der Sozialpolitik," *Archiv für soziale Gesetzgebung und Statistik,* 10 (Berlin, 1897): 1–48.

——— "Jüdischer Geist im modernen Wirtschaftsleben," *Die neue Rundschau,* 21 (1910): 585–615.

——— *Die Rationalisierung in der Wirtschaft,* Vortrag auf dem 25. kirchl. soz. Kongress in Düsseldorf, Leipzig, 1928.

——— "Technik und Kultur," *Archiv für Sozialwissenschaft und Sozialpolitik,* 33 (Tübingen, 1911): 305–347.

——— *Die Zukunft des Kapitalismus,* Berlin, 1932.

Spranger, Eduard, *Begabung und Studium,* Deutscher Ausschuss für Erziehung und Unterricht, Leipzig, 1917.

——— *Der deutsche Klassizismus und das Bildungsleben der Gegenwart,* 2nd ed., Veröffentlichungen der Akademie gemeinnütziger Wissenschaften zu Erfurt: Abteilung für Erziehungswissenschaft und Jugendkunde, 3, Erfurt, 1928.

——— "Die drei Motive der Schulreform," M. Siebourg and P. Lorentz, eds., *Monatsschrift für höhere Schulen,* 20 (1921): 260–274.

——— *Gedanken über Lehrerbildung,* Leipzig: Quelle und Meyer, 1920.

——— *Der gegenwärtige Stand der Geisteswissenschaften und die Schule,* Rede gehalten auf der 53. Versammlung deutscher Philologen und Schulmänner in Jena am 27. September 1921, Leipzig, 1922.

——— *Das humanistische und das politische Bildungsideal,* Deutsche Abende im Zentralinstitut für Erziehung und Unterricht, 6, Berlin, 1916.

——— "Mein Konflikt mit der national-sozialistischen Regierung 1933," *Universitas: Zeitschrift für Wissenschaft, Kunst und Literatur,* 10 (1955): 457–473.

——— "Der Sinn der Voraussetzungslosigkeit in den Geisteswissenschaften," *Sitzungsberichte der preussischen Akademie der Wissenschaften: Philosophisch-historische Klasse,* 1929, pp. 2–30.

——— *Wandlungen im Wesen der Universität seit 100 Jahren,* Leipzig, 1913.

——— "Das Wesen der deutschen Universität," *Das akademische Deutschland,* III, 1–38.

——— *Wilhelm von Humboldt und die Reform des Bildungswesens,* Berlin, 1910.

Stern, William, *Studien zur Personalwissenschaft,* pt. I: *Personalistik als Wissenschaft,* Leipzig: J. A. Barth, 1930.

——— *Vorgedanken zur Weltanschauung,* Leipzig, 1915.

Tönnies, Ferdinand, *Gemeinschaft und Gesellschaft,* Leipzig, 1887.

——— *Hochschulreform und Soziologie: Kritische Anmerkungen über Beckers "Gedanken zur Hochschulreform" und Belows "Soziologie als Lehrfach,"* Vermehrter Sonder-Abdruck aus dem *Weltwirtschaftlichen Archiv,* vol. XVI, Jena, 1920.

────── "Die Krisis des Reichsgedankens," *Die neue Rundschau,* 19 (1908): 518–528.

────── *Der Nietzsche-Kultus: Eine Kritik,* Leipzig, 1897.

────── "Troeltsch und die Philosophie der Geschichte," *Schmollers Jahrbuch,* 49 (1925): 147–191.

────── *Das Wesen der Soziologie: Vortrag gehalten in der Gehe-Stiftung zu Dresden am 12. Januar 1907,* Neue Zeit- und Streitfragen, Gehestiftung, 4th annual series, no. 3, Dresden, 1907.

Troeltsch, Ernst, *Die Bedeutung der Geschichte für die Weltanschauung,* Geschichtliche Abende im Zentralinstitut für Erziehung und Unterricht, 10, Berlin, 1918.

────── *Demokratie,* Sonderabdruck aus dem *Kunstwart und Kulturwart,* vol. 32, Schriften des Demokratischen Studentenbundes Berlin, Berlin, 1919.

────── *Deutscher Geist und Westeuropa: Gesammelte kulturphilosophische Aufsätze und Reden,* Hans Baron, ed., Tübingen: Mohr, 1925.

────── *Die Dynamik der Geschichte nach der Geschichtsphilosophie des Positivismus,* Philosophische Vorträge, veröffentlicht von der Kant-Gesellschaft, 23, Berlin, 1919.

────── *Gesammelte Schriften,* vol. IV: *Aufsätze zur Geistesgeschichte und Religionssoziologie,* ed. Hans Baron, Tübingen: Mohr, 1925.

────── *Der Historismus und seine Probleme,* vol. I: *Das logische Problem der Geschichtsphilosophie (Gesammelte Schriften,* vol. III), Tübingen: Mohr, 1922.

────── "Die Krisis des Historismus," *Die neue Rundschau,* 33 (1922): 572–590.

────── *Der Kulturkrieg: Rede am 1. Juli 1915,* Deutsche Reden in schwerer Zeit, 27, Berlin, 1915.

────── *Nach Erklärung der Mobilmachung,* Rede gehalten bei der von Stadt und Universität einberufenen vaterländischen Versammlung am 2. August 1914, Heidelberg, 1914.

────── "Die Revolution in der Wissenschaft," *Schmollers Jahrbuch,* 45 (1921): 1001–1030.

────── *Spektator-Briefe: Aufsätze über die deutsche Revolution und die Weltpolitik 1918–22,* Hans Baron, ed., Tübingen: Mohr, 1924.

────── *Das Wesen des Deutschen: Rede gehalten am 6. Dezember 1914 in der Karlsruher Stadthalle,* Heidelberg, 1915.

Vierkandt, Alfred, "Programm einer formalen Gesellschaftslehre," *Kölner Vierteljahrshefte für Sozialwissenschaften,* 1 (1921): 56–66.

────── "Sozialgeist und Sozialethik der Gegenwart," *Deutsche Rundschau,* 220 (1929): 1–10, 141–148.

────── *Die sozialpädagogische Forderung der Gegenwart,* Sozialpädagogische Abende im Zentralinstitut für Erziehung und Unterricht, 1, Berlin, 1920.

Vossler, Karl, "Nationalliteratur und Weltliteratur," *Zeitwende,* 1 (1928): 13.

———— *Politik und Geistesleben: Rede zur Reichsgründungsfeier im Januar 1927 und drei weitere Ansprachen*, Münchener Universitätsreden, 8, Munich, 1927.

———— *Positivismus und Idealismus in der Sprachwissenschaft*, Heidelberg, 1904.

———— *Die romanischen Kulturen und der deutsche Geist*, Munich, 1926.

———— *Die Universität als Bildungsstätte*, Vortrag gehalten im Deutschen Studentenbund in München am 15. Dezember 1922, Munich, 1923.

Wagner, Adolph, *Agrar- und Industriestaat: Eine Auseinandersetzung mit den Nationalsozialen und mit Professor L. Brentano über die Kehrseite des Industriestaats und zur Rechtfertigung agrarischen Zollschutzes*, Jena, 1901.

———— *Die akademische Nationalökonomie und der Sozialismus*, Rede zum Antritt des Rectorats der Königlichen Friedrich-Wilhelms-Universität in Berlin gehalten in der Aula am 15. Oktober 1895, Berlin, 1895.

———— *Die Entwicklung der Universität Berlin, 1810–1896*, Rectoratsrede, Berlin, 1896.

———— *Staatsbürgerliche Bildung*, Adolf Damaschke, ed., Soziale Zeitfragen: Beiträge zu den Kämpfen der Gegenwart, 59, Berlin: Verlag "Bodenreform," 1915.

Weber, Adolf, *Arbeitskämpfe oder Arbeitsgemeinschaft*, Recht und Staat in Geschichte und Gegenwart, 48, Tübingen, 1927.

———— *Die Aufgaben der Volkswirtschaftslehre als Wissenschaft*, Tübingen, 1909.

———— *Das Ende des Kapitalismus? Die Notwendigkeit freier Erwerbswirtschaft*, 2nd ed., Munich: M. Hueber, 1929.

———— *Sozialpolitik: Reden und Aufsätze*, Munich, 1931.

Weber, Alfred, "Die Bureaukratisierung und die gelbe Arbeiterbewegung," *Archiv für Sozialwissenschaft und Sozialpolitik*, 37 (1913): 361–379.

———— "Deutschland und der Osten," *Die neue Rundschau*, 33 (1922): 337–345.

———— *Deutschland und die europäische Kulturkrise*, Berlin: S. Fischer, 1924.

———— *Deutschland und Europa 1848 und heute*, Die Paulskirche, 1, Frankfurt, 1923.

———— *Das Ende der Demokratie? Ein Vortrag*, Berlin, 1931.

———— *Gedanken zur deutschen Sendung*, Sammlung von Schriften zur Zeitgeschichte, Berlin, 1915.

———— *Ideen zur Staats- und Kultursoziologie*, Alfred Weber, ed., Probleme der Staats- und Kultursoziologie, 1, Karlsruhe: G. Braun, 1927.

———— *Die Krise des modernen Staatsgedankens in Europa*, Stuttgart: Deutsche Verlagsanstalt, 1925.

———— "Neuorientierung in der Sozialpolitik," *Archiv für Sozialwissenschaft und Sozialpolitik*, 36 (1913): 1–13.

———— "Prinzipielles zur Kultursoziologie," *Archiv für Sozialwissenschaft und Sozialpolitik*, 47 (1920–21): 1–49.

Weber, Max, *From Max Weber: Essays in Sociology*, H. H. Gerth and C. Wright Mills, eds., New York: Oxford University Press, 1958.

—— *Gesammelte Aufsätze zur Wissenschaftslehre*, Tübingen: Mohr, 1922.

—— *Gesammelte politische Schriften*, 2nd ed., Johannes Winckelmann, ed., Tübingen: Mohr, 1958.

—— "Die sogenannte 'Lehrfreiheit' an den deutschen Universitäten," *Frankfurter Zeitung und Handelsblatt*, Sept. 20, 1908.

—— *Der Sozialismus*, Vienna, 1918.

—— *Wissenschaft als Beruf*, 2nd ed., Munich, Leipzig: Duncker und Humblot, 1921.

Wertheimer, Max, *Über Gestalttheorie: Vortrag gehalten in der Kantgesellschaft Berlin am 17. Dezember 1924*, Sonderdrucke des Symposion, 1, Erlangen, 1925.

Wiese, Leopold von, "Der Begriff und die Probleme der Volksbildung, soziologisch betrachtet," in L. v. Wiese, ed., *Soziologie des Volksbildungswesens: Schriften des Forschungsinstituts für Sozialwissenschaften in Köln*, I (1921), 3–45.

—— "Europa als geistige Einheit," in A. von Gleichen-Russwurm, et al., eds., *Der Leuchter: Weltanschauung und Lebensgestaltung* (Darmstadt: O. Riechl, 1919), pp. 51–77.

—— "Individualismus und Staatssozialismus," *Die Verhandlungen des dreiundzwanzigsten Evangelisch-sozialen Kongresses abgehalten in Essen vom 28. bis 30. Mai 1912*, nach dem stenographischen Protokoll (Göttingen, 1912), pp. 13–30.

—— *Politische Briefe über den Weltkrieg: Zwölf Skizzen*, Munich, 1914.

—— *Der Schriftsteller und der Staat*, Kleine Schriften des Forum-Verlags, 3, Berlin, Munich, 1918.

—— "Skizze des Aufbaus eines Systems der Beziehungslehre," *Kölner Vierteljahrshefte für Sozialwissenschaften*, 2 (1922): 61–69.

—— "Die Soziologie als Einzelwissenschaft," *Schmollers Jahrbuch*, 44 (1920): 347–367.

—— "Staatssozialismus," *Die neue Rundschau*, 27 (1916): 194–212.

—— *Standesentwicklung und Klassenbildung: Vortrag gehalten im Bund der technisch-industriellen Beamten*, Schriften des Bundes der technisch-industriellen Beamten, 4, Berlin, 1905.

—— *System der allgemeinen Soziologie als Lehre von den sozialen Gebilden der Menschen (Beziehungslehre)*, 2nd ed., Munich, Leipzig: Duncker und Humblot, 1933.

—— "Das Überpersönliche," *Die neue Rundschau*, 28 (1917): 433–445.

—— "Vom Liberalismus der Zukunft," *Die neue Rundschau*, 28 (1917): 865–874.

—— *Das Wesen der politischen Freiheit*, Tübingen, 1911.

Windelband, Wilhelm *Geschichtsphilosophie: Eine Kriegsvorlesung: Fragment aus dem Nachlass*, Wolfgang Windelband and Bruno Bauch, eds., Kantstudien: Ergänzungshefte, 38, Berlin, 1916.

—— *A History of Philosophy*, 2nd ed., New York, 1901.

—— *Die Philosophie im deutschen Geistesleben des 19. Jahrhunderts*, Tübingen: Mohr, 1927.

—— *Präludien: Aufsätze und Reden zur Einleitung in die Philosophie*, 3rd ed., Tübingen: Mohr, 1907.

—— *Der Wille zur Wahrheit*, Akademische Rede zur Erinnerung an den zweiten Gründer der Universität Karl Friedrich Grossherzog von Baden am 22. November 1909, Heidelberg, 1909.

Wundt, Wilhelm, *Die Nationen und ihre Philosophie: Ein Kapitel zum Weltkrieg*, 2nd ed., Leipzig, 1915.

—— *Die Psychologie im Kampf ums Dasein*, Leipzig, 1913.

—— *Über den wahrhaften Krieg*, Rede gehalten in der Alberthalle zu Leipzig am 10. September 1914, Leipzig, 1914.

NOTES

All translations from sources cited in German are my own.

Schmollers Jahrbuch stands for *Jahrbuch für Gesetzgebung, Verwaltung und Volkswirtschaft im Deutschen Reiche* and for its continuation under the title *Schmollers Jahrbuch für Gesetzgebung, Verwaltung und Volkswirtschaft im Deutschen Reich. Archiv* stands for *Archiv für soziale Gesetzgebung und Statistik* and for its continuation under the title *Archiv für Sozialwissenschaft und Sozialpolitik. Das akademische Deutschland*, vol. III, stands for Michael Doeberl, Otto Scheel, et al., *Das akademische Deutschland*, vol. III: *Die deutschen Hochschulen in ihren Beziehungen zur Gegenwartskultur*, Berlin: C. A. Weller, 1930.

Introduction

1. Karl Mannheim, *Ideology and Utopia: An Introduction to the Sociology of Knowledge*, trans. Louis Wirth and Edward Shils (New York, n.d. [1955]), p. 156.

Chapter One

1. J. H. Clapham, *The Economic Development of France and Germany, 1815–1914*, 4th ed. (Cambridge, Eng., 1955), pp. 82, 91, 278.

2. W. H. Bruford, *Germany in the Eighteenth Century: The Social Background of the Literary Revival* (Cambridge, Eng., 1959), pp. 247–253.

3. H. Völcker, ed., *Die Stadt Goethes: Frankfurt am Main im XVIII. Jahrhundert* (Frankfurt, 1932), pp. 85, 89–90. See also Ernst Kohn-Bramstedt, *Aristocracy and the Middle-Classes in Germany: Social Types in German Literature, 1830–1900* (London, 1937), pp. 24–25.

4. W. H. Bruford, *Culture and Society in Classical Weimar, 1775–1806* (Cambridge, Eng., 1962), esp. pp. 53–73, 428–431.

5. *Allgemeines Landrecht für die preussischen Staaten*, pt. II, titles VII–X.

6. A book which has greatly influenced my whole argument is Hans Rosenberg, *Bureaucracy, Aristocracy and Autocracy: The Prussian Experience, 1660–1815* (Cambridge, Mass., 1958). See also Bruford, *Germany*, pp. 266–269.

7. Standard works on the subject of this paragraph: Karl Biedermann, *Deutschland im Achtzehnten Jahrhundert*, vol. II: *Deutschlands geistige, sittliche und gesellige Zustände im Achtzehnten Jahrhundert*, pt. I: *Bis zur Thronbesteigung Friedrichs des Grossen*, 2nd ed. (Leipzig, 1880), pp. 269–434; Friedrich Paulsen, *Geschichte des gelehrten Unterrichts auf den deutschen Schulen und Universitäten vom Ausgang des Mittelalters bis zur Gegenwart*, 2nd ed., I (Leipzig, 1896), 511–550.

8. Biedermann, *Bis zur Thronbesteigung*, p. 428.

9. For this and the following, see Fritz Hartung, *Deutsche Verfassungsgeschichte vom 15. Jahrhundert bis zur Gegenwart*, 2nd ed. (Leipzig, 1922), pp. 74–77; Otto Hintze, *Die Hohenzollern und ihr Werk: Fünfhundert Jahre vaterländischer Geschichte*, 9th ed. (Berlin, 1916), pp. 349–352, 395–400; Rosenberg, *Bureaucracy*, pp. 46–56.

10. For much of the following: Paulsen, *Geschichte des Unterrichts*, 3rd ed., suppl. by Rudolf Lehmann, II (Berlin, 1921), 9–315; Franz Schnabel, *Deutsche Geschichte im neunzehnten Jahrhundert*, vol. I: *Die Grundlagen*, 4th ed. (Freiburg, 1948).

11. Paulsen, *Geschichte des Unterrichts*, II, 192–205.

12. Bruford, *Germany*, p. 235.

13. The passage is cited (in translation) in Kuno Francke, *A History of German Literature as Determined by Social Forces* (New York, 1916), pp. 375–358.

14. Along with Bruford, *Germany*, Paulsen, *Geschichte des Unterrichts*, and Schnabel, *Grundlagen*, see: W. Windelband, *A History of Philosophy*, trans. James H. Tufts, 2nd ed. (New York, 1901), pp. 529–622; Hajo Holborn, "Der deutsche Idealismus in sozialgeschichtlicher Beleuchtung," *Historische Zeit-*

schrift 174 (1952): 359–384; Wilhelm Roessler, *Die Entstehung des modernen Erziehungswesens in Deutschland* (Stuttgart, 1961); Frederic Lilge, *The Abuse of Learning: The Failure of the German University* (New York, 1948), pp. 1–56.

15. Rosenberg, *Bureaucracy*, pp. 202–228; Franz Schnabel, *Deutsche Geschichte im neunzehnten Jahrhundert*, vol. II; *Monarchie und Volkssouveränität*, 2nd ed. (Freiburg, 1949), pp. 198–199.

16. Cited in Rosenberg, *Bureaucracy*, p. 208.

17. Selections from the *Allgemeines Landrecht* are translated in R. R. Palmer, *The Age of the Democratic Revolution: A Political History of Europe and America, 1760–1800*, vol. I: *The Challenge* (Princeton, 1959), pp. 509–512. Comments in Roessler, *Erziehungswesen*, pp. 232–233.

18. Erich Wende, *Grundlagen des preussischen Hochschulrechts* (Berlin, 1930), pp. 23–26, quotes and comments upon pt. II, title XII, paragraphs 1, 2, 67, and 68 of the code, which remained basic for the universities.

19. *Die Idee der deutschen Universität: Die fünf Grundschriften aus der Zeit ihrer Neubegründung durch klassischen Idealismus und romantischen Realismus* (Darmstadt, 1956).

20. Schnabel, *Die Grundlagen*, pp. 408–457; Paulsen, *Geschichte des Unterrichts*, II, 278–315; W. Lexis, ed., *Die Reform des höheren Schulwesens in Preussen* (Halle, 1902), pp. 1–6.

21. Berlin statutes reprinted in Max Lenz, *Geschichte der Königlichen Friedrich-Wilhelms-Universität zu Berlin* (Halle, 1910), IV, 223–263.

22. As in the case of Bonn; see Friedrich von Bezold, *Geschichte der Rheinischen Friedrich-Wilhelms-Universität* (Bonn, 1920), I, 99–100. Other later foundings: Strassburg, Frankfurt, Hamburg, Cologne. Moves, refoundings, or statutory changes: Munich, Tübingen, and Münster. In all these cases, at least, there was room for influence of Berlin model.

23. Friedrich Paulsen, *Die deutschen Universitäten und das Universitätsstudium* (Berlin, 1902), pp. 88–91; W. Lexis, ed., *Das Unterrichtswesen im Deutschen Reich*, vol. II: *Die höheren Lehranstalten und das Mädchenschulwesen im Deutschen Reich* (Berlin, 1904), pp. 4–12; Gerhardt Giese, ed., *Deutsche Schulgesetzgebung* (Langensalza, n.d.[1932?]), pp. 3–15, 63–144, which includes reprint of the unsuccessful Süvern Draft of 1819.

24. Paulsen, *Geschichte des Unterrichts*, II, 327–362, 406–442, 546–555; Lexis, *Reform*, pp. 7–9.

25. Paulsen, *Geschichte des Unterrichts*, II, 323–327, 459–473, 556.

26. R. Hinton Thomas, *Liberalism, Nationalism and the German Intellectuals, 1822–1847* (Cambridge, Eng., 1951), pp. 51–119.

27. Paulsen, *Geschichte des Unterrichts*, II, 473, and II, 473–479 for the following; Alexander Busch, *Die Geschichte des Privatdozenten: Eine soziologische Studie zur grossbetrieblichen Entwicklung der deutschen Universitäten* (Stuttgart, 1959), pp. 53–57; Lexis, *Reform*, p. 10.

28. Paulsen, *Geschichte des Unterrichts*, II, 478, 491–501, 556–558.

29. *Ibid.*, pp. 558–569, 581–584; Lexis, *Reform*, pp. 11–17, 64–67.

30. W. Lexis, ed., *Das Unterrichtswesen im Deutschen Reich*, vol. IV: *Das technische Unterrichtswesen*, pt. I: *Die Technischen Hochschulen* (Berlin, 1904), pp. 3–15, 44–46. See also Paulsen, *Geschichte des Unterrichts*, II, 574–576, 698; Wilhelm Schlink, "Wesen und Gestaltung der deutschen Technischen Hochschulen," *Das akademische Deutschland*, III, 39–52.

31. General point and all quotes in this paragraph: Paulsen, *Geschichte des Unterrichts*, II, 500–501, 557–558, 569–570, 590, 683–687.

32. Basic secondary work: W. Lexis, ed., *Das Unterrichtswesen im Deutschen Reich*, vol. III: *Das Volksschulwesen und das Lehrerbildungswesen im Deutschen Reich* (Berlin, 1904).

33. Carl H. Becker, *Secondary Education and Teacher Training in Germany* (New York, 1931), p. 5.

34. *Ibid.*, pp. 6–8; Thomas Alexander, *The Training of Elementary Teachers in Germany* (New York, 1929), pp. 6–12.

35. Including rough estimate of living expenses at universities: Adolf Beier, ed., *Die höheren Schulen in Preussen (für die männliche Jugend) und ihre Lehrer*, 3rd ed. (Halle, 1909), pp. 1170–1171; Wilhelm Lexis, ed., *Die deutschen Universitäten* (Berlin, 1893), I, 162–164; Lexis, *Unterrichtswesen*, III, 170.

36. Basic secondary sources: Lexis, *Unterrichtswesen*, II, 4–109; Lexis, *Reform*, pp. 1–74.

37. Whole subject of examinations and *Berechtigungen*: Lexis, *Universitäten*, I, 83, 102–104; Lexis, *Unterrichtswesen*, II, 157–172; Paulsen, *Universitäten*, pp. 426–435; Lexis, *Reform*, pp. 1–34, 61–117, which includes historical background.

38. See note 37 above and W. Lexis, ed., *Das Unterrichtswesen im Deutschen Reich*, vol. I: *Die Universitäten im Deutschen Reich* (Berlin, 1904), pp. 52–57; I. Jastrow, "Promotionen und Prüfungen," *Das akademische Deutschland*, III, 219–244; Max Baumgart, *Grundsätze und Bedingungen zur Erlangung der Doctorwürde be allen Fakultäten der Universitäten des Deutschen Reichs* (Berlin, 1884).

39. Lexis, *Reform*, p. 16.

40. Max Weber, *Gesammelte politische Schriften*, 2nd ed., ed. Johannes Winckelmann (Tübingen, 1958), pp. 235–236.

41. Paulsen, *Universitäten*, pp. 149–150.

42. Basic on universities: Paulsen, *Universitäten*, pp. 83–335; Lexis, *Universitäten*, I, 3–168; Lexis, *Unterrichtswesen*, I, 39–57.

43. On the legal situation for Prussia see Walter Landé, *Preussisches Schulrecht: Kommentar* (Berlin, 1933), I, 1–5, 34–39; Conrad Bornhak, *Die Rechtsverhältnisse der Hochschullehrer in Preussen* (Berlin, 1901), esp. pp. 15–22. Arnold Köttgen, *Deutsches Universitätsrecht* (Tübingen, 1933), is more inclusive.

44. Lexis, *Unterrichtswesen*, I, 46; Paulsen, *Universitäten*, pp. 123–127. For ranks stated in military terms (and, for example, *"Cortège-Fähigkeit"*) for various states see Busch, *Geschichte des Privatdozenten*, p. 143.

45. *Ibid.*, pp. 21–23, 106–108; E. Th. Nauck, *Die Privatdozenten der Universität Freiburg i. Breisgau, 1818–1955* (Freiburg, 1956), pp. 139–144.

46. Paulsen, *Universitäten*, p. 101, cites *Norddeutsche Allgemeine Zeitung*, Dec. 5, 1901.

47. Ludwig Bernhard, *Akademische Selbstverwaltung in Frankreich und Deutschland: Ein Beitrag zur Universitätsreform* (Berlin, 1930).

48. On what follows see Lexis, *Unterrichtswesen*, I, 44–48; II, 222–223; III, 170. Paulsen, *Universitäten*, pp. 106–114; F. Eulenburg, *Der "akademische Nachwuchs": Eine Untersuchung über die Lage und die Aufgaben der Extraordinarien und Privatdozenten* (Leipzig, 1908), pp. 111, 134–135; Busch, *Geschichte des Privatdozenten*, pp. 99–101.

49. Paulsen, *Geschichte des Unterrichts*, II, 390.

50. Busch, *Geschichte des Privatdozenten*, pp. 147–148 as an example.

51. Population (46,707,000 for 1885 and 56,862,000 for 1901) and primary school enrollment (8,829,812 for 1901): *Statistisches Jahrbuch für das deutsche Reich*, 24 (1903): 2, 208. Figure of 7.5 million is my estimate on that basis. Primary education was practically universal according to the authoritative J. Conrad, *Das Universitätsstudium in Deutschland während der letzten 50 Jahre* (Jena, 1884), p. 181. Secondary school enrollment (without Alsace-Lorraine) was computed from Lexis, *Unterrichtswesen*, II, 178–183, 194, 196, 198, 201, 203–213. *Progymnasium* counted with gymnasium.

52. Hubert Graven, "Gliederung der heutigen Studentenschaft nach statistischen Ergebnissen," *Das akademische Deutschland*, III, 319.

53. Lexis, *Reform*, pp. 413, 416; Lexis, *Unterrichtswesen*, II, 185; Lexis, *Universitäten*, I, 127.

54. Lexis, *Reform*, p. 416.

55. Wilhelm Ruppel, *Über die Berufswahl der Abiturienten Preussens in den Jahren 1875–1899: Eine statistische Studie* (Fulda, 1904), p. 30.

56. Conrad, *Universitätsstudium*, pp. 49–50; J. Conrad, "Einige Ergebnisse der deutschen Universitätsstatistik," *Jahrbücher für Nationalökonomie und Statistik*, new series, 32 (Jena, 1906): 448.

57. Lexis, *Universitäten*, I, 140–141.

58. Franz Eulenburg, *Die Entwicklung der Universität Leipzig in den letzten hundert Jahren* (Leipzig, 1909), p. 205.

59. Helmuth Plessner, ed., *Untersuchungen zur Lage der deutschen Hochschullehrer*, vol. III: Christian von Ferber, *Die Entwicklung des Lehrkörpers der deutschen Universitäten und Hochschulen 1864–1954* (Göttingen, 1956), pp. 177–178.

60. Statistics in this section are from Clapham, *Economic Development*, pp. 278, 280–281, 283, 285; Gustav Stolper, *The German Economy, 1870–1940: Issues and Trends* (New York, 1940), pp. 38, 41–42.

61. Ernst Rudolf Huber, *Deutsche Verfassungsgeschichte seit 1789*, vol. II: *Der Kampf um Einheit und Freiheit 1830 bis 1850* (Stuttgart, 1960), pp. 610–611. On interpretation of these figures, originally compiled by Veit Valentin, see also Lenore O'Boyle, "Liberal Political Leadership in Germany, 1867–1884," *Journal of Modern History*, 28(1956): 345–346. Valentin's procedure reflects common German usage of "academic" to describe the university-educated, the mandarins.

62. Friedrich Zunkel, *Der rheinisch-westfälische Unternehmer, 1834–1879* (Cologne, 1962), p. 189.

63. L. Rosenbaum, *Herkunft und Beruf der deutschen Abgeordneten 1847–1919* (Frankfurt, 1923), p. 23.

64. O'Boyle, "Liberal Leadership," p. 341. See also p. 343.

65. Rosenbaum, *Herkunft und Beruf*, p. 23.

66. Bruno Gebhardt, *Handbuch der deutschen Geschichte*, vol. III: *Von der Französischen Revolution bis zum ersten Weltkrieg*, 8th ed., ed. Herbert Grundmann (Stuttgart, 1960), p. 305.

67. This and what follows is from Karl Demeter, *The German Officer Corps in Society and State, 1650–1945* (New York, 1965), pp. 22, 54, 89. See also p. 93.

68. The basic secondary work on this subject is Rudolf Lehmann, *Die pädagogische Bewegung der Gegenwart: Ihre Ursprünge und ihr Charakter* (Munich, 1922). See also *Die Pädagogik der Gegenwart in Selbstdarstellungen*, ed. Erich Hahn (Leipzig, 1926); Richard H. Samuel and R. Hinton Thomas, *Education and Society in Modern Germany* (London, 1945).

69. For the following see Paulsen, *Geschichte des Unterrichts*, II, 588–614, 715–772; Lexis, *Reform*, pp. vii–x, 18–34, 70–117.

70. *Die Verhandlungen der Konferenz zur Berathung von Fragen betreffend das höhere Unterrichtswesen in Preussen* (Berlin, 1891); Paulsen, *Geschichte des Unterrichts*, II, 18, 595–598.

71. Otto Schröder, *Aufnahme und Studium an den Universitäten Deutschlands* (Halle, 1908).

72. Arnold Sachse, *Friedrich Althoff und sein Werk* (Berlin, 1928), esp. pp. 48–63, 176–192; Paulsen, *Geschichte des Unterrichts*, II, 696–709.

73. Graven, "Gliederung der Studentenschaft," p. 318. I am told that the technical institutes were sometimes called "plumbers' academies" in German university circles even during the Weimar period. See also Willy Hellpach, *Wirken in Wirren: Lebenserinnerungen*, vol. I: *1877–1914* (Hamburg, 1948), pp. 492–493.

74. Max Dessoir, *Buch der Erinnerung* (Stuttgart, 1946), pp. 206–208; Friedrich Meinecke, *Erlebtes, 1862–1901* (Leipzig, 1941), p. 220; Busch, *Geschichte*

des Privatdozenten, pp. 66–68; Karl Jaspers, *Die Idee der Universität* (Berlin, 1923), p. 77.

75. Ulrich von Wilamowitz-Moellendorff, *Erinnerungen, 1848–1914* (Leipzig, 1928), pp. 294–300; Paulsen, *Universitäten,* pp. 102–103.

76. Sachse, *Althoff,* pp. 168–169. Similar but not identical figures in Paulsen, *Geschichte des Unterrichts,* II, 704.

77. Busch, *Geschichte des Privatdozenten,* pp. 61–105, reflects these anxieties in many anecdotes.

78. Max Oberbreyer, *Die Reform der Doctorpromotion: Statistische Beiträge* (Eisenach, 1878), esp. pp. 10–11, 146–155.

79. Graven, "Gliederung der Studentenschaft," p. 318.

80. E. Horn, *Kolleg und Honorar: Ein Beitrag zur Verfassungsgeschichte der deutschen Universitäten* (Munich, 1897); *Die akademische Laufbahn und ihre ökonomische Regelung: Ein Wort an die Regierung und an die Volksvertretung,* 2nd ed. (Berlin, 1895); Paulsen gives name of anonymous author as G. Runze in *Universitäten,* p. 112. See also Sachse, *Althoff,* pp. 202–211; Lexis, *Unterrichtswesen,* I, 43–47.

81. Paulsen, *Universitäten,* p. 113.

82. For this and what follows see Conrad, "Einige Ergebnisse," pp. 475–477; Busch, *Geschichte des Privatdozenten,* p. 76. See also Eulenburg, *Der "akademische Nachwuchs,"* p. 8.

83. Basic on this whole subject: Busch, *Geschichte des Privatdozenten,* pp. 109–135; Eulenburg, *Der "akademische Nachwuchs."*

84. *Ibid.,* pp. 80, 103–104, 118–119.

85. Nauck, *Privatdozenten der Universität Freiburg,* pp. 72–73.

86. Lexis, *Unterrichtswesen,* I, 51; Busch, *Geschichte des Privatdozenten,* pp. 114–115; *Die Actenstücke des Disciplinarverfahrens gegen den Privatdozenten Dr. Arons,* ed. Leo Arons (Berlin, 1900); I. Jastrow, *Die Stellung der Privatdozenten* (Berlin, 1896), pp. 46–55.

87. Nauck, *Privatdozenten der Universität Freiburg,* pp. 67–70, 145–147; Paulsen, *Geschichte des Unterrichts,* II, 705–710.

88. This impression is based on the autobiographical materials listed in the bibliography. Some striking examples are Dessoir, *Buch der Erinnerung,* pp. 167–218; Hellpach, *Wirken in Wirren,* I, 487–498; Friedrich Meinecke, *Strassburg, Freiburg, Berlin, 1901–1919: Erinnerungen* (Stuttgart, 1949), pp. 176–180; Gustav Radbruch, *Der innere Weg: Aufriss meines Lebens* (Stuttgart, 1951), pp. 75–76; Werner Weisbach, *Und alles ist zerstoben: Erinnerungen aus der Jahrhundertwende* (Vienna, 1937), pp. 160–179. Johannes Flach, *Der deutsche Professor der Gegenwart,* 2nd ed. (Leipzig, 1886), is probably an exaggerated account by a malcontent.

89. *Der Fall Valentin: Die amtlichen Urkunden,* ed. Felix Rachfahl (Munich, 1920), p. xii.

90. Conrad, "Einige Ergebnisse," p. 442. See also Lexis, *Reform*, pp. 412–413, 416–417; Lexis, *Unterrichtswesen*, II, 177–185, 218, 220.

91. Lexis, *Reform*, p. 413; Otto Boelitz, *Der Aufbau des preussischen Bildungswesens nach der Staatsumwälzung* (Leipzig, 1924), p. 160. *Progymnasium* and *Reformgymnasium* (1914) counted with gymnasium.

92. Conrad, "Einige Ergebnisse," p. 441.

93. Graven, "Gliederung der Studentenschaft," p. 319.

94. *Preussische Statistik*, vol. 204 (Berlin, 1908), p. 147 of text.

95. Eulenburg, *Entwicklung der Universität Leipzig*, p. 205.

96. Plessner, *Untersuchungen*, III, 177–178.

97. My groupings and calculations based on *Preussische Statistik*, vol. 204, pp. 154–155 of text.

98. Stolper, *German Economy*, p. 107.

99. *Ibid.*, p. 151.

100. For good discussion of this problem see Rudolf Meerwarth, Adolf Günther and W. Zimmermann, *Die Einwirkungen des Krieges auf Bevölkerungsbewegung, Einkommen und Lebenshaltung in Deutschland (Wirtschafts- und Sozialgeschichte des Weltkrieges. Deutsche Serie*, general editor James T. Shotwell; Stuttgart, 1932). See esp. Adolf Günther, "Die Folgen des Krieges für Einkommen und Lebenshaltung der mittleren Volksschichten Deutschlands," pp. 99–279.

101. This has been something of a tradition in twentieth-century Germany. See for example Alfred Weber, *Die Not der geistigen Arbeiter* (Munich, 1923), p. 47.

102. On this, see Georg Schreiber, *Die Not der deutschen Wissenschaft und der geistigen Arbeiter* (Leipzig, 1923); Weber, *Not der geistigen Arbeiter*, pp. 5–6, 16–23.

103. Friedrich Schmidt-Ott, "Notgemeinschaft der Deutschen Wissenschaft," *Das akademische Deutschland*, III, 603–618; Karl Griewank, *Staat und Wissenschaft im Deutschen Reich: Zur Geschichte und Organisation der Wissenschaftspflege in Deutschland* (Freiburg, 1927), pp. 38–81.

104. Schreiber, *Not der Wissenschaft*, pp. 41–42; *Das akademische Deutschland*, III, 213, 344–345, 457; Walter Schöne, *Die wirtschaftliche Lage der Studierenden an der Universität Leipzig* (Leipzig, 1920); Nauck, *Privatdozenten der Universität Freiburg*, pp. 55–58.

105. *Ibid.*, p. 38.

106. For this and the following: Weber, *Not der geistigen Arbeiter*, pp. 41–48, 52–53.

107. Griewank, *Staat und Wissenschaft*, p. 96; *Mitteilungen des Verbandes der Deutschen Hochschulen*, ed. K. Voigt (Halle), II(1922), 247–266; III(1923), 59; V(1925), 52–53; VII(1927), 99.

108. All enrollment figures in this paragraph given to nearest 1000: Graven, "Gliederung der Studentenschaft," p. 318.

109. Otto Baumgarten, *Die Not der akademischen Berufe nach dem Friedensschluss* (Tübingen, 1919). See also Walter M. Kotschnig, *Unemployment in the Learned Professions* (London, 1937).

110. Carl Dreyfuss, *Occupation and Ideology of the Salaried Employee*, trans. E. Abramovitch (New York, 1938), pp. 288–298.

111. Graven, "Gliederung der Studentenschaft," p. 339.

112. Meerwarth, *Einwirkungen des Krieges*, p. 258.

113. Robert Michels, *Umschichtungen in den herrschenden Klassen nach dem Kriege* (Stuttgart, 1934), p. 80. See also pp. 58–85, which are generally relevant to my argument.

114. Johannes Hohlfeld, ed., *Dokumente der Deutschen Politik und Geschichte von 1848 bis zur Gegenwart*, vol. III: *Die Weimarer Republik 1919–1933* (Berlin, n.d. [1951]), pp. 20–22, 99, 104–108, 124–125. For analysis and political background, see Thomas Alexander and Beryl Parker, *The New Education in the German Republic* (New York, 1929), pp. 3–11; G. Wolff, *Grundschulfragen und Grundschulgegner* (*Schulpolitik und Volksbildung: Schriftenreihe des Preussischen Lehrervereins*, 9; Osterwieck-Harz, 1923), pp. 13–19.

115. Hertha Köllner, *Das Schulprogramm der deutschen Sozialdemokratie* (Langensalza, 1920), pp. 31–57.

116. The articles of the Constitution which in any way pertain to education are those numbered 10, 109, 120, 142–150, and 174; Hohlfeld, *Dokumente*, III, 62, 79, 81, 85–86, 91. For history of the negotiations and comments see Walter Landé, *Die Schule in der Reichsverfassung* (Berlin, 1929), esp. pp. 27–48; Johannes Hoffmann, *Schule und Lehrer in der Reichsverfassung: Ein Kommentar* (Stuttgart, 1921).

117. *Die Reichsschulkonferenz in ihren Ergebnissen*, ed. Zentralinstitut für Erziehung und Unterricht Berlin (Leipzig, n.d.[1920]), pp. 164–165.

118. C. H. Becker, *Gedanken zur Hochschulreform*, 2nd ed. (Leipzig, 1920); Konrad Haenisch, *Staat und Hochschule: Ein Beitrag zur nationalen Erziehungsfrage* (Berlin, 1920); Konrad Haenisch, *Neue Bahnen der Kulutrpolitik: Aus der Reformpraxis der deutschen Republik* (Berlin, 1921); *Die Statuten der preussischen Universitäten und Technischen Hochschulen*, vol. I: *Die grundlegenden Erlasse der Staatsregierung*, ed. Otto Benecke (Berlin, 1929), pp. 9–18.

119. *Ibid.*, p. 11.

120. *Ibid.*, pp. 13–18.

121. *Zentralblatt für die gesamte Unterrichtsverwaltung in Preussen*, 63 (1921): 8–12.

122. Haenisch, *Staat und Hochschule*, pp. 108–111.

123. Konrad Weiss, "Bemerkungen zu den bisherigen Verhandlungen über

das Reichsschulgesetz," *Die Hilfe*, 19 (October 1923): 340–342; Walter Landé, ed., *Aktenstücke zum Reichsvolksschulgesetz* (Leipzig, 1928).

124. Wolff, *Grundschulfragen*, pp. 1–33; Leonhard Froese, ed., *Deutsche Schulgesetzgebung, 1763–1952* (Weinheim, n.d.[1953]), pp. 86–88, for this and the following.

125. Alfred Pottag, ed., *Die Bestimmungen über die Volks- und Mittelschule und über die Ausbildung und die Prüfungen der Lehrer und Lehrerinnen in Preussen*, 25th ed. (Berlin, n.d.[1925]), pp. 1-12. Handbooks on other states are listed in the bibliography. Surveys: Fischer, "Entwicklung der Schulgesetzgebung"; Alexander and Parker, *The New Education*. Public pre-secondary schools (*Vorschulen*) had not existed in southern Germany even before 1918.

126. Eugen Löffler, *Das öffentliche Bildungswesen in Deutschland* (Berlin, 1931), pp. 139–141.

127. Erich Wende, *C. H. Becker: Mensch und Politiker* (Stuttgart, 1959).

128. Alfred Eckardt, *Der gegenwärtige Stand der neuen Lehrerbildung in den einzelnen Ländern Deutschlands und in ausserdeutschen Staaten* (Weimar, 1927), pp. 15–24; Fischer, "Entwicklung der Schulgesetzgebung," pp. 177–179.

129. For this and the following see Pottag, *Bestimmungen Volks- und Mittelschule*, pp. 334–343; Joseph Mayer, *Das höhere Unterrichtswesen in Bayern: Vorschriften-Sammlung* (Munich, 1928), p. 144.

130. Schröder, *Aufnahme und Studium*, p. 5.

131. Pottag, *Bestimmungen Volks- und Mittelschule*, pp. 29–33, 260–275.

132. Willy Hellpach, *Prägung: Zwölf Abhandlungen aus Lehre und Leben der Erziehung* (Leipzig, 1928), pp. 250–253.

133. *Die Neuordnung des preussischen höheren Schulwesens: Denkschrift des Preussischen Ministeriums für Wissenshaft, Kunst und Volksbildung* (Berlin, 1924).

134. Hans Richert, ed., *Richtlinien für die Lehrpläne der höheren Schulen Preussens* (Berlin, 1927).

135. Schröder, *Aufnahme und Studium*, pp. 6–7.

136. *Deutsche Hochschulstatistik*, vol. VII (summer semester, 1931). I compared figures for 1928–1932 and did not find higher ones.

137. *Das akademische Deutschland*, III, 330–331; Boelitz, *Aufbau des Bildungswesens*, p. 160.

138. Graven, "Gliederung der Studentenschaft," pp. 318–319.

139. Becker, *Secondary Education*, pp. 25–28.

140. *Das akademische Deutschland*, vol. I: *Die deutschen Hochschulen in ihrer Geschichte*, pp. 121–124, 199–204, 268–270.

141. Alexander and Parker, *The New Education*, pp. 215–242.

142. Hellmut Volkmann, *Die Deutsche Studentenschaft in ihrer Entwicklung seit 1919* (Leipzig, 1925); J. H. Mitgau, *Studentische Demokratie: Beiträge zur*

neueren Geschichte der Heidelberger Studentenschaft, 2nd ed. (Heidelberg, 1927); *Das akademische Deutschland,* III, 363–384, 451–498.

143. The states did attempt to control the lecture fee system and to lower some rates. They terminated the professors' customary right to set their own fees. But it is hard to see that these things made much difference. I. Jastrow, "Kollegiengelder und Gebühren," *Das akademische Deutschland,* III, 281–283.

144. Calculated on the basis of "active" faculty listed in *Minerva: Jahrbuch der gelehrten Welt,* vol. 23 (Strassburg, 1914) and vol. 30 (Berlin, 1930).

145. *Mitteilungen des Verbandes,* III (1923), 59–60; Dingler, "Privatdozententum," *Das akademische Deutschland,* III, 212–218.

146. Hans Gerber, *Der Wandel der Rechtsgestalt der Albert-Ludwigs-Universität zu Freiburg im Breisgau seit dem Ende der vorderösterreichischen Zeit,* II (Freiburg, n.d. [1952?]), 225–226; Mayer, *Höhere Unterrichtswesen in Bayern,* pp. 3–8; *Statuten der preussischen Universtitäten,* I, 30–41; VI, 5–48.

147. *Mitteilungen des Verbandes,* vol. IV (1924), p. 10. See also vol. II (1922), p. 105.

148. For the corporation's position on all these issues see Karl Brandi, "Vorbildungs und Zulassungsfragen," *Das akademische Deutschland,* III, 257–262; *Mitteilungen des Verbandes,* vol. I (1921), Suppl. 2, pp. 10–15, Suppl. 3, p. 49, vol. II (1922), pp. 104–105, vol. III (1923), p. 62, vol. IV (1924), pp. 8–10, 119–124, vol. V (1925), p. 51, vol. VII (1927), pp. 100, 114–116, vol. VIII (1928), pp. 44–48, vol. IX (1929), p. 105, vol. XII (1932), pp. 66–69.

149. *Ibid.,* vol. XII (1932), pp. 66–69.

150. *Ibid.,* vol. VII (1927), p. 100, vol. VIII (1928), p. 45.

151. *Ibid.,* vol. II (1922), p. 30, vol. I (1921), pp. 29–31, 144–148, Suppl. 3, p. 47, vol. II (1922), pp. 24–30, 42–44, vol. III (1923), p. 61.

152. *Ibid.,* vol. I (1921), p. 29.

153. Wilhelm Schlink, "Rektorenkonferenz und Verband der Deutschen Hochschulen," *Das akademische Deutschland,* III, 592.

154. See the comments of Werner Richter, "Staatliche Wissenschaftsverwaltung," *Das akademische Deutschland,* III, 619–630.

Chapter Two

1. The bibliography describes my general obligations. The lines of descent from Weber and from Troeltsch would make a fascinating study. Gerth's contribution: Hans Gerth, *Die sozialgeschichtliche Lage der bürgerlichen Intelligenz: Ein Beitrag zur Soziologie des deutschen Frühliberalismus* (diss., Frankfurt, 1935).

2. W. H. Bruford, *Culture and Society in Classical Weimar, 1775–1806* (Cam-

bridge, Eng., 1962), pp. 436–440; Wilhelm Roessler, *Die Entstehung des modernen Erziehungswesens in Deutschland* (Stuttgart, 1961), pp. 181–186, 332.

3. Karl Jaspers, *Die Idee der Universität* (Berlin, 1923), pp. 18, 9.

4. See Erich Franz, *Deutsche Klassik und Reformation* (Halle, 1937), pp. 377–402, for the religious influence.

5. Franz Rauhut, "Die Herkunft der Worte und Begriffe 'Kultur,' 'Civilisation' und 'Bildung,'" *Germanisch-Romanische Monatsschrift*, 3 (1953): 81–91.

6. Norbert Elias, *Über den Prozess der Zivilisation*, vol. I: *Wandlungen des Verhaltens in den weltlichen Oberschichten des Abendlandes* (Basel, 1939), pp. 1–64.

7. *Ibid.*, p. 8; Joseph Niedermann, *Kultur: Werden und Wandlungen des Begriffs und seiner Ersatzbegriffe von Cicero bis Herder* (Florence, 1941), pp. 218–219.

8. Wilhelm Windelband, *A History of Philosophy*, trans. James H. Tufts, 2nd ed. (New York, 1901), pp. 529–622; Wilhelm Windelband, *Präludien: Aufsätze und Reden zur Einleitung in die Philosophie*, 3rd ed. (Tübingen, 1907), esp. pp. 135–168. S. Körner, *Kant* (Hammondsworth, 1955), is a concise contemporary statement.

9. Windelband, *History of Philosophy*, p. 580.

10. Eduard Spranger, "Das Wesen der deutschen Universität," *Das akademische Deutschland*, III, 12.

11. Werner Jaeger, *Stellung und Aufgaben der Universität in der Gegenwart* (Berlin, 1924), p. 27.

12. The phrase quoted is a chapter title in Wilhelm Windelband, *Die Philosophie im deutschen Geistesleben des 19. Jahrhunderts* (Tübingen, 1927).

13. Roessler, *Entstehung des Erziehungswesens*.

14. *Wallensteins Tod*, act III, scene 13.

15. Max Weber, *Gesammelte Aufsätze zur Wissenschaftslehre* (Tübingen, 1922), p. 44. Mill's term was "the spiritual sciences."

16. Wilhelm Dilthey, *Pattern and Meaning in History: Thoughts on History and Society*, ed. H. P. Rickmann (New York, 1962).

17. The basic works on German historiography are the writings of Ernst Troeltsch and Friedrich Meinecke, which are cited in the bibliography. See also: Joseph Engel, "Die deutschen Universitäten und die Geschichtswissenschaft," *Historische Zeitschrift*, 189 (1959): 223–378; George G. Iggers, "The Dissolution of German Historism," Richard Herr and Harold T. Parker, eds., *Ideas in History: Essays Presented to Louis Gottschalk by His Former Students* (Durham, N.C., 1965), pp. 288–329.

18. Ernst Troeltsch, *Naturrecht und Humanität in der Weltpolitik: Vortrag bei der zweiten Jahresfeier der Deutschen Hochschule für Politik* (Berlin, 1923), pp. 13–14.

19. See "Wissenschaft," *Der Grosse Brockhaus*, 15th ed. (Leipzig, 1928–1935).

20. Windelband, *Präludien*, pp. 35–36.

21. *Die Idee der deutschen Universität: Die fünf Grundschriften aus der Zeit ihrer Neubegründung durch klassischen Idealismus und romantischen Realismus* (Darmstadt, 1956).

22. Spranger, "Wesen der Universität," p. 4.

23. C. H. Becker, *Vom Wesen der deutschen Universität* (Leipzig, 1925), pp. 1–24.

24. Reinhold Seeberg, "Hochschule und Weltanschauung," *Das akademische Deutschland*, III, 165, 166. See also Theodor Litt, *Wissenschaft, Bildung, Weltanschauung* (Berlin, 1928), p. 3.

25. This argument was very often repeated. For examples see Spranger, "Wesen der Universität," p. 16; Jaspers, *Idee der Universität*, pp. 44–45.

26. *Ibid.*, pp. 7–8, 44.

27. *Ibid.*, pp. 46, 47.

28. Litt, *Wissenschaft, Bildung, Weltanschauung*, pp. 12–13; Seeberg, "Hochschule und Weltanschauung," pp. 166–167; Jaspers, *Idee der Universität*, pp. 15, 44.

29. Georg Simmel, "Der Begriff und die Tragödie der Kultur," *Philosophische Kultur: Gesammelte Essais* (Leipzig, 1911), p. 248.

30. Jaspers, *Idee der Universität*, pp. 23–35, for this whole paragraph.

31. For this and the following see Spranger, "Wesen der Universität," pp. 1–38 and esp. pp. 13–14.

32. Jaspers, *Idee der Universität*, p. 11.

33. Jaeger, *Stellung und Aufgaben*, p. 9.

34. Adolph Wagner, *Die Entwicklung der Universität Berlin, 1810–1896: Rectoratsrede* (Berlin, 1896), p. 10.

35. Spranger, "Wesen der Universität," p. 3.

36. Jaspers, *Idee der Universität*, pp. 64–78.

37. Leonard Krieger, *The German Idea of Freedom: History of a Political Tradition* (Boston, 1957), p. 72.

38. Along with Krieger, see "Rechtsstaat," *Der Grosse Brockhaus*, 15th ed. (Leipzig, 1933).

39. The word stems from Fichte. My use of the term is based in part on Franz Schnabel, *Deutsche Geschichte im neunzehnten Jahrhundert*, vol. I: *Die Grundlagen*, 4th ed. (Freiburg, 1948), pp. 52, 296–299, 410–453.

40. His 1797 "Versuch, die Grenzen der Wirksamkeit des Staates zu bestimmen" is discussed in Schnabel, *Die Grundlagen*, pp. 291–293, and in Jacques Droz, *L'Allemagne et la Révolution Française* (Paris, 1949), pp. 297–309.

41. Friedrich Meinecke, *Weltbürgertum und Nationalstaat: Studien zur Genesis des deutschen Nationalstaates* (Munich, 1908).

42. Friedrich Meinecke, *Das Zeitalter der deutschen Erhebung, 1795–1815*, 3rd ed. (Bielefeld, 1924), p. 2.

43. Ernst Troeltsch, "Die deutsche Idee von der Freiheit," *Die neue Rundschau*, 27 (1916): 50–75; Ernst Troeltsch, *Das Wesen des Deutschen: Rede gehalten am 6. Dezember 1914 in der Karlsruher Stadthalle* (Heidelberg, 1915); Otto Hintze, Friedrich Meinecke, Hermann Oncken, and Hermann Schumacher, eds., *Deutschland und der Weltkrieg* (Leipzig, 1915), pp. 52–90, 617–643; Adolf von Harnack, Friedrich Meinecke, Max Sering, Ernst Troeltsch, and Otto Hintze, *Die deutsche Freiheit: Fünf Vorträge* (Gotha, 1917), pp. 14–39, 79–113.

44. Hajo Holborn, "Der deutsche Idealismus in socialgeschichtlicher Beleuchtung," *Historische Zeitschrift*, 174 (1952): 359–384.

45. Heinrich Rickert, *Über idealistische Politik als Wissenschaft* (Sonderabdruck aus *Die Akademie*; Erlangen, n.d. [1925?]).

46. Eduard Spranger, *Der deutsche Klassizismus und das Bildungsleben der Gegenwart*, 2nd ed. (Erfurt, 1928), p. 22.

47. Troeltsch, "Idee der Freiheit," pp. 71–72.

48. For interpretations of the Revolution of 1848 and its antecedents in the 1830's and 1840's see Schnabel, *Monarchie und Volkssouveränität*, pp. 123–173, 197–209; Krieger, *German Idea of Freedom*, pp. 229–329, 341–348; Rudolph Stadelmann, *Soziale und politische Geschichte der Revolution von 1848* (Munich, 1948).

49. The best collection of anecdotes, though not orderly, is Max von Boehn, *Biedermeier: Deutschland 1815–1847* (Berlin, 1922), esp. pp. 41–49, 352–364.

50. R. Hinton Thomas, *Liberalism, Nationalism and the German Intellectuals, 1822–1847* (Cambridge, Eng., 1951).

51. Paulsen, *Geschichte des Unterrichts*, II, 234, and (for the following) 316–327, 456–473.

52. Heinrich Heffter, *Die deutsche Selbstverwaltung im 19. Jahrhundert: Geschichte der Ideen und Institutionen* (Stuttgart, 1950), pp. 351–352.

Chapter Three

1. Eduard von Hartmann, *Tagesfragen* (Leipzig, 1896), pp. 25–44.

2. Friedrich Meinecke, *Politische Schriften und Reden*, ed. Georg Kotowski (Darmstadt, 1958), pp. 49–50.

3. *Ibid.*, pp. 51, 52.

4. Wolfgang J. Mommsen, *Max Weber und die deutsche Politik, 1890–1920* (Tübingen, 1959), esp. pp. 188–206; Max Weber, *Gesammelte politische Schriften*, Johannes Winckelmann, ed. (2nd ed., Tübingen, 1958).

5. Meinecke, *Politische Schriften*, p. 48.

6. *Ibid.*, p. 43; see also pp. 41, 54.

7. *Ibid.*, p. 59.

8. Friedrich Paulsen, "Parteipolitik und Moral," *Jahrbuch der Gehe-Stiftung zu Dresden*, VI (Dresden, 1901), 132–133.

9. Leopold von Wiese, "Vom Liberalismus der Zukunft," *Die neue Rundschau*, 28 (1917): 870.

10. Esra Bennathan, "Die demographische und wirtschaftliche Struktur der Juden," in Werner E. Mosse, ed., *Entscheidungsjahr 1932: Zur Judenfrage in der Endphase der Weimarer Republik* (Tübingen, 1965), pp. 87–131; Peter G. J. Pulzer, *The Rise of Political Anti-Semitism in Germany and Austria* (New York, 1964), pp. 3–15.

11. Wilhelm Ruppel, *Über die Berufswahl der Abiturienten Preussens in den Jahren 1875–1899: Eine statistische Studie* (Fulda, 1904), pp. 14–15; Hubert Graven, "Gliederung der Studentenschaft nach statistischen Ergebnissen," *Das akademische Deutschland*, III, 326–329.

12. Bennathan, "Demographische und wirtschaftliche Struktur"; E. G. Lowenthal, "Die Juden im öffentlichen Leben," in Mosse, *Entscheidungsjahr*, pp. 51–85; Ruppel, *Berufswahl*, pp. 20–21, 24, 32–33; Alexander Busch, *Die Geschichte des Privatdozenten* (Stuttgart, 1959), pp. 158–160.

13. *Ibid.*, p. 160.

14. Max Dessoir, *Buch der Erinnerung* (Stuttgart, 1946), pp. 156–157.

15. Busch, *Geschichte des Privatdozenten*, p. 160; Bernhard Breslauer, ed. for the Verband der Deutschen Juden, *Die Zurücksetzung der Juden an den Universitäten Deutschlands* (Berlin, 1911), pp. 6–7, 10–14.

16. Pulzer, *Rise of Political Anti-Semitism*; George L. Mosse, *The Crisis of German Ideology: Intellectual Origins of the Third Reich* (New York, 1964), esp. pp. 149–189, 190–203; Fritz Stern, *The Politics of Cultural Despair: A Study in the Rise of the German Ideology* (Berkeley, 1961).

17. Mildred S. Wertheimer, *The Pan-German League, 1890–1914* (New York, 1924), pp. 65–74; Alfred Kruck, *Geschichte des Alldeutschen Verbandes, 1890–1939* (Wiesbaden, 1954), pp. 16–18.

18. Eckart Kehr, *Schlachtflottenbau und Parteipolitik, 1894–1901: Versuch eines Querschnitts durch die innerpolitischen, sozialen und ideologischen Voraussetzungen des deutschen Imperialismus* (Berlin, 1930), pp. 343–348, 360–364.

19. Wolfgang Marienfeld, *Wissenschaft und Schlachtflottenbau in Deutschland, 1897–1906* (Suppl. 2 of *Marine Rundschau*; April, 1957); Abraham Ascher, "Professors as Propagandists: The Politics of the Kathedersozialisten," *Journal of Central European Affairs*, 23 (1963): 282–302.

20. Marienfeld, *Wissenschaft und Schlachtflottenbau*, p. 53.

21. *Ibid.*, p. 108; extensive lists of academic propagandists for naval expansion on pp. 109–115.

22. Schmoller, Dernburg, Delbrück, and others, *Reichstagsauflösung und Kolonialpolitik: Offizieller stenographischer Bericht*, Kolonialpolitisches Aktionskomite, ed. (Berlin, 1907), pp. 16, 17–18.

23. See above, Chapter One, note 87; Dieter Fricke, "Zur Militarisierung des deutschen Geisteslebens im wilhelminischen Kaiserreich: Der Fall Leo Arons," *Zeitschrift für Geschichtswissenschaft,* 8 (1960), 1069–1107.

24. Kurt Rossmann, *Wissenschaft, Ethik and Politik: Erörterung des Grundsatzes der Voraussetzungslosigkeit in der Forschung* (Heidelberg, 1949).

25. Max Weber, "Die sogenannte 'Lehrfreiheit' an den deutschen Universitäten," *Frankfurter Zeitung und Handelsblatt,* 53.262 (Sept. 20, 1908): 1. On the whole atmosphere see Ferdinand Tönnies and Friedrich Paulsen, *Briefwechsel 1876–1908,* ed. Olaf Klose, E. G. Jacoby, and I. Fischer (Kiel, 1961), pp. 324–328.

26. The best secondary accounts on what follows are Paul Mombert, *Geschichte der Nationalökonomie* (K. Diehl and P. Mombert, eds., *Grundriss zum Studium der Nationalökonomie,* vol. II; Jena, 1927), pp. 449–534; Theo Suranyi-Unger, *Die Entwicklung der theoretischen Volkswirtschaftslehre im ersten Viertel des 20. Jahrhunderts* (Jena, 1927), pp. 41–117; Joseph A. Schumpeter, *History of Economic Analysis,* ed. E. B. Schumpeter (New York, 1954), esp. pp. 800–820, 843–855.

27. The basic sources on this organization are Lujo Brentano, *Mein Leben im Kampf um die soziale Entwicklung Deutschlands* (Jena, 1931); Ascher, "Professors as Propagandists." A recent account, good as narrative, though not always convincing in its analysis is Dieter Lindenlaub, *Richtungskämpfe im Verein für Sozialpolitik* (Wiesbaden, 1967), see esp. I, 44–83.

28. Gustav Schmoller, "Wechselnde Theorien und feststehende Wahrheiten im Gebiete der Staats und Socialwissenschaften und die heutige deutsche Volkswirtschaftslehre," *Schmollers Jahrbuch,* 21 (1897): 1387–1408; Gustav Schmoller, *Zwanzig Jahre Deutscher Politik, 1897–1917: Aufsätze und Vorträge* (Munich, 1920), pp. 1–50; Gustav Schmoller, "Die Entstehung der deutschen Volkswirtschaft und der deutschen Sozialreform," *Schmollers Jahrbuch,* 39 (1915): 1609–1640; Adolph Wagner, *Die akademische Nationalökonomie und der Socialismus: Rede zum Antritt des Rektorats* (Berlin, 1895); Lujo Brentano, *Ethik und Volkswirtschaft in der Geschichte: Rede beim Antritt des Rektorats* (Munich, 1901).

29. For examples, see Lujo Brentano, *Die Stellung der Studenten zu den sozialpolitischen Aufgaben der Zeit* (Munich, 1897), esp. pp. 20–22; *Die Verhandlungen des achtzehnten Evangelisch-sozialen Kongresses, nach dem stenographischen Protokoll* (Göttingen, 1907), esp. pp. 17–31 (Schulze-Gävernitz's paper); Arthur Salz, *Die Rechtfertigung der Sozialpolitik: Ein Bekenntnis* (Heidelberg, 1914).

30. Brentano, *Ethik und Volkswirtschaft,* p. 36.

31. Adolph Wagner, *Agrar- und Industriestaat: Eine Auseinandersetzung mit den Nationalsozialen und mit Professor L. Brentano* (Jena, 1901).

32. Cited in Mombert, *Geschichte der Nationalökonomie,* p. 479.

33. Schmoller, *Zwanzig Jahre,* pp. 21–50; Brentano, *Mein Leben,* pp. 97–99.

34. Brentano, *Stellung der Studenten,* p. 21.

35. Lujo Brentano, *Reaktion oder Reform: Gegen die Zuchthausvorlage* (Berlin: Verlag der *Hilfe*, 1899); Lujo Brentano, *Über Syndikalismus und Lohnminimum: Zwei Vorträge* (Munich, 1913); Lujo Brentano, *Wahlprogramm der vereinigten Liberalen und Demokraten Bayerns*, for the Süddeutsche Verband nationalsozialer Vereine (Munich, n.d. [1904]).

36. I. Jastrow, *"Sozialliberal": Die Aufgaben des Liberalismus in Preussen*, 2nd ed. (Berlin, 1894).

37. Joseph Schumpeter, *Wie studiert man Sozialwissenschaft?*, 2nd ed. (*Schriften des Sozialwissenschaftlichen Akademischen Vereins in Czernowitz*, 2; Munich, 1915).

38. Werner Sombart, *Dennoch! Aus Theorie und Geschichte der gewerkschaftlichen Arbeiterbewegung* (Jena, 1900), for this and the following.

39. Werner Sombart, "Ideale der Sozialpolitik," *Archiv*, 10 (1897): 1–48.

40. Ludwig Bernhard, *Unerwünschte Folgen der deutschen Sozialpolitik* (Berlin, 1912).

41. Adolf Weber, *Die Aufgaben der Volkswirtschaftslehre als Wissenschaft* (Tübingen, 1909), pp. 75–76.

42. Schumpeter, *History of Economic Analysis*, pp. 815–819.

43. For comments on what follows see Talcott Parsons, "Capitalism in Recent German Literature," *Journal of Political Economy*, 37 (1929): 31–52.

44. Werner Sombart, "Der Anteil der Juden am Aufbau der modernen Volkswirtschaft," *Die neue Rundschau*, 21 (1910): 145–173; Werner Sombart, "Jüdischer Geist im modernen Wirtschaftsleben," *Die neue Rundschau*, 21 (1910): 585–615; Werner Sombart, "Der Bourgeois einst und jetzt," *Die neue Rundschau*, 24 (1913): 1481–1509. The first edition of Sombart's *Modern Capitalism* came out in 1902. He was revising his ideas for the later edition. For comments and a brief biography see F. X. Sutton, "The Social and Economic Philosophy of Werner Sombart: The Sociology of Capitalism," Harry Elmer Barnes, ed., *An Introduction to the History of Sociology* (Chicago, 1948), pp. 316–331.

45. Sombart, "Der Bourgeois einst," p. 1495.

46. Joseph Schumpeter, *Imperialism, Social Classes: Two Essays*, trans. Heinz Norden (New York, 1955), pp. 3–98. Arthur Salz, *Das Wesen des Imperialismus* (Leipzig, 1921), is a typical mandarin response to Schumpeter, which sees imperialism as the expression of national pride, not an atavism, useful as a counterweight to individualism and dangerous only in the extreme form preferred by the masses.

47. Max Weber, *Der Sozialismus* (Vienna, 1918).

48. Alfred Weber, "Der Beamte," *Die neue Rundschau*, 21 (1910): 1321–1339; Alfred Weber, "Die Bureaukratisierung und die gelbe Arbeiterbewegung," *Archiv*, 37 (1913): 361–379; Alfred Weber, "Neuorientierung in der Sozialpolitik," *Archiv*, 36 (1913): 1–13.

49. Leopold von Wiese, "Individualismus und Staatssozialismus," *Die Ver-*

handlungen des dreiundzwanzigsten Evangelisch-sozialen Kongresses, nach dem stenographischen Protokoll (Göttingen, 1912), p. 13.

50. Brentano, *Ethik und Volkswirtschaft*, pp. 39, 41.

51. Schumpeter, *History of Economic Analysis*, p. 805.

52. Heinrich Herkner, "Der Kampf um das sittliche Werturteil in der Nationalökonomie," *Schmollers Jahrbuch*, 36 (1912): 515–555; Lujo Brentano, "Über Werturteile in der Volkswirtschaftslehre," *Archiv*, 33 (1911): 695–714; Salz, *Rechtfertigung der Sozialpolitik*.

53. Barnes, *History of Sociology*, pp. 209–215. For fascinating Marxist analysis of German sociology as ideology see Georg Lucacz, "Die deutsche Soziologie vor dem ersten Weltkrieg," *Aufbau: Kulturpolitische Monatsschrift*, 2 (1946): 476–489; Georg Lucacz, "Die deutsche Soziologie zwischen dem ersten und dem zweiten Weltkrieg," *ibid.*, pp. 585–600.

54. For what follows, see Ferdinand Tönnies, *Gemeinschaft und Gesellschaft: Abhandlung des Communismus und des Socialismus als empirischer Culturformen* (Leipzig, 1887); Ferdinand Tönnies, "Gemeinschaft und Gesellschaft," in Alfred Vierkandt, ed., *Handwörterbuch der Soziologie* (Stuttgart, 1931), pp. 180–191; Ferdinand Tönnies, "Stände und Klassen," *ibid.*, pp. 617–638; Rudolf Heberle, "The Sociological System of Ferdinand Tönnies: 'Community' and 'Society,' " in Barnes, *History of Sociology*, pp. 227–248. *Gemeinschaft und Gesellschaft* was written before 1881. The first edition in 1887 attracted little notice. A second edition did not follow until 1912; but the third through seventh editions appeared in quick succession between 1912 and 1926. There is a translation: *Community and Society*, trans. Charles P. Loomis (East Lansing: Michigan State University Press, 1957).

55. Tönnies, *Gemeinschaft und Gesellschaft*, pp. 279–280, 288.

56. Tönnies, *Gemeinschaft und Gesellschaft*, p. 287.

57. See Ferdinand Tönnies, "Ferdinand Tönnies," Raymond Schmidt, ed., *Die Philosophie der Gegenwart in Selbstdarstellungen*, III (2nd ed.; Leipzig, 1924), 203–242; Ferdinand Tönnies, "Troeltsch und die Philosophie der Geschichte," *Schmollers Jahrbuch*, 49 (1925): 183–191.

58. Tönnies and Paulsen, *Briefwechsel*. See also Ferdinand Tönnies, "Die Krisis des Reichsgedankens," *Die neue Rundschau*, 19 (1908): 518–528.

59. Tönnies, "Troeltsch und die Philosophie," p. 189.

60. For the following: Ferdinand Tönnies, *Einführung in die Soziologie* (Stuttgart, 1931); Ferdinand Tönnies, *Das Wesen der Soziologie: Vortrag gehalten in der Gehe-Stiftung* (Neue Zeit- und Streitfragen, IV, 3; Dresden, 1907).

61. *Ibid.*, p. 28.

62. See Georg Simmel, "Das Problem der Sociologie," *Schmollers Jahrbuch*, 18 (1894): 1301–1307; Rudolf Heberle, "The Sociology of Georg Simmel: The Forms of Social Interaction," in Barnes, *History of Sociology*, pp. 249–273; Georg Sim-

mel, "Soziologie der Über- und Unterordnung," *Archiv*, 24 (1907): 477–546, esp. the concise definitions on p. 477.

63. Georg Simmel, "Über das Wesen der Sozial-Psychologie," *Archiv*, 26 (1908): 285–291.

64. An extreme example is Othmar Spann, "Klasse und Stand," *Handwörterbuch der Staatswissenschaften*, 4th ed., V (Jena, 1923), 692–705. Leopold von Wiese, *Standesentwicklung und Klassenbildung* (Berlin, 1905), is more sophisticated.

65. Max Weber, *From Max Weber: Essays in Sociology*, trans. and ed. H. H. Gerth and C. Wright Mills (New York: Oxford University Press, 1958), pp. 193–194.

66. *Ibid.*, pp. 200, 239, 240, 242–243, 416, 428, 436.

67. Ernst Troeltsch, *Nach Erklärung der Mobilmachung: Rede gehalten bei der von Stadt und Universität einberufenen vaterländischen Versammlung am 2. August 1914* (Heidelberg, 1914), pp. 9, 10.

68. Erich Marcks, *Wo stehen wir?* (Ernst Jaeckh, ed., *Der Deutsche Krieg*, 19; Stuttgart, 1914), p. 20.

69. The three paragraphs in order: *ibid.*, p. 27; Alois Riehl, *1813–Fichte–1914; Rede am 23. Oktober 1914* (*Deutsche Reden in schwerer Zeit*, 7; Berlin, 1914), p. 17; Johann Plenge, *Der Krieg und die Volkswirtschaft* (*Kriegsvorträge der Universität Münster i.W.*, 11/12; Münster, 1915), pp. 187–188.

70. Rudolf Kjellén, *Die Ideen von 1914: Eine weltgeschichtliche Perspektive* (*Zwischen Krieg und Frieden*, 29; Leipzig, 1915).

71. Rudolf Eucken, *Lebenserinnerungen: Ein Stück deutschen Lebens* (Leipzig, 1921), p. 99. See also Klaus Schwabe, "Zur politischen Haltung der deutschen Professoren im ersten Weltkrieg," *Historische Zeitschrift*, 193 (1961): p. 604.

72. Probably the most serious presentation of the German case is Otto Hintze, Friedrich Meinecke, Hermann Oncken, and Hermann Schumacher, eds., *Deutschland und der Weltkrieg* (Leipzig, 1915).

73. Ernst Troeltsch, *Der Kulturkrieg: Rede am 1. Juli 1915* (*Deutsche Reden in schwerer Zeit*, 27; Berlin, 1915).

74. *Erklärung der Hochschullehrer des Deutschen Reiches*, Berlin, Oct. 23, 1914. See also Kulturbund deutscher Gelehrter und Künstler, *Briefwechsel zwischen den Herren Yves Guyot und Daniel Bellet und Herrn Lujo Brentano*.

75. Marcks, *Wo stehen wir?*, p. 18.

76. Werner Sombart, *Händler und Helden: Patriotische Besinnungen* (Munich, 1915), pp. 64, 14.

77. *Ibid.*, pp. 19, 20.

78. Wilhelm Wundt, *Die Nationen und ihre Philosophie: Ein Kapitel zum Weltkrieg*, 2nd ed. (Leipzig, 1915).

79. *Ibid.*, pp. 49–56; Sombart, *Händler und Helden*, pp. 10-11, 20-22.

80. Adolf von Harnack, Friedrich Meinecke, Max Sering, Ernst Troeltsch, and Otto Hintze, *Die deutsche Freiheit: Fünf Vorträge* (Gotha, 1917).

81. Friedrich Meinecke, *Deutsche Kultur und Machtpolitik im englischen Urteil: Rede am 12. April 1915* (*Deutsche Reden in schwerer Zeit*, 29; Berlin, 1915), esp. pp. 25–27.

82. Alfred Weber, *Gedanken zur deutschen Sendung* (Berlin, 1915).

83. Sombart, *Händler und Helden*, p. 65.

84. *Ibid.*, p. 101.

85. *Ibid.*, p. vi.

86. Friedrich Meinecke, *Die deutsche Erhebung von 1914: Aufsätze und Vorträge*, 2nd ed. (Stuttgart, 1914); Heinrich Herkner, *Krieg und Volkswirtschaft: Rede am 26. Februar 1915* (*Deutsche Reden in schwerer Zeit*, 19; Berlin, 1915), esp. pp. 28–30; Plenge, *Krieg und Volkswirtschaft*, p. 189; Rudolf Eucken, *Die weltgeschichtliche Bedeutung des deutschen Geistes* (Ernst Jaeckh, ed., *Der Deutsche Krieg*, 8; Stuttgart, 1914); Paul Natorp, *Der Tag des Deutschen: Vier Kriegsaufsätze* (Hagen, 1915); Wundt, *Die Nationen*, pp. 131, 134–146; Riehl, *1813–Fichte–1914*, pp. 17, 20.

87. The best secondary sources on the subject are Schwabe, "Haltung der Professoren"; Fritz Fischer, *Griff nach der Weltmacht: Die Kriegszielpolitik des kaiserlichen Deutschland 1914/18*, 2nd ed. (Düsseldorf, 1962), pp. 178–202.

88. *Unabhängiger Ausschuss für einen Deutschen Frieden*, in the pamphlet collection at Bayerische Staatsbibliothek, Munich.

89. *Wortlaut der sich gegen Annexionen richtenden Delbrückschen Eingabe*, circulated by Unabhängiger Ausschuss, available at Bayerische Staatsbibliothek, Munich.

90. Mommsen, *Weber*, pp. 241–251, as an example.

91. Meinecke, *Politische Schriften*, p. 217.

92. *Ibid.*, pp. 214–215, 219.

93. It is fascinating to follow this process in *ibid.*, pp. 76–251.

94. Leopold von Wiese, "Staatssozialismus," *Die neue Rundschau*, 27 (1916): 194–212; Wiese, *Politische Briefe über den Welt-Krieg: Zwölf Skizzen* (Munich, 1914), pp. 79-85 and esp. pp. 84–85; Wiese, "Vom Liberalismus," pp. 865–874; Wiese, *Politische Briefe*, pp. 93–101.

95. Hans Delbrück, "Professor Below als Vorkämpfer der Vaterlandspartei," *Preussische Jahrbücher*, 172 (1918): 126–129.

96. Weber's growing bitterness during the war may be followed in Mommsen, *Weber*, pp. 207–279, and in Weber, *Politische Schriften*, pp. 109–191, 211–431.

97. *Ibid.*, pp. 212–213, 318, 285, 290, 150–151 for the five paragraphs. "Calculation" consistently italicized by Weber.

Chapter Four

1. Bonn's pamphlet *Sozialisierung* (Munich, n.d. [1919]) was published by the *Verlagsabteilung der Deutschen Volkpartei*. Georg Kerschensteiner (prewar *Freisinn*) may also have voted People's Party in Bavaria.

2. S. D. Stirk, *German Universities through English Eyes* (London, 1946), p. 29, claims (without source citation) that "in the state of Baden, after fourteen years of government by Social Democrats, there were in the universities of Heidelberg and Freiburg and at the Technische Hochschule at Karlsruhe, only three professors who were Social Democrats." This seems very plausible. At Berlin, Freiburg, Heidelberg, and Munich, I found Radbruch, Lederer, Aster, and Mannheim, plus (on a lower level of distinction) the Marxist theoretician Heinrich Cunow and the party historian August Müller. In his *Neue Bahnen der Kulturpolitik* (Berlin, 1921), Konrad Haenisch mentioned Cunow and Müller together with five other men as Social Democrats who had been called to Prussian universities and technical institutes between 1918 and 1921, when there was some incentive to make Social Democratic appointments.

3. The most important primary and secondary sources on modernist politics during the Weimar period are Friedrich Meinecke, *Politische Schriften und Reden*, ed. Georg Kotowski (Darmstadt, 1958), pp. 254–401; Friedrich Meinecke, *Nach der Revolution: Geschichtliche Betrachtungen über unsere Lage* (Munich, 1919); Ernst Troeltsch, *Spektator-Briefe: Aufsätze über die deutsche Revolution und die Weltpolitik 1918/1922*, Hans Baron, ed. (Tübingen, 1924); Max Weber, *Gesammelte Politische Schriften*, 2nd ed. Johannes Winckelmann (Tübingen, 1958), pp. 436–548; Waldemar Besson, "Friedrich Meinecke und die Weimarer Republik," *Vierteljahrshefte für Zeitgeschichte*, 7 (1959): 113–129; Eric C. Kollman, "Eine Diagnose der Weimarer Republik: Ernst Troeltschs politische Anschauungen," *Historische Zeitschrift*, 182 (1956): 291–319; Wolfgang J. Mommsen, *Max Weber und die deutsche Politik, 1890–1920* (Tübingen, 1959), pp. 280–367.

4. Wilhelm Kahl, Friedrich Meinecke, and Gustav Radbruch, *Die deutschen Universitäten und der heutige Staat* (Tübingen, 1926), pp. 38–39 for the resolution. Troeltsch had died in 1923, Max Weber in 1920.

5. Troeltsch, *Spektator-Briefe*, p. 52, p. v (Meinecke speaking); Meinecke, *Politische Schriften*, p. 282. On monarchist sentiments among modernists, see also *ibid.*, p. 406.

6. *Ibid.*, p. 412.

7. Meinecke, *Nach der Revolution*, p. 44.

8. Hans Delbrück, *Ludendorffs Selbstporträt* (Berlin, 1922); Hans Delbrück, *Kautsky und Harden* (Berlin, 1920); Hans Delbrück, "Der Stand der Kriegs-

schuldfrage," *Zeitschrift für Politik*, 13 (1924): 293–319. Weber, *Politische Schriften*, pp. 476–485, is the best modernist statement on war guilt.

9. Bonn, *Sozialisierung*; Max Weber, *Der Sozialismus* (Vienna, 1918); Joseph Schumpeter, "Sozialistische Möglichkeiten von heute," *Archiv*, 48 (1921): 305–360.

10. Ernst von Aster, *Marx und die Gegenwart* (Tübingen, 1929).

11. Meinecke, *Politische Schriften*, p. 409.

12. Troeltsch, *Spektator-Briefe*, pp. 90–91, 139.

13. Karl Vossler, *Politik und Geistesleben (Münchener Universitätsreden*, 8; Munich, 1927), pp. 4, 8.

14. Gerhard Anschütz, *Drei Leitgedanken der Weimarer Reichsverfassung* (Tübingen, 1923), p. 31.

15. With Bonn, the notion functions as an unstated category. With Weber, it is explicit: Alfred Weber, *Die Krise des modernen Staatsgedankens in Europa* (Stuttgart, 1925); M. J. Bonn, *Die Krisis der europäischen Demokratie* (Munich, 1925); M. J. Bonn, *Die Auflösung des modernen Staates* (Berlin, 1921); M. J. Bonn, "Die wahre Weltrevolution," *Die neue Rundschau*, 34 (1923): 385–394.

16. Max Weber, *Politische Schriften*, pp. 486–489; Mommsen, *Weber*, pp. 333–386, which is not confined to Weber; Meinecke, *Politische Schriften*, p. 432.

17. Examples: Meinecke, *Politische Schriften*, pp. 446–452; Alfred Weber, *Das Ende der Demokratie? Ein Vortrag* (Berlin, 1931); Robert Holtzmann, *Reichsverfassung und Gegenwart: Rede 9. Juli 1932, Universität zu Berlin* (Berlin, 1932); Willy Helpach, *Politische Prognose für Deutschland* (Berlin, 1928), pp. 118–203.

18. Hermann Oncken, *Unser Reich: Rede bei der Gedächtnisfeier zur Wiederkehr des Tages der Reichsgründung* (Heidelberg, 1921), p. 21; Meinecke, *Nach der Revolution*, p. 63; Troeltsch, *Spektator-Briefe*, p. 310; Alfred Weber, "Geist und Politik," *Die neue Rundschau*, 37 (1926): p. 341.

19. Meinecke, *Nach der Revolution*, pp. 70–71; Meinecke, *Politische Schriften*, pp. 403, 387.

20. *Ibid.*, p. 403.

21. For this and the following, see Meinecke, *Nach der Revolution*, pp. 63–66; Ernst Troeltsch, *Demokratie: Sonderabdruck aus dem Kunstwart und Kulturwat (Schriften des Demokratischen Studentenbundes Berlin*; Berlin, 1919), pp. 9-10.

22. Meinecke, *Politische Schriften*, p. 412.

23. For this and the following see Ernst Troeltsch, "Deutsche Bildung," Ernst Troeltsch, *Deutscher Geist und Westeuropa: Gesammelte kulturphilosophische Aufsätze und Reden*, ed. Hans Baron (Tübingen, 1925), pp. 169–210; Meinecke, *Politische Schriften*, pp. 389–392.

24. Hans Delbrück, "Von der Bismarck-Legende," *Historische Zeitschrift*, 133 (1925-1926): 69–82.

25. Ernst Cassirer, *Die Idee der republikanischen Verfassung: Rede zur Verfassungsfeier am 11. August 1928* (Hamburg, 1929), p. 31. See also Troeltsch, *Demokratie*, p. 10.

26. *Rektorwechsel an der Friedrich-Wilhelms-Universität zu Berlin am 15. Oktober 1919* (Berlin, 1919), p. 21; Carl Neumann, *Vom Glauben an eine kommende nationale Kunst* (Heidelberg, 1919); p. 3; Michael Doeberl, *Sozialismus, soziale Revolution, sozialer Volksstaat* (Munich, 1920), p. 98; Eduard Meyer, *Rede zur Gedächtnisfeier des Stifters der Berliner Universität König Friedrich Wilhelm III, 3. August 1920* (Berlin, 1920), p. 31.

27. Gustav Roethe, *Festrede des Geheimen Regierungsrates Professor Dr. Gustav Roethe gehalten zur Bismarck-Gedenkfeier in der Singakademie zu Berlin am 11. April 1920* (Berlin, n.d. [1920]), p. 11; Karl Alexander von Müller, *Deutsche Geschichte und deutscher Charakter* (Stuttgart, 1926), p. 161; Georg von Below, *Einleben in die Verfassung oder Verfassungsänderung* (Langensalza, 1926), p. 36.

28. Examples: Walter Otto, *Deutschlands Schuld und Recht* (Marburg, 1919); Siegmund Hellmann, *Die politischen Wirkungen des Friedens von Versailles* (Munich, 1921); Karl Alexander von Müller, *Volk in Not!* (Munich, n.d. [1912]); M. Sering, *Das Friedensdiktat von Versailles und Deutschlands wirtschaftliche Lage* (Berlin, 1920).

29. Willy Andreas, *Die Wandlungen des grossdeutschen Gedankens: Rede zur Reichsgründungsfeier der Universität Heidelberg 18. Januar 1924* (Berlin, 1924); Willy Andreas, *Die Räumung der besetzten Gebiete: Rede bei der Feier am 1. July 1930 gehalten im Schlosshof* (Heidelberger Universitätsreden, 10; Heidelberg, 1930).

30. Various "cases": Konrad Haenisch, *Staat und Hochschule: Ein Beitrag zur nationalen Erziehungsfrage* (Berlin, 1920), pp. 95–99; Richard H. Samuel and R. Hinton Thomas, *Education and Society in Modern Germany* (London, 1949), pp. 127–128; Edward Yarnall Hartshorne, Jr., *The German Universities and National Socialism* (Cambridge, Mass., 1937), pp. 684–685.

31. Samuel and Thomas, *Education and Society*, p. 127; Willy Hellpach, *Wirken in Wirren: Lebenserinnerungen*, vol. II: *1914–1925* (Hamburg, 1949), pp. 169–171.

32. Roethe, *Festrede 11. April 1920*, p. 12.

33. *Mitteilungen des Verbandes der Deutschen Hochschulen*, ed. K. Voigt (Halle), III (1923), 62.

34. For this and the following see Hellpach, *Wirken in Wirren*, II, 173–178.

35. *Zentralblatt für Unterrichtsverwaltung*, 64, 363–364. The Corporation was indignant, of course; see *Mitteilungen des Verbandes*, II (1922), 221–223.

36. Quoted in Hellpach, *Wirken in Wirren*, II, 171. Further information on the case on pp. 171–173 of that volume and in *Beschluss der philosophischen*

Fakultät Heidelberg vom 16. Mai 1925 in der Angelegenheit des Privatdozenten Dr. Gumbel (Heidelberg, n.d. [1925]).

37. *Ibid.*, pp. 7, 3, 4.

38. *Mitteilungen des Verbandes*, XI (1931), 30–31, 46–47.

39. Meinecke, *Politische Schriften*, p. 391.

40. *Beschluss der philosophischen Fakultät*, p. 7.

41. Friedrich Heilbronn, "Hochschule und auswärtige Politik," *Das akademische Deutschland*, III, 143–152.

42. Hans Rothfels, *Die Universitäten und der Schuldspruch von Versailles: Zum 28. Juni 1929: Eine ungehaltene akademische Rede* (*Königsberger Universitätsreden*, 5; Königsberg, 1929), p. 7.

43. Rudolf Smend, "Hochschule und Parteien," *Das akademische Deutschland*, III, 153–162, esp. pp. 155 and 158 for terminology.

44. Aloys Fischer, "Das Verhältnis der Jugend zu den sozialen Bewegungen und der Begriff der Sozialpädagogik," in A. Fischer, ed., *Jugendführer und Jugendprobleme: Festschrift zu Georg Kerschensteiners 70. Geburtstag* (Leipzig, 1924), p. 221; Sering, *Friedensdiktat*, pp. 45–46; Roethe, *Festrede 11. April 1920*, p. 7.

45. Georg Steinhausen, "Der Materialismus als Verfallserscheinung," *Deutsche Rundschau*, 204 (1925): 255–268.

46. Müller, *Deutsche Geschichte*, p. 26.

47. *Ibid.*, p. 55. For examples of his terminology see pp. 50, 53, 83, 84.

48. Georg von Below, *Die Hemmnisse der politischen Befähigung der Deutschen* (Langensalza, 1924), p. 21. Category dominates whole essay.

49. Eduard Meyer, *Spenglers Untergang des Abendlandes* (Berlin, 1925), p. 23.

50. Below, *Einleben in die Verfassung*, p. 40.

51. Below, *Hemmnisse*, pp. 18, 19; Below, *Einleben*, p. 19; Doeberl, *Sozialismus*, p. 12; Müller, *Deutsche Geschichte*, pp. 60–61, 158.

52. Erich Marcks, *Deutsches Schicksal* (Leipzig, 1921), pp. 5, 14; Gustav Roethe, *Deutsche Dichter des 18. und 19. Jahrhunderts: Ein vaterländischer Vortrag* (Berlin, 1919), p. 25.

53. Walther Lotz, *Kollektivbedarf und Individualbedarf* (*Sitzungsberichte der Bayerischen Akademie der Wissenschaften, Philosophisch-historische Abteilung*, vol. for 1929, no. 2; Munich, 1929), p. 6.

54. *Reichsgründungsfeier der Friedrich-Wilhelms-Universität zu Berlin am 18. Januar 1925* (Berlin, 1925), p. 14. Italics are Seeberg's.

55. Felix Rachfahl, *Preussen und Deutschland in Vergangenheit, Gegenwart und Zukunft* (Tübingen, 1919).

56. Doeberl, *Sozialismus*.

57. For examples of upper-house schemes and related "reform" proposals, see Doeberl, *Sozialismus*, pp. 77–78; Below, *Einleben*; Georg von Below, *Deutsche Reichspolitik einst und jetzt* (Tübingen, 1922). In 1927, the Corporation of

German Universities protested against the poor representation of the universities in the Economic Council and demanded that the government take some action to do justice to the importance of German professors in the life of the nation: *Mitteilungen des Verbandes*, VII (1927), 102.

58. Heinrich Triepel, *Die Staatsverfassung und die politischen Parteien: Rede bei der Feier der Erinnerung an den Stifter der Berliner Universität, am 3. August 1927* (Berlin, 1927), p. 28, p. 31.

59. Meyer, *Rede zur Gedächtnisfeier*, p. 15; Doeberl, *Sozialismus*, p. 98; Otto, *Deutschlands Schuld und Recht*, pp. 78–79.

60. Neumann, *Vom Glauben*, p. 13; Below, *Hemmnisse*, p. 46; Müller, *Deutsche Geschichte*.

61. Roethe, *Festrede 11. April 1920*, p. 13.

62. Carl H. Becker, *Gedanken zur Hochschulreform* (Leipzig, 1919), pp. 5–9.

63. Friedrich von der Leyen, "Gedanken zur Hochschulreform," *Deutsche Rundschau*, 184 (1920): 249.

64. Georg von Below, *Soziologie als Lehrfach: Ein kritischer Beitrag zur Hochschulreform* (Munich, 1920).

65. Ferdinand Tönnies, *Hochschulreform und Soziologie: Kritische Anmerkungen über Becker's 'Gedanken zur Hochschulreform' und Below's 'Soziologie als Lehrfach'* (Jena, 1920); Leopold von Wiese, "Die Soziologie als Einzelwissenschaft," *Schmollers Jahrbuch*, 44 (1920): 347–367.

66. For the following see *Kölner Vierteljahrshefte für Sozialwissenschaften*, 1 (Munich, 1921): 5–11, 47–55, and 56–66 (for announcements by Wiese and Vierkandt); Leopold von Wiese, "Skizze des Aufbaus eines Systems der Beziehungslehre," *ibid.*, 2 (1922): 61–69; Leopold von Wiese, *System der Allgemeinen Soziologie als Lehre von den sozialen Gebilden der Menschen (Beziehungslehre)*, 2nd ed. (Munich, 1933); Leopold von Wiese, "Beziehungslehre," *Handwörterbuch der Soziologie*, pp. 66–81; J. Milton Yinger, "The Systematic Sociology of Leopold von Wiese," in Harry Elmer Barnes, ed., *An Introduction to the History of Sociology* (Chicago, 1948), pp. 274–286.

67. Wiese, *System der Soziologie*, pp. 7–8, 53, 32–37.

68. Ernest Mannheim, "The Sociological Theories of Hans Freyer," Barnes, ed., *History of Sociology*, pp. 362–373.

69. Othmar Spann, "Klasse und Stand," *Handwörterbuch der Staatswissenschaften*, 4th ed., V (Jena, 1923), 692–705; Bartholomew Landheer, "The Universalistic Theory of Othmar Spann and His School," in Barnes, *History of Sociology*, pp. 385–399; Theo Suranyi-Unger, *Die Entwicklung der theoretischen Volkswirtschaftslehre im ersten Viertel des 20. Jahrhunderts* (Jena, 1927), pp. 73–77.

70. Werner Sombart, ed., *Soziologie* (Berlin, 1923), pp. 5–16.

71. Emil Lederer, "Der Zirkulationsprozess als zentrales Problem der ökono-

mischen Theorie," *Archiv*, 56 (1926): 1–25; Emil Lederer, *Planwirtschaft* (Tübingen, 1932).

72. Robert Liefmann was particularly fond of such unnecessary labels; see Robert Liefmann, *Wirtschaftstheorie und Wirtschaftsbeschreibung* (Tübingen, 1929). Even a perfectly respectable history of German economics cannot avoid these fashions; see Suranyi-Unger, *Entwicklung der Volkswirtschaftslehre*, esp. pp. 66–67, 96–101.

73. Otto von Zwiedineck-Südenhorst, "Zum Schicksal der Sozialpolitik in Deutschland," *Schmollers Jahrbuch*, 47 (1924): 77–142; Götz Briefs, "Über das Verhältnis des Proletarischen zum Sozialistischen," *Kölner Vierteljahrshefte für Soziologie*, 3 (1923): 99–109, esp. pp. 108–109; Götz Briefs, *Wirtschaftsverfassung und Gesellschaftsordnung (Akademische Schriftenreihe der Technischen Hochschule Charlottenburg, 2; Berlin-Charlottenburg, 1929).

74. Götz Briefs, "Gegenwartsfragen des deutschen Wirtschaftslebens," Philip Witkop, ed., *Deutsches Leben der Gegenwart* (Berlin, 1922), p. 294; see also p. 297.

75. Arthur Salz, *Macht und Wirtschaftsgesetz: Ein Beitrag zur Erkenntnis des Wesens der kapitalistischen Wirtschaftsverfassung* (Leipzig, 1930); Adolf Weber, *Sozialpolitik: Reden und Aufsätze* (Munich, 1931); Adolf Weber, *Arbeitskämpfe oder Arbeitsgemeinschaft* (Tübingen, 1927); Adolf Weber, *Wirtschaft und Politik (Münchener Juristiche Vorträge, 6; Munich, 1925); Adolf Weber, *Das Ende des Kapitalismus? Die Notwendigkeit freier Erwerbswirtschaft*, 2nd ed. (Munich, 1929); Hermann Schumacher, "Gegenwartsfragen des Sozialismus," *Schmollers Jahrbuch*, 44 (1920): 1–28; Robert Liefmann, *Geschichte und Kritik des Sozialismus* (Leipzig, 1922), esp. pp. 185–187.

76. Leopold von Wiese, "Sozialpolitik," *Handwörterbuch der Staatswissenschaften*, 4th ed., VII (Jena, 1926), 612–622.

77. For the following see Werner Sombart, *Die Rationalisierung in der Wirtschaft: Vortrag auf dem 25. Kirchl. soz. Kongress* (Leipzig, 1928); Werner Sombart, *Die Zukunft des Kapitalismus* (Berlin, 1932).

78. Werner Sombart, *Beamtenschaft und Wirtschaft: Vortrag gehalten auf dem Mitteldeutschen Beamtentag, 1927* (Berlin, 1927), pp. 19–20.

79. Wolfgang Hock, *Deutscher Antikapitalismus: Der ideologische Kampf gegen die freie Wirtschaft im Zeichen der grossen Krise* (Frankfurt, 1960).

80. Weber, *Politische Schriften*, p. 429.

81. Moritz Julius Bonn, *Nationale Kolonialpolitik (Schriften des Socialwissenschaftlichen Vereins der Universität München*, 5; Munich, 1910).

82. Emil Lederer, "Zur Soziologie des Weltkrieges," *Archiv*, 39 (1914): 347–384; Emil Lederer, "Die Umschichtung des Proletariats," *Die neue Rundschau*, 40 (1929): 145–161.

83. Franz Oppenheimer, *Die sociale Frage und der Sozialismus: Eine kritische*

Auseinandersetzung mit der marxistischen Theorie (Jena, 1912); Franz Oppenheimer, *Richtungen der neuen deutschen Sociologie* (Jena, 1928).

84. Ernst von Aster, "Zur Kritik des deutschen Nationalismus," *Die neue Rundschau*, 36 (1925): 1–15; Aster, *Marx*, pp. 32–36.

85. Aster, "Zur Kritik," pp. 8, 15.

86. Ernst von Aster, "Metaphysik des Nationalismus," *Die neue Rundschau*, 43 (1932); 40–52; Ernst von Aster, "Die Krise der bürgerlichen Ideologie," *Die neue Rundschau*, 42 (1931): 1–13; Aster, *Marx*, esp. pp. 17–18.

87. "Ferdinand Tönnies," *Die Philosophie der Gegenwart in Selbstdarstellungen*, III (2nd ed.; Leipzig, 1924), 203–242; "Leopold von Wiese," *Die Volkswirtschaftslehre der Gegenwart in Selbstdarstellungen*, II (Leipzig, 1929), 187–239.

88. Leopold von Wiese, ed., *Soziologie des Volksbildungswesens (Schriften des Forschungsinstituts für Sozialwissenschaften in Köln*, 1; Munich, 1921), pp. 3–45, 200–215, 552–568.

89. Roberto Michels, "Intellectual Socialists," in George B. de Huszar, ed., *The Intellectuals: A Controversial Portrait* (Glencoe, 1960), pp. 316–321.

90. Lujo Brentano, *Der Judenhass (Wege zur Verständigung*, 1; Berlin, 1924); Karl Vossler, *Politik und Geistesleben (Münchener Universitätsreden*, 8; Munich, 1927), pp. 19–21.

91. Sigmund Freud, *Selbstdarstellung*, 2nd ed. (Vienna, 1936), p. 8.

92. Meinecke, *Politische Schriften*, pp. 341–342.

93. Golo Mann, "The German Intellectuals," in Huszar, *The Intellectuals*, pp. 459–469.

94. Lujo Brentano, *Walter Rathenau und seine Verdienste um Deutschland* (Munich, n.d. [1922]), p. 19.

95. Paul Natorp, *Sozialidealismus: Neue Richtlinien sozialer Erziehung*, 2nd ed. (Berlin, 1922), p. 2; Alfred Vierkandt, *Die sozialpädagogische Forderung der Gegenwart* (Berlin, 1920), p. 9.

96. Alfred Weber, "Deutschland und der Osten," *Die neue Rundschau*, 33 (1922): 337–345; Alfred Weber, *Deutschland und die europäische Kulturkrise* (Berlin, 1924).

97. Alfred Weber, *Deutschland und Europa, 1848 und heute (Die Paulskirche*, 1; Frankfurt, 1923), p. 20.

98. Alfred Vierkandt, "Sozialgeist und Sozialethik der Gegenwart," *Deutsche Rundschau*, 220 (1929): 1–10, 141–148, esp. pp. 4–8; Ernst Treoltsch, "Die geistige Revolution," *Kunstwart und Kulturwart*, 34 (1921): 233.

99. Gerhard Ritter, *Bismarcks Reichsgründung und die Aufgaben deutscher Zukunft: Sonderabdruck aus der Breisgauer Zeitung vom 20. Januar 1928* (Freiburg, n.d. [1928]), p. 23; Vierkandt, "Sozialgeist und Sozialethik," pp. 1–3.

100. Friedrich Meinecke, "Ein Gespräch aus dem Herbste 1919," in Meinecke, *Nach der Revolution*, pp. 107–144. The quotes from this essay that follow are from pp. 110–112.

101. Fischer, "Verhältnis der Jugend," p. 209.

102. Ernst Robert Curtius, *Der Syndikalismus der Geistesarbeiter in Frankreich* (Bonn, 1921).

103. Robert Michels, *Umschichtungen in den herrschenden Klassen nach dem Kriege* (Stuttgart, 1934), esp. pp. 58–85 on the intellectual upper class; Alfred Weber, *Die Not der geistigen Arbeiter* (Munich, 1923).

104. *Ibid.*, pp. 9–11; Rudolf Meerwarth, Adolf Günther, and W. Zimmermann, *Die Einwirkungen des Krieges auf Bevölkerungsbewegung, Einkommen und Lebenshaltung in Deutschland* (Stuttgart, 1932), p. 279; Georg Schreiber, *Die Not der deutschen Wissenschaft und der geistigen Arbeiter* (Leipzig, 1923), pp. 45–48.

105. Bonn, "Die wahre Weltrevolution," p. 394; Rudolf Eucken, *Lebenserinnerungen: Ein Stück deutschen Lebens* (Leipzig, 1921), p. 109.

106. Weber, *Not der geistigen Arbeiter*, pp. 6, 12, 8, 13, 12, 14, 23–24, 40.

107. Hermann Oncken, "Politik als Kunst," *Handbuch der Politik*, 3rd ed., vol. I: *Die Grundlagen der Politik*, ed. Gerhard Anschütz, et al. (Berlin, 1920), pp. 8–14; quote from p. 14.

108. Gerhard Ritter, *Gneisenau und die deutsche Freiheitsidee* (Tübingen, 1932), pp. 35–36.

109. Friedrich Meinecke, "Drei Generationen deutscher Gelehrtenpolitik," *Historische Zeitschrift*, 125 (1922): 248–283.

110. Alfred Weber, "Geist und Politik," p. 337.

111. Paul Natorp, *Genossenschaftliche Erziehung als Grundlage zum Neubau des Volkstums und des Menschentums* (Berlin, 1920), pp. 15–16.

112. Hermann Güntert, *Deutscher Geist: Drei Vorträge* (Bühl-Baden, 1932), p. 14.

113. For the following see Hellmut Volkmann, *Die Deutsche Studentenschaft in ihrer Entwicklung seit 1919* (Leipzig, 1925); George L. Mosse, *The Crisis of German Ideology: Intellectual Origins of the Third Reich* (New York, 1964), pp. 268–272.

114. Willy Hellpach, *Prägung: Zwölf Abhandlungen aus Lehre und Leben der Erziehung* (Leipzig, 1928), pp. 235–240; *Zentralblatt für die gesamte Unterrichtsverwaltung in Preussen*, 69 (1927): 325–327; Erich Wende, *C. H. Becker: Mensch und Politiker*, pp. 252–267.

115. Paul Ssymank, "Organisation und Arbeitsfeld der Deutschen Studentenschaft," *Das akademische Deutschland*, III, 363.

116. *Mitteilungen des Verbandes*, VII (1927), 101; Eduard Norden, *Bericht über das Amtsjahr 1927/28 erstattet bei der Rektoratsübergabe* (Berlin, 1928).

117. Smend, "Hochschule und Parteien," pp. 158–162.

118. Karl Dietrich Bracher, *Die Auflösung der Weimarer Republik: Eine Studie zum Problem des Machtverfalls in der Demokratie*, 4th ed. (Villingen, 1964), pp. 146–149.

119. Kurt Sontheimer, *Antidemokratisches Denken in der Weimarer Republik: Die politischen Ideen des deutschen Nationalismus zwischen 1918 und 1933* (Munich, 1962).

120. Fischer, "Verhältnis der Jugend," pp. 210–211, 223.

Chapter Five

1. Georg Simmel, *Der Krieg und die geistigen Entscheidungen: Reden und Aufsätze,* 2nd ed. (Munich, 1917), pp. 14–15; Theobald Ziegler, "Auf der Schwelle des neuen Jahrhunderts," *Neue deutsche Rundschau,* 11 (Berlin, 1900): 1–17.

2. W. Stern, *Vorgedanken zur Weltanschauung* (Leipzig, 1915).

3. For this and the following, see Rudolf Eucken, *Geistige Strömungen der Gegenwart* (Leipzig, 1904), pp. 1–10, quote being on p. 4; Rudolf Eucken, *Die geistigen Forderungen der Gegenwart,* 3rd ed. (Berlin, 1918), esp. the introduction; Rudolf Eucken, *Lebenserinnerungen: Ein Stück deutschen Lebens* (Leipzig, 1921), pp. 61–117.

4. *Ibid.,* p. 66.

5. *Ibid.,* p. 108; Eucken, *Geistige Strömungen,* p. 2; Eucken, *Lebenserinnerungen,* p. 117.

6. Karl Jaspers, *Die Idee der Universität* (Berlin, 1923), pp. 68–74; Hermann Paul, *Gedanken über das Universitätsstudium: Rede beim Antritt des Rektorats der Ludwig-Maximilians-Universität gehalten am 11. Dezember 1909* (Munich, 1909); Ziegler, "Auf der Schwelle"; Theobald Ziegler, *Der deutsche Student am Ende des 19. Jahrhunderts,* 10th ed. (Leipzig, 1908); Karl Weinhold, *Rede beim Antritt des Rektorats gehalten in der Aula der Königlichen Friedrich-Wilhelms-Universität zu Berlin am 15. Oktober 1893* (Berlin, 1893), pp. 13–16; Werner Jaeger, *Stellung und Aufgaben der Universität in der Gegenwart* (Berlin, 1924), p. 20.

7. *Ibid.,* pp. 3–8.

8. Erich Marcks, *Die Universität Heidelberg im 19. Jahrhundert: Festrede zur Hundertjahrfeier, am 7. August 1903* (Heidelberg, 1903), p. 43.

9. Eduard Spranger, "Das Wesen der deutschen Universität," *Das akademische Deutschland,* III, 12, 33; Jaspers, *Idee der Universität,* pp. 61, 64, 48; Friedrich Meinecke, *Erlebtes 1862–1901* (Leipzig, 1941), pp. 99–100, 119, and p. 100 for quote; Max Scheler, "Von zwei deutschen Krankheiten," A. von Gleichen-Russwurm et al., *Der Leuchter: Weltanschauung und Lebensgestaltung* (Darmstadt, 1919), pp. 186, 187.

10. Eucken, *Geistige Strömungen,* p. 5. See also Georg Steinhausen, *Deutsche Geistes- und Kulturgeschichte von 1870 bis zur Gegenwart* (Halle, 1931), pp. 265–277; Eucken, *Lebenserinnerungen,* pp. 117, 77.

11. Meinecke, *Erlebtes, 1862–1901,* p. 167.

12. Koenraad Swart, *The Sense of Decadence in Nineteenth-Century France* (The Hague, 1964).

13. Frederic Lilge, *The Abuse of Learning: The Failure of the German University* (New York, 1948), pp. 84–130.

14. Richard H. Samuel and R. Hinton Thomas, *Education and Society in Modern Germany* (London, 1949), pp. 17–35.

15. Karl Heinrich Höfele, "Selbstverständnis und Zeitkritik des deutschen Bürgertums vor dem ersten Weltkrieg," *Zeitschrift für Religions- und Geistesgeschichte*, 8 (1956): 40–56.

16. Werner Weisbach, *"Und Alles ist zerstoben": Erinnerungen aus der Jahrhundertwende* (Vienna, 1937), p. 187.

17. Ernst Troeltsch, "Deutsche Bildung," in Ernst Troeltsch, *Deutscher Geist und Westeuropa: Gesammelte kulturphilosophische Aufsätze und Reden*, ed. Hans Baron (Tübingen, 1925), p. 169.

18. Werner Sombart, "Technik und Kultur," *Archiv*, 33 (1911): 305–347.

19. For music examples and terms, see pp. 342–347.

20. Leopold von Wiese, "Das Überpersönliche," *Die neue Rundschau*, 28 (1917): 436.

21. Leopold von Wiese, *Der Schriftsteller und der Staat* (Berlin, 1918), pp. 19, 21–22.

22. Georg Simmel, "Persönliche und sachliche Kultur," *Neue deutsche Rundschau*, 11 (1900): 700–712; Georg Simmel, "Der Begriff und die Tragödie der Kultur," *Philosophische Kultur: Gesammelte Essais* (Leipzig, 1911), pp. 245–277; Georg Simmel, *Der Krieg und die geistigen Entscheidungen: Reden und Aufsätze*, 2nd ed. (Munich, 1917); Georg Simmel, *Der Konflikt der modernen Kultur: Ein Vortrag*, 2nd ed. (Munich, 1921).

23. Alfred Weber, "Die Bedeutung der geistigen Führer in Deutschland," *Die neue Rundschau*, 29 (Berlin, 1918): 1249–1268.

24. An orthodox and a modernist example: Reinhold Seeberg, "Hochschule und Weltanschauung," *Das akademische Deutschland*, III, 168–170; C. H. Becker, *Vom Wesen der deutschen Universität* (Leipzig, 1925), pp. 32–34.

25. "Georg Kerschensteiner," in Erich Hahn, ed., *Die Pädagogik der Gegenwart in Selbstdarstellungen* (Leipzig, 1926), pp. 45–96.

26. For the following, see Kerschensteiner's *Die gewerbliche Erziehung der deutschen Jugend* (Darmstadt, 1901); *Staatsbürgerliche Erziehung der deutschen Jugend* (Erfurt, 1901); *Begriff der Arbeitsschule*, 3rd ed. (Leipzig, 1917); "Das öffentliche Unterrichtswesen im Volksstaate," *Die neue Rundschau*, 30 (1919): 1171–1187; *Die Seele des Erziehers und das Problem der Lehrerbildung* (Leipzig, 1921); and *Das einheitliche deutsche Schulsystem: sein Aufbau, seine Erziehungsaufgaben*, 2nd ed. (Leipzig, 1922).

27. *Ibid.*, p. 13. See also pp. 121–123.

28. Kerschensteiner, *Seele des Erziehers*, pp. 18–23.

29. *Ibid.*, p. 78.

30. Kerschensteiner, "Das öffentliche Unterrichtswesen," p. 1180.

31. Kerschensteiner, *Das einheitliche Schulsystem*, p. 102, and "Das öffentliche Unterrichtswesen," pp. 1175–1179.

32. Compare Kerschensteiner, *Gewerbliche Erziehung*, with his *Begriff der Arbeitsschule*, pp. 60–75, and *Das einheitliche Schulsystem*, pp. 6–7, 256–259 (ref. to Simmel on p. 257).

33. Kerschensteiner, *Staatsbürgerliche Erziehung*, quote being from p. 15. See also Kerschensteiner, *Begriff der Arbeitsschule*, pp. 2, 14–17, 44–48, and *Das einheitliche Schulsystem*, pp. 5–6, 213–225, 240.

34. Kerschensteiner, *Staatsbürgerliche Erziehung*, p. 48.

35. Rudolf Lehmann, *Die pädagogische Bewegung der Gegenwart: Ihre Ursprünge und ihr Charakter* (Munich, 1922), is the best account. See also Hahn, *Pädagogik der Gegenwart*.

36. Rudolf Virchow, *Lernen und Forschen: Rede beim Antritt des Rectorats an der Friedrich-Wilhelms-Universität zu Berlin gehalten am 15. Oktober 1892* (Berlin, 1892).

37. Paul, *Gedanken über das Universitätsstudium*; Wilhelm von Christ, *Reform des Universitätsunterrichtes: Rede beim Antritte des Rektorats der Ludwig-Maximilians-Universität gehalten am 21. November 1891* (Munich, 1891); Ziegler, *Der deutsche Student*; Alfred Weber, "Bedeutung der geistigen Führer," p. 1263.

38. Rudolf Lehmann, "Kultur und Schule der Gegenwart," *Die neue Rundschau*, 19 (1908): 753, 754, 755.

39. *Ibid.*, pp. 759, 760.

40. Kurt Wolzendorff, *Die Universität in der Demokratie (Flugschriften der Frankfurter Zeitung*; Frankfurt, 1919), p. 26.

41. Carl H. Becker, *Gedanken zur Hochschulreform* (Leipzig, 1919); Haenisch, *Staat und Hochschule: Ein Beitrag zur nationalen Erziehungsfrage* (Berlin, 1920), esp. pp. 108–111.

42. Leopold von Wiese, ed., *Soziologie des Volksbildungswesens (Schriften des Forschungsinstituts für Sozialwissenschaften in Köln*, 1; Munich, 1921), pp. 3–45, 200–215, 552–568, quote being from p. 556.

43. Paul Natorp, *Genossenschaftliche Erziehung als Grundlage zum Neubau des Volkstums und des Menschentums* (Berlin, 1920).

44. Jonas Cohn, *Erziehung zu sozialer Gesinnung* (Langensalza, 1920), pp. 9, 11, 12.

45. Alfred Vierkandt, *Die sozialpädagogische Forderung der Gegenwart (Sozialpädagogische Abende im Zentralinstitut für Erziehung und Unterricht*, 1; Berlin, 1920), p. 13.

46. Friedrich Meinecke, *Politische Schriften und Reden*, ed. Georg Kotowski (Darmstadt, 1958), pp. 385–392.

47. Vierkandt, *Sozialpädagogische Forderung*, pp. 4, 10–11.

48. *Ibid.*, pp. 7–9, 22–24.

49. *Ibid.*, pp. 24–27.

50. Max Scheler, "Universität und Volkshochschule," Wiese, ed., *Soziologie des Volksbildungswesens*, pp. 153–191.

51. Becker, *Gedanken*, pp. 5–9, 24–29.

52. Haenisch, *Staat und Hochschule*, pp. 110–111.

53. Aloys Fischer, "Arbeiten und Lernen: Psychologische Betrachtungen zur heutigen Schulreformbewegung," *Das Arbeitsprinzip im naturwissenschaftlichen Unterricht: Zweites Jahrbuch der Pädagogischen Zentrale des Deutschen Lehrervereins* (Leipzig, 1912), pp. 1–61.

54. Ferdinand Jakob Schmidt, *Volksvertretung und Schulpolitik* (Berlin, 1919), p. 53. My translation is as clear as the original: "Der Gegenstand dieses Bildungsprozesses in erster Linie ist nicht die individuelle Wissensbildung, sondern die höchste, wesensgleiche Bestimmung des Menschen: die geistige Persönlichkeitsbildung zur sittlichen Freiheit," and so on.

55. *Ibid.*, pp. 27, 28–29.

56. Gustav Cohn, "Über Fakultäten, deren Vereinigung und Trennung," *Schmollers Jahrbuch*, 29 (1905): 18; Eduard Spranger, "Die drei Motive der Schulreform," *Monatsschrift für höhere Schulen*, 20 (1921): 260–274.

57. *Ibid.*, pp. 268, 270, 273.

58. Eduard Meyer, *Die Aufgaben der höheren Schulen und die Gestaltung des Geschichtsunterrichts* (Berlin, 1918), pp. 1–45.

59. Friedrich von der Leyen, "Gedanken zur Hochschulreform," *Deutsche Rundschau*, 184 (1920): 249.

60. Spranger, "Drei Motive," p. 267; Spranger, *Begabung und Studium* (Leipzig, 1917), p. 28.

61. *Ibid.*, pp. 75, 76.

62. Ulrich von Wilamowitz-Moellendorff, *Der griechische und der platonische Staatsgedanke* (Berlin, 1919).

63. Eduard Spranger, *Gedanken über Lehrerbildung* (Leipzig, 1920).

64. Wilhelm Kahl, *Geschichtliches und Grundsätzliches aus der Gedankenwelt über Universitätsreformen: Rede zur Gedächtnisfeier, am 3. August 1909* (Berlin, 1909), p. 24.

65. George L. Mosse, *The Crisis of German Ideology: Intellectual Origins of the Third Reich* (New York, 1964), pp. 153–170. Mosse associates the whole education reform movement with volkish attitudes. This seems to me inappropriate, at least in the case of such modernists as Kerschensteiner, Paul Östreich, and Gustav Wyneken.

66. For the following, see: Friedrich von der Leyen, *Deutsche Universität und deutsche Zukunft: Betrachtungen* (Jena, 1906); Friedrich von der Leyen, "Aufgaben der Universität," *Die neue Rundschau*, 19 (1908): 1249–1258; Leyen,

"Gedanken zur Hochschulreform"; Carl Neumann, "Neue Aufgaben der deutschen Universitäten: Auslandskurse und Pflege der deutschen Kultur," *Deutsche Rundschau,* 177 (1918): 33–51.

67. Werner Jaeger, *Humanismus und Jugendbildung: Vortrag gehalten in der Versammlung der Freunde des humanistischen Gymnasiums, am 27. November 1920* (Berlin, 1921), p. 13.

68. *Ibid.,* pp. 38–39, 41, 43.

69. Eduard Spranger, *Das humanistische und das politische Bildungsideal (Deutsche Abende im Zentralinstitut für Erziehung und Unterricht,* 6; Berlin, 1916).

70. Meyer, *Aufgaben der höheren Schulen,* pp. 69–89; Eduard Meyer, *Humanistische und geschichtliche Bildung: Vortrag gehalten in der Vereinigung der Freunde des humanistischen Gymnasiums . . . am 27. November 1906* (Berlin, 1907); Albert Rehm, *Der Weltkrieg und das humanistische Gymnasium: Ein Wort zur Abwehr und Verständigung* (Munich, 1916); Eduard Norden, *Die Bildungswerte der lateinischen Literatur und Sprache auf dem humanistischen Gymnasium: Vortrag gehalten in der Versammlung der Vereinigung der Freunde des humanistischen Gymnasiums . . . am 25. November 1919* (Berlin, 1920); Gustav Roethe, *Humanistische und nationale Bildung, eine historische Betrachtung: Vortrag gehalten in der Vereinigung der Freunde des humanistischen Gymnasiums . . . am 6. Dezember 1905* (Berlin, 1906); see Roethe's version of the anti-utilitarian argument on p. 8.

71. Standard texts and essays by German historians of philosophy: Wilhelm Windelband, *Die Philosophie im deutschen Geistesleben des 19. Jahrhunderts* (Tübingen, 1927); Traugott K. Oesterreich, "Die philosophischen Strömungen der Gegenwart," in Paul Hinneberg, ed., *Die Kultur der Gegenwart,* pt. I, sec. VI: *Systematische Philosophie,* 3rd ed. (Leipzig, 1921), pp. 352–395; Erich Becher, *Deutsche Philosophen* (Munich, 1929), pp. 279–306; Max Scheler, "Die deutsche Philosophie der Gegenwart," in Philipp Witkop, ed., *Deutsches Leben der Gegenwart* (Berlin, 1922), pp. 127–224; Raymund Schmidt, ed., *Die Philosophie der Gegenwart in Selbstdarstellungen,* 7 vols. (Leipzig, 1922–29).

72. For the following see Wilhelm Windelband, *Präludien: Aufsätze und Reden zur Einleitung in die Philosophie,* 3rd ed. (Tübingen, 1907), esp. pp. 135–168; Ernst Cassirer, *Der kritische Idealismus und die Philosophie des 'gesunden Menschenverstandes'* (Hermann Cohen and Paul Natorp, eds., *Philosophische Arbeiten,* I, 1; Giessen, 1906).

73. Walter M. Simon, *European Positivism in the Nineteenth Century* (Ithaca, 1963).

74. See, for example, Windelband, *Philosophie im deutschen Geistesleben,* pp. 60–66.

75. Karl Vossler, *Positivismus und Idealismus in der Sprachwissenschaft* (Heidelberg, 1904); A. Riehl, *Plato: Ein populär-wissenschaftlicher Vortrag*

(Halle, 1905), p. 33; Friedrich Meinecke, *Strassburg, Freiburg, Berlin 1901–1919: Erinnerungen* (Stuttgart, 1949), pp. 22 and 90–91 for quotes.

76. On German historiography see Josef Engel, "Die deutschen Universitäten und die Geschichtswissenschaft," *Historische Zeitschrift*, 189 (1959): 223–378; Theodor Schieder, "Die deutsche Geschichtswissenschaft im Spiegel der Historischen Zeitschrift," *Historische Zeitschrift*, 189 (1959): pp. 1–72.

77. For Lamprecht's views see Karl Lamprecht, *Moderne Geschichtswissenschaft: 5 Vörtrage* (Freiburg, 1905), and *Zwei Reden zur Hochschulreform* (Berlin, 1910). On the controversy see Georg von Below, *Die deutsche Geschichtsschreibung von den Befreiungskriegen bis zu unseren Tagen: Geschichte und Kulturgeschichte* (Leipzig, 1916); Karl Lamprecht, *Die historische Methode des Herrn von Below: Eine Kritik (Beigabe zur Historischen Zeitschrift*, vol. 82, no. 2; Berlin, 1899). For comments see Friedriche Meinecke, *Erlebtes 1862–1901* (Leipzig, 1941), pp. 194–195.

78. Terms: Lamprecht, *Moderne Geschichtswissenschaft*, pp. 76–77.

79. Lamprecht, *Zwei Reden*, p. 44.

80. Meinecke, *Erlebtes*, p. 195.

Chapter Six

1. Ernst Cassirer, "Der Begriff der symbolischen Form im Aufbau der Geisteswissenschaften," in Fritz Saxl, ed., *Vorträge der Bibliothek Warburg 1921–1922* (Berlin, 1923), pp. 11–39; Ernst Cassirer, *Der kritische Idealismus und die Philosophie der "gesunden Menschenverstandes"* (Hermann Cohen and Paul Natorp, eds., *Philosophische Arbeiten*, vol. I, no. 1; Giessen, 1906).

2. Wilhelm Windelband, *Die Philosophie im deutschen Geistesleben des 19. Jahrhunderts*, 3rd ed. (Tübingen, 1927), pp. 83–84.

3. For a neo-Kantian attack on Mach see Richard Hönigswald, *Zur Kritik der Machschen Philosophie: Eine erkenntnistheoretische Studie* (Berlin, 1903).

4. Hans Vaihinger, "Wie die Philosophie des Als Ob entstand," Raymund Schmidt, ed., *Die Philosophie der Gegenwart in Selbstdarstellungen*, II (2nd ed.; Leipzig, 1923), 183–212.

5. Alois Riehl, *Friedrich Nietzsche: Der Künstler und Denker: Ein Essay* (Stuttgart, 1897).

6. *Wissenschaftliche Weltauffassung: Der Wiener Kreis (Veröffentlichungen des Vereins Ernst Mach*, 1; Vienna, 1929), pp. 14, 29.

7. Carl Stumpf, *Vom ethischen Skeptizismus: Rede zur Gedächtnisfeier* (Berlin, 1908); Wilhelm Wundt, *Erlebtes und Erkanntes* (Stuttgart, 1920), pp. 382–399.

8. Theodor Lipps, *Philosophie und Wirklichkeit* (Heidelberg, 1908), p. 38;

Moritz Geiger, *Die Wirklichkeit der Wissenschaften und die Metaphysik* (Bonn, 1930); Julius Ebbinghaus, *Über die Fortschritte der Metaphysik* (Tübingen, 1932), p. 6.

9. Examples: Friedrich Kuntze, *Der morphologische Idealismus: Seine Grundlagen und seine Bedeutung* (Munich, 1929); Ferdinand Jakob Schmidt, *Der philosophische Sinn: Programm des energetischen Idealismus* (Göttingen, 1912). Schmidt says in his *Kant der Geistesherold einer neuen Menschheitsepoche:* "Was [Kant] die Philosophie der praktischen Vernunft nannte, ist der Anhub der metaphysischen Totalitätswissenschaft des Geistes. Seit Kant gibt es eine neuweltliche Philosophie, und ihre grosse Aufgabe ist die fortschreitende Entwicklung des willensgeistigen Denkverfahrens, der Ganzheitlichkeit, der willensgeistigen oder freiheitschöpferischen Humanitätsidee und des willensgeistigen Produktionsystems der geschichtlichen Gesittungswelt" (pp. 66–67).

10. In addition to the general essays on the history of German philosophy which are cited in Chapter Five, see the following primary sources for the Baden school: Wilhelm Windelband, *Präludien: Aufsätze und Reden zur Einleitung in die Philosophie,* 3rd ed. (Tübingen, 1907), essays no. 1, 2, 5, 10, 11, 13; Heinrich Rickert, *Kant als Philosoph der modernen Kultur: Ein geschichtsphilosophischer Versuch* (Tübingen, 1924); Paul Natorp, *Philosophie und Pädagogik: Untersuchungen auf ihrem Grenzgebiet* (Marburg, 1909); Paul Natorp, *Sozial-Idealismus: Neue Richtlinien sozialer Erziehung,* 2nd ed. (Berlin, 1922); Jonas Cohn, *Der Sinn der gegenwärtigen Kultur: Ein philosophischer Versuch* (Leipzig, 1914).

11. Windelband, *Präludien,* p. vi.

12. For general background, see Gardner Murphy, *An Historical Introduction to Modern Psychology,* with a supplement by Heinrich Klüver (New York, 1929).

13. "Carl Stumpf," *Die Philosophie der Gegenwart in Selbstdarstellungen,* ed. Raymond Schmidt, V (Leipzig, 1924), 205–265, esp. pp. 232–261.

14. G. E. Müller, *Komplextheorie und Gestalttheorie: Ein Beitrag zur Wahrnehmungspsychologie* (Göttingen, 1923).

15. The standard line in capsule form: Traugott Konstantin Oesterreich, "Die philosophischen Strömungen der Gegenwart," in Paul Hinneberg, ed., *Die Kultur der Gegenwart,* pt. I, sec. IV: *Systematische Philosophie,* 3rd ed. (Leipzig, 1921), pp. 370–374.

16. Murphy, *Modern Psychology*: Emphasis upon emergence of quantitative methods and upon transition from structural approach (static topography of mental states: Locke, Wundt) to functional conceptions (dynamic analysis of mental processes, observation of organism's active reactions and adjustments). No contradiction between functionalism and quantification in this scheme. Various German psychologists given credit for functionalist orientations. For startling contrast, see supplement by Klüver, pp. 417–455 and esp. pp. 417–422, which describes recent German psychology "from the inside": antiquantitative,

antipositivist, standard remarks about "wholes," and use of Lamprecht's theories on supposed transition from an age of dissociation to one of synthesis.

17. Wilhelm Wundt, *Die Psychologie im Kampf ums Dasein* (Leipzig, 1913).
18. On the crisis of the humanistic disciplines see H. Stuart Hughes, *Consciousness and Society: The Reorientation of European Social Thought, 1890–1930* (New York, 1959), esp. pp. 183–248; Georg G. Iggers, "The Dissolution of German Historism," Richard Herr and Harold Parker, eds., *Ideas in History: Essays Presented to Louis Gottschalk by His Former Students* (Durham, N.C., 1965), pp. 288–329.
19. On Dilthey see Wilhelm Dilthey, *Gesammelte Schriften*, vol. VII: *Der Aufbau der geschichtlichen Welt in den Geisteswissenschaften*, ed. B. Groethuysen (Leipzig, 1927), pp. 79–188; H. A. Hodges, *Wilhelm Dilthey: An Introduction* (London, 1944); Wilhelm Dilthey, *Pattern and Meaning in History: Thoughts on History and Society*, ed. H. P. Rickmann (New York, 1962); Carlo Antoni, *Vom Historismus zur Soziologie*, trans. W. Goetz (Stuttgart, n.d. [1950]), pp. 7–56. On the others see Georg Simmel, *Die Probleme der Geschichtsphilosophie: Eine erkenntnistheoretische Studie* (Leipzig, 1892); Windelband, *Präludien*, pp. 355–379; Heinrich Rickert, *Kulturwissenschaft und Naturwissenschaft: Ein Vortrag* (Freiburg, 1899), based on his *Grenzen der naturwissenschaftlichen Begriffsbildung*; Max Weber, *Gesammelte Aufsätze zur Wissenschaftslehre* (Tübingen, 1922). Dilthey continued to develop his ideas until his death in 1911. His *Construction of the Historical World in the Geisteswissenschaften* came out in 1910; his *Types of Weltanschauung and Their Development in the Metaphysical Systems* followed in 1911.
20. Rickert, *Kulturwissenschaft*, p. 67.
21. Weber, *Wissenschaftslehre*, esp. pp. 44–45 for Knies, pp. 49–56 for Wundt, and pp. 70–86 for comments on Münsterberg's distinction between "objectifying" and "subjectifying" knowledge.
22. *Ibid.*, p. 112, from "Plisch und Plum": "Wer sich freut, wenn wer betrübt, macht sich meistens unbeliebt."
23. Max Weber, "Über einige Kategorien der verstehenden Soziologie," Weber, *Wissenschaftslehre*, 2nd ed. Johannes Winckelmann (Tübingen, 1951), pp. 427–474.
24. For the following see Heinrich Rickert, *Die Philosophie des Lebens: Darstellung und Kritik der philosophischen Modeströmungen unserer Zeit* (Tübingen, 1920); Wilhelm Windelband, *Der Wille zur Wahrheit: Akademische Rede* (Heidelberg, 1909); Georg Simmel, *Der Konflikt der modernen Kultur: Ein Vortrag*, 2nd ed. (Munich, 1921); Georg Simmel, "Persönliche und sachliche Kultur," *Neue deutsche Rundschau*, 11 (1900): 700–712. See also "Lebensphilosophie," *Der Grosse Brockhaus*. Comments: Kurt Sontheimer, *Antidemokratisches Denken in der Weimarer Republik: Die politischen Ideen des deutschen Nationalismus zwischen 1918 und 1933* (Munich, 1962), pp. 65–72 and elsewhere.

25. Rudolf Eucken, *Erkennen und Leben* (Leipzig, 1912).

26. Ernst Troeltsch, *Die Bedeutung der Geschichte für die Weltanschauung* (Berlin, 1918); Ernst Troeltsch, *Die Dynamik der Geschichte nach der Geschichtsphilosophie des Positivismus* (Berlin, 1919); Ernst Troeltsch, "Naturrecht und Humanität in der Weltpolitik," in Ernst Troeltsch, *Deutscher Geist und Westeuropa: Gesammelte kulturphilosophische Aufsätze und Reden*, ed. Hans Baron (Tübingen, 1925), pp. 3–27; Ernst Troeltsch, *Der Historismus und seine Probleme*, book I: *Das logische Problem der Geschichtsphilosophie* (Tübingen, 1922); Ernst Troeltsch, "Die Krisis des Historismus," *Die neue Rundschau*, 33 (1922): 572–590.

27. Wilhelm Windelband, *Geschichtsphilosophie: Eine Kriegsvorlesung: Fragment aus dem Nachlass*, ed. Wolfgang Windelband, Bruno Bauch (*Kantstudien: Ergänzungsheft*, 38; Berlin, 1916).

28. Troeltsch, "Krisis des Historismus," pp. 584–585, 586.

29. Ernst Troeltsch, *Humanismus und Nationalismus in unserem Bildungswesen: Vortrag gehalten in der Versammlung der Vereinigung der Freunde des humanistischen Gymnasiums am 28. November 1916* (Berlin, 1917); Ernst Troeltsch, *Demokratie* (*Schriften des Demokratischen Studentenbundes Berlin*; Berlin, 1919); Ernst Troeltsch, "Der neue Geist," *Kunstwart und Kulturwart*, 33 (1919): 27–31; Ernst Troeltsch, "Die geistige Revolution," *Kunstwart und Kulturwart*, 34 (1921): 227–233; Ernst Troeltsch, "Deutsche Bildung," in Troeltsch, *Deutscher Geist*, pp. 169–210.

30. Troeltsch, "Der neue Geist," pp. 30–31.

31. Ernst Troeltsch, *Spektator-Briefe: Aufsätze über die deutsche Revolution und die Weltpolitik 1918/22*, ed. Hans Baron (Tübingen, 1924), pp. 48–49.

32. Troeltsch, "Die geistige Revolution," p. 231.

33. *Ibid.*, pp. 232, 233.

34. Troeltsch, *Demokratie*, p. 11.

35. Troeltsch, "Deutsche Bildung," pp. 175, 176, 177.

36. *Ibid.*, pp. 178–179, 184.

37. *Ibid.*, p. 185.

38. Rudolf Lehmann, "Die Bedeutung der Erziehungswissenschaft für die Gegenwart," *Preussische Jahrbücher*, 183 (1921): 211.

39. *Ibid.*, p. 217.

40. Alfred Vierkandt, *Die sozialpädagogische Forderung der Gegenwart* (Berlin, 1920), pp. 5, 14–17, 19, and 26 for terms in this paragraph.

41. *Ibid.*, pp. 9–10, 20.

42. Theodor Litt, *Berufsstudium und "Allgemeinbildung" auf der Universität* (Leipzig, 1920); Theodor Litt, *Nationale Erziehung und Internationalismus* (*Sozialpädagogische Abende in Zentralinstitut für Erziehung und Unterricht*, 3; Berlin, 1920).

43. Werner Richter, *Wissenschaft und Geist in der Weimarer Republik*

(*Arbeitsgemeinschaft für Forschung des Landes Nordrhein-Westfalen: Geisteswissenschaften*, 80; Cologne, 1958), pp. 9–25, p. 17 for quote.

44. Max Weber, *Wissenschaft als Beruf*, 2nd ed. (Munich, 1921).

45. *Ibid.*, p. 21.

46. *Ibid.*, p. 25.

47. *Ibid.*, p. 32.

48. Karl Jaspers, *Max Weber: Rede bei der von der Heidelberger Studentenschaft veranstalteten Trauerfeier* (Tübingen, 1921), p. 11.

49. Willy Hellpach, *Wirken in Wirren: Lebenserinnerungen*, II (Hamburg, 1949), 184–190.

50. Information on Kahler in the essays by Salz and Troeltsch cited below in notes 52 and 53.

51. Erich von Kahler, *Der Beruf der Wissenschaft* (Berlin, 1920), pp. 39, 53.

52. Arthur Salz, *Für die Wissenschaft gegen die Gebildeten unter ihren Verächtern* (Munich, 1921), p. 94. Title adapted from F. E. D. Schleiermacher's anonymous "Über die Religion: Rede an die Gebildeten unter ihren Verächtern" (1799).

53. Ernst Troeltsch, "Die Revolution in der Wissenschaft: Eine Besprechung von Erich von Kahlers Schrift gegen Max Weber: 'Der Beruf der Wissenschaft' und der Gegenschrift von Arthur Salz: 'Für die Wissenschaft gegen die Gebildeten unter ihren Verächtern'," *Schmollers Jahrbuch*, 45 (1921): 1001–1030.

54. *Ibid.*, p. 1007.

55. Eduard Spranger, *Der gegenwärtige Stand der Geisteswissenschaften und die Schule: Rede gehalten auf der 53. Versammlung deutscher Philologen und Schulmänner in Jena am 27. September 1921* (Leipzig, 1922), pp. 5–6, 33.

56. *Ibid.*, p. 33.

57. *Ibid.*, pp. 44–45.

58. *Ibid.*, pp. 31–32.

59. *Ibid.*, p. 44.

60. *Ibid.*, p. 15.

61. *Ibid.*, p. 37.

Chapter Seven

1. Heinrich Rickert, *Kant als Philosoph der modernen Kultur: Ein geschichtsphilosophischer Versuch* (Tübingen, 1924), p. 20.

2. *Ibid.*, p. 31.

3. *Ibid.*, p. 121.

4. *Ibid.*, p. 128.

5. The slogans cited are the titles of Rickert's chapters 11 and 12.

6. Most of the mandarin accounts of German philosophy (which have been cited earlier) were written by "critical realists." I am drawing upon them a

good deal in what follows. I am also using Erich Becher, *Grundlagen und Grenzen des Naturerkennens* (Munich, 1928); Hans Driesch, "Philosophie und positives Wissen," in A. von Gleichen-Russwurm et al., *Der Leuchter: Weltanschauung und Lebensgestaltung* (Darmstadt, 1919), pp. 337–366; Hans Driesch, *Grundprobleme der Psychologie: Ihre Krisis in der Gegenwart* (Leipzig, 1926).

7. Becher, *Grundlagen und Grenzen*, p. 66.

8. I struggled briefly with Edmund Husserl, "Ideen zu einer reinen Phänomenologie und phänomenologischen Philosophie," *Jahrbuch für Philosophie und phänomenologische Forschung*, I (Halle, 1913), 1–323.

9. Max Scheler, "Die deutsche Philosophie der Gegenwart," in Philipp Witkop, ed., *Deutsches Leben der Gegenwart* (Berlin, 1922), p. 129.

10. Werner Jaeger, *Stellung und Aufgaben der Universität in der Gegenwart* (Berlin, 1924), pp. 26–27.

11. Becher, *Grundlagen und Grenzen*, pp. 17–24; Driesch, "Philosophie und positives Wissen," pp. 354–357.

12. Max Frischeisen-Köhler, "Die Philosophie der Gegenwart," in Max Dessoir, ed., *Lehrbuch der Philosophie*, vol. I: *Die Geschichte der Philosophie* (Berlin, 1925), p. 554.

13. Driesch, "Philosophie und positives Wissen," p. 342.

14. Becher, *Grundlagen und Grenzen*, pp. 68–82.

15. G. E. Müller, *Komplextheorie und Gestalttheorie: Ein Beitrag zur Wahrnehmungspsychologie* (Göttingen, 1923).

16. For the following, see: Max Wertheimer, *Über Gestalttheorie: Vortrag gehalten in der Kantgesellschaft Berlin am 17. Dezember 1924* (Sonderabdrucke des Symposion, 1; Erlangen, 1925); Max Wertheimer, *Drei Abhandlungen zur Gestalttheorie* (Erlangen, 1925); Wolfgang Köhler, *Gestalt Psychology* (New York, 1929).

17. *Ibid.*, p. 119, for example. Köhler was consciously writing for a hostile audience, which made for clear writing and some restraint. Wertheimer's *Über Gestalttheorie* is only about twenty pages long, and almost every page contains examples of the pictorial language I am referring to.

18. Wertheimer, *Über Gestalttheorie*, p. 7, emphasis his.

19. Wertheimer, *Drei Abhandlungen*, pp. 164–184.

20. Kurt Lewin, *Die Entwicklung der experimentellen Willenspsychologie und die Psychotherapie* (Leipzig, 1929).

21. E. R. Jaensch, *Einige allgemeinere Fragen der Psychologie und Biologie des Denkens, erläutert an der Lehre vom Vergleich* (E. R. Jaensch, ed., *Arbeiten zur Psychologie und Philosophie*, 1; Leipzig, 1920).

22. "Richard Hönigswald," in Hermann Schwarz, ed., *Deutsche Systematische Philosophie nach ihren Gestaltern* (Berlin, 1931), pp. 191–223; Richard Hönigswald, *Die Grundlagen der Denkpsychologie: Studien und Analysen* (Munich, 1921).

23. Eduard Spranger, *Lebensformen: Geisteswissenschaftliche Psychologie und Ethik der Persönlichkeit*, 4th ed. (Halle, 1924), esp. pp. vii-xv, 3–20. Ten thousand copies of this book had been printed by 1924. See also Eduard Spranger, *Der gegenwärtige Stand der Geisteswissenschaften und die Schule* (Leipzig, 1922), pp. 14–27; Gardner Murphy, *An Historical Introduction to Modern Psychology* (New York, 1929), pp. 443–455 (Klüver's supplementary chapter).

24. Spranger, *Der gegenwärtige Stand*, pp. 20–21.

25. Spranger, *Lebensformen*, p. viii.

26. William Stern, *Studien zur Personalwissenschaft*, part I: *Personalistik als Wissenschaft* (Leipzig, 1930), esp. pp. iii-vii, 1–26; Murphy, *Modern Psychology* pp. 422–426 (Klüver).

27. Stern, *Personalistik*, p. vii.

28. Felix Krueger, *Über Entwicklungspsychologie: Ihre sachliche und geschichtliche Notwendigkeit* (Leipzig, 1915); Murphy, *Modern Psychology*, pp. 434–437 (Klüver).

29. Matthias Meier, *Der Seelenbegriff in der modernen Psychologie*, (Munich, n.d. [1921]), p. 5.

30. *Ibid.*, pp. 7, 21, 23, and 24 for successive paragraphs.

31. *Ibid.*, pp. 23, 21.

32. Ernst von Aster, *Die Psychoanalyse* (Berlin, 1930).

33. The three are: Oswald Bumke, *Eine Krisis der Medizin: Rede gehalten bei der Übernahme des Rektorats am 24. November 1928 (Münchener Universitätsreden*, 13; Munich, 1929), pp. 7–8; Oesterreich, "Die philosophischen Strömungen," p. 373; and Alois Wenzel, *Das unbewusste Denken* (Karlsruhe, 1927).

34. Traugott Konstantin Oesterreich, *Grundbegriffe der Parapsychologie* (Pfullingen in Württemberg, 1921); Hans Driesch, *Parapsychologie: Die Wissenschaft von den "okkulten" Erscheinungen: Methodik und Theorie* (Munich, 1932). See also Hans Driesch, *Grundprobleme der Psychologie: Ihre Krisis in der Gegenwart* (Leipzig, 1926).

35. Hans Rosenberg, *Die Entwicklung des räumlichen Weltbildes der Astronomie (Kieler Universitätsreden*, 11; Kiel, 1930), p. 27.

36. Eduard Kohlrausch, *Die geistesgeschichtliche Krise des Strafrechts: Rede zum Antritt des Rektorats* (Berlin, 1932); Martin Dibelius, *Urchristentum und Kultur (Heidelberger Universitätsreden*, 7; Heidelberg, 1928); Emil Gotschlich, *Hygiene, Zivilisation und Kultur (Heidelberger Universitätsreden*, 8; Heidelberg, 1929).

37. Friedrich Kuntze, *Der morphologische Idealismus: Seine Grundlagen und seine Bedeutung* (Munich, 1929); Dietrich von Hildebrand, *Metaphysik der Gemeinschaft: Untersuchungen über Wesen und Wert der Gemeinschaft* (Augsburg, 1930).

38. Heinrich Weber, *Das Sozialisierungsproblem in der Forstwirtschaft: Rektoratsrede* (Freiburg, 1931), p. 25.

39. Vinzenz Schüpfer, *Die Bedeutung des Waldes und der Forstwirtschaft für die Kultur im Wandel der Zeiten* (*Münchener Universitätsreden*, 10; Munich, 1928), p. 30.

40. Examples: Wilhelm Pinder, *Reden aus der Zeit: Schriften zur deutschen Lebenssicht* (Leipzig, 1934); Eugen Lerch, *Romain Rolland und die Erneuerung der Gesinnung* (Munich, 1926), p. 17.

41. Bumke, *Krisis der Medizin*, pp. 4, 7, 8, 9.

42. Friedrich Schürr, *Sprachwissenschaft und Zeitgeist: Eine sprachphilosophische Studie* (*Die neueren Sprachen*, suppl. 1 to vol. XXX; Marburg, 1922), pp. 30, 79.

43. For example, Reinhard Demoll, *Der Wandel der biologischen Anschauungen in den letzten hundert Jahren: Rede zum Antritt des Rektorates, am 21. November 1931* (*Münchener Universitätsreden*, 23; Munich, 1932).

44. Paul Mombert, *Geschichte der Nationalökonomie* (Jena, 1927), pp. 532–533.

45. Werner Sombart, ed., *Soziologie* (Berlin, 1923), pp. 5–16.

46. Werner Sombart, *Die drei Nationalökonomien: Geschichte und System der Lehre von der Wirtschaft* (Munich, 1930). The concluding section of the second edition of Sombart's *Modern Capitalism* appeared in 1927.

47. Sombart, *Drei Nationalökonomien*, pp. 85–88 for dissolution argument.

48. Otto Hintze, "Troeltsch und die Probleme des Historismus," *Historische Zeitschrift*, 135 (1926–1927): 188–239; Felix Rachfahl, *Staat, Gesellschaft, Kultur und Geschichte* (Jena, 1924).

49. Erich Rothacker, "Gedanken über nationale Kultur," *Zeitschrift für Deutsche Bildung*, 1 (1925): 8–15.

50. Kurt Breysig, *Die Geschichte der Seele im Werdegang der Menschheit* (Breslau, 1931).

51. Friedrich Meinecke, "Kausalitäten und Werte in der Geschichte," *Historische Zeitschrift*, 137 (1927–1928): 1–27.

52. Karl Vossler, *Die Universität als Bildungsstätte: Vortrag gehalten, am 15. Dezember 1922* (Munich, 1923), p. 14.

53. Karl Jaspers, *Die Idee der Universität* (Berlin, 1923), pp. 49, 79.

54. *Ibid.*, pp. 61, 63.

55. Leopold von Wiese, "Umrisse eines Versuches der Synthese des Volksbildungswesens," in Leopold von Weise, ed., *Soziologie des Volksbildungswesens* (*Schriften des Forschungsinstituts für Sozialwissenschaften in Köln*, 1; Munich, 1921), p. 554; Emil Lederer, "Zur neueren geldtheoretischen Literatur," *Archiv*, 47 (1920–21): 876–888; Ferdinand Tönnies, "Troeltsch und die Philosophie der Geschichte," *Schmollers Jahrbuch*, 49 (1925): 183.

56. Theodor Litt, *Wissenschaft, Bildung, Weltanschauung* (Berlin, 1928);

Eduard Spranger, "Das Wesen der deutschen Universität," *Das akademische Deutschland*, III, 33.

57. Werner Jaeger, *Stellung und Aufgaben der Universität in der Gegenwart* (Berlin, 1924), pp. 25–26.

58. Reinhold Seeberg, "Hochschule und Weltanschauung," *Das akademische Deutschland*, III, 178. Spranger took the same line in "Wesen der Universität," p. 13.

59. Eduard Spranger, "Die drei Motive der Schulreform," *Monatsschrift für höhere Schulen*, 20 (1921): 260–274.

60. Jaspers, *Idee der Universität*, pp. 1, 3.

61. *Ibid.*, pp. 6–7.

62. Examples: Karl Vossler, *Sprachgemeinschaft und Interessengemeinschaft* (*Sitzungsberichte der Bayerischen Akademie der Wissenschaften, philosophisch-philologische und historische Klasse*, vol. for 1924, no. 1; Munich, 1924); Jonas Cohn, *Befreien und Binden: Zeitfragen der Erziehung überzeitlich betrachtet* (Leipzig, 1926), p. 80.

63. Ernst Troeltsch, *Naturrecht und Humanität in der Weltpolitik: Vortrag bei der zweiten Jahresfeier der Deutschen Hochschule für Politik* (Berlin, 1923), pp. 12–13.

64. Karl Vossler, *Die romanischen Kulturen und der deutsche Geist* (Munich, 1926); Gustav Neckel, *Germanen und Kelten: Historisch-linguistisch-rassenkundliche Forschungen und Gedanken zur Geisteskrisis* (Heidelberg, 1929).

65. Ernst Robert Curtius, *Französischer Geist im neuen Europa* (Stuttgart, 1925), pp. 268–270.

66. *Ibid.*, pp. 275, 291.

67. Fritz Strich, "Natur und Geist der deutschen Dichtung," in Fritz Strich and Hans H. Borcherdt, eds., *Die Ernte: Abhandlungen zur Literaturwissenschaft, Franz Muncker zu seinem 70. Geburtstage* (Halle, 1926), p. 29.

68. Fritz Strich, *Dichtung und Zivilisation* (Munich, 1928), pp. 172, 79, 89, 102.

69. Hugo von Hofmannsthal, *Das Schrifttum als geistiger Raum der Nation* (Munich, n.d. [1927]), pp. 27, 29–30, 31.

70. Carl H. Becker, *Secondary Education and Teacher Training in Germany* (New York, 1931).

71. *Staatsbürgerliche Erziehung*, ed. F. Lampe and G. H. Franke for the Zentralinstitut für Erziehung und Unterricht (Breslau, 1924).

72. Willy Hellpach, *Wirken in Wirren: Lebenserinnerungen*, II (Hamburg, 1949), 157–222; Willy Hellpach, *Die Wesensgestalt der deutschen Schule* (Leipzig, 1925); Willy Hellpach, *Politische Prognose für Deutschland* (Berlin, 1928), p. 149 for quote.

73. Albert Rehm, *Zum Kampf um das Reichsschulgesetz* (Langensalza, 1925).

74. Aloys Fischer, *Erziehung als Beruf* (Leipzig, 1922), pp. 40–41; Eduard Spranger, *Der deutsche Klassizismus und das Bildungsleben der Gegenwart*, 2nd

ed. (*Veröffentlichungen der Akademie gemeinnütziger Wissenschaften zu Erfurt, Abteilung für Erziehungswissenschaft und Jugendkunde*, 3; Erfurt, 1928), p. 6; Werner Jaeger, "Die geistige Gegenwart der Antike," in Werner Jaeger, ed., *Die Antike: Zeitschrift für Kunst und Kultur des klassischen Altertums*, V (Berlin, 1929), 167–186.

75. Gustav Roethe, *Wege der deutschen Philologie: Rede zum Antritt des Rektorats* (Berlin, 1923); Eduard Spranger, *Der Anteil des Neuhumanismus an der Entstehung des deutschen Nationalbewusstseins: Rede zur Reichsgründungsfeier zu Berlin* (Berlin, 1923); Albert Rehm, *Die Antike und die deutsche Gegenwart* (Munich, 1923).

76. Albert Rehm, *Neuhumanismus einst und jetzt: Rede zum Antritt des Rektorates gehalten in der Aula am 29. November 1930* (*Münchener Universitätsreden*, 22; Munich, 1931), pp. 19, 20–21; Rehm, *Die Antike*, pp. 11, 35 and p. 50 for quote.

77. E. Schwartz, *Rede zur Reichsgründungsfeier der Universität München* (*Münchener Universitätsreden*, 2; Munich, 1925), pp. 4, 12.

78. *Die Ausbildung der höheren Lehrer an der Universität: Denkschrift der philosophischen Fakultät der Friedrich-Wilhelms-Universität Berlin* (Leipzig, 1925).

79. Rehm, *Die Antike*, pp. 20–21.

80. Erich Jaensch, *Neue Wege der Erziehungslehre und Jugendkunde: Zur philosophischen Grundlegung der Pädagogik* (*Veröffentlichungen der Abteilung für Erziehungswissenschaft und Jugendkunde der Akademie gemeinnütziger Wissenschaften zu Erfurt*, 9; Erfurt, 1928).

81. Theodor Litt, *Führen oder Wachsenlassen: Eine Erörterung des pädagogischen Gundproblems*, 3rd ed. (Leipzig, 1931); Theodor Litt, *Möglichkeiten und Grenzen der Pädagogik: Abhandlungen zur gegenwärtigen Lage von Erziehung und Erziehungstheorie* (Berlin, 1926), pp. 1–88.

82. *Ibid.*, p. 83.

83. Georg Kerschensteiner, *Der Begriff der staatsbürgerlichen Erziehung*, 5th ed. (Leipzig, 1923); Georg Kerschensteiner, *Autorität und Freiheit als Bildungsgrundsätze* (Leipzig, n.d. [1924]); Georg Kerschensteiner, *Theorie der Bildung* (Leipzig, 1926).

84. Kerschensteiner, *Begriff der staatsbürgerlichen Erziehung*, pp. 45, 69.

85. Cohn, *Befreien und Binden*, p. vi.

86. *Ibid.*, p. 52.

87. *Ibid.*, pp. 72–73, p. 77. For a fuller exposition of Cohn's views on the cultural crisis, see also: Jonas Cohn, *Der Sinn der gegenwärtigen Kultur: Ein philosophischer Versuch* (Leipzig, 1914).

88. Cohn, *Befreien und Binden*, pp. 78, 79.

89. Aloys Fischer, "Psychologisch-ethische Vorfragen der Heimaterziehung," in

Walther Schönichen, ed., *Handbuch der Heimaterziehung* (Berlin, 1923), pp. 27–105, esp. pp. 103–104 for this and the following.

90. Aloys Fischer, "Das Verhältnis der Jugend zu den sozialen Bewegungen und der Begriff der Sozialpädagogik," in Aloys Fischer, ed., *Jugendführer und Jugendprobleme: Festschrift zu Georg Kerschensteiners 70. Geburtstag* (Leipzig, 1924), pp. 209–306, quote being from p. 230.

91. Fischer, "Psychologisch-ethische Vorfragen," p. 104; Fischer, "Verhältnis der Jugend," p. 231.

92. *Ibid.*, p. 223; Aloys Fischer, *Die kulturellen Grundlagen der Erziehung* (Erlangen, 1925), pp. 40, 25–26.

93. Spranger, *Der deutsche Klassizismus*, pp. 5, 10–11.

94. Theodor Litt, *Die Philosophie der Gegenwart und ihr Einfluss auf das Bildungsideal* (Leipzig, 1925).

95. Fischer, *Die kulturellen Grundlagen*, pp. 48, 52–54; Aloys Fischer, *Arbeits- und Erlebnispädagogik* (Vienna, 1932), pp. 9, 7, 12–15.

96. *Ibid.*, pp. 23, 22.

97. Aloys Fischer, "Unsere Zeit und die Mission der Pädagogik," in A. Fischer, T. Litt, H. Nohl, and E. Spranger, eds., *Die Erziehung: Monatsschrift für den Zusammenhang von Kultur und Erziehung in Wissenschaft und Leben*, 1 (Leipzig, 1925/26): 1–7.

98. Ulrich Peters, "Zum Geleit," in Ulrich Peters, ed., *Zeitschrift für Deutsche Bildung*, 1 (Frankfurt, 1925): 1–7.

99. Rehm, *Die Antike*, pp. 55–57; Spranger, *Der deutsche Klassizismus*, pp. 8, 17–18; Carl H. Becker, *Vom Wesen der deutschen Universität* (Leipzig, 1925), pp. 42–44.

100. For the following: Alfred Weber, *Ideen zur Staats- und Kultursoziologie* (Alfred Weber, ed., *Probleme der Staats- und Kultursoziologie*, 1; Karlsruhe, 1927); Alfred Weber, "Prinzipielles zur Kultursoziologie," *Archiv*, 47 (1920–21): 1–49; Alfred Weber, "Kultursoziologie," *Handwörterbuch der Soziologie*, pp. 284–294.

101. Max Scheler, "Von zwei deutschen Krankheiten," in A. von Gleichen-Russwurm, et al., *Der Leuchter: Weltanschauung und Lebensgestaltung* (Darmstadt, 1919), pp. 161–190.

102. Max Scheler, *Die Formen des Wissens und die Bildung* (Bonn, 1925), pp. 1–10.

103. *Ibid.*, pp. 11–39; Max Scheler, *Die Wissensformen und die Gesellschaft* (Leipzig, 1926), pp. i–xi, 1–57; Max Scheler, *Philosophische Weltanschauung* (Bonn, 1929), pp. 1–14, 47–57.

104. Max Scheler, "Weltanschauungslehre, Soziologie und Weltanschauungssetzung," *Kölner Vierteljahrshefte für Sozialwissenschaften*, 2 (1922): 18–33.

105. I am not considering Mannheim's early essay on the "Structural Analysis of Epistemology" or his debunking critique of "Conservative Thought." Rather,

the following essays seem to me most characteristic of his methodological position: "On the Interpretation of 'Weltanschauung'," in Karl Mannheim, *Essays on the Sociology of Knowledge*, ed. Paul Kecskemeti (London, 1952), pp. 33–83 (this essay was written in 1921); "Historismus," *Archiv*, 52 (1924): 1–60; "Das Problem einer Soziologie des Wissens," *Archiv*, 53 (1925): 577–652; *Die Gegenwartsaufgaben der Soziologie: Ihre Lehrgestalt* (Tübingen, 1932), pp. 17–21; *Ideology and Utopia: An Introduction to the Sociology of Knowledge*, trans. L. Wirth and E. Shils (New York, n.d. [1955]), including the 1936 English version, which was itself an expansion of the 1929 original in German, and the essay "Wissenssoziologie" from the 1931 *Handwörterbuch der Soziologie*.

106. Mannheim, *Ideology and Utopia*, p. 276.

107. Mannheim, "Historismus," p. 4.

108. Mannheim, *Ideology and Utopia*, p. 102.

109. *Ibid.*, p. 295.

Conclusion

1. For this whole paragraph see Karl Dietrich Bracher, *Die Auflösung der Weimarer Republik: Eine Studie zum Problem des Machtverfalls in der Demokratie*, 4th ed. (Villingen, 1964), pp. 146–149.

2. Walter H. Kaufmann, *Monarchism in the Weimar Republic* (New York, 1953), p. 237, cites *Der Rote Aufbau*, 1930, no. 10, pp. 529f for the following figures: Of 2.5 million young people who entered the German political system as new voters between 1928 and 1930, 1.6 million voted for Hitler's party. That reflects on their teachers.

3. Karl Jaspers, *Man in the Modern Age*, trans. E. and C. Paul (London, 1933). The German original, *Die geistige Situation der Zeit*, was first published in 1931.

4. Aloys Fischer, *Über Sinn und Wert geschichtlicher Bildung in der Gegenwart: Rede gehalten, am 18. Januar 1932* (Münchener Universitätsreden, 24; Munich, 1932).

5. Ernst Robert Curtius, *Deutscher Geist in Gefahr* (Stuttgart, 1932).

6. Ernst Hoffmann, *Die Freiheit der Forschung und der Lehre: Rede, am 17. Januar 1931* (Heidelberger Universitätsreden, 12; Heidelberg, 1931).

7. *Mitteilungen des Verbandes der Deutschen Hochschulen*, ed. K. Voigt, 12 (November 1932): 150–151.

8. Eduard Spranger, "Mein Konflikt mit der national-sozialistischen Regierung 1933," *Universitas: Zeitschrift für Wissenschaft, Kunst und Literatur*, 10 (1955): 457–473, quote on p. 457. This article is the classic portrait of the mandarin reaction to National Socialism, the most revealing primary source in the field.

9. For the following, see Karl Dietrich Bracher, Wolfgang Sauer, and Gerhard Schulz, *Die nationalsozialistische Machtergreifung: Studien zur Errichtung des totalitären Herrschaftssystems in Deutschland 1933/34*, 2nd ed. (Cologne, 1962), pp. 308–326, 565–570; Edward Yarnall Hartshorne, *The German Universities and National Socialism* (Cambridge, Mass., 1937).

10. *Ibid.*, pp. 87–100.

11. Ernst Nolte, "Zur Typologie des Verhaltens der Hochschullehrer im Dritten Reich, *Aus Politik und Zeitgeschichte: Beilage zur Wochenzeitung Das Parlament*, November 17, 1965, p. 10. Nolte makes some very useful distinctions in this article; but I think he underestimates the responsibility of orthodox scholarship itself. See also Wilhelm Roepke, "National Socialism and the Intellectuals," in George B. de Huszar, ed., *The Intellectuals: A Controversial Portrait* (Glencoe, 1960), pp. 346–353; Max Weinreich, *Hitler's Professors: The Part of Scholarship in Germany's Crimes Against the Jewish People* (New York, 1946); Rolf Seeliger, *Doktorarbeiten im Dritten Reich: Dokumentation mit Stellungnahmen (Dokumentenreihe Braune Uuniversität*, 5; Munich, 1966). Weinreich is one-sided. Seeliger usefully calls attention to the role of some rather distinguished *Doktorväter* in the production of "brown" dissertations.

12. On this and the whole situation see Klaus Epstein's review of Friedrich Meinecke, *Ausgewählter Briefwechsel*, ed. Ludwig Dehio and Peter Classen (Stuttgart, 1962), in *History and Theory*, 4 (1964): 78–96.

13. *Bekenntnis der Professoren an den deutschen Universitäten und Hochschulen zu Adolf Hitler und dem nationalsozialistischen Staat*, ed. Nationalsozialistischer Lehrerbund Deutschland/Sachsen (Dresden, n.d. [1933]). Jaensch, Krueger, and Freyer were among the signers. Some other names are also familiar; but full first names were rarely given, which suggests caution.

14. Spranger, "Mein Konflikt," pp. 462, 465.

15. Friedrich Meinecke, *The German Catastrophe: Reflections and Recollections*, trans. Sidney B. Fay (Cambridge, Mass., 1950), pp. 115–121.

16. *Ibid.*, and Friedrich Meinecke, *Politische, Schriften und Reden*, ed. Georg Kotowski (Darmstadt, 1958), p. 484, for example.

17. Helmut Arntz for the Presse- und Informationsamt der Bundesregierung, *Tatsachen über Deutschland*, 5th ed. (Wiesbaden, 1962), p. 12.

INDEX